Industry in England

Originally published in 1912, *Industry in England* provides a complete history of industry and industrial changes in England from pre-Roman times to modern England as it stood in the early twentieth century. Using Gibbins' previous text *The Industrial History of England* as a base, this work aims to tackle economic and industrial questions in relation to social, political and military contexts in detail to present a full picture of what life in England was like at the time these industrial changes took place and how this influenced industry. This title will be of interest to students of History.

T0347864

Industry in England

Historical Outlines

Henry De Beltgens Gibbins

First published in 1912
by Charles Scribner's Sons

This edition first published in 2016 by Routledge
2 Park Square, Milton Park, Abingdon, Oxon, OX14 4RN
and by Routledge
711 Third Avenue, New York, NY 10017

Routledge is an imprint of the Taylor & Francis Group, an informa business

© 1912 Henry De Beltgens Gibbins

Publisher's Note
The publisher has gone to great lengths to ensure the quality of this reprint but points out that some imperfections in the original copies may be apparent.

Disclaimer
The publisher has made every effort to trace copyright holders and welcomes correspondence from those they have been unable to contact.

A Library of Congress record exists under LC control number: 17007160

ISBN 13: 978-1-138-19265-2 (hbk)
ISBN 13: 978-1-315-63978-9 (ebk)
ISBN 13: 978-1-138-19266-9 (pbk)

INDUSTRY IN ENGLAND

HISTORICAL OUTLINES

BY

H. DE B. GIBBINS, LITT.D., M.A.

SOMETIME UNIVERSITY (COBDEN) PRIZEMAN IN POLITICAL ECONOMY, OXFORD
AUTHOR OF "THE INDUSTRIAL HISTORY OF ENGLAND" AND
"THE HISTORY OF COMMERCE IN EUROPE"

WITH MAPS, TABLES, AND A PLAN

SEVENTH EDITION, REVISED

NEW YORK
CHARLES SCRIBNER'S SONS
1912

TO MY WIFE

OF INDUSTRIAL HISTORY AND
SOCIAL REFORM

"... *The Sibyl offers her books, in which the future
is forecast, to the Roman statesman, according to the
legend. The price is refused twice, and, after each repulse,
she destroys irrevocably one of the volumes, demanding
the same price for the third. This is what Bacon called
the wisdom of the ancients, and the moral is plain.*"

JAMES E. THOROLD ROGERS

PREFACE

IN 1890 the author published a small book, entitled *The Industrial History of England*, which met with a somewhat undeserved success, and has rapidly gone through several large editions. It was described in the first preface as "an attempt to relate in a short, concise, and simple form the main outlines of England's economic and industrial history," meant "to serve as an introduction to a fuller study of the subject, and as a preliminary sketch which the reader can afterwards, if he wishes, fill in for himself from larger volumes;" and it seems to have attained its object of awakening popular interest, to some extent, in a very important branch of national history. But it had all the faults of a brief outline, and contained errors of fact and of expression which no one has regretted more sincerely than the author. It has therefore been my endeavour, in this larger work, to produce a History of Industry of a more satisfactory character, while at the same time retaining the essential features that characterised the earlier effort. As before, I have attempted, as far as possible, in the brief limits of a work like this, to connect economic and industrial questions with social, political, and military movements, since only in some such mutual relation can historical events obtain their full significance.

The Industrial History of England has been taken, on the whole, as the basis of this book, and the arrangement

b   vii

of periods and chapters has been but slightly altered; but the original book has been entirely re-written, and so much new matter has been added that the present volume is quite three times the size of the first essay. Fresh maps have been drawn, new tables of statistics added, and footnotes have been given for every statement of any importance.

The first period also, up to the Norman conquest, contains entirely new matter, involving a certain amount of original work. For some time it has appeared to me that the results of archæological and antiquarian research into the pre-historic period have not been sufficiently utilised in dealing with our industrial history, and that the origin of the manor, in especial, derives added light from these investigations. It has therefore been my endeavour to weave into the story of industrial progress several of the results arrived at by investigators of pre-historic conditions, believing, as I do, that the many centuries of industrial human life which elapsed before our written history began must have left upon our nation some traces of their course. At the same time, I have not wished to emphasise the pre-historic period unduly, and have therefore confined the remarks upon it to a very limited space. But I hope that the "survey of the origin of the manor," in § 32, may be some contribution to the discussion of the subject.

Throughout the book I have tried to review the industrial life of England as a whole, and to present a general survey of it throughout its gradual development. In this respect *Industry in England* differs from most works of the kind, for they have generally been devoted either to some special period or some special aspect, or have dealt

with industry only as a branch of the national commerce. I
have endeavoured to give full weight to the views of other
writers, especially on disputed points,[1] but have also indicated my own (though with considerable diffidence) where
there seemed reason to differ from them. I do not suppose
that I have succeeded in being impartial, for, though
impartiality is the ideal, it is also the will o' the wisp of
the historian, and generally deserts him when he needs it
most; but I have at least endeavoured to give reasons for
my conclusions. And while in some points I differ, no
one admires more than myself the work of such historians
as Dr Cunningham and Professor Ashley, whose names I
venture specially to mention, because I wish gratefully to
acknowledge the magnitude of the help rendered to me, as
to all students, by their recent contributions to industrial
history. My obligations to them are, I trust, acknowledged
as often as possible in the footnotes, but mere references of
that kind cannot convey by any means adequately the
extent to which a student like myself has benefited from
their researches.

As regards the footnotes generally, every endeavour has
been made to acknowledge all the sources which have been
consulted, and any omission in this respect the author
sincerely regrets. Considerable difficulty was occasioned
by my change of residence during the completion of the
book, and a consequent compulsory recourse to different
libraries; and the indulgence of readers and critics is
therefore asked for any omission or error thereby caused
It might also be added that this book has been written in

[1] As, *e.g.*, The Peasants' Revolt, the condition of the Labourer in the
fifteenth century, the Poor Law of Elizabeth, the Assessment of Wages,
&c., &c.

the intervals of a very busy life, and out of reach of any special collection of works on industrial subjects or of any of the greater libraries of the kingdom.

I cannot conclude without paying a tribute to the memory of the late Professor J. E. Thorold Rogers, to whom I showed, as a mere beginner in his special subject, the proofs of the first few chapters of the little book (*The Industrial History of England*) from which this larger volume has developed. To his kindly encouragement and to the inspiring teaching of his economic works, I owe whatever knowledge I possess of that side of our national history which is of such vast importance to a citizen of modern England.

H. DE B. GIBBINS

PREFACE TO THE SECOND EDITION

THE very favourable reception and rapid sale of this book have necessitated the issue of a second edition within a few months of the publication of the first. Only a few verbal corrections have been made, but I should like to quote the following explanation from the preface to the fifth edition of my earlier work, the *Industrial History of England*:

"It has been said that I write with a prejudice against the owners of land : but this is not the case. The landed gentry of England happen, for some centuries, to have held the predominant power in the State and in society, and used it, not unnaturally, in many cases to further their own interests. It is the duty of an historian to point this out, but it need not, therefore, be thought that he has any special bias against the class. Any other class would have certainly done the same, as, for instance, mill-owners did among their own *employés* at the beginning of this century, and as, in all probability, the working-classes will do, when a further extension of democratic government shall have given them the opportunity. It is a fault of human nature that it can rarely be trusted with irresponsible power, and unless the influence of one class of society is counterbalanced more or less by that of another, there will always be a tendency to some injustice. I trust that my readers will bear this in mind when reading the following pages, and will believe that I intend no unfairness to the landed gentry of England, who have done much to promote the glory and stability of their country."

H. DE B. GIBBINS

CONTENTS

PERIOD I

EARLY HISTORY, FROM PRE-HISTORIC TIMES TO THE NORMAN CONQUEST

CHAPTER I

PRE-ROMAN BRITAIN

SECTION   PAGE
1. Industrial History 3
2. The English Nation and Country 3
3. The Aboriginal Inhabitants of Britain 5
4. Their Social and Economic Condition 7
5. The Bronze Age and the Celtic Immigration . . . 8
6. Résumé: The Peoples of Early Britain 10
7. Their Social and Economic Condition 10
8. The Celts in the time of Pytheas 11
9. Foreign Trade of Britain 14
10. Internal Trade: Roads and Rivers 16
11. Physical Aspect of Pre-Roman Britain 17

CHAPTER II

ROMAN BRITAIN

12. The Roman Occupation 21
13. Roman Roads 22
14. Roman Towns in Britain 23
15. The Romans and Agriculture 25
16. Celtic and Non-Roman Influence in Agriculture . . . 27
17. Commerce and Industry in Roman Britain . . . 31

CHAPTER III

THE SAXON PERIOD

18. The Saxon Invasions 34
19. The Saxon Village and its Inhabitants 37
20. Village Life 38
21. Methods of Cultivation 40

SECTION		PAGE
22. Isolation of Villages. Crafts and Trades. Markets	. .	41
23. Foreign Commerce and the Danes	. . . .	43
24. Summary of Trade and Industry in the Saxon Period	. .	46

CHAPTER IV

THE MANOR AND THE MANORIAL SYSTEM

25. The Interest of the Question as to the Origin of the Manor	.	47
26. The Mark Theory and the Manor .	. . . .	48
27. Criticisms of the Mark Theory	. . . . .	49
28. Vinogradoff's Evidence on the Manorial System	. . .	52
29. Evidence from Manorial Courts and Customs	. . .	55
30. The "Customary" Tenants	. . . . .	56
31. The Evidence of Village Communities	. . .	57
32. A Survey of the Origin of the Manor	. . . .	58
33. The Feudal System	. . . . . .	60

PERIOD II

FROM THE NORMAN CONQUEST TO THE REIGN OF HENRY III

(1066-1216 A.D.)

CHAPTER V

DOMESDAY BOOK AND THE MANORS

34. The Survey ordered by William I.	. . . .	65
35. The Population given by Domesday	. . . .	66
36. The Wealth of various Districts .	. . . .	68
37. The Manors and Lords of the Manors	. . . .	70
38. The Inhabitants of the Manor	. . . . .	71
39. The Condition of these Inhabitants	. . . .	73
40. Services due to the Lord from his Tenants in Villeinage .	.	74
41. Money Payments and Rents	. . . .	74
42. Free Tenants. Soke-men .	. . . . .	75
43. The Distinction between Free and Unfree Tenants	. .	76
44. Illustrations of Manors from Domesday .	. . .	78
45. Cuxham Manor in the Eleventh and Thirteenth Centuries	.	79
46. Description of an Eleventh Century Village	. . .	80
47. The Decay of the Manorial System	. . . .	84

CHAPTER VI

THE TOWNS AND THE GILDS

48. The Origin of the Towns .	. . . . .	86
49. Rise of Towns in England	. . . . .	87
50. Towns in Domesday	. . . . .	88

CONTENTS

SECTION   PAGE

51. Special Privileges of Towns 89
52. How the Towns obtained their Charters . . . 90
53. The Gilds and the Towns. Various kinds of Gilds . . 91
54. How the Merchant Gilds helped the Growth of Towns . . 93
55. How the Craft Gilds helped Industry 94
56. Life in the Towns of this time 96

CHAPTER VII

MANUFACTURES AND TRADE : ELEVENTH TO THIRTEENTH CENTURIES

57. Economic Effects of the Feudal System 98
58. Foreign Trade. The Crusades 100
59. The Trading Clauses in the Great Charter . . . 101
60. The Jews in England 103
61. Manufactures in this Period : Flemish Weavers . . . 104
62. Economic Appearance of England in this Period. Population.
    The North and South 106
63. General Condition of the Period 108

PERIOD III

FROM THE THIRTEENTH TO THE END OF THE FIFTEENTH CENTURY, INCLUDING THE GREAT PLAGUE

(1216-1500)

CHAPTER VIII

AGRICULTURE IN MEDIÆVAL ENGLAND

64. Introductory. Rise of a Wage-earning Class . . . 111
65. Agriculture the Chief Occupation of the People . . . 112
66. Methods of Cultivation. The Capitalist Landlord and his Bailiff.
    The "Stock and Land" Lease 113
67. The Tenants' Communal Land and Closes . . . 115
68. Ploughing 116
69. Stock, Pigs, and Poultry 116
70. Sheep 117
71. Increase of Sheep-farming 118
72. Consequent Increase of Enclosures . . . 119

CHAPTER IX

THE WOOLLEN TRADE AND MANUFACTURES

73. England's Monopoly of Wool 120
74. Wool and Politics 121
75. Prices and Brands of English Wool 124
76. English Manufactures 125

SECTION   PAGE
77. Foreign Manufacture of Fine Goods 126
78. Flemish Settlers teach the English Weavers. Norwich   127
79. The Worsted Industry 129
80. Gilds in the Cloth Trade 130
81. The Dyeing of Cloth 131
82. The Great Transition in English Industry . . . 131
83. The Manufacturing Class and Politics 132

CHAPTER X

THE TOWNS, INDUSTRIAL VILLAGES, AND FAIRS

84. The Chief Manufacturing Towns 134
85. Staple Towns and the Merchants 135
86. Markets 138
87. The Great Fairs 140
88. The Fairs of Winchester and Stourbridge . . 142
89. English Mediæval Ports 144
90. The Temporary Decay of Manufacturing Towns . . . 145
91. Growth of Industrial Villages. The Germs of the Modern Factory System 146

CHAPTER XI

THE GREAT PLAGUE AND ITS ECONOMIC EFFECTS

92. Material Progress of the Country. 149
93. Social Changes.   The Villeins and the Wage-paid Labourers . 150
94. The Famine and the Plague 151
95. The Effects of the Plague on Wages 152
96. Prices of Provisions 155
97. Effects of the Plague upon the Landowners . . . 156
98. Large and Small Holdings : the Yeomen . . . 157
99. The Statute of *Quia Emptores* 158
100. The Emancipation of the Villeins 159

CHAPTER XII

THE PEASANTS' REVOLT OF 1381, AND THE SUBSEQUENT CONDITION OF THE WORKING CLASSES

101. The Place of the Revolt in English History . . . 161
102. New Social Doctrines 162
103. The Coming of the Friars. Wiklif . . . 163
104. The Renewed Exactions of the Landowners . . . 164
105. Social and Political Questions 165
106. The Mutterings of a Storm 167
107. The Storm Breaks Out 168
108. The Result of the Revolt 170
109. The Condition of the English Labourer . . . 172
110. Purchasing Power of Wages 175
111. Drawbacks 177

CHAPTER XIII

THE CLOSE OF THE MIDDLE AGES

SECTION   PAGE

112. The Nobility 180
113. The Country Gentry 182
114. The Yeomen 183
115. Agriculture and Sheep-farming 184
116. The Stock and Land Lease 186
117. The Towns and Town Constitutions 187
118. The Gilds and Municipal Institutions 189
119. The Decay of Certain Towns 190
120. The Commercial and Industrial Changes of the Fifteenth
    Century 192
121. The Close of the Middle Ages 194

PERIOD IV

FROM THE SIXTEENTH CENTURY TO THE EVE OF THE INDUSTRIAL REVOLUTION

(1509-1716)

CHAPTER XIV

THE REIGN OF HENRY VIII., AND ECONOMIC CHANGES IN THE SIXTEENTH CENTURY

122. Henry VIII.'s Wastefulness 199
123. The Dissolution of the Monasteries 202
124. Results of the Suppression 203
125. Pauperism 205
126. The Issuing of Base Coin 206
127. The Confiscation of the Gild Lands 207
128. Bankruptcy and Rapacity of Edward VI.'s Government . 209
129. The Agrarian Situation 211
130. The Enclosures of the Sixteenth Century . . . 213
131. Evidence of the Results of Enclosing 215
132. Other Economic Changes. The Finances . . . 218
133. Summary of the Changes of the Sixteenth Century . . 220

CHAPTER XV

THE GROWTH OF FOREIGN TRADE

134. The Expansion of Commerce. The New Spirit . . . 223
135. Foreign Trade in the Fifteenth Century 224
136. The Venetian Fleet 225
137. The Hanseatic League's Station in London . . . 227

SECTION   PAGE
138. Trade with Flanders. Antwerp in the Fifteenth and Sixteenth
     Centuries   228
139. The Decay of Antwerp and Rise of London as the Western
     Emporium   230
140. The Merchants and Sea-Captains of the Elizabethan Age in the
     New World   231
141. Remarks on the Signs and Causes of the Expansion of Trade   .   232

CHAPTER XVI

ELIZABETHAN ENGLAND

142. Prosperity and Pauperism   234
143. The Restoration of the Currency.   235
144. The Growth of Manufactures   236
145. Monopolies of Manufacturing Towns   239
146. Exports of Manufactures and Foreign Trade   .   .   .   240
147. The Flemish Immigration   241
148. Monopolies   242
149. The Revival of the Craft Gilds   246
150. Agriculture   247
151. Social Comforts   250
152. The Condition of the Labourers   251
153. Assessment of Wages by Justices.   The First Poor Law   .   253
154. The Working of the Assessment System   .   .   .   255
155. The Law of Apprenticeship   259
156. The Elizabethan Poor Law   260
157. Population   263

CHAPTER XVII

PROGRESS OF AGRICULTURE IN THE SEVENTEENTH AND EIGHTEENTH
CENTURIES

158. Résumé of Progress since Thirteenth Century   .   .   .   265
159. Progress in James I.'s Reign.   Influence of Landlords   .   .   266
160. Writers on Agriculture. Improvements. Game   .   .   267
161. Drainage of the Fens   268
162. Rise of Price of Corn and of Rent   269
163. Special Features of the Eighteenth Century. Popularity of
     Agriculture   270
164. Improvements of Cattle, and in the Productiveness of Land.
     Statistics   271
165. Survivals of Primitive Culture. Common Fields .   .   273
166. Great Increase of Enclosures   274
167. Benefits of Enclosures as Compared with the Old Common Fields   275
168. The Decay of the Yeomanry   276
169. Causes of the Decay of the Yeomanry   278
170. The Rise in Rent   279
171. The Fall in Wages   280

CHAPTER XVIII

COMMERCE AND WAR IN THE SEVENTEENTH AND EIGHTEENTH CENTURIES

SECTION   PAGE

172. England a Commercial Power 284
173. The Beginnings of the Struggle with Spain . . . 285
174. Cromwell's Commercial Wars and the Navigation Acts . . 286
175. The Wars of William III. and of Anne 288
176. English Colonies 290
177. Further Wars with France and Spain 291
178. The Struggle for India 293
179. The Conquest of Canada 295
180. Survey of Commercial Progress during these Wars . . 296
181. Commercial Events of the Seventeenth Century (Banking—the Bank of England, National Debt, Restoration of the Currency) 299
182. Other Important Commercial Events (Darien Scheme, Union of England and Scotland, Methuen Treaty, Speculation and the South Sea Bubble) 801

CHAPTER XIX

MANUFACTURES AND MINING

183. Circumstances Favourable to English Manufactures . . 805
184. Wool Trade. Home Manufactures. Dyeing . . . 805
185. Other Influences Favourable to England. The Huguenot Immigration 807
186. Distribution of the Cloth Trade 808
187. Coal Mines 810
188. Development of Coal Trade: Seventeenth and Eighteenth Centuries 811
189. The Iron Trade 812
190. Pottery 814
191. Other Mining Industries 815
192. The Close of the Period of Manual Industries . . . 816

PERIOD V

THE INDUSTRIAL REVOLUTION AND MODERN ENGLAND

CHAPTER XX

THE EVE OF THE REVOLUTION

193. Industry and Politics. Landowners and Merchant Princes . 821
194. The Coming of the Capitalists 824
195. The Class of Small Manufacturers 826
196. The Condition of the Manufacturing Population . . 827

SECTION PAGE
197. Two Examples of Village Life 328
198. Condition of the Agricultural Population . . . 331
199. Growth of Population 332
200. England still mainly Agricultural 334
201. The Domestic System of Manufacture . . . 336

CHAPTER XXI

THE EPOCH OF THE GREAT INVENTIONS

202. The Suddenness of the Revolution and its Importance . . 341
203. The Great Inventors 343
204. The Revolution in Manufactures and the Factories . . 347
205. The Growth of Population and the Development of the Northern
Districts 349
206. The Revolution in the Mining Industries . . . 352
207. The Improvements in Communications 354
208. The Nation's Wealth and its Wars 356

CHAPTER XXII

WARS, POLITICS, AND INDUSTRY

209. England's Industrial Advantages in 1763 . . . 358
210. The Mercantile Theory 359
211. The Mercantile Theory in Practice 361
212. English Policy towards the Colonies 364
213. Attempts to raise a Revenue from America . . . 367
214. Outbreak of War 368
215. The Great Continental War 370
216. Its Effects upon Industry and the Working Classes . . 372
217. Politics among the Working Classes 376
218. Political Results of the Industrial Revolution . . . 378

CHAPTER XXIII

THE FACTORY SYSTEM AND ITS RESULTS

219. The Results of the Introduction of the Factory System . . 381
220. Machinery and Hand Labour 383
221. Loss of Rural Life and of Bye-Industries . . . 385
222. Contemporary Evidence of the New Order of Things . . 387
223. English Slavery. The Apprentice System . . . 388
224. The Beginning of the Factory Agitation 391
225. Efforts towards Factory Reform 392
226. Richard Oastler 393
227. Factory Agitation in Yorkshire. For and Against . . 395
228. Ten Hours' Day and Mr Sadler 397
229. The Evidence of Facts 398
230. English Slavery 400
231. The Various Factory Acts 403
232. How these Acts were Passed 404

CHAPTER XXIV

THE CONDITION OF THE WORKING CLASSES

SECTION   PAGE
233. Disastrous Effects of the New Industrial System   .   .   407
234. The Allowance System of Relief   408
235. The Growth of Pauperism and the Old Poor Law   .   .   410
236. The Poor Law and the Allowance System   .   .   .   412
237. Restrictions upon Labour   415
238. The Combination Acts   416
239. Growth of Trades Unions   419
240. The Working Classes Fifty Years Ago   421
241. Wages   424

CHAPTER XXV

THE RISE AND DEPRESSION OF MODERN AGRICULTURE

242. Services Rendered by the Great Landowners   .   .   .   427
243. The Agricultural Revolution   430
244. The Stimulus caused by the Bounties   .   .   .   433
245. Agriculture under Protection   435
246. Improvements in Agriculture   436
247. The Depression in Modern Agriculture   439
248. The Causes of the Depression (lack of capital, rents, lack of adaptability, lack of education and scientific methods)   .   441
249. The Labourer and the Land   445
250. The Condition of the Labourer   447
251. The Present Condition of British Agriculture .   .   .   450

CHAPTER XXVI

MODERN INDUSTRIAL ENGLAND

252. The Growth of our Industry   454
253. State of Trade in 1820   455
254. The Beginnings of Free Trade   456
255. Revolution in the Means of Transit   .   .   .   458
256. Modern Developments   459
257. Our Colonies   461
258. England and other Nations' Wars   463
259. Present Difficulties. Commercial Crises   464
260. Commercial Crises since 1865   466
261. The Recent Depression in Trade   467
262. The Present Mercantile System. Foreign Markets   .   .   469
263. Over-production and Wages   470
264. The Power of Labour. Trades Unions and Co-operation. Labour Politics   471
265. The Necessity of Studying Economic Factors in History   .   473

LIST OF MAPS

1. PHYSICAL ASPECT OF ENGLAND IN SAXON AND NORMAN
   TIMES . . . . *To face page* 65

2. PLAN OF A TYPICAL VILLAGE . . . *On page* 84

3. THE DISTRIBUTION OF WEALTH IN ENGLAND IN 1503 *To face page* 196

4. THE DISTRIBUTION OF WEALTH IN ENGLAND IN 1636 ,, 263

5. INDUSTRIAL ENGLAND, 1700-1750 (SHOWING POPU-
   LATION AND MANUFACTURES) . . . ,, 350

6. INDUSTRIAL ENGLAND IN 1895 (SHOWING POPULATION
   AND MANUFACTURES) . . . ,, 454

PERIOD I

EARLY HISTORY, FROM PRE-HISTORIC TIMES
TO THE NORMAN CONQUEST

A

INDUSTRY IN ENGLAND

CHAPTER I

PRE-ROMAN BRITAIN

§ 1. *Industrial History.*

THE history of a nation's industry must necessarily date
back to pre-historic times and to the earliest stages of national
life. For the history of industry is the history of civilisation,
and a nation's economic development must, to a large extent,
underlie and influence the course of its social and political
progress. Hence it has been aptly remarked [1] that there is
no fact in a nation's history but has some traceable bearing
on the industry of the time, and no fact that can be
altogether ignored as if it were unconnected with industrial
life. " The progress of mankind is written in the history
of its tools ; " [2] and to the economic historian the transition
from the axehead of stone to that of bronze is quite as
important as a change of dynasty ; and certainly, in its way,
it is as serious an industrial revolution as the change from
the hand-loom to machinery. There are, indeed, few studies
more interesting than that in which we watch how a nation
developes in economic progress, passing from one stage of
industrial activity to another, till at length it reaches the
varied and multitudinous complexity of toil that forms our
present system of industry and commerce. During this
progress the necessities of its trade and manufactures bring
it into contact with the politics of other nations in a manifold
and often a curious variety of ways, and thus political history
gains fresh interest and a clearer light from causes which, in
themselves, are often neglected as obscure or insignificant.

§ 2. *The English Nation and Country.*

Now, in dealing with the history of England, or indeed

---

[1] Cunningham, *Growth of Industry*, I. p. 7.
[2] Walpole, *Land of Home Rule*, p. 15.   3

with that of any other nation, there are two fixed data which must always be considered first, namely, the people and their country. So much has been said about the special fitness of the people and country of England for the pursuits of industry and commerce that we are apt to forget that this fitness has only been discovered in very recent times, and that, till the days of Elizabeth, the English were far behind several other European nations, if not in economic development, at any rate in economic supremacy. It is, in fact, useful to remind ourselves that England is not inhabited by a naturally inventive nation,[1] and that we owe most of our progress in the arts and manufactures to foreign influences. The causes, moreover, of English supremacy and commerce in the nineteenth century are almost as recent as that supremacy itself, and, with one great exception—the application of steam-power to industry—reside more in the natural advantages of the country than in the natural ingenuity of the nation.

But since the dawn of history both people and country have undergone many and remarkable changes, and, indeed, few things are more essential to an adequate understanding of the English people and their economic progress than a recognition of the fact that they consist of an exceedingly mixed population. Like a palimpsest which has been used over and over again, the general surface of English characteristics presents to the historical inquirer, in a more or less blurred condition, the traces of Teutonic, Roman, Celtic, and even pre-historic races, who have each contributed their quota to the economic progress of the nation and to the physical peculiarities of the individual. To take but one instance, the agricultural development of this country was for centuries profoundly affected by the manorial system, and in the village community upon which this was based we can see survivals of each of the waves of conquest which passed over the land, while beneath and below them all remain, as crystallised relics of a pre-historic age, strange customs and habits of a primitive race that lead us back in thought to the earliest dawn of civilised institutions.

It will not, therefore, be altogether out of place if we attempt to obtain some slight idea of those early races who

[1] Rogers, *Econ. Interp. of History*, ch. xiii.

inhabited England long before it had gained its present name, or had even received its Romanised-Celtic appellation of Britannia. For whole races of mankind are rarely, if ever, entirely annihilated; "the blood of the conquerors must in time become mixed with that of the conquered; and the preservation of men for slaves and women for wives will always insure the continued existence of the inferior race, however much it may lose of its original appearance, manners, or language."[1] The pre-historic populations of the British Isles left traces for centuries upon our agricultural industry and village customs, so that the more detailed study and wider recognition of their survivals into modern times are not merely the idle interest of an unscientific curiosity. The strange persistence of early or inferior races and institutions amid the most devastating wars and most overwhelming invasions is one of the most remarkable features of history;[2] and the intelligent recognition of this fact in recent times has done much to enlarge and correct our conceptions of human progress. Many an agricultural labourer of to-day shows in the cast of his features and shape of his head a continuity of descent from the pre-historic inhabitants of his native land beside which the pedigree traced from a Norman noble fades into the insignificance of modernity.

§ 3. The Aboriginal Inhabitants of Britain.

Now, at the earliest period to which the written records of classical writers take us back, there seems to have been living in Britain a population originating from no less than three stocks. "The civilised Gauls had settled on the eastern coasts before the Roman invasions began, and were to spread across the island before the Roman conquest was complete. The Celts of an older migration were established towards the north and west, and ruled from the Gaulish settlements as far as the Irish Sea; and here and there we find traces of still older peoples who are best known as the tomb-builders and the constructors of the pre-historic monuments."[3] Of these three stocks the aboriginal was

---

[1] Elton, Origins, ch. i.   [2] Cf. Dawkins, Early Man in Britain, p. 331.
[3] Elton, Origins, p. 93.

that of the Iberians or Ivernians, the oldest Neolithic race known in Europe, a small, dark-haired, dolichocephalic people. These were already retreating before an immigration of Celtic peoples, but seem to have also amalgamated with the immigrating race to a considerable extent, and, being thus preserved from absolute extinction, have survived to our own day.[1] These aborigines were known to the Romans under the name of Silures,[2] and, like the Goidels of the first Celtic immigration,[3] were in the Neolithic stage of culture. Their industry and mode of life has been reconstructed for us with marvellous care and fidelity by the labours of Professor Boyd Dawkins.[4] He concludes that the population was probably large, and divided into tribal communities, who certainly possessed fixed habitations—not only caves, but log-huts and wooden houses—and, though living principally on their flocks and herds and the game of the vast forests, they were by no means unacquainted with the arts of agriculture. The implements by which their building and agricultural operations were carried on were only of stone, but they seemed to have been used very skilfully. Indeed, the use of the stone axe marks a distinct epoch in the history of industry, for by it man was enabled "to win his greatest victory over nature," by cutting down the trees of the vast primeval forests in order to make a clearing for tilling the ground and building his house. The arts of spinning and weaving[5] were also introduced into Europe and Britain in the Neolithic age, and were preserved, in the more remote districts, with but little variation until the quite modern introduction of more complicated machinery. Flint-mining and pottery-making were also carried on, and the art of boat-building[6] had proceeded sufficiently to allow of voyages being made [in canoes] from France to Britain and from Britain to Ireland. It is also evident that the Neolithic tribes of Britain had

---

[1] Cf. Rhys, Celtic Britain, p. 275.—"Skulls are harder than consonants, and races lurk behind when languages slink away. The lineal descendants of the Neolithic aborigines are ever among us, possibly even those of a still earlier race."

[2] Tac., Agric., c. xi.   [3] Cf. Rhys, Celtic Britain, p. 213.
[4] Early Man in Britain, ch. viii. p. 290.   [5] Ib., p. 275.   [6] Ib., p. 290.

commercial intercourse one with another, though of course only in the rude and primitive form of barter ;[1] for stone axes and other implements are found distributed over districts very far removed from the places in which they were made. That this sort of traffic was carried on over considerable distances is also proved from the fact that axes of jade[2] are found in Britain where that material was quite unknown.

§ 4. *Their Social and Economic Condition.*

The social condition of the people in this period seems to have been very much like that of the tribes of Central Africa at the present time. They were divided into tribal communities, generally at war one with another, though each tribe probably obeyed its own chief, " whose dominion was limited to the pastures and cultivated lands protected by his fort, and extended but a little way into the depths of the forests, which were the hunting ground common to him and his neighbours." Each community inhabited a sort of clearing in the forests that overspread the land, and grew a few patches of flax for spinning or small-eared wheat for food ;[3] but the flocks and herds must have constituted their chief property. From the possession of such property social differences must very early have arisen ; and the variation in the size and shape of their burial places goes to show that even in those pre-historic times property was by no means equally distributed.

The flocks and herds here mentioned consisted of pigs, sheep, goats, and oxen, all of which were domesticated in the Neolithic period. Of oxen, two or three breeds were known in Europe, though in Britain " the small, delicately-shaped Celtic shorthorn "[4] was the sole domestic ox as late as the English conquest. In the fields there were no less than eight kinds of cereals (including varieties of wheat, barley, and millet) and " several of our most familiar seeds and fruits [*e.g.*, peas, apples, pears, plums] grew in the Neolithic gardens and orchards,"[5] though all were

---

[1] *Cf.* Solinus, c. 24, speaking of the Silures of Wales in Roman times : "They will have no markets or money, but give and take in kind, getting what they want by barter and not by sale."

[2] *Early Man*, p. 281.　　[3] *Ib.*, p. 272.　　[4] *Ib.*, p 297.　　[5] *Ib.*, p. 301.

smaller and nearer to their wild forms than those now known. Since this Neolithic age we have done little but progress on lines which the primitive workers of Britain and Europe began. " To the Neolithic peoples we owe the rudiments of the culture which we ourselves enjoy. The arts which they introduced have never been forgotten, and all subsequent progress has been built upon their foundation. Their cereals are still cultivated by the farmer, their domestic animals still minister to us, and the arts of which they possessed only the rudiments have developed into the industries —spinning, weaving, pottery-making, mining—without which we can scarcely recognise what our lives would be."[1]

§ 5. *The Bronze Age and the Celtic Immigration.*

The Neolithic age survived in remote parts of Britain almost unchanged into Roman times, for the Silures who fought so desperately against the Romans in Wales were still in this stage of culture.[2] But, disregarding these exceptional tribes, it is clear that culture, civilisation, and industry all made vast and rapid strides when the Bronze age succeeded that of stone, and the little stone axes were superseded by those of metal. Whether the Celts of the first Celtic immigration brought implements and weapons of bronze with them, as Professor Boyd Dawkins seems to think,[3] or whether these Celts were, like the Iberians, still in the stone age of culture when they first came to Britain,[4] it is certain that, before the second Celtic immigration took place the bronze age had long since begun. And the bronze axe marked a new epoch. The forest trees were now more easily cut down, and further clearings were made for agricultural operations. Wild animals became scarcer with the invasion of the forests, and men had to rely less upon the chase and more upon agriculture for their food. With the progress of agriculture came a step upward in civilisation. Habitations, too, became larger and were better built;[5] the arts of spinning and weaving both flax and wool were carried on more successfully;[6] the harvest

[1] *Early Man*, p. 308.   [2] Elton, *Origins*, p. 138.   [3] *Early Man*, p. 342.
[4] So Taylor, *Origin of the Aryans*, p. 128.   [5] *Early Man*, p. 352.
[6] *Ib.*, p. 359.

was now gathered with bronze reaping-hooks;[1] and the smith became an important craftsman with a comparatively large array of tools.[2] Mining was now more easily carried on, and it is probable that Cornish tin, and Irish and Welsh gold,[3] were worked by the natives of Britain and found their way to the Greek and Phenician traders of the Mediterranean through Gaul to the port of Massilia. As yet these southern merchants had not yet ventured as far as our coasts, and the adventurous voyage of Pytheas (B.C. 330 ?) was yet to come. But the inhabitants of the Britain of this period were possessed of an appreciable degree of civilisation. "It is clear," says Elton,[4] "that they were not mere savages, or a nation of hunters and fishers, or even a people in the pastoral and migratory stage. The tribes had learned the simpler arts of society, and had advanced towards the refinements of civilised life. . . . They were, for instance, the owners of flocks and herds ; they knew enough of weaving to make clothes of linen and wool ; and without the potter's wheel they could mould a plain and useful kind of earthenware. The stone *querns* or hand-mills, and the seed-beds in terraces on the hills of Wales and Yorkshire, show their acquaintance with the growth of some kind of grain, while their pits and hut-circles prove that they were sufficiently civilised to live in regular villages."

The Bronze age was succeeded by that of Iron, but the pre-historic Iron Age in Britain was probably of much shorter duration than that of bronze.[5] " It is represented principally by the contents of an insignificant number of tombs, and by numerous isolated articles." But now the small isolated communities of the Neolithic age are becoming welded together into larger bodies, obedient to one rule ; [6] civilisation becomes much higher, and commerce

[1] *Early Man*, p. 360.   [2] *Ib.*, p. 385.
[3] *Ib.*, p. 421.   [4] *Origins*, p. 145.
[5] Dr Evans places the beginning of the bronze age in Britain between 1400 and 1200 B.C., and thinks that iron swords were used in the south of Britain soon after the fourth or fifth century B.C. In the third or second century B.C. bronze had practically fallen into disuse for cutting implements.—Evans, *Ancient Bronze Implements*, pp. 471, 472.
[6] *Early Man*, p. 426.

increases, till at length we come out of the mists of antiquity into the clearer dawn of history, and the pre-historic period is at an end.

§ 6. *Résumé: The Peoples of Early Britain.*

We have thus seen that originally, during the greater part of the stone age, Britain was inhabited by the short, dark, Iberian race, and that towards the end of that period it was invaded by a tall and fair Celtic people, who either brought with them, or before long acquired, implements and weapons of metal.[1] It is also probable[2] that there were two Celtic invasions of Britain, the first that of the Goidels, who spread into Scotland and Ireland, often amalgamating with the aborigines, and the second that of the Brythones, who seized the more fertile portions of the island, in the south and south-east, and drove the others before them into the west and north. These Brythones included the Gaulish tribes mentioned by Cæsar[3] as having crossed over from Belgic territories into Britain not very long before his own invasion of that country, "though there are signs that an immigration from Belgium had been proceeding for several generations" previously.[4] There were thus, for some time before the Roman invasion of Cæsar (B.C. 55), peoples of three different stocks living together in Britain. There were the more or less civilised Gauls in the eastern portions, who had come over long before the Roman period, and gradually, both before and during the Roman occupation, spread across the island in a northerly and southerly direction. Then there were, in the north and west of the island, the civilised Celts of an older migration, whose territories stretched from the Gaulish settlements to the Irish Sea, and included both Goidels and Brythones. And, lastly, here and there in many localities, among the other tribes, we constantly come upon survivors of the older and pre-historic tribes of a much remoter period.

§ 7. *Their Social and Economic Condition.*

It must not, however, be imagined that any uniform

---

[1] Taylor, *Origin of Aryans*, p. 80.   [2] Rhys, *Celtic Britain*, p. 213, and map.
[3] *B. G.*, ii. 4, and v. 14.   [4] Elton, *Origins*, p. 102.

description will apply to the industrial or social development of these different races. They were all in various stages of civilisation, and though commercial, and possibly social, intercourse between them was not uncommon, they remained for centuries with their distinguishing features unobliterated. The oldest races were in the pre-metallic stage ;[1] the British Celts were in the later Bronze period on their first arrival, and possibly became acquainted with the use of iron later, while the more recent Gaulish arrivals were certainly familiar with iron implements and weapons. We are prepared, therefore, to find great dissimilarity of culture among the varied population of Britain in the pre-Roman period. The oldest races were really little other than savages in their mode of life—at any rate, in those remote regions to which they had retreated before the successive Celtic invasions. Where they had come in contact with their more civilised neighbours they were, however, probably not so wild or degraded as the descriptions of Greek and Roman writers of that day seem to imply.[2] But they do not seem to have had regular towns, houses, or fields, though they kept flocks and herds. They depended very largely on hunting for their subsistence, and also on the natural products of the woods, such as wild fruits and nuts. Dion Cassius mentions their strange refusal to eat the fish with which British rivers were at that time swarming, and it is curious to notice, as showing how pre-historic customs have persisted into our own time, that in certain Irish and Highland localities this prejudice still exists.[3]

§ 8. *The Celts in the time of Pytheas.*

The condition of the Celtic invaders has already been alluded to in the remarks made above[4] on the industries of the Bronze Age, but we may here briefly add the information derived from the observations of the Greek explorer Pytheas, who started from the Greek colony of Massalia (Marseilles) about 330 B.C. to explore " the Celtic countries " of the north. He was commissioned by a committee of the

[1] Elton, *Origins*, p. 122.
[2] *Cf.* Dion Cassius (Xiphiline), lxxvi. 12; Claudian, *B. Getic,* 417; Solinus, c. 4.　　　　[3] Elton, p 165.　　　[4] Above, p. 8.

Massalian merchants to discover the sources of the lucrative tin trade, the secret of which had hitherto been jealously guarded by the Carthaginians, who monopolised it. The narrative of his voyage is for us of peculiar interest, for its fragments contain the first notices of what was then an almost unknown land ;[1] while the fact that the Massalians thought the tin trade of such importance as to warrant the expense of an exploring expedition is a proof of the activity of the foreign commerce of pre-historic Britain. Pytheas, on reaching Britain, which he first touched on the shores of Kent, not only landed there, but travelled over part of the country on foot to collect information about the tin trade. He almost certainly went westward, passing through what is now Wiltshire and South Hampshire— then a great forest district — to Cornwall. " Here he found the country of the tin, which was dug out of the ground in mines with shafts and galleries. The people were very hospitable, their commerce with foreign merchants having civilised them and softened their manners."[2] The tin thus mined was carried six days' journey to an island called Ictis,[3] whence the traders from Gaul conveyed it across the Channel into Gaul, and finally down the Rhone in barges to Massalia. Besides tin-mining, Pytheas found a fairly considerable agriculture, observing " an abundance of wheat in the fields," though, owing to the moist nature of the climate and lack of regular sunshine, the sheaves had to

[1] The statements of Pytheas, recorded as they are only by his critics, have been received both in ancient and modern times with considerable scepticism, but there seems, after a careful review of them, little reason to doubt their substantial accuracy. See especially C. R. Markham's paper on *Pytheas, the discoverer of Britain*, in *The Geographical Journal*, Vol. I. No. 6, where his observations are vindicated from a geographical standpoint.

[2] *Cf.* Diodorus Siculus, c. 22. This account was almost certainly taken from Timaeus, who derived it from Pytheas.

[3] Where "Ictis" was situated is still a subject of controversy. Elton thinks it was Thanet (p. 35-37), Sir E. Bunbury and Captain Markham think it was St Michael's Mount. Professor Rhys (*Celtic Britain*, 46, 47) inclines to Thanet. This latter view certainly explains Caesar's story that the tin " nascitur in mediterraneis regionibus," and also explains why Pytheas on touching the coast at Kent had to travel westwards, seeing on his way the temple of Stonehenge, very early reports of which reached the Greek. But Elton doubts his being in those parts.

be thrashed in "great barns."[1] The natives possessed also "cultivated fruits, a great abundance of some domesticated animals but a scarcity of others, and made a beverage from wheat and honey,"[2] the "metheglin" of some country districts in the present day. That the state of agriculture was, however, very backward in some districts (probably those occupied by the older inhabitants), we gather from Posidonius,[3] who visited Britain in the first century B.C., and related that the " people have mean habitations made chiefly of rushes or sticks, and their harvest consists in cutting off the ears of corn and storing them in pits underground," using it from day to day. But, on the other hand, agriculture was well advanced in the Gaulish settlements of the South and East. "The British Gauls," says Elton,[4] "appear to have been excellent farmers, skilled as well in the production of cereals as in stock-raising and the management of the dairy. Their farms were laid out in large fields without enclosures or fences, and they learned to make a permanent separation of the pasture and arable, and to apply the manures which were appropriate to each kind of field. The plough was of the wheeled kind, an invention that superseded the old ' overtreading plough ' held down by the driver's foot." A remarkable proof of their advanced knowledge was shown in the practice of marling. " They relied greatly on marling and chalking the land. The same soil, however, was never twice chalked, as the effects were visible after standing the experience of fifty years. The effect of the ordinary marl was of even longer duration, the benefit being visible in some instances for a period of eighty years." Many varieties of marl were used—the lime-marl, chalk-marl, the red, dove-coloured, sandy, and pumice varieties being all mentioned by Pliny. They had two varieties of cattle—the small Welsh breed or "Celtic shorthorn " and the Kyloe or Argyllshire variety—as well as sheep, pigs, and fowls.[5] It is worthy of notice, in view of landed customs which we shall have to note in later times, that there is no trace among them of co-operative husbandry.

---

[1] Strabo, iv., v. 5. (*Cas.* 201). [2] *Ib.* [3] See Diodorus, v. 21.
[4] Elton, pp. 115-116. [5] *Ib.*, pp. 116-117.

The Gauls were likewise expert not only in agricultural but also in textile manufactures of a simple kind in cloth and linen. "They wove their stuffs for summer, and rough felts or druggets for winter wear,[1] which are said to have been prepared with vinegar, and to have been so tough as to resist the stroke of a sword. They had learned the art of using alternate colours for the warp and woof, so as to bring out a pattern of stripes and squares," and obviously of dyeing the materials.

We see, then, from a survey of the various inhabitants of Britain in pre-Roman times, that they had reached in some parts a very fair degree of industrial development, especially in agriculture, though in other districts they were equally backward. Manufactures and mining [2] were in progress, and the latter had given rise to what must have been for those times a considerable foreign commerce, though this was confined to the southern coasts. It is not easy, perhaps, to gain a general survey of the country, because the conditions of culture in the various districts and among the different races were so diverse, and this diversity was at once a consequence and a cause of the difficulties of communication. But though we cannot in this period make any industrial generalisations, we may be certain that its industrial conditions left some marks on future ages, and that any consideration of post-Roman civilisation and customs —especially in the permanent and abiding influences of agriculture—must necessarily be imperfect if it fails to take into account the survivals of the pre-historic period.

§ 9. *Foreign Trade of Britain.*

It was the conquest of Gaul that brought the Romans of Julius Cæsar's day close to the shores of Britain, and it was mainly from the reports of Gaulish traders that Cæsar derived not only his knowledge of that country but also his

---

[1] Elton, pp. 110, 111.

[2] The tin districts of the time of Pytheas and Posidonius, *i.e.* in the third and first centuries B.C., are given by Elton, p. 33, as Dartmoor, the country round Tavistock and round St Austell, the southern coast of Cornwall, the district round St Agnes on the north coast, and between Cape Cornwall and St Ives.

desire to conquer it. The Romans evidently thought the conquest worth making for the sake of the possible wealth that might accrue from it, for the inhabitants of Britain were hardly formidable enough politically to threaten the Roman frontiers in Gaul. Probably they expected more from the island than they actually obtained,[1] and, as Elton remarks,[2] "the ultimate conquest was doubtless hastened by the dream of winning a land of gold and a rich reward of victory." But although we may admit that the Romans entertained exaggerated hopes, we may glance for a moment at the actual state of trade in Britain in the days before their arrival.

It is obvious, in the first place, that the Phenicians and Carthaginians, and—after the voyage of Pytheas—also the Greeks, would not have made their long and dangerous voyages to Britain for tin unless the supplies of that metal had been sufficiently large to make it well worth their while, especially as it was procurable also in Spain. Hence the British tin trade must have been of considerable dimensions for those times. It is equally obvious that the foreign traders must have brought other goods to exchange for tin, since the British were in that stage of civilisation when barter comes naturally to the uncommercial mind, and the use of coined money was little understood.[3] Besides tin, it is certain that the gold which is found with tin in Cornwall, and the silver which is also mingled with the lead, formed articles of export. Iron was also exported,[4] especially when the Gauls of the later immigration began to work the mines of the Weald of Kent. Besides metals, we find mention of agricultural and pastoral produce, corn and barley, cattle and hides; and the trade in the special British breed of hunting dogs,[5] both with Gaul and Rome, was of some importance. The pearl fishery, of which we hear so much from Bede, was probably greatly exaggerated, since Tacitus mentions British pearls only to slight them, and it is improbable that it should not have continued till

---

[1] Tac., *Agric.*, 12.   [2] *Origins*, p. 293.
[3] For these imports, see p. 16.   [4] Cæsar, B. G., v. 12.
[5] Martial, *Epigram.* xiv. 200; Claudian, *Stil.*, iii. 301.

much later times if it had been lucrative. On the other hand, the slave trade was an important feature, especially after the Roman conquest. Among the most ancient articles of commerce was almost certainly amber, of which small quantities were found on certain portions of the British coast ; but the British supply is too small to account for the great quantity found in the *tumuli*,[1] and hence it must have formed an important article of import from the North Sea and Baltic shores. Very probably the Phenician and other traders found it a useful medium of exchange, and under the Roman Empire the import from the Ostians [2] was sufficient to bear a tax which yielded a small revenue.[3] Ivory, bracelets (and certainly other ornaments), glass, and " such-like petty merchandise," are all mentioned by Strabo [4] as being imported, and his statements indicate the kind of trade that must have gone on for centuries before his time. Weapons of all kinds would find a ready sale in the island, while furs and the skins of wild animals, of which there were very large numbers in Britain, were exported. Speaking generally we may say that, although the Britains were able to manufacture implements, weapons, pottery, and clothing for themselves, yet the foreign trade was necessarily an exchange of foreign manufactured articles for raw produce, and continued for many centuries to be of this nature.

§ 10. *Internal Trade : Roads and Rivers.*

The means of communication by which trade was carried on internally were the rivers, the " ridge ways "[5] or roads on the open ground at the top of ridges of hills—of which the High Street in the Lake district, afterwards a Roman road, is a very good example—and other rough tracks. The first road-makers were the wild animals migrating to early pastures and the savages who followed them.[6] But the place of rivers in the commercial history of the early and middle ages was most important, since, till good roads were made,

[1] *Cf.* Elton, p. 63.
[2] They occupied the district near the mouth of the Elbe, though Dr Latham places them further east.
[3] Strabo, iv. 278.   [4] *Ib.*   [5] *Social England*, vol. i. p. 88.
[6] Thorold Rogers, *Econ. Int. of History*, p. 490.

carriage by water was far less troublesome and expensive than by land,[1] and it has been well remarked[2] that the rivers Thames and Severn were of prime importance to the development of early British trade.[3] Down these rivers the British trader floated in his frail coracle or "curragh" of hides, and even ventured to cross over from the western coasts to Ireland.[4] The people of the southern and Cornish shore had, however, ships of oak of a much more seaworthy character, and evidently, from Cæsar's account,[5] were skilful and daring navigators. They traded chiefly with Northern and Western Gaul.

§ 11. *Physical Aspect of Pre-Roman Britain.*

Having gained some idea of the industry and commerce of early Britain, it is now time to glance briefly at the physical condition of the country which the Romans were about to conquer. We are struck at once by the fact that its appearance was vastly different from the aspect which it wears to-day. The typical English landscape of the present, with its smiling pasturage, neat hedges, and well-tilled fields, simply did not then exist, or, at any rate, was to be seen only in a few favoured spots. Whereas to-day the cultivable and cultivated area includes the greater part of the surface, it was at that time only a small fraction of it. Forests and scrub, fen, moor, and marsh occupied most of the land. "A cold and watery desert" is Elton's description of it,[6] and though his expression is exaggerated, it is nearer the truth than another writer's fanciful epithet[7] of a "land of sunshine and pearls." Britain was certainly far more rainy then than now, owing

---

[1] So, too, in Europe the main commercial routes followed in France the Rhine, and in Germany the Rhone and Danube; see my *Commerce in Europe*, §§ 68, 69. [2] *Social England*, vol. i. p. 89.

[3] In this commerce coins were probably not much used, and it is supposed that no British coins were struck before 200 B.C., though some are said to appear to be "centuries older than Cæsar's first expedition." Later on the various chiefs seem to have struck silver and other coins for their own tribes in imitation of Gallic and Roman money. *Cf.* Evans, *Coins of the Ancient Britons*, for a subject which we cannot discuss properly here.

[4] Elton, p. 232. [5] Cæsar, B. G., iii. 9, 13.
[6] *Origins*, p. 218. [7] In *Social England*, vol. i. p. 89.

to the influence of the vast forests which covered the land, and consequently also it was more foggy. "The ground and atmosphere were alike overloaded with moisture. The fallen timber obstructed the streams; the rivers were squandered in the reedy morasses, and only the downs and hill-tops rose above the perpetual tracts of wood." [1] It was these downs and hill-tops on which the earliest inhabitants, unable to clear the forests effectually with their feeble axes, necessarily practised the first elements of agriculture,[2] and it is here that their traces are most abundant. The gradual clearing away of the woodland in later, and especially in Roman, times drew the agriculturist down into the river valleys. The extent of forest was immense. In the South there were more than a hundred miles of the "Andredsweald" between Hampshire and the Medway, and many miles more in the opposite direction into Dorset and Wiltshire. In the Severn valley was the forest of the Wyre, around the modern Worcester, extending right over Cheshire, and the forest of Arden nearly covered all Warwickshire. Another huge wood lay between London and the Wash; the Midlands from Lincoln to Leicester and from the Peak to the Trent were occupied by miles of forest, of which Sherwood and Charnwood are only fractional and fragmentary remains. Yorkshire and Lancashire were wild wastes of moorland and scrub, and most of the country was regarded as a desert that lay between Derby Peak and the Roman Wall.[3]

The marshes and swamps were also of considerable extent in many low-lying parts that have since been drained and reclaimed. Notably this was the case with the Romney Marsh on the coast of Kent, which, when Caesar came to Britain, was a morass invaded every day by the tide as far as Robertsbridge in Sussex.[4] The low-lying parts of Essex, Surrey, and

[1] Elton, p. 218.

[2] Green, *Making of England*, p. 8; and Gomme, *Village Community*, pp. 75-95, who deals fully with the "terrace cultivation" on the hills.

[3] The above description is based on Green's vivid picture in the *Making of England*, pp. 10-12.

[4] Elton, p. 103.

Kent below London were then "extensive flats covered with water at every tide,"[1] and the Thames estuary invaded a district almost as large as the Wash. The valley of the Stour[1] was also covered by the sea for many miles above the present tidal limit, while the Wash extended northwards nearly to Lincoln and westwards to Huntingdon and Cambridge. The lower reaches of the Trent formed another huge marsh, and its basin generally was one of the wildest and least frequented parts of the island.[2]

In this comparatively wild and uncultivated condition of the country, it is easy to believe that wild animals were exceedingly numerous. In fact, they existed till far into the period of modern history. Wolves and bears were met in the vast forests for centuries after the Roman and Saxon invasions, and only gradually became extinct.[3] The wild boar was very common, and so late as Henry II.'s reign was hunted on Hampstead Heath, where also were chased the wild cattle whose descendants are now regarded as curiosities in the famous herd at Chillingham Park. A sign of the infrequency of human habitation in certain districts is seen in the numbers of beavers that built their colonies on the streams, remaining in remote parts till the twelfth century.[4] Indeed, it is evident that the Britain of pre-Roman days must have been, on the whole, a very wild and savage country, many parts of which had scarcely even been trodden by the foot of man. Yet, as we have seen, there were already in some places, especially in the South-East, many marks of civilisation and progress in industrial arts, and when the Romans came to the island they found many tribes and settlements that were considerably advanced in agricultural and domestic industries, though, on the other

---

[1] Airy, in *Athenæum*, 1683, on the Claudian Invasion of Britain.

[2] *Making of England*, p. 75.

[3] Martial (*Epigr.*, vii. 34), mentions the Scotch bear, and Boyd Dawkins (*Cave Hunting*, p. 75), thinks the native British bear was not extinct till the tenth century A.D. Frequent mention of wolves is found in mediæval documents—*e.g.*, in the account rolls of Whitby Abbey, temp. Ric. II., and they probably were not extinct in England till the end of the fifteenth century. (Newton, *Zoology of Ancient Europe*, p. 24), and in Scotland much later.

[4] Girald. Cambrensis, *Itin. Wall*, ii. 3.

hand, there were others but little removed from savagery. We shall probably be right in supposing that the divergences of culture were very strongly marked, and that a considerable distinction was to be found between the skilled Gaulish farmer of Kent and the wild pre-Aryan inhabitants of the North and West.

CHAPTER II

§ 12. *The Roman Occupation.*

THE two expeditions of Julius Cæsar in the years 55 and
54 B.C.—the first of which was certainly a failure and the
second very nearly so—were followed by almost a century
of repose from foreign invasion. It was not till ninety
years after Cæsar's earlier attempts that the Romans, led
on this occasion by Aulus Plautius, and aided by German
auxiliaries, again invaded Britain (A.D. 44). But this time
they came to stay, and although the conquest proved
perhaps more difficult than they had anticipated, it was
under successive generals accomplished at last. The year
70 A.D. may be taken, for convenience, as the date when
the power of the most stubborn of the natives was effectually broken, and though much fighting remained to be
done, the conquest was practically complete. For seventy
years after the victories of Julius Agricola (A.D. 70-84)
there was peace, and had it not been for the incursions of
the Picts and Scots by land, and of the Saxon pirates by
sea, the peace would have been almost uninterrupted. The
Romans remained as the rulers of Britain for three centuries
and a half, and then the exigencies of self-defence in other
regions of the Empire compelled them to retire. The last
legions left the island in 407 A.D.[1]

It is difficult to estimate the exact effect of their occupation. While some very able writers[2] have found reason
to believe that it had lasting effects both on the political,
municipal, industrial, and especially on the agricultural
development of the country, others have regarded it merely
as a military administration, similar (as we are told with a
rather wearisome paucity of example) to that of the French

[1] Green, *Making of England*, p. 24. The date 410 A.D. is that of the
letter bidding Britain provide for its own defence.

[2] As *e.g.* Coote, in his *Romans in Britain.*

in Algeria.[1] It would probably be nearer the truth to compare the Roman position with that of the English in India, making due allowance for differences of civilisation and of policy. The Romans could no more settle in Britain on account of the cold than we can settle in India on account of the heat. So, too, if the English were to withdraw from India after three hundred years of occupancy (and they will probably retire before that period), the net effect of their presence would be much the same as that of the Romans here. The influence in both cases has been only skin deep, and though it touches the upper classes of the natives very effectually, it hardly affects the lower. Well-to-do British youths went to study and "see life" in Rome, just as well-to-do Hindu and Mahommedan youths come to London, and with much the same result. Prominent natives were occasionally entrusted in Britain with Roman administration, as they are similarly entrusted by us in India. After all, it is mainly the efforts of industry which survive. The customs, laws, and language disappear, and the roads and bridges remain. These, with a number of ruined fortresses, lighthouses,[2] drainage works, and towns which had sprung from camps, are the most important relics of the Roman occupation in Britain.

§ 13. Roman Roads.

We will speak of the roads first, because, especially now, in an age of railways, their importance cannot be over-estimated. They were not all by any means first built by the Romans, but represent in many cases adaptations of and improvements upon Celtic, or even still more ancient,[3] roadways. The roadway over High Street, near Winder-mere, is such an one. But the main function of the Roman roads was, after all, military, and therefore we find them made sometimes more with a view to the military import-ance of certain strategic connections than to the require-ments of commerce. At the same time, after these roads

---

[1] Green, *Making of England*, p. 7, and Pearson, *History of England*, i. 55.
[2] As at Dover, and the Richborough beacon.
[3] *Cf.* Thorold Rogers, *Econ. Interpr. of History*, p. 490.

had been once made, whatever their original purpose may
have been, they were eagerly used by traders, who were
also thankful for the military protection which the roads
enjoyed. "The Roman plan," says Elton,[1] "was based on
the requirements of the provincial government, and on the
need for constant communication between the Kentish ports
and the outlying fortresses on the frontiers." Hence several
of the routes fell into comparative desuetude when the
strategic need for them was gone, and only those which
afforded the greatest facilities for commerce were kept up.
The needs of industry frequently outlive those of war. In
mediæval times we find four great highways traversing the
kingdom of England, and representing "a combination of
those portions of the Roman roads which the English adopted
and kept in repair, as communications between their principal cities." These four great highways were [2] :—

(1.) *Watling Street* (to use its later name), from Kent
to London, and then *viâ* St Albans and Northampton to
Chester and on to York, bifurcating then northwards to
Carlisle and to near Newcastle.

(2.) *The Fosse Way*, from the Cornish tin-mines through
Bath and Cirencester to Lincoln, crossing Watling Street
at High Cross between Coventry and Leicester.

(3.) *Ermin Street*, a direct route from London to Lincoln
through Colchester and Cambridge, and sending out
branches to Doncaster and York.

(4.) *Ikenild* or *Ickenield Street*, whose course is somewhat obscure, and is often confused with Ryknild Street,
which latter led from the Severn valley and Gloucester to
Doncaster. The *Ikenild Street* came from Norwich and
Bury St Edmunds to Dunstable, thence to Southampton,
with branches to Sarum and the western districts.

§ 14. *Roman Towns in Britain.*

Of these, which are commonly called the four *Roman*
ways, the Ikenild Street was almost certainly an ancient

---

[1] *Origins*, p. 327, where the military system of roads is fully explained.

[2] *Cf.* Elton, *Origins*, p. 326, and Guest, *The Four Roman Ways, Archæol.
Journ.*, xiv. p. 99, and also Cooper King in *Social England*, vol. i. pp. 49-51,
who adds others.

British pathway, possibly adapted and used by the Romans, while Ermin Street is thought not to have been Roman south of Huntingdon. There was, however, an important Roman road from London to Richborough (Rutupiæ) on the Kentish coast, then the chief military and commercial port for intercourse with Gaul, and strongly fortified, where on dark nights a beacon always shone to guide ships across the channel. Along all the roads there were frequent fortresses and stationary camps, and it is in many cases from these camps that our English towns have grown up.[1] The towns were divided (constitutionally) into four classes, and the division helps us to understand their relative importance. First came the *coloniæ*, inhabited by Roman veterans, and enjoying the same laws and customs as Rome itself. There were nine of these—Richborough and Reculver, guarding the now filled-up channel of Thanet to the Thames; London, an important trading centre from Celtic times; Colchester; Bath, then as now a noted sanatorium; and Gloucester, Caerleon-on-Usk, Chester, Lincoln, and Chesterfield, all of military importance. Next came the *municipia*, where the inhabitants had the rights of Roman citizens, making their own laws and electing their own magistrates. There were only two of these— York, the northern capital, quite as important in those times as London; and Verulamium (St Albans), which guarded the entrances to the Midlands. Third in order came those towns, ten in number, which had the *Latin right* and elected their own magistrates, and lastly came the *stipendiary* towns, which were governed by Roman officials, and had to pay tribute. This class included all towns not mentioned above—that is to say, nearly the whole population of Britain.[2]

It has been truly said that "the type of every Roman city was the camp,"[3] but it is equally true that "a Roman camp was a city in arms,"[4] in which the soldiers corresponded to the colonists and settlers of more modern times. "The

---

[1] About 218 Roman stations are known in Britain. *Soc. England*, vol. i. p. 62.

[2] Lingard, *Hist. of Eng.*, i. p. 50; Wright, *Celt, Roman, and Saxon*.

[3] Pearson, *Hist. of Eng.*, i. 43.   [4] Elton, *Origins*, p. 310.

ramparts and pathways of the camps developed into walls and streets, the square of the tribunal into the market-place, and every gateway was the beginning of a suburb, where straggling rows of shops, temples, rose-gardens, and cemeteries were delivered from all danger by the presence of a permanent garrison. In the centre of the town stood a group of public buildings, containing the court-house, baths, and barracks, and it seems likely that every important place had a theatre or a circus for races and shows."[1] There were fifty-nine towns[2] that might be called Roman, but the bulk of the population was engaged in agriculture and resided in the country districts, and therefore it is to rural industry that we must now turn our attention.

§ 15. *The Romans and Agriculture.*

It seems doubtful whether the Romans ever settled in sufficient numbers to alter permanently the conditions of agricultural industry, except in a few very favourable neighbourhoods. In the first place the climate was against them, just as it is against the English in India, though from a totally different reason. Just as no Englishman could tolerate life in India without the ever-moving punkah, so no Roman could reside in his English villa unless it was carefully heated by hot-water pipes.[3] Nor did the land offer a chance of making great wealth. "The great number of villas whose remains can still be traced is a proof that the lords of the soil were in easy circumstances, while the fact that the structures were commonly of wood, raised upon a brick or stone foundation, is an argument against large fortunes."[4] The surface of the country, too, was still wild and unreclaimed in many parts, and not suitable for advanced agriculture. The river-valleys, which contain a richer and more fertile soil, were only gradually being cleared of the primeval forest that encumbered them, for it is a significant fact that it is mainly in the natural clearings of the uplands that the population concentrated itself at the close of the Roman rule, and it is over these districts that the ruins of the

[1] Elton, *Origins*, p. 311.   [2] Marcianus, *Heracleota*, ii. 14.
[3] Green, *Making of England*, pp. 7 and 45.
[4] Pearson, *History of England*, i. 52

villas or country houses of the Roman landowners are most thickly planted.[1]   Besides all this, the distance of Britain from the centre of the Roman world was sufficient to prevent a large influx of Roman settlers, and hence it is not at all surprising to find that most of the Roman monuments and inscriptions in our island refer mainly to matters of a military and official character.

At the same time there can be no doubt that those districts where the few Roman settlers did build their villas must have enjoyed many industrial advantages over the more barbarous portions of the island.   Traces of those villas,[2] with their Italian inner courts, colonnades, and tesselated pavements are still found, the household buildings being surrounded by an outer wall, against which were probably built the rude huts of the British peasantry or serfs who tilled the foreigner's land.   But it is not certain that these Roman farmers were responsible for the peculiar features that afterwards distinguished English agricultural and manorial life, and very possibly too much importance has been attached to Roman influence in this respect.   It is going too far to say that, during the Roman period, " England became an agricultural country," and that " the agricultural system then established remained during and after the barbarian invasions." [3]   We know that even before the arrival of Cæsar the Gallic Britons of the south-east were comparatively good farmers (p. 13), and it is sufficient to admit that their agriculture was further developed after the Roman conquest, without assuming the introduction of the Roman agricultural system.

The majority of the remains of Roman villas are found in the southern counties,[4] and, however great their influence undoubtedly was here, it did not extend very far into the interior.   The fact that Britain became celebrated for its export of corn [5] may be taken in more than one way.   Some have regarded it as a proof of good agriculture under Roman influence, others as merely showing that the population was

---

[1] Green, *Making of England*, p. 9.

[2] Wright, *Celt, Roman, and Saxon*, p. 243 and pp. 227 *sq.*

[3] Ashley, Introduction to Coulanges' *Origin of Property in Land*, p. xxiv.

[4] Professor Ashley mentions this himself, p. xxvi.   [5] *Cf. ib.*, p. xxv.

so small that it could not consume all the corn it grew. In any case, " the great private estates surrounding the villas of wealthy landowners, and cultivated by dependants of various grades—*coloni*, freedmen, and slaves " [1]—cannot have been numerous enough to influence the agricultural development of the country as a whole. Had this been the case, we should almost certainly find more traces than we do of the Roman implements of husbandry,[2] which are well-known and continue in use at the present day, with very little difference in their structure, in those countries where Roman influence was most deeply felt. But, as a matter of fact, as Mr Seebohm shows,[3] though he draws a different conclusion therefrom, one of the main features of English husbandry was the plough-team of eight oxen, common to the agriculture of England, Wales and Scotland, but certainly not Roman in origin. Moreover, the remains of the homesteads and houses of early English villages show us that Roman influence never extended very markedly into agricultural buildings. "The villager in his wattle and daub, and the lord in his oak-rooted hall, carry us back to primitive economics within which there is no room for the great commercialism of the Roman world," [4] and it is a significant fact in this connection that the art of making bricks, and building in brick, introduced by the Romans, was never taken up by the agricultural population as a whole, but became extinct after the Roman occupation till its revival in the fifteenth century.[5]

§ 16. *Celtic and Non-Roman Influence in Agriculture.*

The same conclusion—that the Roman occupation had little practical influence with the agricultural industry of the country, except in a few favoured districts [6]—is forced upon

[1] Ashley, as above, p. xxv.
[2] *E.g.* the wheel-plough ; *cf.* Gomme, *Village Community*, p. 277.
[3] Seebohm, *Village Community*, p. 388.
[4] Gomme, *Village Community*, p. 46.
[5] Thorold Rogers, *Econ. Interp. of Hist.*, p. 279.
[6] The extent of the Romanised area is often exaggerated. The North and West were almost untouched by Romans, and no villas are found north of Aldborough in Yorks. See F. T. Richards in *Social England* i. p. 24.

us again by a review of the philological and ethnological evidence, which has hitherto been almost disregarded by economic historians. Where Roman power was greatest in Britain was in the creation of a national government. It hardly so much as entered the life of the agricultural village communities,[1] in which, in spite of the influence of the Romanised towns, the mass of the population of Britain continued to dwell from the first dawn of civilisation till the advent of the factory system and its concomitants. Rome had probably no more effect on the agricultural life of the people of Britain than England has on the methods of the peasant population of India, and when we hear that Britain exported large quantities of corn in the Roman era, we merely note that India exports equally large quantities to England at the present day, without inferring therefrom that the Hindu ryot has adopted English agricultural methods. The agricultural history of our country begins, not with the Roman invasion, but with the pre-historic efforts of those ancient hill-tribes,[2] whose industrial relics still remain for our investigation, and who cultivated their hill-sides in terraces, because these were the only clearings that emerged from the all-pervading primeval forest. This is the reason why the population, even at the close of the Roman period, was most numerous in the uplands.[3] The hillmen gave way to the Celts, though their traces are still among us, and the Celts, with their superior culture, developed agriculture probably almost up to the level at which it was found at the Saxon conquest, and at which it remained for many centuries afterwards. The philological evidence on this point is of considerable interest. An extraordinary number of words in our present language referring to agricultural implements and industry are of Celtic origin, and those are said to be "not a twentieth of what might be alleged."[4] A few instances

---

[1] *Cf.* Gomme, *ut supra*, p. 133.

[2] For a careful investigation of this evidence see Gomme, *Village Community*, pp. 71, 83-95.   [3] Green, *Making of England*, p. 8.

[4] Garnett, in the *Journal of the Philological Society*, i. 171. Among others he instances :—bran (skin of wheat), cabin, gusset (*cf.* Welsh, *cwysed*, ridge or furrow), threave (a bundle of sheaves, W., *drefa*), bill, fleam (W., *flaim*, a cattle lancet), wain, wall, trace, stook (of corn), gavelock (a fork), park (=a field), filly, fog (=fog-grass), basket, &c., &c. *Measures* of

are given in the footnote, and it should also be noticed, as showing the permanence of ancient populations in the rural districts, that many rural or "provincial" terms [1] are Celtic in origin. The survivals of curious customs connected with land, and the evidence of folk-lore generally, must be left to the archæologist; [2] but the student of industrial history cannot fail to notice the persistence of ancient populations, even in a subject condition, and their influence upon industrial life. Very possibly it is to this persistence that the backwardness of English agriculture for so many centuries is largely due. Learning little from the Roman, the native inhabitants of Britain had little to teach the Saxon. Even now, at the close of the nineteenth century, in the remoter districts of Ireland the heir of centuries of Celtic civilisation may be seen ploughing with his rude plough fastened to his horse's tail,[3] while in the Isle of Man a farmer of the present generation sacrificed one of his cattle at the cross roads to cure a plague which was destroying the others.[4] The ethnological evidence has of late been carefully studied, and distinct traces of an earlier (non-Aryan) population have been found in many places, the distinguishing characteristics of this early race being their dark hair, dark eyes, dark skin, and small stature. Such traces are seen in such varying localities as the counties comprising the ancient Siluria — Glamorgan, Brecknock, Monmouth, Radnor, and Hereford—in Cornwall and Devon, and in Gloucester, Wiltshire, and Somerset.[5] We may

grain show Celtic origin—*e.g.*, windle (Lancs. dialect for a measure, from W., *gwyntell*, a basket) hoop (Yorks. for a quarter peck), hattock (Yorks. for a shock of corn), peck (*cf.* W., *peg*). Also flannen (Hereford for flannel), frieze, brat (Yorks. for "pinafore," *cf.* W., *brat*=clout; rag), mesh (*cf.* W., *masg*, a stitch), borel (O.E. for coarse cloth, *cf.* bureler), lath, &c., may be instanced for textile industry. Probably a careful investigation of rural dialects would furnish many more.

[1] Besides provincialisms given above, *cf.* Yorks. *toppin*, a crest or ridge; *sile*, a strainer; Northern *stook*, a shock of corn; Somerset, *soc*, a ploughshare, on which last *cf.* Schrader, *Sprachvergleichung* (Eng. trans.), p. 288.

[2] *Cf.* Gomme, *ut supra*, chs. v. and vi.

[3] The author heard this stated publicly by a Notts farmer who was an eye-witness during a visit to Ireland.

[4] Walpole, *Land of Home Rule*, p. 190 n. This farmer was alive in 1893.

[5] Elton, *Origins*, p. 137, with which *cf.* the note on p. 57 of Cunningham's *English Industry and Commerce*, vol. i.

expect to find survivals in the west, but it is more surprising to discover them still existing in the eastern fen country and in the Midlands—especially round about Derby, Stamford, Leicester, and Loughborough [1] — for here we know, from place names and other evidence, that the Saxon and Danish conquerors settled in overwhelming numbers. But this merely proves how hard it is to destroy a subject population,[2] and if the non-Aryan, pre-Celtic inhabitants of early Britain have thus survived, a fortiori must we make allowance for the survival of the Celtic races who succeeded and conquered them, only to be in turn conquered themselves. The Celtic race, in spite of some modern appearances to the contrary, possesses, under certain circumstances,[3] a considerable power of amalgamation with other races without entirely losing its distinctive characteristics. They amalgamated as conquerors with the Iberians,[4] and as conquered with the Saxon and Scandinavian,[5] and the most recent historian of the Isle of Man, where their influence is so strongly marked, has called attention to their place in the history of culture. "We live in a time when the Celtic race is gradually disappearing. Those parts of Europe where Celtic blood is predominant are those where population is decreasing (as in Ireland) or with difficulty maintained (as in France). Yet we ought not, in consequence, to forget the great part which the Celt has played in history, or the influence which the Celt has exercised in the civilisation of the world."[6] Hitherto, certainly, the economic historian has neglected to note his influence[7] upon English agriculture, an influence which, though at first in favour of progress up to a certain point, was probably afterwards rather conservative

---

[1] Elton, u. s.

[2] Cf. also S. Walpole, Land of Home Rule, p. 14, and also p. 21, for description of the Celtic and Iberian population as existing in the undisturbed isolation of the Isle of Man in Roman times.

[3] As now in the United States.   [4] Walpole, ib., p. 14.

[5] Strikingly so in the Isle of Man, which affords a very favourable field for ethnological study; cf. Walpole, ib., p. 76.   [6] Ib., p. 41.

[7] Though some admit the survival of many of the Celtic and pre-Celtic population (cf. Ashley, preface to F. de Coulanges' Origin of Property in Land, p. 36), they forget the influence which these must have exercised.

or even retrogressive. If it is true, as Professor Ashley puts it,[1] that "under the Celtic, and therefore under the Roman, rule, the cultivating class was largely composed of the pre-Celtic race," and that "the agricultural population was but little disturbed,"[2] it seems clear that the economic influence of such a population must have been very marked. Such indeed we shall find afterwards to be the case, when we come to investigate more closely the manorial system as it appeared in Anglo-Saxon and Norman times.

§ 17. Commerce and Industry in Roman Britain.

But before proceeding to the Saxon period we must in conclusion give a short glance at trade and industry under the Romans. The *pax Romana* allowed both to develop as far as they were at that time likely to do, and, though never a rich country, in this early time[3] Britain was certainly not a land of poverty. Agriculture went on, as it had done before the Romans came,[4] and as it was sure to do under a peaceful regime, while mining seems to have been even more vigorously carried on than of old. Lead was mined in the Mendip Hills, Derbyshire, and elsewhere, and became so abundant that its output was limited by law; copper in Anglesey and Shropshire; iron in the Forest of Dean, Hereford, and Monmouth; coal, though only for home use, in Northumberland; and in some parts a little silver.[5] The roads also threw those parts of the country through which they passed open to trade and intercourse, though on the other hand in later periods nothing is more striking than the self-contained character of the villages, and their comparative isolation one from the other.[6] The harbours of the south and south-east coast did a busy trade with Gaul, whose merchants acted as intermediaries between Britain and the outer world. The chief British exports seem to have been, besides corn and the minerals already

---

[1] Ashley, preface to F. de Coulanges' *Origin of Property in Land*, p. 37.
[2] *Cf.* also Gibbon, *Decline and Fall*, ch. xxxviii.
[3] *Cf.* F. T. Richards in *Soc. England*, vol. i. p. 93.
[4] *Cf.* O. M. Edwards in *Social England*, vol. i. p. 87.
[5] F. T. Richards in *Social England*, vol. i. p. 92.
[6] *Cf.* the case of Bampton, quoted by Gomme, *V. C.*, p. 160.

referred to, cattle and sheep, the skins and furs of wild
animals, wild beasts themselves for the Roman games,
hunting dogs, and a large number of slaves. Kentish oysters
were also known in Rome. Most of the ordinary clothing
and textile fabrics for domestic use were made in the island
itself,[1] and so too were the coarser kinds of pottery, and
great quantities of bricks and tiles. The imports consisted
of a limited supply of the finer kinds of cloth and pottery
for the use of the upper classes, of wine, and ivory, amber,
and all kinds of metallic ornaments.[2] Exports were almost
certainly in excess of imports, since, like all provinces subject to the Roman rule, Britain had to pay heavy taxes to
its conquerors. These included the *tributum,* or property and
income-tax; the *annona,* a fixed quantity of corn for the
Roman armies in Britain and on the Continent; and
portoria, or import duties.[3] The collection of the last-
named was made at the harbours with which our coasts
abounded,[4] though the fact that these harbours were so
numerous, and the ships of that time so light that they
could run in almost anywhere, probably caused a large
amount of smuggling. In this connection it should be
noticed that many towns standing on rivers, now inac-
cessible to our large ships, were used as ports for sea-going
vessels, both in Roman and in mediæval times. Such were
Exeter, Lincoln, Nottingham, York, and a host of others.[5]
The rivers themselves also formed natural highways into
the interior, which were used far more then than now[6] in
proportion to the amount of trade carried on. As regards
the population, it is impossible to form an exact estimate.
Cæsar[7] speaks of " an infinite number of people " as living

---

[1] They also knew how to dye these in purple, scarlet, and other colours.
Pliny, *Hist. Nat.,* xvi. 8; xxii. 26.

[2] The Britons were very fond of these, using brass and iron, if they could
not get gold. *Social England,* vol. i. p. 103.

[3] F. T. Richards in *Social England,* vol. i. p. 21. A five per cent. legacy
duty was also levied on those who had the Roman franchise.

[4] Euminius, *Pan. Constant.,* c. 11. and *cf.* "Innumerable ports, some
since silted up and forgotten, some perhaps buried in the German Ocean."
Thorold Rogers, *Six Centuries,* p. 153.

[5] *Social England,* vol. i. p. 205.

[6] *Cf.* examples of their use in Continental traffic in my *Commerce in
Europe,* §§ 68, 69, and *cf.* § 26.   [7] Cæsar, *B. G.,* vi. 12.

in the south-east, and the story of the sack of Verulamium, when 70,000 Romans are said to have been massacred,[1] although the number is probably exaggerated, yet shows that the towns at least were populous. The condition of agriculture and trade also, which was more flourishing than it became for some time after the Saxon conquests, would lead us to suppose a fairly numerous population, though the unreclaimed and wooded nature of much of the country prevented it from being by any means dense. But, on the whole, it was a fairly flourishing province and people on which the Saxons descended.

[1] Tacitus, *Ann.*, xiv. 33.

CHAPTER III

§ 18. *The Saxon Invasions.*

THE development of Roman Britain, after proceeding for three and a half centuries, was gradually checked by the weakness of the Roman power. As everyone knows, Rome had in the fifth century enough to do in defending the Continental portions of her empire without troubling about an outlying province like Britain. The Romans were compelled to leave Britain to its fate, and their legions had to quit its shores. But years before they went the Eastern and South-Eastern coast of the island had been harried by pirates of Teutonic race, "the second wave of the Aryans," and a special officer had to be appointed to keep them in check. He was known as the Count (*Comes*) of the Saxon shore,[1] and had command of a squadron and a line of nine forts extending from Brancaster on the Wash to Pevensey on the coast of Sussex. Besides these Saxon pirates, the Picts and Scots raided the country, venturing on one occasion (368 A.D.) as far south as the banks of the Thames, and, thus harassed both by sea and land, the unfortunate Britons might well cry out, "The barbarians drive us to the sea; the sea to the barbarians; we are massacred or must be drowned."

In course of time the barbarians conquered the country. The conquest was the result not of one but of a series of invasions and expeditions, which, beginning at first as mere piratical raids, assumed by the middle of the fifth century the more serious aspect of victorious colonisation and migration.[2] Into the details of that conquest we have not time to go, but it has been picturesquely and minutely

---

[1] *I.e.*, the shore infested by the Saxon pirates, not that colonised by the Saxons, as some think. *Cf.* Stubbs, *Const. Hist.*, I. c. iv. p. 19, and Freeman, *Norman Conquest*, I. p. 11.   [2] Stubbs, *Const. Hist.*, I. iv. p. 59.

described by the graphic author of the *Making of England.*
It is, however, interesting to note that the expeditions of
the Saxon invaders were, as much perhaps from the nature
of the country as from the manner of their inception, independent and separate one from the other. When the "East
Saxons" landed in Essex, proceeding as they did up the
valleys of the Colne and Stour, they found a junction with
the invaders of Kent (even had they wished one) blocked
by a gigantic forest, which prevented further progress south-
ward.[1] But, leaving the manner and details of the conquest to others, it is of prime importance to the economic
historian to discover how far the Saxons destroyed or left
undisturbed the inhabitants of the conquered country. Here
we come at once to disputed ground. Some have thought
that they practically made a clean sweep of all the institutions, both Roman and British, which they found, and
began history afresh with Teutonic customs and manners
both in political and industrial life.[2] "The Britons fled
from their homes;[3] whom the sword spared famine and
pestilence devoured : the few that remained either refused
or failed altogether to civilise the conquerors." This view
is based upon the exaggerated statements of mere ecclesiastical historians like Bede and Gildas, who had a natural
prejudice against the heathen Saxons, and wished to draw a
dark picture of the sufferings of their church. It is adopted
also by those who like to make picturesque generalisations
from striking but insufficient data, and who take the utter
devastation of places like Andredes-Ceaster as typical of
what happened to the whole country.[4] A truer view is that
which, while admitting the disappearance of many of the
upper class, the Romans and Romanised Britons, infers from
a number of very different facts the survival of the great
mass of the British population. "The common belief that
the Celtic population of Britain was exterminated or driven
into Wales and Brittany by the Saxons has absolutely no

[1] Epping and Hainault forests are its relics now. *Cf.* Airy, *Hist. of
Eng.*, p. 9.

[2] So Stubbs, I. iv. p. 61, who heads one paragraph "general desolation."

[3] *Ib.*

[4] So Green, whose judgment seems here at fault, *Short History*, pp. 10,
11 ; and his numerous followers—*e.g.*, Airy, *Hist. of Eng.*, p. 10.

foundation in history"; [1] and the great Gibbon, fully as he describes the havoc wrought by the Saxons in art, religion, and political institutions, carefully points out that this does not imply the extirpation of the subject population itself. "Neither reason nor facts," he says, "can justify the unnatural supposition that the Saxons of Britain remained alone in the desert which they had subdued. After the sanguinary barbarians had secured their dominion, it was their interest to preserve the peasants as well as the cattle of the unresisting country. In each successive revolution the patient herd becomes the property of its new masters, and the salutary compact of food and labour is silently ratified by their mutual necessities." [2]   Or, as a less celebrated author concisely puts it, the object of the Saxon invaders was not "to settle in a desert, but to live at ease, as an aristocracy of soldiers, drawing rent from a peaceful population of tenants," [3] and we may add, as time went on, assisting in the calm pursuits of peace themselves.

The facts of archæology, ethnology, and language, to some of which we have already referred, and the curious survivals and customs of the manorial system, to which we shall come presently, bear out this supposition. It is certain, for instance, that there is a large proportion of Celtic and pre-Celtic blood in the population even of the east of England as well as of the west, and the English language itself, which has been called "the tongue of one people spoken by another," is regarded by some as further confirmatory evidence. [4] Women and slaves were sure to have been kept alive rather

[1] Pearson, *Hist. of Eng.*, I. p. 99.   [2] *Decline and Fall*, ch. xxxviii.
[3] Pearson, *Hist. of Eng.*, I. p. 101. *Cf.* also Ashley (preface to F. de Coulanges' *Origin of Property in Land*, p. 32.), "the destruction of Roman or Romanised land*owners* is not inconsistent with the undisturbed residence upon the rural estates of the great body of actual labourers."

[4] F. York Powell in *Social England*, Vol. I. p. 132. On the other hand, Prof. Cunningham, *Growth of Industry, &c.*, Vol. I. p. 60, thinks there must have been "a general displacement of population to allow of the introduction of a new speech"; but there are plenty of historical cases to prove the contrary. There is no general law regulating the survival of languages; sometimes that of the conqueror, sometimes that of the conquered prevails. *Cf.* Walpole, *Land of Home Rule*, p. 76, and Taylor, *Origin of the Aryans*, p. 209. The Celtic language did not prevail in France, though the Celtic race has remained. The destruction of the

than uselessly massacred ; and, in fact, we may readily believe that the land was continuously tilled "in the same fashion and chiefly by people of the same stock " from the time when the Romans came, or before it, till the close of the middle ages and the more modern changes in agriculture.[1] It has been well observed that whereas the Roman settler always remained outside the life of the British village community, the Saxon forced his way into it,[2] and the whole development of English social and industrial history is dominated by this fact—the intrusion of a conquering element into a conquered community.[3] Thus the manor, as we shall see, presents to us two main elements, the seigneurial and communal, the relations of tenants to their lord and to each other. The only difficulty is to distinguish the origin of each.

§ 19. *The Saxon Village and its Inhabitants.*

For the present, let us glance at the inhabitants of the ordinary English village as we find them much later when the struggles of invader and invaded have ceased, and both are living peacefully together. It is at the village that we must look, not at the town, for the Saxon disliked urban life and was essentially a dweller in villages.

The divisions of its inhabitants have been admirably summarised by Mr York Powell[4] in the following manner : First came the gentry, including the thegen (landlord or " squire ") and parish priest. The *thegen* lived on his own land and paid for it by special duties to the king, to whose following (*comitatus*) he belonged ; the priest also lived on the land—*i.e.*, the glebe with which his patron (probably the thegen) had endowed the village church. Next came the farmer-class of yeomen or *geneats*, corresponding to

Christian religion, on which, with others, Freeman and Cunningham also rely to prove the disappearance of the pre-Saxon population, means very little. Nothing is more frequent than change of religion by half-civilised peoples, as witness the triumphs of Islam, while, on the other hand, the Christian Church in Roman Britain was only the religion of the few, and the extent of its influence has been greatly exaggerated by the interested statements of ecclesiastical historians.

[1] York Powell, *ut supra.* [2] Gomme, *Village Community*, pp. 41, 60, 147.
[3] *Cf.* Vinogradoff, *Villeinage*, p. 303, who implies this, though not in so many words. [4] *Social England*, Vol. I. p. 124.

tenant-farmers, freemen who farmed their own land, or perhaps farmed their lord's, working for the landlord as well as paying rent to him. Thirdly came the peasant class of *cotsetlas*, or cottagers, and *geburs* or copyholders, the former being labourers with five acres of land to support them instead of receiving wages, and the latter copyholders bound to heavy services or " task-work " for their lord. The fourth class were the labourers, such as herdsmen, barnkeepers, and woodwards, who were serfs, and were paid partly in food and clothes, and partly, if they were village officials, by certain perquisites and dues. Distinct from them were the *free* village tradesmen, such as the hunter, fowler, smith, carpenter, potter, pedlar, and travelling merchants,[1] who either took service under a lord or pursued their occupation independently.

We have, therefore, here several classes whom we may classify as follow :—

I. *Gentry* (" of gentle rank "), including (1) the thegen, (2) the priest.

II. *Freemen*, including (1) the geneat, and (2) the tradesmen.

III. *Unfree* men, including (1) the cotsetla, (2) the gebur, (3) the labourers and serfs.

To which we should add, as quite distinct from the others, the small class of *slaves* (not serfs), such as the women-servants and menials about the house of the squire or yeoman. These formed a small, and, as time went on, a diminishing class, though for centuries the export trade in slaves was a dismal feature of English commerce.

§ 20. *Village Life.*

The life of the villages was very much the same in Anglo-Saxon times as it has always been in agricultural districts, and must, in its broad features, always continue to be. We need only make allowances for differences of degree in agricultural progress. It is very fully pictured to us in the illuminated manuscripts of the period, and in

---

[1] Those, of course, had their houses in some town, but travelled from village to village selling their wares.

the Bayeux tapestry. The early part of the year was taken up with ploughing, digging, and sowing, and the approach of the lambing season ; then came the hay and grain harvest and sheep-shearing ; while the autumn brought with it extensive preparations for winter in the way of killing and salting cattle for food in the winter months and storing wood for fires. During the winter itself threshing and winnowing went on, and most of the smith's and carpenter's work was postponed till then, while in the houses the women were busy weaving and making rough and homely garments for their men. The most noticeable features in rural life from these early times right up to the sixteenth century, and even later, were the absence of winter roots for cattle, and of coal for their masters. Roots, and even carrots and parsnips, were then unknown to the farmer,[1] and it was consequently impossible for him to keep his cattle through the cold weather. Hence they had to be killed and salted, and could never attain to the excellence of our modern breeds. The absence of coal involved the use of large quantities of firewood in our cold climate, and hence there was a continual and increasing encroachment upon the forests. Fish and game were fortunately plentiful, and helped to relieve the monotony of salt meat, and eels were a very favourite food,[2] being found in greater numbers then than now owing to the numerous fens and marshes that occupied so many districts. Though it was impossible to keep cattle in any great numbers through the winter, oxen were used for ploughing, and also for food, and sheep were valued for their wool, which, " from the earliest records," formed an article of export to Flanders,[3] and was afterwards much more largely produced. Large numbers of swine were kept,[4] since the rearing and maintenance of these was far more economical than that of cattle, as they could feed on

[1] Rogers, *Six Centuries*, p. 78.
[2] So much so that rent was often paid by a stipulated quantity of eels. *Social England*, Vol. I. p. 207.
[3] Thorold Rogers, *Six Centuries*, p. 78, and see also Macpherson, i. 288.
[4] P. H. Newman in *Social England*, Vol. I. p. 213, and see the illumination in the Cottonian MSS.

the acorns and beech-mast found in unlimited quantities in the forests. "Pannage," or food for swine, is frequently mentioned in Domesday, being given as for over thirty thousand hogs in Hertfordshire and over ninety thousand in Essex. Beekeeping was an important industry, the honey being used both for mead and flavouring.[1]

§ 21. *Methods of Cultivation.*

As regards agriculture, it is noticeable that at one time extensive culture was common,[2] as at Lauder,[3] but it gradually was given up in favour of the intensive system. Special fields were set apart for cultivation in common as permanent arable land on the open field system, and numerous survivals thereof are found in England even to the present day, as at Laxton in Notts, in Cambridgeshire, and elsewhere.[4] Both the two-field and the three-field system were employed, one field lying fallow and the other being under crop according to the former method, while, under the latter, two out of three fields were under crops and the third lay fallow.[5] Though the two-field system, or a modified form of it,[6] was not uncommon, the three-field one became eventually more usual. The crops grown included wheat, rye, oats, and barley, with beans and pease. The fields were not enclosed, except by temporary fences, which were removed after harvest so that the cattle might feed, and strips of land belonging to various owners and tenants lay intermingled[7] with those occupied by the others, being only marked off by "balks" of untilled land. A villein generally possessed a pair of oxen along with his holding, but probably the various small tenants combined their teams in order to do their ploughing more effectively,[8] the normal team being, as we saw, of eight oxen.[9] Most of the operations of agriculture were performed in common,

[1] York Powell, *Soc. Eng.*, Vol. I. p. 124; for swine, *cf. ib.*, p. 213.
[2] Cunningham, i. p. 20.　[3] So Cunningham, but *cf.* Gomme, *V. C.*, p. 150.
[4] Seebohm, *Village Community*, 1-13.
[5] See the diagram and explanation in Cunningham, i. 71.
[6] At least in Germany, *cf.* Hanssen, *Agrarhist. Abh.*, i. 178. In some districts of England also both systems existed side by side.
[7] *Laws of Ine*, 42 (Thorpe, i. 129).　[8] Cunningham, i. 73.
[9] Seebohm, *V. C.*, p. 388.

or by men whom the village community as a whole paid, or rather supported, and who did certain work, such as thatching, swine-herding, or ploughing, in return for their keep.[1] This common system of agriculture naturally produced only poor results, and prevented improvement by individual enterprise, but it sufficed for the simple requirements of those days, and was in harmony with the economic ideas of the age.

§ 22. *Isolation of Villages. Crafts and Trades.*

Each of the separate communities living in these villages, or in the small towns that were now growing up,[2] was on the whole very much cut off from its neighbours. Partly because of the disunion and conflicts that for many years prevailed among the various Saxon conquerors, and partly owing to the difficulties of intercommunication when the Roman roads were no longer kept up, and from many other causes, the villages were very much disinclined for mutual intercourse, and endeavoured to be, as far as possible, each a self-sufficing economic unit, obtaining their food and clothing, coarse and rough though it generally was, from their own flocks and herds and from their own land. Hence only the simplest arts and domestic manufactures were carried on by the people at large, such as the crafts of the iron and coppersmith, the shoemaker, and the carpenter. It is, however, proper to notice the important part which the monasteries played as centres of industrial life. The larger monasteries, such as those of St Edmunds or Glastonbury, were great industrial centres,[3] and it was the monks, or the foreign workmen introduced by them, who brought to a high degree of perfection the arts of embroidery and weaving, and of glass and metal work for ornamental purposes.[4] St. Dunstan,[5] among others, is said to have encouraged metal work. But the great mass of the people cared little for such arts.

[1] Cunningham quotes instances from Saxon and Welsh sources on p. 74 of vol i., *Growth of English Industry.*
[2] On the growth of towns, see later, p. 86 *et seq.*
[3] A. L. Smith in *Social England*, Vol. I. p. 207.
[4] Cunningham, *Growth of Industry*, i. 78.
[5] Will. of Malm., *Vita S. Dunstani*, ch. ix. p. 262 ; Stubbs' *Memorials of St Dunstan* (ed. 1874).

But however strongly a community may desire—or feel it necessary—to be self-sufficing, it can never be so entirely. Differences of soil, of mineral wealth, and of other advantages cause one community to lack that which another has in abundance. Salt, for instance, was very largely in request (as we have seen) for salting meat for winter use, and some idea of the importance of the salt manufacture of that period may be obtained from the fact that in six shires no less than 727 salt works are named in Domesday as paying rent to their lords. But it cannot be universally procured in England, any more than iron and other necessaries of life. Hence internal trade, however limited, was still sure to arise, and we find evidence of its recognised existence in the laws of Ine,[1] which require that "chapmen" should trade before witnesses. This proves the existence of a distinct class of traders, and it is also certain that local markets likewise existed. At first these were always held on the neutral boundaries between the territories of two or more villages or communities,[2] the place of the market being marked by a boundary stone, the origin of the later "market cross." Sunday seems to have been the usual market day, till the influence of the church altered it to Saturday.[3] Sometimes also, besides these local markets, larger ones were held at stated times during the year in well-known localities, and the shrines of saints were among the most frequented spots for this purpose. These fixed markets often developed into towns. Thus the origin of Glasgow may be traced to the fair held at the shrine of St Ninian (570 A.D.),[4] and many other instances of the religious origin, not only of fairs but also of towns themselves, might thus be quoted. These markets were productive of great revenue to the lord of the manor in which they were held ; that at Taunton [5] brought in

---

[1] Laws of Ine, 25 ; Thorpe, i. 118.

[2] A good example of this is Moreton-in-Marsh, an ancient market town situated on the boundaries of the four counties of Oxford, Gloucester, Worcester, and Warwick. The fact is recorded by a stone, known as the "four shires' stone," and situated about a mile from the present town along the London road.

[3] Craik, British Commerce, i. 74.   [4] Cunningham, i. 90.

[5] For Taunton market dues, cf. Thorpe, Dip. Ang., 235; and Social England, i. 208.

£2, 10s. a year in fees, and that at Bedford £7, and we shall have occasion to mention them as factors in the growth of towns in another chapter (pp. 87, 89).

It seems that in the early days of the Saxon settlement, trade at the markets and fairs was largely carried on by simple bartering of commodities. Mere barter, however, is tedious and cumbersome ; and although up to a late period of the Saxon settlement a large proportion, though not the whole, of English trade proceeded in this fashion,[1] the use of coined money for the purposes of exchange became common in the ninth century, while in 900 A.D. regular money payments are recorded as being made by tenants to their landlords.[2] And when we come to the levy of Danegeld (991 A.D.), it is clear from the very imposition of such a tax that metallic money must have been widely diffused and in general circulation.

§ 23. *Foreign Commerce and the Danes.*

Trade of all kinds had suffered a severe blow when the Romans quitted Britain, but even during the Saxon period English merchants still carried on a certain, though limited, amount of foreign commerce. This commerce was greatly stimulated by the Danish invasions and settlements. It is a curious fact that so many of the names of towns and places on our coast have Scandinavian forms, as *e.g.*, those terminating in -*ness*, -*vick*, and -*by*, and it is said to show that our maritime trade, not only in the Danish districts, but even outside them, was mainly in the hands of northern traders.[3] But this is not surprising when we remember that the Danes, before ever they came to England, were most enterprising navigators, as is shown by their very early commerce with Russia and the East,[4] their colonisation of Iceland (874 A.D.), and their discoveries of Greenland (985 A.D.) and the east coast of North America.[5]

---

[1] *Cf.* Craik, *Hist. Brit. Commerce*, i. 83, 84. Slaves and cattle were used as media of exchange. [2] Cunningham, *Growth of Industry*, i. 112.
[3] The point is noted by A. L. Smith in *Social England*, i. p. 201.
[4] Cunningham, i. 84.
[5] *Cf.* fully Mallet's *Northern Antiquities*, ch. ix., and the supplementary chapter in Bohn's edition, p. 244.

Though they were cruel and savage pirates, they were traders also, and, when they had settled down, as they did in such large numbers in the North and East of England,[1] they formed an active industrial and mercantile population, and often became merchants of great importance.   To the Danes also we may trace the beginnings of some of our towns,[2] since their merchants required fixed centres for their commerce. " The Danes and Northmen," says Professor Cunningham,[3] " were the leading merchants, and hence it was under Danish and Norse influences that the villages [which afterwards became towns] were planted at centres suitable for commerce, or that well-placed villages received a new development." Besides this they were instrumental in causing English trade to develope with the North of Europe, and, generally speaking, gave a needed stimulus to navigation, which the Saxons for some unaccountable reason neglected as soon as they settled down in England.   A sign of their influence is seen in the " doom " or decree, probably of the tenth century, which provided that " if a merchant thrived so that he fared thrice over the sea by his own means, then was he of thegen-right worthy "[4]—and this thegen-right gave him a comparatively high rank.   The settlement of German

---

[1] Their presence is still so clearly perceptible in the place-names, provincial words, and the physique of the population of these districts, that we need not further enlarge upon the abiding nature of their influence. It will be sufficient to note briefly the extent of the "Danelagh" (as given by F. York Powell, *Soc. Eng.*, i. p. 145).

Middlesex and Essex, Saxon land chiefly settled by Danes.
Norfolk and Suffolk, East English land   do.   do.
Bucks, Northants, ⎫ Land of the English of the March,
Herts,   Beds, ⎬ settled chiefly by Danes, but also by
Cambs,   Hunts, ⎭ Northmen.
Lincoln, Leicester, ⎫ Land of the English of the March, settled
Derby,   Notts, ⎬ chiefly by Northmen.
Stamford district, ⎭
Yorks and part of Durham, North English land settled chiefly by
        Northmen.

[2] The five Danish boroughs of Derby, Nottingham, Lincoln Leicester, and Stamford had a most complete municipal constitution.

[3] *English Industry and Commerce*, i. 88.

[4] *Ranks*, 6 ; Thorpe, i. 193.   It was probably passed in Athelstan's reign, Craik, i. 66.

merchants in London,[1] pointing to an increasing continental traffic, also dates from the time of Ethelred the Unready (about 1000 A.D.).

Much of this foreign trade, such as it was, and it certainly was not very great, lay in the quantities of precious metals and stuff for embroideries which were imported for use in the monasteries (p. 41). A good list of such imports is given by the merchant who is supposed to speak in Ælfric's Saxon *Dialogues*.[2] He mentions purple, silk, gems, ivory, gold, dyed stuffs, dyes, wine, oil, brass, tin, glass, and sulphur ; while the dangers of the foreign traders calling are pithily expressed in his remark, that "sometimes I suffer shipwreck with the loss of all my goods, scarcely escaping myself." Besides the imports mentioned here we may add furs and skins (which came gradually to be imported instead of exported, as wild animals died out in England), weapons of war, and iron-work. The exports which were exchanged for these were chiefly raw products, including wool—which afterwards became more and more important—cattle, and horses,[3] with tin, lead, and possibly iron. There was a very large export trade in slaves, and their prices are recorded in the laws of the period.[4] Bristol was a great centre of this sad traffic,[5] and remained so till the twelfth century, and English and Danish slaves formed an important merchandise in the markets of Germany. The devout Gytha, Earl Godwin's wife, is said to have shipped whole gangs, especially of young and pretty women, for sale in Denmark.[6] As in many modern instances, her piety was not allowed to prejudice her pocket. As regards the travels of English merchants, we know that they went as far as Marseilles, and frequented the great French fairs of Rouen and St Denis[7] in the ninth century ; while, rather earlier, we have a most interesting document, our

[1] Craik, *Hist. Brit. Comm.*, i. 68.
[2] See Thorpe, *Analecta Anglo-Saxonica*, p. 101.
[3] These are mentioned in a law of Athelstan, Craik, i. 71.
[4] *Leges Wallice*, II. xvii. 30, 31, and II. xxii. 13. The price was one pound of silver, or a pound and a half "if brought from across the sea."
[5] William of Malmesbury, *Vita Wlfstani*, ii. 20, and Craik, i. 71.
[6] Pearson, *Hist. of Eng.*, i. 287.   [7] Cunningham, i. 80.

first treaty of commerce in fact,[1] dated 796 A.D., by which
Karl the Great, or Charlemagne, as he is sometimes called,
grants protection to certain English traders from Mercia.
In King Alfred's days, one English bishop is said to have
"penetrated prosperously" as far as India,[2] bearing the
King's gifts to the shrine of St Thomas, on the Malabar
coast, but this is an isolated case, and though Alfred tried
to encourage navigation by his care for the navy,[3] and by
his interest in the adventurous voyages of Othere and
Wulfstan,[4] the fact remains that foreign merchants, including Jews,[5] came to England in greater numbers than the
English ventured abroad.

§ 24. Summary of Trade and Industry in the Saxon Period.

Taking a general survey of the period between the Saxon
and the Norman conquests, we see that crafts and manufactures were few and simple, being limited as far as possible
to separate and isolated communities.   The fine arts, and
works in metal and embroideries, were confined to the
monasteries, which also imported them.   The immense
mineral wealth of the island in iron and coal was practically
untouched.   Trade, both internal and foreign, was small,
though it developed as the country became more peaceful
and united.   The great mass of the population was engaged
in agriculture, and every man had, so to speak, a stake in
the land and belonged to a manor or an overlord.   A landless
man was altogether outside the pale of social life.   Land,
in fact, was the basis of everything,[6] and it is for this reason
that it is so important to understand the conditions of
tenure and the whole land system of that age.   Hence we
must occupy a short time in the discussion of the origin of
the manorial system, which at the close of the Saxon period
we find in force throughout the country.

[1] Haddan and Stubbs, *Councils*, iii. 496.
[2] So William of Malmesbury, *Gesta Pontif.*, ii. 80.
[3] *Cf.* Craik, *Hist. Brit. Commerce*, i. 65.   [4] In his *Orosius.*
[5] Craik, *British Commerce*, i. 63, 64.
[6] Stubbs, *Const. Hist.*, I. ch. v. pp. 74, 79.

CHAPTER IV

THE MANOR AND THE MANORIAL SYSTEM

§ 25. *The Interest of the Question as to the Origin of the Manor.*

THE question of the origin of the English manor, however abstract and academic it may at first appear, is in reality one of the most interesting of all social topics. When the manor is clearly distinguished as a social factor in the historical period, it always involves two elements—the seigneurial and the communal, the lord on the one hand, and on the other his dependants, who do their work and hold their land in common. The question, therefore, at once arises as to which of these two elements is the older? Is the manor the result of the subjection of an originally free community to an overlord, or was there always, even in the beginnings of social life, a dependent and servile population who tilled the land for the benefit of others? According as history decides one way or the other, it will influence our views on the land question in general, including the discussions even of the present day. From one point of view we shall be inclined to think that the present system of private property in land is the system which, in one form or another, has existed from the beginning, and is the outcome of social forces which have their justification in the earliest pages of history. From another point of view we may hold that property in land did not exist at all in early times, but that the land was held in common for the good of all, while the ownership of it was vested only in the nation, so that the present system of private owner-ship is the degenerate outcome of centuries of appropriation of common property by individuals, whose title to it was in many cases more or less doubtful. Hence reformers like Henry George maintain that we ought to revert to common ownership of land as being the only natural condition and basis of social and economic life, though, on the other hand, so great an authority as Sir Henry Maine has declared that the change from common to private ownership is the sign of an advancing civilisation. Whatever view we hold, it is obvious that the question of the origin of the manor and of property in land is of more than usual interest.

§ 26. *The Mark Theory and the Manor.*

During the present century, owing to the valuable labours of a number of German and English historians,[1] some writers have come to the conclusion (though it is much disputed) that in very early times, before the Germanic tribes, afterwards called English, had crossed over to England, or perhaps even before they had settled down in Europe, all land was held in common by various communities. Each community contained a few families, or possibly a whole tribe. The land occupied by this community had been cleared away from the original forests or wastes where they had settled,[2] and was separated from that of other communities by a boundary or *mark*, a name which in course of time came to be applied not to the boundary but to the land itself thus portioned off.[2] Within this *mark* was the primitive village or township, where each member of the community had his house, and where each had a common share in the land. This land was of three kinds :—(1) The *forest* and *waste* land, from which the mark had been originally cleared, useful for rough natural pasture, but quite uncultivated ; (2) The *pasture* land, including, perhaps, *meadows*,[3] sometimes enclosed and sometimes open, in which each mark-man looked after his own hay, and stacked it for the winter. This land was sometimes divided into allotments for each member ; (3) The *arable* land, which also was divided into allotments for each mark-man. But a man's rights, whether in the allotments or in the common pastures and forests, were of the nature of usufruct only, his title to absolute ownership being merged in the general title of the

[1] Including Kemble, K. Maurer, Stubbs, Freeman, Gneist, Maine, and especially G. F. von Maurer and Hanssen. For a careful summary of the views of each see Vinogradoff's able *Introduction* in his *Villeinage in England.*

[2] Stubbs, *Const. Hist.*, i. p. 49, ch. iii., who gives a good summary of the mark system. [3] Stubbs, *Const. Hist.*, i. 49.

tribe, which, however, he of course shared with the rest.[1] To settle any question relating to the division or use of the land, such as the choice of the meadow, the rotation of crops, or the allotment of the shares of land, or to decide any other business of common importance, the members of the mark, or *mark-men*, met in a common council called the *mark-moot*[2]—an institution of which relics are said to have survived for many centuries.[3] This council, and the mark generally, formed, it was said, the political, social, and economic unit of the early English tribes, but now this view is not supported by scholars, except as regards agricultural arrangements. The mark probably did not exist in the form just sketched out when these tribes first occupied England, though there may have been some modification of it introduced. It had probably already undergone considerable transformation towards what is called the manorial system and private ownership.[4] But those who hold the *mark* theory maintain that many traces of it still remain even now. Our commons,[5] still numerous in spite of hundreds of enclosures, the manorial courts,[6] and the names of places ending in -*ing*—a termination which implies a family settlement[7]—are evidences which remain among us even at the close of the nineteenth century. And, of course, it is to the *mark* system that the communal element in our early and mediæval English agriculture is supposed to be due.

§ 27. *Criticisms of the Mark Theory.*

Leaving for the moment the consideration of the truth or inaccuracy of the *mark* theory, we find, at any rate at the time when the Saxon settlement in England had been completed, that a very different system prevailed, namely, the *manorial* system. The word "manor" is a Norman word for the Saxon "township" or community,[8] and it differs

---

[1] Stubbs, *Const. Hist.*, i. p. 49.

[2] Stubbs, i. p. 51. The word mearcmot (found A.D. 971) was instanced by Kemble, but Anglo-Saxon scholars do not think that *mark* in this connexion means more than a "boundary." *Cf.* Earle, *Land Charters*, p. 45.

[3] Stubbs, p. 84.   [4] *Ib.*, p. 75.   [5] *Ib.*, p. 84.   [6] *Ib.*

[7] Stubbs, *Const. Hist.*, I. ch. v. p. 81; Taylor, *Words and Places*, 132.

[8] So Ordericus Vitalis, iv. 7; see Stubbs, *Const. Hist.*, I. ch. v. p. 89, and ch. ix. p. 273.

D

from the *mark* in that the *mark* was a group of households or persons organised and governed on a communal and democratic basis, while in the manor we find an autocratic organisation and government, whereby a group of *tenants* (not independent "markmen") acknowledge the superior position and authority of a "lord of the manor." The great feature of the manor is, in fact, this subjection to a lord, who owned absolutely a certain portion of the land therein and had rights of rent (paid in services, food, or money, or in all three) over the remainder. On the other hand the tenants had certain rights as against the lord,[1] but these and the questions connected with these we must leave till later.

Such are the distinctive features of the mark and the manor. The point to be now considered is : how did the one result from the other ? It seems very probable that the manorial system must have been the result of conquest, but if so, who were the conquerors that imposed it upon their subjects ? Were they the Anglo-Saxons, or the Romans, or the pre-Roman invaders of Britain ? If the conquerors were the Saxons, then it follows that they themselves had already developed beyond the mark system before they came to these islands. It was at one time thought that the manorial system grew up in the later periods of the Saxon conquest, but received the form, with which mediæval documents make us familiar, only shortly before the Norman rule, and assumed many of its features under Norman influence. But it is now more generally accepted that the manorial system was in existence as the prevailing form of social organisation very soon after the Saxon invasion.[2]

---

[1] Vinogradoff, *Villeinage in England*, pp. 174, 176.

[2] This is the net result of Mr Seebohm's valuable labours. He thinks that the Roman villa presents all the essential features of an English manor, and thus implies that the Saxon lords of the manors merely stepped into the shoes of their Roman predecessors. In an essay more recent than his book on the *Village Community*, he seems inclined to ante-date the feudal side of the manorial system still further. "The British village community was already a good deal feudalised" *before* the Saxon conquest ; possibly (under the influence of Belgic Gauls of the S.E.) even before the Roman conquest. See his valuable critique of Vinogradoff in the *English Historical Review*, Vol. VII., No. 27 (July 1892).

Certainly we have hardly any satisfactory evidence of the mark itself in England, though, as we noted just above, survivals of its influence are found. And, indeed, many authorities of great weight have gone so far as to deny that the mark ever had any existence, whether in England or Europe, except in the mistaken theories of Teutonic historians. Those who reject the mark theory do so largely because they argue that the servile and dependent cultivators of the manorial system lead us back, not to an originally free, but to an originally servile population. They deny that the communal element is ever seen where it can be proved that the cultivating group are proprietors ; it is only found among dependants or tenants, not among free men. " Where the cultivating group are in any real sense proprietors they have no corporate character, and where they have a corporate character they are not proprietors." [1] They combat, moreover, the very facts and quotations from ancient writers upon which advocates of the mark theory base their inferences. Apart from the powerful work of Mr F. Seebohm in his *Village Community*, perhaps the most concise and certainly the most violent attack upon the holders of the mark theory is that made by Fustel de Coulanges in his essay on the *Origin of Property in Land*.[2] He first challenges the meaning given to certain passages of Cæsar and Tacitus [3] by G. F. von Maurer, and then tries to show that in early German law *mark* means " a boundary " primarily, and secondly a piece of private property, and that private property in land

---

[1] W. J. Ashley, criticising Maine in Note A to his own *Introduction* to F. de Coulanges' *Origin of Property in Land*, p. xlvii.

[2] It first appeared in *Revue des Questions Historiques*, April 1889, and is published separately in English in Mr Ashley's translation above referred to.

[3] The main passages are Cæsar, *B. G.*, vi. 21-23, and Tacitus, *Germ.*, c. 26, upon which *e.g.* our English authority Stubbs bases his remarks in *Const. Hist.*, I. c. ii. But it seems to me that de Coulanges, although he makes out a good case against von Maurer on some points, emphasises unduly Cæsar's words *cogunt*, compel, and *principes*, chiefs, in saying they mean "chiefs arbitrarily disposing of the soil of which alone they are owners." But in their natural sense the words merely imply that the people fall in with the arrangements made by their "chief men," and for all we know, the people may merely have deputed certain chief men to carry out the customary division of land desired by the community.

was the assumption upon which all early German law is based. But M. de Coulanges' criticisms, valuable as they are, do not disprove altogether the existence of some form of common ownership of land in the remoter periods of Teutonic or of British history ; for the proof of this common owner-ship lies more in survivals and customs [1] than in stray references in legal documents. And Professor Lamprecht, a follower of von Maurer, was quite right in pointing out [1] that nothing depends on the *word* " mark " itself. It matters very little after all whether we find the word in documents or not ; it even matters very little whether the mark ever existed as it is depicted by von Maurer or Stubbs. The fact remains that there are extensive evidences of communal ownership (as well as tenancy) in English manors, and these evidences point back to a state of things which the theory of private property in land and a dependent body of cultivators in the earliest times cannot satisfactorily explain.

§ 28. *Vinogradoff's Evidence on the Manorial System.*

The most recent, and certainly one of the most learned, investigators of this difficult question has concluded, as the result of his researches, that " the communal organisa-tion of the peasantry is more ancient and more deeply laid than the manorial order. Even the feudal period shows everywhere traces of a peasant class living and working in economically self-dependent communities under the loose authority of a lord, whose claims may proceed from political sources, and affect the semblance of ownership, but do not give rise to the manorial connection between estate and village." [3] The so-called manorial system con-sists in the peculiar connection of two entirely distinct agrarian bodies or parties [4]—the community of villagers cultivating their own fields, and the home-estate (some-times loosely called the demesne) of the lord " tacked on to " this settlement. This expression " tacked on " gives the key to the solution of the question. The manorial

[1] As shown *e.g.*, in Gomme's *Village Community.*
[2] In *Le Moyen Age*, June 1889, p. 131.
[3] Vinogradoff, *Villeinage*, pp. 408, 409.   [4] *Ib.*, p. 404.

system, as we find in late Saxon and Norman times, contains a seigneurial element which has evidently been superimposed upon an originally communal element. Originally there was an *independent* village community (whether living exactly according to the "mark" system or not does not matter), but in later times we find a dependent community working for a home-farm, which is the lord's. How did the independent community become subject to this lord? The holders of the older "mark" theory seem to have supposed that the subjection was due to political and social causes gradually enhancing the power of some local man of note or authority. "The relation of dependence on a lord may have been entered into by a free landowner for the sake of honour or protection";[1] and there are abundant evidences of this "commendation" of weaker men to those who were politically and socially more powerful[2]—though, as a matter of fact, the practice was generally the result of the police organisation, not of the land system.[3] "The man who had land judged the man who had not,"[4] and there was a constant assimilation going on between the really servile dependents of a lord and the smaller landowners. But however the practice of commendation arose, it undoubtedly had great effect in reducing the originally free status of many of the smaller landowners. At the same time, the main features of the manorial subjection to a lord are probably due more to the influence of conquest than to that of social or judicial requirements, though these latter cannot be neglected or minimised. The number of servile dependents is too large to be accounted for by peaceful influences. Moreover, it has been till recently overlooked that in many cases the services rendered by dependants were rendered not to a lord living on a *home* farm, but to one living at some considerable distance.[5] This is specially

---

[1] Stubbs, *Const. Hist.*, vol. I. ch. v. p. 79; *cf.* also p. 273.
[2] Especially in Domesday; see Ellis, *Introd. to Domesday*, i. 64-66.
[3] Stubbs, *ut ante*, p. 79, note, and p. 189.
[4] *Ib.*, p. 189. The landless man was compelled to choose a lord for his surety and protector, *ib.*, p. 153.
[5] Vinogradoff, *Villeinage*, p. 405.

the case in the furnishing of provisions for the lord's table and other wants, for we constantly find that provisions were sent by the dependents to a castle a long way off. There is also the matter of the *firma unius noctis*,[1] as it is called, the payment of "provisions for one night" made to the king's household by a borough or village, which seems to point to a community "standing entirely by itself and taxed to a certain tribute, without any superior land-estate necessarily engrafted upon it." Vinogradoff thinks this implies an over-lordship exacting tribute, but not the close manorial relationships which we see under a later system. Again, the fact that the lord's demesne land is often found in strips, mixed up with the strips of the peasantry (p. 82), seems also to imply a time when the tenants or subject class did not collect to work for the lord upon a separate home farm, as we find them doing later, but merely devoted one part of their labour upon their own ground in the common fields to the use and payment of the lord.[2] This shows an intermediate stage between the tribute paid by a practically self-dependent community (as in the case of the *firma unius noctis*) and the services rendered when the village was linked more closely with a manorial estate.[3] Once again, we note the existence of a special class of servants [4] "who collect and supervise the dues and services of the peasants" in early times, but who are not to be found so frequently in the thirteenth and fourteenth centuries, when the number of "home farms" was becoming greater. Besides these special servants (radmen, rodknights or riding-bailiffs), we also note that in many cases the "free" tenants or *socmen* (see p. 75) have a kind of supervision over the rest while they are doing some of the services for the lord, and their position indicates that, though the village is already set to work for the lord, it manages this work as much as possible by itself as a self-dependent community.[5]

---

[1] Vinogradoff, *Villeinage*, p. 405, and see Pearson, *Hist. of Eng.*, vol. I., Appx. D. Thus the community of Badwen in Essex rendered a payment of eight nights, Soham and Fordham in Cambs. gave three nights, and many other instances are found in Domesday.

[2] Vinogradoff, *Villeinage*, p. 406.   [3] *Ib.*, p. 406.

[4] *Ib.*, p. 407.   [5] *Ib.*, p. 407.

§ 29. *Evidence from Manorial Courts and Customs.*

All this seems to imply the subjection of originally free communities to an overlord, a subjection that proceeded first by reducing them to a more or less loose and tribute-paying relationship, and later by the introduction of a resident lord on a home farm (the demesne), or at least of a home farm superintended by a bailiff representing a lord. The internal constitution of the manor gives the strongest evidence for this original freedom. In the manorial courts (p. 80) the tenants were the jurors and suitors, while the lord or his steward was not the judge, but merely the recorder of their decisions. It was the suitors and jurors, the tenants in fact, who constituted the court and pronounced the judgments.[1] It was not till much later, under Norman influence, that the status of the tenants in their own courts became debased, and the lord or his bailiff was regarded as the judge.[2]

Another very important piece of evidence, showing that ceremonies, which have been erroneously regarded as proving the original servility of tenants prove in reality their original freedom, is the manorial form of surrender and admittance. When a tenant was admitted into his holding " in base tenure," the steward handed to him a rod. This was till lately thought to symbolise the lord's authority, but Vinogradoff shows [3] that, on the contrary, it was a survival of the old custom, requiring that important transactions should be performed before witnesses and a middleman, and that the steward had taken the place of the middleman and did not really represent the lord at all.[4] A case like this shows us at once how archaic are the constitutions and customs of the village community, and how easily, when these customs are no longer understood, they may be erroneously construed as evidences of seigneurial power.

[1] Vinogradoff, *Villeinage*, p. 370.
[2] It may be added that the village as a body frequently acts as an organised community in disposing of rights connected with the soil. *Cf.* the case of Brightwaltham, Vinogradoff, p. 359. [3] *Villeinage*, pp. 372, 373.
[4] *Cf.* Gomme, *Vill. Comm.*, p. 191, who quotes a similar transference of a rod, or twig, in the Malmesbury village community. The twig here (as in the other cases mentioned by Vinogradoff) represents the land itself, certainly not a lord's authority.

§ 30. *The " Customary " Tenants.*

The position of " free " tenants (p. 75) in the later manors is, again, a matter of some difficulty. It is as erroneous to imagine that at (say) the time of Domesday there was no intermediate grade between the lord and his serfs or villeins, as it is to hold that all the Saxons and those who came over with them were entirely free. In Domesday we find traces of a large number of tenants of various degrees of freedom, and it is these traces, together with those derived from the legal procedure of the Norman period, that Vinogradoff has explained with masterly insight. It is now pretty evident that the classification of society into villeins and freedholders is comparatively late and artificial,[1] and that between these two distinct classes there was a third class, and a very large one, of " customary "[2] freeholders, who had *originally* formed the great mass of the peasantry.[3] The Anglo-Saxon world was ordered and governed by custom to an extent quite unappreciated by the Norman lawyer and surveyor, and hardly to be realised at all by Englishmen of the present day. But this " customary " life, and all that it implied, was perfectly well understood by the inhabitants of the village who lived under it. The villagers cared nothing for abstract legal definitions of tenure and status, though they all knew the conditions under which they and their forefathers held their land. But the Normans, with their fixed ideas of " free " and " unfree " tenancies, tried to reduce everyone into one of these two sharply-defined categories,[4] and hence it comes that " villeinage " must not be taken too literally as a clear definition of a tenant's status or tenure, but we must remember that it was really " a complex mould into which several heterogeneous elements had been fused."[5] Hence

---

[1] *Villeinage*, pp. 132, 177.

[2] The word *custumarius* is found in *Rot. Hundred.*, ii. 422, 507a.

[3] Vinogradoff, p. 220.

[4] The fact that *free* men in Kent and on the Danish manors of Essex were all classed by Domesday as *villani* shows what mistakes the Normans made. Vinogradoff, p. 208.

[5] Vinogradoff, p. 177; *cf.* also " The life of the villein is chiefly dependent on custom, *which is the great characteristic of mediæval relations* and which stands *in sharp contrast* with slavery on the one hand and freedom on the other."

it is certain that many men who in Domesday are classed as "villeins" were for all intents and purposes "free" men, who either merely rendered services, not always necessarily servile, as a condition of holding land, or who, in addition to holding perfectly free land, held also some other land in villeinage, and thus became confused altogether with villeins. There is little doubt that the free holdings in the manors represent, in many cases, free shares in a village community, upon which the manorial structure has been superimposed.[1]

§ 31. *The Evidence of Village Communities.*

We have, therefore, many reasons for believing that the original condition of the subject manorial villages had been at an earlier period that of free communities. But if so, can we not find traces of such communities in England? Were they all extinct at the time of Domesday? Recent writers certainly incline to the belief that individually and collectively villeins were more free in Saxon than in Norman times,[2] but it has been stoutly denied[3] that there are any free village communities to be found later than the Norman conquest, or, indeed, previous to it. Only communities peopled by *villeins* are mentioned. But we have already seen that Domesday is an unsatisfactory guide in questions of status,[4] and there is good reason to doubt whether these villein communities were quite so devoid of freedom as the Norman surveyors described them. In the cases of Chippenham and Malmesbury, at least, Mr Gomme[5] gives very remarkable evidence of their being free communities in the time of Domesday, and much later also, and the various other instances which he quotes in his valuable work[6] certainly tend to prove very clearly, by their relics

[1] Vinogradoff, p. 353. *Cf.* Bracton, *De Leg.*, ch. xi. *f.* 7 (i. p. 53, ed. Twiss). Of course there were also other causes of free tenements, as— *e.g.*, commutation, but this is one cause which cannot be overlooked.
[2] Vinogradoff, p. 135.
[3] Seebohm, *Village Comm.*, p. 103; Ashley, *Econ. Hist.*, i. 18, and in his introd. to F. de Coulanges.   [4] Vinogradoff, p. 208.
[5] *Village Comm.*, pp. 173-200, and see p. 195 specially for the quotation from Domesday.
[6] See especially ch. vi. on "Tribal Communities in Britain," ch. vii.

and survivals, that, as Vinogradoff also concludes the free
village community existed in these islands, as it did elsewhere, before the manorial system was superimposed or
"tacked on to" it.

§ 32. *A Survey of the Origin of the Manor.*

Having come to this conclusion, which must necessarily
influence any view which we take of the manorial system,
we may now venture to set forth a comprehensive though
brief survey of the origin of the village community, with
its seigneurial and communal elements, which we find in
historic times. This I do with considerable diffidence—for
I am well aware of the conflicting theories already pro-
pounded—but a review of the facts, placed in due perspective and exhibiting an orderly development, may have
its advantages. To begin with, we see, on looking back
into the mists of prehistoric antiquity, that a large [1] non-
Aryan population existed in these islands in the Neolithic
stage of culture. They had already made some small
advances in agriculture, and had passed,[2] or were rapidly
passing, from the tribal [3] to the village community—a
transition [4] which is natural as the development of agriculture necessitates a closer connection with the soil than
the more or less unsettled tribal stage allows. Upon the
state of society thus formed, or forming, descended successive waves of Aryan invaders in the shape of the Celtic
immigrants to Britain. At first, no doubt, the Aryan
tribes, with the pride so characteristic of the earlier Aryan
races, took but little part in the cultivation of the land,
but preferred to leave it to the conquered and subject
Iberians, exercising only a loose overlordship over the more
remote village communities.[5] (This accounts for the survival, centuries later, of the customs already mentioned, that

Transitional types of the village community in Britain, ch. viii. The *Final*
type; also ch. iii. Methods of dealing with British evidence.

[1] Boyd Dawkins, *Early Man*, pp. 290, 306.   [2] Elton, *Origins*, p. 145.

[3] Boyd Dawkins, *Early Man*, p. 272.

[4] *Cf.* the similar transition from tribe to village in India; Tupper,
Punjab Customary Law, ii. p. 28. The tribal community persisted longer
in Wales; *cf.* Gomme, *V. C.*, p. 63.

[5] Gomme, *V. C.*, p. 71.

suggest, even in the later manors, a much looser tie between lord and dependants than afterwards existed.) But as time went on we know that the Celtic invaders, especially the most recent of them (p. 13), themselves made very considerable progress in agriculture, and thus the agrarian bond between the subject and the conquering races became closer and closer. Then came the Roman occupation, but we have already seen that, after making full allowance for the undoubted extent of Roman influence in other directions, its effect upon the village community and its agriculture can only have been on a level with our own influence upon the villages of India. When the Romans took away their military and administrative forces, the Celtic and non-Aryan communities remained much as they had been before the Romans came.[1] The Roman did not enter into the life of the village community as did Celt or Saxon. He was above it and not of it. But when the Saxons came, their influence was felt at once. Terrible as they were in their destruction of the upper classes, especially those of the towns, they did not seek to destroy the peasantry of the rural districts,[2] any more than the successive conquerors of India (who could be to the full as cruel as the Saxons ever were) have obliterated the villagers of the Punjab.[3] On the contrary, their own agrarian development (p. 39) was much the same as that of the land they invaded. The village community received, therefore, certainly no check from this fresh invasion. What happened was that the Celt and Iberian were debased in status in some cases, where the conquerors made their first settlements, but were left in the remoter parts of the country pretty much as before, though with a continual tendency to fresh debasement as time went on and the conquest proceeded. They helped to form the large and mixed class of servile dependants whom we find later. The Saxons themselves brought slaves and dependants with them, for it is absurd to suppose them all free and equal.[4] And no doubt the

[1] *Cf.* Gomme, *V. C.*, pp. 60, 63.   [2] Gibbon, *Decline and Fall*, ch. xxxviii.
[3] Lord Metcalfe, quoted by Gomme, *V. C.*, p. 60.
[4] There were almost certainly larger and smaller private estates ; Stubbs, *Const. Hist.*, vol. I. ch. v. pp. 52, 73. For slaves, *cf.* p. 78.

leaders and their chief followers occupied from the first period of the invasion a high position in the social and economic scale.[1] But there were also large numbers of free Saxon soldiers [2] who settled down on the land which they and their chiefs had taken, and it is to this class— and to the Danes who came later—that we owe the numerous "free tenants" of the later manor. It is pretty evident also that the amount of freedom was greater in Saxon times than in Norman,[3] and consequently greater in the earlier portion of the Saxon period than in the later. Much also was left to custom and tradition in the relations of lord and dependant. Then finally came the Norman conquest, with its stricter feudalism, its inelastic ideas of status and tenure, and its great work of firm organisation and consolidation. The tie between the lord and his dependants had been growing closer, more personal, and, if we may say so, more "residentiary," all through the Saxon period, and the Norman conquest accentuated this development, raising the lord, debasing the dependant, and fusing into one the numerous varying grades of villeinage. And so we arrive at last at the manor of historic times, with all those various influences and survivals within it that were the heritage of Iberian, Celt, and Saxon, but which history could not record.

§ 33. *The Feudal System.*

In the next period we shall find this manorial system consolidated and organised under the Norman rule, and may therefore defer a detailed description of a typical manor till then. Here we may add, however, that the manor, especially in its social, judicial, political, and non-economic relations, is closely connected with the feudal system. But it must be remembered that feudalism, and all that it implied, had already begun in England some considerable time before the Norman conquest; and as the manor afforded a convenient unit, political as well as social,

[1] Stubbs, *Const. Hist.*, Vol. I. pp. 73, 55, 149.
[2] The division of the land among the conquering host is seen in Stubbs, *ut ante*, pp. 71, 72.   [3] Vinogradoff, *Villeinage*, p. 135.

for the estimation of feudal duties and services, the lord of the manor tended to become more and more a feudal chief. In the primitive Saxon constitution the political unit had been the *free man*, but later, as land passed from being public to private property, the sign of freedom became the possession of land. The landless man had to select a lord, and the "land becomes the sacramental tie of all public relations." [1] The lords of the manors became nominally the protectors, but really the masters, of the freemen around them, who were poor, and only had a small piece of land. The practice of commendation [2] for judicial or defensive purposes, and the granting of judicial powers [3] to the larger landowners, all tended in the same direction, while the frequent incursions of the Danes probably threw the smaller free tenants still more under the influence of the greater local landowners, who would offer them their protection in return for manorial services. When, therefore, William the Norman conquered England, he did not, as is still often supposed, impose a feudal system upon the people. The system was there already, developed from the manors, and the Norman kings only organised and crystallised it still further. [4]

[1] Stubbs, *Const. Hist.*, I. ch. vii. p. 167.
[2] Stubbs, i. 79, and the valuable note there relating to the practice in Domesday.
[3] *E.g.*, *sac* and *soc* (Stubbs, i. 184).
[4] *Cf.* Pearson, *Hist. of Eng.*, i. 283, 284

PERIOD II

FROM THE NORMAN CONQUEST TO THE REIGN OF HENRY III.

(1066-1216 A.D.)

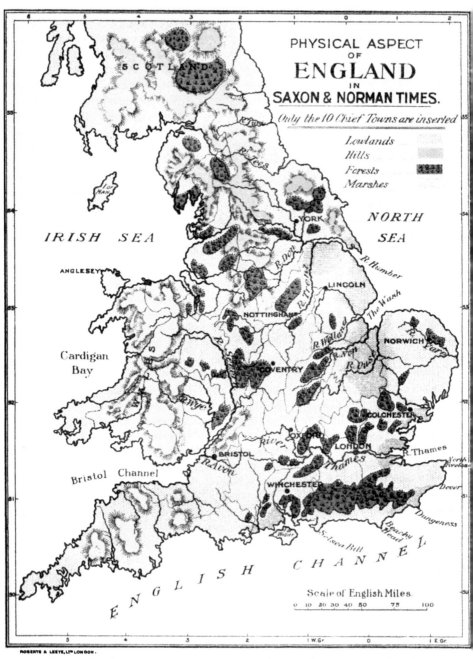

PHYSICAL ASPECT
OF
ENGLAND
IN
SAXON & NORMAN TIMES.

Only the 10 Chief Towns are inserted

Lowlands
Hills
Forests
Marshes

SCOTLAND

IRISH SEA

NORTH SEA

ANGLESEY

Cardigan Bay

YORK

LINCOLN

R. Humber

The Wash

NOTTINGHAM

NORWICH

COVENTRY

R. Welland

R. Ouse

COLCHESTER

OXFORD

LONDON

R. Thames

BRISTOL

Bristol Channel

R. Avon

River Thames

WINCHESTER

Dover

Dungeness

Beachy Head

Selsea Bill

ENGLISH CHANNEL

Scale of English Miles.
0 10 20 30 40 50   75   100

NOTE.—For the features here noted compare the remarks on pages 17, 69 and 107.

CHAPTER V

DOMESDAY BOOK AND THE MANORS

§ 34. *The Survey ordered by William I.*

IT was very natural that when William the Norman had conquered England he should wish to ascertain the capabilities of his kingdom, both in regard to military defence and for purposes of taxation, and that he should endeavour to gain a comprehensive idea of the results of his conquest. He therefore ordered a grand survey of the kingdom to be made, and sent commissioners into each district to make it. These officials were bidden to make a long list of enquiries about all the estates in the realm, including the following points :—The name of each manor; who held it in the time of King Edward the Confessor; how many " hides " there were in the manor,[1] or, in other words, the rateable value of the estate; how many ploughs there were on the estate, whether belonging to the lord or the villeins; how many villeins, homagers, cottars, or slaves there were; how many free tenants and tenants in socage (*socmen*); how much wood, meadow, and pasture; and the number of mills and fish ponds. They were further to enquire what had been added to or taken away from the estate—that is, the depreciations and improvements ; the gross value in the time of King Edward (T.R.E.), the present value in the time of King William (T.R.W.) ; how much each free man or socman had, and whether any advance could be made in the value. The results of this great survey, taken separately in counties, were then sent to Winchester, then the capital city, and there methodised, enrolled, and codified as we now

---

[1] It is almost impossible to fix the value of the hide as a measurement. It was never expressly determined, nor is it so fixed in Domesday ; Ellis, *Introd.*, i. 145 *sqq.* ; Birch, *Domesday*, 229. Cunningham (i. 120) puts it at 60 to 80 modern acres under crop, or an area of 120, including land fallow, under the then system of agriculture.

see them.[1] The inquisition was probably commenced in the year 1085, and completed in the year following. It contains the earliest and most reliable statistics for English industrial history, and it is to be regretted that no adequate general table or analysis of this great work has yet been made by a competent economic authority, or that historians do not use it more copiously for gaining a knowledge of the social and economic conditions of the time. For this latter purpose it is absolutely unrivalled.

§ 35. The Population given by Domesday.

Before presenting a few main features gathered from the large mass of facts thus recorded, it may be well to remark that of the 40 counties into which England is now divided, six are not included in the survey. Those omitted are Monmouth, Northumberland, Cumberland, Westmoreland, Durham, and Lancashire. But of these Lancashire had not yet been made a separate county, and part of it therefore appears in the survey of Yorkshire and Cheshire. Monmouth was at that time entirely Welsh, and the other counties—those in the North—were still desolate and wasted by the ruthless severity of William's well-known devastation (1069-70 A.D.). After his march from the Humber to the Tyne, not one inhabited village was to be seen on the road between York and Durham, and many of those whom the sword had spared died of starvation in the nine years' famine which followed this dreadful punishment.[2] The more westerly parts of the North were hardly yet conquered at the time of the survey. The statistics of the other 34 counties are, however, pretty full; and from them we gather that the total population must have been, in round numbers, rather under two million persons. The population actually given[3] is 283,242, but this only includes the able-bodied men, and it should be multiplied by five to give the general total of actual inhabitants. This multiplication gives about 1,400,000, and allowing

---

[1] Birch, *Domesday*, p. 25 ; Ellis, i. 153 ; see also Note A.

[2] Pearson, *Hist. of Eng.*, i. 361, and Freeman, *Norman Conquest*, iv. 292, v. 42.

[3] See Ellis, *Introduction to Domesday*, Vol. II. p. 514.

for omissions or careless enumeration (as *e.g.* in Yorkshire[1]), we may say not much more than 1,800,000 for the whole land. Small as this number may seem, it was not greatly increased for several centuries.[2]

The population of the different counties is interesting, and is exhibited in the following tables, first in order of actual numbers, and secondly in order of density proportionate to the area of each county. It will be noticed at once that the eastern and southern counties were the most populous at that time, as was to be expected in a period when the number of the population depended, much more closely than it does now, upon the yield of agricultural produce and the development of agriculture generally.

I. Table of Actual Population in Different Counties, as given in Domesday.

County.	Popula-tion.*	County.	Popula-tion.*
1 Norfolk - -	27,087	18 Berks - -	6,324
2 Lincoln - -	25,305	19 Notts - -	5,686
3 Suffolk - -	20,491	20 Cornwall - -	5,438
4 Devon - -	17,434	21 Bucks - -	5,420
5 Essex - -	16,060	22 Hereford - -	5,368
6 Somerset - -	13,764	23 Cambridge -	5,204
7 Kent - -	12,205	24 Shropshire -	5,080
8 Sussex - -	10,410	25 Herts - -	4,927
9 Wilts - -	10,150	26 Worcester - -	4,625
10 Hampshire -	9,032	27 Surrey - -	4,383
11 Northamps -	8,441	28 Bedford -	3,875
12 Gloucester -	8,366	29 Staffordshire -	3,178
13 Yorks -	8,055	30 Derbyshire -	3,041
14 Dorset - -	7,807	31 Huntingdonshire	2,914
15 Oxford - -	6,775	32 Cheshire - -	2,349
16 Leicestershire -	6,772	33 Middlesex - -	2,302
17 Warwick - -	6,574	34 Rutland - -	862

* It must be remembered the figures represent only able-bodied males.

---

[1] See *Domesday, f.* 302 A, about the manors "ad Prestune"—"sixteen are cultivated by a few men, but how many men there are is not known."

[2] Pearson, *Hist. of England*, i. 377.

II. TABLE OF COUNTIES according to Proportionate Density
of Population.

COUNTY.	Acres per person.*	COUNTY.	Acres per person.*
1 Suffolk - -	46	18 Warwick - -	87
2 Norfolk - -	50	19 Sussex - -	89
3 Essex - -	61	20 Notts - -	92
4 Middlesex - -	66	21 Gloucester -	93
5 Lincoln - -	69	22 Devon - -	94
6 Oxfordshire -	71	23 Hereford - -	99
7 Northamps -	74	24 Cambs - -	100
8 Leicester - -	75	25 Worcestershire -	102
9 Berkshire - -·	76	26 Surrey - -	105
10 Somerset - -	76	27 Rutland - -	110
11 Bedfordshire -	76	28 Cornwall - -	158
12 Hunts - -	78	29 Shropshire -	166
13 Kent - -	79	30 Staffs. - -	204
14 Dorset - -	81	31 Derby - -	216
15 Herts - -	82	32 Cheshire - -	279
16 Wilts - -	85	33 Yorks - -	497
17 Bucks - -	86	34 Hants - -	1011

* Fractions omitted.

It is in some respects, perhaps, rather remarkable that the
first three most populous counties are Suffolk, Norfolk, and
Essex; but this seems to have been due to the wool (and
other) trade with Flanders and the Continent, for it must
be remembered that at that time the eastern counties' ports
were much frequented. Next to these in population come
the Southern and Midland counties.

§ 36. The Wealth of various Districts.

The distribution of wealth among the various counties
is also interesting, as may be seen from the following table
of the twenty-one leading counties of that time, with the
approximate value of the rents paid by the manors therein,
deduced from Domesday.[1] Here the Eastern and Southern

---

[1] This table is compiled from data given (for another purpose) by Pearson, Hist. of Eng., Vol. I., Appx. D. Though necessarily only approxi
mate, it still seems fairly reliable.

counties rank highest, Kent coming first, then Essex, Norfolk, and Sussex, while Oxford takes rather a higher place, and Middlesex (excluding London) a low one. The table is as follows :—

Order.	COUNTY.	Approx. Rental.		
		£	s.	d.
1	Kent - - - -	5717	6	7
2	Essex - -	4784	16	8
3	Norfolk - - -	4514	11	7
4	Sussex - - -	3436	12	0
5	Oxford - - -	3242	2	11
6	Devon - - -	3220	14	3
7	Gloucester - - -	2827	6	8
8	Dorset - - -	2656	9	8
9	Berks - - -	2460	16	1
10	Northamps - -	1843	0	7
11	Bucks - - -	1813	7	9
12	Herts - - -	1541	13	11
13	Surrey - - -	1524	4	9
14	Warwick - -	1359	13	8
15	Bedford - - -	1096	12	2
16	Worcester - -	991	0	6
17	Hunts - - -	864	15	4
18	Middlesex - -	754	7	8
19	Leicester - - -	736	3	0
20	Cornwall - - -	662	1	4
21	Derby - - -	461	4	0

Generally speaking, then, we may say that the east and south of England contained the richest, best tilled, and most populous parts of the country. Their downs and wolds afforded good pasturage for sheep and cattle, while the woods in every district formed excellent fattening grounds for swine, of which large numbers were kept. The hollows at the foot of the downs in the south and west, the river flats of the eastern counties, and the low gravel hills in other parts contained the best and easiest land to work. The chief towns [1] were London, Bristol, Norwich, Lincoln,

[1] Curiously enough, London, Bristol, and Winchester do not appear separately in the survey, but are only mentioned casually. For other important towns, cf. p. 89.

Oxford, York, Exeter, and Winchester; and Dover was also a place of considerable importance. But they were almost insignificant if we compare them with their modern dimensions. York had only some 1600 houses;[1] Norwich boasted not more than 1320 burgesses; and it has been estimated that, generally speaking, from 7000 to 10,000 people in all was "the population of a first class town."[2] They were, in fact, trading centres rather than seats of manufacturing industry. Although comparatively unimportant at the time of Domesday, they began to increase very much in prosperity soon afterwards. There are 9250 manors enumerated in Domesday, and all except the towns above mentioned were practically what we should now call villages of no great size.

§ 37. *The Manors and Lords of the Manors.*

Of course each of these manors, after the Norman Conquest, was held by a "lord," who in turn held it more or less remotely from the King. It is, in fact, the distinguishing feature of the Conquest, that William the Norman made himself the supreme landowner of the country, so that all land was held under him.[3] He himself also, as a private landowner, held a large number of manors, which were farmed by his bailiffs, and for each of these manors he was therefore in a double sense the lord. But the majority of the manors in the country were held by his followers, the Norman nobles, and nearly all of them had several manors each. Now it was impossible for a noble to look after all his manors himself, even if he had wished it, since by William's cautious policy their lands had been assigned to them in various widely separated districts,[4] and some of them, again, had so many manors that personal supervision was impossible.[5] Nor was it always advisable to leave them merely to the care of bailiffs, and, therefore, naturally the great landowners used to sub-let some of their manors to

---

[1] Cunningham, *Growth of Industry*, i. 166.
[2] Pearson, *Hist. of Eng.*, i. 381.
[3] Taswell-Langmead, *Const. Hist.*, ch. ii. p. 49; Stubbs, I. ch. ix. p. 274.
[4] Stubbs, i. p. 272.
[5] Robert of Mortain held the largest number—viz., 793; but Odo of Bayeux had 439, and Alan of Brittany 442. The ancient demesne of the Crown consisted of 1422. Ellis, i. 225, 226.

other tenants—often to Englishmen who had submitted to the Norman Conquest. The nobles who held their land direct from the King were called *tenants-in-chief*, and those to whom they sub-let it were called *tenants-in-mesne*. But when a noble let a manor to a tenant-in-mesne, this tenant then for all practical purposes took his place, and became the " lord " of that manor. Thus, then, we find various kinds of manors—some owned directly by the King, others by the great nobles, and others again held by tenants-in-mesne. For instance, in the Domesday of Oxfordshire,[1] we find that one Milo Crispin, a tenant-in-chief, held a large number of manors from the King, but also let many to sub-tenants, that of Cuxham, *e.g.*, being let to Alured, who was therefore its lord. So, too, in Warwickshire, the manor of Estone (now Aston) was one of those belonging to William Fitz-Ansculf, but he had let it to Godmund, an Englishman, who was therefore " lord of the manor of Estone." In many cases the lordship of a manor was vested to a monastery or abbey; in fact, it is said that the Church held rather more than one-fifth of the whole land of the kingdom.[2]

§ 38. The Inhabitants of the Manor.

The lord of the manor was a person of great importance, but of very varying social position. The great nobles, such as Odo of Bayeux, whose rent roll was well over £3000 a year (an enormous sum for those days), or Robert of Mortain, who numbered his manors not by the score but by the hundred, held, of course, a rank equal to the noblest and richest of the Dukes of the present day. But there was a large number of lesser nobles, whose income varied from £300 to £500 a year, and also many county gentlemen, as we should call them, who, though tenants-in-chief and lords of manors, had a comparatively small income.[3]

---

[1] See the survey for Oxfordshire in any reprint.

[2] Pearson reckons : the Crown held $\frac{1}{4}$, the Church $\frac{7}{20}$, and the barons the remaining $\frac{1}{2}$; *Hist. of Eng.*, i. 383.

[3] " Five to twenty pounds a year was no uncommon income for a gentleman " (Pearson, *Hist. of Eng.*, i. 384), but this must be multiplied by 20 at least to give any idea of its value in modern figures.

Besides the lord himself (whether King, noble, or sub-
tenant), with his personal retainers, and generally a parish
priest or some monks, there were three distinct classes of
inhabitants—(1) First came the *villani* or villeins, who
formed about 38 per cent.[1] of the total population recorded
in Domesday, and were by far the most numerous and
widely-spread class.[2] Their holdings differed in size, but on
the average we may take them as occupying a *virgate* or
yardland, which is equivalent to some 30 acres of arable
land, and, of course, their holdings were scattered in plots
among the common fields of the manor.   The villeins also
had a house in the village, and were often called *virgarii*
or *yardlings*, from holding a virgate of land.   (2) Next to
the villeins came the *cottars*, or *bordars*,[3] a class distinct
from and below the former, who probably held only some
5 or 10 acres of land and a cottage, and did not even
possess a plough, much less a team of oxen apiece, but had
to combine among themselves for the purpose of ploughing.
They form 32 per cent. of the Domesday population.
Finally came (3) *the slaves*, who were much fewer in
numbers than is commonly supposed, forming only 9 per
cent. of the Domesday population.[4]   Less than a century
after the Conquest these disappear, and merge into the
cottars.   They should not be confused with either villeins
or bordars, but Ellis is probably right in supposing that
the *servi* correspond to the Saxon *theow* or *esne*, while the
villeins correspond to the *ceorls* or churls, and that under
the Norman system there was a continual approximation
going on between them, the churls becoming degraded, and
the position of the theows being improved, so that both
were brought nearer together in the social scale.[5]

---

[1] The percentages are given by Seebohm, *Village Community*, p. 86.

[2] Ellis tabulates 108,407 (*Domesday*, ii. 511).

[3] See Ellis, *Domesday*, ii. 511, and Birch, *Domesday*, pp. 141 and 154;
also Ashley, *Economic History*, I. i. p. 18. Ellis tabulates 82,119 bordars,
1749 " coseets," and 5054 *cotarii*. The terms *coseet, cotsedae, coscez, cozets,
coteri, cotmanni, cotarii* seem to be used more or less of the same class.
The exact status of the bordar and cottar has been the subject of much
discussion, but probably the real distinction between them was very slight.

[4] In Ellis (ii. 511), 25,156 *servi*.

[5] *Cf.* Birch, *Domesday*, p. 170 ; Stubbs, *Const. Hist.*, I. xi. p. 428.

§ 39. *The Condition of these Inhabitants.*

The chief feature of the social condition of these classes of people was that they were subject to a lord. They each depended upon a superior, and no man could be either lordless or landless, for all persons in *villeinage*, which included every one below the lord of the manor, were subject to a master, and bound to the land, except, of course, " free tenants " (p. 75). But even against their lord the villeins had certain rights which were to be recognised; [1] and they had, besides, many comforts and little responsibility, except to pay their dues to their lord. Moreover, it was possible for a villein to purchase a remission of his services, and become a " free tenant ; " or he might become such by residing in a town for a year and a day, and being a member of a town gild, as long as during that period he was unclaimed by his lord.[2] And in course of time the villein's position came to be this—he owed his lord the customary services (p. 75) whereby his lord's land was cultivated ; but his lord could not refuse him his customary rights in return— " his house and lands, and rights of wood and hay " [3]—and in relation to every one but his lord he was a perfectly free citizen. His condition tended to improve [4] (at least in an economic sense), and by the time of the Great Plague (1348) a large number of villeins had become actually free, having commuted their services for money-payments.[5] What these services were we shall now explain. But, finally, it should be pointed out that the state of villeinage and of serfage was practically the same thing in two aspects ; the first implying the fact that the villein was bound to the soil, the second that he was subject to the master. A serf

---

[1] Vinogradoff, *V. in E.*, pp. 174, 176. The lord could even be fined for not fulfilling his village duties. Gomme, *Vill. Comm.*, p. 117.

[2] Stubbs, *Const. Hist.*, I. ch. xi. p. 421.

[3] Stubbs, II. xvi. p. 453.

[4] Seebohm in *Eng. Hist. Review*, July 1892, vol. vii. 27, p. 457, who agrees with Thorold Rogers. Dr Stubbs and others hold a quite contrary view (*Const. Hist.*, i. p. 427), but this is because they take into account only the legal status, not the economic condition of the villein.

[5] Rogers, *Six Centuries*, p. 253. The process of commutation had probably begun before the Conquest. Ashley, *Econ. Hist.*, I. ch. i. p. 22.

was not a slave; and, as we saw above, *slaves* became extinct soon after the Norman Conquest.

§ 40. *Services due to the Lord from his Tenants in Villeinage.*

Under the manorial system rent was paid in a very different manner from that in which it is paid to-day, for it was a rent not so much of money, though that was employed, as of services. The services thus rendered by tenants in villeinage, whether villeins or cottars, may be divided, although they present much variety, into *week-work*,[1] and *boon-days* or work on special days.[2] The week-work consisted of ploughing or reaping, or doing some other agricultural work for the lord of the manor for two or three days in the week, or at fixed times, such as at harvest; while *boon-day* work was rendered at times not fixed, but whenever the lord of the manor might require it, though the number of boon-days in a year was limited.[3] When, however, the villein or cottar had performed these liabilities, he was quite free to do work on his own land, or, for that matter, on anyone else's land, as indeed the cottars frequently did, for they had not much land of their own, and, therefore, often had time and labour to spare. It was from this cottar class with time to spare that a distinct wage-earning class,[4] like our modern labourers, arose, who lived almost entirely by wages. We shall hear more of them later on, but at the time of the Conquest not many such existed.

§ 41. *Money Payments and Rents.*

It was also usual for a tenant, besides rendering these servile services, to pay his lord a small rent either in money or kind, generally in both. Thus, on Cuxham manor,[5] we find a villein (or serf) paying his lord ½d. on November 12th every year, and 1d. whenever he brews. He also pays, in

---

[1] "Wic-weorce," *Rectitudines*, 375 (Schmid).
[2] Seebohm, *V. C.*, 41, 78.   [3] At least by custom; Seebohm, p. 79.
[4] Thorold Rogers, *Hist of Agric.*, ii. 329, with his customary completeness, gives many instances of rates at which these farm servants were hired, including ploughmen, carters, shepherds, gardeners, cowherds, &c., &c
[5] Thorold Rogers, *Six Centuries*, p. 40.

kind, 1 quarter of seed-wheat at Michaelmas; 1 peck of wheat, 4 bushels of oats, and 3 hens on November 12th; also 1 cock and 2 hens, and 2d. worth of bread every Christmas. His *services* are—to plough and till ½-acre of the lord's land, to give 3 days' labour at harvest, and other days when required by the bailiff. This was the rent for about 12 or 15 acres of land (half a virgate), and, upon a calculation of the worth of labour and provisions at that time (end of thirteenth century), it comes to about 6d. an acre for his land and 3s. a year for his house and the land about it (*curtilage*).

§ 42. *Free Tenants. Soke-men.*

So far mention has been made only of tenants in villeinage; but in the Domesday Book we find another class of tenants, called free,[1] who had to pay a fixed rent, either in money or kind, and sometimes in labour. This rent was fixed and unalterable in amount, and they were masters of their own actions as soon as it was paid. They were not like the villeins, bound to the soil, but could transfer their holdings, or even quit the manor if they liked. They were, however, subject to their lord's jurisdiction in matters of law, and hence were called *soke-men* (from *soke* or *soc* = jurisdiction exercised by a lord).[2] They also were bound to give military service when called upon, which the villeinage tenants had not to give. If they had any services to render, these were generally commuted into money payments; and here we may observe that there was a constant tendency[3] from the Conquest to the time of the Great Plague (1348) towards this commutation. Villeins also could, and did frequently, commute their labour rents for money rents.

In Domesday we find that the Eastern and East-central counties[4] were those in which " free " tenants or soke-men

---

[1] *Liberi homines, sochemanni; cf.* Seebohm, *V. C.*, pp. 87, 88.   [2] *Ib.*

[3] The whole of the services, both week-work and boon-days, are found occasionally commuted as early as 1240; Ashley, *Econ. Hist.*, I. c., i. p. 31. Complete commutation became general by the reign of Edward II. Rogers, *Six Centuries*, p. 218.

[4] Ellis gives 10,097 *liberi homines*, of which more than half (5344) were

were most prevalent. There they form from 27 to 45 per
cent. of the inhabitants of those parts, though, taking all
England into view, they only form 4 per cent. of the total
population.[1] It is almost certain that they were of Danish
or (later) of Norman origin ; for it is in the Danish
districts that they are chiefly found, and their position is
exceptional and privileged. The number of free tenants,
however, was constantly increasing, even among tenants in
villeinage, for the lord often found it more useful to have
money, and was willing to allow commutation of services ;
or, again, he might prefer not to cultivate *all* his own land
(his *demesne*), but to let it for a fixed money rent not only
to a freeman but to a villein [2] to do what he could with it,
and thus the villein became a free man, while the lord
was sure of a fixed sum from his land every year, whether
the harvest were good or bad.

§ 43. *The Distinction between Free and Unfree Tenants.*

The classification of the inhabitants of the manors which
we have just examined is based upon the classification of
Domesday. But, like that of Domesday, though clear in
its main features, it is rough and even artificial. In fact,
being drawn up for the purposes of a fiscal survey, the
Domesday inquirers classed the various kinds of tenants
under heads " too few and simple to be accurate." In
Domesday the demesne land is distinguished from land
held " in villeinage," and the Book does not recognise free
tenants (*libere tenentes*) on land in villeinage, because, for
the purposes of the survey, such tenants were practically
villeins, and, therefore, " unfree." But, as a matter of fact,
there were in those times many people whom Domesday
regarded simply as *villani* who were really more free than
ordinary villeins.[3] But this the Norman surveyors, and

in Suffolk ; also 2041 *liberi homines commendati* (1895 in Suffolk), and no less
than 23,072 *sochemanni. Introd.*, pp. 511-514.

[1] See also the maps in Seebohm, *V. C.*, p. 86.

[2] Ashley, *Econ. Hist.*, I. i. p. 27, who quotes the case of Ralph de Diceto
in *Domesday of St Paul's*, 114.

[3] For instance, free men often took, in addition to their own land, a
villein holding with the services attached to it, but still preserved their
personal freedom.

the Norman lawyers of the same period, could not understand.[1] They were inclined to follow the theory of Roman Law, which recognised no middle position between freedom and slavery. As a matter of fact, we notice after the Conquest a continual attempt to degrade the villein in the eyes of the law by accentuating all the servile elements in his condition, and ignoring the very numerous elements that betoken some kind of freedom.

It is no wonder, then, that we find a persistent tradition, to which modern investigation gives no slight support, to the effect that the freedom of the villein was greater in Saxon than in Norman times.[2] It is even held [3] that the privileged *socmen* represent a state of freedom that at one time was the normal condition of villeins. However this may be, we may arrive with some certainty at the conclusions already indicated [4] : (1) An analysis of the legal evidence of Norman times shows that the classification of society into villeins (or " unfree " men) and freeholders is comparatively late and artificial.[5] (2) For there existed between these two clearly-marked classes a large body of " customary " freeholders,[6] and from these customary holders the ranks of the villeins were constantly recruited, as the legal minds of the day tended to debase the condition of freedom which the customary holders possessed. But (3) originally the customary freeholders formed the main bulk of the population.

Now, the work of the statesmen and lawyers of Norman times tended to change the " customary " freedom of the villein into an almost complete servitude from the legal point of view.[7] But, on the other hand, economic forces were at work which tended inevitably to give the villein more and more practical, if not legal, freedom. The advantages of a settled government, the extension of commerce and manufactures, and the prosperity gained thereby under

---

[1] Domesday even regarded the free men in Kent and in Danish manors in Essex as *villani*. Vinogradoff, *V. in E.*, p. 208.

[2] Vinogradoff, *V. in E.*, p. 135, though Seebohm rather doubts it ; see his criticism in *Eng. Hist. Review*, July 1892, p. 449.

[3] Vinogradoff, p. 136.

[4] P. 56.

[5] *Villeinage in England*, pp. 177, 220.

[6] See p. 56 above.

[7] *Cf.* Vinogradoff, *V. in E.*, p. 45, and note.

the cover of the law and order established very soon after the Conquest, all gave back to the villein tenants on the economic and industrial side far more than the lawyers took away in legal definitions and status.[1] The economic effects of the new industry, commerce, and prosperity became the source of a practical freedom,[2] which existed none the less surely though it was persistently ignored by the lawyers ; and this practical freedom grew greater and greater, till at last, in spite of legal definitions, villeinage became a state more of antiquarian than of actual interest. The Peasants' Revolt of 1381 opened the eyes of England to this fact, and from that year the death-knell of villeinage as a practical institution was already sounded.

§ 44. *Illustrations of Manors from Domesday.*

But this is greatly to anticipate the story of industrial development. We must return to the manors of Norman days, and it will perhaps be well to give two illustrations drawn from the Domesday Book (eleventh century) and from bailiffs' accounts of a later period (end of thirteenth century).

First, we will take a manor in Warwickshire in the Domesday Survey [3] (1089)—Estone, now Aston, near Birmingham. It was one of a number belonging to William, the son of Ansculf, who was tenant-in-chief, but had let it to one Godmund, a sub-tenant, or tenant-in-mesne. The Survey runs—"William Fitz-Ansculf holds of the King Estone, and Godmund of him. There are 8 hides.[4] The arable employs 20 ploughs; in the demesne the arable employs 6 ploughs, but now there are no ploughs. There are 30 villeins with a priest, and 1 bondsman, and 12 bordars (*i.e.*, cottars). They have 18 ploughs. A mill pays

---

[1] This follows the view of Seebohm (*cf.* his remarks in *Eng. Hist. Rev.*, July 1892, p. 457).

[2] A serf or villein could in later days even become a knight, as did Sir Robert Sale, or a bishop, as did Grostête of Lincoln. Rogers, *Six Centuries*, p. 32.

[3] *Domesday* of Warwick, *q.v.*

[4] A *hide* varied in size, and was (after the Conquest) equal to a *carucate*, which might be anything from 80 to 120 or 180 acres. See Cunningham, *Growth of Eng. Industry*, i. 120, and *cf. note* 1, p. 65 above.

three shillings. The woodland is three miles long and half-a-mile broad. It was worth £4 ; now 100 shillings."

Here we have a good example of a manor held by a sub-tenant, and containing all the three classes mentioned before in this chapter—villeins, cottars, and slaves (*i.e.*, bondsmen). The whole manor must have been about 5000 acres, of which 1000 were probably arable land, which was of course parcelled out in strips among the villeins, the lord, and the priest. As there were only 18 ploughs among 30 villeins, it is evident that some of them at least had to use a plough and oxen in common. The demesne land does not seem to have been well cultivated by Godmund the lord, for there were no ploughs on it, though it was large enough to employ six. Perhaps Godmund, being an Englishman, had been fighting the Normans in the days of Harold, and had let it go out of cultivation, or perhaps the former owner had died in the war, and Godmund had rented the land from the Norman noble to whom William gave it.

§ 45. *Cuxham Manor in the Eleventh and Thirteenth Centuries.*

Our second illustration can be described at two periods of its existence—at the time of Domesday and 200 years later. It was only a small manor of some 500 acres, and was held by a sub-tenant from a Norman tenant-in-chief, Milo Crispin. It is found in the Oxfordshire Domesday, in the list of lands belonging to Milo Crispin. The Survey says : " Alured [the sub-tenant] now holds 5 hides for a manor in Cuxham. Land for 4 ploughs ; now in the demesne, 2 ploughs and 4 bondsmen. And 7 villeins with 4 bordars have 3 ploughs. There are 3 mills of 18 shillings ; and 18 acres of meadow. It was worth £3, now £6." Here, again, the three classes of villeins, cottars or bordars, and slaves are represented. The manor was evidently a good one, for though smaller than Estone, it was worth more, and has three mills and good meadow land as well. Now, by the end of the thirteenth century this manor had passed into the hands of Merton College, Oxford, which then represented the lord, but farmed it by means of a bailiff. Professor Thorold Rogers gives us a description of it,[1] drawn from the annual accounts of this bailiff, which he examined along with many others from other manors. We find one or two changes have taken place, for the bondsmen have entirely disappeared, as indeed they did in less than a century after the Conquest all through the land. The number of villeins and bordars has increased, for there are now 13 villeins and 8 cottars and 1 free tenant. There is also a prior, who holds land (6 acres) in the manor but does not live in it ; also two other tenants, who do not live in the manor, but hold "a quarter of a knight's fee " (here some 40 or 50 acres)— a knight's fee [2] comprising an area of land varying from 2 hides to 4 or even 6 hides, but in any case worth some £20. As the Cuxham land was good, the quantity necessary for the valuation of a fee would probably be only the small hide or carucate of 80 acres, and the quarter of it, of course, 20 acres or a little more. The 13 serfs hold 170 acres, but the 8 cottars only 30 acres, including their tenements. The free tenant holds 12¾ acres, and Merton College as lord of the manor some 240 acres of demesne. There are now two mills instead of three, one belonging to the prior and the other to another tenant. There were altogether, counting the families of the villeins and cottars, but not the two tenants of military fees, about 60 or 70 inhabitants, the most important being the college bailiff and the miller.

§ 46. *A Village of the Eleventh Century.*

Now in both these country manors, as in all others, the central feature would be the dwelling of the lord, or manor-house. It was substantially built, and served as a court-house for the sittings of the *court baron* and the *court leet.*[3]

---

[1] *Six Centuries,* p. 41.

[2] It is very difficult to state exactly what a knight's fee really was; Stubbs, *Const. Hist.,* I. xi. p. 431. *Cf.* Pearson, *Early and Middle Ages,* i. 375, and ii. 463, who puts it at about 5 hides, or a rental of £20.

[3] *Manorial Courts.*—The *court baron* was composed of a kind of jury of freeholders, and was concerned with civil proceedings. The *court leet* was composed of all tenants, both free and serf, who acted as a jury in criminal cases, minor offences, and so forth. Both courts were presided

If the lord did not live in it, his bailiff did so, and perhaps the lord would come occasionally himself to hold these courts, or his bailiff might preside. Near the manor-house generally stood the church, often large for the size of the village, because the nave was frequently used as a town-hall for meetings or for markets.[1] Then there would be the house of the priest, possibly in the demesne ; and after these two the most important building was the mill, which, if there was a stream, would be placed on its banks in order to use the water-power. The rest of the tenants generally inhabited the principal street or road[2] of the village, near the stream, if one ran through the place. The average population of an eleventh century village must have been about 150 persons.[3] The houses of these villages were poor and dirty, not always made of stone, and never (till the fifteenth century) of brick,[4] but built of posts wattled and plastered with clay or mud,[5] with an upper storey of poles reached by a ladder. The articles of furniture would be very coarse and few, being necessarily of home manufacture ; a few rafters or poles overhead, a bacon-rack, and agricultural tools being the most conspicuous objects. Chimneys were unknown, except in the manor-houses, and so too were windows, and the floor was of bare earth. Outside the door was the " mixen," a collection of every kind of manure and refuse,[6] which must have rendered the village street alike unsavoury, unsightly, and

over by the lord of the manor or his bailiff. Thus local discipline and law was concentrated in the hands of the inhabitants of the parish themselves, and the manorial courts were a very useful means of education in local self-government. Unfortunately their power, utility, and educational influence declined with the decay of the whole manorial system. *Cf.* Rogers, *Six Centuries*, pp. 63 and 420 ; Stubbs, *Const. Hist.*, I. xi. 399 ; Maitland, *Select Pleas*, I. lxv. ; and Vinogradoff, *V. in E.*, pp. 362, 365, and ch. v. of Essay II.

[1] Rogers, *Six Centuries*, p. 66.   [2] Gomme, *Vill. Comm.*, p. 173.
[3] We can easily compute this by dividing the Domesday population (283,342) by the number of manors (9250), which gives about 30 able-bodied men per village, or 150 persons if we multiply by five.
[4] Rogers, *Econ. Interpretation of History*, p. 279.
[5] *Cf.* Gomme, *Vill. Comm.*, p. 44.
[6] This is very noticeable in certain villages of the Belgian Ardennes— *e.g.*, Sommière, near Dinant.

F

unwholesome. But though their life was rude and rough, it seems that the villagers were fairly happy, and, considering all things, not much worse off than their descendants are now.[1] Of course it is very difficult to compare the life of different ages, especially of periods so diverse as the eleventh or thirteenth century and the nineteenth. But it would be true to say that a mediæval labourer was often better off as regards food [2] than the unskilled labourer of to-day, though, on the other hand, he may have been worse clad and worse housed. One thing, perhaps, balances another. Yet probably the social life of the mediæval village, with its active manor courts and parish councils, was more interesting than that of a nineteenth century country parish, and the villager, though a villein, had a greater voice in parish affairs than his modern representative, except quite recently, possessed.

It is necessary, in order to complete our sketch of the manorial system from the time of the Conquest onwards, to understand how the land was divided up. We may say that there were seven kinds of land altogether. (1) First came the lord's land round about the manor-house, the *demesne* land, which was strictly his own, and generally cultivated in early times by himself or his bailiff. All other land held by tenants was called *land in villeinage.* (2) Next came the arable land of the village, held by the tenants in *common fields.*[3] Now these fields were all divided up into many strips, and tenants held their strips generally in quite different places, all mixed up in any order [4]

---

[1] I am inclined to follow the view of Thorold Rogers in this (*cf. Six Centuries*, pp. 68, 69), with whom Dr Cunningham, after all, practically agrees (*Eng. Industry*, i. 275). In estimating comparative prosperity, we must regard the *possibilities* of each age, and how far the villager attained them then or can do so now. Almost certainly he came nearer to such possibilities as there were than his modern brother does. Hasty denials of mediæval prosperity and comfort only betoken ignorance.

[2] Cunningham, i. 275.

[3] Seebohm, *Vill. Comm.*, pp. 1-27, and the maps there; Gomme, *Village Community*, pp. 194, 166; Cunningham, *Eng. Industry and Commerce*, i. 70, 71.

[4] "A single farmer might have to cut his portion of grass from twenty different places, though the tenants frequently accommodated one another by exchanging allotments when it was convenient to do so." Gomme, *Vill. Comm.*, p. 166.

(*cf.* diagram, where the tenants are marked **A, B, C,** &c.). The lord [1] and the parson might also have a few strips in these fields. There were at least three fields, in order to allow the rotation of crops mentioned before (p. 40). Each tenant held his strip only till harvest, after which all fences and divisions were taken away, and the cattle turned out to feed on the stubble. (3) Thirdly came the *common pasture,* for all the tenants. But each tenant was restricted or stinted in the number of cattle that he might pasture,[2] lest he should put on too many, and thus not leave enough food for his neighbours' cattle. Sometimes, however, we find pasture without stint, as in Port Meadow at Oxford to this day.[3] (4) Then comes the *forest* or *woodland,* as in Estone, which belonged to the lord, who owned all the timber. But the tenants had rights, such as the right of lopping and topping certain trees, collecting fallen branches for fuel, and the right of "pannage"—*i.e.,* of turning cattle, especially swine, into the woods to pick up what food they could. (5) There was also in most manors what is called the *waste*—*i.e.,* uncultivated land, affording rough pasture, and on which the tenants had the right of cutting turf and bracken for fuel and fodder. Then near the stream there would perhaps be some (6) *Meadow land,* as at Cuxham, but this generally belonged to the lord, who, if he let it out, always charged an extra rent (and often a very high one),[4] for it was very valuable as affording a good supply of hay for the winter. Lastly, if the tenant could afford it, and wanted to have other land besides the common fields, where he could let his cattle lie, or to cultivate the ground more carefully, he could occupy (7) a *close,* or a portion of land specially marked off and let separately.[5] The lord always had a close on his demesne, and the chief tenants would generally have one or two as well. The close land was of course rented more highly than land in the common fields.

The accompanying diagram shows a typical manor, held by a sub-tenant from a tenant-in-chief, who holds it of the king. It contains all the different kinds of land, though,

---

[1] Vinogradoff, *V. in E.*, p. 406.   [2] Rogers, *Six Centuries*, p. 90.

[3] *Ib.*, p. 74.   [4] *Ib.*, p. 73.   [5] *Ib.*, p 89.

of course, they did not always all exist in one manor. It also shows the manor-house, church, mill, and village.

THE KING (supreme landlord).

TENANT-IN-CHIEF, owning various manors.

A SUB-TENANT, or tenant-in-mesne, the lord of the manor below.

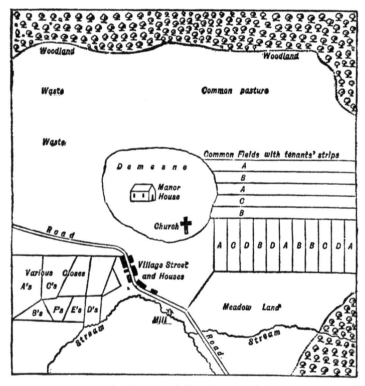

§ 47. *The Decay of the Manorial System.*

Such, then, was the manorial village and the manorial system generally in the eleventh century, and thus it lasted for two or three centuries more. But in course of time it died out, though survivals of it last even to our own day.

The decay of this social and economic system begins most clearly and markedly with the changes made by the Black Death (1348), and by the social revolution which followed it, of which the Peasants' Revolt was the first and most startling symptom (*cf.* ch. xii.). The legislation of Edward I. forms, again, another epoch from which to date the decay of manorial institutions. He laid the foundations of a system of national instead of local regulations for industry, and from that time forward the essentially local arrangements of the manors began to lose both their necessity and their utility.[1] As Dr Cunningham says—" In regard to commerce, manufactures, and to agriculture alike, the local authorities were gradually overtaken and superseded by the increasing activity of Parliament, till, in the time of Elizabeth, the work was practically finished."[2] The essentially local and personal relations of the manor gave way to the more general and impersonal relations of national government and national economy.

[1] Cunningham, *Industry and Commerce*, i. pp. 241-245.   [2] *Ib.*, p. 243.

CHAPTER VI

THE TOWNS AND THE GILDS

§ 48. *The Origin of the Towns.*

As in the case of the village, so also the town, in the modern sense of the word, had its origin in the primitive settlements of the people. The only difference between a town and a village lay, originally, in the number of inhabitants, and in the fact that the town was a more defensible place than the rural settlement, since it probably had a rampart or a moat surrounding it instead of the mere hedges which ran round the villages.[1] It was simply in the Anglo-Saxon period a more strictly organised form of the village community.[2] In itself it was merely a manor or group of manors; as Professor Freeman puts it, one part of the district where men lived closer together than elsewhere.[3] The town had at first a constitution like that of the primitive village, but its inhabitants had gradually gained certain rights and functions of a special nature.[4] These rights and privileges had sometimes been received from the lord of the manor on which the town had grown up[5]; for towns, especially provincial towns, were often at first only dependent manors, which gained safety and solidity under the protection of some great noble, prelate, or the king himself;[6] who finally would grant the town thus formed a charter.[7]

[1] Stubbs, *Const. Hist.*, I. v. 92. The Anglo-Saxons called them "*burh*" —*i.e.*, "boroughs." [2] *Ib.* [3] *Norman Conquest*, v. p. 470.

[4] Thus Lincoln, Stamford, and other towns had certain rights of jurisdiction, *sac* and *soc; Domesday* (Lincoln).

[5] In other cases they were probably the inherited rights of a free community.

[6] Stubbs, *Const. Hist.*, I. v. p. 93, who quotes examples of the *eorles tun, cyninges burh, cyninges tun.*

[7] This charter would give rights of jurisdiction over the citizens, of taking toll, &c.; *cf.* Stubbs, *Const. Hist.*, I. v. 106. Such rights were also granted to private individuals.

§ 49. *Rise of Towns in England.*

Towns first became important in England towards the end of the Saxon period. Saxon England had never been a settlement of towns, but of villages or manors. But gradually towns developed, though differing widely in the circumstances and manner of their growth. Some grew up in the fortified camps of the invaders themselves,[1] as being in a secure position; some arose from a later occupation of the once sacked and deserted Roman towns.[2] Many grew silently in the shadow of a great abbey or monastery.[3] Of this class was Oxford, which first came into being round the monasteries of Osney and S. Frideswide. Others clustered round the country houses of some Saxon king or earl.[4] Several important boroughs owed their rise to the convenience of their site as a port or a trading centre. This was the origin of the growth of Bristol, whose rise resulted directly from trade;[5] and London of course had always been a port of high commercial rank.[6] A few other towns, like Scarborough and Grimsby,[7] were at first only small havens for fishermen. But all the English towns were far less flourishing before the arrival of the Normans than they afterwards became.

The influence of the Danes, however, should be noted as

[1] Especially in the case of the Danes; Cunningham, *Growth of Industry*, i. 91; Green, *Hist. of Eng. People*, i. 207.

[2] Some of the Roman towns never quite lost their continuity of life; *cf.* Jessop, *Studies by a Recluse*, p. 120, who instances London, Chester, Lincoln, and Exeter; *cf.* also Green, *History*, i. 207.

[3] Stubbs, I. v. 93; Freeman, *Norman Conquest*, v. 471; Rogers, *Six Centuries*, p. 103.

[4] Green (*History*, i. 207) evidently follows Stubbs, *u.s.*

[5] From very early times it had an active trade with Ireland; *cf.* Cunningham, *Growth of Industry*, i. 89, note; and Craik, *British Commerce*, i. 72.

[6] Probably it was originally a hill-fort; and its name is said to mean the "hill fort by the water." Its importance in Roman times was very great; Green, *Making of England*, p. 3. In Saxon times it was left much to itself, but hedged in with a ring of Saxon agricultural settlements. Gomme, *Village Comm.*, p. 52.

[7] A fair attended by foreign merchants was held in Saxon times on Scarborough beach; Cunningham, i. 82, *n.* Grimsby merchants are mentioned in Rymer, *Foedera*, II. i. 110, 133. See also Rogers, *Six Centuries*, 104.

promoting the growth of towns. Though undoubtedly pirates, the Danish invaders were often also merchants, and often planted villages at centres suitable for commerce, or stimulated by their trade the growth of places which but for their coming might have remained undeveloped.[1] Moreover, it is the towns of Danish origin that frequently show the most ancient municipal organisation ; as the records of the five "Danish boroughs"—Nottingham, Derby, Lincoln, Stamford, and Leicester—go to prove.[2] Even to-day near the heart of modern London the Church of St Clement Danes reminds us of those rough seafaring men, half pirates half traders, whose patron saint was Clement with his anchor.[3]

§ 50. Towns in Domesday.

If now we once more go back to our great authority, the survey made by William the Norman, we find that the status of the towns or boroughs is clearly recognised, though they are now regarded as held by the lord of the manor "in demesne," or, in default of a lord, as part of the king's demesne.[4] Thus Northampton at that time was a town in the king's demesne ; Beverley was held in demesne by the Archbishop of York.[5] It was possible, too, that one town might belong to several lords, because it spread over, or was an aggregate of, several manors or townships. Thus Leicester[6] seems to have included four manors, which were thus held in demesne by four lords—one by the king, another by the Bishop of Lincoln, another by a noble, Simon de Senlis, and the fourth by Ivo of Grantmesnil, the sheriff. In later times it was held under one lord, Count Robert of Meulan, who had acquired the four portions for himself.

Now, in the Domesday Book there is mention made of forty-one provincial cities or boroughs, most of them being

---

[1] Cunningham, i 88.

[2] Stubbs, *Const. Hist.*, I. ch. v. p. 93. For many years these five towns held together in a confederation which was the backbone of Danish power in the Midlands ; *cf.* Jessop, *Studies*, p. 126.

[3] For Danish influence see York Powell, *Eng. Hist. Review*, No. XVII. p. 134.   [4] Stubbs, *Const. Hist.*, I. xi. 408.   [5] *Ib.*, p. 409.   [6] *Ib.*

the county towns of the present day.[1]   There are also ten fortified towns of greater importance than the others. They are Canterbury, York, Nottingham, Oxford, Hereford, Leicester, Lincoln, Stafford, Chester, and Colchester.[1] London was a town apart, as it had always been, and was the only town which had an advanced civic constitution, being regulated by a port-reeve and a bishop,[2] and having a kind of charter, though afterwards the privileges of this charter were much increased. London was of course a great port and trading centre, and had many foreign merchants in it. It was then, as well as in subsequent centuries, the centre of English national life, and the voice of its citizens counted for something in national affairs.[3] The other great ports of England at that time were Bristol, Southampton,[4] and Norwich,[5] and as trade grew and prospered, many other ports rose into prominence (see p. 144).

There were also other towns which grew up merely as aggregates of traders, and had not acquired as yet any other cohesion than as organised communities. These formed the large class of mere *market towns*, which of course still exist in large numbers, still serving the purpose to which they originally owed their existence without growing much beyond their old proportions.

§ 51. *Special Privileges of Towns.*

It is not till the twelfth century that the towns begin to have an independent municipal history as self-governing boroughs,[6] nor is it till the fifteenth century that we come to advanced municipal life and organisation. But, even at the time of the Norman Conquest, most towns, though small, were of sufficient importance to have a certain status of their own, with definite privileges.[7] The privilege they strove for first of all was generally an immunity from appearing before the Court of Appeal where the king's officer

---

[1] Stubbs, *Const. Hist.*, I. xi. 403.   [2] *Ib.*, p. 404.
[3] *Cf.* Rogers, *Six Centuries*, p. 109.
[4] It was the chief port of Southern England; Rogers, *Six Centuries*, p. 104.
[5] *Ib.*, p. 106. It was famed for its harbour; and, like many another disused port of the east coast, did a large trade with the Netherlands.
[6] Mrs Green, *Town Life*, i. p. 11.   [7] Stubbs, I. xi. 408.

presided and levied his fees;[1] but perhaps the most important privilege was the second one—the immunity from the personal taxation exacted by the officers of the Royal Exchequer, and collected by the sheriff.[2] To gain their points they asked, first, the rights of choosing their own justiciar,[3] or official who should preside in the town court and relieve them from the necessity of appearing at other courts; and then they requested the liberty of taxing themselves, and of composition for taxation—*i.e.*, the right of paying a fixed sum or rent to the Crown, instead of the various tallages, taxes, and imposts that might be required of other places.[4] This fixed sum,[5] or composition, was called the *firma burgi*, and by the time of the Conquest was nearly always paid in money. Previously it had been paid both in money and kind, for we find Oxford paying to Edward the Confessor six sectaries of honey as well as £20 in coin; while to William the Norman it paid £60 as an inclusive lump sum.[6] By the end of the Norman period[7] all the towns had secured the *firma burgi*, and the right of assessing it themselves, instead of being assessed by the sheriff; they had the right also of choosing an officer of their own, instead of the king's bailiff or *reeve*. They had thus their own tribunals, a charter for their customs, and special rules of local administration, and, generally speaking, had gained entire judicial and commercial freedom.

§ 52. *How the Towns obtained their Charters.*

It is interesting to see what circumstances helped forward this emancipation of the towns from the rights possessed by the nobles and the abbeys,[8] or by the king. The chief cause of the readiness of the nobles and kings to grant

---

[1] Jessop, *Studies of a Recluse*, p. 130.   [2] *Ib.*

[3] As in the Charter to London given by Henry I., quoted by Stubbs, *ut ante*, p. 405.   [4] Stubbs, *u. s.*, p. 410.

[5] Ellis, *Introd. to Domesday*, i. 190, gives many examples.

[6] Ellis, *Introd.*, i. 193.   [7] Stubbs, *u. s.*, p. 424.

[8] A noble, bishop, or abbot on whose demesne a town existed of course had the judicial and other rights of a lord of the manor over such a town, and could part with them by giving a charter. Thus Beverley gained its charter, not from the crown, but from Archbishop Thurstan. *Cf.* Stubbs, *Const. Hist.*, I. xi. 411. Manchester remained under its feudal lord till 1846.

charters during this period (from the Conquest to Henry
III.) was their lack of ready money. Everyone knows how
fiercely the nobles fought against each other in Stephen's
reign, and how enthusiastically they rushed off to the
Crusades under Richard I. They could not indulge their
love of fighting, which in their eyes was their main duty,
without money to pay for their fatal extravagances in this
direction, and to get money they frequently parted with
their manorial rights over the towns which had grown up
on their estates.[1] Especially was this the case when a
noble or king was taken prisoner, and wanted the means
of his ransom.[2] In this way Portsmouth and Norwich
gained their charters by paying part of Richard I.'s ransom
(1194). Again, Rye and Winchelsea gained theirs by
supplying the same king (in 1191) with two ships to
aid his Eastern crusade.[3] Many other instances might be
quoted from the cases of nobles who also gave charters
when setting out upon these extraordinary expeditions.
Indeed, the Crusades had a very marked influence in this
way upon the growth of English towns. Some one had to
pay for the wars in which the aristocracy delighted, and it
is well to remember the fact that the expenses of all our
wars—and they have been both numerous and costly—
have been defrayed by the industrial portion of the community. Even the glories and cruelties of that often savage
age of so-called knightly chivalry,[4] which has been idealised
and gilded by romancers and history-mongers, with its
tournaments and torture-chambers, were paid for by that despised industrial population of the towns and villages which
contained the real life and wealth of mediæval England.

§ 53. *The Gilds and the Towns. Various kinds of
Gilds.*

But besides the indirect effect of the Crusades, there
was another powerful factor in the growth and emancipation of the towns after the Conquest. I refer to the
merchant gilds, which were becoming more and more pro-

[1] Cunningham, *Growth of Industry*, i. p. 198.
[2] Green, *History*, i. 212.   [3] See Rymer, *Foedera*, I. 63, 53.
[4] *Cf.* the state of things instanced by Green, *History*, i. 156.

minent all through this period, though the height of their
power was not reached till the fourteenth century. These
merchant gilds were one of four other kinds of gilds,
all of which seem to have been similar in origin. The
earliest gilds are found in Saxon times,[1] and were very
much what we understand by clubs at the present day. At
first they were associations for more or less religious and
charitable purposes,[2] and formed a sort of artificial family,
whose members were bound by the bond not of kinship but
of an oath, while the gild-feast, held once a month in the
common hall, replaced the family gatherings of kinsfolk.
These gilds were found both in towns and villages, but
chiefly in the former, where men were brought more closely
together. Besides (1) the *religious* gilds, we find in
Saxon times (2) the *frith* gilds,[3] formed for mutual assistance in case of violence, wrong, or false accusation, or in
any legal affairs. But this class of gilds died out after the
Conquest. The most important were (3) the *merchant*
gilds mentioned above, which existed certainly in Edward
the Confessor's time, being called in Saxon *ceapemanne* gilds,
and they were recognised at the time of the Conquest, for
they are recorded in Domesday here and there as possessing
lands.[4] The merchant members of these gilds had various
privileges, such as a virtual monopoly of the local trade of
a town, which even outsiders were not allowed to infringe,
and freedom from certain imposts.[5] They had, at any rate at
first, a higher rank than the members of the (4) *craft* gilds.[6]
These last were associations of handicraftsmen, or artisans,
and were separate from the merchant gilds, though also of
great importance. If a town were large enough, each craft
or manufacture had a gild of its own, though perhaps in
smaller towns members of various crafts would form only
one gild. Such gilds were found, too, not only in towns
but in country villages, as is known, *e.g.*, in the case of

---

[1] Stubbs, *Const. Hist*, I. xi. p. 411, who gives an excellent summary. *Cf.*
also Brentano, *History and Development of Gilds*, and Gross, *Gild Merchant*,
for further information.   [2] Stubbs, *ut ante*, p. 412.
  [3] They were possibly earlier than the religious associations. *Cf.* Stubbs,
ut ante, p. 414.   [4] *Ib.*, p. 416.
  [5] Gross, *Gild Merchant*, i. 44.   [6] Stubbs, *ut ante*, p. 417.

some Norfolk villages, where remains of their halls have been found.[1] Their gild feasts are probably represented to this day in the parish feasts, survivals of ancient custom.

§ 54. How the Merchant Gilds helped the Growth of Towns.

Now it was only natural that the existence of these powerful associations in the growing boroughs should secure an increasing development of cohesion and unity among the townsmen. Moreover, the merchant gilds had a very important privilege, which would make many outsiders anxious to join their ranks—namely, that membership in a gild for a year and a day made a villein a free man.[2] Thus the gilds included all the free tenants in a town, and very often the body of free citizens, who, of course, as free men, formed the only really influential class in a town, found themselves, by thus uniting together in a gild, "craft," or "mistery," in a position to gain even greater influence than before. In fact, only those who were members of some gild or "mistery" were allowed to take part in the municipal government of their town.[3] As time went on, and their influence grew, it became the special endeavour of the gildmen to obtain from the Crown or from their lord of the manor wider commercial privileges, such as grants of coinage, the right of holding fairs, and of exemption from tolls.[4] Then they asked for freedom of justice, and for the right of self-government; and it is supposed also that it was possibly the gilds also, as representing practically the town itself, who bought up the *firma burgi*,[5] and thus became their own assessors of taxes. Finally, no doubt, they helped largely in buying a charter, as we have seen, from a king or noble in need of ready money. And so, gradually, and by other steps which cannot now be clearly traced, the emancipation of the towns was won by the gilds; the boroughs became free from their lords' restrictions and dues; till by the end of the twelfth century chartered towns, which were

---

[1] Rogers, *Six Centuries*, p. 417.   [2] Stubbs, *Const. Hist.*, I. xi. p. 417.
[3] Ashley, *Economic Hist.*, II. i. 26.
[4] Stubbs, *Const. Hist.*, I. ix. p. 425.   [5] *Ib.*, p. 416.

very few at the time of the Conquest, became the general rule. In later times, again, the power of the gilds passed to the town corporations.[1]　Yet at no time can we say that the governing body of the town was identical in idea with the merchant gild.[2]　It is true that in time membership of some gild became indispensable to the status of a burgher,[3] but still the gild was theoretically distinct from the municipal body, though practically it was generally one and the same.　The chief result of the gilds and of gild-life was to produce greater unity and cohesion among the townsmen,[4] and thus to awake in them the idea of the corporate unity of municipal life.

§ 55. How the Craft Gilds helped Industry.

So far we have specially noted the work of the merchant gilds, which, as it were, built up the constitution and freedom of the towns.　But the craft gilds did similar work also.　Originally, it is true, the merchant gilds reckoned themselves above the craft gilds; but in later times the two classes came, so to speak, to stand more side by side[5]; and each class of gild occupied the same relation to the municipal government, though very often the members of each might vary greatly in wealth or position[6]—from the poor cobbler, who was yet a member of the shoemakers' gild, to the rich merchant of drapery, who might have held the highest municipal honours.

We must now look for a moment at the work of the artisans' gilds, or craft gilds, which afterwards became very important.[7]　These are found not only in London but in provincial towns.　The London weavers are mentioned as a craft gild in the time of Henry I. (1100 A.D.),[8] and most of these gilds seemed to have existed already for a long period.　The Goldsmiths' Gild claimed to have possessed land before the Norman Conquest, and it was fairly powerful in the days of Henry II. (1180 A.D.), for he found it

[1] Ashley, Econ. Hist., II. i., p. 13.
[2] Stubbs, ut supra, p. 418.　　[3] Ib., p. 425.　　[4] Ib., p. 425.
[5] Ashley, Econ. Hist., II. i. p. 24.　　　　　[6] Ib., p. 25.
[7] They were, perhaps, more often known as "crafts," "misteries," or "companies."　　[8] Cunningham, English Industry (1882), 132.

convenient to try and suppress it.[1]   But it did not receive
the public recognition of a charter till the fourteenth century.   They arose, of course, first in the towns, and originally seem to have consisted of a small body of the leading
men of a particular craft, to whom was confided the regulation of a particular industry, probably as soon as that
industry was thought of sufficient importance to be regulated.
In the fifteenth century they became so universal that every
trade which occupied as many as twenty men in a town had
a gild of its own.[2]   The gild tried to secure good work on
the part of its members,[3] and attempted to suppress the
production of wares by irresponsible persons who were not
members of the craft.[4]   Their fundamental principle was,
that a member should work not only for his own private
advantage but for the reputation and good of his trade—
"for the honour of the good folks of such misteries." [5]
Hence bad work was punished, and it is curious to note
that night-work was prohibited as leading to poor work.[6]
The gild also took care to secure a supply of competent
workmen for the future (and at the same time to restrain
competition) by training a limited number of young people
in its particular industry.   Hence arose the system of each
"master" having apprentices ; and though in earlier times it
does not seem to have been necessary that a person must
pass through an apprenticeship before being admitted a
member of a craft or mistery, in later days this rule was
rigidly enforced.[7]   The gild, moreover, exercised some kind
of moral control over its members, and secured their good
behaviour, thus forming an effective branch of the social
police.[8]   On the other hand, it had many of the characteristics of a benefit society, providing against sickness and
death among those belonging to it, as indeed all gilds did.[9]
At the end of the fourteenth century it is noticeable that

---

[1] Ashley *Econ Hist.*. I. ii. 81.   [2] Ashley, *ut supra*, II. ii. p. 74.
[3] Ashley, *Econ Hist* II. ii. p. 72.   [4] Rogers, *Six Centuries*, p. 107.
[5] See the Royal Order of Edward III., quoted by Bain, *Merchant and
Craft Gilds*, p. 40.
[6] Cunningham, i. p. 314.   [7] Ashley, *Econ. Hist.*, II. ii. p. 84.
[8] Ochenkowski, *England's Wirthschaftl. Entwickelung*, p. 66.
[9] Rogers, *Six Centuries*, pp. 110, 347.

the custom was growing of erecting special "houses" or "halls" for the gilds, these buildings being duly provided with the social and religious appurtenances of kitchen, chapel, and often also almshouses.[1]

These institutions, however, did not apparently only belong to the towns, but were found in country districts also; thus we hear of the carpenters' and masons' rural gilds in the reign of Edward III.[2] Even the peasant labourers, according to Professor Thorold Rogers,[3] possessed these associations, which in all cases served many of the functions of the modern trade unions. Later on (1381) we shall come to a very remarkable instance of the power of these peasants' unions in the matter of Tyler's rebellion.

§ 56. *Life in the Towns of this time.*

The inhabitants of the towns were of all classes of society. There was the noble who held the castle, or the abbot and monks in the monastery, with their retainers and personal dependants; there were the busy merchants, active both in the management of their trade and of civic affairs; and there were artisans and master workmen in different crafts. There were free tenants, or *tenants in socage,* including all the burgesses, or burgage-tenants, as they were called; and there was the lower class of villeins, who, however, always tended to rise into free men as they were admitted into the gilds. To and fro went our forefathers in the quiet, quaint, narrow streets, or worked at some handicraft in their houses, or exposed their goods round the market cross. And in those old streets and houses, in the town-mead and market-place, as a picturesque historian says,[4] amid the murmur of the mill beside the stream, and the notes of the bell that sounded its summons to the crowded assembly of the town-mote, in merchant-gild and craft-gild was growing up that

---

[1] Ashley, *Econ. Hist.*, II. ii. 82. It is also worth noting, as illustrating the close connection between the gilds and municipal life, that at Nottingham the Town Hall is still called the "Guild Hall."

[2] This may be inferred from Rogers, *ut supra*, pp. 236 and 237.

[3] *Ib.*, p. 252. See also his *Econ. Interpret. of History*, p. 306, on Village Guilds.

[4] Green, *History*, i. 212.

sturdy industrial life, unheeded and unnoticed by knight or baron, that silently and surely was building up the slow structure of England's wealth and freedom. This life was fostered by the idea of unity which possessed the townspeople of that day quite as much as it does those of our own time ; and this unity was promoted not only by the gilds but by the possession of town property in common by the towns-men,[1] in the shape of those common fields and pastures that were the relics of the time when the town was merely a village settlement.[2]   In later times we find the townsmen undertaking common enterprises, such as the proper pro-vision of corn or water for the citizens.[3]   The decay of municipal life, however, begins to date from the sixteenth century (or about that period), when commerce and trade were becoming more and more national and less local in character, and consequently national regulations of a more far-reaching character were required.   But, long before municipal or even gild life began to decay, it had done a very important work.   It had caused a radical change in social and political relationships, by its recognition of persons as standing for themselves and not tied to the land or depending on a superior lord.   The association of persons *as* persons had taken the place of the feudal association which was based only on land.[4]   Land was now no longer the basis of everything : a new social and economic force had appeared, and slowly but surely feudalism began to give way before it.

[1] Ashley, *Econ. Hist.*, II. i. 36.   [2] Above, p. 86, and *cf.* p. 48.
[3] More frequently in the fifteenth and sixteenth centuries.   Ashley, *ut supra*, p. 36.
[4] *Cf.* Maurer, *Städteverfassung*, iii. 725.

CHAPTER VII

MANUFACTURES AND TRADE : ELEVENTH TO THIRTEENTH
CENTURIES

§ 57. *Economic Effects of the Feudal System.*

WE shall find that, for some time after the Norman Conquest, English industry does not develope very rapidly, and
that for obvious reasons. The feud that existed between
Norman and Saxon—although, perhaps, partially allayed
by Henry I.'s marriage to an English wife [1]—and the social
disorder that accompanied this feeling, hardly tended to
that quiet and security that are necessary for a healthy
industrial life. The frightful disorders that occurred during
the fierce struggle for the kingdom between Stephen of
Blois and the Empress Maud, and the equally frightful
ravages and extortions of their contending barons, must
have been serious drawbacks to any progress. As the old
annalist remarks—" They fought among themselves with
deadly hatred ; they spoiled the fairest lands with fire and
rapine ; in what had been the most fertile of counties they
destroyed almost all the provision of bread." [2] But this terrible struggle fortunately ended in ruining many of the
barons who took part in it, and in the desirable destruction
of most of their abodes of plunder. The accession of
Henry II. (1154) marks a period of amalgamation between
Englishmen and Normans, not only in social life, but in
commercial traffic and intercourse.[3]

But even when we come to look at the feudal system in
a time of peace, we see that it did not tend to any great
growth of industry. It certainly gave, under a strong
ruler [4] (but only then) some security for person and pro-

---

[1] The reign of Henry I., however, was on the whole peaceful. " He was
a good man, and great was the awe of him : he made peace for man and
deer."—*English Chron.* (Bohn), 1135.   [2] Quoted by Green, *History*, i. 155.
[3] Green, *History*, i. 161   [4] Cunningham, i. 131.

perty, but it encouraged rather than diminished that spirit of isolation and self-sufficiency which was so marked a feature [1] of the earlier manors and townships. In these communities, again, little scope was afforded to individual enterprise, from the fact that the consent of the lord of a manor or town was often necessary for the most ordinary purposes of industrial life.[2] It is true, as we have seen, that when the noble owner was in pecuniary difficulties the towns profited thereby to obtain their charters; and perhaps we may not find it altogether a matter for regret that the barons, through their internecine struggles, thus unwittingly helped on the industry of the land. It may be admitted also, that though the isolation of communities consequent upon the prevalent manorial system did not encourage trade and traffic between separate communities, it yet tended to diffuse a knowledge of domestic manufactures throughout the land generally, because each place had largely to provide for itself.

The constant taxation,[3] however, entailed by the feudal system, in the shape of tallages, aids, and fines, both to king and nobles, made it difficult for the lower classes to accumulate capital, more especially as in the civil wars they were constantly plundered of it openly. The upper classes merely squandered it in fighting. Agriculture suffered similarly, for the villeins, however well off, were bound to the land,[4] especially in the earlier period soon after the Conquest, and before commutation of services for money rents became so common as it did subsequently; nor could they leave their manor [5] without incurring a distinct loss, both of social status, and, what is more important, of the means of livelihood. The systems of constant services to the lord of the manor, and of the collective methods of cultivation, were also drawbacks to good agriculture.[6] Again, in trade, prices

[1] Rogers, *Econ. Interp. History*, p. 283.
[2] *Cf.* the *Court Leet Records of Manchester* (pub. 1884), and Pearson, *Hist. of England*, i. 594.
[3] On taxation, see Stubbs, *Const. Hist.*, I. ch. xiii. pp. 576-586.
[4] On the other hand this had its advantages as giving the agriculturist security of tenure (*cf.* Bracton, *De Leg.*, ch. viii. *f.* 24*b*; Vol. I. p. 198-209 (ed. Twiss).
[5] Except on payment of a fine; *cf.* p. 151, below.   [6] Cunningham, i. 132.

were settled by authority, competition was checked,[1] while merchants had to pay heavy duties to the king, and were very much at the mercy of the royal officials.[2]

§ 58. *Foreign Trade. The Crusades.*

But, on the other hand, the Norman Conquest, which combined the Kingdom of England with the Duchy of Normandy in close political relations, gave abundant opportunities for commerce, both with France and the Continent, and foreign trade certainly received a stimulus from this fact. It was further developed by the Crusades. The most obvious effect of these remarkable expeditions for a visionary success was the opening up of trade routes throughout Europe to the shores of the Mediterranean Sea, and to the East in general.[3] They produced also a considerable redistribution of wealth in England itself, for the knights and nobles that set out for the Holy Land often mortgaged their lands and never redeemed them, or they perished, and their lands lapsed to the crown or to some monastery that took the place of a trustee for the absent owner.[4]

As to foreign trade, our chief authority at this time is the old chronicler, Henry of Huntingdon, whose history was published about 1155 A.D.[5] Like most historians, even of the present day, he says very little about so insignificant a matter as trade, but the single sentence which he devotes to it is probably of as great value as any other part of his book. From it we gather that our trade with Germany was extensive, and that we exported lead and tin among the metals;[6] fish and meat and fat cattle (which seems to point to some improvement in our pastoral economy); and, most important of all, "most precious wool," though at that time the English could not weave it properly for themselves. Our

---

[1] Cunningham, i. p. 230.   [2] Stubbs, *Const. Hist.*, i. p. 522.

[3] The Crusades *opened up* routes rather than followed those already existing ; *cf.* Gibbon, *Decline and Fall*, ch. lviii.

[4] *Cf.* Gibbon, *ut supra.*

[5] Quoted by Craik, *Hist. of Brit. Commerce*, i. 105.

[6] It appears from other authorities also that the export of these two metals must have been large. "The roofs of the principal churches, palaces, and castles in all parts of Europe are said to have been covered with English lead." Craik, *ut supra*, i. 105.

imports, however, were very limited, comprising none of the necessaries of life, and few of its luxuries beyond silver and foreign furs. Other imports were fine woven cloths, used for the dresses of the nobility ; and, after the Crusades began, of rich Eastern stuffs and spices, which were in great demand, and commanded a high price. So, too, did iron, which was necessary for agricultural purposes, as Englishmen had not yet discovered their rich stores of this metal, but had to get it from Spain and the lands on the Baltic shore.[1] Generally speaking, we may say that our imports consisted of articles of greater intrinsic value and scarcity than our exports, and thus were fewer in number, though there must have been some balance to be paid in coin or bullion. But this balance must have been comparatively small, as coined money, though, of course, no longer a rarity, was by no means plentiful, and was very precious. The German merchants certainly paid for English wool in silver.[2]

§ 59. *The Trading Clauses in the Great Charter.*

One great proof of the existence of a fair amount of foreign trade is seen in the clauses which were inserted in the Great Charter (1215), by the influence of the trading class. One enactment secures to foreign merchants freedom of journeying and of trade throughout the realm,[3] and another orders an uniformity of weights and measures [4] to be enforced over the whole kingdom. The growth of town life is seen in the enactment which secures to the towns the enjoyment of their municipal privileges, their freedom from arbitrary taxation, and the regulation of their own trade.[5] The amercement of a freeman, even upon conviction of felony, was never to include his contenement ; nor his wares, if he were a merchant, nor his wainage if a villein.[6] The exaction of forced labour or of provisions and

---

[1] Rogers, *Six Centuries*, pp. 88 and 151.
[2] Henry of Huntingdon, *ut supra*.
[3] John had already promised this at the commencement of his reign. Maitland, *Hist. of London*, i. 73-75. It was again laid down in Clause 41 of the Charter.
[4] Magna Carta, § 35. This had already been enjoined in an Assize of Richard I., and again by that King in 1194 (Hoveden, iii. 263 ; iv. 33).
[5] Magna Carta, § 13.   [6] Magna Carta, § 20.

chattels without payment by the royal officers was also for-bidden,[1] and this must have been a great boon to the agricul-tural population. On the other hand, it is very noticeable that the royal officers are not to take money in lieu of military service from those who are willing to perform the service in person,[2] a regulation which shows that commutation for services, military and otherwise, was now very common.

The general tone of those clauses of the Great Charter which deal with merchants, or with commerce and industry, is certainly remarkable in an age when, on the Continent of Europe at least, the merchant and his calling were generally despised by the "upper classes"; and it is not a little to the credit of the English nobility of that day that they recognised the value of commerce and industry to the nation, and gave them special attention in the agreement which they forced upon King John. Their conduct showed both breadth and liberality, as compared with that of their Continental fellow-peers, who throughout Europe were accustomed to oppress and pillage the trader;[3] nor is it the less creditable because it was actuated by a spirit of enlightened self-interest. The merchant class was now becoming a power in the land, and as such was worth recognising, even by the nobility; and probably some indi-vidual merchants of influence took care that the interests of their class were not neglected in the Charter of the nation.

---

[1] Magna Carta, §§ 28, 30, 31, 23. These clauses raise the whole question of "purveyance," *i.e.*, the prerogative enjoyed by the crown of buying up provisions and other necessaries for the use of the royal household at an appraised valuation, and even without the consent of the owner; also of forcibly impressing the carriages and horses of a subject to do the King's business upon a public road on paying a fixed price. The abuses to which this prerogative gave rise were, of course, many and various, nor was the evil completely suppressed till the prerogative was formally re-signed by Charles II. The prerogative was extended to men's labour as well as their goods. Thus Edward III. granted a commission to William of Walsingham to impress painters for the works at St Stephen's Chapel, Westminster, "to be at our wages as long as shall be necessary," and all such as refused were to be imprisoned by the Sheriff. Edward IV. granted a similar impressment of workers in gold for the royal household. Rymer, t. vi. 417; t. xi. 852; Hallam, *Middle Ages*, iii. 149; Taswell-Langmead, *Const. Hist.*, p. 132.

[2] Magna Carta, § 29.   [3] Taswell-Langmead, *Const. Hist.*, p. 132.

§ 60. *The Jews in England.*

Among the mercantile community, moreover, there was a distinct class which also has special recognition in the Charter, for we find clauses [1] which endeavour to restrict usury as exacted by the Jews—a fact which, while pointing to a not unfamiliar aspect of the Hebrew race, also shows their growing importance as an economic factor in mediæval England. We will, therefore, briefly mention the facts concerning them at this period.

The first appearance of the Jews in England may practically be reckoned as occurring at the time of the Norman Conquest, for immediately after 1066 they came in large numbers from Rouen, Caen, and other Norman towns.[2] They stood in the peculiar position of being the personal property, or "chattels," of the King,[3] and a special officer governed their settlements in various towns. These settlements were called Jewries, of which those at London, Lincoln, Bury St Edmunds, and Oxford were at one time fairly considerable.[4] They were protected by the King (for, being royal "chattels," no one dared interfere with them), and, of course, paid him for their protection. Their general financial skill was acknowledged by all, and William II. employed them to farm the revenues of vacant sees, while barons often employed them as stewards of their estates. They were also the leading, if not the only, capitalists of that time,[5] and must have assisted merchants considerably in their enterprises, though only upon a heavy commission.[6] After the death of Henry I., the security which they had enjoyed was much weakened, in proportion as the royal power declined in the civil wars, and in the twelfth and thirteenth centuries they were in a precarious position. Stephen and Matilda openly robbed them, Henry II. (in 1187) demanded one-fourth of their chattels, and Richard I.

---

[1] Magna Carta, §§ 10 and 11.
[2] Craik, *Hist. British Commerce*, i. p. 94 ; Bourne, *Romance of Trade*, p. 9.
[3] Cunningham, i. p. 145.   [4] *Romance of Trade*, p. 10.
[5] Craik, *British Commerce*, i. 95.
[6] The rate seems to have been 40 per cent. *Cf. Anglo-Jewish Exhibition Papers*, 207.

obtained large sums from them for his crusading extravagances. From 1144 to 1189 riots directed against them
became common, and the Jewries of many towns were
pillaged. In 1194 Richard I. placed their commercial
transactions more thoroughly under local officers of the
crown. John exploited them to great advantage, and levied
heavy tallages upon them, and Henry III. did very much
the same. They were expelled[1] from the kingdom in 1290,
and before this had greatly sunk from their previous position
as the financiers of the crown to that of petty money-lenders
to the poor at gross usury. What concerns us more immediately to notice in this early period of English history
is their temporary usefulness as capitalists in trading transactions at a time when capital was not easily accumulated
or kept in safety, and as a body from whom the crown
could obtain money in times of need without appealing to the
nation at large. Their expulsion seems to have been due
to an outbreak of fanaticism of more than usual virulence.

§ 61. *Manufactures in this Period: Flemish Weavers.*

We now turn from the subject of trade and finance to
that of manufacturing industry. On doing so, we find that
the chief industry is that of weaving coarse woollen cloth.
An industry so necessary as this, and one, too, that can be
carried on in a simple state of society with such ease as a
domestic manufacture, would naturally always exist, even
from the most uncivilised times. This, as we saw above,[2]
had been the case in England. But it is noticeable that,
although Henry of Huntingdon mentions the export of " fine

---

[1] It appears that this expulsion of the Jews was not absolutely complete, and Jewish tradition gives the year 1358 as the date of final expulsion; but in 1410 a Jewish physician, Elias Sabot, was certainly allowed
to practise in England. There seems to have been a certain immigration of Jews to England when they were expelled from Spain by Ferdi-
nand and Isabella (1492), for there are notices of them recovering debts in
English law courts. Their presence in this country was, however, only
first *publicly* sanctioned by Cromwell; and during the Commonwealth and
the reign of Charles II. they came back here in considerable numbers. *Cf.*
Wolf's *Anglo-Jewish Exhibition Papers*, p. 57; and my own *History of
Commerce in Europe*, p. 99; Craik, *British Commerce*, i. p. 129; Cunningham, *Eng. Ind.*, i. pp. 266, 267.

[2] Pp. 6 and 8, above.

wool" as one of the chief English exports, and although England had always been in a specially favourable position for growing wool, her manufacture of it had not developed to any great extent. Nevertheless it was practised as a domestic industry in every rural and urban community, and at this period already had its gilds—a sure sign of growth. Indeed, one of the oldest *craft* gilds was that of the London weavers,[1] of which we find mention in the time of Henry I. In this reign, too, we first hear of the arrival of Flemish immigrants in this country, who helped largely both then and subsequently in the development of the woollen manufacture. Some Flemings had come over indeed in the days of William the Norman, having been driven from Flanders by an incursion of the sea, and had settled at Carlisle. But Henry I., as we read in Higden's Chronicle, transferred them to Pembrokeshire in 1111 A.D. : "Flandrenses, tempore regis Henrici primi, ad occidentalem Walliæ partem, apud Haverford, sunt translati."[2] Traces of them remained till a comparatively recent period,[3] and the names of the village of *Flemingston*, and of the road called the *Via Flandrica*, running over the crest of the Precelly mountains, afford striking evidence of their settlement there, as also does the name *Tucking Mill* (*i.e.*, cloth-making mill, from German and Flemish *tuch*, " a cloth ").[4] Norfolk also had from early times been the seat of the woollen industry, and had had similar influxes of Flemish weavers. Their immigration does not, however, become important till the reign of Edward III., when we shall find that English cloth manufacture begins to develop considerably.[5] In this period, all we can say is that England was more famed for the wool that it grew than for the cloth which it manufactured therefrom, and it had yet to learn most of its improvements from lessons taught by foreigners. Indeed, some have gone so far as to state that weaving as a regular craft was first introduced into England by

[1] Cunningham, i. p. 181.   [2] Higden, in Gale, *Scriptores*, Vol. III. p. 210.
[3] *Cf.* Holinshed's *Chronicle*, 1107.   [4] Taylor, *Words and Places*, p. 186.
[5] Burnley (*Hist. of Wool and Woolcombing*, p. 50) says the distinction between woollen and worsted industry cannot be traced with certainty before the Flemish immigration, though it probably existed in Saxon times.

foreigners at the time of the Norman Conquest,[1] and that
the origin of craft gilds is to be found in the need for combination to protect each other that was felt by these foreign
artisans when they first settled here.[2] But while certain
points, in the history of weavers especially, tend to confirm
this view, it seems unlikely that there were no gilds formed
by Englishmen themselves prior to foreign settlement,
although we may readily admit that it is largely to foreigners,
and especially to the Flemish, that England owes its early
progress in the making of cloth.   It is noticeable also
that Domesday Book gives evidence of a considerable
number of artisans of French or other foreign extraction
living in England at the time of the Conquest.[3]

§ 62. *Economic Appearance of England in this Period.*
Population.

The England of the Domesday Book was very different
from anything which we can now conceive, nor did its
industrial condition change much during the next century
or two.   The population was probably under 2,000,000
in all; for we saw that in Domesday Book only 283,242
able-bodied men are enumerated. These, multiplied by five,
to include women and children, give 1,400,000 of general
population, and allowing for omissions, we shall find two
millions rather over than under the mark.[4] Nor, indeed,
could the agricultural and industrial state of the country
have supported more.[5] This population was chiefly located
in the southern and eastern counties,[6] which were also
politically and socially by far the most important, for the
north of England, and especially Yorkshire, had been laid
waste by the Conqueror in consequence of its revolt in
1068.   The whole country between York and the Tees
was ravaged, and the famine which ensued is said to have

[1] Cunningham, *Growth of Industry,* i. 179, 180 (but *cf.* Ashley, *Econ.
Hist.,* i. 83). 　　　　　　　　　　　　　　　　　　[2] *Ib.*

[3] *E.g.,* at Shrewsbury, *Domesday,* i. 252 a, 1, Gretford, i. 268 a, 1,
Cambridge, i. 189 a, 1.

[4] A calculation three centuries later, based on the assessment for the poll-
tax of 1377, gives 2½ millions (Topham, in *Archæologia,* vii. 337).

[5] *Cf.* Rogers, *Six Centuries,* p. 119.

[6] See the map in Freeman's *Norman Conquest,* iv. p. 101.

carried off 100,000 victims. Indeed, for half a century the land "lay bare of cultivation and of men" for sixty miles northward of York, and for centuries more never fully recovered from this terrible visitation.[1] The Domesday Book records district after district and manor after manor in Yorkshire as "waste."[2] In the North-west of England, now the most densely populated part of the country, and in the East, all was fen, moorland, and forest, peopled only by wild animals and lawless men.[3] Till the seventeenth century, in fact, Lancashire and the West Riding of Yorkshire were the poorest counties in England;[4] and the fens of East Anglia were only reclaimed in 1634. The main ports were London for general trade;[5] Southampton, for the French trade in wines; Norwich, for the export wool trade with Flanders, and for imports from the Baltic; and on the west coast Bristol, which had always been the centre for the western trade in Severn salmon and hides.[6] At one time, too, it was the great port for the trade of English slaves who were taken to Ireland, but William the Norman checked that traffic,[7] though it lingered till Henry II. conquered Ireland. For internal trade, *market towns*, or villages, as we should call them, were gradually springing up. They were nearly always held in demesne by the lord of the manor, who claimed the tolls, though in after years the town bought them of him.[8] Some of these markets had existed from Saxon times, as is seen by the prefix "Chipping" (=*chepinge*, A.S. a market), as in Chipping Norton, Chippingham, and Chepstowe; others date from a later period, and are known by the prefix "Market," as, *e.g.*, Market Bosworth.[9] But these market towns were very small, and, indeed, only some half-dozen towns in the kingdom had a population above 5000 inhabitants. These were London (40,000), York and Bristol (12,000), Coventry and Plymouth (9000), while Norwich, Lincoln, Salisbury,

[1] Freeman, *Norman Conquest*, iv. 272.   [2] *Ib.*, v. 42.
[3] Sim. Dun., *Gest. Regg.*, 1079, p. 85, Hinde.
[4] Rogers, *Six Centuries*, p. 127.   [5] *Ib.*, pp. 122-124.   [6] *Ib*
[7] Freeman, *Norman Conquest*, iv. 625.
[8] Stubbs, *Const. Hist.*, I. xi. 408.
[9] Taylor, *Words and Places*, pp. 394, 395 (ed. 1864).

Lynn, and Colchester had from 5000 to 7000 each.[1] But
nevertheless the settlement made by the Norman Conquest had
the effect of considerably strengthening the growth of towns,[2]
and we shall see more of their importance in the next period.

§ 63. *General Condition of the Period.*

Speaking generally for the whole period after the Conquest, we may say that, though the economic condition of
England was by no means unprosperous, industrial development was necessarily slow. The disputes between Stephen
and Maud, and the civil wars of their partisans, the enormous drain upon the resources of the country caused by
Richard I.'s expenses in carrying on crusades when he
should have been ruling his kingdom, and the equally
enormous taxes and bribes paid by the worthless John to
the Papal See, could not fail seriously to check national
industry. It is no wonder that in John's reign, at the
beginning of the thirteenth century, we hear of great
discontent throughout all the land, of much misery and
poverty, especially in the towns, and of a general feeling
of revolt. That miserable monarch was only saved from
deposition by his opportune death.

Yet with all these evils the economic condition of England, although depressed, was by no means absolutely
unhealthy ; and the following reign (Henry III., 1216-72),
with its comparative peace and leisure, afforded, as we shall
see, sufficient opportunity to enable the people to regain a
position of general opulence and prosperity, An important
change was coming over the industrial history of England
in the twelfth and thirteenth centuries, for now we begin to
see manufacturing and other industries arising side by side
with agriculture as a new phenomenon,[3] and the manufacturer and artisan was making himself felt as a new power
by the side of baron and farmer. This time of quiet progress and industrial growth forms a fitting occasion for the
marking out of a new epoch.

[1] Ashley, *Econ. Hist.*, II. i. p. 11.
[2] Freeman, *Norman Conquest*, v. 472.
[3] Ashley, *Econ. Hist.*, II. ii., p. 99.

PERIOD III

FROM THE THIRTEENTH TO THE END OF THE FIFTEENTH CENTURY, INCLUDING THE GREAT PLAGUE

(1216-1500)

CHAPTER VIII

§ 64. *Introductory. Rise of a Wage-earning Class.*

THE long reign of Henry III., although occasionally troubled by internal dissensions among the barons, was, upon the whole, a prosperous and peaceful time for the people in general, and more especially for those whom historians are pleased to call the lower classes. For by this time a remarkable change had begun to affect the condition of the serfs or villeins, a change already alluded to, by which the villeins became free tenants, subject to a fixed money rent for their holdings. This rent was rapidly becoming a payment in money and not in labour,[1] for, as we saw, the lords of the manors were frequently in want of cash, and were ready to sell many of their privileges. The change was at first gradual, but by the time of the Great Plague (1348), money rents were becoming the rule rather than the exception, and though labour rents were not at all obsolete, it was an ill-advised attempt to insist upon them unduly that was the prime cause of Wat Tyler's insurrection (1381). Before the Plague, in fact, villeinage in the old sense was becoming almost extinct, and the peasants, both great and small, had achieved a large measure of freedom. The richer villeins had developed into small farmers, while the poorer villeins, and especially the cottars, had formed a separate class of agricultural labourers, not indeed entirely without land, but depending for their livelihood upon wages paid for helping to cultivate the land of others. The rise of this class, which lived by wages and not by tilling their own land, was due to the

---

[1] The entries in the *Hundred Rolls* show us that at the end of the thirteenth century the process of substituting money payments for actual service had gone a long way ; Cunningham, *Growth of Industry*, i. 218.

III

fact that cottars and others, not having enough land of their own to occupy their whole time, were free to hire themselves to those who had a larger quantity. Especially would they become labourers at a fixed wage for the lord of a manor when he had commuted his rights to the unpaid services of all his tenants for a fixed money rent. Of course this change came gradually, but its effect is seen subsequently in the difficulties as to wages expressed in the Statutes of Labourers, difficulties which first became serious after the Great Plague. At the end of the thirteenth century we can trace three classes of tenants—(1) Those who had entirely commuted their services for a fixed money rent ; (2) those who gave services or paid money according as their lord preferred ; and (3) those who still paid entirely, or almost entirely, in services.[1]

§ 65. *Agriculture the Chief Occupation of the People.*

Throughout the whole of this period the vast majority of the population were continuously engaged in agricultural pursuits, and this was rendered necessary owing to the very low rate of production consequent upon the primitive methods of agriculture. The production of corn was only about four,[2] or sometimes eight, bushels per acre, and this naturally had the effect of keeping down the population, at this time still only between 1,500,000 and 2,000,000.[3] It is a remarkable fact that even the inhabitants of the towns used at harvest-time to go out into the country to get agricultural work, and people often migrated from one district to another for the same pnrpose,[4] just as Irish agricultural labourers of to-day are accustomed to cross over to England for the harvesting. Some attention was being paid to sheep farming, and noticeable progress in this branch of industry took place later. One order of monks in particular,

---

[1] See the *Hundred Rolls ; Rot. Hund.*, ii. 636, ii. 324, and ii. 494.

[2] Rogers, *Six Centuries*, p. 119.

[3] But *cf.* the discussion between Seebohm and Rogers in *Fortnightly Review*, II., III., IV., where Seebohm seems to think 5,000,000 possible in 1346.

[4] Rogers, *Hist. Agric.*, i. 63.

the Cistercians,[1] used to grow large quantities of wool; and, indeed, England had almost a monopoly of the wool trade with Flanders (p. 120). But the great increase of sheep-farming occurs rather later, at the beginning of the sixteenth century.[2]

§ 66. *Methods of Cultivation. The Capitalist Landlord and his Bailiff. The "Stock and Land" Lease.*

The agriculture of the early part of this period is described to us by various writers, of whom we may specially notice three—Walter de Henley, Robert Grosseteste of Lincoln, and a third author whose name is unknown. The most noticeable of these is certainly Walter de Henley, whose treatise, called "*La Dite de Hosbanderie,*" and written in French, is still preserved in many manuscripts.[3] There is little doubt that he wrote in the early part of the thirteenth century, and his treatise remained the standard work on agriculture till the appearance of Fitzherbert's in 1523. The treatise by Grosseteste of Lincoln is called *Reules Seynt Robert*, and was written about 1240 A.D., for the guidance of the Countess of Lincoln in managing her estate and also her household.[4] It consists of twenty-eight practical maxims, but is more concerned with the household than the farm. The anonymous work, called *Husbandry*,[5] seems to have been specially written for landowners, who at this period were beginning to take care that the accounts of their estates were presented to them in writing, and it lays down the proper methods of drawing up and presenting the accounts, the receipts and outlay necessary on an estate, and the probable returns from both land and stock. It has a special interest, because it was in the reign of Henry III. that the system of keeping accurate agricultural accounts first came into vogue,[6] and it is owing to this fact

[1] Cunningham, *Growth of Industry*, i. 196 and 547.
[2] More's *Utopia*, p. 41.
[3] *E.g.*, Oxford, Bodleian, *Douce*, 98 ; Merton, cccxi. ; British Museum, *Add.* 6159, and several others. [4] Pegge, *Life of Grosseteste*, 95.
[5] Several MSS. exist; *e.g.*, Merton, Oxford, cccxxi. ; British Museum, *Add.* 6159.
[6] Cunningham, *English Industry*, i. 272 ; Rogers, *Six Centuries*, 48. Of course it is on these accounts that Rogers' unique *History of Agriculture and Prices* is based.

that it has been possible to gain a very clear idea of the agricultural economy of England in the Middle Ages.

If we look at a typical manor, we shall find that the arable land in it seems to have been divided fairly equally between the landlord and the manorial tenants, and before the Great Plague the landlord appears to have been not merely a rent-receiver, but a capitalist who cultivated his land by the aid of a bailiff, subject very often to his own personal supervision. Now, the business of a manor was very elaborate, and required a great deal of supervision, and we have an account of the various officers on a large estate given in a small work called *Senescalcia.*[1] We find three officers specially mentioned—the Seneschal, Bailiff, and "Praepositus." The seneschal was employed on large estates, consisting of many manors, to visit the manors in turn and see that the bailiff of each did his duty; he therefore had to know the details and customs of each estate, and what it ought to produce, in order that his lord might receive his full dues from it. The bailiff was the representative of the lord in single manors, and had the responsibility of cultivation of the soil of the demesne land and of agricultural operations generally; while the "praepositus" was the chief man among the villeins, and shared the responsibility of cultivation with the bailiff, as representing the interests of the tenants. The bailiff had to keep accurate accounts to present to his lord or the seneschal, and it is from these accounts, which were kept with wonderful clearness, neatness, and accuracy, that we derive our knowledge of the agriculture of this period.

Tenancies were, of course, of various kinds, as we have already seen (pp. 71, 75), but there is one which came into vogue about this time that specially deserves our attention. In many cases, especially on lands owned by monasteries, the land was held on the "stock and land lease" system,[2] whereby the landlord let a certain quantity of stock with the land, for which the tenant, at the expiration of his lease, had to account either in money or kind. An instance of this kind of lease was the practice of the landlord letting

---

[1] Cunningham, i. 222.   [2] Rogers, *Hist. Agric. and Prices,* i. 25.

cows to dairy farmers.[1] In mediæval times the person to whom cows were leased for dairy purposes was the *deye*, *i.e.*, dairyman or dairymaid.[2] The stock and land lease plan [3] was favourable to the tenant, for it supplied his preliminary want of capital, and if he was fortunate, allowed him often to make considerable profits, and even eventually to purchase an estate for himself.

§ 67. *The Tenant's Communal Land and Closes.*

It must always be remembered, however, that most of the arable land in a manor was " communal," *i.e.*, each tenant held a certain number of furrows or strips in a common field, the separate divisions being merely marked by a piece of unploughed land, where the grass was allowed to grow. The ownership of these several strips was limited to certain months of the year, generally from Lady Day to Michaelmas, and for the remainder of the year the land was common pasture. This simple and rudimentary system was utterly unsuited to any advanced agriculture. The tenants, how- ever, also possessed " closes," some for corn, others for pasture and hay. The rent of a close was always higher than that of communal land, being eightpence instead of sixpence per acre, which seems to have been the usual annual charge.[4] Besides the communal arable land and his close, the husbandman also had access to two or three kinds of common of pasture—(1) a common close for oxen, kine, or other stock, pasture in which is stinted both for landlord and tenant ; (2) the open (" champaign " or " champion ") country, where the cattle go daily before the herdsmen ; (3) the lord's outwoods, moors, and heaths, where the tenants are stinted but the lord is not.[5] Thus the tenant had valuable pasture rights, besides the land he actually rented. But the system of holding arable land in strips must have been very cumbrous and have caused many disputes, since often a tenant would hold a short lease on one strip and a longer lease on another, or

---

[1] Rogers, *Hist. Agric.*, i. 330.
[2] The rent charged for cows was 5s. per annum. Rogers, *Hist. Agric.*, i. 25.   [3] For an example, see below, p. 186.
[4] Rogers, *Hist. Agric.*, iv. 96.   [5] *Ib.*, iv. 93.

confusion of ownership would arise, while in many ways tenure was made insecure, and no encouragement was given to advanced agriculture.

§ 68. *Ploughing.*

As regards the cultivation of the land, it was generally ploughed three times a year.[1] Ordinary ploughing took place in the autumn, the second ploughing in April, the third at midsummer. The furrows were, according to Walter de Henley, a foot apart, and the plough was not to go more than two fingers deep. The ploughing and much other work was done by oxen, which are recommended both by Walter de Henley and by Fitzherbert as being cheaper than horses, and because they could also be used for food when dead.[2] The hoeing was undertaken by women, who also worked at harvest time in the fields. In *Piers the Plowman's Crede* (about 1394 A.D.) we have a description of a small farmer ploughing while his wife leads the oxen : "His wife walked by him with a long goad, in a cutted cote cutted full high." [3]

An average yield of something more than six bushels per acre is what Walter de Henley thinks necessary to secure profitable farming.[4] The chief crops seem to have been wheat, barley, and oats.[5]

§ 69. *Stock, Pigs, and Poultry.*

As to stock, the amount kept was generally rather large, and the agriculturist of the thirteenth century was fully alive to the importance of keeping it,[6] since most of his profit came therefrom. Oxen, as we saw, were kept for the plough and draft, but not much stock was fatted for the table, especially as it could not be kept in the winter. There was no attempt to improve breeds of cattle, for the scarcity of winter food (winter roots being unknown till much later) [7] and the general want of means for resisting

---

[1] Rogers, *Hist. Agric.*, i. 270 *n.*, and 329.

[2] Walter de Henley, quoted in *Hist. Agric.*, i. 328 ; and Fitzherbert, quoted *ib.*, iv. 41.

[3] Line 433.   [4] Rogers, *Hist. Agric.*, i. 270, note.

[5] *Ib.*, i. 26.   [6] *Ib.*, i. 36, and 46-59, and p. 21.   [7] *Ib.*, i. 52.

the severities of the winter helped to keep all breeds much upon the same level.[1] On the other hand, swine were kept in large numbers,[2] for every peasant had his pig in his sty, and, indeed, probably lived on salt pork most of the winter. Care was taken with the different breeds.[3] The whole of the parish swine were generally put in summer under the charge of one swineherd, who was paid both by the tenants and the lord of the manor.[4] The keeping of poultry, too, was at the time universal, so much so that they were very rarely bought by anyone, and, when sold, were almost absurdly cheap.[5] This habit of keeping fowls, ducks, and geese must have materially helped the peasant in ekeing out his wages, or in paying that portion of his rent which was paid in kind ; as, *e.g.*, in the case of the Cuxham tenant (p. 75) who had to pay his lord six fowls in all during the year. Indeed, " poultry rents " were almost universal.[6]

§ 70. *Sheep.*

This animal is so important in English agriculture that we must devote a special paragraph to it alone. For the sheep was, in the earlier periods of English industrial history, the mainstay of the British farmer, chiefly, of course, owing to the quantity of wool required for export. England had, up to a comparatively recent period, almost a monopoly of the raw wool trade, her only rival being Spain. There were, as mentioned before, a great number of breeds of sheep, and much care was taken to improve them.[7] The fleece, however, was light, being only as an average about two lbs., according to Professor Rogers,[8] and the animal was small. The reason of this was that the attempts of the husbandman to improve his breeds were baffled by

---

[1] Rogers, *Hist. Agric.*, i. p. 52.   [2] *Ib.*, i. 335.
[3] Walter De Henley, quoted in *Hist. Agric.*, i. 336.
[4] The same custom has been observed by the author in Swiss mountain villages, where a common goatherd takes care of the goats of the peasants, being paid so much per goat by each villager, and receiving also board and lodging for a night in turn from each.
[5] Rogers, *Hist. Agric.*, i. 339 ; iv. 58.
[6] *Ib.*, i. 339.   [7] *Ib.*, i. 333.   [8] *Ib.*, i. 53.

the hardships of the mediæval winter, and by the prevalence of disease, especially the rot and scab.[1]   It is probable
that the average loss on the flocks was 20 per cent. a year.
They were generally kept under cover from November to
April, and fed on coarse hay, wheat, and oat straw, or pea
and vetch haulm ;[2] but no winter roots were available.

§ 71. *Increase of Sheep-farming.*

A great increase of sheep-farming took place after the
Great Plague (1348), and this from two causes.[3]   The
rapid increase of woollen manufactures, promoted by Edward
III., rendered wool-growing more profitable, while at the
same time the scarcity of labour, occasioned by the ravages
of the Black Death, and the consequently higher wages
demanded, naturally attracted the farmer to an industry
which was at once very profitable, and required but little
paid labour.   So, after the Plague, we find a tendency
among large agriculturists to turn ploughed fields into
permanent pasture, or, at any rate, to use the same land
for pasture and for crops, instead of turning portions of the
" waste " into arable land.   Consequently, from the beginning of the fifteenth century we notice that the agricultural
population decreases in proportion as sheep farming increases, and the steady change may be traced in numerous
preventive statutes till we come to those of Henry VIII. about
decayed towns, especially in the Midlands, the south, and the
Isle of Wight.[4]   The author of a political song of Henry VI.'s
reign declared that our enemies sneered at English sheep-
farming and thought it lessened our naval power.[5]   Another
cause that, in Henry VIII.'s time, had a distinct influence
in promoting sheep-farming was probably the lack of capital
which made itself felt, owing to the general impoverishment
of England in his wasteful reign, and which naturally turned

---

[1] Rogers, *Hist. Agric.*, i. 31, 334.
[2] Walter de Henley, in Rogers, *Hist. Agric.*, i. 334.
[3] *Cf.* Cunningham, *English Industry*, i. 361.
[4] *Cf.* 6 Henry VIII., c. 6 ; 7 Henry VIII., c. 1 ; 27 Henry VIII., c. 22 ;
and 32 Henry VIII:, cc 18 and 19.
[5] From *Ye Libelle of Englishe Policie*, vv. 36, 37.

farmers to an industry that required little capital, but gave quick returns.[1] We should also add as another cause the rise in prices caused by the discoveries of silver in the New World.

§ 72. *Consequent Increase of Enclosures.*

One consequence of this more extensive sheep-farming was the great increase in enclosures made by the landlords in the sixteenth century.[2] So great were these encroachments and enclosures in north-east Norfolk, that they led, in 1549, to a rebellion against the enclosing system, headed by Ket ;[3] but though more marked perhaps in Henry VIII.'s reign, the practice of sheep-farming had been growing steadily in the previous century. Fortescue, the Lord Chancellor of Henry VI. (about the middle of the fifteenth century), refers to its growth and the prosperity it caused in rural districts [4]—a prosperity, however, that must have been confined only to the great landowners. We receive other confirmation of this from various statutes designed to prevent the rural population from flowing into the towns, as, for example, the Acts of 1 and 9 Richard II. (1377 and 1385), of 17 Richard II. (1394), promoting the export of corn in hopes of making arable land more valuable.[5] Another Act was passed in 1489 (4 Henry VII., c. 16) to keep the rural population from the towns. In fact, it is very clear that at this time a great change was passing over English agriculture, and the old agricultural system was becoming seriously disorganised. But the growth of sheep-farming is also connected with a great economic and industrial development in England—the rise and progress of cloth manufactures and of the weaving industry generally, and to this we must now devote our next chapter.

[1] *Cf.* Rogers, *Six Centuries*, 445.

[2] Rogers, *Hist. Agric.*, iv. 109 ; and Cunningham, *Growth of Industry*, i. 362.

[3] Rogers, *Hist. Agric.*, iv. 124 ; Cunningham, *Growth of Industry*, i. 428.

[4] Sir John Fortescue wrote a treatise called *The Comodytes of England* before 1451 ; and his works were edited by Lord Clement ; *cf.* i. 551.

[5] At the request of the Commons, Richard " granted licence to all his liege people of the realm of England to carry corn out of the same realm to what parts they please them, except to his enemies ; " 17 R. II., c. 7.

CHAPTER IX

§ 73. *England's Monopoly of Wool.*

THE development of the woollen industry in England is interesting and important for two reasons.[1] On the one hand it shows us the origin of the parliar wealth of our country both in the middle ages and later, and on the other it illustrates with great clearness the evolution of our industry generally, an evolution that begins with the rude efforts of prehistoric peoples, passes through the stages of family work and gild work in hand-made industry, till in more recent times it reaches the stage of the machine and the factory. It is also particularly associated with our own country, for in the middle ages England was the chief wool-producing country in the North of Europe. Spain grew wool also,[2] but it could not be used alone for every kind of fabric,[3] and, besides, it was more difficult to transport wool from Spain to Flanders, the seat of the manufacture of that article,[4] than it was to send it across the narrow German Ocean, where swarms of light craft plied constantly between Flanders and the eastern ports of England.[5] Hence England had a practical monopoly of the wool trade,[6] which was due not only to its favourable climate and soil, but also to the fact that even at the worst periods of civil war—and they did not last for long—our island was incomparably more peaceful than the countries of Western Europe. From the thirteenth to the seventeenth century the farmers of Western Europe could not possibly have kept sheep, the most defenceless and tender of domestic

---

[1] Ashley, *Early History of the English Woollen Industry*, p. 1 ; see also Note A. [2] Burnley, *Wool and Woolcombing*, p. 59.
[3] Bonwick, *Romance of the Wool Trade*, p. 346.
[4] Burnley, *Wool and Woolcombing*, p. 58.
[5] Rogers, *Six Centuries*, p. 124. [6] Ashley, *Woollen Industry*, p. 35.

animals, amid the wars that were continually devastating their homesteads; nor, as a matter of fact, did they do so.[1] But in England, especially after the twelfth century, nearly everybody in the realm, from the king to the villein, was concerned in agriculture, and was interested therefore in maintaining peace. Even when the great landlords, after the Plague of 1348, gave up the cultivation of their arable land, they often undertook sheep-farming, and enclosed large tracts of land for that purpose. Hence the export trade in wool became more and more important, and there was always a continual demand for English wool to supply the busy looms of the great manufacturing towns in Flanders, Holland,[2] and even Florence[3] in Italy.

§ 74. Wool and Politics.

The most convincing proof of the importance of the wool trade is seen in England's diplomatic relations with Flanders, which, by the way, afford an interesting example of the necessity of taking economic factors into account in dealing with national history. Flanders was the great manufacturing country of Europe at that time. England supplied its raw material in vast quantities, and nine-tenths of English wool went to the looms of Bruges and Ghent. A stoppage of this export from England used to throw half the population of the Flemish towns out of work, and cause great misery.[4] The immense transactions that even then took place are seen from the fact that a single company of Florentine merchants would contract[5] with the Cistercian monks of England for the whole year's supply of the wool produced on their vast sheep-ranges on the Yorkshire moorlands; for the Cistercian order were among the foremost wool-growers in the country.[6] Now, it is a curious and significant fact that when Edward I., Edward III., and Henry V. premeditated an attack on France, they generally took care to gain the friendship of Flanders first,[7] so as to

---

[1] Rogers, *Econ. Interp.*, p. 9.
[2] Burnley, *Wool and Woolcombing*, p. 60.   [3] *Ib.*, p. 58.
[4] Ashley, *James and Philip von Astevelde*, 84, 91.
[5] *Cf.* Peruzzi, *Commercio e Banchieri di Firenze*, 70, 71.
[6] Burnley, *Wool and Woolcombing*, p. 61.   [7] Rogers, *Econ. Interp.*, p. 9.

use that country as a base from which to enter France, or
at least as a useful ally; and secondly, they paid a large
proportion of the expenses of their French expeditions by
means of a wool-tax in England.   Thus, when Edward III.
opened his campaign against France in 1340, he did so
from Flanders,[1] with special help afforded by a Flemish
alliance.   This king also received annually £60,000 from
the wool-tax alone,[2] and on special occasions even more
Again, it was a grant of 6s. 8d. on each sack of wool
exported that enabled Edward I. in 1275 to fill his
treasury for his subsequent invasion of Wales.[3]   The same
king in 1297 obtained the means for equipping an expedition against France, *via* Flanders, from the same source.
Similarly Henry V. took care to cultivate the friendship of
the Flemish and their rulers before setting out to gain the
French crown, and paid for his expedition by raising taxes
on wool and hides.[4]   We may add to the notices here
given the treaty of 1274 between Edward I. and the
Countess of Flanders, protecting the export of English
wool to Flanders, and the well-known case of Perkin
Warbeck.   This impostor was supported by the dowager
Duchess of Burgundy, and was well received in Flanders,
then ruled by the Archduke Philip.   As Philip, at the
instigation of the Duchess, encouraged Warbeck, Henry
VII. took the step of banishing all Flemings from England
(1493), and as Philip replied by expelling all the English
from Flanders, commercial intercourse between the two
countries was almost entirely suspended.   The result was
that, as Bacon tells us,[5] this interruption "began to pinch
the merchants of both nations very sore," and they besought
their respective sovereigns "to open the intercourse again."
Philip withdrew his support from Warbeck, and the impostor was left without resources, so that his subsequent
appearance in England was a complete failure.   The want
of English wool thus altered the policy of the Flemish
rulers, and before long the "great treaty," or *Intercursus*

[1] Green, *Hist. of England*, i. 411.   [2] *Rot. Parl.*, ii. 200.
[3] Stubbs, *Const. Hist.*, ii. 192, 244.   [4] Rogers, *Six Centuries*, p. 304.
[5] Bacon's *History of King Henry VII.* (ed. by Lumby), p. 144, which
see for full account of Warbeck.

Magnus, was made between the two nations (1496), by which trade was once more allowed to proceed unchecked, and "the English merchants came again to their mansion at Antwerp, where they were received with procession and great joy."[1]

Henry VII. also made a commercial treaty with Denmark[2] (1490), and one with the Republic of Florence, securing to that city a stipulated supply of English wool every year.[3] The enormous revenues also, which from the thirteenth to the fifteenth centuries were exacted from England by the Papal Court, and by the Italian ecclesiastics quartered on English benefices, were transmitted in the shape of wool to Flanders, and sold by the Lombard exchangers, who transmitted the money thus realised to Italy.[4] Matthew Paris estimated the amount of ordinary papal taxation for the year 1245 at a sum of no less than 60,000 marks.[5] The extent of these revenues may also be gathered from the fact that the Parliament of 1343, in a petition against Papal appointments to English ecclesiastical vacancies, asserted that "The Pope's revenue from England alone is larger than that of any Prince in Christendom."[6] And at this very time the deaneries of Lichfield, Salisbury, and York, and the archdeaconry of Canterbury, were all held by Italian dignitaries, while the Pope's collector sent from London 20,000 marks a year to his master at Rome.[7] Now, these impositions were paid out of the proceeds of English wool. It is interesting, too, to find that taxes for King Edward III. were calculated, not in money, but in sacks of wool. In one year (1338) the Parliament granted him 20,000 sacks;[8] in another year (1340) 30,000 sacks.[9] In 1339 the barons had granted him "the tenth sheaf, fleece, and lamb."[10] Early in the fifteenth century

---

[1] Bacon's *History of King Henry VII.*, p. 147.
[2] Rymer, *Foedera,* xii. 381.　　　　[3] *Ib.*, xii. 390.
[4] *Cf.* Cunningham, *English Industry,* i. 194, 271, 378; and Schanz, *Engl. Handelspolitik,* i. 111.
[5] Quoted by Cunningham, *Growth of Eng. Industry* (1 vol. ed. 1882), p. 146.
[6] Green, *Hist. of English People,* i. 408.　　[7] *Ib.*, p. 408.
[8] *Foedera,* ii. 1022, 1049, 1064.　　[9] Stubbs, *Const. Hist.*, ii. 380.
[10] *Ib.*

£30,000 out of the £40,000 revenue from customs and taxes came from wool alone.[1] Once more, as in the days of the Crusades, we are able to see how the Hundred Years' War with France and the exactions of Rome were paid for by the industrial portion of the community, while underneath the glamour of the victories of Edward III. and Henry V. lies the prosaic but powerful wool-sack.

§ 75. *Prices and Brands of English Wool.*

Having now seen the importance of wool as a factor in English industry and in political history, we must proceed to study more closely the facts of the woollen trade, and the manufacture of woollen cloth. The chief growers of wool were the Cistercian monks,[2] who owned huge flocks of sheep. The wool grown near Leominster, in Herefordshire, was the finest of all, and, generally speaking, that grown in Wiltshire, Essex, Sussex, Hampshire, Oxfordshire, Cambridge, and Warwickshire was the best.[3] The poorest came from the North of England and from the Southern downs. There were a number of different breeds of sheep, for care was taken to improve the breed, and it would seem that forty-four different brands of English wool, ranging in value from £13 to £2, 10s. the sack (of 364 lbs.) were recognised both in the home and foreign markets.[4] The average price[5] of wool from 1260-1400 was 2s. 1¾d. per clove of 7 lbs., *i.e.*, a little over threepence a pound, sometimes fourpence. In the middle of this period (1354) the average annual export, according to Misselden,[6] was about 32,000 sacks, which is equal to 11,648,000 lbs., representing a value of some £180,683 yearly.[7] At this time the export trade in wool between England and the Low Countries was not carried on by English merchants, but by foreigners, and chiefly those belonging to what was known as the "Hanse of London."[8] This was not the great Teutonic Hansa, but

[1] Rogers, *Six Centuries*, p. 305.
[2] Cunningham, *Growth of Industry*, i. 547. [3] Rogers, *Hist. Agric.*, i. 383.
[4] *Rot. Parl.*, 32 Hen. VI. [5] Rogers, *Hist. Agric.*, i. 366.
[6] *Circle of Commerce*, 119. [7] *Cf.* Rogers, *Hist. Agric.*, i. 367.
[8] Ashley, *Woollen Industry*, p. 38. Of course the Teutonic Hansa also was engaged in the wool trade.

was an association of merchants from the towns of Rheims, Amiens, and others in North France and Flanders, and even from Paris, who traded with England for English wool.[1] Merchants also came for wool from Cologne, and the men of Cologne had a house in London (distinct from the Teutonic Hansa's house) as early as 1157.[2] These merchants would supply the towns on the Rhine, for many of these cities had flourishing cloth manufactures.[3]

§ 76. English Manufactures.

Now, although Flanders has been mentioned as the chief manufacturing centre for Europe, it must not be supposed that England could not manufacture *any* of the large quantity of wool which it grew. Undoubtedly the people of the Netherlands were at that time the great manufacturers of the world, and were acquainted with arts and processes to which the English were strangers, while for a long time the English could not weave fine cloths : but, nevertheless, there was a considerable manufacturing industry, chiefly of coarse cloths,[4] an industry very widely spread, and carried on in people's own cottages under the domestic [5] system. This industry was encouraged by the Government in occasional, but of course futile, regulations prohibiting the export of wool, in order that it might be used for home manufactures.[6] The chief kinds of cloth made were hempen, linen, and woollen coverings, such as would be used for sacks, dairy-cloths, woolpacks, sails of windmills, and similar purposes.[7] The great textile centres were Norfolk (Norwich)[8] and Suffolk, where, indeed, manufacturing industries had existed long before the earliest records. An idea of their importance may be given from the fact that, in the assessment for the wool-tax of 1341,

---

[1] Ashley, *Woollen Industry*, p. 36.
[2] Lappenberg, *Hans. Stalhof zu London, Urk.*, 2.
[3] Ashley, *Woollen Industry*, p. 38.
[4] *Cf.* Walter of Hemingburgh, *Chronicon*, i. 306 (Eng. Hist. Soc., 1848).
[5] Cunningham, i. 394.
[6] *E.g.*, the Oxford Parliament of 1258 prohibited export of wool. *Cf.* Ashley, *Woollen Industry*, p. 39, and his *Econ. Hist.*, II. ch. iii. p. 194.
[7] Rogers, *Hist. Agric.*, i. 568.
[8] Burnley, *Wool and Woolcombing*, 866.

Norfolk was counted by far the wealthiest county in England after Middlesex (including London).[1] There was also a cloth industry of importance in the West of England, the chief centures being Westbury, Sherborne, and Salisbury.[2] The linen of Aylsham were also celebrated.[3] That there was even some export of cloth as well as raw wool is clear from Misselden's statement,[4] that in 1354 A.D. there was exported 4774½ pieces of cloth, valued at 40s. each, and 806½ pieces of worsted stuff, at 16s. 8d. each.

§ 77. *Foreign Manufacture of Fine Goods.*

But we find rich people used to purchase the fine cloths from abroad[5]—*e.g.*, linen from Liège and Flanders generally, and velvet and silk goods from Genoa and Venice— although there was certainly a silk industry in London, carried on chiefly by women, and protected by an Act of 1455.[6] Misselden[4] mentions the import of 1831 pieces of fine cloth, valued at no less than £6 each. But in the England of which we are now speaking, the textile industries were prevented from attaining a full development from the fact that, though general, they were strictly local; and, moreover, those who practised them did not look upon their handicraft as their sole means of livelihood, but even till the eighteenth century were generally engaged in agriculture as well. The cause of this is connected with the isolation and self-sufficiency of separate communities, previously noted. An evidence of the consequent inferiority of English to Flemish cloth is given by the fact that an Act of 1261 attempts to prohibit the import of spun stuff and the export of wool. Needless to say it was useless. The prices of cloth at this period are interesting, as showing the great difference between the fine (*i.e.*, foreign) and coarse (home) cloths. The average price of linen is 4d. an ell, being as low as 2d., and as high as 8¼d. Inferior woollens sold at 1s. 7½d. a yard, "russet" at 1s. 4d., blanketing at 1s. On the other hand, scarlet cloth (foreign)

[1] Rogers, *Six Centuries*, 115, 116. [2] Rogers, *Hist. Agric.*, i. 570.
[3] Rogers, *Six Centuries*, p. 105. [4] Misselden, *Circle of Commerce*, 119.
[5] Rogers, *Hist. Agric.*, i. 570. [6] 33 Hen. VI., c. 5.

rises to the enormous price of 15s. a yard. Cloth for liveries varied from 2s. 1d. to 1s. per yard. Speaking generally for the period 1260-1400, we may give the average price of the best quality at 3s. 3½d. a yard from 1260-1350, and 3s. 5½d. from 1350-1400 ; while cloth of the second quality fetched 1s. 4½d. in the first period, and 1s. 11¼d. in the second.[1]

§ 78. *Flemish Settlers teach the English Weavers. Norwich.*

It is to Edward III., very largely, that the development of English textile industry is due. It is true that, long before, Henry II. had endeavoured to stimulate English manufacture by establishing a " cloth fair " in the churchyard of St Bartholomew[2] at Smithfield. But English industry had developed slowly till the days of Edward, partly, no doubt, owing to the continual disorder of the preceding reigns. Stimulated, probably, by his wife Philippa's connection with Flanders, he encouraged Flemish weavers to settle in England, and also brought back home some Englishmen who had settled in Flanders and were apparently engaged in the cloth manufacture. Such, at any rate, appears to be the case from a perusal of an anonymous work dealing with this action of Edward III., and entitled *The Golden Fleece.*[3] The account runs thus—

" The wools of England have ever been of great honour and reception abroad, as hath been sufficiently witnessed by the constant amity which, for many hundred years, hath been inviolably kept between the Kings of England and the Dukes of Burgundy, only for the benefit of the wool, whose subjects, receiving the English wool at 6d. a pound, returned it (through the manufacture of these industrious people) in cloth at 10s. a yard, to the great enriching of that state, both in revenue to their sovereign and in em-

---

[1] Rogers, *Hist. Agric.*, i. 568-593, and ii. 536-542.

[2] Ashley, *Woollen Industry*, 65 ; Bonwick, *Romance of the Wool Trade*, 339.

[3] The extract is found in Burnley's *History of Wool and Woolcombing*, p. 61. *The Golden Fleece* was published anonymously in 1599, but treats of an earlier period also.

ployment to their subjects, which occasioned the merchants
of England to transport their whole families in no small
numbers into Flanders, from whence they had a constant
trade to most parts of the world.

"And this intercourse and trade between England and
Burgundy endured till King Edward III. made his mighty
conquests over France and Scotland, when he projected
how to enrich his people and to people his new conquered
dominions; and both these he designed to effect by means
of his English commodity, wool; all which he accomplished,
though not without great difficulties and opposition; for
he was not only to bring back his own subjects home, who
were and who had been long settled in those parts, with
their whole families (many of which had not so certain
habitations in England as in Flanders), but he was also to
invite clothiers over to convert his wools into clothing (and
these were the subjects of another prince), or else the
stoppage of the stream would choke the mill, and then not
only clothing would everywhere be lost, but the materials
resting upon his English subjects' hands would soon ruin
the whole gentry and yeomanry for want of vending their
wools. Now, to show how King Edward smoothed these
rough and uneven passages were too tedious for this short
narrative, though otherwise in their contrivance they may
be found to be ingenious, pleasing, and of great use."

We may note also a statute[1] of the year 1337, which
offers protection to all foreign clothworkers who may settle
in England, and, at the same time, in order to encourage
home manufactures, prohibits, on the one hand, the export
of wool, and, on the other, the import of foreign cloth.
After this date large numbers of foreigners seem to have
come over here,[2] and complaints against them are frequently
made by English cloth manufacturers.[3] But, although
Englishmen naturally felt some jealousy of this foreign
immigration, it resulted in lasting good to the industry and
trade of our country, and undoubtedly increased our wealth
very greatly.

---

[1] The 11 Ed. III., cc. 3, 4.   [2] Ashley, *Woollen Industry*, 47.
[3] Madox, *Firma Burgi*, 284 *n.*, col. 2.

The Flemish weavers settled chiefly in the eastern counties, though we hear of two Flemings from Brabant[1] settling in York in 1336; and shortly before this time one John Kemp,[2] also a Fleming, removed from Norwich, and founded in Westmoreland (1331) the manufacture of the famous "Kendal green." The chief centre, however, of the foreign weavers was naturally Norwich,[3] the Manchester of those days, with a population of some 6000,[4] and the chief industry was that of worsted cloths, so named from the place of manufacture, Worstead. When we speak of worsted cloths, we mean those plain, unpretending fabrics that probably never went beyond a plain weave or a four-shaft twill. The yarn was very largely spun on the rock or distaff, by means of a primitive whorl or spindle, while the loom was but a small improvement on that in which Penelope wove her famous web.[5] There was a great demand among religious orders for sayes and the like, of good quality; plain worsteds were generally worn by the ordinary public.

§ 79. *The Worsted Industry.*

Whether the growth of the worsted cloth industry was connected or not with this particular Flemish immigration we cannot determine, but after the Flemings came it seems to have increased.[6] The manufacture was confirmed to the town of Worstead by a patent of 1315;[7] and in 1328,

[1] Rymer, *Foedera*, ii. 954.   [2] *Ib.*, ii. 823.

[3] Bonwick, *Romance of the Wool Trade*, 366.

[4] Rogers, *Six Centuries*, 117.

[5] Compare two interesting pictures, one of weaving (about A.D. 1130-1174), from M.S. *Trin. Coll. Camb.*, R. 17, 1; and the other of a loom from the Faröe Isles, from Montelius, *Civilisation of Sweden*, both reproduced in Green's *History of the English People*, illustrated edition, vol. I. pp. 171 and 172.

[6] Burnley, *Wool and Woolcombing*, p. 50.

[7] Worsted is first mentioned in official records in the eighth year of Edward II. (1315), when the clothiers of Norwich are accused of making pieces of only 25 yards in length and selling them as being of 30 yards. But, of course, worsted as a material was known long before this period. William Rufus had a pair of stockings of "say," a kind of worsted, which were valued at 3s., a very high price for those days. See Burnley, *ut supra*, 51.

I

also, Edward III. issued a letter patent[1] on behalf of the cloth workers in worsted in the county of Norfolk. The manufacture was already so extensive and important that next year a special "aulnager"[2] (or cloth searcher) was appointed to inspect the worsted stuffs of Norwich and district, who held his office for twenty years. In 1348, however, on the petition of the worsted weavers and merchants themselves, the patent was revoked, and the aulnager removed.[3] But in 1410, after Norwich had gained a new charter (1403), the power of "aulnage" was once more given, at its own request, to its mayor and sheriffs, or their deputies.[4]

§ 80. Gilds in the Cloth Trade.

In the previous period we referred to the origin and growth of the craft-gilds, and it is interesting to note their importance in connection with the woollen industry at this time. As a separate craft, that of the weaver cannot be traced back beyond the early part of the twelfth century ; in the middle of the twelfth century, however, gilds of weavers are found established in several of the larger English towns.[5] At first they were in voluntary association, though acting independently of each other, but it became the policy of the government in the fourteenth century to extend the gild organisation over the whole country, and thus to bring craftsmen together in organised bodies.[6] Elaborate regulations were drawn up for their governance by Parliament, or by municipalities. Now, in London at this date (about 1300), and probably at Norwich and other large towns, the woollen industry was divided into four or five branches—the weavers and burellers, the dyers and fullers, and the tailors (cissores).[7] The weavers and burellers were each in a separate gild, the dyers and fullers together in one, while the tailors formed a third gild of

---

[1] Col. Rot. Pat., 103, 2 Ed. III.   [2] Col. Rot. Pat., 104.
[3] Ib., 156, 22 Ed., III.   [4] Rot. Parl., iii. 637.
[5] The Pipe Rolls of the early years of Henry II. show gilds of weavers in Winchester, Huntingdon, Nottingham, and York. Pipe Rolls, 2-4 Hen. II., ed. 1844.
[6] Ashley, Woollen Industry, p. 17.   [7] Ashley, ib., 27.

their own. But they were all very conscious that they had interests in common, and they were accustomed to act together in matters affecting the industry as a whole, such as, *e.g.*, ordering cloth made in the city to be dyed and fulled in that city, and not sent out to some other town.[1]

§ 81. *The Dyeing of Cloth.*

The dyeing and fulling industry, however, could not have flourished much in England at this time, for English cloths were mostly sent to be fulled and dyed in the Netherlands ;[2] and indeed we cannot consider dyeing as a really English industry till the days of James I., where it will be duly mentioned. At the same time it was not unknown, for it was practised even in early Celtic days ;[3] and we have scarlet, russet, and black cloths of English make in the fourteenth century.[4] Woad, also for dyeing, was imported in John's reign.[5] But the industry was chiefly carried on in the Netherlands, owing to the progress there made in the cultivation of madder, which forms the basis of so many different dyes. This plant has never been at any time largely cultivated in England, and, moreover, the Dutch for several centuries possessed the secret of a process of pulverising the root in order to prepare it for use. Such being the case, there is no wonder that they far excelled the English in the art of dyeing.[6]

§ 82. *The Great Transition in English Industry.*

From the time of this first Flemish immigration in the fourteenth century, we perceive the beginning of an important modification in our home industries. Hitherto England had been almost exclusively a purely agricultural country, growing large quantities of wool, exporting it as raw material, and importing manufactured goods in exchange. But from this period the export of wool gradually

---

[1] *Liber Custumarum,* 127-9 (of 1298 A.D.)

[2] Yeats, *Technical History of Commerce,* p. 147.   [3] Page 14 above.

[4] Yeats, *u. s.,* p. 148.

[5] Madox, *Hist. Exchequer,* 531, 532 (in 12 John). Evidently the home supply of woad, the traditional dye of the ancient Briton, was insufficient.

[6] Yeats, *Tech. Hist.,* p. 151.

declines, while on the other hand our home manufactures increase, until at length they in turn are exported. Now, the beginnings of this export date from the fourteenth century.[1] In fact, manufactured cloth, and not raw wool becomes the basis of our national wealth, and frequently [2] the export of wool is forbidden altogether, so that we may have the more for the looms at home.

A proof of the growing importance of manufacture in this period is the noticeable lack of labourers and the high wages they get, as set forth in an Act of Henry IV. (1406),[3] which points to an increase of weavers in all parts of the kingdom, that takes labourers from other employments. We may also incidentally note from this the growth of a distinct "labour class" living upon wages and not on the land.[4]

§ 83. *The Manufacturing Class and Politics.*

The growing importance of the manufacturing and merchant classes which were now rapidly springing up [5] can be clearly traced in the politics of the Tudor period. In spite of two great drawbacks, the cloth manufacture was progressing. It had naturally been severely checked for a generation or so by the awful national disaster of the Great Plague, which occurred so soon after Edward III. had helped to promote it in England, and which for the time utterly paralysed English industry in all its branches. It had been checked again by the long and useless wars which Edward III. and his successors carried on against France, at enormous cost and with no practical results, but which of course were paid for out of the proceeds of our national industries. But after these two checks it developed steadily, even during the Wars of the Roses; for these wars were carried on almost exclusively by the barons and their retainers, in a series of battles hardly any of which were of

---

[1] Burnley, *Wool and Woolcombing*, p. 66.
[2] By the 4 Hen. VII., c. 11; 22 Hen. VIII., c. 2; 37 Hen. VIII., c. 15.
[3] 7 Hen. IV., c. 17.   [4] Ashley, *Econ. Hist.*, vol. II. p. 101.
[5] We note now the growth of a class of merchants who were not manufacturers, but occupied solely in buying and selling cloth. Ashley, *Woollen Industry*, pp. 58-67.

any magnitude, exaggerated though they have been both by contemporary and later historians.[1] These wars had the ultimate effect of causing the feudal aristocracy to destroy itself in a suicidal conflict, and thus helped to increase the influence of the middle class, *i.e.*, the merchants and manufacturers, as a factor in political life. And thus it became the policy of the Tudor sovereigns, who were gifted with a certain amount of native shrewdness, to hasten the decaying power of the feudal lords by simultaneously supporting, and being supported by, the middle class, and to the alliance thus made between the crown and the industrial portion of the community we owe a rapid increase of commercial prosperity which laid the foundations of the greatness of the Elizabethan age, and of the great mercantile enterprises that succeeded it.

[1] *Cf.* Rogers, *Six Centuries*, 332-334. The Wars of the Roses seem to have had no effect upon wages and prices, even though there may have been some disorganisation; *cf.* Cunningham, i. 402.

CHAPTER X

THE TOWNS, INDUSTRIAL VILLAGES, AND FAIRS

§ 84. *The Chief Manufacturing Towns.*

DURING the period between the Norman Conquest and the middle of the thirteenth century, the towns, as we saw, had been gradually growing in importance, gaining fresh privileges, and becoming almost, in some cases quite, independent of the lord or king, by the grant of a charter. Moreover, they had grown from the mere trading centres of ancient times into seats of specialised industries, regulated and organised by the craft-gilds.[1] This new feature of the industrial or manufacturing aspect of certain towns is well shown in a compilation, dated about 1250, and quoted by Professor Rogers in *Six Centuries of Work and Wages*,[2] which gives a list of English towns and their chief products. Hardly any of the manufacturing towns mentioned are in the North of England, but mostly in the East and South.

The following table gives the name of the town, and its manufacture or articles of sale :—

TOWN.	PRODUCT.	TOWN.	PRODUCT.
(1) *Textile Manufactures.*		**(2) *Bakeries.***	
Lincoln	Scarlet cloth.	Wycombe	Fine bread.
Bligh	Blankets.	Hungerford	„
Beverley	Burnet cloth.	St Albans	„
Colchester	Russet cloth.		
Shaftesbury	Linen fabrics.		
Lewes	„	**(3) *Cutlery.***	
Aylesbury	„	Maxtead	Knives.
Warwick	Cord.	Wilton	Needles.
Bridport	Cord and Hempen fabrics.	Leicester	Razors.

[1] Cunningham, *Growth of Industry*, i. 309, &c.
[2] *Six Centuries*, p. 105. I have classified the list there given.

TOWN.	PRODUCT.	TOWN.	PRODUCT.
(4) *Breweries.*		Corfe	Marble.
Banbury	Brewing.	Cornwall ⎫ towns ⎭	Tin.
Hitchin	,,		
Ely	,,	(6) *Fishing Towns.*	
(5) *Markets.*		Grimsby	Cod.
Ripon	Horses.	Rye	Whiting.
Nottingham	Oxen.	Yarmouth	Herrings.
Gloucester	Iron.	Berwick	Salmon.
Bristol	Leather and Hides.		
Coventry	Soap.	(7) *Ports.*	
Northampton	Saddlery.	Norwich.	
Doncaster	Horse-girths.	Southampton.	
Chester	Skins and Furs.		
Shrewsbury	,,	Dunwich	Mills.

This list is obviously incomplete, for it omits towns like Sheffield and Winchester, both of which were important as manufacturing towns from very early times, though the woollen manufactures of the latter were soon outstripped by those of Hull, York, Beverley,[1] Lincoln, Boston,[1] and especially Norwich.[1] But such as it is the list is curious, chiefly as showing how manufactures have long since deserted their original abodes, and have been transferred to towns of quite recent origin.

§ 85. *Staple Towns and the Merchants.*

It will have been observed that by the time this list was compiled, most towns were either the seat of a certain manufacture or the market where such manufactures were chiefly sold. Now, in the days of Edward I. and Edward II. (1272-1327) several such towns were specially singled out and granted the privilege of selling a particular product, the *staple* of the district, and were hence called *staple towns.* But as the articles of commerce upon which customs were levied were wool, woolfells, and leather, these products are generally meant when speaking of staple goods.[2] The singling out of certain towns was adopted to facilitate the collection of the customs.[3] Besides a number of towns in England, staples were fixed at certain foreign ports for the sale of English goods. At one time Antwerp [4]

[1] Cunningham, i. 181 *n.*   [2] Craik, *Hist. of British Commerce,* i. 120.
[3] Cunningham, i. 287.   [4] Craik, *Hist. Brit. Commerce.* i. 121.

was selected as the staple town for our produce, at another time Bruges,[1] and afterwards St Omer.[2]   A staple was also set up at Calais [3] when we took it (1347), but at the loss of that town in 1558 it was transferred to Bruges.[4]   The staple system thus begun by the first two Edwards was altered and reorganised by Edward III.   His first intention seems to have been to abolish the whole system of staples, at least abroad; and this he did [5] in 1328. But such freedom of trade was not maintained for long. After various alterations and changes, it was in 1353 finally decided (by the 27 Ed. III., st. 2, c. 1) to remove the staple from all or any foreign towns, and to hold it only in certain English towns.   These were Newcastle, York, Lincoln, Norwich, Westminster, Canterbury, Chichester, Exeter, and Bristol in England ; Caermarthen for Wales ; and Dublin, Waterford, Drogheda, and Cork for Ireland. To compensate for the closing of foreign staples, every inducement was held out to foreign merchants to frequent the towns in England, though (with the exception of the years 1353-76) the staple at Calais was allowed to remain.[6] Now, although regulations like these are opposed to our modern ideas of free competition, they were to a certain extent useful in the Middle Ages, because the existence of staple towns facilitated the collection of custom duties, and also secured in some degree the good quality of the wares made in, or exported from, a town.   For special officers were appointed to mark them if of the proper quality and reject them if inferior.[7]

We might add that each staple was, of course, in accordance with the ideas of that time, subject to various regulations, and each staple town had a " mayor of the staple " distinct from the mayor of the town, though afterwards the two offices became united.[8]   There was also an association of " merchants of the staple," who claimed to

---

[1] Rot. Parl., ii. 149 (5), 202 (13).   [2] Rot. Hund., i. 406.
[3] " From the time of Richard II. till 1558 the staple was fixed at Calais." Cunningham, i. 372 n.
[4] Bonwick, Romance of Wool Trade, 172.   [5] 2 Ed. III., c. 9.
[6] Craik, Hist. Brit. Commerce, i. 123.   [7] Cunningham, i. 258.
[8] Gross, Gild Merchant, i. 145.

date as a separate body from the time of Henry III.[1] Certainly there seems to have been some sort of recognised body of English merchants trading with Flanders as early as 1313 A.D., for their "mayor" is mentioned then.[2] Another association of some importance as a trading company was The Company of Merchant Adventurers, incorporated in 1407[3] as a kind of branch of the Mercer's Company. They appear to have had depôts in Exeter and Newcastle, besides their chief place in London,[4] and were engaged in the export of cloth as distinct from raw wool and woolfells, which, of course, formed the business of the Merchants of the Staple.[5] These associations are very interesting as forerunners of those great trading companies, which in later centuries did so much to promote our foreign trade.

Now, these regulations of the staple, and the growth of these trading associations, show pretty clearly the growing importance of commerce in national affairs, and also the increasing prominence of merchants as a distinct and influential class in the community. Their influence arose, of course, from their wealth, and was increased no doubt by the custom of those days, which recognised them as a class apart from the landowners, who were still, with the clergy, almost the only people who were supposed to count for anything in national life. So much were they a special class, that the sovereign often negotiated with them separately.[6] Thus in 1339, when Edward III. was as usual fighting against France, and also, as usual, in great want of money, he was liberally supplied with loans by Sir William de la Pole, a rich merchant of Hull, who acted on behalf of himself and many other merchants.[7] On one occasion he lent the King no less than £18,500, a most enormous sum for those days. Sir Richard Whittington performed similar services for Henry IV. and Henry V.[8]

---

[1] Cunningham, i. 287.   [2] Rymer, *Foedera*, ii. 102.
[3] *Ib.*, viii. 464.   [4] Gross, *Gild Merchant*, i. 153.
[5] *Rot. Parl.*, v. 64 (38), speaks of "their merchandises of wool and woolfell."
[6] Stubbs, *Const. Hist.*, ii. 191, 192.
[7] Craik, *Hist. Brit. Commerce*, i. 172.   [8] *Ib.* i. 174.

The family of Pole, as is well known, rose by their wealth to great rank and power, being created successively Earls, Marquises, and Dukes of Suffolk, and took an important place in the history of the nation. The rise of Pole and other great merchants to the ranks of the nobility marks a most noticeable social development in English history, for it shows how the peerage has been from almost the earliest times recruited from commerce, while in many other European countries it was impossible for anyone connected with trade to become one of the *noblesse*. By avoiding this irrational exclusiveness, our nation has to some extent also avoided the fatal evils which in other countries have befallen an aristocracy of a more rigid type.

§ 86. *Markets*

Besides the staple towns, another class was formed by the country market towns, many of which exist in agricultural districts to-day in much the same fashion as they did six centuries ago. The control and regulation of the town market was at first in the hands of the lord of the manor,[1] but by this period it had mostly been bought[2] by the corporation or by the merchant gild, or by both, and was now one of the most valued of municipal privileges. The market-place was always some large open space within the city walls, such as, for instance, exists very noticeably in Nottingham to this day. London had several such spaces, of which the names Cornhill, Cheapside, and the Poultry still remain. The capital was indeed a perpetual market, though of course provincial towns only held a market on one or two days of the week. It is curious to notice how these days have persisted to modern times. The Wednesday and Saturday market of Oxford has existed for at least six centuries,[3] if not more, and so has that of Nottingham. The control of these markets was undertaken by the corporation for various purposes.[4] The first of these was to

---

[1] Stubbs, *Const. Hist.*, i. p. 426, and Rogers, *Hist. Agric.*, i. 141.
[2] Stubbs, *Const. Hist.*, I. xi. p. 408 *sqq.* implies this.
[3] Rogers, *Six Centuries*, p. 138.
[4] Ashley, *Econ. Hist.*, II. i. p. 19; also see the Nottingham *Borough Records*, iii. 62.

prevent frauds and adulteration of goods, and for this purpose special officers were appointed,[1] as in the staple towns, or like the "aulnager" of Norwich mentioned before. This was possible in a time when industry was limited and the competitive idea was as yet unborn, and one cannot help thinking that it must have been of great use to purchasers, provided only that these officers were incorruptible, which was not always the case. The second object of the regulators of the market was to keep prices at a "natural level," and to regulate the cost of manufactured articles. The price of provisions in especial was a subject of much regulation, but our forefathers were not very successful in this point, laudable though their object was. The best example of such regulation is found, perhaps, in the Act 13 Rich. II., st. 1, c. 8 (1389-90), which ordains—" Forasmuch as a man cannot put the price of corn and other victuals in certain," the justices of the peace shall every year make proclamation "by their discretion, according to the dearth of victuals, how much every mason, carpenter, tiler, and other craftsmen, workmen, and other labourers by the day shall take by the day, with meat and drink or without meat and drink, and that every man shall obey such proclamations from time to time, as a thing done by statute." Finally, provision is made for the correct keeping of the *assize*, or *assessment* from time to time, of the prices of bread and ale. The earliest notice of an "assize" in England is found in the Parliament Rolls for 1203,[2] but the practice is probably much older, and the most ancient law upon the subject is the 51st Hen. III. (A.D. 1266), the "Assisa Panis et Cerevisiæ." The assize of bread was in force till the beginning of the nineteenth century, and was only then abolished in London.[3]

The "assize" arranged by statute was, of course, a national matter, but many local regulations were in force.

---

[1] *Gilds* usually seem to have appointed their own officers, except the gilds of those who were engaged in providing food and drink. In these cases the officers (such as "ale conners" and "flesh conners") were appointed by the *borough* authorities. *Cf.* Ashley, *Econ. Hist.*, II. i. p. 30.

[2] 5 John ; *cf.* Craik, *Hist. Brit. Commerce*, i. 137.

[3] *Ib.*, p. 137.

Strict laws were also made [1] against the practices of fore-stalling, engrossing, or regrating of provisions, *i.e.*, buying them in such quantities or at such times as to control a future market ; for there seems to have been an idea—not perhaps altogether irrational—in the minds of our ancestors that it was something unseemly to manipulate the market in the case of commodities of such universal consumption as articles of food. Nor were the laws against these practices finally removed from the Statute Book till towards the end of the eighteenth century. [2]

§ 87. *The Great Fairs.*

Now, besides the weekly markets there were held annually in various parts of the kingdom large fairs, which often lasted many days, and which form a most important and interesting economic feature of the time. They were necessary for several reasons, since the ordinary trader could not and did not exist in the small villages, in which it must be remembered most of the population lived, nor could he even find sufficient customers in a town of that time, for very few contained over 5000 inhabitants; and because the inhabitants of the villages and towns could find in the fairs a wider market for their goods, and more variety for their purchases. Moreover, as has been well remarked,[3] since the stream of commerce was too weak in those days to penetrate constantly to all parts of the country, this occasional concentration of trade in fairs was distinctly advantageous for industry. The result was that these fairs were frequented by all classes of the population, from the noble and prelate to the villein,[4] and hardly a family in England did not at one time of the year or another send a representative, or at least give a commission to a friend, to get goods at some celebrated fair. They afforded an oppor-tunity for commercial intercourse between inhabitants of all parts of England, and with traders from all parts of

---

[1] *Cf.* the Statute *De Pistoribus*, of 51 Hen. III. (or perhaps 13 Ed. I.) till the 5 and 6 Ed. VI., c. 14 and 15.

[2] 12 Geo. III., c. 71. [3] W. Roscher, *Engl. Volkswirthschaftlehre*, 133.

[4] Rogers, *Six Centuries*, p. 148

Europe. They were, moreover, a necessity arising from the economic conditions of a time when transit of goods was comparatively slow, and when ordinary people disliked travelling frequently or far beyond the limits of their own district. The spirit of isolation which is so marked a feature of the mediæval town or village [1] encouraged this feeling, and except the trading class few people travelled about, and those who did so were regarded with suspicion. Till the epoch of modern railways, in fact, fairs were a necessity, though now the rapidity of locomotion and the facility with which goods can be ordered and despatched, have annihilated their utility and rendered their relics a nuisance. But even in the present day there are plenty of people to be found in rural districts who have rarely, and sometimes never, been a dozen miles from their native village. As late as the eighteenth century several fairs of great importance were still in full vigour, as we may see from a list given by that ingenious compiler, Malachy Postlethwaite.[2] He mentions—" (1) Stourbridge Fair near Cambridge, beyond all comparison the greatest in Britain, perhaps in the world ; (2) Bristol, two fairs, very near as great as that of Stourbridge ; (3) Exeter ; (4) West Chester ; (5) Edinburgh ; also several marts, as : Lynn, Boston, Beverley, Gainsborough, Howden, &c. ; (6) Weyhill Fair, and (7) Burford Fair, for sheep ; (8) Pancrass Fair in Staffordshire, for saddle horses ; (9) Bartholomew Fair in London, for lean and Welsh black cattle ; (10) St Faith's in Norfolk, for Scots runts ; (11) Yarmouth fishing fair for herrings, the only fishing fair in Great Britain, or that I have heard of in the world, except the fishing for pearl oysters near Ceylon in the West Indies ; (12) Ipswich butter fair ; (13) Woodborough Hill near Blandford in Dorset, famous for West country manufactures, Devonshire kersies, Wiltshire druggets, &c. ; (14) two cheese fairs at Atherstone and Chipping Norton ; with innumerable other fairs, besides weekly markets for all sorts of goods, as well our own as of foreign growth."

[1] Rogers, *Econ. Interp.*, p. 283.
[2] Postlethwaite, *Dict. of Trade and Commerce* (ed. 1774), s. v. *Fair.*

§ 88. *The Fairs of Winchester and Stourbridge.*

Fairs were held in every part of the country at various times of the year. Thus there was a fair at Leeds,[1] which for several centuries served as a centre where the wool-growers of Yorkshire and Lancashire met English and foreign merchants from Hull and other eastern ports, and sold them the raw material that was to be worked up in the looms of Flanders. But there were a few great fairs that eclipsed all others in magnitude and importance, and of these two deserve special mention, those at Winchester and Stourbridge. (1.) That at *Winchester* was founded in the reign of William Rufus, who granted the Bishop of Winchester leave to hold a fair on St Giles' Hill for one day in the year.[2] Henry II., however, granted a charter for a fair of sixteen days. It was mainly, though by no means entirely, for wool and woollen goods. During this time the great common was covered with booths and tents, and divided into streets called after the name of the goods sold therein, as, *e.g.,* " The Drapery," " The Pottery," " The Spicery." Tolls were levied on every bridge and roadway to the fair, and brought in a large revenue to the Bishop. The fair was of importance till the fourteenth century, for in the *Vision of Peres the Plowman,* Covetousness tells how

> " To Wye [3] and to Winchester I went to the fair." [4]

But it declined from the time of Edward III., chiefly owing to the fact that the woollen trade of Norwich and other eastern towns had become far more important, while on the other hand Southampton was found to be a more convenient spot for the Venetian [5] traders' fleet to do business.

(2.) *Stourbridge Fair.*—But the greatest of all English fairs, and that which kept its reputation and importance

---

[1] Bourne, *Romance of Trade,* p. 62.

[2] Kitchin, *Winchester (Historic Towns),* pp. 63, 161, and Ashley, *Econ. Hist.,* I. ii. p. 100.

[3] Probably Weyhill in Hampshire.

[4] For a very full account of the Fair see Warton's long note on this line in his *History of English Poetry,* § viii.

[5] Below, p. 225.

the longest, was the Fair of Stourbridge, near Cambridge.[1] It was of European renown, and lasted three weeks, being opened on the 18th of September.[2] Its importance was due to the fact that it was within easy reach of the ports of the east coast, such as Lynn, Colchester, and Blakeney, which at that time were very accessible and much frequented.[3] Hither came the Venetian and Genoese merchants, with stores of Eastern produce—silks and velvets, cotton, and precious stones. The Flemish merchants brought the fine linens and cloths of Bruges, Liège, Ghent, and other manufacturing towns. Frenchmen and Spaniards were present with their wines; Norwegian sailors with tar and pitch; and the mighty traders of the Hansa towns exposed for sale furs and amber for the rich, iron and copper for the farmers, and flax for the housewives, while homely fustian, buckram, wax, herrings, and canvas mingled incongruously in their booths with strange far-off Eastern spices and ornaments. And in return the English farmers —or traders on their behalf—carried to the fair hundreds of huge wool-sacks, wherewith to clothe the nations of Europe, or barley for the Flemish breweries, with corn and horses and cattle also. Lead was brought from the mines of Derbyshire, and tin from Cornwall; even some iron from Sussex, but this was accounted inferior to the imported metal. All these wares were, as at Winchester, exposed in stalls and tents in long streets, some named after the various nations that congregated there, and others after the kind of goods on sale. This vast fair lasted down to the eighteenth century in unabated vigour, and was at that time described by Daniel Defoe, in a work now easily accessible to all,[4] which contains a most interesting descrip-

[1] This Stourbridge or Sturbridge is now almost in Cambridge itself, the relics of the fair being held in a field near Barnwell, about a mile and a half from the city. In ancient times it was very easy for merchants to come up the river Ouse in barges or light boats, as water-transport was much more used then than now, and even the sea-going ships were very light craft. Probably a Flemish merchant would find no difficulty in sailing all the way from Antwerp to Cambridge in a light ship.

[2] The description which follows is based on Rogers, *Hist. Agric.*, i. 141-143.   [3] Rogers, *Six Centuries*, p. 124.

[4] In his *Tour through the Eastern Counties* (1722); *Tour*, i. 91, or p. 164 in Cassell's *National Library* Edition.

tion of all the proceedings of this busy month. It is not much more than a hundred years ago that the Lancashire merchants alone used to send their goods to Stourbridge upon a thousand pack horses,[1] but now the pack-horses and fairs have gone and the telegraph and railway have taken their place.

§ 89. *English Mediæval Ports.*

In the last paragraph mention was made of the east coast having ports of great prominence in this period. It will be convenient here to notice what were the chief ports of England, and to remark how few of them have retained their old importance. The chief port was of course London, which has always held an exceptional position, and the other principal ports were on the east and south coast.[2] Southampton was from early times the chief southern harbour, and next to it Dartmouth, Plymouth, Sandwich, and Winchelsea, Weymouth, Shoreham, Dover, and Margate. They were connected with the trade in French and Spanish goods. On the western coast Bristol was almost the only port much frequented, being the centre and harbour for the western fisheries, and also a place of export for hides and the cloth manufactures of the western towns. In the fifteenth century Bristol fishermen penetrated through the Hebrides to the Shetland and Orkney Islands and to the northern fisheries, where they found that the Scarborough men had preceded them.[3] On the eastern coast, indeed, Scarborough was one of the most enterprising ports.[4] Boston, Hull, Lynn, Harwich, Yarmouth, and Colchester were also very flourishing, and were concerned in the Flemish and Baltic trade.[5] Further north Newcastle was the centre for the coasting trade in coal,[6] and Berwick was a fisherman's harbour. But the southern and eastern ports were the most frequented, as being suitable to the light and shallow

---

[1] Toynbee, *Industrial Revolution*, p. 55.
[2] *Cf.* Cunningham, i. 258 ; Rogers, *Six Centuries*, 122.
[3] Rogers, *Six Centuries*, p. 124.
[4] For the making of a pier there, *cf.* Statute 37 Hen. VIII., c. 14.
[5] Rogers, *Six Centuries*, p. 124.   [6] *Ib.*

craft that did a coasting trade, or ran across to the Continent in smooth weather.

The extent of piracy was, however, a great drawback to the prosecution of trade by sea, and formed a danger which in these days we can only inadequately realise.[1] Organised bands of pirates, called the "Rovers of the Sea," ravaged our coasts in the reign of Henry VI.[2] It was quite a common occurrence for Scarborough to be attacked by Scotch, French, and Flemish pirates[3]; and even large towns like London and Norwich made plans of defence against possible attacks from such enemies.[4] Merchant vessels had to sail together in fleets for the sake of security; both Henry IV. and Henry VI. empowered merchants in the coast towns to organise defensive schemes[5]; and the protection of merchant shipping also occupied the attention of Henry VIII.[6] In fact, for many centuries piracy was the curse of our maritime trade.

§ 90. *The Temporary Decay of Manufacturing Towns.*

We have now noticed the chief markets, fairs, ports, and manufacturing towns of mediæval England, and it will be seen that commercial prosperity was certainly developing. So, too, were home manufacturing industries, but their growth brought about a curious effect in the decay of certain towns, and the rise of industrial villages in rural districts. To the decay of towns we find frequent reference in the Statutes of Henry VI., Henry VII., and his successor, *i.e.*, from 1490 or 1500 onwards. This decay was due to several causes, among others to the heavy taxation caused by wars with France,[7] to the growth of sheep-farming mentioned above, and also to the fact that the industrial disabilities imposed upon dwellers in towns, in consequence

---

[1] *Cf. The Paston Letters*, i. 114.
[2] *Rot. Parl.*, iv. 350 (42), 376 (29). [3] *Rot. Parl.*, iii. 162 (46).
[4] Denton, *Fifteenth Century*, pp. 87, 89.
[5] Rymer, *Foedera*, viii. 438, 439, 455. [6] *Ib.*, xiii. 326.
[7] In 1433 Parliament in voting a tenth and fifteenth had to remit £4000 to poor towns, among which Yarmouth and Lincoln are noted. *Rot. Parl.*, iv. 425. *Cf.* also *R. P.*, v. 5 and v. 37 for other remissions. For other evidences of decay see *Rot. Parl.*, vi. 390, 438, and 514; Statutes 27 Hen. VIII., c. 1; 32 Hen. VIII., c. 18, and others.

K

of the corporate privileges of the gilds, now far exceeded the
advantages of residence there. The days of usefulness for
the gilds had gone past; their restrictions, especially as to
apprentices and journeymen,[1] were now felt only to cramp
the rising manufacturing industries. Hence we find the
manufacturers of the Tudor period were leaving the towns
and seeking open villages instead, where they could develope
their trade free from the vexatious restrictions of old-
fashioned corporations. Of course laws were passed to
check this tendency, and to confine particular industries to
particular towns. Thus, in Norfolk, no one was to "dye,
shear, or calendar cloth" anywhere but in the town of Norwich[2]; no one in the northern counties was to make
"worsted coverlets" except in York.[3]

§ 91. *Growth of Industrial Villages. The Germs of the Modern Factory System.*

Such protective enactments were, however, as protective
enactments must generally be, utterly in vain. Henry VII.
tried [4] to remedy the supposed evil by limiting the privileges of interference of the gilds in causing their ordin-
ances to be first approved by the Chancellor or Justices;
but even this step was useless. Manufactures were slowly
and surely transferred to country villages,[5] and in several
industries a kind of modern factory system can be traced
at this time. Master manufacturers, weary of municipal
and gild-made restrictions, organised in country places little
communities solely for industrial purposes, and so arranged
as to afford greater scope for the combination and division
of labour.[6] The system of apprenticeship was a powerful
element in this scheme, and supplied ready labour for these
small factories. The goods were made not as formerly only

---

[1] *Cf.* Statute 28 Hen. VIII., c. 5.
[2] *Cf.* the 5 Hen. VIII., c. 4; 14 and 15 Hen. VIII., c. 3; and 26 Hen.
VIII., c. 16.
[3] 34 and 35 Hen. VIII., c. 10.   [4] 19 Hen. VII., c. 7.
[5] Mrs Green, *Town Life*, ii. 88, says that this removal was in search of
water-power (*e.g.*, in Yorkshire and Gloucestershire). But a more powerful reason was the tyranny of the gilds; Gross, *Gild Merchant*, i. 52.
[6] *Cf* Ashley, *Woollen Industry*, p. 75, and Gross, *u. s.*

for local use, but for the purposes of trade and profit throughout the kingdom. The master was bound to his workmen rather more closely than the mill-owner of the present day to his " hands," for the spirit of personal sympathy and obligation still survived in these small labour communities, nor was there any wide social gulf fixed between master and man.[1] But the germs of the modern system were there; for this new system was not that of mere cottage industry, as had been the rule in previous periods, but a system of congregated labour organised upon a capitalistic basis by one man—the organiser, head, and owner of the industrial village—the master clothier.

It is, perhaps, interesting to note in this place the exemplification of the four systems or stages through which manufacturing industry usually passes.[2] They may be called—(1) The family system, under which each worker produces separately, aided only by his wife and children; (2) the system of production under the supervision and arrangements of gilds, as we have already seen, and where small " masters " employ a few men to work with them as journeymen and apprentices, while they as manufacturers sell their own goods to the public; (3) the domestic system, which is much the same as the one previous, except that the master manufacturer is no longer a merchant to the public,[3] but simply produces, on a large scale, for purchase by dealers; and lastly (4) we have the factory system of modern times, which is familiar to all. Now the growth of the domestic system and of the great master clothiers may be dated from the middle of the fourteenth century,[4] and it extended through the fifteenth to the eighteenth century.[5] We see now clothiers in a large way of business who buy the wool, cause it to be spun, dyed, and finished, and then sell it to drapers or merchants, who retail it to the public.[6] The great sheep farmers were often clothiers, and made up into cloth the wool they grew.[7]

Among these famous "master clothiers" we read of men like

[1] Cf. Ashley, Woollen Industry, p. 74.
[2] Cf. Held, Zur socialen Geschichte Englands, 541 sq.
[3] Ashley, Woollen Industry, p. 73.
[4] Ib., 81.
[5] Ib., 73.
[6] Ib., 81.
[7] Ib., 80.

John Winchcombe, or " Jack of Newbury," as he was called, of whom it is recorded that a hundred looms always worked in his house,[1] and who was rich enough to send a hundred of his journeymen to Flodden Field in 1513.[2]   His kerseys were famous all over Europe.[3]   It was from communities such as these that the villages of Manchester, Bolton, Leeds, Halifax, and Bury took their rise, and afterwards developed into the great factory towns of to-day.   But these work-shops, large though they seemed then, were utterly insig-nificant compared with the huge factories of modern times, where the workmen are numbered in thousands, and are to the capitalist-employer, or joint-stock company that owns the mill, merely a mass of human machines, more intelli-gent though not so durable as other machines, and possessed of an unpleasant tendency to go out " on strike," for reasons that usually appear to their employer insufficient and sub-versive of the whole industrial system.   However, the in-dustrial system is not subverted, though the workmen can hardly be said to be upon the same pleasant footing with their employers as they used to be in the old industrial village.   But even in those days things did not always go smoothly, and there are traces [4] of the existence of a very badly paid class of workmen in manufacturing towns.

[1] Burnley, *Wool and Woolcombing*, p. 69.   In 1549 the English envoy at Antwerp advises the Protector, Somerset, to send to Antwerp for sale a thousand pieces of "Winchcombe's kersies."

[2] Bischoff, *Woollen and Worsted Manufacture*, i. 55.

[3] Burnley, *ut supra*, p. 69.

[4] Mrs Green, *Town Life*, ii. 101.   The wages were only one penny a day, which was low even for those times.

CHAPTER XI

§ 92. *Material Progress of the Country.*

IN the preceding chapters we have attempted to give an idea of the state of industry and commerce in England in the Middle Ages. We now come to a most important landmark in the history of the social and industrial condition of the people—viz., the Great Plague of 1348 and subsequent years. Almost two centuries had elapsed since the death of Stephen (1154) and the cessation of those great civil conflicts which harried England in his reign. These two centuries had witnessed on the whole a continuous growth of material prosperity. The wealth of the country had increased ; the towns had developed, and their development was partly the effect and partly the cause of the growth of a prosperous mercantile and industrial middle class, who regulated their own affairs in their gilds, and also had a voice in municipal management. No doubt it was true that in the fourteenth century municipal life was still on a small scale,[1] but much progress had been made since the twelfth century. Already it was a great advantage to be a " burgher," for the towns opened up to the artisan and shopkeeper a way to take their place among people of privilege.[2] But the country at large was still mainly devoted to agricultural and pastoral pursuits, and the mass of the people were engaged in tilling the ground or feeding cattle. The mass of the people, too, were now better fed and better clothed than those of a similar class on the Continent, and though there were social discontents at intervals, there was nothing in England so terrible and so outrageous as the " Jacquerie " revolt in France. The industrial factor, moreover, was making itself more and more felt in national and

[1] Mrs Green, *Town Life*, i. 13.   [2] *Ib.*, i. 181.

political life, for industrial questions assumed a hitherto unsuspected importance when a large proportion of the House of Commons was formed of burghers directly interested in trade and manufactures.[1]

§ 93. *Social Changes. The Villeins and Wage-paid Labourers.*

Besides the growth of material prosperity in these two centuries, we find that the commutation of villeinage services into money payments to the lord of the manor—a tendency frequently commented upon—had been growing apace.[2] This commutation had been going on for a long time, in fact, ever since the Conquest, if not before, and the villeins had in many cases freed themselves not only from labour dues, but from the vexatious customary fines or " amercements " which they had to pay to the lord of the manor on certain social occasions—such as the marriage of a daughter, or the education of a son for the Church.[3] But of course this freedom was not complete, though it is important to notice its growth, for we shall see that it formed the occasion of a great class struggle some years after the Great Plague.

There is another feature which is also of importance, and which had come more and more into prominence during the past two centuries. I refer to the increase in the numbers of those who lived upon the labour of their hands, and were employed and paid wages like labourers of the present day. It has been mentioned before that they arose from the cottar class, from the small tenants and landless cottagers,[4] who had not enough land to occupy their whole time, and who were therefore ready to sell their labour to an employer. These two features—the commutation of labour-dues for money payments and the rise of a wage-paid labouring class—are closely connected, for it was natural that, when the lord of a manor had agreed to receive money from his tenants in villeinage instead of labour, he

---

[1] Mrs Green, *Town Life*, i. 72.   [2] Ashley, *Econ. Hist.*, II. ii. 265, 267.

[3] The ordination of villeins had become so common that the constitutions of Clarendon were inclined to restrict it. *Cf.* Stubbs, *Const. Hist.*, I. ch. **xi**. p. 431 ; and *Const. Clar.*, 16.   [4] Ashley, *Econ. Hist.*, II. ii. p. 267.

should have to obtain other labour from elsewhere and pay for it in the money thus received by commutation. The tendency of these social changes was greatly in favour of the villeins, whose social condition had steadily improved,[1] and whose tenancy in villeinage was fast losing its originally servile character. Neither were the villeins, whether comparatively well-to-do yeomen or agricultural labourers, so much bound to the manor as formerly, for in proportion as their labour services were no longer necessary, their lord would let them leave the manor and seek employment, or take up some manufacturing industry, elsewhere. It had always been possible for the villeins or serfs to do this on payment of a small fine (*capitagium*),[2] and it is certain that, as money-payments became increasingly the fashion, the lord would not object to receiving this further payment, unless perchance he required a good deal of labour to be done upon his own land.

§ 94. *The Famine and the Plague.*

The position of the labouring class had been further improved by the effects of the famines which occurred in the early years of the fourteenth century.[3] Of course they suffered great hardships, and their numbers were considerably thinned, but at the same time this loss of life and diminution in their numbers caused their services to become more valuable in proportion to their scarcity, and they gained a rise of some 20 per cent. in wages.[4] From this date till the coming of the Great Plague, some thirty years later, they and the rest of the English people enjoyed a period of great prosperity.[5] It was on the whole a " merry England" on which the Great Plague suddenly broke. The prosperity of the people was reflected in the splendour and brilliancy of the court and aristocracy, while the national pride had been increased by the recent capture of Calais (1347), and by the other successes in the French war,[6] which brought

[1] Stubbs, *Const. Hist.*, II. ch. xvi. p. 454.
[2] Bracton, *De Leg.* (ed. Twiss), ch. x. *f.* 6*b* p. 49.
[3] *Cf.* Stowe, *Annals*, for 1314 and 1315 A.D. ; and Rogers, *Six Centuries*, p. 217.   [4] Rogers, *ib.*, p. 218.   [5] *Ib.*, 219
[6] Green, *History of English People*, i. 429.

not only glory but occasionally wealth, in the shape of
heavy ransoms. But in 1348 the prosperity and pride of
the nation was overwhelmed with gloom. The Great
Plague came with sudden and mysterious steps from Asia
to Italy, and thence to Western Europe and England,
carried some say by travelling merchants, or borne with its
infection on the wings of the wind. It arrived in England
at the two great ports of Bristol and Southampton [1] in
August 1348, and thence spread all over the land. Its
ravages were frightful. Whole districts were depopulated,
and about one-third of the people perished.[2] Norwich and
London, being busy and crowded towns, suffered especially
from the pestilence, and though the numbers of the dead
have been grossly exaggerated by the panic of contemporaries and the credulity of modern historians,[3] there can
be no doubt that the loss of life was enormous.[4] The
plague fell alike upon the dwellers in the towns, with their
filthy, undrained streets,[5] and upon the labourers working in
the open fields amid the fresh air and the sunshine. The
same fate came to all. "The fell mortality came upon them,
and the sudden and awful cruelty of death winnowed them."[6]

§ 95. *The Effects of the Plague on Wages.*

The most immediate consequence of the Plague was a
marked scarcity in the number of labourers available ;[7] for

[1] Henry of Knighton's *Chronicle*, ii. p. 61, ed. Lumby.

[2] Rogers (*Six Centuries*, p. 223) thinks one-third died; Cunningham
(*English Industry*, i. 304) thinks nearly half; Denton (*England in Fifteenth
Century*, p. 98) more than half.

[3] It was asserted by the fourteenth century chroniclers, and has often
been repeated since, that nearly 60,000 people died in Norwich alone.
Green (i. 429) says "thousands of people" died at Norwich. As a matter of
fact, the whole county of Norfolk, including that city, hardly contained
30,000 people. *Cf.* Rogers, *Six Centuries*, p. 223.

[4] *Cf.* Jessop, *Coming of the Friars*, p. 193, who shows that half the parish
priests of certain districts died during that year. The *Chronicle of St
Alban's* alone records (ii. 369) the death of more than forty-seven monks.

[5] *Cf.* Denton, *Fifteenth Century*, 103.

[6] This wonderfully vivid sentence is from Henry of Knighton's *Chronicle*,
u. s., ii. p. 63.

[7] "There was such a want of servants in work of all kinds that one would
scarcely believe that in times past there had been such a lack." Henry of
Knighton's *Chronicle*, *u. s.*, ii. p. 64.

being of the poorest class they naturally succumbed more readily to famine and sickness. This scarcity of labour naturally resulted in higher wages. The landowners began to fear that their lands would not be cultivated properly, and were compelled to buy labour at higher prices than would have been given at a time when the necessity of the labourer to the capitalist was more obscured. Hence the wages of labourers rose far above the customary rates. In harvest-work,[1] for example, the rise was nearly 60 per cent. and what is more, it remained so for a long period; while the rise in agricultural wages generally was 50 per cent.[2] So it was also in the case of artisans' wages, in the case of carpenters, masons, and others.[3] It seems that the upper classes and employers of that day very strongly objected to paying high wages, as they naturally do. The king himself felt deeply upon the point. Without waiting for Parliament to meet, Edward III. issued a proclamation[4] ordering that no man should either demand or pay the higher rate of wages, but should abide by the old rate. He forbade labourers to leave the land to which they were attached, and assigned heavy penalties to the runaways. Parliament assembled in 1350 and eagerly ratified this proclamation, in the laws known as the *Statutes of Labourers.*[5] But the demand for labour was so great that such legislative endeavours to prevent its proper payment were fortunately ineffective. Runaways not only found shelter, but also good employment and high wages.[6] Parliament fulminated its threats in vain, and in vain increased its penalties by a later[7] statute of 1360, ordering those who asked more than the old wages to be imprisoned, and, if they were fugitives, to be branded with hot irons. For once the labourer was able to meet the capitalist on equal terms. Moreover, the effects of the Plague were not limited to those occasioned by the great

---

[1] Rogers, *Six Centuries*, p. 234.   [2] *Ib.*, p. 237.   [3] *Ib.*, 234-237.

[4] On the 18th of June 1349 (23 Ed. III.); *cf.* Rymer, *Foedera*, III. i. 198, who apparently places it a year too late.

[5] The 25 Ed. III., stat. ii. c. 1, and later 31 Ed. III., stat. i. c. 6, and 34 Ed. III., cc. 9, 10, 11.

[6] Knighton's *Chronicle, ut supra*, p. 64.   [7] 34 Ed. III., cc. 9, 10, 11.

visitation of 1348, for there were two or three other outbreaks of pestilence in subsequent years.[1] Thus the scarcity of labourers was felt more and more keenly by their former employers, and the landowners naturally did their best to compel them to work.[2] The class of free labourers and tenants who had commuted their services for money payments was oppressed, and "the ingenuity of the lawyers who were employed as stewards on each manor was exercised in trying to restore to the landowners that customary labour whose loss was now severely felt."[3] Former exemptions and manumissions were often cancelled, and labour services again demanded from the villeins.[4] The result was inevitably a gradual union of labourers and tenants of all classes against landowners and employers— the beginnings, in fact, of a social struggle, in which we recognise the unfortunate modern tendency of "a hostile confrontation of labour and capital." Combinations and confederacies of labourers became frequent,[5] and the strife grew more and more bitter, till the crisis came at last, and open revolt took place. "The difficulties of the manorial lords would be renewed with every subsequent visitation of the Plague, and the pressure on villeins to render actual service would become more severe, until at last it resulted in the general outbreak of the peasants in 1381."[6] Nor were the social troubles thus caused in any great degree diminished by the successes of Edward III. and the Black Prince in France, or even by the conclusion of peace at Bretigny (1360). Indeed, it must be obvious to anyone who considers how wars are paid for, that military success, unless it is a great deal more productive than was that of Edward III., really only makes matters worse, owing to the financial burdens which it imposes upon the people. And

---

[1] In 1361 and 1369. *Annals of England* (Parker), pp. 196, 197.

[2] Thus, the penalties are far more severe in the 34 Ed. III., c. 9, 10, 11, than in previous statutes.

[3] Green, *History*, i. 432.

[4] *Cf.* Stubbs, *Const. Hist.*, II. ch. xvi. 455.

[5] The villeins "gather themselves together in great routs, and agree by such confederacy that everyone shall aid other to resist their lords," &c., &c. Stat. 1 Rich. II., c. 6.

[6] Cunningham, *Growth of Industry*, i. 357.

as a matter of fact, misery and discontent continued, even after the Peace of Bretigny, to increase day by day.[1]

§ 96. *Prices of Provisions.*

We must stop, however, to note the more economic effects of the Black Death. Now, although there was a great rise in the price of labour, the price of the labourers' food did not rise in proportion. The price of provisions, indeed, was but little affected,[2] for food did not then require much manual labour in its production, and hence the rise of wages would not be much felt here. What did rise was the price of all articles that required much labour in their production, or the cost of which depended entirely upon human labour. The price of fish, for instance, is determined almost entirely by the cost of the fisherman's labour, and the cost of transit. Consequently we should under these circumstances expect a great rise in the price of fish,[3] and such indeed was the case. So, too, there was an enormous increase in the prices [4] of tiles, wheels, canvas, lead, iron-work, and all agricultural materials, these being articles whose value depends chiefly upon the amount of labour spent over them, and upon the cost of that labour. Hence, both peasant and artisan gained higher wages, while the cost of living remained for them much the same ; while those who suffered most were the owners of large estates, who had to pay more for the labour which worked these estates, and more too for the implements used in working them. It has, however, been pointed out,[5] on the other hand—and with some truth—that the lords of the manors must have gained a great deal, in the years during and immediately after the Plague, from the fees of "heriots"[6]

---

[1] Green, *History*, i. 438.

[2] Grain, meat, poultry, etc., retain much the same prices as before the Plague, or are only a little dearer. Rogers, *Six Centuries*, 239.

[3] *Ib.*, 240.   [4] *Ib.*, 238.

[5] By Jessop, *The Black Death in E. Anglia*, in *The Coming of the Friars*, p. 255, who also thinks that the rise in wages had begun *before* the Plague, and was merely accelerated by it.

[6] The "heriot" was a payment from "a dead man to his lord"; the "relief" was paid by the son before he could succeed to his father's lands. See Stubbs, *Const. Hist.*, i. pp. 261 and 24 *note*, 157.

and "reliefs" which they received consequent upon so many tenants' holdings changing hands through death. But any sums of money thus gained came of course only from a transitory condition of affairs, while the rise of wages and (in some cases) of prices was more permanent. We may, however, legitimately suspect, as an inference from modern cases, that the lords of the manors and the employers made the most of their hardships, in the hopes that arrears of taxation might be lightened by Parliament.[1]

§ 97. *Effects of the Plague upon the Landowners.*

The fact that the larger landowners found the cost of working their land doubled or even trebled caused important economic changes. Before the Plague the cost of harvesting upon a certain estate, quoted by Professor Rogers,[2] was £3, 13s. 9d.; afterwards it rose to £12, 19s. 10d. Moreover, the landlord had to consent to receive lower rents,[3] for many tenants could not work their farms profitably with the old rents and the new prices for labour and implements. And, as rent is paid out of the profits of agriculture, it became obvious that smaller profits must mean lower rents. Now, in this state of things the landlord had two courses open to him. He could turn off the tenant and cultivate all his land himself, or he could try to exist upon the smaller income gained from lower rents. It was obviously impossible for him to cultivate all his land himself, for he would have to employ a large number of bailiffs for his various manors, and trust to their honesty to do their best for him. He therefore decided to allow his tenants to pay him a smaller rent. What is more, he in many cases decided under the circumstances to give up farming altogether, and to let even the lands which he had reserved for his own cultivation.[4] The landlords, in fact,

---

[1] Jessop, *ut supra*, p. 256.   [2] *Six Centuries*, p. 241.

[3] In the words of Henry of Knighton's *Chronicle* (*ut supra*, ii. p. 65), the lords had "either entirely to free them, or give them an easier tenure at a small rent, so that homes should not be everywhere irrecoverably ruined and the land everywhere remain entirely uncultivated."

[4] This became even more frequent in the next century—the fifteenth. Stubbs, *Const. Hist.*, iii. 552. The new tenants were known as *firmarii*

had not, apparently, either the ability or the inclination to superintend agriculture under these changed conditions, and ceased trying to work their land themselves. One great result of the Plague, therefore, was that landlords to a large extent gave up capitalist farming upon their own account, and let their tenants cultivate the soil upon the modern tenant-farming method. There was, in fact, a complete change introduced into the agricultural system, the foundations of the modern arrangement of comparatively large farms,[1] held by tenants and not by small owners, were laid, and the present distinction between the farmer and the labourer was more clearly established.[2]

§ 98. *Large and Small Holdings: the Yeomen.*

This change in the agricultural situation also operated in other ways. Concurrently with the greater development of the modern system of tenant farmers, there is reason to believe[3] that the Plague caused in many places the concentration of several estates into one, in cases where numerous deaths had resulted in the succession of a single heir to the estates of his stricken relatives, and thus the tendency towards the combination of large estates in few lands was strengthened, and the great landowner became more clearly distinguished from his neighbours. "The gentry became richer and their estates larger." But at the same time there was also an undoubted tendency towards the multiplication of small holdings, both those in the hands of tenants and of owners, so that the class of peasant-farmers and yeomen greatly increased in numbers.[4]

The circumstances of the time favoured these, for the rise in the price of labour was not so severely felt by this class, since they could and did use the unpaid labour of their families upon their holdings.[5] Then, when they had

(*i.e.*, those who paid a *firma* or fixed rent), "fermors," or "farmers." Ashley, *Econ. Hist.*, II. ii. 267.

[1] Stubbs, *Const. Hist.*, I. ch. xvi. 400 ; Rogers, *Hist. Agric. and Prices,* i. 667.   [2] *Ib.*

[3] Jessop, *The Black Death in East Anglia*, in *The Coming of the Friars,* p. 251.

[4] Rogers, *Six Centuries*, p. 241.   [5] *Ib.*

tided over the immediate results of the Plague, they took larger holdings as they grew richer. They were helped in this by the stock and land lease system already referred to (p. 114), which gave them the use of a larger quantity of agricultural capital than they could otherwise have commanded. But when the tenant-farmer's wealth increased he found himself able, as a rule, to keep his own stock.

§ 99. *The Statute of Quia Emptores.*

It also would appear that, independently of the effects of the Plague, the number of substantial yeomanry (some of whom helped later to swell the numbers of the country gentry) was increasing from another cause. Little more than half a century before the Black Death, the Crown had thought it necessary to introduce the well-known Statute of *Quia Emptores*. This enactment[1] was intended to prevent the practice of "subinfeudation," whereby the tenants of the greater lords received other and smaller tenants on condition of their rendering to them feudal services similar to those which they themselves rendered to their original lords. The Statute of *Quia Emptores*[2] purposed to check this process by providing that in any case of alienation of land to a sub-tenant, this sub-tenant should hold it, not of the other tenant, but of the superior lord or real owner. The intention undoubtedly was to prevent the alienation of land, but, as so often happens with legislative enactments, the actual result was of a directly opposite character. The tenant who, previously, had been compelled to retain in any case at least so much of his holding as enabled him to fulfil his feudal obligations to his overlord, was now able (by a process similar to the modern sale of "tenant right") to transfer both land and services to new holders.[3] The estates thus transferred, however large or small they might be, were now held directly of the Crown or superior lord; and the class of

---

[1] Stubbs, *Const. Hist.*, II. ch. xv. p. 180; Taswell Langmead, *English Const. Hist.*, pp. 62, 138, 228.

[2] The king (Edward I.) enacted this "by the instance of his magnates only" (*ad instantiam magnatum regni sui*) on July 8th, 1290 (18 Ed. I., c. 1).

[3] Green, *History*, i. 336.

small gentry and freeholders grew steadily from this time both in numbers and importance. The Plague assisted the tendency of the Statute, and an important social change was thereby wrought. " The facilities thus given to the alienation and subdivision of lands; the transition of the serf into the copyholder, and of the copyholder by redemption of his services into a freeholder; the rise of a new class of ' farmers,' as the lords ceased to till their demesne by means of bailiffs, and adopted instead the practice of leasing it at a rent or ' farm ' (*firma*) to one of the ' customary ' tenants; the general increase of wealth which was telling on the social position, even of those who still remained in villeinage—all undid more and more the earlier process which had degraded the free ceorl of the English Conquest into the villein of the Norman Conquest, and covered the land with a population of yeomen, some freeholders, some with services that every day became less weighty and already left them virtually free." [1]   The yeomanry of England formed henceforth for several centuries an important factor in national life, and their decline was a national misfortune. [2]

§ 100. *The Emancipation of the Villeins.*

In fact, the gradual amelioration of the conditions of villeinage or serfage received a forcible impetus from the Great Plague.   Those villeins who had not already become free tenants, and especially those who lived on wages, [3] shared in the advantages now gained by all who had labour to sell.   Their labour was more valuable, and they were able with their higher wages to buy from their lord a commutation of those exactions which interfered with their personal freedom of action, [4] with their right to sell their labour to other employers, or with their endeavours to reach a better social position.   Serfage or villeinage gradu-

---

[1] The extract, which gives a good summary of the conclusions of other writers, is from Green, *History of the English People*, i. 420.

[2] For this decline, see below, p. 276.

[3] Rogers, *Six Centuries*, p. 242.

[4] " Money payments were substituted for service." Stubbs, *Const. Hist.*, II. ch. xvi. p. 454.

ally became practically a mere form,[1] though the landowners, supported by the lawyers,[2] interposed many obstacles in the path of emancipation, and a great Revolt
was necessary to enable the villeins to show their power.
This revolt and its result must now engage our attention.[3]

[1] Stubbs, *Const. Hist.*, II. ch. xvi. p. 254. "It was by a mere legal
form that the villein was described as less than free."

[2] *Ib.*, p. 455. The lawyers seem to have been against the freedom of
villeins ever since the Norman Conquest. *Cf.* Vinogradoff, *Villeinage in
England*, pp. 134, 150, &c., &c.

[3] Of course villeinage did not die out all at once ; nor would it be necessary for me to say so, were it not for the perversity of certain critics, who
imagine that, because I attach great importance to the Plague and the
Peasant's Revolt, I maintain that villeinage ceased suddenly. For sur
vivals, see later, p. 171.

CHAPTER XII

THE PEASANTS' REVOLT OF 1381, AND THE SUBSEQUENT CONDITION OF THE WORKING CLASSES

§ 101. *The Place of the Revolt in English History.*

THE Revolt to which allusion has just been made has been described by one of our greatest and most careful historians [1] as " one of the most portentous phenomena to be found in the whole of our history"; nor has the criticism [2] of those who have endeavoured to minimise its results succeeded in depriving it of its historical importance. "The extent of the area over which it spread, the extraordinary rapidity with which intelligence and communication passed between the different sections of the revolt, the variety of cries and causes which combined to produce it, the mystery that pervades its organisation, its sudden collapse and its indirect permanent results, give it a singular importance both constitutionally and socially." [3] It is therefore of interest to note the various influences which produced such an uprising, and to examine the various grievances which the villeins of the fourteenth century endeavoured to redress by such revolutionary methods. The revolt was undoubtedly serious, and would certainly have had far more sanguinary consequences, had it occurred later than it actually did. Fortunately the working classes of England were not so utterly ground down beneath the heel of their superiors as was the case across the Channel, and they resented their

---

[1] Stubbs, *Const. Hist.*, II. ch. xvi. p. 449.

[2] *Cf.* Ashley's criticism of *J. E. Thorold Rogers* in *The Political Science Quarterly*, Vol. IV., No. 3, September 1889. Also Cunningham, *Growth of English Industry*, Vol. I. p. 360. But these historians practically admit all that Rogers really wished to prove, as my quotations show. See below, p. 172.

[3] Stubbs, *ut ante*, p. 450.

injuries sooner, otherwise England might have witnessed a few centuries later that volcanic upheaval of a slow peasantry, enraged by ages of seigneurial oppression, which burst with such terrific and long-contained violence over eighteenth century France. Fortunately, also, the upper classes of England seem to have taken warning in time from what happened in 1381, and did not in actual fact, whatever they may have said and thought, proceed to such foolish extremities as would have infallibly endangered both their property and their position.

§ 102. *New Social Doctrines.*

By no means the least important among the effects of the Great Plague was the spirit of independence which it helped to raise in the breasts of the villeins and labourers, more especially as they now gained some consciousness of the power of labour, and of its value as a prime necessity in the economic life of the nation.[1]   There was, indeed, a revolutionary spirit in the air in the last quarter of the fourteenth century, and the villeins could not help breathing it.   The social teaching of the author of *Piers the Plowman*, with his outspoken denunciation of those who are called the upper classes,[2] the bold religious preaching of Wiklif and the wandering friars, and the marked political assertion of the rights of Parliament by the "Good Parliament"[3] of 1376, were all manifestations of this spirit.   It was natural, too, that, feeling their power as they did, the villeins should become restive when they heard from the followers of Wiklif that, as it was lawful to withdraw tithes from priests who lived in sin, so "servants and tenants may withdraw their services and rents from their lords that live openly a cursed life."[4]

---

[1] *Cf.* Gower, *Vox Clamantis*, in Stubbs, *u. s.*, ii. p. 454, where he describes hired labourers of the period of the Revolt, and accuses them of wishing to have too much of their own way.

[2] See below, p. 167.   I have treated this more at length in *English Social Reformers*, pp. 5-25.

[3] Stubbs, *Const. Hist.*, II. ch. xvi. pp. 428-433.   "It marked the climax of a long rising excitement," p. 428.

[4] Wiklif, *English Works* (E.E.T.S.), p. 229, *Of Lords and Servants.*

§ 103. *The Coming of the Friars.   Wiklif.*

Such, indeed, was the teaching that Wiklif promulgated, and it was carried throughout all England by that great association of wandering friars which he founded under the title of the "poor priests."[1]   These men were like the mendicant friars who had come to England a century before[2] to work in the poorer parts of the English towns; though Wiklif's priests generally wandered out[3] into the isolated and remote country villages, and spread abroad the independent doctrines and the revolutionary spirit of the times.   Spending their lives in moving about among the "upland folk," as the country people were called, clad in coarse, undyed, brown woollen garments, they won the confidence of the peasants, and what is more, helped them to combine in very effectual unions.[4]   They served as messengers between those in different parts of the country, having passwords and a secret language of their own.[5]   Their preaching was similar to that of the celebrated priest of Kent, John Ball, who for twenty years before the great rising (1360-80) openly spoke words like these—"Good people, things will never be well in England so long as there be villeins and gentlemen.   By what right are they whom we call lords greater than we ?   On what grounds have they deserved it ?   Why do they hold us in serfage ?   They have leisure and fine houses : we have pain and labour, and the wind and rain in the fields.   And yet it is of us and our toil that these men hold their estate."   These searching questions as to the rights of the lords, and the bold but true statement

---

[1] Green, *History*, i. 474.

[2] The Black Friars of Dominic came in 1221, and the Grey Friars of Francis in 1224.   Jessop, *Coming of the Friars*, 32, 34.   The Dominicans were "trained men of education addressing themselves mainly to the educated classes"; the Franciscans appealed to the lowest and poorest class, and worked in the slums of the towns of those days.   *Ib.*, 28, 21.

[3] Friars and "poor priests" were found everywhere ; *cf.* Wylie, *England under Henry IV.*, ch. xvi.

[4] These unions or confederacies are complained of and prohibited (uselessly) by the Statute 1 Rich. II., c. 6 (1377).

[5] See the message of John Ball (himself, of course, a priest) to the commons of Essex, quoted in Skeat's Preface to *Piers the Plowman*, p. xxvi., and Green's *History*, i. p. 475.

that it was the villeins and labouring classes who supported
—and paid for—their high estate, came closely home to
the peasants. They were influenced also by the independent religious views of the Lollards,[1] which encouraged independent thought in other ways. And this independence of
social and religious tenets was hardly calculated to make
the villeins bear with equanimity the exactions of their
lords after the Great Plague.

§ 104. *The Renewed Exactions of the Landlords.*

For it must be remembered that the Great Plague did
not emancipate the villeins, nor cause the landowners to
give up farming on their own account immediately. The
process, of course, took a few years, and in these few years
the landowners made desperate efforts to avoid paying
higher wages than formerly for labour. As it had now
become costly, they insisted more severely upon the per-
formance by their tenants of such labour dues as were not
yet commuted for money payments.[2] They even tried to
make those tenants who had emerged from a condition of
villeinage to a free tenancy return back to villeinage again,[3]
with all its old labour dues and casual services. If a man
could not prove by legal documentary evidence that he
held his land in a free tenancy, the landowner might pretend he was a villein tenant, and subject to all a villein's
services, although these services might long ago have been
commuted for a money rent without any legal formality.[4]

---

[1] Note the complaints against Lollard teaching in the Statute 2 Henry
V., I. c. 7.

[2] As Stubbs puts it — "The villeins ignored the Statute [*i.e.*, of
labourers], and the lords fell back upon their demesne rights over the
villeins" (*Const. Hist.*, II. ch. xvi. p. 455). The point of view of the
lords is expressed, plaintively enough, in the Statute 1 Rich. II., c. 6—
"The villeins and land-tenants in villeinage who owe services and customs
to the said lords have now lately withdrawn and do daily withdraw their
services and customs," &c., &c.

[3] "The old rolls were searched, the pedigree of the labourer was tested
like the pedigree of the peer, and there was a dread of worse things coming" (Stubbs, *ut ante*, p. 455).

[4] This was no doubt the cause of the particular animosity shown against
manorial documents, which in many cases the villeins tried to burn; *cf.*
Walsingham, *Hist. Angl.*, i. 455.

There is much reason to believe, moreover, that they abused their power of inflicting "amercements," or fines, upon their tenants in the manor courts for trivial breaches of duty.[1] So at least Wiklif[2] and the author of *Piers the Plowman*[3] tell us. The villeins naturally resisted this attempt to make a retrograde movement, which would force them back into the old bondage from which they had redeemed themselves;[4] the free tenants[5] supported them, for they knew their turn would come next if the serfs failed; and the labouring classes in the towns—many of whom had kinsmen in the country, or had been villeins once themselves—eagerly joined the movement[6] also, in hopes of bettering their position generally.

§ 105. *Social and Political Questions.*

Meanwhile, other social and political grievances contributed to the general uneasiness. The state of the kingdom, instead of allaying, merely increased the undercurrent of discontent among the lower classes. The Statutes of Labourers,[7] by their endeavours to reduce the rates of wages to the old level of the days before the Plague, or to keep the multitudes of wandering labourers in search of work tied down to their own particular localities, only succeeded in widening the gulf and increasing the bitterness between rich and poor. Many of Edward's French conquests had been lost since the Peace of Bretigny; the Plague had come again with renewed devastations; the Parliament

---

[1] *Cf.* Ashley, in his essay on *Thorold Rogers* in the *Political Science Quarterly*, Vol. IV., No. 3, p. 399, who mentions this very point, though he criticises severely Rogers' view of the case. Also *cf.* Ashley, *Econ. Hist.*, II. ii. 265.

[2] Wiklif, *English Works* (E.E.T.S.), *Of Lords and Servants*, p. 233—"Lords many times do wrongs to poor men by unreasonable amercements."

[3] *Piers Plowman*, Passus C., ix. l. 37 (Skeat's ed., i. p. 197), "When ye amercyn any man let mercy be taxer."

[4] "With the teaching of Wiklif in the air, it was natural that the villeins should become restive." Ashley, *Pol. Science Quarterly*, IV., No. 3, p. 399.

[5] "The irritation spread to the whole class, whether bond or free." Stubbs, *Const. Hist.*, II. xvi. 455.

[6] *Ib.*, p. 456.   [7] Above, p. 153.

had unwisely (1376 and 1379) sought to enforce the
Statutes of Labourers still more stringently;[1] the king
himself was sinking into a premature old age, the victim of
his own profligacy and of the designing ministers and
avowed mistresses who surrounded him. His debts and
the expenses of his French wars had become a fatal burden
upon his own country. His continual levies of tenths and
fifteenths upon the produce of the kingdom, especially upon
wool, and his taxation of exports and imports, were seriously
draining the resources of the nation.[2] To meet the expenditure on war abroad, and on luxury at the court, a poll-tax of
a groat a head was ordained among the last acts of the dying
king,[3] who passed away at last in June 1377, robbed of
his rings even on his death-bed by his mistress, Alice
Perrers.[4]

Richard II., who succeeded to the throne, was a child of
only eleven years of age. The war with France was still
going on, bringing continual disasters and defeats to the
English troops even on our own shores;[5] and at last, to
meet its expenses, Parliament, meeting at Northampton on
November 5th, 1380, granted the famous poll-tax which
was the immediate cause of the Peasants' Revolt.[6] The
tax was now made 12d. instead of a groat (4d.), as it had
been previously,[7] and was levied on every person above
fifteen years of age.[8] Although it was graduated, its lowest
limit was yet three times the previous tax, and it was collected also in the most odious manner, for the troops who
had just returned from France, after the conclusion of peace
in January 1381, were clamorous for pay, and, to meet

[1] Above, p. 153.
[2] *Rot. Parl.*, ii. 310 ; Stubbs, *Const. Hist.*, II. xvi. 424.
[3] *Rot. Parl.*, ii. 364.   It was granted by Parliament on February 22, 1377.
[4] Green, *History*, i. 470.
[5] In July and August 1377, the French ravaged the Isle of Wight, and
burned Hastings and Rye, and in August 1380 they ravaged the whole of
the south coast. *Annals of England* (Parker), sub anno.
[6] *Rot. Parl.*, iii. 88-90.
[7] A graduated poll-tax had been granted in 1379, the lowest tax being
a groat on every person over sixteen years of age, while earls paid £4.
Rot. Parl., iii. 57, 58.
[8] Prince, *Parallel History*, i. 659 (ed. 1842) ; Hume's *History of England*,
iii. 6 (ed. 1818).

their demands, the ministers borrowed a large sum from foreign merchants, assigning them this tax in return, and allowing them to appoint their own collectors.[1]

§ 106. *The Mutterings of a Storm.*

This new oppression brought the discontent of the people to a climax. But the discontent had long been making itself felt, and was only waiting for a definite opportunity to burst forth into flame. As we saw,[2] the poorer villeins and labourers had long since banded together in trades unions of a secret sort, while the "poor priests" of Wiklif and the "begging friars"[3] had long been wandering from village to village, carrying the messages of the angry peasants from one to another, and preaching social reform, if not social equality. Quaint letters in rude rhyme passed through the peasant ranks—the voice of "Piers the Plowman" was making itself heard. Here is an epistle[4] from John Ball, issued from the prison into which he had been thrown, to the people of Essex—"John the Shepherd, sometime St Mary's priest of York and now of Colchester," it ran, "greeteth well John Nameless, and John the Miller, and John the Carter, and biddeth them beware of guile in the town and stand together in God's name; and he biddeth Piers the Plowman go to his work, and chastise well Hob the Robber[5]; and take with you John True-man and all his fellows and no more; and look sharp and go ahead (loke scharpe you to go on heved) and no more." Some rhyme follows, and the letter concludes—"And so biddeth John Truman and all his fellows." It is obvious that this letter contains a message clearly intelligible to those for whom it was meant, but of no meaning to others, while the obscure references to "Piers the Plowman" would be easily interpreted by the proper readers thereof. Another letter runs—

---

[1] The story of the collectors' alleged misbehaviour is well known.
[2] Above, p. 163.   [3] *Chron. Angl.*, p. 312.
[4] Quoted in Skeat's Introduction (p. xxvi.) to *Piers the Plowman*.
[5] This probably meant that the agricultural labourer is to rise against the lord who was "robbing" him of his rights.

> " John Ball
> Greeteth you all.
> And doth for to understand
> He hath rung your bell.
> Now right and might !
> Will and skill !
> God speed every dele ! " [1]

Such were the hidden messages and passwords that were whispered from one villein to another, or carried by wandering friars, throughout the length and breadth of the land, till at length the storm broke, and all at once, in Yorkshire and Lancashire, in Suffolk and Essex, in Kent and in Devon, north, west, east, and south,[2] the peasantry of England rose as one man against their masters.

§ 107. *The Storm Breaks Out.*

The simultaneous nature of the rising leaves us no doubt that it was preconcerted. The collectors of the poll-tax seem to have been openly opposed first in Essex,[3] and when Sir Thomas Belknap, a judge, was sent to punish the rioters, he was obliged to flee for his life. Almost at the same time a workman, named Wat or Walter the Tyler,[4] killed a collector who, it is said, insulted his daughter.

According to documents in the Public Record Office, " a cry was raised that no tenant should do service or custom to the lords as they had aforetime done," [5] and immediately bands of town workmen in some cases, and of rustics in others, assembled together under the leadership of men with assumed names, such as Jack the Miller and Jack Straw. In Kent they burst open the gaols, seized William de Septvanz the Sheriff, and compelled him to deliver up the taxation rolls, which were promptly burnt.[6] But these acts were not the immediate object of the villeins. After

[1] Part.

[2] " Far more rapidly than the news could fly," says Stubbs, II. xvi. 450.

[3] Walsingham, i. 454. Stubbs, *ut supra*, 457.

[4] It seems to have been really *John* Tyler of Dartford who did this, but Wat Tyler of Maidstone is often confused with him. *Cf.* Stubbs, p. 456, *note.*

[5] *Cf. Annals of England* (Parker, Oxford, 1876), p. 203.

[6] *Arch. Cant.*, iii. 76.

releasing John Ball from Maidstone Gaol, they proceeded, as all know, to London, demanding not merely the abolition of the unjust poll-tax, but (what is significant as showing the real nature of the rising) also the relief of the rural population from the exactions of their lords.[1]   It is significant also to note how many clergy were in the ranks of the insurgents, for in indictments made after the rising [2] we find the chaplain of one church, the sacristan of another, and the clerk of a third, charged with heading mobs that sacked stewards' houses and burnt court-rolls.[3]   The mass of peasants and others assembled at Blackheath on June 12th, 1381, entered London the following day, then seized the Tower, and murdered the Archbishop of Canterbury and the King's Treasurer.   On the 14th the men of Essex met Richard at Mile End, and on the 15th the men of Kent had a conference with him at Smithfield, when their chief leader, Wat the Tyler, was slain by the Lord Mayor of London.[4]

The details of those meetings are almost too well known to need repetition here.   But the demands of the men of Essex prove clearly the real origin of the movement.   "We will that you free us for ever, us and our lands," they asked, "and that we be never named or held as villeins." "I grant it," said the King, with regal diplomacy, and the peasants believed him.[5]   He gave the same promise to the men of Kent, and it was only after receiving his letters of emancipation [6] that the reformers returned to their homes, though the rising was not yet entirely at an end, for one party certainly remained in arms up to July 1st.[7]

But the peasants learned very soon how vain a thing it

---

[1] They demanded (1) abolition of bondage, (2) a general pardon, (3) abolition of tolls, (4) the commutation of villein services.   See Richard II.'s patent revoking manumissions; Rymer, *Foedera*, iv. 216.

[2] *Cf. Annals*, p. 204; *Rot. Parl.*, iii. 108.

[3] These were the records of the manorial courts held by the lords of the manors. *Rot. Parl.*, iii. 116; Walsingham, *Hist. Angl.*, i. 455.

[4] Stubbs, *Const. Hist.*, ii. p. 458.

[5] Walsingham, *Hist. Angl.*, i. 459.

[6] "We release you from all bondage." Walsingham, i. 466, 467, and *cf.* 473.

[7] *Annals of England*, p. 204, *note*.

was to put their trust in princes. Within a fortnight (on June 30th) Richard issued a proclamation that *all* tenants, whether villeins or free, should render all accustomed services as heretofore;[1] and on July 2nd he formally annulled the charters of freedom,[2] a step that was subsequently sanctioned by Parliament when it met again on November 5th (5 Richard II., c. 6). Special commissioners were sent into the country to punish the insurgents,[3] and it would seem that as many as 1500 persons were executed by their orders.[4] Everywhere the peasants and their leaders were put down by the severest measures. Richard marched through Kent and Essex with an army of 40,000 men, ruthlessly punishing all resistance.[5] " Villeins you were," he cried, as the men of Essex claimed from him his own royal promise ; " villeins you were, and villeins you are. In bondage you shall abide, and that not your old bondage, but a worse ! "[6] At St Alban's John Ball was hanged on July 15th,[7] and so, too, was another leader, one Grind-cobbe, as he was called. But as he died Grind-cobbe uttered the words, which, in spite of king and lords, at last came true—" If I die, I shall die for the cause of the freedom *we have won*, counting myself happy to end my life by such a martyrdom."[8]

§ 108. *The Result of the Revolt.*

And, as a matter of fact, the peasants in reality gained their point. They had to shed their own blood, but they won in the end. The landowners in Parliament certainly refused any notion of compromise at first ; they even prayed the King to ordain " that no bondman nor bondwoman (*i.e.*, no villein) shall place their children at school, *as had been done*, so as to advance their children in the world by their

---

[1] Rymer, *Foedera*, iv. 126. [2] *Ib.*
[3] Richard himself had to interfere to repress their severity. Rymer, *Foed.*, iv. 133.
[4] *Annals*, p. 205 ; Stubbs, quoting *Mon. Evesh.*, p. 33, says that in all 7000 insurgents were executed.
[5] Green, *History*, i. 484.   [6] Walsingham, *Hist. Angl.*, ii. 18.
[7] Stubbs, *Const. Hist.*, ii. p. 452, *note.*
[8] Green, *History*, i. 485.

going into the church."[1]   They even asked that lords might reclaim villeins from the chartered towns,[2] but the king had the sense to refuse both petitions.   The poor priests, unlicensed preachers, or "Lollards," were ordered to be arrested or held in strong prison "until they justify themselves according to the law and reason of Holy Church."[3] But after the first year or two, all these efforts fortunately proved abortive.   Villeinage rapidly became practically extinct, and commutation of labour services for money rents became more and more common.[4]   Evidence of this is seen in the whole tone of the writings of Fitzherbert, the author of a well-known work, " On Surveyinge," who, about 1530, instead of regarding the surviving instances of villeinage as quite the natural thing, laments over its continuance as a disgrace to the country—a marvellous change of attitude since the fourteenth century.[5]   Almost the last cases of survival occurred under Elizabeth,[6] who enfranchised the bondmen on royal estates in 1574, though a few later notices of the custom appear.   No doubt some traces of the old order remained for centuries; indeed, it would have been strange if such had not been the case.   Although, for instance, the old manorial system is long since dead, its relics survive among us to-day, and *courts leet* are still held in many places.   Yet no one contends that the manor survives as in the fourteenth century.   But, speaking broadly, the peasants achieved their object; the labours of John Ball, Tyler, and Grinde-cobbe were not altogether futile; and the century that followed the Great Revolt was, on the whole, one of considerable prosperity for the English labourer.[7]

---

[1] *Rot. Parl.*, iii. 294, 296.   [2] *Ib.*
[3] 5 Ric. II., st. 2, c. 5.   [4] Stubbs, *Const. Hist.*, II. ch. xvi. 463.
[5] *Cf.* Cunningham, i. p. 360, who, however, thinks villeinage did not die out so quickly.
[6] Rymer, *Foed.*, xv. 731.
[7] In this account of the Peasants' Revolt I find myself in agreement with the general conclusions of Thorold Rogers, though the careful reader will notice that none of the references in the footnotes refer to his works, but are taken from other authorities.   Some modern economic historians have criticised (with more or less severity) the conclusions of this eminent authority, but, curiously enough, when their own theories are looked into,

§ 109. *The Condition of the English Labourer.*

After this great insurrection came a time of considerable prosperity for the English labourer, and it lasted all through the fifteenth century. Food was cheap and abundant; wages were amply sufficient. In fact, soon after the Revolt a statute of 1388 complains of them being " outrageous and excessive." [1]   True, the employers ot

they merely confirm those held by Thorold Rogers, at least in their broad outlines. Professor W. J. Ashley has an elaborate criticism of Rogers' work in general and his theory of the Peasants' Revolt in particular in the *Political Science Quarterly*, Vol. IV., No. 3, and roundly accuses Rogers of belonging to the " cataclysmic school " (p. 400) of history, of seeking after dramatic effect rather than absolute truth, and of not being " guided by the idea of gradual, reasonable, undramatic development " in history (p 407). Unfortunately for this criticism, however, human history, even on its economic side, refuses to be either gradual, undramatic, or even consistently reasonable. If it were, it would not be human, though it might be academic — a dubious gain.   There have been sudden and dramatic developments often enough, as witness the discovery of the New World, and its conquest by the Spaniards ; or the rise of Napoleon ; or the ver; dramatic (not to say theatrical) French Revolution.   The Industrial Revolution in England was rightly called by Toynbee a revolution and not an evolution, for it presents a sudden and by no means gradual development. And the Peasants' Revolt was certainly one of the " dramatic " developments of our social history.   It is impossible to read contemporary documents without noticing the important place it took in the minds of those who lived through it, short though it was ; and I am prepared to follow Bishop Stubbs in his estimate of it rather than attempt to minimise its importance. As to the cause of the revolt as set forth by Stubbs and Rogers, Professor Ashley says (*P. S. Q.*, p. 399), "*Certainly* no evidence has yet been adduced that can be regarded as confirming it." This is utterly to ignore the words of Wiklif, " *Piers the Plowman*," and the preambles to the statutes of the day.   As a matter of fact, however, Professor Ashley quotes them himself, and admits from them practically all Rogers' conclusions as to the origin of the Revolt. Dr Cunningham (*Growth of English Industry*, i. 359-360) does the same, and, of course, both declare that the Revolt failed. Dr Cunningham says that in the fifteenth century services were still rendered by villeins (i. 360), and thinks this fact alone proves the failure. Of course services continued to be rendered, but they were on a very different footing than in the days before the Revolt.   From 1381 onwards we find them no longer flourishing but decaying, and within one hundred years they are practically, and in two hundred almost entirely, extinct.   Considering how many relics of the old manorial system survive in the nineteenth century, is it not a little remarkable that villeinage died out so rapidly? No historian in his senses would say that services ceased immediately after the Revolt, but we need not deny that from that time forward they began to die out more rapidly than before.

[1] 12 Rich. II., cc. 3-7, preamble—"The servants and labourers will not

labour still tried, by various petitions and Acts,[1] to enforce the Statute of Labourers, but they were practically unsuccessful, and prosperity seems to have been progressive and continuous till the days of Henry VIII. The wages of a good agricultural labourer, before the Plague, have been calculated at £2, 7s. 10d. per year as an average,[2] including the labour of his wife and child; after the Plague his wages would be £3, 15s., and the cost of his living certainly not more than £3, 4s. 9d. An artisan, working 300 days a year, would get, say, £3, 18s. 1½d. before 1348, and after that date £5, 15s. 7d., which was so far above the cost of maintenance as to give him a very comfortable position.[3] By the day[4] wages were for agricultural labourers 4d. a day, and for artisans, 6d. His working day, too, was probably not excessive,[5] for although the legal day was one of about twelve hours[6] for agricultural labourers, it is pretty certain that, as in other cases, the statutes were generally evaded. Rents were low, and these low rents were one great cause of the prosperity of the new yeoman or tenant farmer class (p. 157) that had arisen after the collapse of the capitalist landowners in consequence of the Plague—a class which remained for at least two centuries the backbone of English agriculture.

Several recent historians, however, have taken a view of the labourer's life in the fifteenth century that by no means agrees with the pleasant condition of things which the statistics of wages seem to indicate. Instead of accepting the fifteenth century as an era of great prosperity, they have endeavoured to paint from various sources a very different

serve and labour without outrageous and excessive hire, and *much more than hath been given in any time past.*" The Act then goes on to fix wages. Surely this is a sign of the practical success of the Peasants' Revolt.

[1] For example, 7 Henry IV., c. 17 ; 23 Henry VI., c. 12 ; 11 Henry VII., c. 22, and others.

[2] Rogers, *Hist. Agric.*, i. 290, 684, 689, and iv. 757.   [3] *Ib.*

[4] Rogers, *Six Centuries*, p. 327.

[5] Rogers infers from various grounds (*Hist. Agric.*, iv. 755) that the working day was of only eight hours, chiefly arguing from the heavy payments for overtime. Dr Cunningham (1-477) thinks the contrary, and quotes the Acts of 11 Hen. VII, c. 22, and 6 Hen. VIII., c. 3.

[6] See the two Acts just quoted.

and very gloomy picture. When it is pointed out that
wages were high both for artisans and labourers, while the
prices of food were particularly low, it is contended on the
other hand that the high wages were only those paid by
the day, that yearly wages were much lower, and that even
for day labourers employment was not constant.[1] The balance of advantage is said to lie with the modern artisan.[2]
If we take the "common servant in husbandry," it is said,
we find[3] he is only paid 20s. 8d. a year, and his wife only
14s., though their food is provided; and even the bailiff
only gets 26s. 8d. a year, with 5s. extra for clothing, and
his food as well.   But it must be remembered that the
statute which prescribes these rates is, of course, laying
down the minimum rates,[4] and there is not the slightest
doubt that far higher wages were habitually paid, not
merely for the work of a few days or weeks, but for work
extending over a whole year.   This, at any rate, is clear
enough in the case of artisans, for at Windsor in 1408 we
find carpenters getting 6d. and 5d. a day for 365 days in
the year,[5] which shows that they were paid an annual
wage at a daily rate, even including Sundays and holidays.
We find similar high wages at York, while at Oxford men
were paid full rates and fed by the College as well.[6]   As
for agricultural labourers, it must be noted that the
majority of them lived in their master's house,[7] when they
did not happen to be the sons of small tenants, or tenants
themselves,[8] who had their land to fall back upon.   Those
who lived in their master's house would certainly be well
fed while there,[9] for food was both abundant and cheap.
Even the minimum basis of wages just quoted (20s. 8d.
per year) cannot be called low, when we remember that it
represents between £12 and £13 of our money,[10] in addition to good board and lodging.   Many an agricultural

---

[1] Cf., e.g., Cunningham, Growth of English Industry, i. 348, 349.
[2] Ib., 349.   [3] In the 11 Henry VII., c. 22.
[4] Rogers, Six Centuries. p. 389.   [5] Ib., 328.
[6] Ib., 328.   [7] Froude, History of England, i. p. 5.
[8] Rogers, Hist. Agric., i. 689, 691. [9] Froude, History, i. 21.
[10] Taking the now generally admitted multiple of twelve to compare
prices of to-day with those of the fifteenth century; cf. Rogers, Six
Centuries, p. 539, 172; Froude, History, i. 26.

labourer in the last decade of the nineteenth century would be only too glad to obtain such payment.[1]   Nor need we be surprised that the bailiff only gets 31s. 8d. .(equivalent to some £19) a year, always supposing that his employer kept within the statute, though this is unlikely ; for it is characteristic of the Middle Ages that superior servants and workmen were paid but little above the average of those whom they superintended.[2]   But, as a matter of fact, there are plenty of instances of bailiffs getting far higher wages, such as from £3 and £5 to over £9 per annum.[3]   And when we come to consider that the average income of a country gentleman[4] was only about £20 per annum in Henry VI.'s days, it is evident that the bailiff was very well paid indeed, and that there was even no such enormous disproportion between the effective incomes of the labourer and the squire as there is to-day.

§ 110. *Purchasing Power of Wages.*

But it is useless to mention the rates of wages unless we can estimate at the same time their purchasing power ; and when we do so, we see that they were amply sufficient, even taking the statutory rates, to purchase for the labourer and artisan an abundance of good and cheap food.   An artisan earning 5d. or 6d. a day, or an agricultural labourer earning 3d. or 4d.,[5] could get plenty of bread, beef, and beer at very low prices.   For beef was only ½d. a pound, and mutton ¾d. ;[6] strong beer only 1d. a gallon, and table-beer a half-penny.[7]   The price of corn averaged a little under 6s. a quarter,[8] and other kinds of grain were equally cheap ;

---

[1] In Notts from £7 to £16 per annum are wages quoted in *Royal Commission on Labour Report*, Agric. Labourer, I. B. V. 127.

[2] It certainly was so with artisans. Rogers, *Hist. Agric.*, iv. 502-504.

[3] See wages quoted from manorial accounts by Rogers, *Hist. Agric.*, i. 287, iv. 119 (where the statutory wages are also mentioned).

[4] This was the income qualifying a country gentleman to be a J.P. by the 18 Henry VI., c. 11.

[5] These wages are those laid down by the 6 Hen. VIII., c. 3, the lower rates being paid in the winter.   [6] Stow's *Chronicle*, p. 568.

[7] *Assize of Brewers*, from a MS. in Balliol College, Oxford, quoted by Froude, *History*, i. 24.

[8] The average from 1260-1400 A.D. is 5s. 10¾d. a quarter ; from 1401 to 1540 it is 5s. 11¾d. Rogers, *Six Centuries*, p. 330.

chickens cost 1d. or 2d., and a pig or goose only 4d.[1]   The cheapness of provisions is seen from the fact that 6d. or 8d. a week was an ordinary estimate for the board of a workman,[2] and 2d. a day or 1s. a week was liberal.[3]   Indeed, the good food enjoyed by the "common people" was the wonder of all foreigners.   "What common folk in all this world may compare with the commons of England in riches, freedom, liberty, welfare, and all prosperity?" is the question in one of Henry VIII.'s State papers;[4] and chroniclers tell us that the food of "artificers and husbandmen consisteth principally in beef, and such meat as the butcher selleth, that is to say, mutton, veal, lamb, pork, whereof one findeth great store in the markets adjoining";[5] while "souse, brawn, bacon, fruit, pies of fruit," and "fowls of sundry sorts" were to be found in most workmen's homes.[6]   Surely it is sufficient evidence of the prosperity of the working classes when food of this description was so easily within their reach.   In fact, it is pretty clear that the close of the fourteenth century witnessed the beginning, and the fifteenth century the continuance, of an era to which the oppressed labourer of later times might well look back with admiration and regret. Holidays were frequent,[7] and if a man lost his wages during them, there was generally plenty of extra work, well paid, in harvest time[8] to compensate for loss of time elsewhere. The Saturday half-holiday, lost subsequently and only recently restored, seems to have been universal.[9]   In the leisure time thus falling to his lot, the agricultural labourer could work upon the land which then invariably went with

[1] Stafford, *State of the Realm*, quoted by Froude, *History*, i. 23.
[2] Rogers, *Six Centuries*, p. 328.   [3] *Ib.*, p. 329.
[4] *State Papers*, Henry VIII., Vol. II. p. 10.
[5] Harrison, *Description of England*, p. 282.
[6] *Ib.*   He adds, "in feasting it is incredible what meat is consumed and spent."   His book was written in the sixteenth century, but it shows that the condition of the working classes was fairly good even then, after the troubles of Henry VIII.'s reign, and therefore was probably quite as good in the fifteenth century.
[7] Froude, *History*, i. 28, reckons one day in every twenty; and it is evident that sometimes holidays were paid for. Rogers, *Six Centuries*, 327.
[8] Mowers could then get 8d. a day. *Privy Purse Expenses of Henry VIII.* (Froude, i. 28).
[9] Mrs Green, *Town Life in the Fifteenth Century*, ii. 133.

his cottage, while in every parish there were large ranges of commons, waste-land and forest, which gave him fuel for nothing, where his pigs might pick up mast and acorns or his geese feed freely, and where, if he had a cow, he might send her to graze. "So important was this privilege considered, that when the commons began to be largely enclosed, Parliament insisted that the working-man should not be without some piece of ground on which he could employ his own and his family's industry."[1] The "allotments" of the nineteenth century labourer, with their sometimes excessive rentals,[2] are a poor recompense for such privileges. In those days, if contemporary evidence goes for anything, England was once in reality "Merrie England," and life, even if unrefined, was coloured with broad, rosy English health.[3]

§ 111. *Drawbacks.*

There were, however, of course, several drawbacks in this pleasant era, as more than one critic has lately told us.[4] The ordinary hardships of human life were in many respects greater than they are now—disease was more deadly, and the risks of life more numerous; but from this very fact the extremes of poverty and wealth were less widely distinguished and less acutely felt; and, although it cannot be asserted that people did not occasionally die of want in very bad times, yet the grinding and hopeless poverty, just above the verge of actual starvation, so often prevalent in the present time, did not belong to mediæval life. The chief ordinary hardships to be encountered were in the winter, for, owing to the absence of winter roots, stock could not be kept except in limited quantities,[5] and the

---

[1] By the Act 31 Eliz., c. 7, every cottage was to have *four acres* of land attached to it. For the points of the above description, *cf.* Froude, *History*, i. 28.

[2] Rents of 35s. an acre, 22s. 6d. an acre, 11s. for one rood, 21s. for nearly half-an-acre, are quoted in *Statistics of Midland Villages* (1891-2) in the *Economic Journal*, Vol. III., No. 9.

[3] Froude, *History*, i. 46.

[4] *Cf.* Denton, *Fifteenth Century*, 105; Jessop, *Coming of the Friars*, 89, &c. (who, however, seems to refer to the thirteenth century); and Cunningham, i. 346, 347.   [5] Rogers, *Six Centuries*, 78.

M

only meat procurable was that which had been previously salted.[1] It is certain that much of mediæval disease is traceable to the excessive use of salted provisions. The houses, too, were rudely built of mud, clay, or even wattled material, for brickmaking was a lost art, and stone was only used for the manor-houses and the dwellings of the wealthy.[2] But food, as we saw, was abundant and cheap, and the cost of living was not more than one-tenth of what it is at the present day.[3] Nor were the houses quite so poorly furnished as some would have us think. Pictures, hangings, cushions, and feather beds were not unknown in the houses of plain country parsons with a salary of something like £6 a year.[4] It is probable that even the houses of the peasants were, compared with the degree of luxury and comfort then attainable, no worse furnished proportionately than they are now; and anyone who has seen Ann Hathaway's cottage at Stratford-on-Avon must admit that, as buildings, the dwellings of the labourer of to-day are often no improvement on those of the sixteenth century.

But two hardships there undoubtedly were, which perhaps were more severe in mediæval times than now. They were famine [5] and plague. The accounts of mediæval famines have no doubt been much exaggerated,[6] and those that occurred were chiefly local, but it is obvious that when means of communication were less perfect than they are now, individual villages might often suffer severely, while in other parts of the country there was plenty. Yet after all it is doubtful whether there was any more real scarcity than there is to-day; for deaths from sheer starvation are common enough among us even now; and against the evidence of famine must be set the evidence of general

---

[1] Rogers, *Six Centuries*, 95.   [2] *Ib.*, 97.

[3] "A penny in terms of the labourer's necessities must have been nearly equal to the present shilling." Froude, *History*, i. 26.

[4] See the very valuable quotation in Froude, *History*, i. 41, of the furniture of the Parson of Aldington, Kent, from an MS. in the Rolls House. *Cf.* also Stubbs, *Const. Hist.*, III. xxi. 555.

[5] See Cunningham, *Growth of Industry*, i. 346, who quotes Holinshed and Stow.

[6] This is obvious from a comparison of prices, which rarely show such variations as would correspond with the terrible descriptions of chroniclers.

plenty as being the normal condition of existence. No one would say that famines occurred regularly in England in the last decade of the nineteenth century, yet if one merely went by depositions at coroners' inquests a very good case might be made out by a critic of our civilisation. On the other hand, pestilence[1] was undoubtedly more common than now, and, of course, owing to lack of medical skill, more deadly; but to talk of "chronic typhoid in the towns and leprosy all over the country"[2] as the normal state of things, is to give a totally wrong impression of the risks of mediæval life. If our forefathers were more exposed to disease, the rude vigour of their constitutions, and the coarser texture of their nervous system, rendered them more impervious to its ravages. Probably, at least in the rural districts, the risks of life were not much greater than now, and though a great pestilence occasionally swept off its victims with tragic suddenness, there was probably not so much general ill-health and liability to death by easily thrown-off diseases as at the present day.

[1] *Cf.* Rogers, *Six Centuries*, 331, 335-337.
[2] Cunningham, *Growth of Industry*, i. 347, uses these words. Against them may be put Rogers' remark (*Six Centuries*, i. 331) that "if abundant evidence as to the rate of wages and silence as to loss of life [in manorial accounts] are to go for anything, it did not create a sensible void in the number of labourers."

CHAPTER XIII

THE CLOSE OF THE MIDDLE AGES

§ 112. *The Nobility.*

THE period from the Peasants' Revolt (1381) to the first few years of the reign of Henry VIII. (1509-1548) presents many interesting features. In it we come to the close of mediæval life, and begin the more modern history of our country. There are several important changes going on, yet, on the other hand, the main aspects of social life remain the same; for the permanence of social features is characteristic of mediæval times.[1] We may, therefore, take the facts presented in the previous section as giving us the outlines of a picture which, in all important points at any rate, lasted till the first half of the sixteenth century. The lives of the peasants and working classes were probably the same for quite a century. But meanwhile important social and economic changes were taking place.

In the fifteenth century, to take the highest ranks first, the great nobles and feudal lords were at the height of their power and splendour; but their glory was as that of the sun before it sinks suddenly out of sight amid a bank of stormy clouds. Fierce, ambitious, covetous, and unrelenting, greedy both of power and of land, they were nevertheless the political leaders of a people whom they alternately terrorised and cajoled, and they recognised the circumstances which their position entailed.[2] In their huge fortified houses and castles they kept enormous retinues of officers and servants, all arranged in distinct grades and provided with regular allowances of food and clothing.[3] Their households were arranged upon a scale of almost

---

[1] Froude, *History*, i. p. 1.
[2] *Cf.* Stubbs, *Constit. History*, Vol. III. ch. xxi. p. 542.
[3] *Ib.*, p. 538.

royal magnificence,[1] and yet the most accurate accounts [2] of income and expenditure were duly kept and audited. The baron's castle was both a court for the neighbouring squires, smaller nobles and gentry, and a school of knightly accomplishments and culture for their sons, while the huge kitchens and wardrobes afforded a continual market to the agriculturists and tradesmen of the district.[3] His progresses from one establishment to another made him known all over the country, and increased his political prestige and popularity. The houses of the Bishops and other great church dignitaries, and some of the larger monasteries, rivalled those of the barons in their magnitude and influence.[4] The nobility and the great officers of the Church had, in fact, an amount of wealth and power which they have rarely surpassed at any time of their history.

That power was also largely increased [5] in the fifteenth century by the practice of enclosing land, to which we shall refer later at greater length. The nobles saw that land meant both power and wealth, and grasped more and more of it as time went on. The Great Plague and the practical freedom of the villeins had indeed tried them sorely at first, but now a new use for land was springing up,[6] with a new system under which the services of their villeins were no longer required. I refer to the growing demand for wool, not only for foreign export but for home manufacture.[7] The growth of home manufactures encouraged sheep-farming on a large scale, and sheep-farming led to the change from arable to pasturage which is characteristic of the fifteenth century. So field was added to field, pasture to pasture, enclosure to enclosure, and the great lords rejoiced anew in the wealth derived from their broad acres. The evils of maintenance and livery were increased ; the power of the nobility grew continually, often

---

[1] *Cf.* Denton, *Fifteenth Century*, pp. 265-272.

[2] Stubbs, *u. s.*, p. 539. [3] *Ib.*, p. 541. [4] *Ib.*, p. 543.

[5] S. R. Gardiner, *Students' History of England*, i. 321.

[6] It was hardly because of the exhaustion of the soil that landowners turned arable into pasture, as Mr Gardiner (*ut supra*) seems to suppose. The land got rest under the system of fallow.

[7] *Cf.* Mrs Green, *Town Life in the Fifteenth Century*, i. 44.

at the expense of their poorer neighbours;[1] the Crown,
till the accession of Henry VII., was far too weak
to control the barons that stood round it; the great
families plundered the country,[2] until at last, quarrelling
among themselves for place and power, they became their
own destruction, and assured their speedy ruin and decay
in those suicidal conflicts known as the Wars of the Roses.

§ 113. *The Country Gentry.*

Next to the greater nobility, and constituting in some
measure a link between these and the yeomen, came the
large body of knights and squires or country gentry,[3] allied
to the nobility by claims of birth and descent, very often
as ancient as those of the haughtiest baron, but by their income and rural habits often not far removed from a well-to-
do farmer.   The income[4] of a knight ,might be placed at
£200 a year, of a squire £50, and while a substantial
yeoman could rarely attain the former sum, he might easily
surpass the latter.[5]   The household of the country gentleman was modelled on that of his greater neighbour, the
noble, and was often in consequence more elaborate than
we should have supposed necessary for his rank.[6]   But food
was abundant and cheap, and money wages were not high,
while very often the servants were his own poor relations.[7]
In the cultivation and management of his estate the knight
or squire found occupation and amusement; and his share
of public duty, both in county court and in musters and
arrays, was by no means light.[8]   He was hardly ever
merely an "absentee landlord," but "lived of his own" on
his own land, while a journey to London was the event of
a lifetime, and not an annual occurrence.   His life was
simple and rough—nay, even, according to our modern ideas,

---

[1] *Cf. Paston Letters* (ed. Arber), Vol. I. 13-15, and Denton, *Fifteenth
Century.* pp. 296-301.

[2] *Cf.* Gardiner, *Students' Hist. of England,* i. 321 and 323.

[3] Stubbs, *Const. Hist.,* III. xxi. p. 544.

[4] From the *Black Book of Edward IV.* (Stubbs, *u. s.,* p. 538).

[5] So we conclude from the well-known case of Latimer's father; Latimer,
First Sermon before King Edward, in the Preface to the *Northumberland
Household Book,* p. xii.

[6] Stubbs, *Const. Hist.,* III. xxi. p. 548.   [7] *Ib.*   [8] *Ib.*

coarse; but he generally did his duty according to his light, and knew pretty thoroughly the needs and the business of his agricultural neighbours; and when at last he was laid to rest in the village church where he had worshipped in pious but easy-going fashion all his days, he was probably regretted by the people of the manor far more than many a greater but less useful man.

§ 114. *The Yeomen.*

Next to the country gentry came that large and sturdy class of yeomen who, for some centuries, formed the real strength of English rural life. Their importance begins to be marked from the reign of Henry II. (1154-1189) onwards,[1] but in the fifteenth century they had come more than ever to the front. They are recognised by the election act [2] of 1430 A.D., which conferred the county franchise on every "forty shilling freeholder," though forty shillings by no means represented the income of a substantial yeoman. Their ranks were strengthened, after the economic changes to which I have before alluded, by the newer class of tenant farmers, who now, together with the smaller owners and freeholders, made up what is called the yeomanry.[3] In this class there was every gradation of income, from that of the forty shilling freeholder to that of the rich tenant farmer, who rivalled perhaps the squire himself, though of course a freeholder might equally be a rich man and the tenant farmer barely worth a couple of pounds. The yeomanry, by the income and social position of its richer members, was connected with the gentry; by its agricultural occupations, and by the poverty of the smaller tenants and freeholders, with the labourers and poorer tenants in villeinage.[4] Thus from baron to villein there was a closely-connected gradation of ranks, though the word "villein" had practically lost all its old significance, and after the reign of Richard II. is never found in the Statute books.[5] Freeholder, tenant, and

---

[1] Stubbs, *u. s.*, p. 552.

[2] The famous statute 8 Henry VI., c. 7, which was not repealed till the 14 Geo. III., c. 58.

[3] Stubbs, *Const. Hist.*, III. xxi. p. 552.　　　　[4] *Ib.*, p. 554.

[5] Froude, *Hist. of England*, i. p. 12.

villein alike were now merged into the yeomanry, except in those cases where a man had become merely an agricultural labourer. Politically, they were a very important element, for the forty shilling franchise must have included nearly all of them, and though the country gentry monopolised Parliamentary representation, their election depended on their yeoman constituents.[1] It was the yeomanry, too, who served on juries, chose the coroner, attended the sheriff's court, and assembled with arms which they themselves provided in the muster of the forces of the shire [2] to follow their King, if need were, across the Channel, and win victory and glory for their leader on the battlefields of France.[3]

§ 115. *Agriculture and Sheep-farming.*

The condition of the labourer we have seen already, and we may now therefore turn to the condition of the chief industry with which he was connected. Agriculture, as regards its methods, was still more or less stationary, but important changes were taking place, both among the tillers of the soil and in the uses to which the land was put. We have noticed the growth of the tenant farmer and yeoman and the emancipation of the villein, and now we note the appearance of the sheep farmer on a large scale. For his appearance in this century there was indeed more than one cause. In the first place, the silent but steady growth of home manufactures [4] since the days of Edward III.[5] had by this time begun to create a considerable home market for wool, in addition to the already existing market among the manufacturers of Flanders. That was no doubt the chief cause. But, besides this, sheep-farming offered to landlords a cheaper and easier method of using their land than other branches of industry, from the fact that it required

---

[1] Stubbs, *u. s.*, p. 557.   [2] Stubbs, *u. s.*, p. 552.

[3] *Cf.* the remarks on yeomanry in war in Green's *History*, i. p. 421.

[4] As evidence of this growth we may quote from a treatise by Sir John Fortescue, *Commodities of England* (written some time before 1451), where he mentions English "woollen cloth ready made at all times to serve the merchants of any two kingdoms."

[5] Above, p. 127.

comparatively little labour. This would be a great consideration, for labour had now become so dear, and the
services of villeins so irregularly and rarely paid [1] since the
great Revolt, that landowners were only too ready to turn
to any industry where villein labour was not required.
Hence we shall not be surprised to find a large increase of
sheep-farming in the fifteenth century, an increase which
caused foreigners to jest and English rhymers to lament,
because (it was said) we cared more for sheep than for the
ships of our navy. "Where are our ships, what are our
swords become? Our enemies bid us for a ship set a
sheep," [2] was the cry, though, like most political cries, it
was doubtless only partially true. Other complaints were
uttered as time went on, especially as the enclosures of
land made by landowners caused widespread distress in
many districts,[3] and the wheat-growing interest of that day
was sufficiently strong to induce the government to frame
enactments which anticipated the Corn Laws of a later
date. The wheat-growers, as opposed to the sheep-farmers,
declared that their industry required encouragement, and
complained that the price of wheat was too low. Whether
there was very much truth in this outcry may be doubted,
since at no time of our history has cheap bread roused
anything but complaint in the British farmer's breast ; but,
at any rate, the export of British corn was encouraged,[4] in
contradiction of a still earlier policy, while the import of
foreign corn was prohibited [5] unless the price of home-
grown wheat was 6s. 8d. a quarter. In justice to the
government, however, it should be added that mere protection was not the only object of these Corn Laws, though,

[1] We find tenants in villeinage quitting the manor without leave, and
tallages refused to the lords (Denton, *Fifteenth Century*, p. 113), nor were
manorial dues paid : "now they pay nothing" is the complaint; *cf.*
Blomfield's *History of Launton, MS.*, quoted by Denton, *u. s.*, p. 114.

[2] From the political poem (of about 1435) called *The Libelle of English
Policie*, 36, 37.

[3] See below, p. 213.

[4] By the 17 Richard II., c. 7; the 4 Henry VI., c. 5; and the 15 Henry
VI., c. 2. Previously to this the 34 Edward III., c. 20, had prohibited
the export.

[5] By the 3 Edward IV., c. 2.

of course, they were passed by a Parliament at that time composed almost exclusively of landowners ; but that legislators
sought to encourage thereby the growth of tillage as opposed
to pasture in order that the rural population might not be
compelled to leave the land.   Not only for agricultural, but
also for military reasons, it was important to prevent the
depopulation of rural districts, which, in some cases, sheep-
farming seemed to imply ; and therefore it is interesting
to notice how "servants and labourers" were directed to
practice with the bow and arrow on Sundays and holidays
instead of playing football, dice, and skittles, and other
unprofitable games.[1]

§ 116. *The Stock and Land Lease.*

Apart from sheep-farming, however, and the consequent
change from tillage to pasturage,[2] things went on much as
before in agriculture, and very few changes were made.
The "stock and land" lease system was still in operation,
and we have a very good example of its working in the
middle of the fifteenth century.[3]   The example is from a
farm at Alton Barnes in Wiltshire, in the year 1455 A.D.
The rental was £14, and the "stock" includes corn, and
both live and dead stock.   The corn was valued at the
price of the local market when the tenant took the farm
over, being altogether £11, 8s. 6½d. ; the live stock consisted of 5 horses, 11 oxen, 3 cows and a bull, 2 heifers and
2 yearlings, 571 sheep, and was valued at £64, 15s. 4½d. ;
and the dead stock came to £3, 15s. 2d., including farm
implements and some household utensils.   By the terms of
the lease the tenant has to restore every article and animal
enumerated (or its value) in good condition, though the
landlord guarantees his tenant against any loss of sheep
amounting to over 10 per cent. of their number.   Sometimes
this guarantee involved a severe loss to the landlord,[4] who
also was responsible for repairs, trade losses, and "poor
years,"[5] so that perhaps it is not surprising that land-

---

[1] 1 Richard II., c. 7.   [2] Stubbs, *Const. Hist.*, III. xxi. p. 611.
[3] Rogers, *Hist. Agric.*, iii. 705-708.
[4] See example in Rogers, *Six Centuries*, p. 285.   [5] *Ib.*, p. 286.

owners were not eager to give such leases if they could do better, and as time went on they fell into disuse. The value of land rose rapidly in the fifteenth century,[1] and people of good means and position were anxious to buy it for the sake of the social and other advantages it entailed,[2] as well as for the profits derivable from wool growing. Rent, too, rose rapidly,[3] and the smaller tenants and yeomen began to feel the competition of large farmers and sheep breeders. But still the great mass of land was held in the old common fields, with their curiously intermixed strips belonging to different tenants,[4] and the great majority of the rural labourers had a piece of land,[5] either of their own or as a holding, wherefrom to supplement their wages. A landless labourer was not yet the rule, while most men could still feel themselves, in some measure at least, active and real sharers in the life of their village community. The old institutions of primitive days were not yet dead,[6] though enclosures and legislation were soon to do their best to kill them. They were giving way to more modern requirements, but still they retained many relics of the past; and though, undoubtedly, it is owing to their persistence that the slow progress of agricultural methods is due, and though it was necessary they should go, one cannot help regretting that the disintegration of the old village community took much of value and interest from the social side of the labourer's life.

§ 117. *The Towns and Town Constitutions.*

When we turn now from the country to the towns we find that here again the fifteenth century is marked by

[1] Rogers, *Six Centuries*, p. 288.
[2] *Cf.* Stubbs, *Const. Hist.*, III. xxi. pp. 610, 611. Among the advantages of landowners may be mentioned a lower rate of taxation, the county franchise, legal protection from absolute forfeiture. Forfeited lands could be restored to the heirs of the dispossessed, whereas a merchant's property once forfeited was gone for ever.   [3] See below, p. 213.
[4] The difficulties caused to landlords by this system are shown in mediæval accounts. *Cf.* Rogers, *Six Centuries*, pp. 286, 287.
[5] Above, p. 177.
[6] *Cf.* Gomme, *Village Community*, ch. viii., where instances of survivals of much *later* date are given.

growth and change.   It has been already remarked that it
was not till the twelfth century that the towns have any
independent municipal life as boroughs at all,[1] while even
in the fourteenth century this municipal life was on a small
scale;[2] but in the fifteenth century wealth was accumulating[3]
and the towns growing more important, till, at the close
of the period, they emerge in something very like their
modern form as corporations.[4]   If we take, for example, the
period between the reigns of Henry III. (1216-1272) and
Henry VII. (1488-1509) we find that the amount of
growth is very considerable.   In the earlier part of the
period[5] the towns had indeed gained their charters, with
the rights of holding their own courts under their own
officers, the right of compounding for their payments to
the crown in the shape of the *firma burgi*,[6] and collecting
this among their citizens, and they had gained the recognition of the merchant and craft gilds that had so important a
share in their municipal life.   But these rights and privileges
were only a commencement of a growth towards a larger
freedom.   In the later years of the period we find that the
typical constitution of the town is the modern one of a
close corporation of mayor, aldermen, and council,[7] with
more or less clearly defined organisation and precise
numbers, and certainly with greater and more independent
self-governing powers.   The "bailiff" has been replaced
by the "mayor," and the town constitution gains by the
change a unity hitherto unknown ; the merchant and craft
gilds have become merged into the corporation and take
part in the municipal government; yet exactly how and
when these changes took place it is most difficult to say
It is, however, very clear that the growth of towns and of
civic constitutions throughout the country was exceeding
varied and irregular.[8]   There is no marked line of development ; sometimes the larger towns received their modern
constitution long before the smaller ; and altogether there
is great diversity of growth.   There is not space here to

---

[1] Mrs Green, *Town Life*, i. p. 11.   [2] *Ib.*, i. p. 13.
[3] *Ib.*, i. p. 15.   [4] Stubbs, *Const. Hist.*, III. xxi. p. 560.
[5] *Ib.*, p. 559.   [6] Above, pp. 90, 93.
[7] Stubbs, *u. s.*, p. 560.   [8] Ashley, *Econ. Hist.*, II. i. p. 11.

discuss the question fully, nor is it necessary for our purpose. It is sufficient to note the development of the towns, and, consequently, of town life, in the fifteenth century, as the beginning of that tendency towards urban attraction which is, perhaps unfortunately, a necessary characteristic of modern industrial progress. But we may devote a passing mention to the connection of the gilds and municipal life.

§ 118. *The Gilds and Municipal Institutions.*

The story of the relations of the merchant gilds to the municipal government on the one hand, and to the craft gilds on the other, is exceedingly complex.[1] Sometimes merchant gilds regarded the craft gilds as rivals, and attempted to suppress them, while at others they sought a surer means of regulating them by including them in their own body.[2] But in the fifteenth century the craft gilds were beginning to decay, at least in the older corporate towns, and were ceasing to be really effective institutions for the wellbeing of the crafts which they professed to regulate.[3] Consequently we need not be surprised at their practical destruction by Somerset in the next century (1547). But the merchant gilds had in many cases become identified with the corporation or governing body of the town to which they belonged, and regulated trade in much the same fashion as before,[4] though trade was now assuming so much larger proportions that it was outgrowing the powers of the regulating bodies. In some cases the name of " merchant gild " died out, as at York, but even then the custom of admitting "freemen" as citizens was exercised, as at Leicester, by the corporation in such a way as to show that the admission was a relic of the powers of the ancient gild.[5] In other places, however, the name and idea of the gild was still preserved, and furnished occasions for city pageants of considerable splendour.[6] But for all practical purposes the merchant gilds had now be-

---

[1] Stubbs, *Const. Hist.* III. xxi. p. 562. [2] Stubbs, *u. s.*, p. 563.
[3] Cunningham, i. p. 464. [4] Stubbs, *u. s.*, p. 564.
[5] *Ib.* [6] As at Preston ; Stubbs, *u. s.*, p. 565.

come identified with the town corporations, and even the gild
"halls" had become the common hall or "town hall" of the
city.[1] The aldermen of the gild became the aldermen of
town wards, and the property of the gild became the property of the town.[2] In London, however, the still existing
"City Companies" represent not merchant but craft gilds,
of which the twelve most important availed themselves in
the fourteenth century of the power to grant livery to
their members, and were then, and are still, distinguished
as the Livery Companies.[3]

§ 119. *The Decay of Certain Towns.*

It will be seen from this short summary, therefore, that
it is to the growth of industry that we owe the development
of our town life and municipal self-government, and that it
is in industrial history that the origin of the towns of
to-day must be sought. In later years towns take an
important share in political history, as well as industrial,
but in the period with which we are now dealing it was not
so. They did not play, either in or out of Parliament, an
important part in the dynastic struggles of the fifteenth
century.[4] Probably they were too much occupied with the
anxieties and responsibilities of their own development to
care much about outside politics, for we must remember
that in mediæval England the life both of town and village
was very self-centred, and neither citizens or villagers had
much interest in affairs outside their own boundaries. In
any case, many of the English towns at this time seem to
have been in a somewhat depressed condition from the
industrial point of view, however much they might be
advancing municipally and socially. The older corporate
towns seem to have decayed[5] towards the end of the
fifteenth century, however prosperous they may have been
at its beginning, and early in the reign of Henry VIII.[6] it

---

[1] Stubbs, *u. s.*, p. 565. One might cite the example of the Nottingham
"Gild Hall," which is the name still given to the quite modern building
used as a town hall.

[2] Stubbs, *u. s.*, p. 566.   [3] *Ib.*, pp. 566, 567.   [4] Stubbs, *u. s.*, p. 592.

[5] This is evident from the remissions of taxation on towns made in 1496.
Rot. Parl., vi. 514, 438.   [6] Statute 3 Henry VIII., c. 8.

is officially noted that "many and the most part of the cities, burghs, and towns corporate within this realm of England be fallen into ruin and decay." At first sight this would seem rather a startling condition of things, and, in fact, one that is almost inexplicable in view of the growth of industry and commerce which we know to have taken place in this age. But the explanation is not far to seek. First of all, we note that the complaint is made only of the old and corporate towns, and that many newer towns were growing up and flourishing with prosperous manufactures. This was certainly the case with Manchester,[1] Birmingham,[2] and (later) Sheffield;[3] and also with the towns of Leeds, Wakefield, and others in the West Riding of Yorkshire.[4] The fact is that the restrictions made by the gilds in these older towns rendered them obnoxious[5] to the new manufacturers who were everywhere springing up, and who preferred to leave the old cities and carry on their occupations undisturbed elsewhere. Then, again, the heavy taxation necessitated by the wars of Henry VI.'s reign, and the unnecessary but heavy exactions of the grasping Henry VII., had fallen very hardly on the corporate towns, while others had escaped.[6] But still another cause, and one more powerful than either of these, may be assigned. It is that they were at the close of the fifteenth century no longer necessary as places of security for traders and manufacturers.[7] In the troublous days of the Wars of the Roses, and in the old times before them, when the nobility were constantly engaged in private warfare, it would not have been safe for a merchant or a manufacturer, or for anyone with much property and little power,[8] to have lived outside a walled town, as most

[1] Mentioned as a market in the *Rot. Parl.*, vi. 182 a, in Edward IV.'s reign, but in 1542 mentioned in a statute of Edward VI. as a flourishing manufacturing town (5 and 6 Ed. VI., c. 6).

[2] Described by Leland, *Itinerary*, iv. 114.

[3] A company of cutlers was formed here in Elizabeth's reign.

[4] Defoe, *Plan of English Commerce*, 127, 129, refers to these towns having woollen manufactures under Henry VII.

[5] *Cf.* Cunningham, *Growth of Industry*, i. 452, 455, 461, and above, p. 146

[6] *Ib.*, i. 461.   [7] *Cf.* Froude's remarks, *History*, i. 9.

[8] For instances of oppression by great nobles, see Denton, *Fifteenth Century*, pp. 296-301, and the *Paston Letters* (ed. Arber), Vol. I. 13-15.

of them then were. A master workman could not then
have migrated with any safety into a country district, either
to obtain water-power or to evade gild-made regulations.
But now that the Wars of the Roses were over, and the Crown
had proved strong enough to establish peace and security
throughout the greater part of the kingdom, one great use of
the older towns as centres of security for manufactures and
trade had become unnecessary; they begin to decline in
importance, though commerce and industry are progressing;
while newer centres take their place, or urban industrial
occupations are spreading even into rural districts. Thus the
pacification of the kingdom, which was the work of Henry
VII. and the Tudors, and which has lasted with but one
serious outbreak into our own times, prevented what might
otherwise have happened too prematurely, namely, that concentration of population into the towns which is one of the
greatest difficulties of the present age.

§ 120. *The Commercial and Industrial Change of the Fifteenth Century.*

Meanwhile, as we have hinted, manufactures and commerce in the fifteenth century, in spite of the decay of
certain towns, were certainly progressing. The woollen
manufacture received a great impetus from Henry VII.,
who, as Edward III. had done, encouraged foreigners to
settle in England in order to instruct English artisans.[1]
He directed his attention specially to the West Riding of
Yorkshire and the towns of Leeds, Wakefield, and Halifax;
and about the same time the export of wool [2] was forbidden in order that there might be plenty of material
for making woollen cloth. In the East of England, Norwich and the county of Norfolk [3] generally still remained a
flourishing seat of manufactures both of woollen and worsted

---

[1] Defoe, *Plan of English Commerce*, 127, 129.

[2] 4 Henry VII., c. 11. The fact that it was again prohibited by the 22
Henry VIII., c. 2, and the 37 Henry VIII., c. 15, shows that either the
prohibition was useless or that it was only temporary.

[3] *Cf.* the information implied in the Statutes 5 Henry VIII., c. 4, and 14
and 15 Henry VIII., c. 3.

stuffs. There was an active export trade in wool to Italian[1] as well as to Flemish towns, and other foreign commerce was being entered into that was to lead to great developments in the future.[2] In fact, the fifteenth century shows us remarkable progress. It is the beginning in many ways of a new era in more than one branch of industry. For there were at least three great changes that form in themselves a commercial and industrial revolution, almost as important in some ways, though not so striking, as the industrial revolution of the eighteenth century. This series of developments was : (1) the change in agriculture, already commented upon,[3] from tillage to pasturage for the sake of wool-growing; (2) the change from England being merely a wool-growing to a wool-manufacturing country[4]; and (3) the change in foreign commerce,[5] whereby Englishmen, who in the days of Edward III. had allowed nearly all their foreign commerce to be monopolised by foreign merchants, now began to take it into their own hands. Nor should we omit, as factors of considerable importance, the great discoveries made at this time by Columbus and Cabot, though at first these discoveries had but little effect upon English commerce. Henry VII., indeed, seems to have had more foresight in this matter than most of his subjects, for he more than once granted commissions for the discovery and investment of new lands.[6] It was not his fault that England did not take the place of Spain in the New World[7]; but Englishmen were not yet ready for such an enterprise, and perhaps it was as well that they were not. Their success was all the greater for its delay.

[1] Namely, Pisa, Venice, and Florence; Rymer, *Fœdera*, XII. 390.

[2] *E.g.* English merchants are now found (1513) doing business in the Levant, to which they had never traded before. *Cf.* Cunningham, i. p. 438, which see also for the development of shipping and foreign commerce generally.

[3] Above, p. 184.

[4] *Cf.* Mrs Green, *Town Life in Fifteenth Century*, i. p. 44.

[5] *Ib.*, i. p. 122.

[6] Besides his patronage of Cabot (*cf.* Rymer. *Fœdera*, XII. 595) he granted patents of exploration in 1501 and later to various Bristol merchants (*ib.* XIII. 41 and 37).

[7] Burrows, *Commentaries on the History of England*, p. 252, puts it thus. Others are inclined to think Henry might have done more than he did.

§ 121. *The Close of the Middle Ages.*

The close of the 15th century brings us to the close of the Middle Ages. Henceforth we are treading on modern ground, and industry also begins to develope under more modern ideas. The old order changes and the new grows gradually into its place, till at length we of the nineteenth century look back upon mediæval life as upon something not quite akin to ours. We feel ourselves more in touch with the men of the sixteenth and seventeenth centuries than with those of the fourteenth, and naturally so, for there is perhaps a greater gulf fixed between the days of Edward III. and Elizabeth than between the days of Elizabeth and Victoria. The old manorial and feudal land system was dying out; the old ideas of regulating crafts, trade, and commerce were giving way to wider and looser methods, more competitive than heretofore, and of more national comprehensiveness. Merchants were beginning to look beyond the confines of the narrow seas to the riches of the gorgeous East and to the newly found lands of the mysterious West. Industry was shaking off the bonds and trammels of local regulations ; the labourer of the manor no longer feared the authority of his lord, nor the artisan of the town the censure of his gild. Social life also was changing and with it political life as well. The Wars of the Roses had destroyed the great nobles of the past, and now the royal power rested chiefly upon the goodwill of the middle classes.[1] The ideal of this class was a king who would act as a superior kind of chief constable [2] who, by keeping the great men in order would allow their inferiors to make money in peace. Such a king was found in Henry VII. It was not perhaps a very high ideal, but it was practically possible, and under Henry VII. the middle classes prospered. Nor were the lower classes as far as we have been able to judge, less fortunate. Poverty and crime existed, as unfortunately they always will, and there were Poor Laws [3] with penal codes to

---

[1] *Cf.* Gardiner, *Student's History*, i. 357.   [2] *Ib.*, i. 331.

[3] Stubbs, *Const. Hist.*, iii. xxi., pp. 599 and 600, points out how the alms-giving of the clergy, the monasteries and the gilds, as well as general

meet them. But poverty was neither so deep nor so widespread as it is now, nor as it soon became, and the monasteries and gilds (when they did their duty) were possibly quite as efficient as a modern Board of Guardians. On the whole, then, the fifteenth century was a period of prosperity and content, in spite of both civil and foreign wars ; and even the wasteful reign of Henry VI., with its unsuccessful wars with France,[1] and huge subsidies to carry them on,[2] though it made the Government unpopular and caused widespread national discontent and occasional insurrections in Kent and Wiltshire,[3] did not materially injure the general welfare. The king himself, however, was nearly bankrupt.[4] The Wars of the Roses which followed (1455-86) do not seem to have affected the country at large very much, being mostly fought in a series of much exaggerated skirmishes by small bodies of nobles and their followers.[5] So, at least, one might infer from the small effect they had upon wages and prices.[6] They ended in

charity sufficed for the necessities of the poor. Most of the legislation on the subject was directed against idleness and random begging. The statutes of 1388, 1495 and 1504 were among the first attempts at a law of settlement and organised relief. But these acts refer only to professional mendicants, (including pilgrims, friars, and even University scholars) and it is probable that for the poor who remained at home and were not vagrants no such legislation was needed (*ib.* p. 603). It was vagrancy more than unrelieved poverty that was the cause of legislation.

[1] For this war *cf.* the useful summary in Burrows *Commentaries on the Hist. of Eng.*, pp. 215-221 and Green, *History of the English People*, i. pp. 547-563.

[2] *Cf.* Stubbs, *Const. Hist.*, iii., pp. 86-125.

[3] This was the rebellion under Cade, in Kent, (June 1450). It was purely political and has no such social significance as the Revolt of 1381. See Stubbs, *Const. Hist.*, iii. xviii. p. 150. In Wiltshire the Bishop of Salisbury was murdered. *Ib.* p. 152.

[4] *Ib.* pp. 117 and 144.

[5] " Happily a war of barons and their retainers rather than of the nation generally. The towns suffered but little." Burrows, *Commentaries*, p. 222. On the other hand, Denton, *Fifteenth Century*, p. 115, says that the Wars of the Roses were of a most devastating character, and that one-tenth of the population were killed. If so, it is extraordinary that so little effect is noticeable in manorial accounts. The statements of the Chroniclers as to numbers slain must be received in this case, as in that of the Black Death, with the utmost caution.

[6] Rogers, *Six Centuries*, pp. 332-334. "It had no bearing on work and wages," (p. 334)

the ruin of the majority of the feudal aristocracy,[1] and at the same time opened a further path for the influence of the industrial classes, whose favour Henry VII. had the wisdom to court, and in return was supported by them in his policy of weakening the power of the great barons. He encouraged commerce,[2] and secured peace for his kingdom while gaining by rather dubious methods considerable wealth for his treasury.[3]   In his reign the nation prospered,[4] and the Middle Ages came to a close in a progressive and industrious England (1500 A.D.).

But before the next century was completed great changes had taken place, one class at least had received a severe blow, and some of the worst difficulties of modern days had already begun.

[1] For the mutual destruction of the nobles *cf.* Gairdner, *Lancaster and York*, p. 227. It is quite true, however, as Denton remarks (*Fifteenth Century*, p. 261) that the wealth of the few who remained was greatly increased, *e.g.* the peers Buckingham, Northumberland and Norfolk.

[2] *E.g.* by his treaties with Denmark in 1490 (Rymer, *Foedera*, xii. 381) with Florence (*ib.* xii. 390) in the same year, and the " Intercursus magnus " with Flanders in 1496, (*ib.* xii. 578).

[3] He had as much as £1,800,000.   Gardiner, *Student's History of England*, i. 357.

[4] One proof of prosperity is that the nation could never have stood the burden of the French Wars as it did unless it had been fairly prosperous. Another proof is the growth of sheep-farming, which, as said above, indicates growing manufactures.   Yet a third is the making of commercial treaties, as mentioned in note 2.

SPECIAL NOTE.

A study of the map opposite, showing the distribution of wealth in the various counties at the close of the fifteenth and beginning of the sixteenth century, will give a clear idea of the general state of the country. The wealthiest counties were, at this period, nearly all agricultural ; while the north and north-western counties, now so rich, were then among the poorest.   Compare the maps opposite pp. 263, 350, and 454.

ROBERTS & LEETE, LTD LONDON.

WEALTH IN ENGLAND IN 1503.

This Map is based on the assessment of counties made in 1503 by Henry VII., for a special "aid." The table of counties in order of their assessment will be found in Rogers' *Hist. Agric.*, iv. 89. The basis adopted is the number of acres to every £1 of assessment, the richer counties thus having the least number of acres to the £1.

1.	Counties with	200—	500 acres, per £1	...	...	...	Dark Brown.
2.	,,	,,	500— 700 ,, ,, ,,	...	...	...	Dark Green.
3.	,,	,,	700— 850 ,, ,, ,,	...	...	...	Dark Red.
4.	,,	,,	850—1,150 ,, ,, ,,	...	...	...	Light Brown.
5.	,,	,,	1,150—2,200 ,, ,, ,,	...	...	...	Light Red.
6.	,,	,,	over 2,200 ,, ,, ,,	...	...	...	Light Green.

NOTE.—This Map should be compared with that opposite page 263.

PERIOD IV

FROM THE SIXTEENTH CENTURY TO THE EVE
OF THE INDUSTRIAL REVOLUTION

(1509-1760)

CHAPTER XIV

§ 122. *Henry VIII.'s Wastefulness.*

HENRY VIII. came to the throne in 1509. He succeeded
to a full treasury[1] left by his thrifty but grasping father,
who had replenished it by exactions from the general prosperity of the country at the close of the fifteenth century.
But he soon dissipated the whole of these accumulations.
He spent a great deal of money in subsidising the Emperor
Maximilian,[2] and in interfering in foreign affairs, in which
he was not very successful, in the hope of winning for himself a military reputation and a leading place in the ranks
of European powers.[3] His continental wars and alliances
cost him dear, or rather they cost the English people dear,
for he not only exhausted the patience of Parliament by
his requests, but had recourse to other exactions in the
shape of benevolences and fines.[4] His apologists have
endeavoured to prove that personally Henry VIII. was not
extravagant, and that his personal expenses did not greatly
exceed those of his somewhat penurious parent.[5] But the

---

[1] See note 3 above, p. 196.   [2] Green, *History of English People*, ii. 109.
[3] It has been pointed out that he realised this ambition and raised England to "the first rank among European nations" (Burrows, *Commentaries*,
p. 253), and that his foreign policy connected England with the Continent
to the advantage of commerce and the middle classes (p. 257). But no one
can deny that he spent money recklessly in so doing, and it may be doubted
whether the ultimate result was worth this vast expenditure.

[4] He had exhausted the treasury and subsidies very early by his French
wars, 1513-1514 A.D., though at the conclusion he got a large sum of money
from the French king, *Annals of England*, p. 288. *Cf.* Green, *History*,
ii. 93. "The millions left by his father were exhausted, his subjects had
been drained by repeated subsidies." For the later attempts to obtain
money, especially in 1523 and 1525, *cf.* Green, ii. 116, 117, 121, 122.

[5] *Cf.* Froude, *History*, i. 39, who says Henry VII.'s expenses were a little
over £14,000 a year, out of which were defrayed the whole cost of the
king's establishment, expenses of entertaining foreign ambassadors, main-

fact remains that he managed to spend all his father's
accumulations, over a million and three-quarters sterling,
before he had been on the throne many years,[1] that he had
to repudiate his debts,[2] that he was addicted to gambling
in private [3] as well as to spending the nation's money recklessly in public, and that he left to his unfortunate young
son Edward VI. a treasury not only exhausted of cash but
burdened with unpaid debts.[4] Nor can it be denied that
he roused open revolt by his attempts to obtain funds by
ordinary methods;[5] and it was probably the difficulties which
he found in raising money by taxation that formed a very
strong incentive for his spoliation of the monasteries and
debasement of the currency. No doubt some excuse is to
be found for Henry's enormous expenditure in the necessities of foreign politics and the wars with France and Scotland, but even in time of peace his expenditure seems to
have been extravagant. The cost of his household establishments, and those of his children, was simply enormous;
for the establishments of Mary, Edward, and even Elizabeth
were each more costly than the whole annual charge of his
father's household.[6] His extravagance was monumental,

tenance of the Yeomen of the Guard, retinues of servants, and all outlay
not connected with public business. Under Henry VIII. these expenses
were £19,894, 16s. 8d., equal to some £240,000 of our money. But the
question remains, where did all the money go that Henry VIII. obtained
by various means? It has never been properly accounted for, and these
household accounts evidently do not represent his entire expenditure.

[1] *Cf.* Green, ii. 93, where the reference is to 1514 A.D.

[2] By the 35 Henry VIII., c. 12, "all loans made to the king were
remitted and released," and the creditors got nothing. Froude, iv. 13, is
"unable to see the impropriety of this proceeding," apparently regarding
it as only another form of taxation. But the creditors must have thought
differently.

[3] *Cf.* the note in Froude, *History*, i. 30, and the *Privy Purse Expenses of
Henry VIII.*

[4] *Cf.* Froude, *History*, v. 119-123, who details the exhaustion of the
Treasury early in Edward VI.'s reign and Northumberland's desperate
attempts to fill it.

[5] As in the revolts of 1525 in Suffolk and Kent (Green, *History*, ii. 122),
when a tenth was demanded from all the laity and a fourth from the
clergy. The royal demand for money had to be abandoned, *Annals of
England*, p. 293.

[6] Rogers, *Six Centuries*, p. 321; *Hist. Agric.*, iv. 28. The accounts are
preserved in the Record Office.

though where his money went he could not himself discover. Wolsey said of him, "Rather than miss any part of his will, he will endanger one half of his kingdom." [1] As a matter of fact he succeeded in impoverishing the whole of it. [2] Nevertheless, it is curious to notice that Henry VIII. did not by any means entirely lose the popularity of his subjects. He was certainly feared, but he was also loved, and even remained popular in spite of his treatment of his wives and the debasement of the currency. [3] It has shrewdly been remarked that this was because he understood his people thoroughly, knowing exactly how far he could go and how much they would bear. [4] But even without this, though it is probably a very true explanation of the matter, his popularity need cause no surprise to any one who understands the relations of king and people and realises the combined ignorance and superficiality of the mass of mankind. A very cursory glance at history shows us that the best rulers have not always been the most popular; [5] that even Nero had his supporters; and that during a prince's lifetime the outside populace have only the very faintest knowledge of what goes on inside a court, while they base their fluctuating affections or dislikes upon the casual public appearances of a monarch and the untrustworthy rumours which, even in the most democratic country, are the utmost that is allowed to penetrate beyond a privileged Court circle. Moreover, after he had seen how his exactions had angered his people in 1525, Henry took care in future to obtain money by means quite as effectual, but more underhand, and thus avoided another popular outbreak. But the fact of his popularity need not detain us. It does not alter the other facts of his cruelty, selfishness, and robbery.

[1] Quoted by Green, *History*, i. 88.

[2] Even Froude admits this, for he records "the general distress" at beginning of Edward VI.'s reign (iv. 352) owing to the base money and other causes. He admits that Henry's household expenses had doubled since the beginning of his reign (iv. 251).

[3] Burrows, *Commentaries on the History of England*, p. 276.

[4] *Ib.*

[5] *E.g.* William III. of England; *cf.* Macaulay's *History*, ch. xi., and *passim.*

§ 123. *The Dissolution of the Monasteries.*

Having wasted the carefully accumulated treasures of his father, Henry sought for further supplies. They were gained at first by increased taxation, but as this money was spent in the French wars,[1] Henry was soon in difficulties again. Then a great temptation came upon him. The monasteries [2] suggested themselves to him as an easy prey, and he knew that an attack upon them would not displease the growing Protestant party in the country. It is possible that he was even animated by reforming zeal, and, if so, it was fortunate that he was able to satisfy his conscience and to fill his purse at the same moment. The religious houses were in many cases certainly not fulfilling their ancient functions properly,[3] and were often far from being the homes of religious virtue.[4] Excuses and even reasons were easily found ; in 1536 the smaller monasteries with an income below £200 a year were suppressed,[5] and in 1539 the larger ones were similarly treated.[6] In all, about a thousand houses were suppressed,[7] the *annual* income of which was some £160,000, equivalent to more than two millions sterling of our present money.[8] Half a dozen bishoprics and a few grammar schools were founded, some fortifications built, and temporary work found for the unemployed out of the proceeds of this spoliation,[9] in order to blind the eyes of the people at large. But with these

---

[1] Green, *History*, ii. 93.

[2] Reforms had been instituted among the clergy before this, even in Henry VII.'s reign. *Cf.* Froude, *History*, i. 97-99

[3] *E.g.* The duty of relieving the poor is said to have been neglected. Froude, i. 76. For other charges see *ib.* ii. 302, sqq.

[4] *Cf.* the state of things at the Lichfield Nunnery, Froude, ii. 319 ; at Foun tains Abbey, where the Abbot kept six women, *ib.* p. 321, and c. x. generally.

[5] By the Act 27 Henry VIII. c. 28.   [6] Act 31 Henry VIII. c. 13.

[7] Green, *History*, ii. 101 gives 1021 altogether. Bishop Creighton (*Dict. Eng. History*, s.v. *Monasticism*) gives only 616 as the total. "There were 186 Benedictines, 173 Augustinians, 101 Cistercians, 33 of the four orders of friars, 32 Premonstratensians, 28 of the Knights Hospitallers, 25 Gil- bertines, 20 Cluniacs, 9 Carthusians, and a few other orders. The total number of monasteries was 616, and their revenues were approximately valued at £142,914 yearly."

[8] Rogers, *Six Centuries*, p. 322, *Hist. Agric.* iv. 29.

[9] Green, *History*, ii. 201 ; Froude, *History*, ii. 345, iii. 207-10.

paltry exceptions the whole of that vast capital and revenue was granted to courtiers and favourites, sold at nominal prices, or frittered away by the king and his satellites.[1]

§ 124. *Results of the Suppression.*

Although the mass of the people did not protest very vigorously against this piece of royal robbery, many of them witnessed with silent dismay the destruction of ancient institutions that had taken at one time an important share in the national life. It is true that the monasteries had, so to speak, worn themselves out and outgrown their usefulness.[2] Some were deeply in debt, some almost deserted, almost all had misapplied their revenues.[3]   Some reform, at least, was necessary, perhaps even a total suppression, but undoubtedly the worst feature about the whole transaction was the distribution of the spoil.[4]   In any case the country districts, if none other, lost in many instances (though not in all) hospitable and charitable friends; and discontent, eagerly fomented of course by the dispossessed monks,[5] broke out into open insurrection.   The well-known revolt called the Pilgrimage of Grace (1536) was an instance of this, though it had also other causes, connected with the general agrarian change which was then taking place.   These causes may be detailed in the words of those concerned in the rebellion, words which give a very clear insight into the grievances that were vexing men's minds in the rural districts : " The poor people and commons," said one, " be sore oppressed by gentlemen because their living is taken away."[6]   This is vague, but another witness tells us more explicitly in what the oppression consisted.   He mentions " the pulling down of villages and farms, raising of rents, enclosures, intakes of the commons, worshipful men taking yeomen's offices, that is, becoming dealers in farm produce.[7] "   One great reason

[1] Many of the new aristocracy of Henry VIII.'s reign owe their riches to this spoliation. "The Russells and Cavendishes rose from obscurity through the grants of church lands." Green, *History,* ii. 201.

[2] Burrows, *Commentaries,* p. 270.   [3] *Ib.*

[4] *Ib.,* p. 271.   [5] *Ib.,* 272.

[6] Evidence of Geo. Gisborne, *Rolls House, MSS.,* miscellaneous, first series, 132 (Froude).   [7] William Stapleton's evidence, *ib.*

of the discontent is thus clearly seen to be the enclosures, and another was the raising of rents; and grievances like these, coupled with religious feeling, fear of change, and sympathy for the dispossessed monks, were sufficient to give rise to a very considerable outbreak, which was only suppressed with some difficulty.[1] The economic disturbances which resulted, though not so clearly seen, were far more severe. They were acute enough from the mere fact of so much wealth having suddenly changed hands and being spent with reckless prodigality. It is said that one-fifth,[2] or even one-third,[3] of the land in the kingdom was held by the monasteries, and this was now transferred from the hold of the Church into the hands of a new set of nobles and landed gentry, created from the dependants and followers of Henry's court.[4] These were enriched, but the former tenants of the monasteries and the poorer class of labourers suffered greatly.[5] Hence serious results followed. Many of the monastic lands were held by tenants upon the stock and land lease system,[6] spoken of before; but, when these monastic lands were suddenly transferred into the clutches of Henry's new and grasping nobility, or were bought by merchants and manufacturers who only cared for profits,[7] the stock was confiscated and sold off, while the money rent was raised. The new owners did not care for the slow, though really lucrative, system of providing the tenant with a certain amount of stock for his land, but simply wished to get all the money they could without delay. They often evicted the tenantry and lived as absentees on the profits of their flocks.[8] The result was that the poorer tenants were

---

[1] *Annals of England*, p. 302, 303. [2] Green, *History*, ii. 201.

[3] Rogers, *Hist. Agric.*, iv. 113; *Six Centuries*, p. 323, who however seems to think it rather doubtful.

[4] *Cf.* Froude, *History*, iii. 206, where he mentions the *novi homines*.

[5] *Cf.* the contemporary evidence in the *Cole MSS.* (Brit. Museum) xii. fol. 5. *The Fall of Religious Houses*: "They never raised any rent nor took any incomes or fines of their tenants." Again, "If any poor householder lacked seed to sow his land, or bread, corn, or malt before harvest, and came to a monastery, he should not have gone away again without help." Of course, some allowance must be made for the evident friendly bias of the author.

[6] Rogers, *Six Centuries*, p. 323. [7] Froude, *History*, iii. p. 206.

[8] Cunningham, *Growth of Industry*, i. p. 434.

almost ruined, and it seems fairly evident that pauperism was much increased.

§ 125. *Pauperism.*

Whether it is true that the monasteries relieved what poverty there was, or not, or whether in pre-Reformation days the charitable instincts of the general public were more actively encouraged [1] by their religion, may still be a matter of dispute, but there can be no doubt as to the growth of pauperism in the days of Henry VIII. Of course it had existed before, and measures had been passed for its relief,[2] but henceforth it becomes a more noticeable phenomenon, and its difficulties increase instead of diminishing. Its growth was due to the agrarian difficulties of the sixteenth century, especially to the enclosures, and perhaps in some measure to that peculiarly modern development of society by which, as the wealth of the nation increases, it seems to become vested in fewer hands, while the numbers of the poor increase with the accumulation of riches. Be that as it may, legislation was found necessary before the suppression of the monasteries, though the suppression must have given an impetus to the other already existing causes of trouble. Two acts were passed in the middle of Henry's reign. The first (1531) mentions the increase of "vagabonds and beggars," and the crimes they commit, and enacts that the justices, mayors, and other authorities "shall make diligent search and inquiry of all aged poor and impotent persons which live, or of necessity be compelled to live, by alms of the charity of the people"; that they then shall only allow them to beg, after giving them a proper license to do so, within certain limits, while begging outside such limits, or without permission, was to be punished by imprisonment in the stocks and by whipping.[3] The second Act (1536), evidently framed because the first was unsatisfactory, forbids private persons to give money to beggars, but makes provision for a charity organisation fund, to be collected by the church wardens on Sundays and holidays in

---

[1] Froude, *History*, i. 77, and *cf.* iv. 355.
[2] Above, p. 194, note 3.   [3] The 22 Henry VIII., c. 12.

the churches. The parish priest was to keep an account of receipts and expenditure. All idle children, over five years of age, were to be appointed " to matters of husbandry, or other craft or labour to be taught." But for the " sturdy vagabond " there was no mercy ; if found begging a second time, he was to be mutilated by the loss of the whole or part of his right ear ; if caught a third time, to be put to death " as a felon and an enemy of the commonwealth." [1] So the law remained for sixty years ; unrepealed through the reigns of Edward VI. and Mary ; reconsidered, but again formally passed, under Elizabeth. " It was the express conviction of the English nation that it was better for a man not to live at all than to live a profitless and worthless life." [2] But the simple, if sanguinary, measures of the Tudor age were found in later days to be insufficient to cure an evil of which simplicity is unfortunately far from being a characteristic.

§ 126. *The Issuing of Base Coin.*

A few years after the dissolution of the monasteries, Henry was in difficulties again. He dared not ask his Parliament for further supplies so soon after his last piece of plunder, and therefore he betook himself to a still more underhand kind of robbery. In 1527 he had begun to debase the currency,[3] and now he repeated this criminal action in 1543, 1545, and 1546.[4] The process was continued by the guardians of Edward VI., till an almost incredible amount of alloy was added to the coins. Already, in 1549, the debasement had reached six ounces of alloy in the pound of silver ; but in 1551 there were nine ounces, a pound of this base mixture being coined into seventy-two shillings.[5] This debasement forms a landmark in English industrial history, almost as noticeable as events like the

---

[1] The 27 Henry VIII., c. 25.   [2] Froude, *History*, i. 88.

[3] Cunningham, i. 482. He coined a pound of silver of the old touch into 45s. in 1527. See Dr Cunningham's strong remarks on the iniquity of the Tudor kings.

[4] Rogers, *Six Centuries*, p. 342. In 1543 the debasement was 2 ounces of alloy in 12, in 1545 it was 6, in 1546 it was 8. The coinage was reformed by Elizabeth. *Cf. Hist. Agric.*, iv. 186-200.

[5] Rogers, *Six Centuries*, p. 343.

first Poor Law or the Plague.   Its effect was not felt immediately, but it was none the less real.[1]   The chief point
that concerned the labourer was that prices rapidly rose,
but that, as is always the case, the rise of wages did not
coincide with this inflation, and when they did rise, they
did not do so in a fair proportion.   The necessaries of life
rose in proportion of one to two and one-half ; wages,
when they finally rose, only in the proportion of one to one
and one-half.[2]   When too late, it was recognised that the
issue of base money was the cause of dearth in the realm,
and Latimer lamented the fact in his sermons.   Meanwhile,
the mischief had been done.

The government was almost bankrupt, and when Henry
VIII. died he bequeathed to his young son, instead of the
magnificent fortune which his own father had amassed, a
treasury not only empty, but completely overwhelmed in
debt.[3]   These debts were augmented by the " wilful government " of the Duke of Somerset, while the council of nobles
who surrounded the youthful Edward only made matters
worse by their unpatriotic rapacity.

§ 127. The Confiscation of the Gild Lands.

In the very first year of Edward's reign a fresh piece of
robbery was carried out.   This was the confiscation of all
chantries and gild lands, planned by Henry VIII.[4] but
executed by the Protector Somerset.   All lands belonging
to " colleges, chantries, and free chapels," were in 1547
given to the king,[5] and it was professed by the Act that
their revenues would be given to the establishment of

---

[1] Rogers, Six Centuries, p. 344.
[2] Ib., p. 345 ; cf. also Froude, History, v. 95.   "The measure of corn
that was wont to be sold at 2s. or 3s. was at 6s. 8d. in March 1551, and
30s. in March 1552.   A cow that had been worth 6s. 8d. sold for 40s."
[3] See Northumberland's letter to the Council ; MSS. Domestic, Edward
VI., vol. xv. (Froude), where he speaks of "the great debts wherein, for
one great part, he [Edward VI.] was left by his Highnesse's father, and
augmented by the wilful government of the late Duke of Somerset, who
took upon him the Protectorship and government of his own authority."
Of course Northumberland's evidence is not altogether unprejudiced.
[4] In the Act 37 Henry VIII., c. 17. cf. Froude, History, iv., p. 193.
[5] By the Act 1 Edw. VI., c. 14.

grammar schools, the maintenance of vicarages, and the support of preachers. Some portion was so applied—probably to salve the consciences of the spoilers—but by far the greater part was shared among the members of the government or devoted to pay off some of the late King's debts.[1] A portion of the lands so confiscated was the property of the craft-gilds both in town and country, having been acquired partly by bequests from members, and partly by purchase from the funds of the gilds. The revenues derived from them were used for lending, without usury, to poorer members of the gilds, for apprenticing poor children, for widows' pensions, and, above all, for the relief of destitute members of the craft.[2] Thus the labourer of that time had in the funds of the gild a kind of insurance money, while the gild itself fulfilled all the functions of a benefit society. Somerset procured the Act for suppressing them on the plea that these lands were associated with superstitious uses. Only the property of the London gilds was left untouched.

The effects of this confiscation were felt perhaps indirectly more than directly, but were none the less serious. No doubt the landed property of the gilds was largely devoted to the maintenance of masses for departed members of the society, but assistance was also freely given to members in distress, to enable them to tide over hard times.[3] These institutions rather prevented men from falling into pauperism than actually relieved it to any great extent,[4] but the net result was of course much the same. Their suppression certainly must have helped to swell the number of untoward influences that combined at this period to depress the condition of the working classes.

Why this abolition was not more generally resented is a point of some interest. In the first place, the lands of the religious gilds and craft gilds were confiscated together on

[1] *Annals of England*, pp. 316, 317. Froude, *History*, iv., p. 313, remarks :—"The carcase was cast out into the fields and the vultures of all breeds and orders flocked to the banquet."

[2] Rogers, *Six Centuries*, p. 347 ; *Hist. Agric.*, iv. 6.

[3] Cunningham, *Growth of Industry*, i., p. 480.

[4] *Ib.*, p. 481 ; and *cf.* on the other hand Prof. Ashley's remarks in the *Political Science Quarterly*, vol. iv., No. 3, p. 402, who rather minimises the usefulness of the gilds.

the plea above mentioned, and thus the difference between them was confused in the eyes of the Protestant party then in the ascendant. Then, again, the London gilds were spared because of their power,[1] and thus it was made their interest not to interfere with the destruction of their provincial brethren. The nobles were bought off with presents gained from the funds of the gilds. Moreover, the *craft* gilds in the country towns were becoming close corporations, whose advantages were often monopolised by a few powerful members. This led, as we saw,[2] to the manufacture of cloth spreading from the towns into industrial villages in the rural districts, where perhaps the mass of the population, not perceiving the full significance of the Act, did not object to a measure which struck a blow at the town " mysteries."[3] But, nevertheless, a great deal of discontent was aroused. Somerset became very unpopular and insurrections broke out in many parts of the country, the most dangerous being in Cornwall, Devonshire, and Norfolk (1549).[4] They were caused not only by this spoliation but by agrarian discontent as well, added to religious disturbances, but German and Italian mercenaries were introduced to put them down,[5] and the protests of the people were everywhere choked in their own blood.

§ 128. *Bankruptcy and Rapacity of Edward VI.'s Government.*

These insurrections serve to show the anger of the nation at the atrocious rapacity and misgovernment of the nobles who surrounded the boy-king Edward. And indeed the nation had a right to be angry. The government was practically bankrupt,[6] and had to resort to the most desperate measures to obtain money for immediate necessities. The currency had been so debased that they dare not debase it any further, and it only remained to acknowledge the fact openly, to throw the burden of it upon the country, and

---

[1] Rogers, *Hist. Agric.*, iv. 6.   [2] Above, p. 146.
[3] Ashley, in *Political Science Quarterly*, Vol. iv., No. 3, p. 402.
[4] *Annals of England*, p. 318; Froude, *History*, iv. 408, 440-453.
[5] Froude, *History*, iv., pp. 445, 447.   [6] Froude, *History*, v. pp. 9, 110.

to call the existing coinage down to its actual value.[1] "By this desperate remedy every holder of a silver coin lost upon it the difference between its cost when it passed into his hands and its actual value in the market. On the 30th April 1551 the Council passed a resolution that in future the shilling should pass for only ninepence, and the groat (4d) for threepence.[2] At the same time, such was the unabashed audacity of this gang of noble swindlers, they contemplated a fresh issue of base money; [3] but, postponing this wickedness for a time, they had recourse to the great banking firm of the Fuggers at Antwerp, and raised loans at ruinous rates of interest.[4] In the month of May, however, they issued £80,000 of silver coin, of which two-thirds was alloy, and in June £40,000, containing no less than three-quarters alloy. "This was the last grasp at the departing prey, and perhaps it transpired to the world : for so profound and so wide was the public distrust that when the first fall in the coin took effect prices everywhere rose rather than declined, even allowing for the difference of denomination."[5]   Then in August a proclamation was issued by which the shilling passed for no more than six-pence,[6] and again the nation had to bear the loss.

But the difficulties of the Government were far from being at an end, and fresh means had to be devised for extorting money from an exhausted country. As early as 1549 Commissioners had been appointed to make inventories of Church ornaments, jewels, vestments and other property, even including the Church bells [7]; but in the autumn and winter of 1552-3 no less than four commissions were appointed with this object, "to go again over the oft-trodden ground and glean the last spoils which could be gathered from the Churches.[8] Vestments, copes, plate, even the coins in the poor-boxes were taken from the churches in the City of London. A sweep as complete cleared the

[1] Froude, *History*, v. pp. 9-15.
[2] *Ib.*, v. p. 10.   [3] *Ib.*, p. 11.
[4] *Ib.*, p. 11 and p. 112. They had borrowed from Antwerp Jews before, iv. p. 399.
[5] *Ib.*, p. 12.   [6] *Ib.*, p. 13.   [7] In Feb. 1549, *Annals of England*, p. 317.
[8] Froude, *History*, v. p. 119.

parish churches throughout the country."[1]   Other measures as mean and as desperate were also taken, and a subsidy was granted by the Parliament of 1553;[2] but all attempts to fill the treasury were rendered useless by the extraordinary rapacity[3] of the 'Council of the Minority,' the nobles who governed during the minority of Edward VI.   Estates worth half-a-million sterling in the money of those days, or about five millions in the money of our own time, had been appropriated by these ministers,[4] and though the Duke of Northumberland accused his rival Somerset of " wilful misgovernance " and waste of treasure,[5] he himself obtained the suppression[6] of the enormously rich bishopric of Durham, and the whole of its temporalities were granted to him as a County Palatine.   It is no wonder that with ministers such as this the country narrowly escaped ruin, nor could it have passed through this period as well as it did, had it not been for the undercurrent of sound prosperity inherited from the latter end of the fifteenth century.   But the situation was most serious, especially in the rural districts, and these now demand our attention.

§ 129. *The Agrarian Situation.*

Of course, by this time, the symmetry of the old manorial system was almost entirely destroyed[7] by the revolution in agriculture to which we have already alluded, and which was now making itself felt increasingly every day.   It was inevitable that such should be the case, and the ultimate benefit was, no doubt, very great, but the immediate effects were productive of considerable hardship to many of the smaller men.   It is true, as has been pointed out by a great German economist,[8] that, after all, agriculture in this period (apart from the special stimulus of wool-growing)

---

[1] Froude, *History*, v. pp. 120, 121.   [2] Act 7 Edward VI., c. 12.

[3] Froude, *History*, iv. 397, mentions "the waste and luxury" of Edward VI.'s nobles as "the preponderating cause" of the pecuniary difficulties of the time.

[4] Froude, *History*, v. p. 128, and *MS. Domestic*, Edward VI., vol. xix.

[5] See preamble to Act 7 Edward VI. c. 12, inspired by Northumberland.

[6] By the Act 7 Edward VI. c. 17.

[7] Ashley, *Econ. Hist.*, ii. ii., p. 263.

[8] Roscher, *Nationalœkonomie des Ackerbaues*, bk. ii., ch. ii.

was only passing through the second of the three great stages which mark its economic evolution. In these we may distinguish (1) the old open-field husbandry of early times, so closely associated with the manorial system ; (2) convertible husbandry, wherein the land is used for a few years as pasture and then put under crops, a method which necessitates enclosures in order that it may be properly carried out in a systematic and orderly manner ; and (3) the more modern method of rotation of crops, which begins in England much later than the period with which we are now dealing. But the process of this evolution with its resulting enclosures, added to the ever-increasing sheep farms, pressed hardly upon the smaller cultivators ; and in the reigns of Henry VIII. and Edward VI. we cannot help being struck with the terrible discontent and misery of the rural districts. The labourers and small husbandmen were becoming more and more separated from the land, while tenant farmers were ruined with high rents exacted by the new nobility.[1] The landed gentry and nobility, however, profited by this, and the merchants grew rich by their accumulations in foreign trade.[2] But those who depended directly upon the cultivation of the land for their living suffered severely. There had been for some years past a steady rise in the price of wool[3] for export, partly because the manufactures of the Netherlands were so flourishing, and partly owing to a general rise of prices on the Continent since the great discoveries of silver in South America. Land-owners saw that it was more immediately profitable to turn their arable land into pasture and to go in for sheep farming on a large scale.[4] They therefore did three things. They evicted as

---

[1] *Cf.* Latimer's *Sermons* (in 1548) in Froude, *History*, iv. p. 356. " You landlords, you rent raisers, I may say you steplords ! that which heretofore went for 20 or 40 pounds by the year, now is let for 50 or 100 pounds : and thus is caused such dearth that poor men which live of their labour cannot with the sweat of their faces have a living."

[2] " Michele, the Venetian, says that many London merchants were worth as much as £60,000 in money ; the graziers and the merchants had made money while the people had starved." Froude, *History*, vi. 78.

[3] Rogers, *Hist. Agric.*, iv. 718 ; the average from 1401 to 1540 was 6s. 2½d. per tod, and from 1541-82, it was 17s. 4d. per tod.

[4] *Cf.* Froude, *Ch. History*, iv. 349.

many as possible of their smaller tenants, so that, as Sir Thomas More tells us, "in this way it comes to pass that these miserable people, men, women, husbands, orphans, parents with little children are all forced to change their seats, without knowing where to go."[1] Then they raised the rents of the larger tenants, the yeomen and farmers, so that, as Latimer mentions, land for which his father had paid £3 or £4 a year, was in 1549 let at £16, almost to the ruin of the tenant.[2] Thirdly, the large land-owners took from the poor their common lands by an unscrupulous system of enclosures.[3] Wolsey had in vain endeavoured to stop their doing this,[4] for he had sagacity enough to perceive how it would pauperize the labourers and others who had valuable rights in such land. But enclosures and evictions went on in spite of his enactments, with the inevitable result of the social disorders already alluded to.[5]

§ 130. *The Enclosures of the Sixteenth Century.*

In speaking of the enclosures made at this time it must be remembered that they were of three kinds.[6]   (1) There was the enclosing of the lord's demesne, which the lord had a perfect right to carry out if he thought it would improve his land, and of which no one could very well complain. There was also (2) the enclosing of those *strips* of land belonging to the lord of the manor which lay intermixed

[1] *Utopia*, p. 64 (Morley's edn.) : the whole of the first part of the *Utopia* is well worth reading for a description of the social and industrial troubles of the time.

[2] Latimer, *First Sermon before Edward VI.*

[3] *Cf.* Lever, *Sermon in the Shroudes* (Arber's edn.) 39 ; Russell, *Ket's Rebellion*, 50, 51 ; Fitzherbert, *Surveyinge*, ch. viii. ; Strype, *Eccles. Mem.*, ii. pt. ii. 360 (referring to 1548), and the evidence quoted below, pp. 214-217.

[4] *Decree in Chancery*, July, 1518 (Brewer, *Calendar of State Papers*, ii. 1054, No. 3297).

[5] The most important of these risings took place in Norfolk, where enclosures had been made upon a tremendous scale. Ket, a tanner of Norwich, took the lead (in 1549) of a large body of some 16,000 tenants and labourers, who demanded the abolition of the late enclosures and the reform of other local abuses. The Earl of Warwick defeated the petitioners in a battle, put down the rising, and hanged Ket at Norwich Castle. The farmers and peasantry were thus cowed into submission. *Cf.* full details in Froude, *History*, iv. 440-453.

[6] Ashley, *Econ. Hist.*, II. ii. p. 285.

with the strips of the tenants in the open fields. To the enclosing of these was again no legal or moral objection to be made, if properly carried out, though it had always been the custom for them to lie alongside the others and share the common cultivation. The exceedingly scattered character of the several lands in the common fields of manors must have been a serious inconvenience to the landowner, especially if he was non-resident, since he had to employ, in addition to his own labour of supervision, the charge and risk of a collector of rents, and moreover often could not recover arrears unless the precise ground from which the rent issued was known and defined, which often was not accurately done.[1] There was therefore considerable inducement to enclose strips and, if possible, to throw them together contiguously. But there was, in so doing, a considerable opportunity of taking a piece of a tenant's land at the same time, and there can be no doubt, from the nature of the complaints made, that this was frequently done.[2] But it was (3) the third kind of enclosures that did the most harm and caused the bitterest outcry ; that is, when the commons and even the tenants' own strips were taken from them. It is true that by the old statute of Merton[3] (1235-6) —a law passed by a parliament of landlords—landowners had been permitted to appropriate portions of the " waste " over which the free, and even the villein, tenants had certain rights of pasturage and turbary, provided that the lord left a " sufficient quantity " of common land for the use of the tenants. But since there was no precise rule as to what constituted a sufficient quantity, it is easy to see that enclosing landlords could do very much as they liked ; and by this time the statute had been forgotten and was entirely neglected. Everywhere complaints are heard of the action of the landowners. But before giving some contemporary evidence upon the subject we will pause for

---

[1] Rogers, *Six Centuries*, pp. 286, 287.

[2] More, *Utopia*, p. 64 (Morley's edn.) says : " when an insatiable wretch resolves to enclose ground, the owners as well as the tenants are turned out of their possessions by tricks or by main force, or being wearied-out by ill-usage they are forced to sell them."

[3] The 20 Henry III., c. 4.

a moment to notice which portion of rural England suffered most from these enclosures.

Professor Ashley [1] has given a very complete account of the enclosures which took place between 1470 and 1600 A.D., and from his investigations it seems that they may be divided into five classes, according to their magnitude in various counties—(1) A very large portion of Suffolk, Essex, and Kent was enclosed; almost two-thirds of Hertfordshire and Worcestershire, a third of Warwick (chiefly in the west of the county), and almost all of Durham, though this latter was enclosed after the Restoration. (2) The counties of Northampton, Shropshire, the southern half of Leicester, East Norfolk, and the Isle of Wight were enclosed to a large extent, but not quite so much as those first mentioned; and (3) sporadic or scattered enclosures were made in the rest of Norfolk, the south of Bedfordshire, and north of Wiltshire. (4) The remaining counties were hardly disturbed by the prevailing desire, *i.e.*, the counties of Yorkshire, Oxford, Nottingham, South Wiltshire, and Buckingham. There remains (5) a group of counties about which not enough information is available (Surrey, Sussex, Hants, Dorset, Somerset, Stafford, Cheshire, Lancashire, Westmoreland, and Cumberland), and we may therefore conclude that enclosures did not take place there to any great extent. It will be seen that it was chiefly the Eastern and South-eastern counties where enclosures were made most largely, probably because they offered the greatest facilities for sheep-rearing and more careful agriculture. The progress of enclosures [2] spreads itself over four centuries, and vitally changed the mediæval rural economy; but it was most rapid in the two periods from 1470 to 1530 A.D., and, much later, from 1760 to 1830 A.D. About the former of these two periods we will now give some contemporary evidence.

§ 131. *Evidence of the Results of Enclosing.*

Such evidence is found both in popular songs and parliamentary documents. An old ballad of the sixteenth century complains:

[1] Ashley, *Econ. Hist.*, II. ii. p. 286.
[2] *Cf.* Ashley, *Econ. Hist.*, II. ii. pp. 285, 286.

> "The towns go down, the land decays,
>   Great men maketh now-a-days
>   A sheep-cote in the church" ;[1]

and this points to the growth of sheep-farming, to which
all other considerations had to give way.   It led also to
the " engrossing " of farms, or the occupying of a large
number of farms merely for the purposes of pasture.   A
petition of 1536 complains of the "great and covetous
misusages of farms within the realm, which misusages," it
says, " hath not only been begun by divers gentlemen, but
also by divers and many merchant adventurers, cloth-
makers, goldsmiths, butchers, tanners, and other artificers,
and unreasonable, covetous persons which doth encroach
daily many farms, more than they can occupy, in tilth of
corn—ten, twelve, fourteen, or sixteen farms in one man's
hands at once."[2]   It goes on to say that " in time past
there hath been in every farm a good house kept, and in
some of them three, four, five, or six ploughs kept and
daily occupied to the great comfort and relief of your
subjects, poor and rich.   But now, by reason of so many
farms engrossed in one man's hands, which cannot till them,
the ploughs be decayed, and the farmhouses and other
dwellings, so that when there was in a town twenty or
thirty dwelling-houses, they be now decayed, ploughs and
all the people clean gone, and the churches down, and no
more parishioners in many parishes, but a neatherd and a
shepherd, instead of three score or four score of persons."
The same complaint is made by Sir Thomas More, who
speaks[3] of the increase of pasture as " peculiar to England,"
by which " your sheep may be said now to devour men,
and to unpeople not only villages but towns."   Land-owners,
and " even those holy men the abbots," he says, " stop the
course of agriculture, destroying houses and towns, reserv-
ing only the churches and enclosed grounds, that they may
lodge their sheep in them."   The result was a terrible increase of pauperism, for men " would willingly work, but

---

[1] *Now-a-dayes*, a ballad (Ballad Society) lines 157-160.
[2] *Rolls House MS.*, *miscellaneous*, second series, 854 (Froude).
[3] *Utopia* (Morley's edn.), p. 64.

can find none that will hire them, for there is no more occasion for country labour, to which they have been bred, when there is no arable ground left."[1]   In fact, the evils were so great that attempts were made to deal with them by legislation ;[2] but they were, of course useless.   "It remains certain," says Froude, speaking of Edward VI.'s reign, "that the absorption of the small farms, the enclosure system, and the increase of grazing farms, had assumed proportions mischievous and dangerous.   Leases as they fell in could not obtain renewal ; the copyholder, whose farm had been held by his forefathers so long that custom seemed to have made it his own, found his fines or his rent quadrupled, or himself without alternative expelled.   The Act against the pulling down of farmhouses had been evaded by the repair of a room which might be occupied by a shepherd, or a single furrow would be driven across a meadow of a hundred acres, to prove that it was still under the plough.   The great cattle-owners, in order to escape the sheep statutes, held their stock in the names of their sons or servants ; the highways and villages were covered in consequence with forlorn and outcast families, now reduced to beggary, who had been the occupiers of comfortable holdings ; and thousands of dispossessed tenants made their way to London, clamouring in the midst of their starving children at the doors of the courts of law for redress which they could not obtain."[3]   A commission was appointed in 1548 to enquire into this distressing state of things, and it resulted in a petition which shows a gloomy picture of rural England.   "The population was diminished, the farmer and labourer were impoverished, villages were

---

[1] *Utopia*, p. 65.   The preamble to the 25 Henry VIII., c. 13, recites all the evils here mentioned.

[2] *Cf.* Act 7 Henry VIII., c. 1, for reconstruction of farm-buildings, and 27 Henry VIII., c. 22, on same subject ; also 25 Henry VIII., c. 13, that no one shall keep more than 2000 sheep, or occupy more than two farms.

[3] Froude, *History*, iv. p. 353, who quotes as authorities Becon's *Jewel of Joy* ; Discourse of Bernard Gilpin in Strype's *Memorials* ; Instructions to the Commissioners of Enclosures, *Ibid* ; Address of Mr Hales, *Ibid* ; and a Draft of an Act of Parliament presented to the House of Commons in 1548, *MS. Domestic*, Edward VI. State Paper Office ; also Lever's *Sermons* in Strype's *Memorials.*

destroyed, the towns decayed, and the industrious classes throughout England in a condition of unexampled suffering." The fault lay in the upper classes, "the nobles, knights, and gentlemen," who by no means fulfilled their duties as "shepherds to the people, surveyors and overseers to the king's subjects," although, as the petition justly remarks, their position "had given them sufficient provision that without bodily labour they might attend thereto."[1] Greed and poverty walked side by side, and while wealth was increasing with the few, the many were suffering terribly from the general change that was passing over both agriculture and society at large.

§ 132. *Other Economic Changes.   The Finances.*

In fact, it becomes evident that the old mediæval system of industry was breaking up in England. The new life created by the Renaissance was causing a keener and more eager spirit among all classes of men. Competition began to operate as a new force, and men made haste to grow rich.[2] The merchants were becoming bolder and more enterprising in their ventures.[3] The discoveries of America by Columbus (1492) and by Cabot (1497), and of the sea-route to India by Vasco di Gama (1498), had kindled a desire to share largely in the wealth of these newly accessible countries. At home the lords of the manors no longer remained in close personal relationships with their tenants, but regarded their estates merely as commercial speculations from which it was their business only to draw as much profit as possible.[4] The tenants were certainly no longer villeins, but were nominally independent and had certain rights. But the lords of the manors had small respect for rights that were only guarded by custom ; and evicted or stole land from their tenants to such an extent that multitudes of dispossessed and impoverished villagers flocked to the towns.

---

[1] *MS. Domestic*, Edward VI., vol. 5, State Paper Office; (Froude, *History*, iv. p. 367).

[2] *Cf.* Froude, *History*, iv. 510, who shows how the haste for riches caused fraud in the woollen cloth trade.

[3] See next chapter.   [4] Froude, *History*, vi. 109, 110.

"The poor are robbed on every side," said a preacher[1] of the day before the court, "and that of such as have authority; the robberies, extortions, and open oppressions of those covetous cormorants, the gentlemen, have no end nor limits nor banks to keep in their vileness. For turning poor men out of their holdings they take it for no offence, but say the land is their own, and turn them out of their shrouds like mice."

Many small tenants and labourers, too, could be found wandering from place to place, begging or robbing.[2] "Thousands in England," says the same preacher, "through such [i.e. the landlords] beg now from door to door who have kept honest houses."[3] The old steady village life, with its isolation and strong home ties, was undergoing a violent transition. Constant work and regular wages were becoming things of the past. The labourer's wages would not purchase the former quantity of provisions under the new high prices caused by the debasement of the currency and by the discoveries of silver from 1540 to 1600;[4] for wages, though they ultimately follow prices, do so very slowly, and not always even then proportionately.

At the same time the nation was almost in the throes of bankruptcy. Edward VI.'s ministers were in a chronic condition of financial exhaustion. Money was constantly being raised by loans, by confiscations, and by subsidies, but the universal peculation of everyone connected with the court made it disappear like flowing water.[5] The expenses of the king's household were in 1549 more than one hundred thousand pounds,[6] then an enormous sum, and more than five times those of Henry VII. The labourers and artificers of all kinds employed by the Government called in vain for their wages,[7] while the daily supplies for

---

[1] Bernard Gilpin, quoted in Froude, *History*, iv. 359.

[2] Hence the very severe Act 1 Edward VI. c. 3, reducing 'loiterers' and vagrants to slavery; but it was repealed soon as being too harsh, and the Act of 1536 was revived by the 3 and 4 Edward VI. c. 16.

[3] *Ut supra.*

[4] *Cf.* Rogers, *Six Centuries*, pp. 343-345, but also Cunningham *English Industry*, i. pp. 483-487; also Anderson, *Commerce*, ii. 166.

[5] Froude, *History*, iv. 397.   [6] *Ib.*

[7] *Ib.*, p. 398.

the common necessities of the Government itself were provided by loans at 13 per cent. from Antwerp Jews, the
heavy interest on which was paid in the proceeds of the sale
of bells and lead robbed from the churches and chantries.[1]
"Never before, and never since, has an English Government
been reduced to shifts so scandalous." Queen Mary, when
she first came to the throne attempted to economise,[2]
but afterwards her strong religious convictions induced
her to strip the already embarrassed treasury of half its
remaining revenues in order to re-establish a Roman priesthood,[3] while her misplaced affection for her Spanish hus-
band made her force the nation into an unnecessary and
expensive war, besides wasting enormous gifts of money
upon Philip himself.[4] When Elizabeth came to the throne
she succeeded to what was practically a bankrupt inherit-
ance.[5] Yet with all this there was wealth in the country,
and when we come to speak of Elizabethan England, we
shall find that, after all, the nation itself was not quite so
poor as the Governments which had done their best to
ruin it.

§ 133. *Summary of the Changes of the Sixteenth Century.*

Such were the circumstances which accompanied and
produced so great an economic transition in this period.
They resulted in the pauperization of a large portion of the
working classes, and in the impoverishment of the small
farmers. On the other hand, the new nobles and landowners gained considerable wealth.[6] The merchants also
were exceedingly flourishing,[7] and foreign trade was growing. In summing up, then, we may say that the suppression of the monasteries and the creation of a new nobility
from the adventurers of Henry VIII.'s court, who obtained
most of the monastic wealth; the debasement of the coinage

---

[1] Froude, *Hist.*, iv. pp. 399, 400.
[2] *Ib.* vi. p. 108.   [3] *Ib.*   [4] *Ib.*, pp. 80, 82, 109 *note*.   [5] See below, p. 234.
[6] A correspondent of Sir William Cecil, speaking of their wealth, calls
them "the meaner sort." *The Distresses of the Commonwealth*, addressed to
the Lords of the Council, December 1558. *Domestic MSS.*, Elizabeth, vol.
i. (Froude, vi. 110), *cf.* also Froude, *History*, vi. 78.
[7] Above, p. 212, *note* 2.

and the exaltation in prices aided largely (1540—1600) by the discovery of new silver mines in South America;[1] the rise in the price of wool both for export and home manufacture, coupled with the consequent increase in sheep farming,[2] and the practice of enclosure of land—all produced most important economic changes in the history of English labour and industry.   To these we must add, towards the end of the sixteenth century, the great immigration of Flemings, chiefly after 1567, owing to the continual persecutions of Alva and other Spanish rulers.[3]   This gave a great impetus to English manufactures, its effects, however, being chiefly felt in the seventeenth century, when another immigration took place.[4]   Finally, in the sixteenth century were laid the foundations of our present commercial enterprise and maritime trade, by the voyages of Drake and other great sea-captains of Elizabeth's time.[5]   Their expeditions, it is true, were mainly buccaneering exploits, but they created a spirit of maritime enterprise that bore good fruit in the following reigns.   Nor indeed was trade even in the previous centuries entirely insignificant, but had considerably developed, as the next chapter will show.   But meanwhile the state of society in England gave grave cause for uneasiness to the thinkers and serious statesmen of the day.   " They beheld the organisation of centuries collapse, the tillers of the earth adrift without employment, villages and towns running to waste, landlords careless of all but themselves, turning their tenants out upon the world when there were no colonies to fly to, no expanding manufactures[6] offering other openings to labour.   A change in the relations between the peasantry and the owners of the soil, which

[1] Anderson, *Commerce*, ii. 166 ; Seebohm, *Era of Protestant Reformation*, p. 228.

[2] Seebohm, p. 49 ; Rogers, *Hist. Agric.*, iv. 718.

[3] The edict which bore in time "its fatal fruit in the Alva persecutions," was issued by the Emperor on April 29th, 1550; and almost immediately Flemings began to emigrate to England.   Froude, *History*, iv. pp. 533-536.

[4] See below, p. 241.   [5] See below, p. 231.

[6] Froude is referring to the enormous manufacturing industry of the nineteenth century, beside which, of course, the growing manufactures of the sixteenth sink into insignificance.

three hundred years have but just effected, with the assistance of an unlimited field for emigration, was attempted harshly and unmercifully, with no such assistance, in a single generation.   Luxury increased on one side, with squalor and wretchedness on the other as its hideous shadow.   The value of the produce of the land was greater than before, but it was no longer distributed." [1]   In fact, with the growth of modern influences in thought, religion, industry, and trade, there came those modern evils which seem to be their inevitable accompaniment ; and we feel that in very truth, both for good and ill, the genius of the sixteenth century was more akin to that of the nineteenth than to that of any previous age.

[1] Froude, *History*, iv. 360.

CHAPTER XV

THE GROWTH OF FOREIGN TRADE

§ 134. *The Expansion of Commerce. The New Spirit.*

JUST as the beginning of the sixteenth century marks what may be called an economic revolution in the home industries of the country, so too it marks the beginning of international commerce upon the modern scale. The economic revolution, of which the new agricultural system and the practice of enclosures were the most striking features, was a change from the old dependent, uncompetitive, and regulated industrial system, to one under which Capital and Labour grew up as separate forces in the form in which we recognise them now. Labour had become virtually independent[1] since the Peasants' Revolt of 1381, and at the same time it felt consciously that it was in opposition to capitalist and land-owning interests. In its desire for freedom it had also begun to shake off even its self-imposed restrictions, and the power of the gilds had rapidly waned.[2] A new and eager spirit came with the Renaissance and the Reformation, a spirit which on the economic side showed itself in the development of competition, the shaking off of old restraints, and in more daring and far-seeing enterprises. Especially was this the case among the merchants, fired as they were by the great discoveries of the latter end of the fifteenth century,[3] and hence we notice, throughout the sixteenth century and especially at its close, that our foreign trade becomes more extensive than it had ever been before, and the foundations of our present international commerce were securely laid.

[1] *Cf.* Seebohm, *Era of the Protestant Reformation*, p. 49.
[2] Above, pp. 189, 208, 209.
[3] Seebohm, *Era of the Protestant Reformation*, p. 5.

§ 135. *Foreign Trade in the Fifteenth Century.*

At this point we must look back for a moment at our foreign trade before this new epoch. Although our enterprises were by no means large, there was yet a fairly considerable trade done in the fifteenth century with the countries in the west of Europe, *i.e.* France, Spain, Portugal, and the Baltic lands, and especially with the Low Countries.[1] As England was then almost entirely an agricultural country,[2] our chief export was wool for the Flemish looms to work up;[3] but the corn laws show that there was also other agricultural produce exported;[4] and likewise some mineral products. In fact England supplied nearly all Western Europe with two most important metals, tin[5] and lead; the former coming chiefly from Cornwall and the latter from Derbyshire,[6] though in neither case exclusively from those counties. Bodmin was the chief seat of the tin trade. Our huge mineral wealth in coal and iron was hardly yet touched, even for home use, and hardly any was exported.[7] Our imports were numerous and varied, their number being balanced by the greater bulk and value of our exports of wool and lead.

A fair amount of trade was done with Portugal and Spain, which sent us iron and war-horses;[8] Gascony and other parts of France sent their wines;[9] rich velvets, linens, and fine cloths were imported from Ghent, Liège, Bruges, and other Flemish manufacturing towns.[10] The ships of

---

[1] See the preamble to the 12 Henry VII., c. 6 (A.D. 1497), which mentions the trade to all these countries.

[2] Seebohm, *Era of Protestant Reformation*, p. 229.

[3] For its importance, *cf.* p. 122, and Bacon's *History of Henry VII.* there referred to.

[4] Above, p. 185.

[5] *The Libelle of English Policie*, about 1436 (fifteenth century), mentions "cloth, wolle, and tynne" as exports.

[6] Rogers, *Six Centuries*, p. 151; *Hist. Agric.*, i. 599.

[7] Coal was, however, used to a small extent, and brought by sea to London; *cf.* Craik, *British Commerce*, i. 147; it also seems in the sixteenth century to have been exported; *cf.* Froude, *History*, iv. 522, in a quotation from a letter of Wm. Lane, merchant, of London, to Sir William Cecil, *MS. Domestic*, Edward VI., Vol. xiii.

[8] Rogers, *Hist. Agric.*, i. 142, 144.

[9] Rogers, *Six Centuries*, p. 151, and *Hist. Agric.*, i. 142-144.   [10] *Ib.*

the Hansa merchants brought herrings, wax, timber, fur, and amber from the Baltic countries; and Genoese traders came with the silks and velvets and glass of Italy.[1] All these met one another, as we saw before, in the great fairs, as at Stourbridge, or in London, the great trading centre of England and afterwards of the Western world.

§ 136. The Venetian Fleet.

But our most important trade in the fourteenth and fifteenth centuries centred round the annual visit of the Venetian fleet to the southern shores of England. This was a great company of trading vessels, which left Venice every year upon a visit to England and Flanders.[2] Our English vessels did not at this time often venture into the Mediterranean, and so all the stores of the Southern European countries, and more especially the treasures of the East, came to us through the agency of Venice.[3] Laden with silks, satins, fine damasks, cottons, and other then costly garments, together with rare Eastern spices, precious stones, and sweet wines,[4] this fleet sailed slowly along the shores of the Mediterranean, trading at the ports of Italy, South France, and Spain, till it passed through the Straits of Gibraltar, and at length came up the Channel and reached our southern ports. When it had reached the Downs, the fleet broke up for a time, some vessels putting in at Sandwich, Rye, and other towns, and a large number stopping at Southampton, while others went on to Flanders.[5] Several days, sometimes weeks, were spent in exchanging their valuable cargoes for English goods, chiefly wool, the balance being paid over in gold; and then the various portions of the great fleet would re-unite again and set sail

---

[1] Rogers, Six Centuries, p. 151; and Hist. Agric., i. 142-144.

[2] Hence the Venetians themselves called it the "Flanders Fleet," and it first sailed in 1317; cf. Cunningham, i. 381, note.

[3] Cf. Craik, British Commerce, i. 165.

[4] Cf. Libelle of English Policie:—

"The great galleys of Venice and Florence
Be well laden with things of complacence,
All spicery and of grocers' ware
With sweet wines, all manner of chaffer, . . . " &c.

[5] Cunningham, English Industry, i. 381.

for Venice, from which city they were often absent for nearly a twelvemonth.[1] This annual visit was very convenient for English traders, before our own merchants ventured far away from our coasts. But it is a sign of the increased commercial enterprise of England in the sixteenth century that the visit then became unprofitable, and the last time[2] the Venetian fleet came to our shores was in 1587.

Besides this annual visit of the Fleet, there was also a large number of Italian merchants residing permanently in London, and engaged apparently in internal as well as foreign trade. They are mentioned in an Act[3] of 1484, which enumerates Venetians, Genoese, Florentines, Apulians, Sicilians, and natives of Lucca, complains of their competition with native English merchants, and seeks to impose upon them various restrictions. The Florentines in London were engaged in banking, and had carried on this business since the days of Edward III., if not before;[4] the Genoese were skilled in the manufacture of weapons of war, and also imported materials, such as woad and alum, that were used in the English cloth manufactures;[5] while the Venetians were, as we saw, engaged chiefly in the importation of foreign cloths and spices. But in course of time these foreign merchants found that Englishmen were beginning to engage in their own trade themselves, and even, as this trade increased, made voyages to Italy, or actually settled in Italian towns. They had begun to do so in the fifteenth century,[6] and had a consul of their own at Pisa, the chief port for English wool;[7] and early in the sixteenth century we find English merchants visiting the Greek islands[8] and the Levant.[9] Thus the monopoly of the Italian visitors to England was gradually broken through, and English merchants took part in the active traffic of the Mediterranean ports.

[1] Bourne, *Romance of Trade*, p. 101.
[2] The Fleet was in that year wrecked off the Isle of Wight; Sir W. Monson (who was an eyewitness), *Naval Tracts*, iv.
[3] The 1 Richard III., c. 9; *cf.* also Craik, *British Commerce*, i. 185.
[4] *Cf.* Cunningham, *English Industry*, i. 379.
[5] *Ib.*, i. 380.   [6] *Ib.*, i. 378.
[7] Rymer, *Foedera*, xii. 390; and *cf.* Cunningham, i. 438.
[8] Rymer, *Foedera*, xiii. 353; xiv. 424.   [9] *Ib.*, xiv. 389.

§ 137. *The Hanseatic League's Station in London.*

While our commerce was, however, not yet so greatly developed, there existed in England another important institution carried on by foreign merchants, this time from Germany. The Hansa, or Hanseatic League, originated in very early times among some of the leading trading towns of Germany,[1] such as Hamburg and Lübeck ; and after a time these towns formed themselves into a League for mutual protection amid the constant wars and piracy of those early days, and became a sort of federal union.[2] In the fifteenth century the League had grown so large and powerful that seventy cities belonged to it, and it had branches or depôts in every important town of Northern Europe.[3] Of course there was a large branch at London, in the "Steelyard," on which spot the Cannon Street Station now stands.[4] This branch had existed from very early times, and a warehouse was there in which the German merchants stored their goods. In Richard II.'s time this building was enlarged, and so it was again in the reign of Edward IV. Round it dwelt the foreign merchants, who formed quite a little colony in the very heart of mediæval London. Here they held a kind of chamber of commerce, presided over by an alderman, with two co-assessors and nine council-men, and meeting regularly on Wednesday mornings in every week.[5] The Steelyard colony existed for some hundreds of years, and taught many valuable lessons in commerce to our English merchants. It provided for us a regular supply of the produce of Russia, Germany, and Norway, especially timber and naval stores, and also corn when our English harvest fell short.[6] But as our own merchants grew more

[1] The "men of the Emperor" are mentioned in King Ethelred's laws (*De Institutis Londinii*, Thorpe, i. 300) as living in London, but this was probably before the Hansa was formed.

[2] The chief authority for the history of the Hansa in England is Lappenberg's *Urkundliche Geschichte des Hansischen Stahlhofes zu London* (Hamburg, 1851), but a good popular history now exists in English in H. Zimmern's *Hansa Towns*.

[3] Craik, *British Commerce*, i. 180.

[4] Zimmern, *Hansa Towns*, p. 187.

[5] Werdenhagen, quoted in Bourne's *Romance of Trade*, p. 99.

[6] Craik, *British Commerce*, i. 235.

prosperous, and their commerce extended, they became jealous of the German colony. Attacks were made upon it by London mobs,[1] and Edward VI. actually (in 1551) rescinded its charter.[2]   That was the beginning of the end.   Mary restored it for a time,[3] but towards the close of Elizabeth's reign (1597) it was finally abolished.[4]   This, too, was another sign of the growth of our own foreign trade.

§ 138. *Trade with Flanders.   Antwerp in the Fifteenth and Sixteenth Centuries.*

We have mentioned before how the eastern ports and harbours of England used to swarm with small, light craft that plied all the summer through between our own country and Flanders.   We have seen, too, that this continuous trade was due to the fact that we supplied the Flemish looms with wool.   Up to the fifteenth century the chief, but by no means the only, Flemish emporium to which our English ships plied, was Bruges,[5] but in the sixteenth century this town quite lost its former glory, and Antwerp [6] took its place.   The change was partly due to the action of Maximilian, the Emperor, to whom Henry VIII. was afterwards allied, and who, in revenge for a rebellion in which Ghent and Bruges took part, caused the canal which connected Bruges with the sea to be blocked up at Sluys [7] (1482), and thus English and other ships were compelled to direct their course to Antwerp, which was rapidly becoming a great and flourishing port. Antwerp remained without a rival till near the close of the sixteenth century, and every nation had its representatives there.[8]   Our own consul, to use a modern term, was, at the

---

[1] Craik, *British Commerce*, i. 233.

[2] *Ib.*, i. 233-235.   [3] *Ib.*, i. 234.

[4] Anderson, *Chron. Deduct. Commerce*, ii. 145.

[5] The English merchants at Bruges were organised into a kind of gild or company, and allowed to elect a mayor of their own, *Rot. Stap.*, 27-46 Edward III., m. 11, *Tower Records*, Record Office.   This was in 1359. See Appendix C. to Cunningham, *English Industry and Commerce*, vol. i.

[6] The "mansion" of the English merchants at Antwerp is mentioned by Bacon, *Life of Henry VII.* (p. 147, ed. Lumby).

[7] Anderson, *Chron. Deduct. of Commerce*, i. 511, 520.

[8] *Ib.*, p. 521.   It also derived much importance from the trade carried

close of the fifteenth century, Sir Richard Gresham; and later, in the reign of Henry VIII., his celebrated son, the financier and economist, Sir Thomas Gresham.[1] The fact of our having these representatives there is again a proof of the growth of trade in the sixteenth century. An Italian author, Ludovico Guicciardini (who died in 1589), gives in his *Description of the Netherlands* a very precise account of our own commerce with Antwerp at this period, and it is interesting to note how varied our commerce had by this time become. This is what he says as to our imports: "To England Antwerp sends jewels, precious stones, silver bullion, quicksilver, wrought silks, gold and silver cloth and thread, camlets, grograms, spices, drugs, sugar, cotton, cummin, linens, fine and coarse serges, tapestry, madder, hops in great quantities, glass, salt-fish, metallic and other merceries of all sorts; arms of all kinds, ammunition for war, and household furniture."[2] As to our exports, he tells us: "From England Antwerp receives vast quantities of coarse and fine draperies, fringes and all other things of that kind to a great value; the finest wool; excellent saffron, but in small quantities; a great quantity of lead and tin; sheep and rabbit skins without number, and various other sorts of the fine peltry (*i.e.* skins) and leather; beer, cheese, and other provisions in great quantities; also Malmsey wines, which the English import from Candia. It is marvellous to think of the vast quantity of drapery sent by the English into the Netherlands."[3]

This list is sufficient to show an extensive trade, and we shall comment upon one or two items of it in the next chapter. Here we need only remark upon the great growth of English manufactures of cloth, and on the fact that English merchants now evidently traded in the Levant.

on by the Portuguese after the discovery of the sea route to India. *Cf.* Craik, *British Commerce*, i. 215.

[1] The lives of Richard Gresham (1485?-1549) and of Thomas Gresham (1519?-1579) are well given by Charles Welch in the new *Dictionary of National Biography*.

[2] Extract in Macpherson's *Annals of Commerce*, ii. 131.

[3] *Ib.*, ii. 131.

§ 139. The Decay of Antwerp and Rise of London as the Western Emporium.

But the prosperity of Antwerp did not last quite a century. Like all Flemish towns, it suffered severely under the Spanish invasion and the persecutions of the notorious Alva. In 1567 it was ruinously sacked, and its commerce was forced into new channels, and the disaster was completed by the sacking of the town[1] again in 1585. Antwerp's ruin was London's gain. Even in 1567, at the time of the first sacking, and earlier still,[2] many Protestant Flemish merchants and manufacturers fled to England,[3] where, as Sir Thomas Gresham promised them, they found peace and welcome, and in their turn gave a great impulse to English commercial prosperity. Throughout Elizabeth's reign, in fact, there was a continual influx of Protestant refugees to our shores, and Elizabeth and her statesman had the sagacity to encourage these industrious and wealthy immigrants.[4] Besides aiding our manufactures, as we shall see later, they aided our commerce. In 1588 there were 38 Flemish merchants established in London, who subscribed £5000 towards the defence of England against the Spanish Armada.[5] The greatness of Antwerp was transferred to London, and although Amsterdam[6] also gained additional importance in Holland, London now took the foremost position as the general mart of Europe, where the new treasures of the two Americas were found side by side with the products of Europe and the East.

---

[1] Craik, *British Commerce*, i. 260 ; Anderson, *Commerce*, ii. 125, 159.

[2] In 1560 Philip's envoy reported to his master that "ten thousand of your Majesty's servants in the Low Countries are already in England with their preachers and ministers." Green, *History*, ii. 389. *Cf.* also Froude, *History*, iv. 535.

[3] Anderson, *Chron. Deduct. of Commerce*, ii. 159 says, "About a third part of the manufacturers and merchants who wrought and dealt in silks, damasks, taffeties, bayes, sayes, serges, and stockings, settled in England, because England was then ignorant of those manufactures."

[4] Letters patent were granted on 5th November 1565, permitting the "strangers" settled at Norwich to manufacture "such outlandish commodities as hath not been used to be made within this our realm of England." Burnley, *Wool and Woolcombing*, p. 67.

[5] Bourne, *Romance of Trade*, p. 115.   [6] Anderson, *Commerce*, ii. 159.

§ 140. *The Merchants and Sea-Captains of the Elizabethan Age in the New World.*

It is thus of interest to note how the great Reformation conflict between Roman Catholic and Protestant in Europe resulted in the commercial greatness of England. Interesting, also, is the story of the expansion of commerce in the New World, owing to the attacks of the great sea captains of those days—Drake, Frobisher, and Raleigh—as well as of numberless privateers, upon the huge Catholic power of Spain.[1] These attacks were perhaps not much more than buccaneering exploits, but the leaders of them firmly believed that they were doing a good service to the cause of Protestantism and freedom by wounding Spain wherever they could. And possibly they were right. Their wondrous voyages stimulated others, likewise, to set out on far and venturesome expeditions.[2] Men dreamt of a northern passage to India, and although Hugh Willoughby's expedition failed, one of his ships under Richard Chancellor reached Archangel,[3] and thus opened up a direct trade with Russia; so that in 1554 a company was formed specially for this trade.[4] Sir John Hawkins voyaged to Guinea and Brazil, and engaged in the slave-trade between Africa and the new fields of labour in America.[5] It was, too, in Elizabeth's reign that the merchants of Southampton [6] entered upon the trade with the coast of Guinea, and gained much wealth from its gold dust and ivory. Bristol fishermen sailed across the dreaded Atlantic to the cod-fisheries of Newfoundland,[7] and at the close of Elizabeth's reign English ships began to rival those of other nations in the Polar whale-fisheries.[8]

---

[1] *Cf.* Froude, *History*, ix. pp. 30, 303, 338, 485; also Green, *History*, ii. pp. 422-425, on the " sea-dogs " and Drake.

[2] A short summary of the deeds of Frobisher, Drake, and Cavendish is given in Craik, *British Commerce*, i. 245-256. See also Hakluyt's *Voyages*.

[3] Hakluyt, i. 246.   [4] *Ib.*, i. 265.   [5] Craik, *Brit. Commerce*, i. 243.

[6] Craik, *British Commerce*, i. 222, notes that trading voyages both to Brazil and Guinea become common after 1530.

[7] They had done so in Edward VI.'s reign, and the fisheries are mentioned in the 2 and 3 Edward VI., c. 6. But only fifteen ships from England were engaged in the fisheries in 1577 as compared with 150 from France. Craik (quoting Hakluyt), *British Commerce*, i. 259.

[8] Craik, *British Commerce*, i. 259, ii. 29.

This reign witnessed also the rise of the great commercial companies. The company of Merchant Adventurers had indeed existed since 1407, if not before,[1] having been formed in imitation of the Hanseatic League. The Russian Company of 1554 was formed upon the model of this earlier company; and later came the foundation of the great East India Company. The last was due to the results of Drake's far-famed voyage round the world,[2] which took three years, 1577-80. Shortly after his return it was proposed to found " a company for such as trade beyond the equinoctial line," but a long delay took place, and finally a company was incorporated for the more definite object of trading with the East Indies.[3] The date of this famous incorporation was 1600, and in 1601 Captain Lancaster made the first regular trading voyage on its behalf. To this modest beginning we owe our present Indian Empire.[4]

§ 141. *Remarks on the Signs and Causes of the Expansion of Trade.*

Now, if we look at the broad features that mark the growth of sixteenth century trade, we shall see that it was closely connected with England's decision to abide by the Protestant cause. It was that which won her the friendship of the Flemish merchants; it was the religious disturbances in Flanders that gained for London the commercial supremacy of Europe; it was our quarrel with Roman Catholic Spain that inspired the voyages of Drake and Hawkins, and thus caused others to venture forth into new and perilous seas, over which in course of time English merchants sailed almost without a rival. And, as we have shown, the signs of the expansion of England are seen in events

---

[1] Rymer, *Foedera*, viii. 464. It was an offshoot of the Mercers Company, which originated from the Brotherhood of St Thomas of Canterbury. *Cf.* 12 Henry VII., c. 6.

[2] *Cf.* Froude, *History*, xi. pp. 121-158.

[3] Craik, *British Commerce*, i. 251; Macpherson, *History of the European Commerce with India*, pp. 72-82; Stevens' *Dawn of British Trade to the East Indies* contains a reprint of the minutes of the Company.

[4] For the history of the Company, see ch. xviii., below.

such as the fall of the Hansa settlement in London, and the cessation of the visits of the Venetian fleet. On the other hand, the rapid growth of the port of Bristol[1] in the west witnessed to fresh trade with the New World, and the progress of Boston and Hull[2] on the east coast is significant as showing the development of our Northern and Baltic trade, even to the extent of rivalling the great Hansa towns.[3] A great stimulus had arisen, and England was now taking a leading position among the nations of the world. It has been well remarked,[4] that in the course of the long reign of Elizabeth the commerce and navigation of England may be said to have risen " through the whole of that space which in the life of a human being would be described as intervening between the close of infancy and commencing manhood. It was the age of the vigorous boyhood and adolescence of the national industry, when, although its ultimate conquests were still afar off, the path that led to them was fairly and in good earnest entered upon, and every step was one of progress and buoyant with hope." We will now survey the condition of the country that was thus setting forth upon a new and active career.

[1] The Bristol merchants were most active in sending out exploring and trading expeditions ; cf. Cunningham, *Eng. Ind.*, i. 445-448 ; Rogers, *Hist. Agric.*, iv. 84.

[2] They had always been important ; cf. p. 144.

[3] In fact a Company for trading in the Baltic, called the Eastland Company, was formed in 1579, and was a competitor of the Hansa, which formerly had had the monopoly in that sea. *Cf.* Macpherson, *Annals of Commerce*, ii. 164.

[4] Craik, *British Commerce*, i. 239.

CHAPTER XVI

§ 142. *Prosperity and Pauperism.*

THE reign of Elizabeth is generally regarded as prosperous, and so upon the whole it was. But she had come to the throne with a legacy of debt from her father,[1] Henry VIII., and from her father's counsellors, who guided her young brother, Edward VI. Nor had Mary helped to alleviate it. "The minority of Edward," remarks Froude,[2] "had been a time of mere thriftless waste and plunder, while east, west, north, and south the nation had been shaken by civil commotions. The economy with which Mary had commenced had been sacrificed to superstition, and what the hail had left the locusts had eaten." This unfortunate Queen, for whom no historian can fail to have a sentiment of the sincerest pity, believing that the spoliation of the monasteries by her father had caused the wrath of Heaven to descend upon her realm, stripped the Crown of half its revenues to re-establish the clergy and to force upon the country a form of religion which it had made up its mind to reject. But it is only fair to remark that the religious persecution in Queen Mary's reign has been much exaggerated, for it would appear that not more than three hundred persons were actually burnt at the stake as Protestants, and, even including those who died in prison, the total seems not to have exceeded four hundred.[3] But the power of the Romish queen was less than her will, and she certainly lost both the confidence and affection of her people. Her treasury was exhausted, the nation financially ruined, and in the latter years of her reign famine and plague had added their miseries to other causes of suffering.[4] Elizabeth

---

[1] Froude, *History*, vi. 108. [2] *Ib.*
[3] Froude (quoting Burghley), *History*, vi. 102.
[4] *Ib.*, vi. 109, and (famine), p. 29.

came to the throne not only with the national purse empty, but with heavy debts owing to the Antwerp Jews,[1] added to a terribly debased currency and a dangerous undercurrent of social discontent. It is to her credit as a sovereign that at her death danger from this last source had passed away.[2] This was partly due to the growth of wealth and industry throughout the kingdom, to the great gains of our foreign trade, and to the rapid expansion of our manufactures. But pauperism was now a permanent evil, and legal measures had to be taken for its relief.[3] One abiding cause of it was the persistent enclosures which still went on, together with the new developments in agriculture. Nevertheless, before the close of her reign the bulk of the people became contented and comfortable, owing to the prolonged peace which prevailed. The merchants and landed gentry,[4] or at least the new owners of the soil, were rich ; the farmers and master-manufacturers were prosperous ; even the artisans and labourers were not hopelessly poor, especially among the upper working classes. But there was a greater tendency towards the modern conditions of continuous poverty among those less fortunately situated.

§ 143. The Restoration of the Currency.

There was, however, one great reform introduced in Elizabeth's reign which benefited the whole nation, and the working classes by no means least of all. The restoration of the currency put wages and prices upon an assured basis, and from that time to this both master and man, whether paying or receiving wages, knew exactly what each was giving and receiving. No measure of Elizabeth's reign has received more deserved praise than the reform of the coinage, though the praise is due not so much to the Queen, who made a considerable profit out of the transaction, but

---

[1] There was about £200,000 owing to the Jews at 14 and 15 per cent. Froude, vi. p. 118.

[2] For discontent at the beginning, cf. Froude, vii. p. 9.

[3] See below, p. 260.

[4] The old nobility were scanty and weak, the new were richer ; Froude, vi. 109.

to the people at large, who had the good sense to bear
cheerfully the loss and expense it involved in order to
obtain a lasting gain.   The whole mass of base money was
estimated, somewhat roughly, at some £1,200,000 sterling.[1]
On the 27th of September 1560, the evils of an uneven
and vitiated currency were explained by a proclamation, in
which the Queen stated that the crown would bear the
cost of refining and recoining the public moneys if the
nation would bear cheerfully its share of the loss, and the
people were invited to bring in and pay over in every market
town, to persons duly appointed, the impure money they
possessed.   The total amount thus collected was 631,950
pounds in weight, and for this £638,000 in money was
paid by the receivers of the Mint.   It yielded when melted
down 244,416 pounds of silver, worth, under the new
coinage system, £733,248 sterling.   After paying for the
cost of collection, refining, reminting, and other expenses,
there was a balance of over fourteen thousand pounds in
favour of the Queen.   "Thus was this great matter
ended, and the reform of the coin cost nothing beyond
the thought expended upon it."[2]

This important question being now disposed of, we may
turn to the condition of the industries of Elizabethan England, and first we must notice the steady growth of manufactures in a land hitherto mainly agricultural.

§ 144. *The Growth of Manufactures.*

The economic transition before alluded to (p. 131), by
which England had developed from a wool-exporting into a
wool-manufacturing country, had in Elizabeth's reign been
almost completed.   The woollen manufacture had become
an important element in the national wealth.   England no
longer sent her wool to be manufactured in Flanders,
although much of it was still dyed there.[3]   It was now

---

[1] Froude, *History*, vii. p. 6.

[2] For the whole transaction see Froude, *History*, vii. pp. 2-9, and the
Lansdowne MSS., 4 ("Charges of refining the base money received into
the Mint, with a note of the provisions and other charges incident to the
same ").

[3] This continued till James I.'s reign ; Craik, *British Commerce*, ii. 33.

worked up at home, and the manufacturing population was not confined to the towns only, but was spreading all over the country;[1] and both spinning and weaving afforded direct employment for an increasing number of workmen, while even in agricultural villages they were frequent bye-industries. The worsted trade, of which Norwich was still the centre, spread over all the Eastern counties.[2] The broad-cloths of the West of England took the highest place among English woollen stuffs.[3] Even the North, which had lagged so far behind the South in industrial development, ever since the harrying it underwent at the hands of William the Norman, began now to show signs of activity and new life. It had, in this period, developed special manufactures of its own, and Manchester[4] cottons and friezes, York coverlets,[5] and Halifax cloth[6] now held their own amongst the other manufactures of the country. There are several signs of the progress of manufactures in this period, two of which deserve special attention. We find that it was becoming increasingly the practice for a master-manufacturer to employ a number of men working at looms, either in their own houses, or more or less under the master's control. So numerous had such employers become,

[1] A well-known historian (Fuller, *Church History* (ed. 1655), p. 142) has given us a list of the chief seats of the cloth trade and its distribution in the seventeenth century, which will illustrate this period also. In the East of England he mentions Norfolk and the Norwich fustians; in Suffolk the bayes of Sudbury; in Essex the Colchester bayes and serges; and also the broad-cloths of Kent. In the West he notices the Devonshire kersies, Welsh friezes, and the cloths of Worcester and Gloucester. In the South Somerset was known for the Taunton serges, and Hampshire, Berkshire, and Sussex are all mentioned as having manufactures of cloth. In the North the "Kendal Greens" of Westmoreland, and the manufactures of Manchester and Halifax, in Lancashire and Yorkshire respectively, are duly noted. From this list it is evident that the manufacturing industry was very widely spread, and must often have been carried on by agriculturists as a bye-industry in agricultural districts. It had not yet become specialised.

[2] *Cf.* the 14 and 15 Henry VIII., c. 3, and the 26 Henry VIII., c. 16, which show that Lynn and Yarmouth also had manufactures.

[3] Fuller, *ut supra.*

[4] *Cf.* the 5 and 6 Edward VI., c. 6. The "cottons" were at that time a kind of woollen manufacture.

[5] Mentioned in the 34 and 35 Henry VIII., c. 10.

[6] Fuller, *ut supra.*

that in the reign of Queen Mary, an "Act touching weavers" was passed,[1] whereby it was sought to remedy this condition of things. The beginnings of the factory system evidently did not commend themselves to sixteenth-century statesmen. The Preamble to the Act sets forth very clearly the state of things in the manufacturing industry at this time. "The weavers of this realm," it says, "have, as well in this present Parliament as at divers other times, complained that the rich and wealthy clothiers do in many ways oppress them—some by setting up and keeping in their houses divers looms, and keeping and maintaining them by journeymen and persons unskilful, to the decay of a great number of artificers which were brought up in the said science of weaving, with their families and households—some by engrossing of looms in their hands and possession, and letting them out at such unreasonable rents that the poor artificers are not able to maintain themselves, much less to maintain their wives, families, and children—some also by giving much less wages and hire for weaving and workmanship than in times past they did, whereby they [*i.e.* the workmen] are forced utterly to forsake their art and occupation, wherein they have been brought up." The Statute then goes on to enact that "no person using the feat or mystery of clothmaking shall keep or retain or have in their houses and possession any more than *one* woollen loom at a time," if they live outside a city, borough, or market town; nor shall they "directly or indirectly receive or take any manner of profit, gain, or commodity by letting or setting any loom," on pain of a fine of twenty shillings. Weavers who live in the towns are not to have more than two looms. The intention of the Act obviously was to prevent the cloth-manufacture from falling into the power of large capitalist-employers, such as the millowners of the present day; and though, of course, such an Act was in the end powerless to arrest the progress of a system which necessarily resulted from the development of industry, it is certainly interesting as showing how far that development had already proceeded.

---

[1] The 2 and 3 Philip and Mary, c. 11.

The time of the factory with its capitalist master and hundreds of "hands" had not yet arrived, but already this glimmer of dawn was announcing the approaching day.

§ 145. *Monopolies of Manufacturing Towns.*

Another important sign of the growth of manufactures is seen in the fruitless attempts made in the sixteenth century to confine a particular manufacture to a particular town. This is a sure indication that the manufacture of that article was increasing in country districts, and that competition was operating in a new and unexpected way upon the older industries. An example of this may be seen in the monopoly granted by Parliament in Henry VIII.'s reign [1] (1530) to Bridport in Dorsetshire, "for the making of cables, hawsers, ropes, and all other tackling." This monopoly was granted upon the complaint made by the citizens of Bridport, that their town "was like to be utterly decayed," owing to the competition of "the people of the adjacent parts," who were therefore by this monopoly forbidden to make any sort of rope. The only result of this measure, however, was to transfer the rope-making industry from Dorset to Yorkshire, and Bridport was in a worse plight than before.

In the same reign (1534) the inhabitants of Worcester, Evesham, Droitwich, Kidderminster, and Bromsgrove, then almost the only towns in Worcestershire, complained [2] that "divers persons *dwelling in the hamlets, thorps, and villages* of the county made all manner of cloths, and exercised shearing, fulling, and weaving within their own houses, to the great depopulation of the city and towns." A monopoly was granted to the towns, the only result of which was that they became poorer than before, a great portion of the local industry being transferred to Leeds. A little later (1544) the citizens of York complain [3] of the competition of "sundry evil-disposed persons and apprentices," who had "withdrawn themselves out of the city into the country," and competed with York in the manufacture

[1] 21 Henry VIII., c. 12.   [2] *Cf.* the 25 Henry VIII., c. 18.
[3] *Cf.* the 34 and 35 Henry VIII., c. 10.

of coverlets and blanketings. York obtained a monopoly, but her manufactures gained nothing thereby. These monopolies granted to towns should not be confused with others granted to individuals for trading purposes. Of this other class we shall speak later. The monopolies of towns here mentioned are, however, interesting as illustrating the growth of manufactures in all parts of the kingdom, and useful as showing the futility of merely protective enactments.

§ 146. *Exports of Manufactures and Foreign Trade.*

Besides these monopolies, we have ample evidence of the growth of our cloth manufactures in the statements made by the historian Guicciardini (1523-89), as to our exports to Antwerp. "It is marvellous," he says,[1] "to think of the vast quantity of drapery sent by the English into the Netherlands, being undoubtedly one year with another above 200,000 pieces of all kinds, which, at the most moderate rate of 25 crowns per piece, is 5,000,000 crowns, so that these and other merchandise brought by the English to us, or carried from us to them, may make the annual amount to more than 12,000,000 crowns," which is equivalent to some £2,400,000. The evidence of the Elizabethan writer Harrison[2] on this point is also interesting. "The wares that they (*i.e.* merchants) carry out of the realm are for the most part broad-cloths and kersies of all colours; likewise cottons, friezes, rugs, tin, wool, our best beer, baize, fustian, mockadoes (tufted and plain), lead, fells, etcetera; which, being shipped at sundry ports of our coasts, are borne from thence into all quarters of the world, and there either exchanged for other wares or ready money, to the great gain and commodity of our merchants." Here it will be seen how important a place English cloth manufactures take in Harrison's somewhat confused list of exports; while the other commodities mentioned, such as lead and skins or fells, show that the older staples of our

---

[1] Quoted in Macpherson, *Annals of Commerce*, ii. 127.

[2] Harrison, *Description of England*, Book III. ch. iv., edition 1557; pages 10 and 11 in the *Camelot Series edition.*

trade were still worthy of notice. Harrison also makes a very interesting remark upon the direction as well as the character of our foreign trade, which is well worth quoting. " Whereas in times past," he says,[1] " their chief trade was into Spain, France, Flanders, Danske (Denmark), Norway, Scotland, and Ireland only, now in these days, as men not contented with these journeys, they have sought out the East and West Indies, and made now and then suspicious voyages, not only unto the Canaries and New Spain (*i.e.*, Spanish America), but likewise into Cathay, Muscovy, and Tartaria, and the regions thereabout, from whence, as they say, they bring home great commodities. But alas ! " he adds, " I see not by all their travel that the prices of things are any whit abated." The rise in prices, however, was not due, as Harrison thought it was, to the increase of trade, but to other causes upon which we have already commented. One other remark of his is worth attention, as showing not only the growth of commerce but the importance of the merchant class in the social life of the country : " They often change estate with gentlemen, as gentlemen do with them, by a mutual conversion of one into the other."[2] At one time this would have been impossible, but this mention of the fact shows us how far the old order had changed.

§ 147. *The Flemish Immigration.*

English progress in manufactures and trade was also about this time greatly aided by the arrival of Dutch and Flemish Protestant refugees who fled from the persecutions of Roman Catholic rulers to a more tolerant country. This immigration of foreign Protestants had begun, as we saw,[3] some time before the days of Elizabeth, but it increased in numbers soon after Elizabeth's accession, when the death of Mary had relieved England from the fear of Romish persecution. A numerous body of Flemings came over in 1561, and starting from Deal, spread to Sandwich, Rye,

---

[1] Harrison, *Description of England*, Book III. ch. iv., edition 1577 ; pages 10 and 11 in the *Camelot Series edition.*

[2] *Ib.*, p. 9, Camelot edition.   [3] Above, p. 221, *note* 3.

and other parts of Kent.[1] Another body settled in Norwich, and over Norfolk generally.[2] In 1570 there were 4000 natives of the Netherlands in Norwich alone.[3] There was also an important settlement in Colchester.[4] After the sack of Antwerp in 1585, the immigration largely increased. The new arrivals introduced or improved many manufactures, such as those of silk, cutlery, clock-making, hats, and pottery.[5] But the greatest improvements they made were in weaving and lace-making. They greatly developed "every sort of workmanship in wool and flax."[6] The lace manufacture was introduced by refugees from Alençon and Valenciennes into Cranfield (Beds.), and from that town it extended to Buckinghamshire, Oxfordshire, and Northamptonshire; while other immigrants founded the manufacture of the well-known Honiton lace in Devon.[7] It is interesting thus to notice how much we owed to foreign teachers in earlier times, for the reigns of Edward III., Elizabeth, and later of Charles II., were all signalised by large influxes of people from the Low Countries, bringing with them increased skill and often considerable capital.

An interesting testimony to the influence of these refugees is afforded by Harrison[8] in his *Description of England*. Speaking about our wool, he remarks: "In time past the use of this commodity consisted for the most part in cloth and woolsteds, but now, *by means of strangers succoured here from domestic persecution*, the same hath been employed unto sundry other uses; as mockados, bays, vellures, grograines, &c., whereby the makers have reaped no small commodity."

§ 148. *Monopolies.*

The influences above mentioned all tended to promote the growth of our manufactures, and there was, besides, considerable industrial progress. It is noticeable, however,

---

[1] *Romance of Trade*, p. 114; Lecky, *History of Eighteenth Century*, i. 191; Boys, *History of Sandwich*, p. 740; and Cunningham, *Eng. Ind.*, ii. 36.

[2] Moens, *The Walloons* (Huguenot Society), 18, 79, 264.

[3] Bourne, *Romance of Trade*, p. 115.   [4] Cunningham, ii. 37.

[5] Bourne, *Romance of Trade*, p. 114.   [6] *Ib.*, p. 115.   [7] *Ib.*

[8] Book III. ch. viii., ed. 1577; Camelot series ed., p. 155.

that in the Elizabethan period there arises an eager discussion about monopolies. The fact that this question was
now raised is sufficient to indicate the growth of a competitive spirit almost unfamiliar to mediæval industry,
and to show that industrial life was growing stronger
and more .self-assertive. Merchants and manufacturers
alike were beginning to resent more keenly the interference of government with industry, and more especially
that form of state interference which took the shape of
granting either to individuals or to a corporation the
exclusive right of producing or trading in any particular
commodity. A strong feeling is manifested against the
possessors of monopolies, and in the closing years of Elizabeth's reign there took place in Parliament that celebrated
debate in which both the monopolies and their holders
were severely attacked. No doubt there was, as usual, a
fair amount of political exaggeration and partisan statement
introduced—for we need not imagine that the Elizabethan
members of parliament were other than human—but there
is also no doubt that a real grievance underlay the complaints then made. A member spoke of the "burden of
monstrous and unconscionable substitutes to the monopolitans
of starch, tin, fish, cloth, oil, vinegar, salt, and I know not
what—nay, what not? The principallest commodities of
my town and country are ingrossed into the hands of these
bloodsuckers of the common-wealth;"[1] and the general
feeling of the House of Commons was so strong, that
Elizabeth thought it best to annul the monopolies then
existing, though she was almost certainly within the legal
limits of her prerogative in originally granting them. Her
successor, however, James I., used his prerogative to create
so many new monopolies that Parliament again protested
in 1609, and he also revoked them all. But after the
suspension of Parliamentary government in 1614, they
were granted again, till in 1621 their existence was one of
the main grievances which the House of Commons then
brought before the king.[2] At a conference with the House

---

[1] D'Ewes, *Complete Journal of the Houses of Lords and Commons*, 646.
[2] *Cf.* Craik, *British Commerce*, ii. 23.

of Lords the Commons offered to prove "that the patents of gold and silver thread, of inns and alehouses, and power to compound for obsolete laws, of the price of horse-meat, starch, cords, tobacco-pipes, salt, train-oil, and the rest were all illegal; howbeit they touched not the tender point of prerogative, but, in restoring the subjects' liberty, were careful to preserve the king's honour." [1]   Three patents or monopolies were more particularly complained of: (1) that of inns and hostelries, (2) that of alehouses, and (3) that of gold and silver thread.[2]   The first two were monopolies granting to individuals the power of licensing inns and taverns, and had led to great abuses, though it is said in defence of the patent that the original intention was to place these houses under some kind of supervision in order to check evils that were admittedly rife in them.[3]   The monopoly of the manufacture of gold and silver thread, granted to Sir Giles Mompesson, was looked upon with disfavour as tending to exhaust the stock of the precious metals in this country.[4]   King James warmly condemned these and all other monopolies, asserting that it made "his hair stand upright" to think how his people had been robbed thereby,[5] and, though he waited three years before doing anything decisive, they were all abolished in 1624.[6] The evil was not yet, however, by any means entirely suppressed, for it took another shape, monopolies being granted by Charles I. to corporations,[7] though not to individuals.   His object was to increase the royal revenue, to which purpose indeed almost every expedient was applied that had any colour of legality.   In this he was certainly successful, for he obtained considerable sums of money, receiving in one year £20,000 for soap alone.[8]   But great

[1] Rushworth, *Historical Collections*, i. 24.
[2] *Cf.* James I.'s speech in Rushworth's *Hist. Collections*, i. 26.
[3] Cunningham, *Growth of English Industry*, ii. 158.
[4] *Ib.*, ii. 159, and Gardiner, *History*, iv. 18.
[5] See his hypocritical but amusing speech quoted by Craik, *British Commerce*, ii. 27, 28.
[6] Statute 21 James I., c. 3.
[7] See Colepepper's speech below; and Dowell, *Taxation and Taxes in England*, i. 244.
[8] Gardiner, *History*, viii. 75.

discontent was caused by monopolies of such common and necessary articles, and it was seen that the form of a "corporation" was only a cloak for individuals to increase their private gains. In the Long Parliament, Colepepper exclaimed indignantly, after reciting numerous grievances against the "monopolisers":[1] "Mr Speaker, they will not bate us a pin; we may not buy our own clothes without their brokerage. These are the leeches that have sucked the commonwealth so hard, that it is become almost hectical. And some of these are ashamed of their right names; they have a wizard to hide the brand made by that good law in the last Parliament of King James; they shelter themselves under the name of a corporation; they make bye-laws which serve their turn to squeeze us and fill their purses." The system, however, of granting these patents to corporations did not cease either then or subsequently under Cromwell and Charles II., but the government took care only to grant monopolies for such purposes as did not cause an outburst of popular feeling.[2] The system has in fact never entirely ceased, for the modern practice of granting patents for a limited time to inventors of new processes is only a modification of the old monopolies, and was prevalent two hundred years ago as well as now.[3] But what is noticeable in the seventeenth century is the almost universal acceptance of the principle of monopoly as opposed to competition, except in those cases where monopoly was clearly seen to be injurious to the common welfare. The people might object to a monopoly of soap or salt[4] because they felt its effects directly; but they considered it quite just and proper that a company like the East Indian should have a monopoly of Asiatic trade. Even when the Commons came into conflict with the Crown it was to them a question more of constitutional than of economic importance; they

---

[1] *Parl. Hist.*, ii. 656.

[2] *Cf.* also Cunningham, *Growth of Industry*, ii. 168.

[3] The Act of 1624 abolishing ordinary monopolies yet granted them for twenty-one years to new industries, and to new processes for fourteen years. 21 James I., c. 3.

[4] For that on salt, *cf. Parl. Hist.*, i. 1205; Strafford's *Letters*, i. 193; and Gardiner, *History*, viii. 285.

were trying to regain rights which had been for some time in abeyance, and to check the menacing growth of royal prerogative. As for the Crown, from Elizabeth onwards, there can be little doubt, although historians have sought to excuse its action by suggesting that it had at heart the proper regulation of industry,[1] that in most cases all that was aimed at was an increase of royal revenue or a ready and easy means of rewarding royal favourites.[2] There were of course, exceptions; and occasionally genuine attempts were made to improve some languishing industry[3] by the doubtful method of a monopoly, but the requirements of the royal purse were the usual guide in matters of this kind. Gradually, however, the general acquiescence in the monopoly system which marks this period gave way before the progress of the spirit of competition, and though it was left to the statesmen of the nineteenth century to perceive that industry is best left as far as possible unhampered by government intervention, we hear but little of this particular form of state regulation as trade and industry expanded.

§ 149. *The Revival of the Craft Gilds.*

We have mentioned in speaking of monopolies that one excuse for them was that the state might seek thereby to regulate or supervise particular industries. Whether the State actually did so or not, it seems to have been thought necessary to return to some institution such as the old craft-gilds, which had practically been annihilated by the confiscation of their lands under Edward VI.'s guardian, Somerset.[4] Certainly in Elizabeth's reign the gilds were useless, and powerless to exercise any real influence over the crafts which they were supposed the represent[5] But

---

[1] *Cf.* Gardiner, *History of England*, iv. 7, anc see his whole chapter (xxxiii.) on the monopolies.

[2] The monopoly of sweet wines granted by Elizabeth to Essex was such a case.

[3] *E.g.*, the patent granted to Cockayne for dyeing and dressing-cloth; Cunningham, *Growth of Industry*, ii. 165.

[4] See above, p. 208.

[5] See the petition in 1571 by fourteen London crafts; Clode, *Early Hist. of Merchant Taylors*, p. 204.

under this queen there came a sort of revival, or at least a reconstruction of the old system. New companies were incorporated for many trades, the ostensible reason being the supervision of the quality of the wares produced in that trade. The real cause, however, was no doubt the existence of such "companies" among the Flemish and other immigrants,[1] who, as we saw, came to England in such large numbers at this time. Since these foreigners had their own associations and met in their own "halls" or gild houses,[2] it is not surprising that English manufacturers and merchants, either from feelings of jealousy or imitation, or both, should wish to have similar and privileged organisations. But these new institutions differed from the old craft-gilds in several ways. They no longer derived their authority from municipalities, but from the Crown or from Parliament. "They were constituted from outside, not from inside the town."[3] Moreover, they were associations of capitalists, or of capitalist employers, rather than of craftsmen, as the old gilds used to be, and were obliged to pay heavily for their patents or charters.[4] Again, various trades were often combined in one company, and there was often no pretence of supervising the wares of all the trades thus associated,[5] though in some few cases the companies were empowered to exercise supervision over the quality of goods. Thus the haberdashers, saddlers, curriers, and shoemakers had supervisory rights, and in London these rights seem to have been exercised with some effect.[6] In the rural districts, however, supervision, even when supposed to exist, was very lax. Still, the revival of these companies is interesting as a kind of continuation, though on considerably different lines, of the gilds of mediæval times.

§ 150. *Agriculture.*

But we must turn now from manufacturing progress to what was then still the greatest industry of the country,

---

[1] *Cf.* Cunningham, *Growth of Industry*, ii. 47, and the note there.
[2] *Ib.*, quoting Morant, *Essex*, i. 77.   [3] Cunningham, *ut supra*, *q.v.*
[4] The upholsterers of London paid £100 to Elizabeth for their charter; *ib.*, ii. 48.   [5] *Ib.*
[6] *Cf.* Act 5 Eliz., c. 8, § 31, and Cunningham, ii. 48.

and glance at the condition of agriculture in Elizabethan England. Here the advance had been slow, but yet it was substantial, and a proof of progress is to be noticed in the fact that towards the end of the sixteenth century competition was making itself felt among tenants for farms. Competitive rents [1] had been hitherto almost entirely unknown in England, but now were becoming more frequent, resulting of course in a rise of rent. But the competition itself in this case shows progress, [2] and this would also seem to be indicated by the comfortable condition of the yeomanry in this period. [3] The growth of our manufactures helped of course to promote sheep-farming, not only (as before) on the part of great landowners, but even of ordinary, moderate farmers. Upon this point Harrison mentions an important fact [4]: " And there is never an husbandman (for now I speak not of our great sheep-masters, of whom some one man hath 20,000) but hath more or less of this cattle (sheep) feeding on his fallows and short grounds, which yield the finer fleece." The same writer also mentions that sometimes grazing was preferred to tillage, because it required less care and capital, but he does not lay so much stress on this as would lead us to suppose that this change was regarded as so great an evil as it was formerly. [5] He seems to think it rather characteristic of a "mean gentleman" to change arable land into pasture, for he speaks [6] of "a mean gentleman who hath cast up all his tillage because he boasteth how he can buy his grain in the market better cheap than he can sow his land," and adds that "the rich grazier often doth also upon the like device, because grazing requireth a smaller household and less attendance and charge." [7] But besides grazing and sheep-farming, which had long since risen into importance, our agriculture had improved in several respects. Here foreign influence,

---

[1] *Cf.* Norden's *Surveyor's Dialogues* (first edition, 1607), and Rogers, *Hist. Agric. and Prices*, v. 42, 43.   [2] *Ib.*, v. 43.

[3] Harrison, *Description of England*, Camelot series edition, p. 12.

[4] *Ib.*, p. 156.

[5] Cunningham, *Growth of Industry*, ii. 52, thinks the mischief of over-much grazing declined at the close of the sixteenth century. *Cf.* also Froude, *History*, vii. p. 10.   [6] Harrison, *u. s.*, p. 36.   [7] *Ib.*

especially that of the Low Countries,[1] is again visible. Already a change in the mode of cultivation had been brought about, not so great as that which took place in the two succeeding centuries, but still quite perceptible. A larger capital was brought to bear upon the land,[2] the breed of horses and cattle was improved,[3] and more intelligent use was made of manure and dressings.[4] It was said that "in Queen Elizabeth's days good husbandry began to take place."[5] In addition to these improvements, the coming of the Flemings and Dutch introduced several new vegetables. The refugees cultivated in their gardens carrots, celery, and cabbages, which were previously either unknown or very scarce in this country,[6] and from the garden these plants were introduced into the farm.[7] The most important service to agriculture, however, was the introduction of the hop, which is said to have been brought to England by some Flemish as early[8] as 1524, and later in the century, in Elizabeth's reign, the hop gardens of Kent had already become famous,[9] and have remained so ever since. As regards wheat, it is noticeable that its price was now rising considerably, but was subject to remarkable fluctuations, varying from 5s. to 25s. a quarter[10] in the last half of the sixteenth century. The average price, however (from 1540 to 1582), was 13s. 10½d., a considerable increase upon that of the previous century and a half, when (from 1401 to 1540) it was only a farthing under six shillings.[11] This may have been due to the Elizabethan corn laws[12] or possibly

---

[1] Rogers, *Hist. Agric. and Prices*, v. 45, 64. He also mentions that this influence was first to be noticed in the eastern counties of England, because they had close business connections with Holland and Flanders. *Cf.* also Harrison, *Description of England*, p. 26, Camelot edition.

[2] Green, *History of England*, ii. 387.   [3] *Ib.*

[4] *Cf.* Gervase Markham's works, *The English Husbandman* (1613), and the *Farewell to Husbandry* (4th edition, 1649), and remarks in Rogers, *Hist. Agric.*, v. 52.

[5] Dymock, *Samuel Hartlib, his Legacy*, p. 52 (1651).

[6] Rogers, *Hist. Agric.*, v. 57.   [7] *Ib.*, v. 50.

[8] Bourne, *Romance of Trade*, p. 29.

[9] *Ib.* They were also grown in Norfolk, Suffolk, and Essex; Norden, in Rogers, *Hist. Agric.*, v. 44.

[10] Rogers, *Hist. Agric. and Prices*, iv. 270, 271.   [11] *Ib.*, Tables, iv. 292.

[12] Cunningham, *Growth of Industry*, ii. 54, 55.

to the increase of population; but, however that may be, it
had the effect of encouraging tillage once more.   But the
great advance in agriculture had not yet come.   That was
reserved for the next two centuries.   Meanwhile the greater
part of rural England was going on in much the same
old ways.   In spite of numerous enclosures, the primitive
common field system was still in vogue among ordinary
husbandmen,[1] and the innate conservatism of the agriculturist was only here and there disturbed by the efforts of a
few adventurous spirits who were introducing new plants
and new methods.

§ 151. Social Comforts.

All this increase of the national wealth in commerce,
manufactures, and industry produced important changes
in the mode of living.   The standard of comfort became
higher.[2]   Food became more wholesome.   As agriculture
improved and animals could be kept through the winter
with greater ease, salt meat and salt fish no longer formed
the staple food of the lower classes for half the year.
Brickmaking [3] had been re-discovered about 1450, and
by the time of Elizabeth the wooden or wattled houses
(p. 81) had generally been replaced, at least among all but
the poorer class, with dwellings of brick and stone.[4]   The
introduction of chimneys and the lavish use of glass also
helped to improve the people's dwellings ;[5] and, indeed, the
houses of the rich merchants, or the lords of the manors,
were now quite luxuriously furnished.[6]   Carpets had
superseded the old filthy flooring of rushes ; pillows and
cushions were found in all decent houses ;[7] and the

---

[1] Rogers, *Hist. Agric.*, v. 49, illustrates this from the survey of Gam-
lingay (Cambs.), made for Merton College, Oxford, in March 1602.

[2] See Harrison, *Description of England*, Bk. III. ch. i. ed. 1577: "Of
the food and diet of the English."—Camelot edn., pp. 84-106.

[3] Rogers, *Econ. Interpretation of History*, p. 279.

[4] See Harrison, *Description of England*, Bk. II. ch. x. edn. 1577, Camelot
edn., p. 117.

[5] *Ib.*, pp. 116 and 119 of Camelot edn.

[6] *Ib.* "The furniture of our houses also exceedeth, and is grown in
manner even to passing delicacy."

[7] *Ib.*, p. 118, Camelot edn. (for carpets), p. 119 (pillows, etc.).

quantity of carved woodwork[1] of this period shows that men cared for something more than mere utility in their surroundings. The lavishness of new wealth was seen, too, in a certain love of display, of colour, and of "purple and fine linen," which characterises the dress of the Elizabethan age.[2] The old sober life and thought of mediæval England had been entirely revolutionised by the sudden opening of the almost fabulous glories of the New World, and men revelled joyously in the new prospects of the wealth of the wondrous West. There was, moreover, now far greater security of life and property than of old, and consequently the old fortified castles of mediæval days had disappeared, as the need for fortification of residences passed away, and the nobility and gentry now sought comfort and magnificence rather than strength and security in their abodes.[3] And with this increased security and the growth of wealth we notice also the growth of capitalism[4] and of a capitalist class, so that the merchant of Elizabeth's days was able to engage in enterprises far larger than those of his predecessors. But yet there were the seeds of pauperism in the land, and all the wealth of the merchants and the adventurers of Elizabethan England did not prevent the sure and inevitable Nemesis that followed upon the crimes and follies of Elizabeth's father and his court.

§ 152. *The Condition of the Labourers.*

For it is impossible, in glancing at the condition of labour in the days of Elizabeth, to forget the disastrous economic changes wrought by the actions of Henry VIII. and his followers. Compared with the fifteenth century, the poverty of the wage-earners in Elizabeth's reign was often great indeed, though even then not so bad as it subsequently became. It was not that the working classes, as a whole, were badly off in the Elizabethan age, for there was undoubtedly a fair amount of prosperity; but there

---

[1] Green, *History*, ii. 391, notices this.
[2] Harrison, *u. s.*, Bk. III. ch. ii., edn. 1577. Camelot edn., pp. 107-112.
[3] *Cf.* Green, *History*, ii. 392.
[4] Cunningham, *Growth of Industry*, ii. 6.

were greater extremes amongst them than before, and a
larger number of indigent in their ranks. Many of the
petty copy-holders who had been dispossessed of their lands
by the enclosures of previous years had fallen into beggary ;[1]
the less provident of the labourers had lost their mediæval
curtilages and plots of land in the same way,[2] and therefore
there was a more numerous class now dependent for their
livelihood on wages only.[3] Consequently there was often
a large number of unemployed wage-earners, and fluctuations in employment became more seriously and more
acutely felt. Contemporary writers complain that the rich
were still often encroaching on the poor man's land,[4] as
they have frequently done since Scriptural times ; and the
labouring man was often too poor to buy himself corn [5]—
a state of things which did not occur so frequently when
everyone had some share in the land and did not depend
on wages only. A great loss must also have been felt by
the working classes in the abolition of the old gilds and
the decay of the old customs associated with them. The
merry gild-feast was no longer a feature of village life,[6] and
holidays and festivals were reduced to a lesser number.[7]
From this time forward we shall not find much advance in
the lot of the labourer. One of his most prosperous periods
was fast approaching its close, and on the whole the next
two centuries show a steady deterioration.

Of course the condition of labour will be best seen by taking
examples of the wages then given. In Elizabeth's reign, then,
we may reckon [8] the yearly wages of an agricultural labourer

[1] Froude, *History*, vii. p. 9.
[2] Rogers, *Hist. Agric. and Prices*, iv. 755.   [3] *Cf.* the Act 31 Eliz., c. 7.
[4] Harrison, *Description of England*, Bk. II. ch. 7, ed. 1577; p. 19, Camelot edn.
[5] *Ib.*, Bk. III. ch. i. ; page 96, Camelot edn.
[6] *Ib.*, Bk. II. ch. v., edn. 1577 ; p. 78, Camelot edn. : "The superfluous numbers of wakes, guilds, fraternities, churchales are well diminished and laid aside." Harrison approved of their abolition, it seems. But *cf.* Blomfield's *Norfolk*, iii. 185, who says, "The poor of the parish always were partakers with them," which shows that they helped to relieve pauperism.
[7] Harrison also thought these "very well reduced." But he was a clergyman, not a labourer. *Description, ut supra.*
[8] Rogers, *Hist. Agric. and Prices*, iv. 737, 738.

at about £8, 4s., and the cost of living, which now included house rent, formerly unknown, at £8, thus leaving a very narrow margin for contingencies. Daily wages were [1] (in 1563)—for artisans, 8d. a day in winter and 9d. in summer; for labourers, 6d. in winter and 7d. in summer, and in harvest-time occasionally 8d. or even 10d. This is not very much more than the wages paid at the close of the fifteenth century [2] (viz., artisans 3s. a week and labourers 2s.), but the price of food had risen almost to three times the old average, while wages had only risen [3] in the proportion of 1 to 1·72. Moreover, a new system was in this reign introduced for arranging wages.

§ 153. *Assessment of Wages by Justices.*

The celebrated Statute,[4] by which this system of the legal arrangement of wages was introduced, has rightly been called a monumental work of legislation.[5] " Taken in conjunction with the Poor Law of the same year, which was, however, subsequently modified, it forms a great system for controlling both the employed and the unemployed; all the experience of preceding reigns is gathered together, and the principal statute was so well framed that it continued to be maintained for more than two centuries." [6] It certainly had an immense, controlling influence upon the destinies of the working classes, though opinions have differed widely as to whether that influence was beneficial or otherwise. Before discussing this point, however, we will briefly examine the provisions of this famous Act.

The preamble is remarkable in that, unlike all previous Statutes of Labourers, it shows a tender concern for the welfare of the labourer, and expresses a fear that his wages may occasionally be too low. It states that " the wages and allowances rated and limited in many of the said

---

[1] From the proclamation of Elizabeth for the county of Rutland in 1563. Rogers, *Hist. Agric.*, iv. 121.

[2] Above, p. 173.   [3] Rogers, *Hist. Agric.*, iv. 757.

[4] The Act 5 Eliz., c. 4 (1563).

[5] Cunningham, *Growth of Industry*, ii. 38.   [6] *Ib.*

statutes (*i.e.*, the old Statutes of Labourers) are in divers places too small and not answerable to this time, respecting the advancement of prices of all things belonging to the said servants and labourers," and "the said laws cannot conveniently, without the great grief and burden of the poor labourer and hired man, be put into good and due execution." This sudden change of attitude on the part of the legislature is most instructive, and even has its humorous side. It shows a complete change of tactics in dealing with the working classes, but one cannot help feeling some lurking doubt as to whether all these honeyed words were genuine. After all, the object of this statute was the same as that of the older ones, namely, to give fixity to wages ; and it is so unusual to find one class legislating in favour of another without some adequate motive that one cannot help thinking that there was something behind all this generosity. Nor is the motive far to seek. It was to place the regulation of wages not merely in the hands of Parliament, whose methods were necessarily slow and cumbersome, but in the hands of the employers of labour, or at least in the hands of a class who would sympathise with employers. Briefly, wages were in future to be fixed by the justices of the peace in quarter sessions, and both employers and employed were bound to abide by the assessments thus made. There could be little doubt that the employers would abide by them readily enough, for the local justices of the peace were sure to be either employers themselves or drawn from the same rank in life ; and the severe penalties imposed upon those who disobeyed the assessment were hardly likely to be incurred by any except the working classes. The generous preamble of the Statute thus resulted in an enactment which, if it could only be enforced, was likely to place the workmen entirely at the mercy of their employers. Of course employers might be, and no doubt often were, men of good and honest heart, and wishful to do the best for their labourers; but it was, to say the least, placing a great temptation in their way to give them the authority to fix a rate of wages to which all were compelled by law to adhere. It is true that this assessment of wages was no hard and fast rule, but was to vary itself with the fluctuations in the prices of provisions ; and the inventors of this kindly scheme expressed a pious hope that "it might yield the hired person, both in the time of scarcity and in the time of plenty, a convenient proportion of wages." But it is to be noted that they added nothing to the statute to make this hope effectual in practice. All they remark is that the justices should take into account, in fixing wages, the price of food " and other circumstances necessary to be considered "—a somewhat vague recommendation ; and the " hired person " had very little voice in the matter.

It may be going too far to characterise this assessment scheme—as one outspoken writer does—as " a conspiracy concocted by the law and carried out by the parties interested in its success," [1] and we may give the employers and legislators of Elizabethan days credit for the highest and kindest intentions in a general sort of way ; but no one except a Utopian optimist can shut his eyes to the fact that this ingenious system gave even the best of employers a direct interest in keeping the assessment of wages for his district as low as possible ; and, human nature being what it is, no one can be surprised if his pocket often tended to get the better of his generosity. And, as a matter of fact, this was of course the case. It is absurd to talk about our forefathers as if they were more than human ; and experience of human nature shows that it is liable to succumb to temptations far less than those which the Act of Elizabeth placed before its administrators.

§ 154. *The Working of the Assessment System.*

Modern historians are nothing if not controversial, and consequently no one need be surprised to find that this Statute is alternately belauded as having been intended to do a real kindness to the working classes and decried as a legal conspiracy to do them an injury. This aspect of the question has been already dealt with sufficiently, but the same

[1] Thorold Rogers, *Six Centuries*, p. 398.

controversy exists as to whether the Act was ever properly effective. It is amusing to find apologists for it declaring that, after all, it was never really enforced ;[1] and, amid the usual contradictions of economic as of other history, it is occasionally hard to find the truth. But it certainly seems to be the case that, in spite of the continued increase in the price of the necessaries of life, the wages of labour did conform to the justices' assessments, and that these assessments were too low to give the labourer an opportunity of really comfortable subsistence.[2] The effect of the Statute was not felt so keenly as long as his wages were supplemented by the ownership of a small plot of land or by rights of common ; but when the enclosures of the eighteenth century took these away from him, the labourer was indeed badly off.[3] At any rate, if the intention of the Act of 1563 was really to raise wages, it was a failure in this respect, for " the machinery it created " (as an historian naively remarks [4] who takes a very favourable view of it) "had not sufficed to raise wages according to the scarcity of the times " in the century following. This is not surprising ; the marvel would have been that wages should have risen when the administrators of the Act were so closely interested in keeping them down. But there can be no dispute that, whether owing to the assessment or not, wages steadily declined in the sixteenth and seventeenth centuries, taken as a whole, as the following tables [5] will show, though, of course, in so long a time there were naturally periods of slight improvement. The only question that arises is : how was it that for once a Statute of Labourers achieved its object when similar statutes had in previous reigns been so ineffectual ?

The reasons for this are several. The labourer had been already weakened (as we saw [6]) in the reigns of Elizabeth's father and brother by the debasement of the currency, the change from tillage to sheep-farming, and the

[1] Cunningham, *Growth of Industry*, ii. 199, 200.
[2] Rogers, *Six Centuries*, p. 353.   [3] *Ib.*
[4] Cunningham, *Growth of Industry*, ii. 195.
[5] Compiled from Rogers, *Six Centuries*, ch. xiv. pp. 387-398.
[6] Above, pp. 206-218.

TABLE OF ASSESSMENTS IN SIXTEENTH AND SEVENTEENTH CENTURIES.
(DAILY WAGES.)

Year.	County.	Agricultural Labour.			Artisans.		Price of Corn per qr.	Remarks.
		Summer.	Winter.	Harvest.	Summer.	Winter.		
1533 (June)	England generally	4d.	...	...	6d. to 7d.	...	7/8	
1564 (June)	Rutland	7d.	6d.	8d. to 10d.	9d.	8d. Master Workmen about 1/-	19/9¾	
1593 (April)	Yorks (E. Riding)	5d.	4d.	8d. to 10d.	8d.	7d.	18/4¼	
1593	Chester	4d.	...	...	6d.	...	18/4½	
1597	Do.	4d.	...	...	6d.	...	56/10½	{Famine year, but wages do not rise accordingly. The wages are calculated from a yearly basis.
1610 (April)	Rutland	7d.	6d.	8d. to 10d.	9d. to 10d.	8d.	40/4	This assessment lasted till 1684.
1651	Essex	1/2 to 1/	...	1/6 to 1/10	1/5 to 1/6	1/2 to 1/6	51/4	A rise in wages.
1661 (Easter)	Do.	1/2	1/-	1/6 to 1/10	...	1/2 to 1/4-	70/6	Fall : purchasing power reduced.
1682	Suffolk	1/-	10d.	1/8 to 10d.	1/6	1/4	43/8	
1684 (April)	Warwick	8d.	7d.	1/- to 8d.	1/- to 8d.	11d. to 7d.	42/0½	Fall in wages.
1725 (May)	Lancs.	10d. to 1/-	9d. to 10d.	1/3 to 10d.	1/- maximum	...	46/1	

Note.—Dr Cunningham, *Growth of English Industry,* ii. 43, 195, 359, remarks that the assessment of wages was practically inoperative at almost all times. He quotes the preamble to the Act 1 James I., c. 6, which complains that Elizabeth's Act was in 1604 not regarded, and seems to think that altogether it had little effect. It is quite possible that assessments were not *regularly* made, and when made were occasionally adhered to, but in face of the fact that so many exist (*cf.* Rogers, *Hist. Agric. and Prices,* v. 618 and vi. 685, and Cunningham, *Growth of Industry,* ii. 199, *notes*), it seems certain that they must have been made fairly often, and even if not *strictly* adhered to, they would form a kind of standard to which wages generally would approximate. At any rate, it is a significant fact that real wages were exceedingly low during the latter part of the sixteenth and early part of the seventeenth century (Cunningham, *u. s.,* ii. 43), and that wages were never raised by Elizabeth's Act (*ib.,* ii. 195); and in Henry Best's *Rural Economy in Yorkshire* in 1641 (*ib.,* ii. 198) it is mentioned that "the constable is to let them (*i.e.,* master and servant) know what the statute will allow," which seems to show that, even when not absolutely adhered to with strictness, the statute had a very considerable influence in regulating wages. Later in the eighteenth century it fell into desuetude, like other regulations of industry, though it was never forgotten (*cf.* the second resolution of the famous meeting of the Berkshire justices at Speenhamland; Cunningham, *u. s.,* ii. 494. But for this see below.

R

numerous enclosures of land. These all had their due effect upon his condition. But there were two other causes of equal power operating at the same time. (1) The conditions of industry had already largely changed; men were less bound to the land than formerly, having been in some cases driven off it by sheep-farms and enclosures, and in others attracted from it by the progress of manufacturing industries. There was, therefore, a much larger class than formerly dependent entirely on wages,[1] with no land of their own to fall back upon, and consequently compelled to take what they could get from the nearest employer. This was in itself a source of weakness; and this weakness was increased by another cause. (2) The old unions of workmen had decayed, the craft gilds had become obsolete or effete,[2] and there was nothing to bind the working-classes together in self-defence. The combined action[3] that resulted in the Peasants' Revolt of the fourteenth century had become a thing so completely of the past that it had fallen into oblivion; and not only that, but the law had now been strained into that iniquitous doctrine of "conspiracy" which stamped all efforts of workmen to improve their condition as *ipso facto* illegal. It was accounted as a "conspiracy,"[4] and, therefore, a legal offence, for workmen to enter into any associations to raise, or endeavour to raise, the rate of wages; and workmen who entered into such illegal combinations were punishable by fine or imprisonment. Meetings held for similar purposes were punishable in the same way, while every inducement was given to a workman to turn traitor and betray his fellows by the promise of indemnity to offenders who informed against their associates. For centuries[5] this tyrannical measure disgraced our statute books; and yet we are asked to believe that the legislators, who framed this law and invented the doctrine of conspiracy to supplement the scheme of assessment of wages, were actuated only

---

[1] Above, p. 252.   [2] Above, pp. 189, 207-209, and *cf.* p. 247.
[3] Above, p. 163.
[4] *Cf.* the Act 2 and 3 Edward VI., c. 15, and the 40 Geo. III., c. 106. The clauses 18, 19, and 20 of the 5 Eliz., c. 4, were also strained to support this doctrine; *cf.* Rogers, *Six Centuries*, pp. 397, 399.
[5] Till the 6 Geo. IV., c. 129; see below, pp. 416-420.

by their kindly concern for the welfare of the working man. But, leaving intentions and motives out of the question, it is easy to see how powerfully the foregoing causes must have operated in depressing the condition of the labourer, and thus rendering it easy to enforce the Elizabethan code of labour laws.

§ 155. *The Law of Apprenticeship.*

There are, however, certain clauses in this statute which are noticeable as regulating the apprenticeship system. In agriculture, any person who had half a ploughland in tillage might take a boy to serve as an apprentice in husbandry till he was twenty-one years of age.   In crafts, a period of seven years was laid down as the time of apprenticeship ; and in order that apprenticeship might be a reality in its educational aspect, every master who had more than three apprentices was required to have one journeyman for every apprentice over this number.   By this means masters would be prevented from getting work done by apprentices which ought to be done by more qualified workmen.   These regulations applied to the whole country, and not merely, as in mediæval times, to trades which had gilds. It is interesting to note that certain limitations were made which were evidently intended to benefit the agricultural interest; and once again one cannot refrain from a suspicion that the landed classes, who constituted the majority in Parliament, were not actuated entirely by motives of pure benevolence to others.   We find that persons engaged in agriculture, or in any trades connected therewith (such as smiths, wheelwrights, and also the weavers of linen and household cloth [1]) might take any apprentice they could find.   But artisans in corporate towns and market towns were more restricted ; they could not take any one who was not the son of a freeman of such town, and the apprentice taken by them was not to be withdrawn from agriculture ; while merchants and shopkeepers in corporate towns were restricted to the sons of " forty-shilling freeholders," and

---

[1] See § 23 of the 5 Eliz., c. 4.   This shows how manufactures and agriculture were often combined.   See above, p. 237, and note there.

those in market towns to the sons of "sixty-shilling freeholders." It has been said that "as a scheme of technical
education the regulations for artisans were admirably suited
to the needs of the times"; [1] and there is no doubt that in
many respects these regulations were beneficial. But it is
always a suspicious circumstance when legislators belonging
to any particular class introduce restrictions that would
naturally benefit the interests of their own order; and it is
very obvious that what was sought in these apprenticeship
clauses was quite as much the convenience of the agricultural interest as the promotion of a scheme of technical
education. Neither the landed gentry nor the agriculturists
whom they represented need be blamed for their action.
Any other class in their position would no doubt have done
the same. But it is superfluous, not to say absurd, to
imagine that Elizabethan Parliamentarians were actuated,
any more than other men, solely by a desire for the welfare
of others.

It should be added, when considering the effects of the
apprenticeship system as thus laid down under Elizabeth,
that in after years there grew up a vast number of trades
that were never touched by this Act at all, since it only
applied to those actually in existence at the time of its
passing. The trades which arose in later times were outside its operations altogether, and were usually known as
the "incorporated trades," because they were regulated not
by this Act but under patents granted to those who invented
a new manufacture or improved an old one.

§ 156. *The Elizabethan Poor Law.*

Closely connected with all this industrial regulation,
which we have now briefly reviewed, was the new legislation rendered necessary by the steady increase of pauperism
—a phenomenon all the more remarkable because it was
also accompanied by a rapid growth of national wealth.
The spectacle of Dives and Lazarus existing side by side is
in our own day so common as to excite little remark; and
the poor-rate is regarded with the same equanimity—or

[1] Cunningham, *Growth of Industry*, ii. 41.

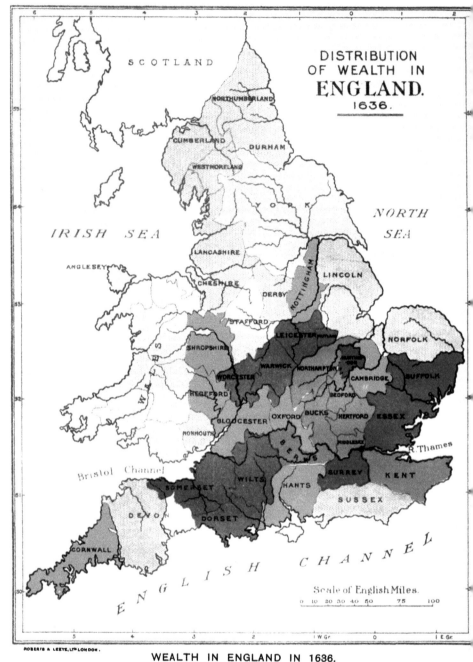

DISTRIBUTION OF WEALTH IN ENGLAND. 1636.

ROBERTS & LEETE, LTD LONDON.

WEALTH IN ENGLAND IN 1636.

This Map is based on the well-known assessment for ship money, and gives the assessment per square mile. It should be compared with that opposite page 196.

1.	Counties assessed at £6 to £7 per square mile					...	Dark Brown.
2.	,,	,,	£5 to £6	,,	,,	...	...	Dark Green.
3.	,,	·	,,	£4 to £5	,,	,,	...	....	Dark Red.
4.	,,	,,	£3 to £4	,,	,,	...	...	Light Brown.
5.	,,	,,	£2 to £3	,,	,,	...	...	Light Red.
6.	,,	,,	under £2	,,	,,	...	...	Light Green.

hopelessness—as the charges for water or police. But it was still of sufficient novelty in the reigns of Henry VIII. and his children to cause English legislators considerable uneasiness. We have already seen (pp. 195, 205) how it was dealt with in former days, and later, in the last year [1] of Edward VI., two collectors were appointed in every parish, whose business it was to obtain from every person of substance a promise of alms for the relief of the poor, to enter such promises in a book and collect the money, and to relieve the poor with it. In the beginning of Elizabeth's reign it was found that further pressure was needed to make people give, and therefore in 1563 another Act [2] was passed, by which a person who was unwilling to contribute to the relief of the poor, and who would not be affected even by the exhortations of his bishop, had to appear before the Justices of the Quarter Sessions and submit to a tax or assessment imposed upon him by them, or be thrown into prison. The provision for the relief of the poor was, in fact, altogether changing in character. It was no longer a free act of Christian charity, but a compulsory contribution towards the mitigation of a social evil, a contribution of the same nature as the nineteenth century poor-rate. There was now "only a step from the process under which a reluctant subscriber to the poor law was assessed by the Justices, and imprisoned on refusal, to a general assessment of all property." [3] This step was taken by the celebrated Poor Law of Elizabeth [4] in 1601. This famous and long-lived [5] Act prescribed the levy of a compulsory poor-rate in every parish, designated the kind of property on which the rate was to be levied, and inflicted penalties on those who disobeyed its provisions. Work was to be provided for those who would or could work, and relief for those who could not; poor children were to be trained to some craft; and the idle were to be punished. Such was the remarkable Act with which, as has been so justly pointed out, the history of English labour has been

---

[1] By the 5 and 6 Ed. VI., c. 2.   [2] The 5 Eliz., c. 3.
[3] Rogers, *Six Centuries*, p. 420.   [4] The 43 Eliz., c. 3.
[5] It was only meant, however, at first to be temporary, but it was renewed in the next Parliament, and at last made permanent by the 16 Charles I., c. 4.

ever since its enactment most intimately associated.[1] At this space of time it is hard to look upon it with eyes unprejudiced, either favourably or unfavourably ; but possibly the best comment upon it has been supplied by its own subsequent history, which has never been able to record its success. One of its greatest defects has been the lack of any adequate system of providing employment for the poor, and this has been the weak point of the whole English Poor-Law code. Work was indeed meant to be provided by this Act of 1601, but its local administrators never set themselves seriously to raise a fund and find such work for the unemployed[2] by providing a stock of hemp, wool, iron, and other materials.[3] The training of children as parish apprentices led to their ill-treatment,[4] and the system of providing relief from the rates developed into one of the most foolish of abuses.[5] With these points we shall deal later, as their full effect becomes more visible ; but there is one which requires notice before we go any further.

In the third clause of this historic Act there is a provision, that if a parish is not rich enough to maintain its own poor entirely, the deficiency, if any, in the rates shall be supplemented from the rest of the hundred.[6] This seems at first sight a reasonable provision, and was probably inserted by the framers of the Act as requisite in view of a very possible contingency. It was not acted upon at first to any great extent,[7] but subsequently it became a favourite instrument of employers of labour for reducing wages, first by lowering them in their own parish to such a point that it was necessary to give the labourer an enormous amount of relief out of the rates, and then by throwing the burden of this relief upon surrounding parishes.[8] The use thus made of this clause in after years was certainly ingenious, for a large proportion of a labourer's wages would thus come out of the pockets of the general public, while a corresponding saving was effected

---

[1] Rogers, *Six Centuries*, p. 421. For various views see Cunningham, *Growth of Industry*, ii. 58-61, and Fowle, *Poor Law*, p. 58.

[2] Cunningham, *Growth of Industry*, ii. 61.

[3] *Cf.* the 18 Eliz., c. 3.   [4] See below, p. 388.   [5] Below, pp. 412-414.

[6] 43 Eliz., c. 3, § 3.   [7] Fowle, *Poor Law*, p. 58. [8] Below, p. 412.

by his employer. The ingenuity of the arrangement is perhaps more conspicuous than its honesty: of that my readers can judge for themselves ; but it merely shows, as has been remarked before, that human nature can rarely resist a temptation which is addressed to its pocket. The action of this apparently innocent clause is seen more clearly in the eighteenth century,[1] but it is well to notice it here, in its place, as a weak spot in an Act that was never particularly strong.

§ 157. *Population*.

We may now conclude our survey of Elizabethan England with a brief notice of the then existing number of inhabitants. The marked improvement in agriculture and the increase of wealth brought with them, at the close of the sixteenth century, an equally marked increase of population. We saw that at the time of Domesday the population of England was under two millions.[2] When the poll-tax of 1377 was levied, in the last year of Edward III.'s reign, it had not much increased, being at most not more than two and a quarter or two and a half millions, according to careful calculations based upon the returns of this tax.[3] But by the end of Elizabeth's reign it had risen rapidly to five million souls,[4] but probably did not increase so quickly during the next hundred and fifty years. The bulk of the population was still in the southern half of the country,[5] although the north was now becoming more prosperous, owing to the extension of manufactures. It will be seen that England was by no means overcrowded, and yet people were found who complained of the increase of population. William Harrison,[6] in his *Description of England*, remarks : " Some also do grudge at the great increase of

[1] Below, pp. 412-414.　　　　　　　　　[2] Above, pp. 66, 106.
[3] Topham, in *Archaeologia*, vii. 337.
[4] Rogers, *Six Centuries*, 463, says still only 2½ millions, but if so it rose very rapidly to 5½ millions by 1688. King, in Davenant's *Works*, ii. 184.
[5] This may be easily seen in the assessment made later by Charles I. for ship-money in 1636. See also Rogers' valuable chapter vii. on *The distribution of wealth in England at different epochs* in his *Economic Interpretation of History*, p. 138 *sqq.* ; and in *Hist. Agric.*, v. 66-125.
[6] Page 125 (Camelot series edition) ; Bk. III., ch. 5, of 1577 edn.

people in these days, thinking a necessary brood of cattle far better than a superfluous augmentation of mankind. But," he adds, severely, " I can liken such men best unto the Pope or the Devil," and adds that in case of invasion they will find " that a wall of men is far better than stacks of corn and bags of money." Even without the fear of invasion before our eyes, it is well for us to-day not to forget this latter sentence in the modern, international race for wealth.

CHAPTER XVII

§ 158. *Résumé of Progress since Thirteenth Century.*

IT will be remembered that great agricultural changes
had taken place since Henry III.'s reign. For a century
or so after his death (1272) the landowner was also a
cultivator, living upon his land and owning a large amount
of capital in the form of stock, which he let out under the
stock and land lease system.[1] But after the Great Plague
(1348) this method of cultivation by capitalist landowners
largely ceased, except in the case of sheep-farming; the
landowner became generally a mere rent receiver; and
agriculture consequently suffered to some extent. Marling,
for instance, fell into disuse, and the breed of sheep, it is
said, deteriorated somewhat.[2] The great feature of the
change was the transformation of large tracts of arable land
into pasture for sheep, and the growth of enclosures for the
sake of the same animal. This process, however, seems to
have ceased to some extent about the last decade of the sixteenth century,[3] and enclosures were afterwards made, as
we shall see, for another reason. The landlords, meanwhile,
rapidly proceeded to raise their rents, till, in the sixteenth
century, extortionate renting became so common that Bishop
Latimer,[4] and Fitzherbert, the author of the useful work on

---

[1] Above, pp. 114, 186.

[2] Rogers, *Six Centuries*, p. 442, who quotes Fitzherbert; and *Hist.
Agric.*, v. 52.

[3] Cunningham, *Growth of Industry*, ii. 52 and 180. He gives 1592 as
about the date of cessation, with a slight increase of enclosures again
about 1597 (Spedding, *Letters and Life of Bacon*, i. 158), but afterwards
enclosures for sheep practically stopped.

[4] *Latimer's Sermons* (Parker Society), p. 99.

surveying,[1] complained about it both in sermons and other writings. For all these reasons English agriculture did not improve very materially between the days of Henry III. and of Elizabeth. But in this queen's reign, as we saw, several improvements were made under the influence of foreign refugees. For the inhabitants of the Low Countries and Holland have been our pioneers not only in commerce and finance, but in agriculture also.[2] It was these people who now introduced into England the cultivation of winter roots[3] (the want of which, it will be remembered, greatly embarrassed the English farmer in the mediæval winter), and in the eighteenth century that of artificial grasses.[4] The introduction of hops also was of great importance.[5]

§ 159. Progress in James I.'s Reign.   Influence of Landlords.

Of course the greatest industrial progress of this period was made in the direction of foreign trade, and in James's reign progress in agriculture was slow as compared with that in commerce, but it was substantial—substantial enough, at any rate, for the landlords to exact an increased competitive rent, as we know from Norden's work, *The Surveyor's Dialogue* (1607).[6] Norden also notes[7] that tenants were eager to take land even at high rents, and this shows that they expected to make good profits. Whether they always made them is another question. But this development of competitive, as contrasted with the old customary, rents is certainly worthy of attention. It was, however, complained that the action of the landlords tended to discourage progress, for when a tenant wished to renew a lease he was threatened with dispossession if he did not pay an increased rent for the very improvements he had made himself.[8]

---

[1] Rogers, *Hist. Agric.*, v. 41.   [2] *Hartlib's Legacy*, p. 54, and *passim*.
[3] Weston, *Discourse of Husbandrie used in Brabant* (1652), p. 25 ; Worlidge, *Systema Agriculturæ*, p. 46 ; Rogers, *Six Centuries*, p. 453.
[4] Rogers, *Six Centuries*, p. 453.   [5] Rogers, *Hist. Agric.*, iv. 57.
[6] *Dialogue*, p. 9.
[7] *Ib.* Norden, by the way, is corroborated by Best, author of *Rural Economy in Yorkshire in* 1641, p. 129. Lands (he says) which had let formerly at 2s., then at 2s. 6d., and again at 3s., had now risen to thrice as much.   [8] See the Preface to *Hartlib's Legacy*, probably by Dymock.

Still, from the facts given by Norden, and also by another writer—Markham, the author of *The English Husbandman* (1613)—it is evident that there was considerable improvement, development, and variety now shown in English agriculture.[1] Arable farming was prosecuted with increased energy,[2] and both to farmers as well as to merchants the seventeenth century brought increased prosperity.[3] The special, characteristic feature of the seventeenth century is the utilisation of the fallow for roots,[4] though these had been known in gardens in the previous century.[5] The most fertile land was to be found in Huntingdon, Bedford, and Cambridge shires, the next best being in Northampton, Kent, Essex, Berkshire, and Hertfordshire.[6] Land was still largely cultivated in common fields,[7] and was, of course, much subdivided. But the practice was now increasing of making enclosures, not as before, for the sake of sheep-farming, but in order to carry on an improved method of tillage.[8] It was recommended by agricultural writers,[9] and their recommendations seem to have been widely adopted, though it is very doubtful whether many of those who enclosed land had personally read their books, for agriculture owes but little to literature. The enclosures thus made for tillage certainly conduced to the improvement of agriculture, though in many cases it is to be feared that the interests of those who had a right to common lands were disregarded, and both the seventeenth and eighteenth centuries witnessed steady progress.

§ 160. *Writers on Agriculture. Improvements. Game.*

One noticeable improvement is the attention now paid to the various kinds of manures,[10] on which subject Markham

---

[1] See Rogers, *Hist. Agric.*, v. pp. 40 to 65.

[2] Cunningham, *Growth of Industry*, ii. 185.

[3] Rogers, *Six Centuries*, 459.   [4] *Ib.*, 468.   [5] Above, p. 249.

[6] Markham, quoted by Rogers, *Hist. Agric.*, v. 55.

[7] It remained so in numerous instances till after the middle of the eighteenth century. Toynbee, *Industrial Revolution*, p. 39.

[8] Cunningham, *Growth of Industry*, ii. 181.

[9] *Hartlib's Legacy*, p. 54; Worlidge, *Systema*, p. 10; Taylor, *Common Good*, p. 13.

[10] Cunningham, *Growth of Industry*, ii. 185; Rogers, *Hist. Agric.*, v. 52.

was the first to write specially, though there are several other authors who have dealt with it.[1] The fact that agriculture was now made the topic of various treatises proves that important development was taking place. Besides the works already mentioned, we have the *Systema Agriculturæ* by Worlidge, a farmer of Hampshire, the second edition of which appeared in 1675. He is a strong advocate of enclosures, as against the old common field system, on the plea that the former is more conducive to high farming ; but he also is in favour of small holdings thus enclosed.[2] Though at first local and somewhat spasmodic, and hindered no doubt by uncertainty of tenure[3] and by the landlord's power of appropriating the results of increased skill on the part of the tenant, under the head of "indestructible powers of the soil," yet the progress made was sufficient to increase very largely the population of England,[4] an increase aided also by the growth of manufactures. A curious fact in the agriculture of the seventeenth century may be here mentioned in passing—that is, the existence of a very large amount of waste land, and the use made of it for purposes of breeding game.[5] At that time it is evident that killing game was not the exclusive right of the landowners, but was a common privilege. Large quantities of game were sold, and at a cheap price, and "fowling" must evidently have been an important item in the farmer's and labourer's means of livelihood.

§ 161. *Drainage of the Fens.*

A most important feature in the development of agriculture in the Eastern counties was the drainage of the fens—*i.e.*, all that large district which extends inward from the Wash into the counties of Lincoln, Cambridge, Northampton, Huntingdon, Norfolk, and Suffolk. This district

---

[1] Blith, *Husbandry*, 60 ; Plato, *Jewel House*, 21. For an excellent account of these writers on agriculture see Rogers, *Hist. Agric.*, v. pp. 40 to 65, frequently copied by other authors.

[2] Rogers, *Hist. Agric.*, v. 62.

[3] Plattes, essay on Husbandry, quoted by Rogers, *Hist. Agric.*, v. 56.

[4] Rogers, *Six Centuries*, p. 463 ; *Hist. Agric.*, v. 64.

[5] Rogers, *Hist. Agric.*, v. 27.

had been partly reclaimed by the Romans, and had been for a time a fertile country.[1] But in the time of the Domesday Book it was once again a mere marsh, owing to incursions of the sea, which the English at that time had not the ability to prevent. Although even in 1436, and subsequently, partial attempts had been made to reclaim this vast area, the first effectual effort was begun only in 1634, by the Earl of Bedford, who received 95,000 acres of the reclaimed land as a reward for his undertaking.[2] The contract was fulfilled under the superintendence of the engineer Vermuyden, a Dutchman, in 1649, and a corporation was formed to manage the "Bedford level," as it was now called, in 1688. The reclaiming of so much land naturally increased the prosperity of the counties in which it stood, and their agriculture flourished considerably in consequence, Bedfordshire for instance being now the most exclusively agricultural county in the kingdom. Similar operations were effected in Hatfield Chase.[3]

§ 162. *Rise of Price of Corn and of Rent.*

The price of corn, meanwhile, was now steadily rising. From 1401 to 1540—*i.e.*, before the rise in prices and the debasements of the coinage—the average price had been a farthing under six shillings per quarter;[4] after prices had recovered from their inflation, and settled down to a general average once more, taking the price from 1603 to 1702, corn was forty-one shillings per quarter.[5] The average produce had apparently declined, or, at any rate, had not increased since the fifteenth and before the improvements of the seventeenth century. In the former period it was about twelve bushels per acre,[6] and in

---

[1] See article on *Bedford Level* in Chambers' *Encyclopædia* (ed. 1888), and Denton, *Fifteenth Century*, pp. 140-141; also Smiles, *Lives of the Engineers*, Vol. I., p. 10.

[2] See more fully Gardiner, *History of England*, ch. lxxxiv., Vol. VIII., p. 295. As the rent was, after the draining, about 30s. an acre, the earl's reward was very substantial.

[3] *Ib.*, Vol. VIII. p. 292. This was in 1626, and Vermuyden was knighted for his efforts (1629); *cf.* Smiles, *Lives of the Engineers*, Vol. I., for Life and Works of Vermuyden.   [4] Rogers, *Hist. Agric.*, iv. 292.

[5] *Ib.*, v. 276.   [6] Rogers, *Econ. Interp.*, p, 53.

the fourteenth century eleven bushels ;[1] but Gregory King, writing in the seventeenth century, only gives ten or eleven bushels as the average of his time.[2] His estimate, however, is doubted.[3] At the same time, rent had risen from the sixpence per acre of the fifteenth century to four shillings,[4] according to Professor Rogers,[5] or even 5s. 6d., according to King,[6] who says the gains of the farmer of his time were very small, and that rents were more than doubled between 1600 and 1699. We will reserve the topic of the rise of rent, however, for a separate section, and keep to the agricultural developments of the period.

§ 163. *Special Features of the Eighteenth Century.*
Popularity of Agriculture.

As the use of winter roots had been the special feature of the seventeenth century, so the feature of the eighteenth was the extension of artificial pasture and the increased use of clover, sainfoin, and rye-grass ;[7] not, of course, that these had been hitherto unknown, but now their seeds were regularly bought and used by any farmer who knew his business. At first, like all other processes of agriculture, the development was very slow and gradual, but it went on steadily nevertheless. A great stimulus to progress was given by the fact that the English gentlemen of the eighteenth century developed quite a passion for agriculture as a hobby, and it became a fashionable pursuit for all people of any means, citizens and professional men joining in it as a kind of bye-industry, in addition to the farmers and landowners, who made it their business.[8] Arthur Young, the great agricultural writer of this century, declares that " the farming tribe is now made up of all classes, from a duke to an apprentice." It should also be added that in the eighteenth

---

[1] Rogers, *Six Centuries*, pp. 476 and 442.
[2] In Davenant's *Works*, ii. 217.   [3] Rogers, *Hist. Agric.*, v. 783.
[4] Taylor, the author of the *Common Good* (1652), gives (p. 15) 3s. 4d. per acre as a typical rent in his time.
[5] *Hist. Agric.*, v. 92.
[6] Quoted in Rogers, *Hist. Agric.*, v. 92, who gives 4s. 1½d. as the average rental of the Belvoir estate.
[7] Rogers, *Six Centuries*, p. 468.   [8] *Ib.*, p. 470.

century more capital was being applied to the pursuit
of agriculture. The wealth gained by the commercial
progress of the day was largely put into the land, and the
great revolution that now took place in English agriculture
was carried on under the influence of men of wealth.[1] But
two important mistakes were made in the eighteenth century,
and they have not ceased to exist in the nineteenth, increasing very largely the distress under which English
agriculture has for some time (1895) been labouring. They
are the mistakes of occupying too much land with insufficient
capital, and of not keeping regular and detailed accounts.[2]
Improvements also were not universal, but were often confined, at least at first, to scattered parts of the country.[3]
Progress was to begin with (say from 1700 to 1760)[4] rather
slow, but afterwards became very rapid, and wealthy landowners made great efforts to improve their estates, succeeding
also thereby in raising their rents and increasing their profits.[5]
They thus became in a way the pioneers of agricultural progress, the principal result of their efforts being seen in the increased number and quality of the stock now kept on farms.

§ 164. *Improvements of Cattle, and in the Productiveness
of Land. Statistics.*

The extended cultivation of winter roots, clover, and
other grasses naturally made it far easier for the farmer to
feed his animals in the winter; and the improvement in
stock followed closely upon the improvement in fodder.[6]
The abundance of stock, too, had again a beneficial result

[1] Cunningham, *Growth of Industry*, ii. 362.
[2] Arthur Young, quoted in Rogers, *Six Centuries*, p. 471.
[3] Toynbee, *Industrial Revolution*, p. 41.   [4] *Ib.*, p. 45.
[5] Cunningham, *Growth of Industry*, ii. 363, 364, following Young, praises
these wealthy landowners for their efforts, and expresses surprise that
later writers have attacked such men for raising rents and for other reasons.
No doubt the landowners are entitled to every praise for their spirited
efforts, but to call a man (as Young practically does) the greatest of
patriots for following the obvious course of enlightened self-interest is
little less than absurd. A landlord who makes a profit out of his land by
improvements in husbandry deserves such a title as little, or as much, as a
manufacturer who derives a handsome profit from a new machine.
[6] Rogers, *Six Centuries*, p. 475.

in the production of increased quantities of manure, and the utilisation of fertilisers was more scientifically developed. The useful, though costly, process of marling was again revived, and was advocated by Arthur Young; soils were also treated with clay, chalk, or lime.[1] So great was the improvement thus made, that the productiveness of land in the eighteenth century rose to four times that of the thirteenth century, when five bushels or eight bushels of corn per acre was the average.[2] Stock, also, was similarly improved; an eighteenth century fatted ox often weighed over 800 lbs.,[3] while hitherto, from the fourteenth to the end of the seventeenth century, the weight had not been usually much above 400 lbs. The weight of the fleece of sheep had also increased quite four times.[4] Population being even then small, a considerable quantity of corn was exported, the British farmer being also protected from foreign competition by the corn laws (made in Charles II.'s reign),[5] forbidding importation of corn, except when it rose to famine prices. Young[6] estimated the cultivated acreage of the country at 32,000,000 acres, arable and pasture being in equal proportions, whereas King[7] had put it at only 22,000,000 in the seventeenth century; its value (at thirty-three and one-half years' purchase) was, says Young, £536,000,000. The value of stock he places at nearly £110,000,000, and estimates the wheat and rye crop at over 9,000,000 quarters per annum, barley at 11,500,000 quarters, and oats at 10,250,000 quarters. The rent of land had risen in Young's time to nearly ten shillings an acre.[8]

[1] Rogers, *Six Centuries*, p. 476.

[2] *Ib.*, 477; *cf.* also Young, who gives 25 bushels an acre (in 1770), while in France it was only 18 bushels. *Travels in France*, i. 354.

[3] *Cf.* Eden, *State of the Poor*, i. 334; Toynbee, *Industrial Revolution*, 44, but Rogers, *Six Centuries*, p. 477, gives 1200 lbs.   [4] *Ib.*, p. 477.

[5] See the 22 Charles II., c. 13, by which a duty of 16s. a qr. was placed on wheat when at or below 53s. 4d., and a duty of 8s. when it was between 53s. 4d. and 80s. a qr. Other kinds of grain were similarly treated. We have seen that the average price of wheat at this time was 41s. a qr.: hence the effect of this law may be easily perceived.

[6] *Northern Tour*, iv. 340-341, but *cf. Eastern Tour*, iv. 455.

[7] *Observations upon the State and Condition of England*, 1696; printed in Chalmers' *Estimate*, p. 52.

[8] *Cf.* Rogers, *Six Centuries*, p. 477; but also *cf. Hist. Agric.*, v. 29.

§ 165. *Survivals of Primitive Culture. Common Fields.*

With all these improvements, however, rural England, even as late as the middle of the eighteenth century, retained in its husbandry many traces of a more primitive state of things. Again and again the permanence of ancient institutions and methods surprises us, here as elsewhere, just as Arthur Young was surprised in his tours through his own country. Thus at Boynton (Yorks) Young found remains of extensive culture ;[1] in other cases the old two-field or three-field system was carried on ; as, for instance, near Ecclesfield in Hallamshire, and at Beverley in Yorkshire.[2] Throughout considerable districts, in fact, the agrarian system of the middle ages still remained in force ;[3] and naturally, compared with the newer methods of agriculture, it yielded but poor results. " Never," says Arthur Young, " were more miserable crops seen than the spring ones in the common fields ; absolutely beneath contempt."[4] The causes of this backward state of things were many, but all naturally arose from the difficulties inherent in the common field system when some of those who used it had surpassed their co-workers in agricultural progress.[5] For one thing the same course of crops was nearly always necessary, and no proper rotation was feasible, the only possible alteration being to vary the proportions of different white-straw crops.[6]

A man of enterprise was therefore greatly hindered ; for if he worked with his neighbours in these open fields he was compelled to follow a traditional but unprogressive course of husbandry against his better judgment. Then, again, much time was lost by labourers and cattle travelling to many dispersed pieces of land from one end of the parish to another.[7] There were continuous quarrels among neighbours about rights of pasture in the meadows,

[1] *Northern Tour*, ii. 7.   [2] *Ib.*, ii. 1, *cf.* also i. 126.
[3] Toynbee, *Industrial Revolution*, p. 39.
[4] *Southern Tour*, p. 384 (ed. 1772).
[5] *Cf.* Toynbee, *Indust. Revolution*, p. 40, and Cunningham, *Growth of Industry*, ii. p. 370.
[6] Toynbee, *Indust. Revolution*, p. 40.
[7] Young, *View of the Agriculture of Oxfordshire*, p. 100.

and in the stubbles after the harvest; and the question of boundaries was another fruitful source of dispute; for we are told that in some common fields there were no "baulks," or strips of unused land to divide the holdings, and men would plough by night to steal a furrow from their neighbours.[1]   Hence it is not surprising that those who followed the new agriculture also encouraged the practice of enclosures.   The old methods had to give way to the new, and these were hardly possible on unenclosed land ; and therefore we note, together with the progress of agriculture, a simultaneous increase in the amount of land enclosed.

§ 166. *Great Increase of Enclosures.*

The abolition of the old system was necessary, but the manner in which it was carried out was often disastrous.   The enclosures made by the landowners were frequently carried on with little regard to the interests of the smaller tenants and freeholders, who, in fact, suffered greatly ;[2] and in the present age English agriculture is, in a large measure, still feeling the subsequent effects of this change, especially in regard to the size of holdings, while many people are advocating a partial return to small farms, cultivated, however, with the improved experience given by modern agricultural progress.   Certainly this was not the first occasion on which the landowners had made enclosures and encroached upon the common lands of their poorer neighbours, and not merely upon the waste ;[3] but the rapidity and boldness of the enclosing operations at the end of the eighteenth century far surpassed anything in previous

---

[1] Young, *View of the Agriculture of Oxfordshire*, p. 239 ; Toynbee, *Indust. Rev.*, p. 40.

[2] "Though we cannot pretend to estimate the extent of the evil, there is no reason to doubt its reality.   Enclosure was carried on by means of private bills; these were passed through Parliament without sufficient inquiry and when many of the inhabitants were quite unaware of the impending change or powerless to resist it." Cunningham, *Growth of Industry*, ii. 486.

[3] Arthur Young found that out of 37 parishes which had been enclosed there were only 12 in which the labourers had not been injured. *Annals of Agriculture*, xxxvi. 513.

times. Between 1710 and 1760, for instance, only 334,974 acres were enclosed;[1] but between 1760 and 1843 the number rose to 7,000,000.[2]

§ 167. Benefits of Enclosures as Compared with the Old Common Fields.

The benefits of the enclosure system were, however, unmistakable, for the cultivation of common fields under the old system[3] was, as Arthur Young assures us, miserably poor. This system produced results far inferior to those gained on enclosed lands, the crop of wheat in one instance being, according to Young, only seventeen or eighteen bushels per acre, as against twenty-six bushels on enclosures.[4] Similarly, the fleece of sheep pastured on common fields weighed only 3½ lbs., as compared with 9 lbs. on enclosures.[5] It is noticeable, too, that Kent, where much land had for a long time been enclosed, was reckoned in Young's time the best cultivated and most fertile county in England.[6] Norfolk, also, was pre-eminent for good husbandry,[7] in its excellent rotation of crops and culture of clover, rye-grass, and winter roots, due, said Young in 1770, to the division of the county chiefly into large farms.[8] " Great farms have been the

[1] Toynbee, *Industrial Revolution*, 38, 39.

[2] *Ib.*, quoting Shaw Lefevre, *The English and Irish Land Question*, p. 199. *The General Report on Enclosures*, p. 46 (Board of Agriculture), gives 4,187,056 as the acreage enclosed from Queen Anne's reign to 1805 only. See also Hammond, *The Village Labourer*.

[3] It may be well to summarise it again briefly. The arable land of each village under this system was still divided into three great strips, subdivided by "baulks" three yards wide. Every farmer would own one piece of land in each strip—probably more—and all alike were bound to follow the customary tillage; this was to leave one strip fallow every year, while on one of the other two wheat was always grown, the third being occupied by barley or oats, pease or tares. The meadows, also, were still held in common, every man having his own plot up to hay harvest, after which the fences were thrown down, and all householders' cattle were allowed to graze on it freely, while for the next crop the plots were redistributed. Every farmer also had the right of pasture on the waste.

[4] At Risby, Yorks; see *Northern Tour*, i. 160-162.

[5] *Northern Tour*, iv. 190.

[6] *Eastern Tour*, iii. 108-109 ; *Northern Tour*, i. 292.

[7] *Eastern Tour*, ii. 150.   [8] *Ib.*, ii. 160,161.

soul of the Norfolk culture." These would have been impossible without enclosing land, and it is clear that great
advantages were derived from this practice. Essex, again,
was a county notable for its progressive husbandry, and
one of the first in which turnips were introduced as a root
crop ;[1] and Essex had been noted for its enclosures for
many generations.[2]   But, in spite of these advantages,
there was one gloomy feature in this new agricultural epoch
which cannot be lightly passed over. I refer to the decay
of the yeomen, who, at one time, were the chief glory of
the agricultural life ot mediæval England.

§ 168. *The Decay of the Yeomanry.*

For centuries the yeoman had held an honoured position
in English history, and as lately as the reign of Elizabeth,
he is alluded to in sympathetic and admiring terms by the
descriptive Harrison. "This sort of people," he says, "have
a certain pre-eminence and more estimation than labourers
and the common sort of artificers, and these commonly live
wealthily, keep good houses, and travel to get riches. They
are also for the most part farmers to gentlemen, or at the
leastwise artificers; and with grazing, frequenting of markets,
and keeping of servants, do come to great wealth, insomuch
that many of them are able to, and do, buy the lands of
unthrifty gentlemen, and often setting their sons to the
schools, to the Universities, and to the Inns of Court, or
otherwise leaving them sufficient lands whereon they may
live without labour, do make them by those means to
become gentlemen. These were they that in times past
made all France afraid. And albeit they be not called
'master,' as gentlemen are, or 'Sir,' as to knights apper-
taineth, but only 'John' and 'Thomas,' yet have they
been found to have done very good service. The kings of
England in foughten battles were wont to remain among
them (who were their footmen), as the French kings did

---

[1] In 1694. See quotation from Houghton, *Collections in Husbandry and
Trade* in the *Encyclopædia Britannica, s. v.* Agriculture.
[2] Above, p. 215.

amongst their horsemen, the prince thereby shewing where his chief strength did consist." [1]

The decline of this sturdy body of small farmers forms a sad interlude in the growing prosperity of the country, and is due to a combination of various causes. Among these we may place the "Statute of Frauds," of 1677, not indeed as a primary cause, but as having a weakening effect upon the position of the yeomen, and contributing in some degree to assist other causes which made themselves felt more keenly in the eighteenth century. By this somewhat high-handed Act [2] it was decreed that after July 24th, 1677, all interests in land whatsoever, if created by any other process except by deed, should be treated as tenancies at will only, any law or usage to the contrary notwithstanding. The intention, apparently, of those who passed this law— an intention which in the end resulted successfully—was to extinguish all those numerous small freeholders who had no written evidence to prove that they held their lands, as they had done for centuries, on condition of paying a small fixed and customary rent. [3]   This Act certainly succeeded in dispossessing many of the class at which it was aimed ; but there were yet a certain number against whom it was inoperative ; hence, at the end of the seventeenth century, twenty years or so after it was passed, Gregory King is able to estimate that there were 180,000 freeholders in England, including, of course, the larger owners. [4]   But by the time of Arthur Young these also had disappeared, or at least were rapidly disappearing, [5] and he sincerely regrets "to see their lands now in the hands of monopolising lords." [6]   This view is the more remarkable as coming from Arthur Young, because he was an ardent advocate of the new agriculture and large farms ; but as a

[1] Harrison, *Description of England*, Bk. III. ch. iv. (edn. 1577), page 13, Camelot Series edn.

[2] The 29 Charles II., c. 3.   [3] *Cf.* Rogers, *Hist. Agric.*, v. 15, 87.

[4] See Macaulay, *History of England*, ch. iii., who thinks this too high, and suggests 160,000.

[5] In 1787 they had practically disappeared in most parts of the country. Young, *Travels in France*, i. 86, ii. 262 (edn. 1793).

[6] Young, *Inquiry into the Present Price of Provisions and Size of Farms* (1773), pp. 126, 139.

practical man he could see what a loss the vanished yeoman was to his country. The curious thing about their disappearance is its comparative rapidity.[1] Of course many yeomen existed at the beginning of the nineteenth century, and a few still remain at the end of it; but there was a sudden and remarkable diminution in their numbers during the century just before Arthur Young wrote (1700-1800). At the close of the seventeenth century a writer on the *State of Great Britain*[2] was able to say that the freeholders of England were "more in number and richer than in any country of the like extent in Europe. £40 or £50 is very ordinary, £100 or £200 in some counties is not rare; sometimes in Kent and in the Weald of Sussex, £500 or £600 per annum, and £3000 or £4000 stock." The evidence, says an eminent economist,[3] is conclusive that up to the Revolution of 1688 the yeomen freeholders were in most parts of the country an important feature in social life.

We may therefore well inquire into the reasons of their decay.

§ 169. *Causes of the Decay of the Yeomanry.*

The cause was partly political and partly social. After the revolution of 1688, the landed gentry became politically and socially supreme,[4] and any successful merchant prince —and these were not few—who wished to gain a footing, sought, in the first place, to imitate them by becoming a great landowner; hence it became quite a policy to buy out the smaller farmers,[5] who were often practically compelled to sell their holdings. At the same time, the custom of primogeniture and strict settlements prevented land from being much subdivided, so that small or divided

---

[1] Toynbee, *Industrial Revolution*, p. 59, whom see for his special chapter on the decay of the yeomanry.

[2] Chamberlayne, *State of Great Britain*, Part I., Book III. p. 176 (edn. 1737). First published in 1669.

[3] Toynbee, *u. s.*, p. 60. [4] Toynbee, *Industrial Revolution*, p. 62.

[5] *Ib.*, 63, 64, who quotes Laurence's *Duty of a Steward* (1727), p. 36. Cunningham, *Growth of Industry*, ii. 379, says they were not bought out then, but his assertion seems unsupported by any adequate evidence. He admits, however, that "in subsequent years they were forced to sell."

estates rarely came into the market for the smaller freeholders to buy.[1] It is also certain that this result was
accelerated by the fact that small farms no longer paid
under the old system of agriculture, and the new system
involved an outlay which the yeoman could not afford.[2]
The yeomanry were superseded by capitalist farmers and
agricultural labourers.[3] Farming on a large scale became
more necessary, and this again assisted in extinguishing the
smaller men, for large enclosures were made by the landed
gentry in spite of feeble opposition from the yeomen,[4] who,
however, could rarely afford to pay the law costs necessary
to put a stop to the encroachments of their greater neighbours. Later on, at the beginning of the nineteenth century
(especially in 1801) the burden of the ever-increasing poor-
rates—a direct consequence of the Poor Law and assessment
system introduced by the Act of Elizabeth [5]—largely aided in
their ruin, for since the labourers were not and could not be
maintained by the wages which their employers paid them,
it followed that the small holders were taxed for the benefit
of the large farmers.[6] The finishing stroke to a rapidly
decaying class was given by the fall in prices after the great
Continental War (1815), following on the inflation of previous years;[7] and as their small properties came into the
market and no holders of their own class appeared to take
their place,[8] their lands went to swell the large farms that
were now the typical feature of British agriculture. Here
and there an occasional representative of a once large and
worthy body of men still remains (1895), but the English
yeoman of the days of Henry V. and Queen Elizabeth, as a
class, has disappeared entirely.[9]

§ 170. *The Rise in Rent.*

The farmer, meanwhile, was heavily taxed for his land, and
though the high prices which he obtained for his corn up to

[1] Toynbee, *u. s.*, p. 64; and Lecky, *History*, i. 196.
[2] Toynbee, p. 65, and Cunningham, *u. s.*, ii. 480.
[3] Cunningham, ii. 364, 480.
[4] *Cf.* the case of Pickering, Yorks; Marshall's *Yorkshire*, p. 54; Toynbee, *Ind. Rev.*, p. 65. [5] Above, p. 262.
[6] Cunningham, *Growth of Industry*, ii. 478. [7] *Ib.*, p. 479. [8] *Ib.*
[9] *Cf.* also Lecky, *History of the Eighteenth Century*, i. p. 196.

the repeal of the corn laws enabled him to pay it, his rent was certainly at a very high figure. The rise had begun, as we have seen, after the dissolution of the monasteries in the sixteenth century, though in that period it was slow. But Latimer asserts[1] that his father only paid £3 or £4 for a holding which in the next generation was rented at £16, the increased figure being only partially accounted for by the general rise in prices. In the seventeenth century, according to King,[2] rents were more than doubled, and the sixpence per acre of mediæval times must have seemed almost mythical. The Belvoir estate, the property of the Dukes of Rutland, who are spoken of as indulgent landlords, forms a good example of the rise of rent in the two following centuries.[3] In 1692 land is found rented at 3s. 9¼d. an acre, and a little later at 4s. 1½d. By the year 1799 the same land had risen to 19s. 3¾d., with a further rise in 1812 to 25s. 8¾d. In 1830 it was at 25s. 1¾d., but in 1850 had risen to 38s. 8d., that is about ten times the seventeenth century rent. This enormous rise could not have been due solely to increase of skill in agricultural industry, but was partly derived from artificial conditions imposed by the corn laws, and partly from increased economy in production, this economy often meaning the oppression and degradation of the agricultural labourer.

§ 171. *The Fall in Wages.*

This degradation was, if not brought about, yet at least greatly assisted by the system of assessment of wages which we noticed in Elizabeth's reign, a system under which the labourer was forced by law to accept the wages which the justices (generally the landed proprietors, his employers) arranged to give him. It is not the business of an historian to make charges against a class, but to put facts in their due perspective. Therefore without comment upon the action of the justices in this matter I shall merely refer to one or two of these assessments and show their effect upon the condition of labour, especially of agricultural labour,

---

[1] Above, p. 213.   [2] Above, p. 270.
[3] Rogers, *Hist. Agric.*, v. 29; *cf.* also *Six Centuries*, p. 479.

which occupied, till Arthur Young's time, more than one-third of the working-classes.[1] Speaking generally for the end of the sixteenth century, we may quote Professor Rogers' remark, that " if we suppose the ordinary labourer to get 3s. 6d. a week throughout the year, by adding his harvest allowance to his winter wages, it would have taken him more than forty weeks to earn the provisions which in 1495 he could have got with fifteen weeks' labour, while the artisan would be obliged to have given thirty-two weeks' work for the same result."[2] I have already given a table [3] of some of these assessments, and we may take in detail, as an example, the one made by the Rutland magistrates in April 1610. The wages of an ordinary agricultural labourer are put at 7d. a day from Easter to Michaelmas, and at 6d. from Michaelmas to Easter. Artisans get 10d. or 9d. in summer, and 8d. in winter. Now, the price of food was 75 per cent. dearer than in 1564, while the rate of wages was about the same ; and compared with (say) 1495, food was three, or even four, times dearer. Another assessment, in Essex in 1661, allows 1s. a day in winter, and 1s. 2d. in summer, for ordinary labour. But, in 1661, the price of wheat (70s. 6d. a quarter) was just double the price of 1610 (35s. 2½d.). The labourer was worse off than ever. Another typical assessment is that of Warwick, in 1684, when wages of labourers are fixed at 8d. a day in summer, 7d. in winter ; of artisans at 1s. a day. At this period Professor Rogers [4] reckons the yearly earnings of an artisan at £15, 13s. ; of a farm labourer at £10, 8s. 8d., exclusive of harvest work ; while the cost of a year's stock of provisions was £14, 11s. 6d. It is true that at this period the labourers still possessed certain advantages afterwards lost, such as common rights,[5] which, besides providing fuel, enabled them to keep cows, pigs, and poultry on the waste. Their cottages, too, were often rent free, being

[1] That is 2,800,000 out of 8,500,000 in 1769 ; Young, *Northern Tour*, iv. 417-419, 364.

[2] Rogers, *Six Centuries*, p. 390.   [3] Above, p. 257.

[4] *Six Centuries*, p. 395.

[5] Cunningham, *Growth of Industry*, ii. 487 ; and Young, *Annals of Agriculture*, xxxvi. 516.

built upon the waste,[1] while each cottage, by an Act of
Elizabeth,[2] was supposed to have a piece of land attached
to it, though this provision, after being frequently evaded,
was finally repealed in 1775. But yet it is evident that,
even allowing for these privileges, which, after all, were
now being rapidly curtailed, the ordinary agricultural
labourer—that is, the mass of the wage-earning population
—must have found it hard work to live decently. There
was, however, a short interval of higher wages during the
Civil War and the commonwealth,[3] the rise being due not
only to the demand of all sorts of stores for the contending
armies, but also to the demand for men to recruit their
forces.[4] Artisans could get 2s. 6d. a day instead of 6d.,[5]
and the rise thus brought about did not immediately disappear. But prices were still rising steadily, and wages
did not follow them closely enough to prevent great distress
among the working-classes. At the end of the seventeenth
century starvation rates of pay are complained of by the
well-known Sir Matthew Hale [6] (1683), and twenty years
before that the increase of pauperism had necessitated the
passing of that Act of Settlement which afterwards became
so unpleasantly celebrated.[7] There are historians who
maintain that the Elizabethan system of assessment of
wages was not responsible for these evils; but even if not
responsible it certainly encouraged them; and not even
the most enthusiastic admirers of that unfortunate Act can
deny that wages were never affected by it beneficially, but
continued to decline with remarkable persistency.[8] By the

[1] Young, *Farmer's Letters*, i. 205 (edn. 1771).   [2] The 31 Eliz., c. 7.
[3] Rogers, *Hist. Agric.*, v. 98 ; Cunningham, *Growth of Industry*, ii. 194.
[4] See *Parl. Hist.*, ii. 10.
[5] A quotation from *Reasons for a Limited Exportation of Wool*, 1677, in
Smith's *Chronicon Rusticum*, i. 257.
[6] *Provision for Poor* (1683), p. 18.
[7] The 13 and 14 Charles II., c. 12. Briefly it gave a parish power to
remove a new comer within 40 days, and send him back to the parish
where he was legally settled, if he was likely to require relief from the
rates. This practically chained the labourer to his native parish. See
below, p. 416, and *cf.* Fowle, *Poor Law*, p. 64.
[8] Cunningham, *Growth of Industry*, ii. 200, remarks : "During this period
there were considerable fluctuations of prices ; the Cambridge wheat rents
for 1654-5 are at 24s. 9½d., and those for 1658-59 at 52s. 2¼d. Yet though

beginning of the eighteenth century the condition of the labourer had sunk to one of great poverty. The ordinary peasant, in 1725, for instance, would not earn more than about £13 or £15 a year; artisans could not gain more than £15, 13s.; while the cost of the stock of provisions was £16, 2s. 3d.[1] Thus the husbandman who, in 1495, could get a similar stock of food by fifteen weeks' work, and the artisan who could have earned it in ten weeks, could not feed himself in 1725 with a whole year's labour.[2] His wages had to be supplemented out of the rates; and there was but little alteration in these wages till the middle of the eighteenth century. But about that time (1750) he had begun to share in the general prosperity caused by the success of the new agriculture and the growth of trade and manufactures. Whereas in the seventeenth century his average daily wages had been 10¼d., and the price of corn 38s. 2d., in the first sixty years of the eighteenth century wages had risen to 1s., and the price of corn was only 32s.[3] The evil, however, had been done, and although a short period of prosperity, chiefly due to the advance made by the new agriculture and manufactures, cheered the labourer for a time, his condition after the Industrial Revolution deteriorated again rapidly, till we find him at the end of the eighteenth century, and for some time afterwards, in a condition of chronic misery.

the price of corn was doubled in this brief period, the Bedford justices do not seem to have felt called upon to make any new order or to try to enforce a different rate of wages." This is not surprising; it merely illustrates what I have remarked before about the temptations of the Assessment Act to employers (above, pp. 255, 256). Yet Dr Cunningham seems to think the assessment system had no influence on wages.

[1] Rogers, *Six Centuries*, p. 398.   [2] *Ib.*

[3] Toynbee, *Industrial Revolution*, p.67.

CHAPTER XVIII

§ 172. *England a Commercial Power.*

IN glancing over the progress of foreign trade in the time
of Elizabeth, we noticed that our war with Spain was due
to commercial as well as to religious causes. The opening
up of the New World had made a struggle for power in the
West now almost inevitable among European nations; the
new route to India round the Cape of Good Hope, discovered
by Vasco di Gama, made another struggle for commercial
supremacy as inevitable in the far East. But England was
certainly slow in entering the field. As a matter of fact,
she was hardly yet ready either in industry, commerce, or
political power. In the reign of Henry VIII. English seamen had not yet ventured far into the Mediterranean,[1] and
even in the last years of Queen Elizabeth England had
absolutely no possessions outside Europe, for every scheme
of colonial settlement had failed.[2] For a century or more
after the discoveries of Columbus and di Gama, Spain and
Portugal, and a little later on Holland, had practically a
monopoly both of the Eastern and Western trade. But now
a change had come. The Englishmen of the Elizabethan
age cast off their fear of Spain, and entered into rivalry
with Holland, till their descendants finally made England
the supreme commercial power of the modern world. The
history of the seventeenth and eighteenth centuries is a
continuous record of their struggles to attain this object.
War is, in fact, their characteristic feature, and it had
everywhere the same purpose.[3]

---

[1] *Cf.* above, p. 225. Rogers, *Hist. Agric.*, iv. 146, says they had not ventured further than Malaga, quoting a Statute of Henry VIII. (32 Hen.
VIII., c. 14).

[2] Seeley, *Expansion of England*, p. 9.　　　　[3] *Ib.*, pp. 20, 21.

§ 173. *The Beginnings of the Struggle with Spain.*

In the last quarter of the sixteenth century Elizabeth had entered (1577) into an alliance, offensive and defensive, with Holland against Spain.[1] The motive of the alliance was partly religious, but the shrewd queen and her equally shrewd statesmen doubtless foresaw more than spiritual advantages to be gained thereby. After the alliance, Drake and the other great sea-captains of that day began a system of buccaneering annoyances to Spanish commerce.[2] The Spanish and Portuguese trade and factories in the East were considered the lawful prizes of the English and of their allies the Dutch. The latter, as all know, were more successful at first than we were, and soon established an Oriental Empire in the Indian Archipelago. But at the very end of her reign England had prospered sufficiently for Elizabeth to grant charters to the Levant Company (1581),[3] and its far greater off-shoot, the East India Company (1600).[4] Then, when a fresh war with Spain was imminent, England wisely began to plant colonies in North America, at the suggestion of Sir Walter Raleigh;[5] and after one or two other abortive attempts, Virginia was successfully founded by the London Company[6] in 1609, and became a Crown colony[7] in 1624. After this, as every one knows, colonies grew rapidly on the strip of coast between the Alleghany Mountains and the Atlantic. Meanwhile, on the other side of the world the East India Company was slowly gaining ground, and founding English agencies or "factories," that of Surat (in 1612) being the most important.[8] As yet we had not come into open conflict with Spain or Portugal; and, indeed, we owed the possession of Bombay[9] to the marriage of Charles II. with Katherine of Braganza (1662). Then the Company gained from Charles II. the important

---

[1] Green, *History*, ii. 410.

[2] Green, *History*, ii. 424, 425 ; Froude, *History*, viii. 440, ix. 337.

[3] Craik, *History of British Commerce*, i. 251, ii. 19.

[4] *Ib.*, i. 253, ii. 13 *sqq.*   [5] Hakluyt, iii. 243, 263, 280.

[6] The first charter given by James I. was in 1606, but the chief settlement was made in 1609. *Cf.* Cunningham, *Growth of Industry*, ii. 144.

[7] *Ib.*, ii. 146.   [8] *Cf.* Craik, *British Commerce*, ii. 16.

[9] *Annals of England*, p. 473. The Island was handed over to the Company in 1668.

privilege of making peace or war on its own account.[1] It had a good many foes to contend with, both among natives and European nations, among whom the French[2] were as powerful as the Portuguese. But it is curious to note how in every part of the colonial world England has been the last to come to the front. In the New World Spain and France, in the East the Portuguese and Dutch, and later in Africa and Australia the Dutch again—all were before her. For a great colonising power it is remarkable how invariably she has let others lead the way.

§ 174. *Cromwell's Commercial Wars and the Navigation Acts.*

The monopoly of Spain was first definitely attacked as a matter of policy by Cromwell, for the deeds of the Elizabethan seamen were not always recognised by the State. James I. had been too timid to declare war, and Charles I. was too much in danger himself to think of trusting his subjects to support him if he did so. But Cromwell was supported both by the religious views of the Puritans and by the desires of the merchants when he declared war against England's great foe.[3] He demanded trade with the Spanish colonies, and religious freedom for English settlers in such colonies. Of course his demands were refused, as he well knew that they would be. Thereupon he seized Jamaica (1655), though he failed to secure Cuba ;[4] and at any rate succeeded in giving the English a secure footing in the West Indies. He seized Dunkirk also (1658) from Spain (then at war with France),[5] with a view to securing for England a monopoly of the Channel to the exclusion of her former friends the Dutch. Dunkirk, however, was a useless acquisition, and was sold again[6] by Charles II. Not content with victory in the West, Cromwell, with the full consent of mercantile England, declared war against the

---

[1] Craik, *British Commerce*, ii. 101.
[2] Seeley, *Expansion of England*, p. 284.
[3] Seeley, *Expansion*, p. 32 ; Cunningham, ii. 150.
[4] Thurloe, *State Papers*, iv. 40 ; *Annals of England*, p. 452.
[5] *Annals of England*, p. 453.
[6] In 1662, October 27th, for five million livres.

Dutch, who were now more our rivals than our friends. It would have been perfectly possible for the English and the Dutch to have remained upon good terms ; but the great idea of the statesmen and merchants of the seventeenth and eighteenth centuries was to gain a sole market and a monopoly of trade, and therefore they thought the Dutch ought to be crushed. The method adopted was shown in the famous Navigation Act [1] of 1651, which forbade the import or export of any goods between Asia, Africa, America, and England, unless these were carried in English ships manned by English crews. This Act was confirmed by another [2] of 1661, which not only laid down the above conditions, but added that the ships must be English built and owned by Englishmen ; and these Acts continued in operation till early in the nineteenth century. As to their effect, there has been great diversity of opinion ; and speaking solely from the point of view of theoretical economics, there would seem no doubt that they were decidedly harmful, as being an attempt to maintain for a single country a monopoly that would naturally be shared by others. A monopoly generally implies an unnecessary tax upon some portion of the community for the benefit of another portion, and it has been complained that these Navigation Laws benefited the shipping interest at the expense of the rest of the nation.[3] It has further been pointed out (even by writers of that time) [4] that our general commerce was injuriously affected by " lessening the resort of strangers to our ports," and also that after all it did not really increase English trade,[5] but that the Eastland and Baltic trade had actually diminished. Other objections are that the Colonies and also English producers were restricted in their dealings and unable to obtain the best market for some of their products ; [6] and again that, however beneficial their ultimate results may have been, the enormous expenses [7] incurred

[1] Act c. 22 of 1651 (Commonwealth).   [2] Act 12 Charles II., c. 18.
[3] Craik, *British Commerce*, ii. 91.
[4] Roger Coke, *Treatise on Trade* (1671).
[5] Sir Josiah Child, *Treatise on Trade* (1698).
[6] Child, *New Discourse*, p. 115.
[7] Alluded to by Cunningham, *Growth of Industry*, ii. 110.

by the wars with the Dutch which followed them counter-balanced for a long time any advantages which they procured.

But it has been truly urged that the legislators who made these celebrated laws were perfectly aware of all the disadvantages they entailed, but considered[1] that the growth of national power would be on the whole fostered, the reserve for the navy strengthened, and the rivalry of the Dutch in course of time annihilated. And, as a matter of fact, all these things came to pass. More especially it has been contended that they helped to defend the country against foreign foes, although they might hamper trade. For this reason Adam Smith,[2] speaking as a politician and not as an economist, eulogises these Acts in the concise remark : " As defence is much more important than opulence, the Act of Navigation is perhaps the wisest of all the commercial regulations of England." This dictum of so great an economist is worthy of the utmost consideration, for it shows us that there are occasions when economics must give way to politics, and that political economy best bears out its title as a science when it remembers that it is qualified by the attribute " political."

On the whole, then, with all their evils, the Navigation Acts were perhaps not so great a mistake as the nineteenth century economist is at first inclined to suppose. At any rate, Cromwell succeeded in his immediate object. The Dutch were provoked into a war in which their prestige was broken and their trade greatly injured ; and before long the contest between them and the English for the mastery of the seas was practically decided. By the end of the seventeenth century Holland had to own her defeat, and England began distinctly to take the lead in commerce.[3]

§ 175. *The Wars of William III. and of Anne.*

But the wars with Holland were only the beginnings of a larger struggle in which England contended against all

---

[1] Alluded to by Cunningham, *Growth of Industry*, ii. 112.

[2] *Wealth of Nations*, Bk. IV. ch. ii. (ii. 38, Clarendon Press edn.). His whole discussion of them should be read.

[3] *Cf.* Seeley, *Expansion of England*, 86.

Western Europe—a struggle that was to last with comparatively brief intermissions till well into the nineteenth century. The continental wars in which England was engaged after the deposition of James II. were rendered necessary to some extent by the tremendous power of France under Louis XIV. William III. saw it was inevitable for the interests of England that Louis XIV. should be checked, and the war of the Spanish Succession (1702-13) was carried on with the object of preventing that king from joining the resources of Spain to those of his own kingdom. For if he had done so, two disastrous results would have happened. The Stuarts would by his help have been restored to the English throne, and the struggle against absolute monarchy and religious tyranny would unfortunately have been fought over again. Secondly, the growth of English commerce and colonies would have been checked, if not utterly annihilated. Here the real point of contention between England and France was the New World. The Spanish Succession, remote as it seemed, concerned Englishmen, because France threatened by her close alliance and influence with Spain to enter into the Spanish monopoly of the New World and to keep England out of it.[1] Hence the most practical results of the war were seen in the acquisition of colonial power.[2] We were not only preserved from the Stuarts, but also, when the war was finally over in 1713, found ourselves in possession of Gibraltar, now one of the keys of our Indian Empire, and of the Hudson's Bay Territory, Newfoundland, and Nova Scotia (then called Acadia)—the foundations of our present Canadian dominion. England was also allowed by Spain the monopoly of the trade in negroes with Spanish colonies,[3] and to send one ship a year to the South Seas. The war, as far as we were concerned, was a commercial success, though we had to pay rather heavily for it, and were involved in further difficulties in America afterwards.

[1] Seeley, *Expansion of England*, pp. 32 and 33.   [2] *Ib.*
[3] This is known as the "Assiento" contract (Art. 12 of the Treaty of 1713). The English had the monopoly of the slave trade for 30 years, but practically till war broke out again in 1739. The contract was renewed for 4 years in 1748, but not at the Peace of 1763.

T

§ 176. *English Colonies.*

It will be seen that by this time (1713) England had definitely entered the field as a colonial power, and was anxious to extend her colonial possessions. She had not shown any great desire for them in earlier years; in fact, we have already remarked that she was then, as she always has been, the last to enter upon a colonising career. But now England was fired by the example of other nations. The motives, however, for our early schemes of colonisation were rather mixed. It certainly cannot be said that our colonies were a natural "expansion" of the mother country, and the use of this term,[1] expansion, is apt to be misleading; for England was certainly by no means over-populated in the sixteenth or seventeenth centuries. In fact, it was then even complained that colonies would drain away population which we could ill afford to spare.[2] There can be little doubt that one of the main causes of colonial enterprise, especially in its earlier stages, was the desire to gain some share of the gold and silver[3] which Spain had obtained so freely. This, indeed, is a frequent inducement to open up and to take possession of new countries, as has been exemplified in our own time both in Australia and South Africa. Often, however, those who go out to seek gold find something better and more lasting in the natural resources of the country; and it is upon these alone that a really stable colony can be founded. The dream of finding Eldorados passed away after a few futile attempts, and men began to realise that America and the Indies—both East and West—offered enormous facilities for a profitable trade. The profits of trade were undoubtedly the real motives of nearly all our subsequent colonial enterprises, with the exception

[1] The use of this word seems to me almost the only fault of Prof. Seeley's admirable lectures. It implies a kind of growth which really never took place till late in the nineteenth century.

[2] See *Britannia Languens* (1680), p. 173.

[3] Adam Smith, *Wealth of Nations*, Bk. IV. ch. vii. (Vol. II. p. 143, Clarendon Press edn.); and Capt. J. Smith, *History of Virginia*, iii. 3 (*Works*, 407), mentions how this hope of gold animated the first settlers in Virginia. So, too, Sir Walter Raleigh hoped to find gold in Guiana, and Frobisher's expedition of 1577 was entirely to seek for gold. Craik, *British Commerce*, i. 246, 254.

of those which proceeded (as in the case of some of the North American colonies) from the desire to find a country where men could practise freely the varied forms of a new religion. Later on, when these profits were seen to be considerable, the home Government began to formulate a definite scheme of colonial policy, in the supposed interests of the mother country ;[1] and there seems to have been at one time a clearly-defined scheme in the heads of politicians to raise up a number of agricultural dependencies which would exchange their useful products for the numerous manufactures which were now becoming so predominant at home.[2] This scheme approximated more nearly to the relations of England and her colonies—which are all new and hardly yet fully developed countries—in the present day. Such a trading connection is a natural and nearly inevitable state of things, and is almost sure to constitute the normal relationship of colony and parent nation. But in the eighteenth century England very nearly broke off this relationship by ill-judged political action,[3] while in the present day her newer colonies are rather foolishly attempting to do the same without having the excuse of political or economic ignorance to shield them, an ignorance which it might have been hoped that the War of American Independence and other subsequent events would have helped to dispel.

But leaving the motives for the foundation of colonies, we may notice their remarkable growth in the seventeenth century,[4] and pass on to consider the vast struggle in which that growth involved England.

§ 177. *Further Wars with France and Spain.*

All the wars in which England now engaged had some commercial or colonial object in view. People had yet to

---

[1] See all Adam Smith's chapter, *Wealth of Nations*, Bk. IV. ch. vii.; also the very valuable essay on *Colonies and Colony Trade* in M'Culloch's *Dictionary of Commerce*, edn. 1844.

[2] M'Culloch, *Dictionary of Commerce* (*s.v.* Colonies), p. 318, edn. 1844, says this is untrue, at least at first.   [3] See below, pp. 364-370.

[4] See the author's *British Commerce and Colonies*, ch. iv. This being a history of industry, the subject of our colonies can only be very briefly referred to. Besides the American colonies (p. 295, *note*) England now had several of the West Indian islands and factories on the Gold Coast.

learn that the best way to extend a nation's trade is to promote general peace; but, in default of that, it seemed well to provoke a general war. Mistaken as England's policy was, it was no more so than that of her neighbours, for all believed, as many do still, in the sole market theory, and England was compelled to fight against other nations who wished to have a monopoly of trade and colonisation. Moreover, England was provoked into war by the secret " Family Compact " between the related rulers of France and Spain, by which Philip V. of Spain agreed to take away the South American trade from England, and give it to his nephew, Louis XV. of France.[1] The result was a system of annoyance to English vessels trading in the South Seas, culminating in the mutilation of an English captain, one Jenkins,[2] and war was declared openly in 1739. This war merged into the war of the Austrian Succession,[3] which lasted for eight years (1740-48), a matter with which England was in no way directly concerned, but which afforded a good excuse to renew the struggle against the commercial growth of France as well as Spain. We did not gain much by it, except the final annihilation of the hopes of the Stuarts, and a small increase of British power upon the high seas, but yet it was undoubtedly necessary to check the power of France.

After a few years, however, we entered upon another war, the Seven Years' War[4] (1756-63), in which England and Prussia fought side by side against the rest of Europe, and attacked France in particular in all parts of the world. The war was largely caused by the quarrels of the French and English colonists in America, and of the rival French and English companies in India.[5] We cannot here go into the details of it. It is sufficient to say that, after a bad beginning, we won various victories by sea and land, and at

[1] Its main object was the ruin of the maritime supremacy of Britain. Green, *History*, iv. 153.

[2] This story is sometimes declared mythical (*e.g.*, by Seeley, *Expansion*, p. 21), but seems to rest on some foundation.

[3] *Cf.* Green, *History*, iv. 155.

[4] Green, *History*, iv. 175-189; Lecky, *History*, ii. 443, iii. 44.

[5] Seeley, *Expansion*, p. 27, points out how many of these conflicts took place when England and France were nominally at peace

at the close (1763) found ourselves, by the Treaty of Paris, in possession of Canada, Florida, and all the French possessions east of the Mississippi, except New Orleans; and we had also gained the upper hand in India. England held now almost undisputed sway over the seas, and our trade grew by leaps and bounds.

Now, the whole of this series of wars is connected together by a necessary cause, and that is the growing commercial and industrial power of England. This growth was a cause of the English attempt to take a place among other commercial nations, such as the Dutch and Portuguese, and this attempt in turn necessitated an attack upon the monopoly of Spain and the rival power of France. The successful issue of these wars again caused industry and trade to advance more prosperously than ever, till at length, both politically and industrially, England rose to the front rank of European nations. It has also been well pointed out, that in the three wars between 1740 and 1783, the struggle as between England and France was more especially for the New World. In the first war the issue was fairly joined; in the second France suffered a fatal fall; in the third, by assisting the American States, she took a signal revenge.[1] " This is the grand chapter in the history of Greater Britain, for it is the first great struggle in which the (British) Empire fights as a whole, the colonies and settlements outside Europe being here not merely dragged in the wake of the mother country, but actually taking the lead."[2] To the history of these colonial dependencies we must now devote a few words, beginning first with India.

§ 178. The Struggle for India.

Since the founding of Surat and the acquisition of Bombay, the East India Company had also founded two forts or stations, which have since become most important cities, namely, Fort St George, now Madras, and Fort William, now Calcutta.[3] They had become powerful, and

---

[1] Seeley, *Expansion*, p. 31.   [2] *Ib.*, p. 31.
[3] Macpherson, *History of European Commerce with India*, p. 125.

each of the three chief stations had a governor and a small army. The French, however, had also an East India Company,[1] whose chief station was Pondicherry, south of Madras; and the two companies were by no means on friendly terms. When their respective nations were at war in 1746-48, they, too, had some sharp fighting, but it was only when Dupleix,[2] the French Governor of Pondicherry, had gained such remarkable influence in Southern India about 1748, that matters became serious. Dupleix was one of the first Europeans who deliberately involved himself in native politics in order to further his country's interests, and he conceived the idea of the conquest of India. The English traders feared with justice the loss both of their lives and commerce, and open war broke out. The magnificent exertions of Clive and Lawrence, however, defeated the French; Dupleix was recalled in 1754, and quiet was for a time restored.[3] But two years afterwards the Seven Years' War broke out, and India was disturbed again. Suraj-ud-Daula, the ally of the French, took Calcutta and committed the Black Hole atrocity (1757), and he and his allies did their best to drive the English out of Bengal.[4] This province, however, was saved by Clive at the battle of Plassey;[5] Coote defeated the French at Wondiwash or Vandivasu (1760); and Pondicherry was captured by the English in 1761.[6] Finally, in 1765, the East India Company became the collector of the revenues for Bengal, Behar, and Orissa, and thus the English power was acknowledged and consolidated.[7] Our future struggles in India were not with the French, but with native princes. So completely did the French power decline that Napoleon, when he was a young and unknown person, so far from dreaming of the conquest of India (as he did later), actually thought of entering the English East India Company's service in order

---

[1] It was organised by Colbert in 1664, but was very unsuccessful at first; Malleson, *French in India*, pp. 27, 57.

[2] *Cf.* Lecky, *History*, ii. 455; *cf.* Seeley, *Expansion*, p. 30.

[3] Lecky, *History*, ii. 455, 456.   [4] Lecky, ii. 456, 497.

[5] Lecky, *History*, ii. 498.   [6] *Ib.*, ii. 503.

[7] *Ib.*, iii. 478. See Lecky's useful summary of the conduct of the Company in India.

to acquire the wealth of an Anglo-Indian nabob.[1] Nevertheless, for a long time the English were actuated in all their Indian conduct and politics by fear of the French. "Behind every movement of the native powers we saw French intrigue, French gold, French ambition; and never, until we were masters of the whole country, got rid of that feeling that the French were driving us out of it, which had descended from the days of Dupleix and Labourdonnais."[2] East and west the duel with France went on, and the underlying cause of the duel was the evergrowing industrial life of England that burst forth into new colonial ventures beyond the seas.

§ 179. *The Conquest of Canada.*

There was, however, a great struggle for commercial supremacy to be waged against the French in America. It began in 1754. The English had now thirteen flourishing colonies between the Alleghany Mountains and the sea.[3] Behind them, above them, and below them, all was claimed

---

[1] Jung, *Lucien Bonaparte et ses Mémoires*, i. 74 (Seeley).
[2] Seeley, *Expansion*, p. 30.
[3] The following list may be useful; and *cf.* Lecky, *History*, ii. 18 *sqq.*

COLONY.	Date of Foundation.	How Founded.
I. Virginia Group—		
Virginia	1606	By the London Company
Maryland	1632	Charter given to Lord Baltimore
N. and S. Carolina	1663	Proprietors
Georgia	1733	By General Oglethorpe
II. New York Group—		
New York	1664	⎫
New Jersey	1664	⎬ Taken from the Dutch
Delaware	1664	⎭
Pennsylvania	1682	Purchased by Wm. Penn from Charles II.
III. New England Group—		
New Hampshire	1622	⎫
Massachusetts	1628	⎬ Colonised by Puritan Settlers
Rhode Island	1631	⎭
Connecticut	1633	

by France as French territory. It was inevitable that the growth of our colonies should lead to war, and such was actually the case. The French began by driving out English settlers from land west of the Alleghany Mountains; the English retorted by driving French settlers out of Nova Scotia, and tried to make a colony in the Ohio valley.[1] In this latter object they were foiled by Duquesne, the French Governor of Canada, who built Fort Duquesne there in 1754. Shortly afterwards, the next Governor, Montcalm, conceived the idea of linking together Forts Duquesne, Niagara, and Ticonderoga by lesser forts, so as to keep the English in their narrow strip of eastern coast-line. Then the English Government at home took up the matter, and sent out General Braddock with 2000 men to help the colonists.[2] Braddock was defeated [3] and killed (1755), but when the Seven Years' War broke out in the next year, Pitt sent ammunition, men, and money to help the colonists to attack Quebec and Montreal.[4] The war was renewed in Canada with fresh vigour; Fort Duquesne was captured in 1758, Quebec in 1759, and Montreal in 1760 ;[5] and when peace [6] was made at Paris in 1763, England had gained all the French possessions in America, and her colonists were enabled to extend as far as they desired. We unfortunately lost them by a mistaken policy a few years afterwards.

§ 180. Survey of Commercial Progress during these Wars.

We may now make a brief survey of our commercial progress in the seventeenth century. The reign of James I. was noticeable for the rapid growth of the foreign trade which had developed from the somewhat piratical excursions of the Elizabethan sailors. Trading companies were formed in considerable numbers, and among them the Levant Company may be noticed, as making great profits in its Eastern trade.[7] The mercantile class was now growing

---

[1] Lecky, ii. 443. [2] Ib., ii. 444. [3] Ib., ii. 446.
[4] Ib., ii. 494. [5] Ib., ii. 495. [6] Ib., iii. 46.
[7] Craik, British Commerce, ii. 19; cf. also Mun, Discourse of Trade from England to East India.

both numerous and powerful, and a proof of their advance in social position and influence is furnished by the new title of nobility, that of baronet, conferred by James I. upon such merchant princes as were able and willing to pay the needy king a good round sum for the honour.[1] It is interesting, by the way, to notice the figures of trade in his reign. In 1613 the exports and imports both together were about £4,628,586 in value,[2] and a sign of a quickly developing Eastern trade is also seen in the fact that James made attempts to check the increasing export of silver from the kingdom.[3] At this time English merchants traded not only in the East, but with most of the Mediterranean ports, with Portugal, Spain, France, Hamburg, and the Baltic coasts.[4] Ships from the north and west of Europe used in return to visit the Newcastle collieries, which were rapidly growing in value.[5] The English ships were also very active in the new cod fisheries of Newfoundland and the Greenland whale fisheries.[6] The development of English trade is signalised in this century by the appearance of numerous books and essays on commercial questions, of which the works of Mun, Malynes, Misselden, Roberts, Sir Josiah Child, Sir William Petty, Worth, and Davenant may be mentioned as among the most important.[7] The increase in the wealth of the country is shown by the rapid rebuilding of London after the Great Fire,[8] when the loss was estimated at £12,000,000; and Sir Josiah Child, writing in 1665, speaks of the great development of the commerce and trade of England in the previous twenty years.[9] The East India Company was so flourishing that in 1676 their stock was quoted at 245 per cent.[10] Trade with America was equally

---

[1] Gardiner, *History*, ii. 112. The sum was £1080.

[2] Craik, *British Commerce*, ii. 33.

[3] Heavy fines were imposed on foreign merchants for doing this in 1619; Gardiner, *History*, iii. 323.

[4] See Lewes Roberts, *The Merchants' Map of Commerce*: London, 1638; *passim* and especially Pt. ii. p. 257.

[5] Rogers, *Hist. Agric.*, v. 140.   [6] Craik, *British Commerce*, ii. 29.

[7] See Palgrave's new *Dictionary of Pol. Economy* for these.

[8] Craik, *British Commerce* (quoting Child), ii. 83.

[9] Child, *New Discourse on Trade*, written in 1665, and published in 1668.

[10] Craik, *British Commerce*, ii. 101.

prosperous.   New Amsterdam, now New York, was taken
from the Dutch[1] in 1664, and in 1670 the Hudson's Bay
Company received their charter.   But the main commercial
fact of the latter half of the seventeenth century, and of
the eighteenth, was the development of the Eastern trade,
and, as a consequence, of the home production of articles
to be exchanged for Eastern goods.[2]   English ships went as
far as India, to Arabia and to Africa, and traded with the
Spanish colonies in the New World.   The cloth trade
especially was greatly increased,[3] and imports of cloth from
abroad were almost superseded.   This improvement in
English manufactures led to increased trade with our colonial
possessions, especially in the West Indies.[4]   It was partly,
perhaps, this great development of English trade with
both the Western and the Eastern markets that stimulated
the genius of the great inventors to supply our manufacturers with machinery that would enable them to meet
the huge demands upon their powers of production, for, by
1760, the export trade had grown to many times its value
in the days of James I.   Then, as we saw, it was only
some £2,000,000 per annum; in 1703, nearly a hundred
years later, it was, according to an MS. of Davenant's,[5]
£6,552,019; by 1760 it reached £14,500,000.[6]   The
markets, too, had undergone a change.   We no longer
exported so largely to Holland,[7] Portugal, and France, as
in the seventeenth century, but instead, one-third of our
exports went to our colonies.[8]   In 1770, for example,
America took three-fourths of the manufactures of Man-

---

[1] Anderson, *Chron. Deduct. Commerce*, ii. 479, and for the Hudson's Bay
Co., *cf.* Anderson, ii. 514.

[2] Rogers, *Econ. Interpretation of History*, p. 288.

[3] In 1699 the woollen cloth manufacture formed between a half and a
third of the total exports (£2,932,292 out of £6,788,166).   Davenant,
Second Report to Commissioners of Public Accounts; Works, v. 460.

[4] Craik, *British Commerce*, ii. 137.

[5] Quoted in Toynbee, *Industrial Revolution*, p. 56, *note.*   Craik, *British
Commerce*, ii. 155, gives £6,644,103, also from Davenant.   But the figures
are nearly the same.

[6] The exact figure (Craik, *British Commerce*, iii. 10) was £15,781,175,
but of this £1,086,205 came from Scotland.

[7] Craik, *British Commerce*, ii. 155.

[8] Toynbee, *Industrial Revolution*, 57.

chester,[1] and Jamaica alone took almost as much of our manufactures as all our plantations together had done in the beginning of the century.[2]

§ 181. *Commercial Events of the Seventeenth Century.*

This is not a history of Commerce, and, therefore, any mention of commercial facts must here be brief.[3]   But the seventeenth and eighteenth centuries are so marked by commercial progress, and are so crowded with important mercantile events, that we must pause to notice a few of the most remarkable of them.   Among these we may place the humble origin of that marvellous system of banking, which is at once the basis and the apex of the modern mercantile fabric.   Banking first seems to have assumed the importance of a regular business in England early in the seventeenth or late in the sixteenth century.   It was carried on especially by goldsmiths,[4] who often advanced money to the sovereign upon the security of taxes or personal credit.   A pamphlet of 1676, called *The Mystery of the Newfashioned Goldsmiths or Bankers Discovered,* shows how banking and money-lending had become a regular business, and gives the year 1645 as about the time when commercial men began regularly to put their cash in the hands of goldsmiths.   It also states that "the greatest of them (*i.e.,* of the goldsmiths) were enabled to supply Cromwell with money in advance upon the revenues, as his occasions required, at great advantage to themselves." Similarly the famous goldsmith, George Heriot,[5] had frequently obliged James I.   It is well known how the London goldsmiths advanced Charles II. as much as £1,300,000, at 8 to 10 per cent. interest, upon the security of the taxes ; and how (in 1672) he suddenly refused to repay the principal, saying they must be content

[1] Young, *Northern Tour,* iii. 194.
[2] Burke, *Works,* i. 278.
[3] I have treated the strictly commercial facts in another volume, *British Commerce and Colonies, from Elizabeth to Victoria.*
[4] See my article on *Goldsmiths' notes* in Palgrave's *Dictionary of Political Economy.*
[5] *Cf.* the excellent note (B) to Sir Walter Scott's *Fortunes of Nigel.*

with the interest, and closed the exchequer, thus causing a serious commercial panic.[1]

The unsatisfactory method of obtaining loans from goldsmiths and other private persons was partly the cause of William Paterson's project [2] of founding what is now known as the Bank of England (1694). Paterson offered to provide the Government of William III. with £1,200,000, to be repaid by taxation on beer or other liquors, and by rates on shipping, while those who subscribed this money were incorporated into a regular company, which was to receive 8 per cent. interest, and also £4000 a year for management.[3] Thus the matter of loans was first placed upon a proper basis, while the Bank thus formed, and supported by Government credit, took at once a leading position in English commerce. The loan just mentioned [4] was the beginning of a regular National Debt, which may be briefly defined as the system of contracting loans upon the security of the supplies or upon Government credit, and of paying them off gradually in succeeding generations.[5]

The Restoration of the Currency was another event of historical importance. It was due to Montague, the Chancellor of the Exchequer. Although, as we saw, Elizabeth had reformed the standard of the coinage, yet, up to the time of Charles II., silver money was made by simply cutting the metal with shears, and shaping and stamping it with a hammer. It was thus quite easy to clip or shear the coins again without being detected, and then pass them off to an unsuspecting person for their full amount. So the coins became smaller and smaller, and people often found, on presenting them at a bank or elsewhere, that they were only worth half their nominal value. At first, under

---

[1] Cunningham, *Growth of Industry*, ii. 223.

[2] *Cf.* Paterson's own Account of *Transactions in relation to the Bank of England*, 1695; and Craik, *British Commerce*, ii. 124; also (for Paterson) Macaulay, *History*, ch. xxiv.

[3] Craik, *u. s.*, ii. 125; Anderson, *Chron. Comm.*, ii. 604; also Rogers, *First Nine Years of the Bank of England*, should be referred to.

[4] Strictly speaking, the money stolen by Charles II. from the goldsmiths was the first debt, but it was not included till later. Cunningham, *Growth of Industry*, ii. 223.

[5] *Cf.* Cunningham, *u. s.*, ii. 403; Rogers, *Econ. Interp.*, 449.

Charles II., it was thought sufficient to issue new coins with a ribbed or " milled " edge, but the only result of this was that the good coin was melted or exported, and (as is always the case) the inferior money remained at home. ,It was then seen, by Montague and Sir Isaac Newton (the Master of the Mint), that the only way was to call in the old coin-age, and issue an entirely new and true milled currency. The expenses of this recoinage, which cost some two and a half millions, were defrayed by a tax on window-panes.[1]

§ 182. *Other Important Commercial Events.*

Among the important commercial events of this period, one ought certainly to include the Darien Scheme and the Union of England and Scotland, although these belong more fitly to a history of Commerce than of Industry. The Darien Scheme was a project originated by William Paterson, the founder of the Bank of England, who pro-posed to colonise the Isthmus of Darien, and use it as " the key of the Indies and door of the world " for commerce.[2] English capitalists, however, would not support his scheme, and it was denounced by the English Parliament. Never-theless, a company was formed in Scotland, called " The Scottish African and Indian Company," a charter was given it by the Scotch Parliament in 1695, and a capital of £900,000 was ultimately raised, £400,000 coming from Scotland, then a very poor country, and the rest from English and Dutch merchants. The hostility of the East India Company, the Levant Company, and of the Dutch in general, however, never ceased, and it was owing to their influence that, when the ill-fated colony at last set out for Darien in July 1698, the settlers were left quite unaided against the attacks of the Spaniards, who claimed the monopoly of South American trade. In fact, Spanish attacks and the climate, so utterly unsuited for European colonists, sealed the fate of the expedition, and few who went out ever returned. This failure had the most serious

---

[1] Rogers, *Econ. Interp.*, p. 200 ; Craik, *British Commerce*, ii. 127.
[2] For an account of this Company see Burton's *History of Scotland*, ch. viii., and Macaulay's *History of England*, ch. xxiv.

effect in impoverishing the Scotch, who could then ill afford the loss, but there is little doubt that it greatly helped to bring about the subsequent Act of Union [1] between England and Scotland, in which William Paterson was largely concerned (1707). The Union proved of considerable benefit to Scotland, as by it trade between the two countries became free, English ports and colonies were thrown open to the Scotch, and Scotland found a large market for woollen and linen goods and cattle in England.

The woollen cloth trade had now assumed such proportions as to make it worth while to attempt to help it forward still more by a commercial treaty. This treaty is important mainly because at the time it was regarded as a monument of economic wisdom.[2] The date of the Methuen Treaty is 1703, and it was arranged by John Methuen between England and Portugal. It was agreed that British woollen goods should be admitted into Portugal and her colonies, provided that at all times Portuguese wines were admitted into England at two-thirds of the duty (whatever it might be) levied on French wines. The result was a considerable increase of trade with Portugal, but an even greater decrease of trade with France,[3] while the wine-drinking of our upper classes took a very different direction, for port, which had hitherto been almost unknown in England, became the typical drink of the English gentleman, and more port was sent to the United Kingdom than to all the rest of Europe together.[4] It was not till the time of the commercial treaty of 1860 with France that the heavy duties on light French wines were reduced, and with them the duties on French manufactures.[5] Till then, as Gladstone said in his speech on the subject in 1862, "it was almost thought a matter of duty to regard Frenchmen as traditional enemies," not only in politics, but in commerce. This French treaty was only one among the many and great services of Cobden to the commerce of his country.[6]

---

[1] Craik, *British Commerce*, ii. 183; Cunningham, *Growth of Industry*, ii. 411.

[2] Craik, *British Commerce*, ii. 165.   [3] *Ib.*, ii. 166.

[4] Bourne, *Romance of Trade*, 135.

[5] The Methuen Treaty itself lasted till 1831. Craik, *u. s.*, ii. 165.

[6] Morley, *Life of Cobden*, ch. xxvii.

It is noticeable that in this period commerce takes an entirely modern tone. We have seen this in the case of banking, of national finance, and of commercial policy. We now notice it also in the growth of speculation; for the eighteenth century is distinguished by its mania for commercial gambling. It is the era in which the modern company promoter makes his first appearance. Many companies were started, far too numerous to mention here, their promotion being due partly no doubt to the fact that those who had hoarded their money during the previous wars were, in the early part of the eighteenth century, anxious to make profitable use of it. Of these new companies the most famous was the South Sea Company, formed in 1711 to trade with South America, but afterwards partaking more of the nature of a financial company. The directors anticipated enormous profits, and offered to advance the Government £7,500,000 to pay off part of the National Debt.[1] Every one knows the story of their collapse (1721), and the ruin it brought upon thousands of worthy but credulous shareholders. But though the most famous, it was by no means the only, or even the first, project of its kind;[2] for this was a time when all the accumulated capital of the country seemed to run riot in hopes of gaining profits. Hundreds of smaller companies were started every day, and an unhealthy excitement prevailed.[3] One company, with a capital of £3,000,000, was started " for insuring to all masters and mistresses the losses they may sustain by servants"; another " for making salt-water fresh"; a third for " planting mulberry trees and breeding silk-worms in Chelsea Park." One in particular was designed for importing " a number of large jackasses from Spain in order to propagate a larger kind of mule in England," as if, remarks a later writer with some severity, there were not already jackasses enough in London alone.[4]

All this mania for investing capital, however, shows how

---

[1] Cf. Craik, *British Commerce*, ii. 190, and Anderson, *Chron. Commerce*, ii. 614.

[2] Cf. Defoe's *Essay on Projects* (1697), especially pp. 11 to 13.

[3] Cf. Craik and Anderson, *u. s.*

[4] *Ib.*, also Bourne, *Romance of Trade*, 316.

prosperous England had now become, and how great a quantity of wealth had been accumulated, partly by trade, but also by the growth of manufactures, and by improvements in agriculture. Englishmen now felt strong enough to begin another struggle for the monopoly of trade,[1] with the result that fresh wars were undertaken, and the country was heavily burdened with debt. But the wars were, on the whole, a success, though the wish for a monopoly was a mistake. We see, in fact, from this brief review, that the prosperity and development of modern English commerce, as we know it, had now begun. It was due, of course, not to the great wars we had waged for the right of a sole market, but to the fact that we were able to supply the markets of the world with manufactured goods which no other country could then produce.[2] How we were able to do so will shortly be seen, when we come to speak of the Industrial Revolution of the last half of the eighteenth century. Meanwhile, we will glance at the state of our manufacturing industries in the period before this great change.

[1] On the "sole market" theory, see Rogers, *Econ. Interp.*, 323.

[2] This was due very largely to the political troubles of other countries Rogers, *Econ. Interpretation*, p. 289; and below, p. 358.

CHAPTER XIX

MANUFACTURES AND MINING

§ 183. *Circumstances Favourable to English Manufactures.*

IT has been frequently remarked in previous chapters that Flanders was the great manufactory of Europe throughout the Middle Ages, and up to the sixteenth century. Her competition would in any case have been sufficient to check much export of manufactured goods from England, though we had by the sixteenth century got past the time when most of our imports of clothing came from Flanders. But, at the end of the sixteenth century, Flemish competition was practically annihilated, owing to the ravages made in the Low Countries by the Spanish persecutions and occupation.[1] But England did not benefit merely by the cessation of Flemish competition : she received at the same time hundreds of Flemish immigrants,[2] who greatly improved our home manufactures, and thus our prosperity was doubly assisted. The result is seen in the fact that our export of wool diminished, while the export of cloth increased, till at the close of the seventeenth century woollen goods formed two-thirds of our total exports.[3]

§ 184. *Wool Trade. Home Manufactures. Dyeing.*

In the reign of James I. the wool trade is even said to have declined,[4] and certainly we know that little wool can have been exported, for nearly all that produced in England was used for home manufacture. On the other hand, however the same fact shows that the manufacturing industry was

---

[1] Above, p. 230.   [2] Above, pp. 221, 230.
[3] Davenant, *Of Gain in Trade* (1699), p. 47.
[4] Craik, *British Commerce*, ii. 34, who thinks the decline partly due to the effects of the monopoly granted to Cockayne.

rising in importance, for it required all the home-grown wool that could be got; and, in 1648, and again in 1660, the export of British wool was for this reason forbidden,[1] and remained so till 1825. The woollen cloth trade was very largely in the hands of the Merchant Adventurers,[2] against whose methods serious complaints were sometimes made,[3] but the manufacturing industry flourished steadily, and a considerable part of the population was now engaged in it. The usefulness of our climate, too, for this particular manufacture had been discovered, and was now recognised,[4] while the manufacturing industry was likewise aided by the impetus given to dyeing by the exertions of Sir Walter Raleigh. Previously to James I.'s reign most English goods had to be sent to the Netherlands to be dyed,[5] as was explained above; but Raleigh[6] called attention to this fact, and proposed to grant a monopoly for the art of dyeing and dressing. It was by his advice that the export of English white goods was[7] prohibited (1608), a proceeding which caused considerable discussion and controversy.[8] At the same time a monopoly was granted to Sir William Cockayne, giving him the exclusive right of dyeing and dressing all woollen cloths.[9] But the Dutch and German cities immediately retaliated by prohibiting the import of any dyed cloths from England, and great confusion arose. "Cockayne was disabled from selling his cloth anywhere but at home, beside that his cloths were worse done, and yet were dearer, than those finished in Holland. There was a very great clamour, therefore, raised against this new project by the weavers now employed, so that the king was obliged to

---

[1] Scobell, *Acts*, i. 138, and the 12 Charles II., c. 32.

[2] *Cf.* Cunningham, *Growth of Industry*, ii. 120.

[3] Craik, *British Commerce*, ii. 35.

[4] Bishop Burnet remarked this to Davenant; Davenant, *Works*, ii. 235.

[5] Gardiner, *History*, ii. 386.

[6] *Observations concerning the Trade and Commerce of England with the Dutch and other Foreign Nations*; *cf.* Craik, *British Commerce*, ii. 9-12; Smith, *Memoirs of Wool*, ch. xxx., xxxi.

[7] Craik, *British Commerce*, ii. 33.

[8] Smith, *Memoirs of Wool*, ch. xxxi.-xxxvi.

[9] Gardiner, *History*, ii. 386, 387; Smith, *Memoirs of Wool*, ch. xxxi. and notes. It seems doubtful whether Cockayne's patent was granted in 1608-9 or 1616; see Smith, *u. s.*

permit the exportation of a limited quantity of white cloths; and a few years after (1615) for quieting the people he found himself under the necessity of annulling Cockayne's patent."[1]

Thus the monopoly failed in its object, as such attempts usually do, but still it is worth noticing as an instance of what was then the universal policy of subjecting industry to various regulations, either for the benefit of those concerned in the industry itself, or because it was thought that benefit might accrue to the State in general.[2]   The regulation of industry was, in fact, regarded as quite right and necessary, either for purely political purposes,[3] or to maintain the quality of manufactures; and though in modern times the tendency has rather been to get rid of State regulation altogether, there are still a fair number of cases where industry is more or less supervised by the State for the good of the community.[4]

§ 185. Other Influences Favourable to England.   The Huguenot Immigration.

But other influences were at work in the seventeenth century in favour of our home industries.   It becomes more and more apparent that our insular position was specially suitable for the development of manufactures as soon as they made a fair start.   Except for the Parliamentary War, which did not disturb the industry of the country very much—for there is no sign of undue exaltation of prices, or anything else that points to commercial distress[5]—England was free from the terrible conflicts that desolated half Europe in the Thirty Years' War.   Our own Civil War was conducted with hardly any of the bloodshed, plunder, and rapine that make war so disastrous.   But the Thirty Years' War (1619-1648) did not cease till the utter exhaustion of the combatants made peace inevitable, and till every leader who had taken part in the beginning of the

[1] Anderson, *Chron. Deduct. Commerce*, ii. 232.
[2] Cunningham, *Growth of Industry*, ii. 157.
[3] *E.g.*, the export of bullion was prohibited for political reasons.
[4] The Factory Acts of the nineteenth century are an instance of this.
[5] Rogers, *Six Centuries*, p. 432, says agriculture even progressed.

struggle was in his grave. Germany was effectually ruined,[1] and with Germany and Flanders laid low, England had little to fear from foreign competition. And just at this moment the folly of our neighbour, the French King Louis XIV., induced him to deprive his nation of most of its skilled workmen by the Revocation of the Edict of Nantes. His loss was our gain. The Edict in question, passed nearly a century previously, had insured freedom of worship to the French Huguenots, who comprised in their ranks the *élite* of the industrial population. Louis XIV.[2] set to work to exterminate the Protestant religion in France, and began by revoking this Edict (1685). Once more England profited by her Protestantism, and, owing to the religious opinions of her people, received a fresh accession of industrial strength. Some thousands of skilled Huguenot artisans and manufacturers came over and settled in this land.[3] They greatly improved the silk, glass, and paper trades,[4] and exercised considerable influence in the development of domestic manufactures generally. It is said that the immigrants numbered 50,000 souls, with a capital of some £3,000,000.[5] Every one knows how they introduced the silk industry into this country, and how Spitalfields long remained a colony of Huguenot silk-weavers.[6] Their descendants are to be found in every part of England.

§ 186. *Distribution of the Cloth Trade.*

From this time forward the cloth trade, in especial, took its place among the chief industries of the country, largely owing to the fresh spirit infused into it, first by Flemish, and afterwards by French weavers. We have already seen where it chiefly flourished in the sixteenth and seventeenth centuries, and now it became more and more widely distributed.[7]

---

[1] Rogers, *Econ. Interpretation of History*, 287.
[2] See Voltaire, *Siècle de Louis XIV.*, ch. xxxii.
[3] *Cf.* Anderson, *Chron. Deduct. Commerce*, ii. 568.
[4] *Ib.*, ii. 569.   [5] *Ib.*, ii. 569.
[6] Voltaire, *Siècle de Louis XIV.*, ch. xxxii. ; Lecky, *History of the Eighteenth Century*, i. 191.
[7] For the following details, *cf.* Rogers, *Hist. Agric.*, v. 95, and the Act 4 and 5 James I., c. 2.

The county of Kent, and the towns of York and Reading, made one kind of cloth of a heavy texture, the
piece being thirty or thirty-four yards long by six and
one-half broad, and weighing 66 lbs. to the piece.
Worcester, Hereford, and Coventry made a lighter kind of
fabric, while throughout the eastern counties of Norfolk,
Suffolk, and Essex were made cloths of various kinds—
plunkets, azures, blues, long cloth, bay, say, and serges;
Suffolk, in particular, made a " fine, short, white cloth."
Wiltshire and Somerset made plunkets and handy warps;
Yorkshire, short cloths.   Broad-listed whites and reds, and
fine cloths, also came from Wiltshire, Gloucestershire, and
Oxfordshire; and Somerset was famous in the eastern part
for narrow-listed whites and reds, and in the west for
" dunsters."   Devonshire made kerseys and grays, as also
did Yorkshire and Lancashire.   The Midlands furnished
" Penistone" cloths and " Forest whites"; while Westmoreland was the seat of the manufacture of the famous
" Kendal green" cloths, as also of " Carpmael" and " Cog-
ware" fabrics.[1]   It will be seen that the manufacture was
exceedingly extensive, and that special fabrics derived their
names from the chief centre where they were made.   It
may be mentioned here, too, that the value of wool shorn
in England at the end of the seventeenth century was
£2,000,000, from about 12,000,000 sheep (according to
Davenant[2]); and the cloth manufactured from it was
valued at about £8,000,000.   Nearly half a century
later (1741) the number of sheep was reckoned[3] at
17,000,000, the value of wool shorn at £3,000,000,
and of wool manufactured at £8,000,000, showing that
progress in invention had not done much to enhance the
value of the manufactured article.   But in 1774, when
the Industrial Revolution may be said to have fairly begun,
the value of manufactured wool was £13,000,000, the
value of raw wool (£4,500,000) being smaller in proportion.[4]

---

[1] Cf. Rogers, Hist. Agric., v. 95, and the Act 4 and 5 James I., c. 2.
[2] Davenant, Discourse on the East India Trade ; Works, ii. 146.
[3] Burnley, Wool and Woolcombing, p. 79.   [4] Ib.

§ 187. *Coal Mines.*

Turning now from textile manufactures to mining and working in metals, we find that in the seventeenth and eighteenth centuries England was just upon the eve of the most important changes in these industries—changes which, in many places, have entirely transformed the face of the country, and have equally transformed the conditions of industry, and with them the social life of the working classes. It is no exaggeration to say that in its effects, both for good and evil, hardly any other historical event has been of so much importance as the modern improvements in coal-mining. But it cannot be too clearly understood that none of our mining and mineral industries attained any propor-tions worth speaking of till what is known as the Industrial Revolution. Englishmen seem to have had hardly any idea of the vast wealth of coal and iron that has placed them in the forefront of Europe as a manufacturing nation. Never-theless we may just glance at the imperfect methods which our forefathers used up till the eighteenth century. Coal-mining had been carried on fairly extensively by the Romans, as, for instance, the discovery of coal cinders at Aston[1] and other places testifies. Then, like all our in-dustries, it was almost entirely given up, and it was due to the Norman Conquest that coal-mining was revived. That it was practised to some extent in the North is seen from an entry in the *Boldean Book* (a kind of Domesday of the county of Durham, composed in 1183), in which a smith is allowed twelve acres of land for making the iron-work of the carts, and has to provide his own coal.[2] But collieries were not opened at Newcastle till the thirteenth century,[3] in the year 1238. In the next year we find notice of the first public recognition of coal as an article of commerce, and from a charter of Henry III. to the freemen of Newcastle, we may date the foundation of the coal trade.[4] In 1273 this had become sufficiently extensive for the use of coal to be forbidden in London, as there was

[1] Bourne, *Romance of Trade*, p. 174.
[2] Yeats, *Technical History of Commerce*, p. 171.
[3] *Ib.*, p. 172.   [4] *Ib.*

a prejudice against it and in favour of wood as fuel.[1]   In the fourteenth century, again, the monks of Tynemouth Priory engaged in mining speculation, and (1380) leased a colliery[2] for £5.   In the fifteenth century trade was sufficiently important to form a source of revenue, for a tax of twopence per chaldron was placed upon sea-borne coal, and in 1421 an Act had to be passed to enforce this tax.[3] In fact, in the fourteenth and fifteenth centuries coal-mining, although in a rather primitive fashion, became general in Great Britain.

§ 188. *Development of Coal Trade: Seventeenth and Eighteenth Centuries.*

By the seventeenth century it had also become important—important enough for the needy Stuart monarch Charles I. to see in it a chance of revenue.   This king gave to Sir Thomas Tempest and his partners the monopoly of the sale of Newcastle coal for twenty-one years,[4] beginning in 1637, and next year he allowed a syndicate to be incorporated which was to buy up all the coal from Newcastle, Sunderland, and Berwick, and sell it in London for "not more than 17s. a ton in summer, and 19s. in winter" —an extravagant price for those times.   The king got a shilling a ton out of this ingenious scheme,[5] until the Long Parliament finally put a stop to this outrageous monopoly.   Yet the coal trade still formed a favourite source of revenue, and the charge of re-erecting public buildings was defrayed by an additional custom on coals.[6] It was said that early in the seventeenth century the Newcastle trade alone employed four hundred vessels.[7]

But although the coal trade was fairly extensive for that period, it was utterly insignificant compared with its present dimensions, and that for a very good reason.   There was no

---

[1] Yeats, *Technical History of Commerce*, p. 172.   Sea-coal is found to have been brought as far south as Dover as early as 1279 ; *cf.* Rogers, *Hist. Agric.*, i. 422, and ii. 394-397.

[2] Yeats, *Technical History*, p. 172.   [3] *Cf.* Act 9 Henry V., c. 10.

[4] Bourne, *Romance of Trade*, p. 154.

[5] *Ib.*; see also Levy, *Monopoly and Competition.*

[6] Cunningham, *Growth of Industry*, ii. 175.

[7] Craik, *British Commerce*, ii. 32.

means of pumping water out of the mines, except by the old-fashioned air-pump, which was, of course, utterly inadequate. Nor was a suitable invention discovered till the very end of the seventeenth century, when Thomas Savery, in 1698, invented a kind of pump, worked by the condensation of steam.[1] This rather clumsy invention, however, was soon superseded in 1705 by Newcomen's steam pump.[2] But it was not till after the commencement of the Industrial Revolution that steam power was scientifically applied to coal-mines by the inventions of Watt and Boulton (1765 and 1774), which we shall notice in their proper place.[3] Up to that time, also, it was difficult to transport coal into inland districts by road, Newcastle coal being carried to London in ships, and then carried up inland rivers in barges. But these barges could not go high up many rivers at that time, and canals were not yet made. It was difficult, for instance, to get coal to Oxford, for it had first to come to London, then part of the way up the Thames, which was not then navigable so far as Oxford, and then by road. But at Cambridge it was easily procurable, for barges could come right up to the town from eastern ports. Hence it was much cheaper at Cambridge than at Oxford.[4]

§ 189. *The Iron Trade.*

As it had been with coal, so with iron. Only very small quantities of it were mined in the Middle Ages ; it was smelted only by wood,[5] as a rule, and was manufactured in a very rude way. We saw that at the great fairs foreign iron, chiefly from the Biscay coast, was much in demand, as our own supply was utterly insufficient.[6] It was naturally not until we learnt to mine and use our coal properly that we learnt also how to mine and manufacture our iron. Before learning this, English workmen used wood as fuel,

---

[1] Smiles, *Lives of the Engineers* (*Boulton and Watt*), ch. iii. A diagram of Savery's engine is on p. 49.

[2] *Ib.*, chs. iii. and iv., and diagrams, pp. 61 and 73.

[3] Below, p. 352.

[4] Rogers, *Hist. Agric.*, v. 757, 774, 776 ; vi. 560.

[5] *Cf.* the 35 Henry VIII., c. 17 ; and Smiles, *Industrial Biography*, ch. ii.

[6] Above, p. 143.

and it is to this cause that we owe the destruction of most
of the forests which, at the time of Domesday, occupied so
large an area. The extinction of the great forest of the
Sussex Wealden is an example of this.[1] " The waste and
destruction of the woods in the counties of Warwick,
Stafford, Hereford, Monmouth, Gloucester, and Salop by
these iron-works is not to be imagined," a speaker said in
Parliament as late as the beginning of the eighteenth
century ;[2] and as wood was used as house-fuel also, it will
readily be understood what a vast destruction of timber
took place. As early as 1581 the erection of iron-works
within certain distances from London and the Thames
had been prohibited " for the preservation of the woods."[3]

But early in the seventeenth century Dud Dudley, son
of Lord Dudley, began to make use of sea and pit coal for
smelting iron, and obtained (1619) a monopoly " of the
mystery and art of smelting iron ore, and of making the
same into cast works or bars, in furnaces, with bellows."[4]
Dudley sold this cast iron at £12 a ton, and made a good
profit out of it, but at last his works were destroyed by an
ignorant mob.[5] He actually produced seven tons a week,
which was considered a large supply, and shows the comparative insignificance of the industry then. However, it
was only comparatively insignificant, for before the close of
the century it was calculated that 180,000 tons of ore were
produced in England yearly ; and in the eighteenth century
(1719) iron came third in the list of English manufactures,
and the trade gave employment to 200,000 people.[6] There
was, however, still great waste of wood, since a great many
iron-masters did not use coal, and therefore the export and
even the manufacture of iron was discouraged by legislation
to such an extent, that, by 1740, the output had been
reduced to 17,350 tons per annum, barely a tenth of the

[1] *Cf.* Rogers, *Econ. Interpretation*, p. 287 ; and below, p. 314.
[2] Bourne, *Romance of Trade*, p. 177.
[3] M'Culloch, *Commercial Dictionary* (ed. 1844) ; *s.v. Iron*, p. 753.
[4] *Cf.* his book *Metallum Martis*, or *Iron made with pit coale, sea coale,
&c.* (1665) ; and M'Culloch, *Commercial Dict.* (1844), *s.v. Iron* ; also
Smiles, *Industrial Biography*, ch. iii.
[5] *Ib.* ; also Bourne, *Romance of Trade*, p. 176.
[6] *Romance of Trade*, p. 177.

previous amount quoted.[1]   The waste of timber was most noticeable in the Sussex Wealden, the forests of which owe their destruction almost entirely to the iron and glass manufactures.[2]

But about this time another inventor, Abraham Darby, of the famous Coalbrookdale Ironworks,[3] discovered the secret of the large blast-furnace in which both pit-coal and charcoal were used.   He began his experiments as early as 1730, but did not do much for some twenty years. In 1756, however, his works were " at the top pinnacle of prosperity ; twenty and twenty-two tons per week sold off as fast as made, and profit enough." [4]

After Darby came Smeaton, and other inventors, and the Industrial Revolution spread to the iron trade.   We shall see it in operation in our next period.[5]

§ 190. *Pottery.*

As with all other manufactures, so, too, the development of pottery was reserved for the Renaissance of industry in the eighteenth century.   Of course pottery of a kind had always been made in England, especially where the useful soil of Staffordshire formed a favourable ground for the exercise of this art.[6]   But the pottery hitherto manufactured had been rude and coarse, and its manufacture was a strictly domestic and not very widespread industry.[7]   We owe its improvement, as in so many other cases, largely to the efforts of the Dutch and Huguenot [8] immigrants of the sixteenth and seventeenth centuries.   For the Dutch had been great among the potters of Europe, as the renown of Delft-ware still testifies, while France had the honour of being the land of Palissy.   The factories at Burslem, how-

---

[1] *Romance of Trade,* p. 178, and M'Culloch, *Commercial Dict.,* *s.v. Iron.*
[2] Norden, in Rogers, *Hist. Agric.,* v. 44.
[3] Smiles, *Industrial Biography,* ch. v. p. 80.
[4] Bourne, *Romance of Trade,* p. 179.   [5] Below, p. 341, 352.
[6] Bourne, *Romance of Trade,* p. 169.
[7] There were, however, potteries elsewhere than in Staffs., as *e.g.* in Essex ; Pennant (1801), *Journey from London to the Isle of Wight,* i. 53 ; and Lowestoft ware is well known to connoisseurs.
[8] Anderson, *Chron. Commerce,* ii. 569.

ever, owed their origin to the industry of two Germans from Nuremberg, called Elers, from whom an Englishman, Astbury, learnt the secret of producing the red unglazed Japanese ware, and the black Egyptian ware.[1] Burslem, too, was the birthplace of Josiah Wedgwood,[2] born 1730, who first began business in 1752 as manager for a master-potter, but started in business on his own account in 1759, the eve of the Industrial Revolution. His efforts and experiments were magnificent and untiring, and they can be read at leisure in various biographical works. It is sufficient here to say that Wedgwood was the man who first made the art of pottery a science, and before his death, in 1795, he had brought this manufacture to such a pitch of excellence that few improvements have been left for his successors to make, and it rose to be one of the chief industries of the country.[3]

§ 191. *Other Mining Industries.*

There remain one or two industries that require a passing mention, but which were not in the eighteenth century of much importance. As to the metals, the foreign trade in tin and lead has been already mentioned. In the reign of John the tin-mines of Cornwall were farmed by the Jews,[4] and the tin and lead trade must have attained considerable proportions in the fourteenth century, for the Black Prince paid his own expenses in the French wars by the produce of his mines of those metals in Devonshire [5] Copper, also, was mined in the northern counties, and in a statute of 15 Edward III. (1343) we find grants of mines given at Skeldane, in Northumberland ; at Alston Moor, in Cumberland ; and at Richmond, in Yorkshire ; a royalty of one-eighth going to the king, and one-ninth to the lord of the manor.[6] Keswick was at that time a centre of this industry ; but the art of the coppersmith was developed chiefly in Germany.[7] The mines were also very primitive, the approaches being made, not

---

[1] Bourne, *Romance of Trade*, p. 171 ; Smiles, *Self Help*, p. 88.
[2] Smiles, *Self Help*, pp. 88-93.   [3] *Ib.*, p. 92.
[4] Yeats, *Technical History of Commerce*, p. 172.   [5] *Ib.*, p. 173.
[6] *Ib.*, p. 173.   [7] *Ib.*, p. 185.

by shafts, but by adits in the side of a convenient hill.
Another mineral, which is very abundant in England,
especially in Worcestershire and Cheshire, was at this
period hardly utilised. Salt was a necessary of life to the
English householder, for he had to salt his meat for the
winter ; but he did not know how to mine it himself, and
either got it imported from south-west France, or contented
himself with the inferior article evaporated on the sea-
coast, until the end of the seventeenth century.[1]

It has been already mentioned that brick-making was a
lost art from the fifth to the fifteenth century. The first
purchase to be recorded was at Cambridge, in 1449 ; but
before the end of the fifteenth century it became a common
building material in the eastern counties, and in the sixteenth century was generally used in London and in the
counties along the lower course of the Thames.[2]

§ 192. *The Close of the Period of Manual Industries.*

We have now reached a turning-point in English industrial history, and are about to study a period that is in
every way a violent contrast to the centuries which preceded it. We have come to the time when machinery
begins to displace unaided manual labour. Hitherto all our
manufactures, our mining, and, of course, our agriculture,
had been performed by the literal labour of men's hands,
helped but slightly by a few simple inventions. Industry,
too, was not organised upon a vast capitalistic basis, though
of course capitalists existed ; but it would be more correct
to say that hitherto industry had been chiefly carried on by
numbers of smaller capitalists who were also manual workmen, even when they employed other workmen under them.[3]
Only in agriculture had the capitalist class become very far
removed from the labourers.[4] There was certainly no such
violent contrast as now exists between a mill-owner and a
mill-hand in the realm of manufacturing industry,[5] though,

---

[1] Rogers, *Econ. Interpretation*, p. 277.   [2] *Ib.*, p. 279.
[3] *Cf.* Toynbee, *Industrial Revolution*, pp. 72, 53.
[4] Above, pp. 157, 184, 212, 216, 271. Toynbee (p. 71) is wrong in saying "the capitalist farmers were not yet in existence."
[5] Toynbee, *Indust. Rev.*, pp. 71, 53.

of course, this contrast existed between the rich landowner, who received rents, and the poor agricultural labourer, whose labour helped to pay them.   But, speaking of industry generally, it may be said that the absence of machinery kept employers and workmen more upon a common level ; and as large factories, of course, did not exist, industry was carried on chiefly in the workmen's homes, while the work-man was not merely a unit among hundreds of unknown "hands" in a mill, but a person not hopelessly removed in social rank from his employer, who was well acquainted with him, and, like him, worked with his own hands.

But now this old order of things passes away, and a new order appears, ushered in by the whirr and rattle of machinery and the mighty hiss of steam.   A complete transformation takes place, and the life of England stirs anew in the great Industrial Revolution.

PERIOD V

THE INDUSTRIAL REVOLUTION AND MODERN
ENGLAND

CHAPTER XX

THE EVE OF THE REVOLUTION

§ 193. *Industry and Politics. Landowners and Merchant Princes.*

WE are, of course, mainly concerned in this book with industrial facts; but as these underlie all politics and national history, we must pause for a moment to see how the growth of commerce had by this time affected the relations of two great classes: the landowners and their new rivals, the great merchants and the commercial classes generally. Up to the time of the deposition of James II., or the Whig Revolution of 1688, as it is sometimes called,[1] the land-owning class had been practically supreme in social and political influence. But from that time forward, although they still held this high position, their influence was heavily counterbalanced by that of the mercantile classes.[2] The Revolution may have been aristocratic in its origin,[3] but it was certainly democratic in its ultimate results. The capitalists and the commercial magnates were all favoured by the great movement which divided the nation into the two historic parties of Whigs and Tories, for it was that movement which first accentuated their importance in the political life of the nation.[4] That importance was still further increased by a series of significant economic events,[5] already alluded to, which took place shortly after the

[1] Lecky, *History of the Eighteenth Century*, i. 171, remarks that the House of Lords was chiefly Whig, and that the aristocracy really effected this Revolution.

[2] For the mercantile element in politics, *cf.* Lecky, *History*, i. 199, 200.

[3] Lecky (*History*, i. 16, 156) shows that it was an aristocratic movement, but does not indicate quite so clearly its results in bringing into prominence the middle (and, later, even the lower) classes.

[4] "The political influence of the industrial and moneyed classes was greatly increased by the Revolution." Lecky, *History*, i. 201.

[5] Above, pp. 299-304.

Revolution; namely, the foundation of the Bank of England (1694), the new and extended Charter granted to the East India Company in 1693, the beginning of the National Debt in the same year, and the Restoration of the Currency in 1696. The commercial and industrial section of the community was becoming more and more prominent, and the great Whig families who occupied themselves with endeavouring to rule England in the eighteenth century relied for their support upon the middle and commercial classes.[1] The old reverence, however, for the position of a landowner had not yet died out, and the men who had gained their wealth by commerce strove for a higher social position by buying land in large quantities.[2] The time had not yet come when a merchant was on equal terms with a landowner.

In fact, there has always been an extraordinary sentimentalism as regards land among all classes of the English people; and for certain reasons, which, though not entirely baseless, are still somewhat inadequate, a man who has merely inherited a large amount of land (even if he has never attempted to cultivate it) is regarded as superior to one who has amassed a fortune in the industrial or commercial world. And this feeling was stronger in the eighteenth century than it is at the present time, though it is certainly even now by no means extinct. Hence commercial magnates then, as now, or even more than now, bought land, hoping to buy with it social prestige. The James Lowther who was created Earl of Lonsdale in 1784 was the descendant of a merchant engaged in the Levant trade;[3] and the first Earl of Tilney was the son of that eminent man of business, Sir Josiah Child.[4] The daughters of merchant princes were even allowed to marry—and maintain—the scions of a needy aristocracy.[5]

The beginning of this new order of things can be dated with some accuracy by a remark of Sir W. Temple's: "I

---

[1] Lecky, *History*, i. 187.
[2] Toynbee, *Industrial Revolution*, p. 62.   [3] *Ib.*, p. 63.
[4] Defoe, *Complete Tradesman* (ed. 1839, Chambers), p. 74.
[5] Thus, Child's daughter married the Marquis of Worcester; *cf.* Toynbee, *Ind. Rev.*, p. 63.

think I remember," he wrote in the last quarter of the seventeenth century,[1] "the first noble families that married into the city for downright money, and thereby introduced by degrees this public grievance, which has since ruined so many estates by the necessity of giving good portions to daughters." Defoe actually discovered the amazing and revolutionary fact that a man engaged in commerce might be a gentleman, though, no doubt, this bold supposition of his was at first looked upon with incredulity. He says: "Trade is so far from being inconsistent with a gentleman that in England trade makes a gentleman; for, *after a generation or two*, the tradesman's children come to be as good gentlemen, statesmen, parliament men, judges, bishops, and noblemen, as those of the highest birth and the most ancient families."[2] Dean Swift remarked, "that the power which used to follow land had gone over to money."[3] Dr Johnson announced oracularly that "an English merchant was a new species of gentleman."[4] This influx of the merchants into the upper classes was not, however, an entirely new thing, though no doubt it became more noticeable at this time; for Harrison, the well-known describer of Elizabethan England, had long before remarked that, though "citizens and burgesses have next place to gentlemen," yet, "they often change estate with gentlemen, as gentlemen do with them, by a mutual conversion of one into the other."[5]

Now, the Industrial Revolution of the eighteenth century went still further than the political revolution of the seventeenth to gain social and political influence for the commercial classes. It succeeded in destroying the feudal but foolish idea that the landowners alone were to be looked upon as the leaders of the nation. It gave the capitalists and manufacturers a new accession of power, by enormously increasing their wealth. Moreover, it helped to undermine the landed interest by making the manufactures of England

[1] Temple's *Miscellanies*, quoted in Lecky, *History*, i. 193.
[2] Defoe, *Complete Tradesman*, u. s., p. 74.   [3] Swift, *Examiner*, No. 13.
[4] Boswell, *Life of Johnson* (7th edn.), ii. 108.
[5] Harrison, *Description of England*, Book III., ch. iv. (edn. 1577), page 9, Camelot Series edn.

at first equal, and afterwards superior, to her agriculture, so that a rich mill-owner or iron-master became as important as a large landowner. The monopoly of the landed interest was broken by capital. Nowhere perhaps is the contrast between the old and new classes in the last century seen more closely than in Sir Walter Scott's novel *Rob Roy*, where the old Tory squire who held fast to Church and king is contrasted with the new commercial magnate who supported the House of Hanover.[1] But already the commercial element was coming to the front in politics.

In very few periods of English political history was the commercial element so strong as in the early Hanoverian days under the régime of Walpole and Pelham.[2] The questions that excited most interest in Parliament were chiefly those connected with commerce and finance.[3] Burke, writing in 1752, summed up the requirements of a Member of the House of Commons in a plaintive sentence,[4] which illustrates the tendency of the time : " A man, after all, would do more by figures of arithmetic than by figures of rhetoric." A rhetorician himself, he meant, in this utterance, to be sarcastic ; but it would be well if it were possible for orators to remember that two and two can only make four, and that the figures of arithmetic are safer guides for the statesman than the hyperboles of oratory. The introduction of the mercantile element into Parliament, and into the ranks of the aristocracy, though by no means an unmixed blessing, has yet had the healthy effect of keeping the English nobility in touch with the mass of the people,[5] and of connecting all ranks together in the common interests of the national life.

§ 194. *The Coming of the Capitalists.*

Now, although the commercial capitalist was fast coming into prominence as the rival of the landowner,[6] he was

---

[1] This illustration is due to W. Clarke, in *Fabian Essays*, p. 78.

[2] *Cf.* Lecky, *History*, i. 433. [3] *Ib.* [4] Prior, *Life of Burke*, i. 38.

[5] *Cf.* Lecky, *History*, i. 170 *sqq.*, on the English aristocracy ; and also Toynbee, *Industrial Revolution*, p. 63.

[6] Cunningham, *Growth of Industry*, ii. 6, remarks : " From the beginning of the eighteenth century onwards the monied interest has overbalanced the landed interest." This is partially true but the capitalist hardly over-

becoming still more prominent as the master of the workmen whom he employed. For before the Industrial Revolution the capitalist had occupied a comparatively subordinate place.[1] Of course capitalists existed, as they have
always done, but their power was small as compared with
that of their successors to-day.[2] The vast enterprises of
modern industry, such as railways or mills, which often
require so large an expenditure of capital before they can
begin to be in any way remunerative, were practically unknown a century ago. The industrial system was, moreover, far less complicated, far less international, far less
subdivided.[3] Instead of the great capitalist manufacturers
of to-day, who can control the markets of a nation, England
possessed numbers of smaller capitalists,[4] with far less
capital, both individually and in the aggregate, than that
which is now required by a man who undertakes even a
moderate business. The great capitalists of the last century were chiefly the foreign trading companies. But home
manufactures, although greatly developed,[5] were still largely
conducted upon the domestic system, and the small capi-
talist-artisan was a conspicuous feature of that time, just as
the large mill-owner or iron-master is of our own day.
Manufactures were carried on by a number of small master-
manufacturers,[6] who gave out work to be done in the homes
of their employés ; and who often combined agricultural
with manufacturing pursuits.[7] But, nevertheless, there were
signs of the approach of the methods of modern capitalism,
and of production upon a large scale. It was becoming in-

balanced the landowner yet, though he was becoming on more equal terms
with him.

[1] *Cf.* Toynbee, *Industrial Revolution*, p. 52.

[2] Cunningham, *Growth of Industry*, ii. 5, dates the rise of the capitalist
class "from the time of Elizabeth onwards." This is rather to antedate
their coming into prominence.

[3] Adam Smith, *Wealth of Nations*, Bk. I. ch. i., remarks that it is impossible to collect all the workmen in different branches of a manufacture
into the same " workhouse" (*i.e.*, mill). In his time the huge modern
factory was unknown. (*Cf.* Rogers' edition of Smith, Vol. I. p. 6, note.)

[4] Toynbee, *Indust. Revolution*, p. 53.

[5] *Cf.* Smith, *Wealth of Nations*, Bk. I. ch. xi. (Vol. I. p. 260, Clarendon
Press edition).

[6] Toynbee, *Indust. Revolution*, 53.   [7] *Cf.* Rogers, *Hist. Agric.*, v. 810

creasingly the custom to employ a large number of workpeople together under one roof, or at least under the direction and supervision of one great manufacturer. Arthur Young, for instance, mentions a silk mill at Sheffield with 152 hands, a large number in the eighteenth century; a factory at Boynton with 150 hands; and a master-manufacturer at Darlington who ran above fifty looms.[1] Work was also given out by capitalist manufacturers or merchants to workmen to do at home in the villages and towns. These workmen were, like the employés of the present day, entirely dependent upon their employer for work and wages. Thus at Nottingham, in 1750, we find fifty master-manufacturers who "put out" work in this way for as many as 1200 looms in the hosiery trade.[2]

§ 195. *The Class of Small Manufacturers.*

But although the coming of the capitalists was now near at hand, the old order of things was not seriously disturbed till the application of steam power to machinery some years later. There were still many small manufacturers who lived on their own land and worked with their workpeople in their own houses. Defoe, in his *Tour through Great Britain* (made in 1724-26), gives an interesting account of this class at a time when they were in the height of their prosperity, before machinery and steam had even begun to cause their disappearance. Speaking of the land near Halifax, in Yorkshire, he says:[3] "The land was divided into small enclosures, from two acres to six or seven each, seldom more, every three or four pieces of land having a house belonging to them; hardly a house standing out of speaking distance from another. We could see at every house a tenter, and on almost every tenter a piece of cloth or kersie or shalloon. At every considerable house there was a manufactory. Every clothier keeps one horse at least to carry his manufactures to the market; and every one generally keeps a cow or two or more for his family. By this means the

---

[1] Young, *Northern Tour*, i. 134; ii. 8, 467 (ed. 1770).
[2] Toynbee, *Indust. Revolution*, 53; Felkin, *History of Hosiery*, 83.
[3] *Tour*, iii. pp. 144-146.

small pieces of enclosed land about each house are occupied, for they scarce sow corn enough to feed their poultry. The houses are full of lusty fellows, some at the dye-vat, some at the looms, others dressing the cloths; the women and children carding or spinning ; being all employed, from the youngest to the oldest." And Defoe adds a remark which is certainly not applicable either to Halifax or to any other manufacturing town of the present day, for he concludes his description with the words: "not a beggar to be seen, or an idle person."[1]

§ 196. *The Condition of the Manufacturing Population.*

For it is a significant fact that under the old domestic system, simple and cumbrous as it was, the manufacturing population was very much better off than it was for some time after the Industrial Revolution. For one thing, they still lived more or less in the country, and were not crowded together in stifling alleys and courts, or in long rows of bare smoke-begrimed streets, in houses like so many dirty rabbit-hutches. Even if the artisan did live in a town at that time, the town was very different from the abodes of smoke and dirt which now prevail in the manufacturing districts. It had a more rural character.[2] There were no tall chimneys, belching out clouds of evil smoke ; no huge, hot factories with their hundreds of windows blazing forth a lurid light in the darkness, and rattling with the whirr and din of ceaseless machinery by day and night. There were no gigantic blast furnaces rising amid blackened heaps of cinders, or chemical works poisoning the fields and trees for miles around. These were yet to come. The factory and the furnace were almost unknown. Work was carried on by the artisan in his little stone or brick house, with the workshop inside, where the wool for the weft was carded and spun by his wife and daughters,[3] and the cloth was

---

[1] *Tour*, iii. p. 146.

[2] *Cf.* Cunningham, *Growth of Industry*, ii. 480.

[3] At Armley "many persons who have small farms also carry on cloth-making, employing their wives, children, and servants." *Report from the Committee on the state of the woollen manufacture ;* Reports, 1806, iii. 602 · also the quotation from Defoe, just above.

woven by himself and his sons. He had also, in nearly all cases, his plot of land near the house,[1] which provided him both with food and recreation, for he could relieve the monotony of weaving by cultivating his little patch of ground, or feeding his pigs and poultry. The woollen weavers, especially, in all parts of the country appear to have had allotments or large gardens,[2] some of which still exist; and even at the beginning of the nineteenth century there was a large part of the manufacturing population which was not yet divorced from rural employments.[3]

§ 197. *Two Examples of Village Life.*

The old conditions of life in English villages under this domestic system, with its healthy combination of agricultural and manufacturing industry, and its prevalence of bye-industries, are even yet not entirely forgotten, and may be here illustrated by personal testimonies, one from the south and the other from the north of England. A most interesting picture of life in a Hampshire village is thus drawn by the late Professor Thorold Rogers[4] " In my native village [West Meon] in Hampshire, I well remember two instances of agricultural labourers who raised themselves through the machinery of the allowance system [5] to the rank and fortunes of small yeomen. Both had large families, and both practised a bye-industry. The village was peculiar in its social character, for there was not a tenant-farmer in it, all being freeholders or copyholders. There was no poverty in the whole place. Most of the labourers baked their own bread, brewed their own beer, kept pigs and poultry, and had half an acre or an acre to till for themselves as part of their hire. The rector built extensively parsonage, schools, and finally church, from his own means, and, therefore, employment was pretty general.

---

[1] Arthur Young, *Farmer's Letters*, i. 205, and *cf.* Toynbee, *Indust. Rev.*, p. 68.

[2] Cunningham, *Growth of Industry*, ii. 480. I might add from personal observation the case of the place still known as the " Woolsorters' Gardens" at Heaton, near Bradford, Yorks.

[3] Cunningham, *u. s.*, ii. 481

[4] *Six Centuries*, p. 502.   [5] See below, pp. 408, 412-414.

The village mason became a considerable yeoman.   But the
two labourers of whom I am speaking had their allowances,
and lived on their fixed wages, with the profits of their
bye-labour . . . and the produce of their small curtilage."
Thus the prevalence of bye-industries, combined with allotments, gave the labourer and artisan, under the domestic
system, a far better chance of gaining a comfortable and
healthy livelihood than he possessed in those cases where
the factory system had deprived him of these advantages.

   The other picture is from a writer [1] who derives his experience from the northern counties.   Speaking of English
village life, " as it existed in the memory of many now
living," he remarks : " The village combined agricultural
with industrial occupation ; the click of the loom was heard in
the cottages ; the farmyard and the fields, the cottages and
the allotment gardens, made a delightful picture of rural
life.   The land was mainly freehold ; the farmers were of
the yeoman class, and not infrequently combined the calling
of a clothier or master manufacturer along with that of
farming.   The farmer's wife, although born with a silver
spoon, was industrious and thrifty ; with her own hand she
would churn the butter, make the cheese, cure the bacon
and ham, or bake the bread ; her daughters would assist in
spinning the yarn, or knitting the stockings ; and from the
cloths woven under their supervision they would, with the
assistance of the village dressmaker, make their own dresses.
If you entered one of the cottages you would find the master
of the house in the 'chamber,' sitting at the loom, busy
throwing the shuttle, weaving a piece of cloth ; his daughter
would be sitting at the wheel, spinning weft ; and the good
wife would be busy with her domestic duties.   One son
would be out working on the land for the farmer ; another
would be working on the weaver's allotment.   Down in
their little allotment plot they grow their own vegetables,
and a little crop of oats, which they have ground into oat-
meal for making their porridge ; they also keep a pig or
two, and provide their own bacon and ham.   They are on
good terms with the master-manufacturer—that is, the

[1] Thomas Illingworth, *Distribution Reform* (Cassell, London, 1885), p. 81.

gentleman who gives them warp and weft to weave into cloth. He is also a large farmer, and in the hay-harvest and corn-harvest they all have a fine time in the fields, giving a hand to the cutting, the harvesting, and home-carrying of the crops. . . . Their chief articles of food are produced from the land immediately surrounding them. Their means of subsistence and comfort are not to be computed by the amount of their earnings in money-wages, but the produce of their bit of land, and the ease and cheapness with which they can obtain other necessities." [1]

It will thus be seen that the old domestic system had, at least for the working-classes, many advantages, some of which have not been even yet perhaps quite compensated by the undoubted benefits of the Industrial Revolution. It is foolish, as well as inaccurate, to imagine that the past must have been necessarily better than the present; but, on the other hand, it may readily be admitted that there are many single features in it which compare more than favourably with those of to-day, though the general outline of the present may be superior.

Work, for instance, was more regular than it often is at present, for there were fewer commercial fluctuations; [2] fashions did not change so quickly, and the market for homespun fabrics was always steady and assured. The relations between employers and employed were far closer; even the distribution of wealth was comparatively more equal. [3] Wages were somewhat less in money value than at present, but, then, prices of food and rent were only about half what they are now. Arthur Young gives 9s. 6d. as the average weekly wages of an artisan in the North and Midland counties, though in some cases they were much higher, while the average rent for a cottage in the same counties he puts at 28s. 2d. a year, or only 6½d. per week. [4] And it must be remembered that this included

---

[1] The writer means that most of these could be obtained from their own work, or from their neighbours, who practised other bye-industries; cf. pp. 82-83 of the book quoted.

[2] Cf. Toynbee, Indust. Revolution, p. 71. [3] Ib.

[4] Young, Northern Tour, iv. 470-472 (wages), 435-439 (rent); ed. 1770. The wages of hand wool combers in 1747 were 12s. to 21s. a week, according to Burnley, Wool and Woolcombing, p. 159.

a piece of land round the cottage.   Meat, also, was cheap, being from 2½d. to 3¼d. per pound ; and bread 1¼d. a pound.[1]   In fact, we may confidently say that artisans, especially spinners and weavers, were well off about 1760. Adam Smith testifies to this in the *Wealth of Nations.* " Not only has grain become somewhat cheaper," he says, " but many other things from which the industrious poor derive an agreeable and wholesome variety of food have become a great deal cheaper." [2]   And the healthy condition of industry in general is shown by the fact that at the close of the wars with France, by the Peace of 1763, when more than 100,000 men accustomed to war were thrown upon the country, and had to find work or else be supported in some way or other, " not only no great convulsion, but no sensible disorder arose." [3]

§ 198. *Condition of the Agricultural Population.*

Nor was that convenient plenty which was the lot of the manufacturing portion of the people confined only to that section.   The condition of the agricultural labourer, who was generally the worst off of all classes, from being so much under the direct supervision of his master, had considerably improved, together with the general improvement of agriculture spoken of in a previous chapter.   The price of corn had fallen, while wages had risen, though these were less than an artisan's, being, according to Arthur Young's average estimate for the North and Midland counties, about 7s. a week.[4]   But it was generally 8s. or 10s., while the board of a working man may be placed at about 5s. or 6s. a week.[5]   Cottages were occasionally rent free, or, at any rate, only paid a low rent, never more than 50s. or 60s. per year,[6] and generally much less.   Moreover, just as

---

[1] Young, *Northern Tour,* iv. 451 *sqq.*
[2] *Wealth of Nations,* Bk. I. ch. viii. (i. 82, Clarendon Press edn.).
[3] *Wealth of Nations.* Bk. IV. ch. ii. (ii. 43, Clarendon Press edn.).
[4] *Northern Tour,* iv. 445.   The exact average is 7s. 1d.   He gives board as 8d. a day in the North and 10d. in the South.   *Ib.,* iv. 441.
[5] *Cf. A Table of Wages and Prices of Commodities during three important Epochs of English Industry,* by Thomas Illingworth (Bradford).   [6] *Ib.*

artisans added to their earnings by agricultural work, so, too, agricultural labourers increased their wages by such bye-industries as spinning and lace-making.[1] There was an abundance of food, clothing, and furniture.[2] Wheat-bread had almost entirely superseded rye-bread.[3] Every poor family now drank tea, which had formerly been a costly luxury.[4] The consumption of meat was, says Arthur Young, "pretty considerable," and that of cheese "immense."[5] An earlier writer states that the labourers, "by their large wages and the cheapness of all necessaries, enjoyed better dwellings, diet, and apparel in England than the husbandmen or farmers did in other countries."[6] Certainly Arthur Young was struck with the difference between the agricultural population of England and that of France, which latter country he visited shortly before the Revolution,[7] when the misery of the labourer was at its lowest depth, owing to the extortions of the privileged noblesse.

§ 199. *Growth of Population.*

But not only had the condition of the industrial population improved in the period 1700-1750, but their numbers had, as a consequence, also considerably increased. The figures rose from 5,475,000 in 1700 to 6,467,000 in 1750.[8] And now, too, was beginning that great shifting of the centres of population, from the South to the North of England, which is so important a feature in the new industrial epoch. The most suggestive fact of this period is the growth of the population of Lancashire and of the West Riding of Yorkshire,[9] which were rapidly becoming

---

[1] *Cf.* Davies, *Case of Labourers in Husbandry* (1795), p. 83 ; Arthur Young, *Annals of Agriculture,* xxv. 344, 484, and xxxvii. 448.

[2] Smith, *Wealth of Nations,* Bk. I. ch. viii. (Vol. I. p. 82).

[3] Young, *Farmer's Letters,* i. 207, 208 (edn. 1771).

[4] *Ib.,* pp. 200, 297 ; Eden, *State of the Poor,* iii. 710.

[5] Young, *Travels in France,* ii. 313 (ed. 1793, Dublin).

[6] Chamberlayne, *State of Great Britain* (1737), p. 177.

[7] See his *Travels in France.*

[8] See *The Statistical Journal,* xliii. 462.

[9] For the migration of population from Devonshire and the "cider counties" to Yorkshire, *cf.* Massie's *Observations on the New Cyder Tax* (1764),

the seats of the cotton and coarse woollen manufactures. Similarly also Staffordshire and Warwickshire, the pottery and hardware centres, were growing in numbers,[1] and so, too, were Durham and Northumberland, whose coal-fields were now far more developed than before.[2]   On the other hand, the population of the Western and Eastern counties, still large manufacturing centres, had increased very little.[3] But in the North and North-west the increase was enormous.   Between 1685 and 1760 the people of Liverpool had increased tenfold, of Manchester fivefold, of Birmingham and Sheffield sevenfold.[4]   The total population of England had increased from the five millions or so of the Elizabethan period, to not much less than eight millions in Arthur Young's time,[5] and far more of these were in the northern portions of the country than was the case even in Defoe's time.   Defoe said, in 1725, " the country south of the Trent is by far the largest, as well as the richest and most populous."[6]   But forty or fifty years later the shifting towards the North had already made itself felt.[7]   The cause of the great increase of population between 1700 and 1760 is to be found in the rapid increase of national wealth gained by foreign commerce, and in the progress of home manufactures and of agriculture.   These in turn led to a greater demand for labour, and, in consequence, to higher wages.   Increased wealth and higher wages mean increased comfort in living, increased command of food, and consequently better chances of survival among children born of poor parents.[8]   Now, in this period the increase in national wealth was, in spite of foreign wars, enormous ; for if England had to pay heavily for these wars, other countries had to pay more heavily still, and were, moreover

No. 4.   *Cf.* also Toynbee's chapter on *Population* in his *Industrial Revolution*, pp. 32 to 38.

    [1] Toynbee, *Industrial Revolution*, p. 35.
    [2] *Ib.*, p. 35.   [3] *Ib.*, p. 35.
    [4] See the figures in Toynbee, *Ind. Rev.*, p. 36.
    [5] It was 7,428,000 in 1770, and 8,675,000 in 1790.   *Statistical Journal*, xliii. 462.   [6] *Tour*, iii. 57 (7th edn.).
    [7] See Toynbee's careful analysis, *Indust. Rev.*, p. 35.
    [8] *Cf.* Adam Smith, *Wealth of Nations*, Bk. I. ch. viii. (Vol. I. pp. 84, 85, Clarendon Press edn.), on " the liberal reward of labour."

the battle-grounds of contending armies, while our own land was at least free from invasion.

§ 200. *England still mainly Agricultural.*

Of the population of the country at this time the majority were still engaged in agriculture, and the agricultural labourers alone formed one-third of the working classes, while a large number even of the manufacturing classes still worked in the fields for a portion of the year, especially in harvest time.[1] In 1770 England was still mainly an agricultural country, and Arthur Young estimates that the income of the agricultural portion of the nation was larger than that of all the rest of the community. But it must be remembered that by far the largest portion of this income was in the hands of the great landowners and the farmers, the share of the labourer being, of course, much smaller. Arthur Young's estimates must be taken with a certain amount of caution, but they are probably approximately correct, and are certainly interesting as giving us a very fair idea of the distribution of occupations and national wealth just before the Industrial Revolution. Hence I append a small table, giving in round numbers the figures of his estimates.[2] It will be noticed that the number of the population is rather too high, but the proportion of one class to another is probably correct.

INCOMES OF VARIOUS CLASSES.[3]
IN MILLION POUNDS.

5	...	...	...	...	Interest on capital 5
1·5		...	...	...	...	Paupers 1·5
5	...	...	...	...	Military and Official 5
5	...	...	...	...	Professions 5
10		...	...	...	Commercial 10
27			...	Manufacturing 27
66					Agricultural 66

Total = £119,500,000.

[1] *Cf.* above, p. 330.
[2] *Cf.* Arthur Young, *Northern Tour*, iv. 543-547 (ed. 1770).
[3] The lines here are drawn to scale.

POPULATION, IN MILLIONS.

·5	... ...	Paupers ·5		
·5	... ...	Military and official ·5		
·2	... ...	Professional ·2		
·7	... ...	Commercial ·7		
Manufacturing 3			3	
Agricultural 3·6				3·6

Total = 8,500,000.

It will be perceived that the agriculturists, though only about half a million more in numbers than the manufacturing classes, had a far larger proportionate income, in fact, more than double. This was of course partly due to the agricultural improvements of this period, and to the fact, that manufactures were still carried on almost solely by hand, thus giving only a small production from a good many workmen. But the Industrial Revolution rapidly changed all this, and now agriculture is no longer the staple industry of the country. We may here refer to what has been previously mentioned in regard to the agricultural development on enclosed land, and to the superiority of the results of enclosures over those of the common fields.[1] Those farmers and large owners who understood the best way of raising crops prospered, and more and more land was enclosed every year to grow corn (which, by the way, was rapidly rising in price), clover, turnips, and other root-crops. No less than 700 Enclosure Acts[2] were passed between 1760 and 1774. Corn was becoming a more valuable crop owing to the increase of population, and now, for the first time in English history, it became necessary to import it.[3] The old common fields were beginning to disappear, and the working classes also lost their rights of pasturing cattle on the wastes, for wastes now were en-

---

[1] Above, p. 275.

[2] Cunningham, *Growth of Industry*, ii. 476.

[3] The period 1766 to 1773 is said to have been the time when our imports first began to exceed our exports (West, *Price of Corn* (1826), p. 10), but Prothero, *Pioneers of English Farming*, p. 88, says that it was not till 1793 that the imports finally out-balanced the exports.

closed.[1] It must be admitted that the old common-field system produced very poor results,[2] but the loss of his common rights was very disastrous to the labourer, for it drove him from the land at the same time as the growth of manufactures attracted him from it,[3] and thus the labourer became in a few years completely divorced from the soil. At present attempts are being made to attract him back to it by offering him small strips of inferior land at a high rent.[4] This is known as the allotment system. It need scarcely be said that, as at present carried out, it is hardly likely to replace the almost universal allotments of previous times.

§ 201. *The Domestic System of Manufacture*

But in the period we are now speaking of, the period before the great inventions, neither the agricultural labourer nor the manufacturing operative was quite divorced from the land. The weavers, for instance, often lived in the country, in a cottage with some land attached to it.[5] But in other respects there had certainly been changes in the industrial system before 1760. At first the weaver had furnished himself with warp and weft, worked it up, and brought it to the market himself;[6] but by degrees this system grew too cumbersome, and the yarn was given out by merchants to the weaver, and at last the merchant got together a certain number of looms in a town or village, and worked them under his own supervision.[7] But even yet the domestic system, as it is commonly called, retained

---

[1] Toynbee, *Industrial Revolution*, pp. 69, 101.   [2] Above, p. 275.

[3] Or, when they did not attract him away, they took from him to a very great extent his bye-industries of spinning, &c. *Cf.* Cunningham, *Growth of Industry*, ii. 483.

[4] The writer was much blamed for this remark when it was first made in 1890. But he cannot see any reason to alter it. Allotment-land is not usually the best in a parish, though labourers often get very good results from it; and the rents charged are certainly far in excess of those on farmers' land. For rents of allotments and results of labour, see the article by Bolton King, *Statistics of some Midland Villages*, in the *Economic Journal* for March 1893.

[5] "Manufactures were little concentrated in towns, and only partially separated from agriculture." Toynbee, *Indust. Rev.*, p. 53.

[6] Toynbee, *u. s.*, p. 54.   [7] *Ib.*

in many if not in most cases the distinctive feature that
the manufacturing industry was not the only industry in
which the artisan was engaged, but that he generally
combined with it a certain amount of agricultural work in
the cultivation of his own small plot of land.[1] This fact
explains to some extent the comparative comfort of the
operative in this cottage industry, for that they were fairly
well off is the testimony of Adam Smith,[2] in 1776. Commercial fluctuations were few, and the home market was
steady, for manufacturers—which term meant both a master-
manufacturer and an ordinary weaver—worked not so much
for a comparatively unknown and vague " market " as for
some particular customer, or for some well-known local
demand. Instead of the manufacturer going to the merchant, the latter often came to the manufacturer, as did
the London merchants, who came down to the North-
country manufacturers, paid them in cash, and took
away their purchases themselves.[3] On the other hand,
however, we have the picture of the " grass farmers " near
Leeds, as late as 1793, who used to buy the wool they
worked, and go through the whole process of converting it
into cloth, and go to market twice a week to sell it.[4] This
is a good example of the combination of agriculture and
manufactures under the domestic system. It is noticeable
also that capital, though it existed in smaller amounts, was
nevertheless in a larger number of hands.[5] The poet's
vision of " contentment spinning at the cottage door " was
not altogether imaginary, for women and children, as we
have seen, shared in the common task brought home by the
head of the family. The enormous difference between the

---

[1] This had been the case also in Elizabethan times, for § 23 of the Act 5
Eliz., c. 4, shows that the weaving of linen and household cloth was often
combined with agriculture. For cloth-weaving carried on in the mansions
of the nobility and gentry, cf. Rogers, *Economic Interpretation of History*,
p. 84. See also W. Radcliffe's interesting evidence in Baines, *Cotton
Manufacture*, p. 337.
[2] *Wealth of Nations*, Bk. I. ch. viii. (Vol. I. p. 82, Clarendon Press
edition).
[3] Toynbee, *Industrial Revolution*, p. 55.
[4] Young, *Annals of Agriculture*, xxvii. 309.
[5] *Cf.* Toynbee, *Indust. Revolution*, p. 52.

old domestic system and the modern factory methods may be illustrated from the pottery manufacture by a quotation which certainly does not err in affording too bright a view of the former. " In the wilder districts of the moorlands a pot-work would be carried on by the joint exertions of a single man and his son or a labourer. The one dug the necessary clay, the other fashioned and lined the ware, whilst the mother or daughter, when the goods were ready, loaded the panniered asses and took her way to distant town and hamlet till her merchandise was sold. She then returned with shop-goods to the solitary pot-work." [1] This was the domestic system in its most elementary form, and is a curious contrast to the conditions which prevail in the present pottery factories of Staffordshire.

But, even in this simple state of industry, trade was by no means so restricted and hampered as some writers have seemed to suppose. On the contrary, there was, in spite of bad roads,[2] very frequent and considerable internal communication for manufacturing purposes, and this was facilitated by means of the local fairs and markets, the importance of which in those days cannot be easily overrated. Manufacturers would ride a long way to buy wool from the farmers, or at the great fairs already mentioned, such as that of Stourbridge,[3] which was sufficiently considerable even a hundred years ago, or those of Lynn, Boston, Gainsborough, and Beverley, all four of which were celebrated for their wool-sales.[4] This wool was brought home and sorted, then sent out to the handcombers,[5] and on being returned combed was again sent

---

[1] Bourne, *Romance of Trade*, p. 170.

[2] On the subject of roads there is somewhat conflicting evidence. Arthur Young constantly refers to the villainous character of the roads he traversed, at the very time when Henry Homer (in 1767) was praising the improved character of all means of communication (*An Enquiry into the Means of Preserving the Publick Roads*). The apparent discrepancy is probably due to the fact that there was no uniformity in the country, and some roads were much worse than others ; cf. W. C. Sydney, *England in the Eighteenth Century*, ii. 1-43, and Cunningham, *Growth of Industry*, ii. 374-378.

[3] Above, p. 143.   [4] Toynbee, *Industrial Revolution*, p. 55.

[5] Burnley, *Wool and Woolcombing*, p. 159, mentions how master wool-

out, often to long distances, to be spun. It was, for instance, sent from Yorkshire to Lancashire, and gangs of pack-horses laden with wool were always to be met plodding over the hills between these two counties.[1] In the same way silk was sent from London to Kendal and back.[2] When spun, the tops, or fine wool, were entrusted to some shopkeeper to "put out" among the neighbours.[3] Then the yarn was brought back and sorted by the manufacturer himself into hanks, according to the counts and twists. The hand-weavers would next come for their warp and weft, and in due time bring back the piece, which often was sent elsewhere to be dyed. Finally, the finished cloth was sent to be sold at the fairs, or at the local "piece halls" of such central towns as Leeds or Halifax.[4]

Hence it will be seen that there was a considerable diffusion[5] of work under the old system, and it was not necessary for great numbers of people to live close together, or to work in factories upon a large scale. Things were done with greater leisure, and more time was taken over them. It was possible, and it seemed even desirable, to regulate the industries of the country in a manner which now would be regarded as both harmful and futile. For with the Industrial Revolution, English industry outgrew the various regulations and conditions which had been previously placed upon it.[6] The regulations of apprenticeship, for instance, which were supposed to guarantee to some extent

combers would buy wool from the staplers, and give it out to hand wool-combers for combing.

[1] Smiles, *Lives of the Engineers (Metcalfe and Telford)*, p. 31.

[2] Young, *Northern Tour*, iii. 171, 173 (ed. 1770).

[3] So in Huntingdonshire in 1793, A. Young says, "women and children may have constant employment in spinning yarn, which is put out by the generality of the country shopkeepers." *Annals of Agriculture*, xxi. 170 ; *cf.* also Radcliffe in Baines, *Cotton Manufacture*, p. 338.

[4] *Cf.* Toynbee, *Industrial Revolution*, p. 54.

[5] "In 1790 there were thirty cloth factories in Warminster, all busy and prosperous. They were not factories in the present sense, but, rather, clothing shops, in which only the finishing processes were effected, *spinning, carding, warping, and weaving being carried on in cottages over a large area* in the towns and in the country villages, *as fifty or sixty years before in farmhouses.*" Daniell's *History of Warminster* (1879), p. 130.

[6] Cunningham, *Growth of Industry*, ii. 258.

the skill and training of the individual workman, became
obsolete, even in those trades to which they had been
formerly applied, when the introduction of machinery
caused the skill of the workman to become of less importance than the delicacy of the machine.   The old conditions
of industry merely hampered the new factory owners, and,
therefore, were rapidly cast aside.   An entirely new order
of things arose.   With the Industrial Revolution came all
the hurry and stress of modern manufacturing life, and a
complete change took place in the manner and methods of
manufacture.   And now, having seen how things stood
immediately before this great change, we can proceed at
once to the means by which it was brought about.

CHAPTER XXI

THE EPOCH OF THE GREAT INVENTIONS

§ 202. *The Suddenness of the Revolution and its Importance.*

THE change, which has been briefly sketched in the previous chapter, from the domestic system of industry to the modern system of production by machinery and steam power was sudden and violent. The great inventions were all made in a comparatively short space of time, and the previous slow growth of industry developed quickly into a feverish burst of manufacturing production that completely revolutionised the face of industrial England. In little more than twenty years all the great inventions of Watt, Arkwright, and Boulton had been completed, steam had been applied to the new looms, and the modern factory system had fairly begun. Of course this system was not adopted by the country immediately or universally. In some trades the old domestic system persisted longer than in others, and weaving by hand-looms, for instance, was still practised as late as the middle of the nineteenth century.[1] But on the whole the transition was accomplished with comparative rapidity, and, as a consequence, the change in the industrial system brought great misery as well as great economic advantages. Nothing has done more to make England what she at present is—whether for better or worse—than this sudden and silent Industrial Revolution, for it increased her wealth tenfold, and gave her half a century's start in front of the nations of Europe. The French Revolution took place about the same time, and as it was performed

---

[1] Writing in 1885, a Yorkshire author says, "as recently as twenty-five to thirty years ago the manufacture of heavy woollen cloth was done by hand-weaving." Thomas Illingworth, *Distribution Reform*, p. 16. This, however, was hardly general so late.

amid streams of blood and flame, it attracted the attention of historians, many of whom have apparently yet to learn that bloodshed and battles are merely the incidents of history. The French Revolution also succeeded in giving birth to one of the world's military heroes, and a military hero naturally excites the enthusiasm of the multitude. Yet even the French Revolution was the result of economic causes that had been operating for centuries, and which had had their effect in England four hundred years before, at the time of the Peasants' Revolt. These economic causes have been rather kept in the background by most historians, who have preferred to dwell upon the antics of French politicians and revolutionaries, many of whom have gained a quite undeserved importance; and it was hardly to be expected that writers should recognise the operation of such causes in England, more especially as their effects were not accentuated by political fireworks, but were even partially hidden by subsequent events resulting from these effects. Men were blinded, too, by an increase in the wealth of the richer portion of the nation, not even seeing whence that wealth proceeded, and quite ignoring the fact that it was accompanied by serious poverty among the industrial classes.[1] Nor did historians perceive that the world-famous wars in which England was engaged at the close of the last century, and up to 1815, were necessitated by her endeavour to gain the commercial supremacy of the world,[2] after she had invented the means of supplying the world's markets to overflowing. Economic causes were at the root of them all. We shall discuss later the connection between our foreign politics and our industry; and we must not

[1] This is recognised by Cunningham, *Growth of Industry*, ii. 443, who remarks, " while the gains of some of the owners of capital were sometimes enormous, the labourers were forced to a lower level of life." *Cf.* also Toynbee, *Industrial Revolution*, p. 93.

[2] Seeley, *Expansion of England*, ch. ii., only partially recognises this, though he is pre-eminent for his accurate view of the eighteenth century wars. But he attributes too much weight to *colonial* expansion, and not enough to industrial and mercantile influences. England was striving almost as much for a market as for colonial power. See Rogers, *Economic Interpretation*, p. 323, and the chapter (xv.) on colonial trade and markets and wars.

forget that, besides this revolution in manufactures, there was one equally important in agriculture.[1] But with this we must deal afterwards ; at present we must adhere to the subject of the development of industry by the great inventors.

§ 203. *The Great Inventors.*

The transition from the domestic to the factory system was begun by four great inventions. In 1770 James Hargreaves,[2] a carpenter and weaver of Standhill, near Blackburn, patented the spinning-jenny, *i.e.* a frame with a number of spindles side by side, which were fed by machinery, and by which many threads might be spun at once, instead of only one, as had been the case in the old one-thread hand spinning-wheel.[3] Hargreaves first used this " jenny " for some time in his own house, and was at once enabled to spin eight times as much yarn as before by using eight spindles ; but afterwards 16, then 20 and 30 were used, and even 120.[4] In 1771 Arkwright[5] established a successful mill at Cromford on the Derwent, in which he employed his patent spinning machine, or " water-frame," an improvement upon a former invention of Wyatt's, which derived its name from the fact that it was worked by water-power.[6] A few years later (1779) both these inventions were superseded by that of Samuel Crompton, a spinner, but the son of a farmer near Bolton,[7] who added domestic spinning and weaving to agriculture. His machine, the " mule," combined and added to the principles of both the previous inventions, and was called by this name as being the hybrid offspring of its mechanical predecessors.[8] It drew out the roving (*i.e.* the

[1] Below, p. 430.
[2] See *Dictionary of National Biography* (ed. Leslie Stephen) for a concise life.
[3] The jenny was invented about 1764, but not patented till 12th July 1770 : for a description see Baines, *Hist. Cotton Manufacture*, pp. 157-8.
[4] Baines, *Cotton Manufacture*, p. 159.
[5] See *Dict. National Biography* (ed. Leslie Stephen).
[6] Baines, *Cotton Manufacture*, p. 153, and description, pp. 151-153. He first tried horse-power, but it was too expensive.
[7] *Dict. Nat. Biography*, xiii. 148.
[8] Baines, *Cotton Manf.*, p. 197.

raw material when it has received its first twist) by an adaptation of the water frame, and then passed it on to be finished and twisted into complete yarn by an adaptation of the spinning-jenny.[1] This invention effected an enormous increase in production, for nowadays 12,000 spindles are often worked by it at once and by one spinner.[2] It dates from the year 1779, and was so successful that by 1811 more than four and a half million spindles worked by "mules" were in use in various English factories.[3] Like many inventors, Crompton died in poverty[4] in 1827.

These three inventions, however, only increased the power of spinning the raw material into yarn. What was now wanted was a machine that would perform a similar service for weaving. This was discovered by Dr Edmund Cartwright, a Kentish clergyman, and was patented as the "power-loom" in April 1785,[5] though it had afterwards to undergo many improvements,[6] and did not begin to be much used till 1813. But the principle of it was there, and it was one of the most important factors in the destruction of the old domestic system. For at first only spinning was done by machinery, while the weavers could still do their work by hand in the old methods; and, indeed, they continued to do so till a comparatively recent period, and many aged people in Northern manufacturing districts can still remember the old weaving industry, as carried on in the workmen's own houses.[7] But the improvements on Cartwright's invention ultimately did away with the hand-weaver, as the others had abolished the hand-spinner, and the old form of industry was doomed.

Its death-blow, however, was yet to come. Wondrous as

[1] Baines, *Cotton Manufacture*, p. 198.
[2] *Romance of Trade*, p. 188.　　　　　　[3] *Ib.*, p. 189.
[4] *Dict. Nat. Biography*, xiii. 150.
[5] Burnley, *Wool and Woolcombing*, p. 111; Baines, *Cotton Manf.*, 229, 230; *Dict. Nat. Biography*, ix. 221.
[6] Cartwright's own attempts to work his invention were unremunerative, and it was not till 1801 that mills were started at Glasgow, where it was worked successfully. Baines, *Cotton Manufacture*, p. 231; Horrocks of Southport introduced further improvements in 1805 and 1813. Baines, *u. s.*, pp. 234 and 235-237.
[7] *Cf.* previous note on page 341 above.

were the changes introduced by the machines just spoken of, none of them would by themselves alone have revolutionised our manufacturing industries. Power of some kind was needed to work them, and water-power,[1] though used at first, was insufficient, and not always available. It was the application of steam to manufacturing processes which finally completed the Industrial Revolution. In 1769, the year in which Wellington and Bonaparte were born, James Watt took out his patent for the steam engine.[2] It was first used as an auxiliary in mining operations, but in 1785 it was introduced into factories, a Nottinghamshire cotton-spinner[3] having one set up in his works at Papplewick, which had previously been run only by water-power. Of course the enormous advantages of steam over water-power soon became apparent; manufacturers, especially in the cotton trade, hastened to make use of the new methods, and in fifteen years (1788-1803) the cotton trade trebled itself.[4]

It may be here remarked that most of the inventions and improvements were made first in the machinery used for making cotton cloth, and were only subsequently introduced into the woollen manufacture. Thus the spinning jenny, patented in 1770, was not used for woollen cloth-making till 1791 or a little later,[5] though it seems that machinery was used in the woollen cloth trade for some of the preparatory processes, such as carding, and even spinning,[6] about 1793. Moreover, in any trade, the introduction of the new inventions was not either simultaneous or unanimous. Manufactures before the Industrial Revolution were, as we have seen, very widely diffused[7] throughout the country, and consequently in some districts improve-

---

[1] *E.g.* in Boulton's works at Soho ; Smiles, *Lives of Boulton and Watt*, p. 130. Horses were even used. *Ib.*

[2] Smiles, *Lives of the Engineers* (*Boulton and Watt*), p. 98.

[3] Toynbee, *Industrial Revolution*, p. 90.   [4] *Ib.*

[5] Spinning jennies were in use at Barnstaple and Ottery St Mary in 1791 (Young, *Annals of Agriculture*, xv. 494), also machinery at Kendal (*ib.*, xv. 497). Benjamin Gott is said to have first introduced the jenny into the woollen manufacture at Leeds in 1800 ; Bischoff, *Woollen Manufactures*, i. 315.

[6] *Cf.* Young, *Annals of Agriculture*, xxvii. 310.   [7] Above, page 338, 339.

ments were introduced which did not come into use in others till several years later.[1] Nevertheless the great change proceeded on the whole with remarkable rapidity, and nowhere was it more noticeable than in the cotton trade. The manufacture of cotton cloth is comparatively modern in England, for it was probably not introduced until the early part of the seventeenth century,[2] and some confusion is caused in people's minds because "cottons" are heard of before this date,[3] But the "cottons" of earlier times were made entirely of wool,[4] and must have been only a weak imitation of real cotton cloth. In a work[5] by Lewis Roberts, a well-known writer on trade, published in 1641, we read, however: "The town of Manchester in Lancashire must also be herein remembered, and worthily, for their encouragement commended ; . . . . for they buy cotton wool in London that comes first from Cyprus and Smyrna, and at home work the same and perfect it into fustians, vermilions, dimities, and other stuffs, and then return it to London, where the same is vented and sold, and not seldom into foreign parts." Here we have probably the first notice of the making of real cotton cloth ; but even in this case only the weft was cotton thread, while the warp consisted of linen yarn, principally imported from Germany and Ireland ;[6] for there was no machinery in use fine enough to weave cotton only, nor had English weavers the inherited skill of the Oriental workmen. Hence the cotton manufacture did not make much progress, and the amount of cotton wool imported annually at the beginning of the eighteenth century was only about a million pounds ;[7] while the entire

---

[1] Cunningham also notes this : *Growth of Industry*, ii. 450.

[2] See article *Cotton* in M'Culloch's *Commercial Dictionary*, ed. 1844, p. 430 ; also Baines, *Cotton Manufacture*, pp. 89-112 ; see also Note A.

[3] Defoe was thus misled into thinking the cotton manufacture earlier than the woollen ; *Tour*, iii. 246.

[4] This is proved by the Act 5 and 6 Edward VI., c. 6 (1552), which was, "for the true making of *woollen* cloth," and yet includes "the cloths called Manchester, Lancashire, and Cheshire cottons."

[5] *Treasure of Traffic* (1641), p. 32.

[6] M'Culloch's *Commercial Dictionary*, *Cotton*, p. 430.

[7] *Ib.*, Table, p. 432.

value of all cotton goods manufactured in Great Britain at the accession of George III. (1760) was estimated at only £200,000 a year.[1] But the progress of the Industrial Revolution in the cotton trade may be seen from the rapid increase of the import of raw cotton from this time onwards. From a little over one million pounds (weight) it rose rapidly to over four million in 1771-75, between six and eleven million from 1776-84, to eighteen million pounds in 1785, and fifty-six million pounds at the beginning of this century (1800).[2]

§ 204. *The Revolution in Manufactures and the Factories.*

But although the Industrial Revolution was at first most marked in the manufacture of cotton, it rapidly extended to that of woollen and linen fabrics. It is impossible here, as well as unnecessary, to describe all the various modifications and adaptations that were made in the various machines ; we can only refer to the general features of the great change. The most remarkable of these was the sudden growth of factories, chiefly, of course, at first for spinning cotton or woollen yarn. The old factories had perforce been planted by the side of some running stream, often in a lonely and deserted spot, very inconvenient for markets and the procuring of labour ; but necessarily so placed for the sake of the water.[3] Hence at first there was no reason to concentrate large numbers of mill-hands in towns, as is necessary now. Those of my readers who know Yorkshire or Lancashire fairly well, may remember how frequently, in the course of some long country walk near Bradford, Halifax, Leeds, or Manchester, they come upon the ruins of some old mill, crumbling beside a rushing stream, a silent relic of the old days before the use of steam. How wonderful must the first rude inventions have seemed to the workers in those old factories, as the strange new machinery rattled and shook in the quiet country

---

[1] Estimated by Dr Percival, of Manchester ; M'Culloch, *u. s.*, p. 430.
[2] Tables in M'Culloch's *Commercial Dictionary*, p. 432 (ed. 1844).
[3] Above, p. 345 ; *cf.* Taylor, *Modern Factory System*, p. 85.

hollows, and the becks and streamlets ran down to turn the new spindles and looms that were to revolutionise the face of agricultural England. But the old water-mills gave way to others worked by steam power, and now it was no longer necessary to choose any particular site for the works, if only plenty of coal was available. So the new race of manufacturers made haste to run up steam-factories wherever they could. " Old barns and cart-houses," says Radcliffe,[1] who wrote on the new manufactures, " outbuildings of all descriptions were repaired ; windows broke through the old blank walls, and all were fitted up for loom-shops ; new weavers' cottages arose in every direction." The merchants, too, who did not run factories on their own account, but merely purchased yarn, began to collect weavers around them in great numbers, to get looms together in a workshop, and to give out warp themselves to the workpeople.[2] And now the workers began to feel the difference between the old system and the new. Formerly they often used to buy for themselves the yarn they were to weave, and had a direct interest in the cloth they made from it, which was their own property. They were, in fact, economically independent. The new system made them dependent upon the merchant or upon the mill-owner.[3] At first, it is true, they gained a rise in wages, for the increase in production was so great that labour was continually in demand, and every family, says Radcliffe,[4] brought home forty to one hundred and twenty shillings per week. But this did not last very long.[5] The new machinery soon threw out of employment a number of those who had worked only by hand ; it enabled women and children to do the work of

[1] Quoted by Baines, *Cotton Manufacture*, pp. 338, 339. W. Radcliffe's book is entitled, "The Origin of the New System of Manufacture, commonly called ' Power Loom Weaving,' and the purposes for which this system was invented and brought into use fully explained in a Narrative." It was published in 1828.

[2] Toynbee, *Industrial Revolution*, p. 91.

[3] *Ib.* "The system meant a change from independence to dependence " (p. 91).

[4] In Baines, *Cotton Manufacture*, p. 339.

[5] Lecky, *History of the Eighteenth Century*, vi. 205, remarks that the condition of the labourers began to deteriorate about 1792.

grown men; it made all classes of workers dependent upon capitalist employers; and it introduced an era of hitherto unheard-of competition. The coming of the capitalists had become an accomplished fact, and with it began also the exploitation of labour. Of this we shall speak in another chapter.[1] Other national changes now demand our attention.

§ 205. *The Growth of Population and the Development of the Northern Districts.*

Two of the most striking facts of the Industrial Revolution are the great growth and the equally great shifting of the population. These have been already briefly alluded to, but a few further details must now be added. Before 1751 the largest decennial increase of population had been about 5 or 6 per cent.[2] But for each of the next three periods of ten years the increase became rapidly greater, till in 1801 it was 14 per cent. on the previous ten years, and reached even $21\frac{1}{2}$ per cent.[3] in the period 1801 to 1811. This last was the highest rate ever reached in England, and is more than double that recorded in the census[4] of 1881 or 1891. The population of England had been under 7,000,000 in 1760;[5] by 1821 it had risen[6] to about 12,000,000, and at the present moment it is rather more than double that number.[7]

At the same time, the great migration to the North, already begun before the Revolution, was now accelerated and completed. The main cause of it was the utilisation of the coalfields for fuel to turn the new machinery in the factories. Hitherto the counties which contained the vast

[1] Below, p. 381 *sqq.*

[2] *Cf.* the figures for each decennium in the *Statistical Journal*, xliii. 462; also *cf.* Toynbee, *Industrial Revolution*, p. 87, but he is inaccurate.

[3] See the careful tables in M'Culloch's *Commercial Dictionary* (1844), *s. v. Population*; also Lecky, *History of the Eighteenth Century*, vi. 201.

[4] It was 10·8 per cent. in 1871-81, and in 1881-91 only 8·2 per cent. (United Kingdom) *Census Returns*, 1891.

[5] Exact figure 6,736,000 (England and Wales). *Statistical Journal*, xliii. 462.

[6] Exact figure 12,000,236. *Ib.*

[7] Exact figure 27,482,104 (England only) in 1891; *Census Returns.*

coal deposits, to which England owes so much of her progress, had been neglected, but now that the wealth that underlay them was understood,[1] they became the natural home of manufacturing industries.[2]   But it may be noticed that, even previously to the utilisation of coal, industry had been attracted to Lancashire and Yorkshire because these counties, with the numerous streams running down from their moors, offered a better supply of water power than the Southern or Eastern districts.   There is little doubt also that the rainy climate[3] of the North-West of England offered greater facilities for certain branches of the cotton and woollen trades than the drier Eastern counties, at any rate, possessed.   The considerations of physical geography as well as of geology show us that, under the new conditions of manufacture, the North-Western counties were obviously fitted for the great industrial part they were now to play in the life of the nation.

These districts, which in the Middle Ages and even later had, as we saw, been comparatively deserted,[4] now became and have since remained the most populous and flourishing of all.   The centres of the new factory system were now naturally in the North, and thither flocked the workers who had formerly been distributed over England in a much more extensive manner, or who had clustered round the great Eastern and South-Western centres of industry, which before 1760 had excelled the other centre, the West Riding, in prosperity.[5]   But now this was changed.   Before the Revolution, the Eastern counties, more especially about Norwich and the surrounding districts, had been famous for their manufactures of crapes, bombazines, and other fine, slight stuffs.[6]   In the West of England the towns of Brad-

---

[1] Macaulay, *History*, ch. iii., rightly calls them "a source of wealth more precious than the gold mines of Peru."

[2] We may here compare Ramsay's remarks in his *Physical Geology and Geography of Great Britain*, pp. 305, 306 (ed. 1872).

[3] For statistics of rainfall, *cf.* Ramsay, *u. s.*, pp. 197-199.

[4] Above, p. 107 ; *cf.* also Macaulay's well-known but rather exaggerated description of the North of England, *History*, ch. iii.

[5] Defoe's *Tour*, iii. 57 (ed. 1769). Macaulay, *History*, ch. iii., "A constant stream of emigrants began to roll northward."

[6] Toynbee, *Industrial Revolution*, p. 47, summarises these well-known facts.

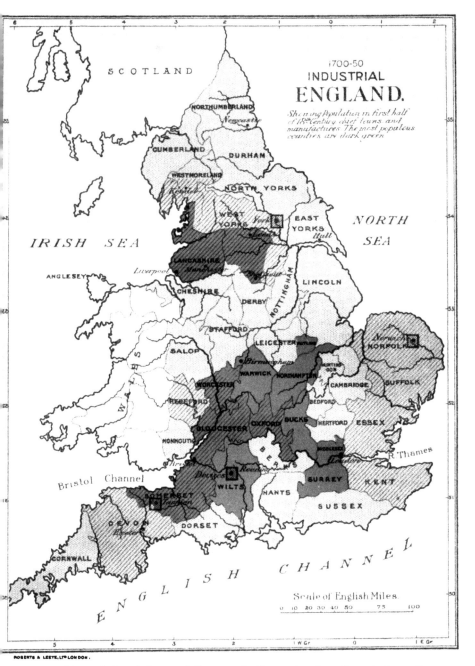

The majority of the population was in the west and south central counties (*dark green*); but Lancs. and the West Riding of Yorks. were increasing. The chief manufacturing centres in (1) Eastern counties, (2) Wilts., (3) Yorks., &c., are shown thus ▨▨▨▨ but it must be remembered that manufactures were very scattered and carried on side by side with agriculture. Several other counties are therefore marked with slanting lines. (Compare the Map opposite page 454.)

ford-on-Avon, Devizes, and Warminster had been manufacturing centres noted for their fine serges ; Stroud had been the centre of the manufacture of dyed cloth,[1] and so was Taunton, for even in Defoe's time (1725) it had 1100 looms ;[2] and the excellence of the Cotswold wool, together with the water power derived from its mountain streams, had done much for the industry of the district.[3] These centres and their productions, then, were far more famous than the third, the West Riding, including the towns of Halifax, Leeds, and Bradford, where chiefly coarse cloths were made.[4] The cotton trade of Lancashire, too, had previously been insignificant, for it is only incidentally mentioned by Adam Smith,[5] though Manchester and Bolton were then, as now, its headquarters. In 1760 only 40,000 persons were engaged in it,[6] while in 1764 the value of our cotton exports was only one-twentieth of our woollen,[7] and only strong cottons, such as dimities and fustians, were made. But now the cotton cities of Lancashire, and the woollen and worsted factories of Yorkshire, far surpass the older[8] seats of industry in wealth and population, while the cotton export has risen to be the first in the kingdom, and the vast majority of the industrial population is now found North of the Trent. These great industrial changes were the direct consequence of the introduction of new manufac-

[1] Toynbee, *Industrial Revolution*, p. 47, and see note 5 on p. 339.
[2] *Tour*, ii. 19 (ed. 1769).
[3] This is pointed out by Toynbee, *Ind. Rev.*, p. 48.   [4] *Ib.*, p. 48.
[5] *Wealth of Nations*, Bk. I. ch. x. (Vol. I. 127, Clarendon Press edn.).
[6] Toynbee, *Industrial Revolution*, p. 49.   [7] *Ib.*, p. 50.
[8] "Woollen cloths, kerseymeres, blankets, etc., formed [in Wiltshire] for a long period a principal manufacture. From the reign of Elizabeth to the close of the eighteenth century, the towns of Wiltshire lying in the valley of the Avon, on the north-west, and in that of the Wily in the south-west, Malmesbury, Chippenham, Bradford, Trowbridge, Westbury, Warminster, Heytesbury, and Wilton, with all the circumjacent villages, were largely employed in the weaving of various kinds of woollen fabrics, and the clothiers were men of wealth and position. This manufacture declined in Wiltshire very rapidly owing to the general adoption of machinery and the power-loom in the great factories of Yorkshire and Lancashire, and to the increasing consumption, throughout England and the Continent, of cotton and linen textures. John Aubrey held that the clothiers suffered in his day, because 'men would take to silk and Indian ware.'" Daniell, *History of Warminster* (1879), p. 130.

turing processes. For the use of steam power in mills necessitated the liberal use of coal, and hence the factory districts are necessarily almost coincident with the great coalfields, as will be seen from any geological map. It is also curious to notice that each coalfield has its own particular manufacture closely associated with it.[1] Thus the Yorkshire coalfield contains most of the towns where the woollen industry prevails, while its southern extension, which descends into Nottinghamshire, includes the cutlery and hardware district of Sheffield and the lace and hosiery of Nottingham. The Lancashire coalfield is almost exclusively surrounded by towns engaged in the cotton trade; the Staffordshire fields are connected chiefly with pottery, and, on their Southern limit, with hardware and machinery; the South Wales coal district is noted for its smelting and ironworks. Moreover, the coal industry had been developed almost simultaneously with the growth of manufactures, and, indeed, one reacted upon the other. It will be convenient here to mention the improvements made in coal-mining and in the iron trade.

§ 206. *The Revolution in the Mining Industries.*

It has been mentioned in a previous chapter[2] that the development of the vast natural resources of our country as regards coal and iron was retarded by the lack of steam power. But with the steam-engines of Watt and Boulton a new era dawned upon coal-mining. In 1774 Watt, after vainly advocating his invention, entered into partnership with Matthew Boulton, a Birmingham man,[3] who devoted all the capital he possessed to the introduction of Watt's engine into practical use. The new engine soon produced a vast change in the manner of pumping water from the mines,[4] just as it also produced other changes in every

---

[1] This is also noticed by H. R. Mill, *Commercial Geography*, pp. 44-46 (ed. 1888), and is, of course, obvious.

[2] Above, pp. 310 to 312.

[3] See Smiles, *Lives of the Engineers* (*Boulton and Watt*), ch. viii., "Their Partnership," p. 146.

[4] See diagram of Watt's pumping-engine for mines in Smiles, *u. s.*, ch. x. p. 180.

manufacture dependent upon the use of coal. Steam-power was used not only to clear the mines of water, but also in sinking shafts,[1] where formerly entrance had often been made only by tunnelling in the side of a hill. It was used, too, in bringing up the coal from the pit, and in many other necessary processes. The result of this application of steam power was soon seen in the general opening up of all the English coal-fields, and the consequent further growth of towns like Newcastle, Sheffield, and Birmingham,[2] whose industries now depend so greatly upon a large supply of coal.

With the great output of coal came an immediate revival of the iron trade, which it will be remembered had greatly declined[3] about 1737 and 1740, for as coal was not available wood had to be used as fuel, and the consequent destruction of forests, especially the Sussex Wealden, had caused legislative prohibitions.[4] The scientific treatment of iron ore in the various processes of manufacture had indeed been improved, but nothing much could be done without coal. This was seen, for instance, by an iron-master, Anthony Bacon, in 1755, who obtained a lease, at the trifling rental of £200 per annum, for ninety-nine years, of a district at Merthyr Tydvil, eight miles long and five broad, upon which he erected both iron and coal works.[5] In 1760 Smeaton's invention[6] of a new blowing apparatus at Dr Roebuck's works at Carron, near Falkirk, did away with the old clumsy bellows ; and the other inventions of the Cranages[7] (1766), of Onions[8] (1783), and of Henry Cort[9] (1784), for which separate treatises must be consulted, brought the manufacture of iron almost to perfection. Whereas about the middle of the eighteenth century we produced only some 18,000 tons of iron annually,[10] and had

---

[1] Bourne, *Romance of Trade*, p. 175.
[2] Both Sheffield and Birmingham only had between 20,000 and 30,000 inhabitants about 1760 ; see Toynbee's table, *Industrial Revolution*, p. 36 ; *cf.* also Lecky, *History of the Eighteenth Century*, vi. 212.
[3] Smiles, *Industrial Biography*, ch. ii. p. 42. [4] *Ib.* ch. ii. pp. 38-42.
[5] *Ib.*, ch. vii. p. 130. [6] *Ib.*, ch. viii. p. 137.
[7] *Ib.*, ch. v. pp. 86-88. [8] *Ib.*, ch. vii. p. 115.
[9] *Ib.*, ch. vii. (all). [10] *Ib.*, ch. v. p. 79.

z

to import at least 20,000 tons,[1] we produced in 1788 as much as 68,000 tons,[2] and the production has gone on steadily increasing to the present time, when some five million tons of iron are obtained annually.[3]

§ 207. *The Improvements in Communications.*

Besides these improvements in mining and machinery, there were also others which, though not perhaps quite so strikingly important, had a considerable influence upon the progress of industry and commerce.   These were the improvements made in the internal communications of the country both by land and water.   It must not be supposed, however, that because improvements were made the state of the roads was so exceedingly bad as it has been the fashion to describe them.   There has been considerable exaggeration as to the difficulties of travelling both in mediæval and later times, and there is plenty of evidence [4] which goes to show that matters were not invariably so bad as might be imagined from descriptions [5] more picturesque than accurate. It is certain that the cost of carriage in mediæval times was cheap, and thus, by implication, that the roads were good. But less care seems to have been shown in maintaining them in later centuries, so that it is quite possible that the roads in England were in better repair in the reign of Edward III. than in that of George III.[6]   Still, even in the eighteenth century, the evidence of Arthur Young [7]—which has been freely misquoted—goes to show that the state of the roads was not by any means so bad as we should imagine if we merely took our picture of them from the complaints made of particularly execrable sections.   The turnpike roads were

[1] Scrivener, *History of the Iron Trade*, pp. 57, 71 ; Smiles, *u. s.*, p. 79, says four-fifths of it came from Sweden.

[2] M'Culloch's, *Commercial Dictionary, s. v. Iron.*

[3] *Year Book of Commerce.*

[4] Rogers, *Six Centuries*, p. 135 ; *Economic Interpretation of History*, p. 483.

[5] *E.g.* in Macaulay, *History*, ch. iii., which has been so freely copied by his inferiors.

[6] Rogers, *Economic Interpretation*, p. 484.

[7] *Cf.* itinerary at end of *Northern Tour*, Vol. IV.

generally in fairly good repair, and it is obvious that matters cannot have been so bad as is supposed, when we consider that in Defoe's time Manchester merchants would send their goods on horses right across England to Stourbridge,[1] or when waggons took silk from London to Kendal,[2] or when live geese were sent to London markets in cartloads from the Fens.[3]

While, however, guarding against receiving an exaggerated impression of the evil state of roads before the end of the eighteenth century, we may notice that about the middle of that period there were great improvements made, insomuch that Henry Homer, writing in 1767, declares (though evidently with rhetorical exaggeration) "there never was a more astonishing Revolution accomplished in the internal system of any country than has been within the compass of a few years in England."[4]   This was due to the erection of turnpikes and levying of tolls under the authority of various Acts of Parliament;[5] and later on there was great development owing to the improved methods introduced by the well-known road-makers, Metcalfe, Telford, and Macadam.[6]

There were also considerable improvements made in carriage by water.   This had been a favourite mode of conveyance in mediæval times, when the rivers were largely used,[7] and it continued to be so till, in the eighteenth century, rivers were supplemented or joined by canals.   A great impetus to canal-making was given by the success of Brindley's efforts in 1758, when he made a canal for the Duke of Bridgewater's colliery at Worsley to Manchester.[8] The importance of this canal was not due to its length, for it was only seven miles long, but to the fact that its construction presented serious engineering difficulties, such as tunnelling through rock and carrying an aqueduct over the

[1] Defoe, *Tour*, i. 94.   [2] Young, *Northern Tour*, iii. 171-173 (ed. 1770).
[3] Defoe, *Tour*, i. 54.
[4] Homer, *The Enquiry into the Means of Preserving the Publick Roads*; *cf*. p. 4 *seq*.
[5] 1 Geo II., c. 11; 5 Geo. I., c. 12; 14 Geo. II., c. 42.   *Cf*. also Smiles, *Lives of the Engineers* (*Metcalfe and Telford*), Vol. III. p. 69.
[6] *Ib.*, *passim*.
[7] Rogers, *Hist. Agric.*, i. p. 663; also i. ch. 27, and v ch. 25.
[8] Smiles, *Lives of the Engineers* (Vol. I., *Brindley*), ch. iii.

River Irwell.[1] Other canals followed. One of ninety-six miles in length, connecting the rivers Trent and Mersey, was finished in 1777 ; Hull and Liverpool were connected by another, and Liverpool with Bristol ; and in 1792 the Grand Junction Canal connected London with Oxford and other important towns in the Midlands.[2] It is curious to notice that on at least one of these early canals, that made from Worsley to Manchester, passengers were conveyed as well as goods. "A branch of useful and profitable carriage, hitherto scarcely known in England, was also undertaken, which was that of passengers. Boats on the model of the Dutch *trek-schuyts*, but more agreeable and capacious, were set up, which, at very reasonable rates and with great convenience, carried numbers of persons daily to and from Manchester along the line of the canal."[3] This branch of traffic has quite died out, and even the carriage of goods by water is now not so frequent as formerly. But it is a matter of regret that waterways are not more used for merchandise in England, as they are in some Continental countries, even where railways are numerous ; for in Belgium,[4] which has quite as many railways in proportion to its size as England, both canals and rivers are very widely used for the transit of goods, and prove of great utility.

§ 208. *The Nation's Wealth and its Wars.*

Of course all these discoveries of new processes in procuring coal and making iron, and the improvements in communication, enormously increased the wealth of England, and at the same time entirely changed the conditions of industry. For they helped the textile manufactures by providing any amount of fuel and machinery, and all these together gave employment to a population that seemed to grow in accordance with the need of the nation for workers.[5]

[1] Smiles, *Lives of the Engineers* (Vol. I., *Brindley*), ch. iii. p. 173.
[2] For a very good summary of the Canals of England and other countries, *cf.* M'Culloch's *Commercial Dictionary* (ed. 1844), *s. v. Canals.*
[3] Aikin, *Description of the Country round Manchester*, p. 116.
[4] This is from the writer's personal observation.
[5] "In the cotton trade," said Sir R. Peel in 1806, "machinery has given birth to a new population," and he ascribed this to early marriages, caused

The new textile and mining industries supplied England with that vast wealth [1] which enabled her to endure successfully the long years of war at the close of last century and the beginning of this. The Industrial Revolution came only just in time, for after the repose of 1763 to 1792, during which this silent Revolution matured and took root, England engaged in a struggle which she certainly could never have supported without a far greater national wealth than she possessed in the first three quarters of the eighteenth century. Even as it was, the year 1815 found a large portion of her people in poverty and distress,[2] while the industrial classes suffered heavily from the taxation which the war imposed.[3] But owing to her industrial development, the war left England at its close, in spite of all her troubles, the foremost nation of Europe in economic development, and consequently first in other matters also. As is the case with most modern contests, this great war originated in economic causes, even to a certain extent in economic mistakes, but it had important effects upon industry, and was largely affected by industrial considerations. Hence we must consider it rather more closely.

by high rate of wages and comfort. Toynbee, *Industrial Revolution*, p. 88, note.

[1] Lecky, *History of the Eighteenth Century*, vi. 218. This is now perceived by most historians, but at one time it was ignored. But it is now recognised that at the time of the Continental War "Pitt's main support lay in the extraordinary financial resources supplied by the rapidly increasing manufactures of England." S. R. Gardiner, *Students' History of England*, p. 835.

[2] This was the time when the Poor Rate was rising year after year, till in 1818 it was over 13s. per head ; see below, p. 422.

[3] Rogers, *Six Centuries*, p. 505.

CHAPTER XXII

WAR, POLITICS, AND INDUSTRY

§ .209. *England's Industrial Advantages in* 1763.

IF we look at the state of the European Powers after the conclusion of the Seven Years' War by the Treaty of Paris in 1763, we shall see that England had achieved a very favourable position for the growth of her internal industries.[1] It is true that together with the rest of Europe she had adopted the policy of endeavouring to secure a sole market[2] for her goods, but though that policy was a mistake, in so far as it aimed at a monopoly, England was not alone in her error, and since other Powers were doing the same, it was just as well that she should hold the lead among them. Moreover, since we are now paying interest upon the heavy national bills which we ran up at that time, we may profitably examine what we gained thereby.

In the first place, England had seriously crippled her powerful commercial rival, France, both in her Indian and American possessions. The French flag had nearly disappeared from the sea.[3] By the Seven Years' War we had gained Canada, Florida, and all the French possessions east of the Mississippi River (except New Orleans); while in India our influence had become supreme, owing to the victories of Clive. French influence in India and America was practically annihilated. Spain, the faithful ally of France, lost with her friend her place as the commercial rival of England in foreign trade. Germany was again being ravaged by the dynastic struggles, in which Frederick

---

[1] Rogers, *Economic Interpretation of History*, pp. 290-291, gives an admirable summary of the state of European powers at this time. *Cf.* also Lecky, *History of the Eighteenth Century*, iii. p. 23, as to the ascendancy of England at this time.

[2] Rogers, *Economic Interpretation*, p. 323.

[3] Lecky, *History*, iii. p. 23.

the Great bore so prominent a part, between the reigning
houses of Austria and Prussia. Holland was similarly torn
by internal dissensions under the Stadtholder William V.,
which gave the rival sovereigns of Prussia and Austria a
chance of making matters worse by their interference. By
1790 the United Provinces had thus sunk into utter insignificance. Sweden, Norway, and Italy were of no account
in European politics, and Russia had only begun to come
to the front. Hence England alone had the chance of
" the universal empire of a sole market." [1]   The supply of
this market, especially in our American colonies, was in
the hands of English manufacturers and English workmen.
The great inventions which came, as we saw, after 1763
were thus at once called into active employment, and our
mills and mines were able to produce wealth as fast as they
could work, without fear of foreign competition.

§ 210. *The Mercantile Theory.*

But in some points our statesmen and merchants made a
mistake in their policy. The commercial mind of England
at this epoch was dominated by what is known as the
Mercantile Theory.[2]   It was a theory that had grown
up naturally out of the spirit of Nationalism, of self-
sustained and complete national life, that was our heritage
from the Renaissance and the Reformation.[3]   It was not
altogether wrong, for its object was national greatness, an
object laudable and harmless enough ; but the believers in
the policy of increasing our national greatness also believed
that it could only be attained in one way, and that was
at the expense of our neighbours. It was not sufficiently
understood that commerce, if properly carried on, is productive of benefit to both the trading parties ; and that
though one side may seem to gain an advantage, there
must be also an advantage to the other side, since other-

---

[1] Rogers, *Economic Interpretation,* p. 291.
[2] *Cf.* Toynbee, *Industrial Revolution,* ch. vii. p. 72 (on *The Mercantile
Theory*); Cunningham, *Growth of English Industry,* ii. pp. 16 *sqq.*
Rogers, *Economic Interpretation of History,* p. 323 ; also Adam Smith,
Wealth of Nations, Bk. IV. chs. i.-viii.
[3] Toynbee, *Industrial Revolution,* p. 76.

wise no one would be willing to trade. The advantages gained by the two parties to a bargain are not always identical or even necessarily similar, but advantage of some kind must exist, for it is the essence of a bargain that each of the contracting parties should benefit by it. The benefit gained by one party may seem to the other insignificant or even illusory, and doubtless it often is; but unless that second party imagined that he was obtaining something at least equivalent to what he gave to the first, he would hardly conclude the exchange. A Hudson's Bay fur-trader is no doubt amused at the folly of the Indian hunter who barters a valuable skin for a few drops of inferior brandy; but so long as the Indian considers the doubtful joys of fire-water superior to the solid merits of the fur of the sable, the bargain is to both commercially profitable. But as long as the principles of barter, which underlie even the most complicated transactions of international commerce, were imperfectly understood, as indeed they still frequently are, it seemed to English legislators and merchants that foreign commerce must result in a loss to one side or the other, unless it was very carefully regulated; and, fearing lest the loss should fall upon them, they naturally took what seemed the best method to avoid it.

Nowhere, perhaps, is this seen more clearly than in the excessive care that was taken to prevent England from losing on the balance of trade by letting gold and silver go out of the country in exchange for foreign commodities. The use of the precious metals in commerce has at all times been imperfectly understood by very many of those who employ them, and by not a few of those who undertake to write about them. Hence it is not surprising to find that politicians and traders from the sixteenth to the eighteenth century believed that the country was suffering a severe loss when it allowed too much bullion to be exported in payment for foreign goods. This loss seemed to occur when the value of our exports did not more or less exactly balance the value of the imports; and when it did not, the difference which England paid to the foreigner in coin or bullion was said to be a national loss, and the

" balance of trade," as it was called, was said to be against us. This was thought to be especially the case in the trade with East India, since large quantities of bullion were exported to buy the Indian commodities which were brought back to England. Only the more thoughtful writers of the seventeenth century perceived that the bullion exported to India was, so to speak, a seed which ultimately brought back a rich harvest in coin by our sale of spices and other Eastern commodities in the European market.[1] But the average politician thought that, in order to secure and retain wealth, it was necessary that on every article exported a balance in coin should eventually be paid to the English dealer ; and hence came those frequent legislative prohibitions of the export of bullion which continued, at least in form, till 1816.[2]

§ 211. *The Mercantile Theory in Practice.*

This is, however, only one example of the results of a theory which maintained that regulation was a vital necessity for commerce. The whole of English industry and commerce was permeated by the influence of this theory. Regulation was its keynote ; but it was regulation with a definite and avowed object. That object was, as hinted above, not only mercantile profit but political power ; and to political power the necessities of industry were to be strictly subordinate. Even in the case just quoted of the export of bullion, there were two motives at work in men's minds : the commercial desire to obtain a visible profit in money, and the political desire to keep in the country an accumulation of treasure, which might be useful in case of war.[3] Of these two motives the political was frequently

---

[1] For this trade see Mun's valuable *Discourse of Trade from England unto the East Indies*, in Purchas's *Pilgrims* (1625) ; also Misselden, *Circle of Commerce* (1623), p. 34 ; Malynes, *Center of the Circle* (1623), p. 114 ; Craik, *British Commerce*, ii. 109, 172-179 ; also Adam Smith, *Wealth of Nations*, Bk. I. ch. v., and Bk. IV. ch. i. (Vol. I. p. 45 and II. 12, Clarendon Press edn.).

[2] Rogers, *Economic Interpretation*, p. 187.

[3] Adam Smith, *Wealth of Nations*, Bk. IV. ch. i. (Vol. II. P. 13, ed. cit.), shows that even in case of war the accumulation of treasure is unnecessary

the stronger, and to this we can trace the whole elaborate series of regulations which were imposed upon English industry and commerce from the days of Richard II.[1] to the beginning of the reign of Victoria. The mercantile system, thus regarded, presents a clear and interesting outline.[2] National power depended, or seemed to politicians to depend, mainly on three things—(1) The accumulation of treasure as a fund in case of emergencies ; (2) the development of shipping as a nursery for the navy ; and (3) the maintenance of an effective population both for commercial and military purposes. To the first requirement we trace the legislative interference with the precious metals already alluded to ; to the second we can trace many statutes regulating the shipping trade, and more especially the famous Navigation Acts[3] of 1651, about which there has been so keen a controversy ; and to the third we may trace, though less distinctly, the attempts of various governments to regulate the agricultural industry of the country, either by encouraging tillage at the expense of pasturage, or by imposing protective duties upon a foreign food supply. This legislative support of agriculture has been attributed[4] to the desire of governments to favour that " kind of employment which was most favourable for the maintenance of a vigorous and healthy race, and the best material for forming a military force." This may have been the case in the days when the English yeoman formed so important a feature in the armies of Henry V. ; but when the success of agriculture was so patently important to the income of the landowners, who for centuries formed the majority of the English Parliament, it is hard to believe that such legislation was not occasionally actuated by motives of obvious self-interest. It is again little less than absurd to regard the Corn Laws as being passed in order to " provide suitable conditions for the constant supply of food,"[5] when they not only notoriously failed in that object, but even prevented its possible accomplish-

[1] *Cf.* Cunningham, *Growth of Industry,* i. 350.
[2] *Ib.,* i. 426, ii. 16.   [3] Above, p 287.
[4] Cunningham, *Growth of Industry,* i. 427.
[5] *Cf.* Cunningham, *Growth of Industry,* ii. 17.

ment. It is quite possible that those who enacted them sincerely believed that the maintenance of a landed aristocracy was necessary to the well-being of the State, and that rents must at all costs be kept up ; but there are few mortals who are not equally convinced of the necessity of their own existence, and fewer still who would not joyfully support a series of measures which appear to be beneficial simultaneously to the public welfare and their private purse.

The Mercantile System, in fact, presents a strange mixture of political expediency and personal gain. Combined with a sincere desire for national progress, there is the irrepressible prompting of class interests. The landowners wanted Protection for agriculture, and the manufacturers wanted Protection for their home industries; and hence we find that while the former acquiesced in the prohibition of the export of wool for the sake of the manufacturing interest, the latter had no objection to the existence of a bounty on the export of corn.[1] Politics, which are at all times beset by the least noble of human passions, were complicated and degraded by the intermixture of commercial interests,[2] and the decline of the mercantile system was due almost as much to the conflicting motives which it could not help bringing into play as to the inherent weakness of a scheme which attempted to regulate a commercial and industrial community which had long outgrown mediæval restrictions.

The scheme of regulation, which was a necessary part of the mercantile system, is seen in every department of industry as well as of commerce, though it was applied much more thoroughly to external than to internal trade.[3] But it has been well remarked that, in an age when it was deemed the duty of the State to watch over the individual citizen in all his relations, and to provide not only for his protection from force and fraud, but even to assure his spiritual welfare, it was after all only natural that the State should attempt to fix a legal rate of wages just as it fixed a legal rate of interest, and that it should try to supervise the production of commodities so as to ensure to its citizens the

---

[1] Toynbee, *Industrial Revolution*, p. 79.   [2] *Ib.*, p. 80.
[3] *Ib.*, p. 75.

manufacture of honest wares.[1] Hence there grew up naturally those restrictions upon industry which are embodied in
the Acts of Apprenticeship and the Assessment of Wages.
The former was supposed to prevent undue competition in a
trade and to provide a suitable number of skilled workmen
capable of turning out honest work,[2] while the latter was to
fix a fair price for a man's labour and to secure a regularity
of wages that would be beneficial to master and man alike.[3]
But the growth of industry and the inevitable tendencies of
human nature rendered the first of these enactments futile
and the second injurious, so that the great economist, who
surveyed the system as it existed at the close of the eighteenth century, could only regard the apprenticeship and
guild laws as causing an obstruction to the freedom of
labour,[4] and the regulation of wages as an oppression of the
poor by the rich.[5] The attempt of legislators to reconcile
public welfare with private interest proved, unfortunately,
unsuccessful.

§ 212. *English Policy towards the Colonies.*

Nowhere, however, were the effects of the mercantile
system so strikingly visible as in the regulations which
were laid upon the trade with our colonial possessions ; and
nowhere do we see more clearly the combination of national
policy with class interests. The purpose, before referred to, of
gaining power and wealth for the nation [6] seemed to English
legislators to require that the colonies should be entirely
subordinate to the mother country, and that their trade and
industry should be regulated so as to increase at once our
political power and our commercial wealth. Legislators
who may have had only a desire to do what seemed best for
the nation politically were supported by merchants whose
private interest it was to keep the colonial trade as far
as possible in their own hands. Hence the trade of the

[1] Toynbee, *Industrial Revolution*, p. 73.
[2] *Cf.* Adam Smith's criticism in *Wealth of Nations*, Bk. I. ch. x., pt. 2
(Vol. I. p. 125, Clarendon Press edn.).
[3] See on this point Dr Cunningham's *Growth of English Industry*, ii. pp.
42-44.   [4] *Ib.*, i. p. 143.
[5] *Ib.*, i. 149 (referring to the effects of the Law of Settlement).
[6] *Cf.* Cunningham, *Growth of Industry*, ii. 153, 154.

colonies was most carefully regulated in the interests of the mother country, though it is only just to observe that in the opinion of Adam Smith the English colonies were more favoured and allowed more extensive markets than those of any other European nation.[1] But England, like all other countries at that date, thought that the greatest benefits of Colonial, or for that matter of any other, trade could only be obtained by securing to itself a monopoly [2] or sole market. " The colonies were regarded merely as markets and farms of the mother country," [3] and Adam Smith was so disgusted at the theory of colonial possessions adopted by English statesmen and merchants, that he remarked bitterly that " to found a great empire for the sole purpose of raising up a people of customers may at first sight appear a project fit only for a nation of shopkeepers." [4] " The maintenance of this monopoly," he adds, " has hitherto been the principal, or more properly, perhaps, the sole end and purpose of the dominion which Great Britain assumes over her colonies." [5]

It has, in fact, been said that the establishment of our American and West Indian colonies was merely a device of the supporters of the Mercantile System, who founded them with the design of raising up a population chiefly agricultural in character, whose commerce should be confined entirely to an exchange of their raw products for our manufactured goods.[6] This, however, is not entirely true. There is not the least doubt that at first the colonists were allowed to carry on a direct intercourse with foreign states, and, in fact, their charters empowered them to do so. The Virginian settlers, for example, established tobacco warehouses in Middleburgh and Flushing in 1620, as depots for their trade with the Continent.[7] It was not till the time of the Navigation Acts (1651 and 1660) that the import and export trade of the colonies was actually mono-

---

[1] Adam Smith, *Wealth of Nations*, Bk. IV., ch. vii. (Vol. II. 155).
[2] *Cf.* Rogers, *Economic Interpretation*, pp. 323, 325, 330.
[3] Toynbee, *Industrial Revolution*, p. 81.
[4] *Wealth of Nations*, Bk. IV. ch. vii. (Vol. II. 196).   [5] *Ib.*, Vol. II. 197.
[6] *Cf.* M'Culloch's *Commercial Dictionary*, *s. v. Colonies* (ed. 1844). The whole article on " Colonies " is worth careful reading.
[7] Robertson's *America*, Book IX. p. 104 (in M'Culloch, *u. s.*).

polised by their mother country. The first of these Acts, as we know, enacted that the trade of the colonists should be carried on exclusively in British or colonial ships, but the second Act[1] went much further than this, for it enacted that certain specified articles—in fact, the chief products of the colonies—should not be exported directly from the colonies to any foreign country, but must be first sent to Britain, and there, in the words of the Act, " unladen, and laid upon the shore," before they could be forwarded to their ultimate destination, if they were meant for any European market. These articles became known by the name of " enumerated articles," and were originally limited to sugar, molasses, ginger, fustic, tobacco, cotton, and indigo ; but afterwards coffee, hides, iron, corn, and lumber were added. Moreover, not content with making the colonists sell their goods only in the English markets, it was enacted further[2] (in 1663) that no goods should be imported into the British colonies unless they were actually first laden and put on board at some British port, so that all commercial intercourse, both of export and import trade, had first to go through British hands. It is quite obvious that, apart from any considerations of national policy, these regulations were dictated by the class interests of British manufacturers and merchants.[3] Even the statesmen of the eighteenth century, apart from the merchants, seem to have thought that the colonies owed everything to England, and that, therefore, it was only fair that they should be exploited in the interests of the mother country.[4] Thus all imports to our colonies from any other country of Europe except England were forbidden, in order that our manufacturers might monopolise the American market.[5] The mercantile policy of our legislators went even further than this, for every attempt was made to discourage the colonists from

[1] The 12 Charles II., c. 18.

[2] M'Culloch, *Commercial Dictionary, u. s.*, p. 318.

[3] The Bristol merchants in especial benefited from these regulations. Hence they talked most glibly about benefiting the mother country ; *cf.* the pamphlet called *An Essay on the State of England* (1697), p. 71, by Cary, of Bristol.

[4] Toynbee, *Industrial Revolution*, p. 81.   [5] *Ib.*

starting manufactures at home. The American woollen industry was interfered with, and the export of woollen manufactures from one colony to another forbidden ;[1] all iron manufactures[2] were suppressed in 1750 ; even colonial hatters were not allowed to send hats from one colony into another.[3] In fact, so far was this principle carried, that Lord Chatham did not hesitate to declare in Parliament that " the British colonists of North America had no right to manufacture even a nail for a horse-shoe."[4] With aggravating restrictions of this character, it was almost certain that sooner or later ill-feeling would arise among the colonists ; and, as a matter of fact, long before the War of Independence, this ill-feeling was gaining ground ; so that the special circumstances which led to the war were only the secondary causes of a movement which was, from the nature of the case, inevitable.

§ 213. *Attempts to raise a Revenue from America.*

Had it not been for the ill-feeling thus caused, circumstances had become, after the defeat of France in the Seven Years' War, very favourable for the building up in America of a colonial empire as rich as that of India, but whose population, unlike that of the East, should consist almost entirely of English settlers. This pleasant vision, however, was never to be realised. The time of separation was approaching. It probably would have come in any case, owing to the mistaken policy of the home Government in regard to colonial trade, but the immediate cause was the attempt made to raise a revenue from the colonies without first gaining their assent thereto, and without allowing them representation at home. The revenue was needed in order to pay for the expenses of the Seven Years' War, in which conflict it cannot be denied that the colonists had received substantial help from their mother country, and had gained substantial benefits. Therefore it did not seem unfair that they should be asked to contribute towards lightening a

[1] Bancroft, *History of the United States*, ii. 284, iii. 478, 566.
[2] *Ib.*, ii. 521, iii. 42.
[3] *Cf.* the 5 George II., c. 22 ; Toynbee, *Industrial Revolution*, p. 81.
[4] Edwards, *West Indies*, Vol. II. p. 566.

burden which had to some extent been incurred on their behalf. Nor, indeed, was the request in itself altogether unreasonable, but the colonists resented the manner in which it was made, and refused to assent to the principle of taxation without representation. The history of the struggle that followed is too well-known to need further repetition.[1] It began with the Stamp Act of 1765, which laid a tax upon the stamps required for legal purposes.[2] This succeeded in irritating the colonists to such an extent that they refused to have any commercial intercourse with the mother country, and so powerful was their opposition that it produced a considerable decline in the colonial trade with England, and English manufacturers themselves requested that the Act might be repealed.[3] This was done in 1776, but the next year the "six duties" were imposed[4] on the ground that it was "expedient that a revenue should be raised in His Majesty's dominions in America." But the opposition of the colonists was so great that it was found impossible to collect the duties, and they were therefore all repealed except that on tea, though a preamble to the Act regarding the tea duty still asserted the right of the home Government to tax its colonies.[5]

§ 214. Outbreak of War.

Then came the refusal of the citizens of Boston to pay even this tax, and their well-known feat of throwing a cargo of tea[6] from the ship that brought it into their harbour (1773). Lord North, the chief minister of George III. at that time, tried to punish the Bostonians by declaring their port closed, and by annulling the charter of Massachussets, their colony.[7] Thus matters went from bad to worse, until, in 1775, all trade with the colonies was forbidden, and the

---

[1] *Cf.* Lecky, *History of the Eighteenth Century*, Vol. III. ch. xii., IV. ch. xiv. and xv., and, of course, Bancroft's *History of the United States*.

[2] *Cf.* Craik, *British Commerce*, iii. 28, and Lecky, *u. s.*

[3] Craik, iii. 30, 31.

[4] So called because they were imposed upon six articles, including glass, tea, paper, red and white lead, painters' colours, and pasteboard. They were estimated to produce about £40,000, for the purpose of paying colonial judges and governors. Craik, iii. 32; Lecky, *History*, iii. 353.

[5] Lecky, *History*, iii. 365.   [6] *Ib.*, iii. 387.   [7] *Ib.*, iii. 397.

rupture with the mother country was completed by the Declaration of Independence on July 4th, 1776. England tried to enforce obedience by military power, but the royal troops were stoutly resisted, and though the fortunes of war frequently varied, and the colonists were often defeated, the result was that they achieved their independence.[1] It should be noted that Spain and France took the opportunity of paying off their ancient grudge against England by helping her colonists against her, chiefly by means of their navies.[2] And it should also be noticed that, in spite of every difficulty, England only just failed to retain her hold upon the colonies, and that if the French had not interfered it is very possible that the colonists would never have succeeded in becoming independent, at any rate not till many years later than they actually did. As it was, however, we lost the opportunity of founding a really great colonial empire, and alienated the sympathies of a large number of our fellow-countrymen. Nevertheless, as has been pointed out,[3] there were great compensations for our loss. As the new nation prospered, our trade with it increased; and as American agriculture developed, the demand for our manufactures in the United States market became greater also; while in the East we were at this time obtaining several new markets hitherto monopolised by Holland. Certainly, from a commercial point of view, the war did our trade very little harm, for soon after it ended we notice a considerable increase in the imports and exports to and from the colonies.[4] But yet no amount of argument about compensation in trade and elsewhere can do away with the fact

---

[1] Apart from Bancroft's great *History of the United States*, few books are more instructive upon the state of feeling in England and America respectively than Thackeray's novel, *The Virginians*.

[2] *Cf.* Lecky, *History*, iv. p. 38. The patriotism of the colonies in thus accepting foreign help after all that England had done for them is an instructive comment upon the supposed bond of sentimental loyalty about which some people talk even now. But the nonsense of sentiment in regard to our colonies is equalled by the bad taste of colonials, who vapour about cutting themselves loose from the old country; *cf.* also Rogers, *Econ. Interpretation*, p. 332.

[3] Caldecott, *English Colonisation and Empire*, p. 57.

[4] *Cf.* Craik, *Hist. Brit. Comm.*, iii. 102.

that England in many ways has suffered a permanent loss from the revolt of the American colonies, and that even for the United States their emancipation has not been an unmixed advantage.

§ 215. *The Great Continental War.*

But although the War of Independence cost us a great deal, it did not seriously affect the development of our home industries. The Industrial Revolution went steadily on, and for just thirty years (1763-93) the country, though not entirely at peace, was yet sufficiently undisturbed to make rapid progress in the new manufacturing methods. But in 1789 the French Revolution broke out, and for over twenty years Europe was plunged into a disastrous and exhausting conflict. At the first outbreak of the Revolution, England looked on quietly.[1] Many men were openly glad that the down-trodden masses of the French nation had overthrown the tyranny of an upper class, whose only idea of their duty in life had been to extort the last farthing from those below them, in order to spend it in irresponsible debauchery. Statesmen like Fox gloried in it;[2] the younger Pitt was anxious not to interfere.[3] But Pitt was forced to act both by capitalists and merchants, who now were equal with the landowners as the two ruling powers of England, and by the landed aristocracy as well. He himself, no doubt, saw that the conquests which the new French Republic was already beginning to make might help France to secure again her old position as the most formidable rival of English commerce.[4] If now this rival could be finally struck down, England was sure of the control of the world's markets. Such, at least, if not his own motives,

[1] Lecky, *History of the Eighteenth Century*, v. p. 445.

[2] *Ib.*, p. 453, and *cf.* pp. 454 to 475.

[3] *Ib.*, pp. 558, 560, and vi. 60.

[4] A hint of English feeling at first that France would suffer a temporary eclipse by the Revolution is given in Lecky, v. 443. But soon the power of the Revolution was to be feared. On the other hand, Napoleon saw equally clearly that France's most serious and persistent rival was England, who was the prime mover of all coalitions against France; *cf. Correspondance de Napoléon I.*, Vol. III. 518-520, and Häusser, *Französische Revolution*, pp. 563-565.

were the considerations that must have been urged upon him by the mercantile party in England. But apart from these commercial interests, the whole body of English constitutional sentiment was arrayed against the excesses of the French Revolutionaries. The aristocracy, the Church, the middle classes, and, in fact, everybody except a few ardent Republicans, were horrified at the brutalities of the Paris mob. Those brutalities were, indeed, worthy of all execration, and yet an excuse may be found for them in the centuries of legalised oppression, rapine, and insult under which the French proletariate had groaned. In England, however, as elsewhere, the excuses which history can make were, if not unknown, at least neither comprehended nor admitted ; though it is somewhat to the credit of the nation that even then the declaration of war came from France and not from England.[1] The immediate cause of a war that was certain to have come sooner or later, was the French invasion of Holland, and after this England was plunged headlong into the great European struggle of Monarchy against Republicanism. Pitt had in this the support of all classes at home. The merchants and manufacturers were only too glad to see their old rival ruined ; the landowners and nobility were, of course, indignant at seeing the " lower classes," even of a foreign nation, rise against their lords, even though their lords perhaps deserved their punishment. But there can be no doubt that the majority of the English people also believed that England was fighting for the great principles of Monarchy and Religion, exemplified, unfortunately, by a foolish king and a corrupted priesthood. The policy of the English Government was certainly approved by the majority of the nation. But the minority, who sympathised with the Revolution, included a certain number of the working classes and others, among whom, especially after the country had felt the first severity of the burdens imposed by the war, a spirit of discontent [2] manifested itself. These

[1] Lecky, *History*, vi. 131, 132.
[2] *Cf.* Lecky, *History of the Eighteenth Century*, v. 448, and Green, *History of the English People*, iv. 314.

manifestations, feeble and somewhat foolish as they were, caused a veritable panic in the country. The Habeas Corpus Act was suspended, and all opposition silenced in imprisonment.[1] In the war, Pitt was indomitable till his death (in 1805), inspiring and subsidising[2] coalitions against France, or guiding England unflinchingly when she had to fight single-handed against the world. At times, as in 1796, Britain was threatened with invasion by the French, and the Irish, or, rather, a certain section of them, assisted[3] her would-be invaders. At another time (1806), English industry was threatened with ruin by Napoleon's Berlin and Milan Decrees, forbidding Continental nations to trade with us.[4] But at last the great inspiring genius of England's enemies was defeated, and the long years of war came to a close in 1815.

§ 216. *Its Effects upon Industry and the Working Classes.*

When peace came at length it found the resources of the nation sorely tried, but not yet exhausted. All classes had suffered somewhat, but the working classes worst of all. Yet the French Revolution, and the consequent wars, had not retarded to a very great extent the development of our industries, though the contest required a large portion of the wealth produced by the new industrial system to pay for it.[5] But in one thing we had had a great advantage over Continental nations, for our island was the only country in which war was not actually going on, and hence our manufactures were undisturbed. Consequently England was by no means so exhausted as the other participants in the struggle, and she had, moreover, the ocean-carrying

---

[1] Green, *History*, iv. 315.

[2] Rogers, *Economic Interpretation*, p. 201, remarks that Pitt "hired the European monarchs in succession, and made very unsuccessful bargains." Elsewhere he is very severe on Pitt (p. 470) for "plunging the country" into this twenty-two years' war. This is not quite fair to Pitt, who seems rather to have tried to avoid war.

[3] *Cf.* Lecky, *History*, VII. chs. xxvii. and xxviii.

[4] *Cf.* my *British Commerce*, pp. 94, 95; *Commerce in Europe*, p. 177; and Craik, *History of British Commerce*, iii. 192, 193.

[5] *Cf.* Lecky, *History*, vi. 218 : Porter, *Progress of the Nation*, i. 188.

trade left secure to her by our undisputed naval supremacy.[1] But yet her finances had been strained to an enormous extent, and before concluding this hasty sketch of the great period of the Continental War, we ought to mention the financial difficulties into which, in spite of commercial prosperity, it plunged our country. None but a rich State could ever have stood the terrible effects of this war as well as England bore them at this time; but even as it was the strain was tremendous. The war actually cost from first to last no less than £831,446,449, and more than £600,000,000 were added to the National Debt.[2] William Pitt, who was then Prime Minister, tried every means of raising money, not only by increasing duties on almost every article that could be taxed,[3] but also by a system of loans. The duties were placed upon spirits, plate, brick, stones, glass, wine, tea, coffee, fruit, hats, horses, and dogs; and these were followed by a heavy income tax,[4] till very soon there were very few articles of any description that were left untaxed. Loans were also raised by the Government upon a system which has since proved very disadvantageous to the country at large,[5] because such easy terms were given to the lenders that practically very little more than 65 per cent. was received for every

[1] Early in the war she gained the mastery of the sea and became the workshop of Europe; Rogers, *Economic Interpretation*, p. 292.

[2] At this period (1793) the revenue from taxation only was £19,845,705, and the expenditure £24,197,070. In 1815 the revenue was £72,210,512, and the expenditure £92,280,180. At the beginning of the war with Russia in 1855 the National Debt was £805,411,690; in 1882 it had been reduced to £754,455,270; and in 1890 to £689,944,027, the annual interest and annuities on which amount to some £25,000,000. *Cf.* W. Hewins' article in the *Co-operative Annual*, 1889. On the Debt generally, see Leone Levi, *History of British Commerce*, Pt. II., ch. iii. Owing to the South African War it had risen in 1903-04 to £798,000,000, or the level of 1870. It now (1911-12) is about £685,000,000.

[3] Rogers, who criticises Pitt's finance very severely, remarks that his taxes were the worst conceivable, because they were nearly all on consumption, trade, and manufactures; *Economic Interpretation*, p. 478. But allowance must be made for the desperate circumstances of the case; *cf.* Leone Levi, *History of British Commerce*, p. 98.

[4] It was 10 per cent. on incomes of £200 and over; Rogers, *Economic Interpretation*, p. 474; and *cf.* Levi, *History of British Commerce*, p. 99.

[5] *Cf.* Lecky's criticism of Pitt's finance, *History*, v. 53; also Leone Levi, *History of British Commerce*, p. 98 (Pt. II., ch. iii.), and p. 102.

£100 nominally subscribed.[1]   Thus between 1793 and
1801 no less than eighteen different loans were raised by
Pitt, but for the nominal capital of £314,000,000 that
were funded as national debt only £202,000,000 were
really received in cash.[2]   Heavy subsidies, amounting to
some £57,000,000, were also given to our continental
allies, chiefly Prussia and Austria. No less than £5,000,000
were sent to German states alone in 1796.[3]   The awful
strain upon the resources of the country naturally led to
severe commercial crises, and even the Bank of England
was directed by the Government to suspend cash payments[4]
of its notes (26th February, 1797). These notes, which now
could not be turned into cash, were nevertheless accepted
loyally by all the principal merchants,[5] and, following their
example, by all classes of the community ; and for more
than twenty years the bank was not permitted to cash its
own notes.[6]   Such was the crisis through which the commerce of the country had to pass, and that it passed
through it successfully says much for English energy and
perseverance.   But if it had not been that the Industrial
Revolution, and the inventions which caused it, had come,
as it were, just in time to increase our national wealth, it
is very doubtful whether the nation could have passed
as successfully as it did through an ordeal so severe as
this.

But the working classes had suffered the most, in spite
of the fact that our manufactures prospered and exports
increased all through the war.   In 1793 the exports were
officially valued at over £17,000,000 ; for every year afterwards they were at least £22,000,000, often more ; in
1800 over £34,000,000, and in 1815 they had quite doubled

---

[1] On some occasions the loan was even issued below £50 per cent;
Rogers, *Economic Interpretation*, p. 452.

[2] Leone Levi, *History of British Commerce*, p. 101.

[3] For exact amounts of foreign loans and subsidies, 1793-1814, see Porter,
Progress of the Nation, ii. 335.

[4] Craik, *History of British Commerce*, iii. 158-164; and Levi, *History of
British Commerce*, Pt. II., ch. i. p. 75.

[5] Craik, *History of British Commerce*, iii. 163.

[6] For the resumption of cash payments in 1819, see Levi, *British Commerce*, pp. 141, 142 (Pt. II., ch. vi.).

their value at the beginning of the war, being then over
£58,000,000 (official value).[1]   But most of the profits
of trade went into the hands of the capitalist manufacturers, while taxation fell with special severity upon the
poor, since taxes were placed on every necessity and convenience of daily life.   Even as late as 1842 there were
over a thousand articles in the customs tariff.[2]   The price
of wheat, moreover, rose to famine height; from 49s. 3d.
per quarter in 1793 to 69s. in 1799, to 113s. 10d. in
1800, and 106s. in 1810.[3]   At the same time wages were
rapidly falling,[4] and thus the burdens of the war fell most
severely upon those least able to pay for them.   But the
poverty of the poor was the wealth of the landowners, who
kept on raising rents continually,[5] and grew rich upon the
starvation of the people; for they persuaded Parliament to
prohibit the importation of foreign corn except at famine
prices,[6] and avoided, as far as possible, even during the
Continental War, the necessary burdens of taxation.[7]   It
was owing to their influence that Pitt raised fresh funds
from taxes on articles of trade, manufacture, and general
consumption.[8]   The result was seen in the deepening distress of the industrial classes, and in 1816 riots broke out
everywhere [9]—in Kent among the agricultural labourers, in
the Midlands among the miners, and at Nottingham among
the artisans, who wreaked their vengeance upon the new
machines which they thought had stolen their bread.   But
the theft must rather be laid to the charge of those who did
not allow them to participate in the wealth they had helped
to create.

[1] Levi, *u. s.*, Appendix, pp. 491, 492.
[2] Levi, *History of British Commerce*, p. 269.
[3] Leone Levi, *British Commerce*, p. 85 (Pt. II., ch. ii.), and p. 145, note.
[4] For further details as to condition of the working classes, *cf.* Rogers,
Six Centuries, p. 505; and Levi, *History of British Commerce*, pp. 145,
146.
[5] Porter, *Progress of the Nation*, i. p. 188.
[6] Below, pp. 434, 435.
[7] Rogers, *Economic Interpretation*, pp. 471, 473, 474.
[8] *Ib.*, p. 470.
[9] *Annual Register*, 58 ; Levi, *History of British Commerce*, p. 146.

§ 217. *Politics among the Working Classes.*

Such were the economic effects of the period of industrial change and foreign war upon English society—the enrichment of the capitalists and landowners on the one hand, but the pauperising of the working classes on the other. So dire was the distress of the workmen that they felt something must be done to make their voice heard effectively in the government of the people. They had tried violence, and that had been put down with a strong hand. Wiser counsels prevailed. William Cobbett,[1] in his *Weekly Political Register* (1803 to 1835), and those who thought like him, taught them to believe that a reform of Parliament would cure their evils by giving them some share in the making of the laws which affected their lives and actions. The influences of the French Revolution and the Industrial Revolution also combined to arouse an active political feeling amongst them ; for the former excited a sympathetic feeling of revolt against unjust oppression, from what source soever it might come, while the latter brought home to them in their daily lives the new and sharp distinctions between the capitalist autocrat and his hundreds of workpeople bound to him only by a cash nexus,[2] who as yet were powerless to resist his endeavours to keep down their wages—powerless because the influence of class interests in legislation [3] had despotically forbidden workmen to combine in unions in their own interests. Indistinctly, but none the less keenly, the working classes began to feel that they too must be consulted in the councils of the nation, and as a preliminary step must gain an influence over political events. But their early endeavours, which were attended by foolish rioting, were sharply and severely repressed, and the legislation following on the Manchester Massacre of 1819, in the shape of the drastic

[1] For this active reformer (*b.* 1762, *d.* 1835), see his *Life*, by Edward Smith (1878), and his own works (*cf.* list at end of his memoir in *Dictionary of National Biography*).

[2] *Cf.* Toynbee, *Industrial Revolution*, pp. 93, 191.

[3] *I.e.*, the Combination Laws, and chiefly the 40 Geo. III., c. 60 (1800), which prohibited all combinations for obtaining an advance in wages or lessening the hours of work.

Six Acts, crushed them for a time.[1]   Still we see in these first rude and abortive efforts of the working classes the beginnings of a definite political policy, which found expression later on in the help given by the masses to the agitation for the Reform Bill of 1832, and still later to the Corn Laws and the Chartist Movement. The results of the Reform Bill, which in its immediate effects seemed only to benefit the middle classes, were very disappointing to working-class politicians,[2] but there was nevertheless among them that deep-seated belief in the ultimate effect of political agitation which has seen its justification, after many years, in the attention now (1895) paid by rival parties in the State to the requirements, or supposed requirements, of the British workman.   But it was the two great Revolutions of a hundred years ago in home industry and foreign politics which first roused the political feelings of the masses, by

[1] This so-called "Massacre" (a term which in this case is grossly misapplied) was only one of a series of riots, originating in a desire for political reform, that occurred in various parts of England. In 1816 there were riots in the agricultural districts of the East of England, and in December of that year others at Spa Fields. In March 1817 the "Blanketeers" caused disturbances at Manchester, and in June there were risings in Derbyshire also. In 1819 there were riots among the working-classes in many places to petition for reform, and proclamations were issued against seditious meetings. The Manchester riot occurred on August 16th, 1819, when the mob was attacked by the yeomanry and one or two persons killed. The "Six Acts" were passed in consequence of these troubles, and may be briefly summarised as follows :—
(1) Nov. 29—Introduced by the Lord Chancellor : An Act to prevent delay in the administration of justice in cases of misdemeanour. (2) Introduced by Lord Sidmouth : An Act to prevent the training of persons to the use of arms and the practice of military evolutions and exercise. (3) An Act for the more effectual prevention and punishment of blasphemous and seditious libels. (4) An Act to authorise justices of the peace in certain disturbed counties to seize and detain arms collected and kept for purposes dangerous to the public peace, and to continue in force till March 25, 1822. (5) Introduced by Lord Castlereagh : An Act to subject certain publications to the duties of stamps on newspapers, and to make other regulations for restraining the abuses arising from the publication of blasphemous and seditious libels. (6) Introduced by Lord Sidmouth in the Lords and (on Nov. 29) by Lord Castlereagh in the Commons : An Act for more effectually preventing seditious meetings and assemblies out of doors, to continue in force for five years (cf. Acland and Ransome's *English Political History*, p. 170).
[2] Toynbee, *Industrial Revolution*, p. 207.

the misery which the War with Republican France inflicted
upon them, and by the new industrial conditions already
brought into play by the introduction of machinery and
accentuated by the effects of that war. A time of industrial
transition is nearly always severe and painful to those who
have to go through it; but the pain and misery of the
great transition in English industry, both manufacturing and
agricultural, was increased tenfold by the terrible foreign
conflict into which England was inevitably plunged. That
transition period, however, brought home to the working
classes, miserable and degraded as they then were, the
necessity of some political reform that would give them a
voice in the management of their own affairs. They were
far too weak then to gain a hearing in Parliament, but as
time went on and their power increased, their voice has
been heard more and more clearly in English politics.

§ 218. *Political Results of the Industrial Revolution.*

Now it is noticeable that the Industrial Revolution,
which caused so much misery to the working classes at
first, gave them in the end much of their present political
power by the very nature of its economic conditions. The
use of machinery worked by steam power necessitated the
concentration of workers into factories, where this power
could easily be supplied to a set of machines; and since
factories, again, to obtain steam power, must be situated
near a convenient supply of coal, it resulted that the
population working in manufactures was compelled to
concentrate itself on the great coal-fields. To this migration of the population to the coal districts of the North and
North-west we have already alluded, and it only remains to
point out here how the growth of great manufacturing
towns, resulting from this process, created immediately the
political question, as to the proper representation of such
large masses of people in Parliament. The system then in
vogue has been described so frequently that it is unnecessary to say more about it, except, perhaps, to point out
the great length of time it took to overcome the influence
of the opposition to reform. One may note, also, the class

jealousy of the great landed proprietors of the House of
Lords against the new manufacturing population that was
demanding admittance into the councils of the nation.
The jealousy was instinctive, and no doubt well founded,
but it has been repaid by the attempts, in later years,
to abolish the House which so adequately represents the
landed interest.   But, however naturally jealous the
landed interest may have been, it was palpably absurb to
refuse to transfer the franchise of Penryn to the huge
town of Manchester, or that of East Retford to Birmingham,[1]
as was the case in 1828, and such exhibitions of opposition
to the inevitable could only arouse the scorn, if not the
anger, of the masses of the people.   But the Reform Bill
was passed at last, and the manufacturing population of the
towns gained the first step in their progress towards
political influence.   It was, however, only a step, and
many more had to be taken before they could be said to be
adequately represented in the life of the nation.   But the
history of their progress towards the franchise is a matter
for the political historian ; the economist need only notice
that the coal mine and the spinning jenny revolutionised
the face of English politics as effectually as the guillotine
changed the course of the politics of France.   Of course
the blood-stained political fireworks of the French Revolution have attracted a larger share of the attention of the
ordinary historian, even in England, than has ever been
given to the less obvious action of industrial forces, but it
is often the case that historians perceive nothing but the
obvious.   Even in dealing with the French Revolution
itself, that favourite theme for those who strive after the
dramatic and picturesque, but are ignorant of all but the
most elementary methods of historical drama or depiction,
the great industrial and economic features of the time are
hopelessly neglected, while page after page is devoted to the
pretentious vapourings of the second-rate philosophers and
pamphleteers of whose works the average Frenchman of
the Revolution was profoundly ignorant.   It is the weakness of literary men to believe that literature is the main

[1] Acland and Ransome's *Political History*. p. 175.

thing in life, and that a pamphlet can change the destiny of a nation. But it is the men who act, and not those who merely talk or write, who bring about great national changes ; and while philosophers were prattling and politicians were orating, the men of action were fighting for the freedom and supremacy of England abroad, or quietly developing her magnificent industrial resources at home. Amid foreign war and political disturbance the miner and the weaver were shaping and changing the future course of the nation. When peace was restored, England had definitely become the workshop of the world, and her industry had definitely completed its transition from the domestic to the factory system. Of this system, with its enormous advantages, but also enormous evils, we must now speak.

CHAPTER XXIII

THE FACTORY SYSTEM AND ITS RESULTS

§ 219. *The Results of the Introduction of the Factory System.*

THE great war which has just been mentioned in the preceding chapter found England at its beginning a nation whose mainstay was agriculture, with manufactures increasing, it is true, but still only of secondary importance. At the commencement of the war English workers spun and wove in their cottages ; at its close they were herded together in factories, and were the servants of machinery. The manufacturing population was rapidly increasing and the agricultural steadily declining.[1] The capitalist element had become the main feature in production, and the capitalist manufacturers the main figures in English industry, rivalling and often overtopping the landed gentry. But a man cannot become a capitalist without capital, and capital cannot be accumulated without labour, though these remarkably obvious facts are constantly forgotten. The large capitalists of earlier manufacturing days obtained their capital, after the first small beginnings, from the wealth produced by their workmen, and from their own acuteness in availing themselves of new inventions. Of the wealth produced by their workmen they took nearly the whole, often leaving their employés only enough to live upon while producing more wealth for their masters. Hence it may be said that capital was in this case the result of abstinence, though the abstinence was on the part of the workman and not of his employer, as we shall shortly see.

This, then, was the immediate result of the factory system : the growth of large accumulations of capital in the hands of the new master-manufacturers, who, with their

---

[1] *Cf.* Porter, *Progress of the Nation*, i. p. 52.

new machinery, undisturbed by internal war, were able to supply the nations of Europe with clothing at a time when these nations were far too much occupied in internecine conflicts on their own soil to produce food and clothing for themselves. Even Napoleon, in spite of all his edicts directed against English trade, was fain to clothe his soldiers in Yorkshire stuffs when he led them to Moscow.[1] It was no wonder that the growth of capital was rapid and enormous. Other results followed. The formerly widespread cottage industry was now aggregated into a few districts, nearly all in Lancashire and Yorkshire, for the sake of the coal which was there so readily available. Not only that, but the workpeople themselves were more closely concentrated in the conditions of their work than they had been before. The factory had become the dominant feature in industry, and that for obvious reasons. For steam can only be generated in a fixed spot, and the motive power furnished thereby can only be distributed over a small area, and thus it became necessary to have all the workpeople close together in one large building. That is the *raison d'être* of the factory system, but even if the necessity for concentration could be obviated by the use of some other motive power, such as electricity, it is doubtful whether manufacturers would alter their arrangements in this respect. For there are also, besides the question of the supply of power, various economies of administration and management, to say nothing of manufacture or purchase and sale, which make the system of working with a number of people together in factories exceedingly advantageous;[2] and these considerations would continue to have weight even if some other motive power than steam were to be in future introduced.

But factories have their disadvantages as well as their uses, and in the early days of the factory system these evils were painfully apparent, at any rate as far as they affected the comfort of the workers. Persons of all ages and both

---

[1] Rogers, *Economic Interpretation*, p. 292.

[2] *Cf.* L. L. Price on *Domestic Industry* in Palgrave's *Dictionary of Political Economy*.

sexes were collected together in huge buildings, under no moral control, with no arrangements for the preservation of health, comfort, or decency.[1]   The enormous extension of trade rendered extra work necessary, and the mills ran all night long as well as by day.   There was as yet no legislation as to the hours or conditions of work.   The machines made " to shorten labour " resulted in many cases in vastly extending it; while in others again they took away all the means of livelihood from the old class of hand-workers with terrible and surprising suddenness.

§ 228. Machinery and Hand Labour.

The substitution of machinery for hand labour progressed, however, with considerable irregularity.   In some cases it took place very rapidly, and caused great distress; in others it came more slowly and with less misery to the worker.   In the hand wool-combing industry, machinery was introduced very slowly, and it was contended that a machine could never accomplish this branch of manufacture with the excellence achieved by manual effort.   It was not till 1840 that the wool-combing machine seriously threatened the hand-comber, and even then many believed it would never supplant him.[2]   But this was an exceptional case ; in most branches of manufacture machinery was introduced very quickly, and the workmen bitterly resented its introduction.   It was useless for economists to point out the ultimate advantages it would confer upon labour ; the workman only saw that it threw him out of employment or lessened his wages.   From his own point of view he was undoubtedly right.   The advantages so praised by economists could not accrue to him immediately, and it was but a poor consolation to reflect that the next generation would reap them, while his own pocket was empty and his cottage bare.   Hence came that fierce, but natural, revolt against the new order of things, which found expression in riots and outrage.   The labourers sought to destroy

[1] Taylor, *Modern Factory System*, pp. 88 (immorality), 169 (insanitary conditions).

[2] Burnley, *Wool and Woolcombing*, p. 166.

the new machinery; and the struggle of what were called
"the iron men," against human beings of flesh and blood,
long continued to be a source of controversy and complaint,
more especially as the workmen saw that the profits[1] made
by these iron men went almost entirely into the hands of
their masters.   In 1812 occurred the Luddite Riots, when
much machinery was destroyed in Nottingham and the
Midland counties; in 1816 they broke out again, and
in 1826 there were riots in Lancashire to destroy the
power looms.[2]   Besides these there were numerous other
acts of violence committed at various times in other parts
of the country.   But it is a remarkable fact that the
greatest of the various riots that occurred at the beginning
of this century had a political rather than industrial origin.
The agitation for the Reform Bill produced far more violence
than the introduction of machinery.   The reasons for this
are easily perceived; for machines were not introduced
simultaneously in all trades, or in all parts of the country,[3]
and therefore the introduction of single machines here and
there only affected a small portion of the working-classes at
any given time; whereas the political issues involved in the
question of Reform were brought before the country as a
whole, and at the same period, and affected everybody
equally.   Perhaps, also, the half-unconscious good sense,
which has at various times been visible among the working
classes, led them to perceive that in the end they would
gain far more by the acquisition of political power than by
the destruction of industrial improvements.

This substitution of machinery for manual labour proceeded, as has been noted in wool-combing,[4] with somewhat
unequal steps.   It occurred far more rapidly and more
markedly in spinning than in weaving; and, even in spinning, the cotton manufacture was affected sooner than the
woollen.[5]   In framework knitting the application of steam-

---

[1] Even Porter (in his *Progress of the Nation*, iii. 3) remarks how great is
the "inequality in the division among the people of the produce of the
national industry"; though he tries to take the most favourable view of
the case.   [2] *Cf.* Taylor, *Modern Factory System*, pp. 157-158.
[3] *Cf.* above, p. 341, note.   [4] Above, p. 383.
[5] *Cf.* generally, Taylor, *Modern Factory System*, pp. 81, 82.

power was long delayed by the great cheapness of labour in that trade, owing to which manufacturers were slow to adopt machinery worked by steam, since it seemed to them that they could not thereby make more profit than they did already.[1] On a general survey of the manufacturers of the country, we may, in fact, say that machinery was used in all branches for spinning[2] by the earlier part of the century, but not for weaving, and it was not till between 1830 and 1840 that the use of weaving machines seriously threatened the hand-looms.[3] The factory system, however, had from the first an indirect influence over the weaver, because the new spinning machines supplied yarn so quickly that weavers no longer used the yarn spun by their wives and children, but bought it from the factories. Hence there was a tendency for them to collect round the new mills,[4] where yarn was so readily obtainable, although they did not actually work in them.

§ 221. *Loss of Rural Life and of Bye-Industries.*

Thus from the first there was that tendency towards concentration of population which is so marked a feature of the Industrial Revolution. This implied also two other changes, both of the utmost importance to the working classes. In the first place their life lost that rural character[5] which had distinguished the domestic system of industry when the weaver worked in his cottage in some village or country town, and varied his manufacturing work with rural occupations. Now he had to live close by the factory, where he and his family worked all day long amid iron machines and stone walls, and the garden and allotment were things of the past. The freedom and independence, too, of the old life were gone, and the sound of the factory bell and the rigidity of the factory hours now formed an unpleasant contrast, which the workers at first

[1] Cunningham, *Growth of Industry*, ii. 620.
[2] *Reports*, 1833, xx. 336.
[3] Cunningham, *Growth of Industry*, ii. 635; Taylor, *Modern Factory System*, p. 81.
[4] *Reports, Miscellaneous*, 1806, iii. 577.　　　　[5] Above, p. 327.

greatly disliked.[1] Restraint and regularity were the features
of the new system, and though they are undoubtedly conducive to increased work, they are not always relished by
the workman.   That is, however, perhaps only a minor
point.   The second great effect of the concentration of
population under the factory system was the loss of bye-
employments.   We have seen already how important these
were[2] in increasing wages; but now they were quite cut
off.   Spinning had been practised by the female members
of almost every household, whether the family was engaged
in agriculture or manufactures; but now the agriculturist
could no longer find a buyer for his homespun yarn, and
the weaver no longer used the produce of his wife's spinning
wheel, but bought it from the factory.   Conversely the
manufacturing artisan no longer went out into the fields
for a little harvest work or supplemented his earnings at
the loom by the produce of his leisure time in his allotment.
The artisan was now confined strictly to the factory, and
the agriculturist strictly to the fields.[3]   There was no over-
lapping of employments; the hum of the spinning-wheel
grew silent in the cottage, and the weaver no longer breathed
the fresh scents of hay and harvest in the country air.
The village lost the artisan, and the artisan lost the village,
while the workers both of country and of town lost a very
real addition to their wages.   Their earnings were now
only what they actually brought home in money from the
mill or farm, and the useful supplements which they had
formerly been able to gain by other work no longer helped
to fill the family purse.   In more ways than one it was a
very real loss, and as even money wages were decreasing,[4]
their lot under the new system could not seem to them
particularly bright.   It is not, therefore, surprising that
men showed their discontent by resisting the introduction
of new machines.

[1] At Ipswich especially, there was a great dislike to factory work;
Reports (1840), xxiii. 196.

[2] Above, pp. 328-330.   [3] *Cf.* also Taylor, *Modern Factory System*, p. 92.

[4] From 1811 to 1842 wages declined, it is said, about 35 per cent.; *cf.*
Reports, 1845, xv. 51 (Muggeridge's figures).   See also Porter, *Progress of
the Nation*, ii. 252, Tables, where spinners, weavers, and labourers show a
marked decrease in wages.

§ 222. *Contemporary Evidence of the New Order of Things.*

A very good idea of the effects of the introduction of the factory system upon the operatives may be formed from a resolution unanimously adopted, after some riots similar to those referred to above, by the magistrates at the quarter sessions of Preston, in Lancashire, and dated November 11th, 1779, wherein it was resolved : " That the sole cause of great riots was the new machines employed in the cotton manufacture : that the county [*i.e.* the manufacturers] had greatly benefited by their erection, and that the destroying them in one county only led to their erection in another ; and that if a total stop were put by the legislature to their erection in Britain it would only tend to their establishment in foreign countries, to the detriment of the trade in Britain." [1] But better than the cold words of a formal resolution is the description of the country round Manchester, published in 1795 by Dr Aikin.[2] He points out what we have already referred to, that " the sudden invention and improvement of machines to shorten labour have had a surprising influence to extend our trade, and also to call in hands from all parts, particularly children for the cotton mills." He says that domestic life is seriously endangered by the extensive employment of women and girls in the mills, for they had become ignorant of all household duties. " The females are wholly uninstructed in knitting, sewing, and other domestic affairs requisite to make them frugal wives and mothers. This is a very great misfortune to them and to the public, as is sadly proved by a comparison of the labourers in husbandry, and those of manufacturers in general. In the former we meet with neatness, cleanliness, and comfort ; in the latter with filth, rags, and poverty." He also mentions the great prevalence of fevers among employés in cotton mills, consequent upon the utterly insanitary conditions under which they laboured. But

---

[1] Quoted in *The History of the Factory Movement,* i. 11, by "Alfred" (Samuel Kydd).

[2] The full title is *A Description of the Country from 30 to 40 miles round Manchester.* John Aikin, M.D. (1747-1822), was a brother of Mrs Barbauld.

nowhere were the evils which accompanied the sudden growth of wealth and of industry so marked as in the case of those miserable beings who were brought to labour in the new mills under the apprentice system. Their life was literally and without exaggeration simply that of slaves.

§ 223. *English Slavery. The Apprentice System.*

When factories were first built there was a strong repugnance on the part of parents who had been accustomed to the old family life under the domestic system to send their children into these places. It was, in fact, considered a disgrace so to do : the epithet of "factory girl" was the most insulting that could be applied to a young woman, and girls who had once been in a factory could rarely find employment elsewhere.[1] Perhaps this was due to the shocking immorality (especially of the masters) in the early factories.[2] It was not until the wages of the workman had been reduced to a starvation level that they consented to their children and wives being employed in the mills. But the manufacturers wanted labour by some means or other, and they got it from the workhouses. They sent for parish apprentices from all parts of England, and pretended to apprentice them to the new employments just introduced.[3] The millowners systematically communicated with the overseers of the poor, who arranged a day for the inspection of pauper children. Those chosen by the manufacturer were then conveyed by waggons or canal boats to their destination,[4] and from that moment were doomed to slavery. Sometimes regular traffickers would take the place of the manufacturer, and transfer a number of children to a factory district, and there keep them, generally in some dark cellar, till they could hand them over to a millowner in want of hands,[5] who would come and examine their height, strength, and bodily capacities,

[1] *History of the Factory Movement*, i. 16.
[2] *Cf.* Gaskell, *The Manufacturing Population of England*, ch. iv.
[3] The Heads of the Bill permitting this (1796) are given in the *History of the Factory Movement*, i. 4, 5.
[4] *Ib.*, i. 17.　　　　　　　　　　　　　　　　　[5] *Ib.*, p. 17.

exactly as did the slave-dealers in the American markets. After that the children were simply at the mercy of their owners, nominally as apprentices, but in reality as mere slaves, who got no wages, and whom it was not worth while even to feed or clothe properly, because they were so cheap, and their places could be so easily supplied. It was often arranged by the parish authorities, in order to get rid of imbeciles, that one idiot should be taken by the millowner with every twenty sane children.[1] The fate of these unhappy idiots was even worse than that of the others. The secret of their final end has never been disclosed, but we can form some idea of their awful sufferings from the hardships of the other victims to capitalist greed and cruelty. Their treatment was most inhuman. The hours of their labour were limited only by exhaustion, after many modes of torture[2] had been unavailingly applied to force continued work. Illness was no excuse: no child was accounted ill till it was positively impossible to force him or her to continue to labour, in spite of all the cruelty which the ingenuity of a tormentor could suggest.[3] Children were often worked *sixteen hours* a day, by day and by night.[4] Even Sunday was used as a convenient time to clean the machinery.[5] The author of *The History of the Factory Movement* writes: " In stench, in heated rooms, amid the constant whirling of a thousand wheels, little fingers and little feet were kept in ceaseless action, forced into unnatural activity by blows from the heavy hands and feet of the merciless overlooker, and the infliction of bodily pain by instruments of punishment, invented by the sharpened ingenuity of insatiable selfishness."[6] They were fed upon the coarsest and cheapest food, often with the same as that served out to the pigs of their master.[7] They slept by

[1] *History of the Factory Movement*, i. pp. 17, 43.
[2] For ghastly examples see the *Memoirs of Robert Blincoe,* or, more conveniently, Taylor, *Modern Factory System*, p. 192. [3] *Ib.*
[4] Alfred, *History of the Factory Movement*, i. 21 ; and Taylor, *Modern Factory System*, p. 196.
[5] Alfred, i. 21.
[6] Alfred, *History of the Factory Movement*, i. 21, 22.
[7] *Memoirs of Blincoe*, quoted by Alfred, *History of the Factory Movement,* i 23 ; also corroborated by other evidence, i. 25.

turns and in relays, in filthy beds which were never cool ;
for one set of children were sent to sleep in them as soon
as the others had gone off to their daily or nightly toil.
There was often no discrimination of sexes ; and disease,
misery, and vice grew as in a hotbed of contagion. Some
of these miserable beings tried to run away. To prevent
their doing so, those suspected of this tendency had irons
riveted on their ankles, with long links reaching up to the
hips, and were compelled to work and sleep in these chains,
young women and girls,[2] as well as boys, suffering this
brutal treatment. Many died, and were buried secretly
at night in some desolate spot, lest people should notice
the number of the graves ; and many committed suicide.[3]
The catalogue of cruelty and misery is too long to recite
here ; it may be read in the *Memoirs of Robert Blincoe*,[4]
himself an apprentice, or in the pages of the Blue-books of
the beginning of this century, in which even the methodical
and dry language of official documents is startled into life
by the misery it has to relate. It is perhaps not well for
me to say more about the subject, for one dares not trust
oneself to try and set down calmly all that might be told
about this awful page in the history of industrial England.
I need only remark, that during this period of unheeded
and ghastly suffering in the mills of our native land, the
British philanthropist was occupying himself with agitating
for the relief of the woes of negro slaves in other countries.
He, of course, succeeded in raising the usual amount of
sentiment, and perhaps more than the usual amount of
money, on behalf of an inferior and barbaric race, who have
repaid him by relapsing into a contented indolence and a
scarcely concealed savagery which have gone far to ruin our

[1] *Cf.* Alfred, *History*, i. 17 ; Taylor, *Modern Factory System*, p. 198 ; *cf.*
also evidence of J. Paterson, overseer, Dundee, before the Sadler Committee, 1832.

[2] Blincoe, quoted in Alfred's *History of the Factory Movement*, i. 23.

[3] *Ib.*, i. 24, 25. No inquests were ever held.

[4] These first appeared in Vol. I. of a periodical called *The Lion*, published by Richard Carlile, 62 Fleet Street, London, but afterwards issued
separately. I have seen a separate copy in the Manchester Free Library ;
cf. also No. 21 of *The Poor Man's Advocate* (Manchester, June 9, 1832) ;
there are copious extracts in Taylor and Alfred, *u. s.*

possessions in the West Indies. The spectacle of England buying the freedom of black slaves by riches drawn from the labour of her white ones, affords an interesting study for the cynical philosopher.

All this time the friends of the negro were harrowing the feelings of the inhabitants of the country in which these daily and nightly cruelties were perpetrated with tales of the sufferings of the unfortunate black men. No notice was taken of the horrors going on under the very eyes of the agitators, till at length the miseries of the factories began to avenge themselves upon a callous population in the shape of malignant fevers, bred from the horribly insanitary conditions of the mills in which these wretched creatures worked.

§ 224. *The Beginning of the Factory Agitation.*

The state of things in factories where large numbers of apprentices were employed became, in fact, so bad that at last something had to be done. In 1802 an Act[1] was passed, by the influence of the first Sir Robert Peel, "for the preservation of the health and morals of apprentices and others employed in cotton and other mills." It is a significant fact that the immediate cause of this bill was the fearful spread through the factory districts of Manchester of epidemic disease, owing to the overwork, scanty food, wretched clothing, long hours, bad ventilation, and overcrowding in unhealthy dwellings of the workpeople, especially the children.[2] The hours of work were 'reduced' to only twelve per day. This Act, however, did not apply to children residing near the factory where they were employed, for they were supposed to be "under the supervision of their parents." The result was that, although the apprentice system was discontinued, other children came to work in the mills, and were treated almost as brutally,[3] though fortunately they were not entirely in the hands of their master. But the evils of this system of child labour were very great.

[1] Act 42 Geo. III., c. 73.
[2] Alfred, *History of the Factory Movement*, i. 27.
[3] *Ib.*, i. ch. iv., and pp. 53, 79, 183, 278-306, ii. 10.

During the whole of the period of 1800 to 1820, and even to 1840, the results of their sufferings were seen in the early deaths of many of the children, and in the crippled and distorted forms of the majority of those who survived.[1] On the women and grown-up girls the effects of long hours and wearisome work were equally disastrous.[2]   A curious inversion of the proper order of things was seen in the domestic economy of the victims of this cheap labour system, for women and girls were superseding men in manufacturing labour, and, in consequence, their husbands had often to attend, in a shiftless, slovenly fashion, to those household duties which mothers and daughters hard at work in the factories were unable to fulfil.[3]   Worse still, mothers and fathers in some cases lived upon the killing labour of their little children, by letting them out to hire to manufacturers, who found them cheaper than their parents.   In fact there was, as one investigator expressed it, "a conspiracy insensibly formed between the masters and the parents to tax them with a degree of toil beyond their strength."[4]

§ 225. Efforts towards Factory Reform.

Meantime, however, the Act of 1802 seems to have become, even as regards apprentices, a dead letter.   White slaves could be bought and sold in England with as much impunity as in the West Indies,—in fact, with more, for by 1815, Wilberforce's wishes as regards trading in slaves had long since become law.   The fact that such sales took place is attested by the debate in the Commons, on June 6th, 1815, introduced by Sir Robert Peel, in which one speaker (Horner) described the sending away of children to distant parishes, and gave an instance in which, "with a bankrupt's effects, a gang of these children had been put

---

[1] Cf. evidence quoted in Alfred, u. s., i. 190, 287, 260, ii. 9.
[2] Cf. evidence in Alfred, u. s., i. 181, 300.
[3] Cf. facts quoted by Engels, Condition of the Working Classes in 1844 (English edition, 1892), pp. 144, 145.
[4] Assistant Commissioner Power, in the famous 1833 Report. Reports, 1833, xx. 604 ; also, cf. Oastler's speech quoted in Alfred, History of the Factory Movement, i. 228, and Sadler's speech, p. 158.

up to sale, and advertised publicly as part of the property.[1]
A still more atrocious instance," he continued, "had been
brought before the court of King's Bench two years ago,
when a number of these boys, apprenticed by a parish in
London to one manufacturer, had been *transferred* [*i.e.*
sold] to another, and had been found by some benevolent
persons in a state of absolute famine." [2]   Facts like these,
even though negroes were not concerned, could no longer
be blinked, and at length, in 1816, a Select Committee of
the House of Commons was appointed to take evidence
upon the state of children employed in the manufactories
of the United Kingdom. Terrible evidence of overwork was
given before this Committee,[3] but the grasp of Mammon was
cruel and relentless ; and now that social reformers were in
earnest, the inevitable opposition of capitalistic greed rose
up in all its power to block the path of humanity.   The
surest block was the barrier of delay.   Further Commissions were asked for by the opponents of factory reform ;
the same kind of evidence as before was repeated in 1819
before a Committee of the Lords ;[4] and when at last
very shame demanded that something should be done, the
ineffectual Act, 59 George III., c. 66, was passed.[5] This
Act, when originally introduced, was meant to apply to all
factories, but it was afterwards limited only to cotton
factories, so that it had only a very partial effect, and was
even then frequently evaded.[6] And in any case the worsted
and woollen mills were not even touched.

§ 226. *Richard Oastler.*

So things went on again as badly as ever for year after
year, and manufacturers grew rich, while children and

[1] Quoted in Alfred's (Samuel Kydd) *History of the Factory Movement,*
i. 43.   [2] *Ib.*, i. 43.
[3] For the nature of the evidence, *cf. History of the Factory Movement,*
Vol. I., ch. iv.   [4] *Ib.*, i 77.
[5] R. W. Cooke-Taylor in *The Factory System and the Factory Acts* (1894)
remarks, p. 61, "It was generally ignored or evaded."
[6] It provided (1) nine years to be limit of age for child employment.
(2) Twelve hours' day for those under sixteen years.   (3) Time to be
allowed for meals.   (4) Ceilings and walls to be washed with quicklime
twice a year.

young people of both sexes were beaten and overworked to make their profits; and philanthropists riding home late at night from heated meetings, after discussing the wrongs of the black slaves, looked with cheerful and ignorant complacency at the great factory windows blazing with light, and accepted them as signs of prosperity, little heeding or little knowing the misery and cruelty that prevailed within their walls. It was, however, one of these friends of the negro, and one who had often had such a midnight ride, who was suddenly aroused to the fact that actual slavery in the most literal sense was going on in England while he was agitating for its abolition abroad. Richard Oastler [1] was the man whose eyes were thus opened, a Yorkshireman by birth, and one well acquainted with the industries of the busy West Riding. He was once in 1830 staying at the house of a friend who lived at Horton Hall, near Bradford, and who was a large manufacturer. As Oastler was talking to him one night about his slavery reforms, his friend John Wood remarked to him: [2] "I wonder you have never turned your attention to the factory system."—"Why should I?" replied the young abolitionist, "I have nothing to do with factories."—"Perhaps not," was the answer, "but you are very enthusiastic against slavery in the West Indies, and I assure you that there are cruelties daily practised in our mills on little children, which I am sure if you knew you would try to prevent." And then he went on to describe to his astonished hearer the horrors of the factories. Even in his own mill Wood confessed that little children were worked from six in the morning till seven at night, with a break of only forty minutes, while in many other mills no rest at all was allowed; and that various cruel devices were employed to goad them on to

[1] He was born in 1789, and had succeeded his father as steward to Mr Thornhill on his Yorkshire estates, living at Fixby Hall, near Huddersfield. It is curious that no proper biography of him exists. In Palgrave's *Dictionary of Political Economy*, however, I have given a short summary of the main facts of his life; *cf.* also Taylor's *Biographia Leodiensis*, pp. 499-503; Hodder's *Life of the Earl of Shaftesbury*, i. 214-216, 304; ii. 189. 211; iii. 249; and "Alfred's" *History of the Factory Movement, passim.* Oastler died in 1861.

[2] See the conversation in Alfred's *History*, i. 95-97.

renewed labour. They were fined, beaten with sticks and straps and whips ; and the girls were also often subjected to shocking indecencies.[1]

§ 227. *Factory Agitation in Yorkshire. For and Against.*

Oastler, when once he saw what was going on about him in his own country, made no delay in entering upon a warfare that was to last for many a weary year, and bring many a trial and disaster. The very next day[2] he wrote a long letter to the great Yorkshire daily paper, the *Leeds Mercury*, in which he took for his text the old, foolish, and utterly untrue statement, "It is the pride of Britain that a slave cannot exist on her soil," and proved very conclusively that slavery could and did exist in a most dreadful form. He pointed out that thousands of children, both male and female, from six to fourteen years of age, and chiefly girls, were compelled to labour thirteen to sixteen hours a day, under the lash of an overseer, in the mills of Bradford, Morpeth, Halifax, Huddersfield, and many other northern towns. This sudden revelation of English slavery created a remarkable sensation, but, of course, called forth a very powerful opposition. The simplest thing was to deny the existence of any such evils, and denials accordingly became remarkably frequent. A keen newspaper correspondence arose, chiefly in the columns of the *Leeds Mercury;* and from this controversy Oastler emerged triumphant, with all his facts proved over and over again, while confirmation of his statements began to pour in from every part of Yorkshire. Before a month had passed, a meeting of the worsted spinners of Bradford was called by some of the principal firms in that town (November 22nd), in order to promote legislation on the subject, and a petition was drawn up to be forwarded to Parliament. A similar agitation now arose in Lancashire, and a bill was laid before the Commons by Lord Morpeth to reduce the hours of labour and raise the limit of age for work in mills.[3] Hope seemed to be dawn-

[1] See the conversation in Alfred's *History*, i. 96.
[2] *Cf. The Leeds Mercury :* Oastler's letter is dated September 29th, 1830.
[3] For all the above, see Alfred's *History*, i. 104-107.

ing for the children of the factories, when suddenly the manufacturers of Halifax and district struck the first note of opposition in a counter petition.[1] They set forth the "unimpeachable character for humanity and kindness" possessed by manufacturers as a class; the impossibility of making profits if hours were reduced; the overpowering force of foreign competition (almost non-existent then as compared with to-day); the general hardships of a manufacturer's lot, owing to taxation and other difficulties; and finally, "the pernicious tendency of all legislative enactments upon trade and manufactures," or, in other words, the necessity of following the golden rule of *laissez faire*.

I have quoted the arguments of this petition because they are in brief a summary of the arguments which were then employed, are now employed, and probably always will be employed against any interference between master and man. In this case the law had only been invoked to step in between master and child; but that mattered little; the "liberty of the subject" and "freedom of contract" were questions too sacred to be trifled with. It was indeed soon seen that these arguments of the millowners and their friends were by no means lacking in cogency, for the proposed legislation upon the working of factories was modified to such an extent as to make it almost useless, and, in any case, the measure was to be applied to cotton mills only.[2] Oastler felt that the day was lost, and said as much in a public letter to the *Leeds Intelligencer* of October 20, 1831, a letter which shows cruel disappointment of heart, indeed, but yet is as full as ever of fire and hope for the future.[3] Incidentally it is curious to note, from a passage in this letter, that the Factory Reformers of that day were accused of being opposed to the abolition of negro slavery, and were said to be getting up a factory agitation "in order to turn the attention of the nation away from West Indian slavery."[4] But in spite of calumny, prejudice, and

[1] Alfred, *History*, i. 109 *sqq.*
[2] So the 1 and 2 William IV., c. 39; and *cf.* Taylor, *Factory System and Factory Acts*, p. 63.
[3] See it almost in full in Alfred's *History*, i. 118.
[4] *Ib.*, i. 119.

the savage opposition of vested interests, the words of Richard Oastler rang forth undauntedly to the working classes of Yorkshire : " Let no promises of support from any quarter sink you to inactivity. Consider that you must manage this cause yourselves. Collect information and publish facts. Let your politics be : Ten hours a day, and a time book." [1]

§ 228. *Ten Hours' Day and Mr Sadler.*

At this time Oastler was living at Fixby Hall, Huddersfield, and from his position as a Tory and a Churchman, as he describes himself, could not at first see his way to working actively among the mill hands, who were mostly " Radicals and Dissenters." But now he saw that no barriers of class, or creed, or politics could be allowed to interfere in this cause, and from henceforth decided to throw in his lot with the factory workers, come what might. He was assisted, from the political side, by men like J. Hobhouse and M. T. Sadler, both Members of Parliament, warmly attached to his cause, and it was decided that Sadler should lead the question in the House of Commons. It would be tedious to go through all the phases of the great Ten Hours' Agitation in and out of Parliament,[2] and therefore it must suffice to mention that Sadler at length introduced a Ten Hours' Bill into the Commons late in 1831, and moved its second reading in March 1832, in a speech [3] of eminent moderation and judgment. He pointed out the existence of child-slavery in England, and the causes of it, mainly in the poverty, but partly in the inducements to laziness, of the parents. Many parents were unable to get work themselves, and thus were compelled to hire out their children to the brutalities and hardships of factory work. Some parents, demoralised by the old Poor Law, selfish and brutalised by custom, purchased idleness for themselves at the cost of their children's health and strength. In some

---

[1] Alfred's *History*, i. 122.

[2] See Alfred's *History*, i. 125 *sqq.*

[3] *Cf.* Taylor, *Factory System and Factory Acts* (1894), p. 64. The speech is given in full in Alfred's *History*, i. 151 *sqq.*

districts, so great was the demand for children's labour, that an indispensable condition of marriage among the working classes was the certainty of offspring,[1] whose wages—beginning at six years old—might keep their inhuman fathers and mothers in idleness. Well might Sadler exclaim:[2] " Our ancestors could not have supposed it possible— posterity will not believe it true—that a generation of Englishmen could exist, or had existed, that would work lisping infancy of a few summers old, regardless alike of its smiles or tears, and unmoved by its unresisting weakness, twelve, thirteen, fourteen, sixteen hours a day, and through the weary night also, till, in the dewy morn of existence, the bud of youth was faded and fell ere it was unfolded." But, to our eternal disgrace as a nation, that generation of Englishmen existed, and Mr Sadler told the House, detail by detail, of the evils and outrages of the whole abominable system. Excessive hours, low wages, immorality, ill-health, —all were enumerated, and then he continued: " Then, in order to keep them awake, to stimulate their exertions, means are made use of to which I shall now advert, as a last instance of the degradation to which this system has reduced the manufacturing operatives of this country. Children are beaten with thongs, prepared for the purpose. Yes, the females of this country, no matter whether children or grown up—and I hardly know which is the more disgusting outrage—are beaten, beaten in your free market of labour as you term it, like slaves. The poor wretch is flogged before its companions—flogged, I say, like a dog, by the tyrant overlooker. We speak with execration of the cartwhip of the West Indies, but let us see this night an equal feeling rise against the factory thong in England."[3]

§ 229. *The Evidence of Facts.*

Of course, it is needless to say that such an equal feeling did not arise, not, that is, with anything like the cry of horror that arose over negro slavery. The hours of black slaves' labour in our colonies were at that very time carefully

---

[1] Alfred's *History*, i. 158.   [2] *Ib.*, i. 161.   [3] *Ib.*, i. 183.

limited by law[1] to nine per day for adults, and six for young persons and children, while night work was simply prohibited. But for white slaves no limit was to be fixed, nor was the arm of the law to interfere. Though Sadler's bill was read a second time, and was referred to a committee, nothing much was done. But the evidence given before this committee at length produced some effect. Oastler's tactics of publishing the facts had now been taken up unwittingly by Parliament itself, and the facts given before Sadler's committee[2] were terrible enough to cause a shudder of shame to run through the country. Yet, after all, the shame was only felt by a minority; the nation, as a whole, was not yet touched. And very soon Mr Sadler lost his seat[3] in the House of Commons, in the election after the great Reform Bill of 1832, and the factory hands were thus left without a Parliamentary advocate of any influence. But now a new leader appeared in the person of Lord Ashley, afterwards Earl Shaftesbury, who undertook to bring forward once more the Ten Hours' Bill. Lord Ashley's life may be read elsewhere,[4] but we may pause to look, though only for a moment, at the revelations of slavery brought to light by the Sadler Committee.[5]

In the first place the Committee received the satisfactory assurance from one witness that the youngest age at which children were employed was never under five.[6] But from five years onwards it was the custom to employ them, from about five o'clock in the morning till as late as ten o'clock at night,[7] during the whole of which time they were on their feet, with a short interval for dinner.[8] The children were generally cruelly treated, so cruelly that they dare not, for their lives, be too late at their work in a morning.[9] One witness stated that he had seen children, whose work it was to throw a bunch of ten or twelve cordings across their hand and take them off, one at a time, so weary as

[1] By the Orders in Council of November 2, 1831.
[2] *Cf.* Taylor, *Factory System and Factory Acts*, p. 65.   [3] *Ib.*, p. 65.
[4] See the excellent *Life*, in 3 vols., by Mr Hodder.
[5] See ch. xii. of Alfred's *History*, Vol. I.
[6] *Ib.* i. 275.   [7] *Ib.* i. 276.
[8] *Ib.* i. 277 (quotation from evidence).   [9] *Ib.* i. 278.

not to know whether they were at work or not, and going through the mechanical actions without anything in their hands.[1] When they made mistakes in this state of fatigue they were severely beaten by the spinner whom they helped or by the overlooker. Several cases of deaths, through such beating and blows, were given in evidence. "The children were incapable of performing their day's labour well towards the end of the day; their fate was to be awoke by being beaten, and to be kept awake by the same method."[2] "At a mill in Duntruin," continued the same man, who gave this evidence,[3] "they were kept on the premises by being locked up while at work, they were locked up in the bothies (sleeping-huts) at night; they were guarded to their work and guarded back again. There was one bothy for the boys, but that did not hold them all, so there were some of them put into the other bothy along with the girls." Sometimes the elder children tried to escape from such miserable and degraded surroundings. When caught, as they generally were, they were inhumanly flogged, or sent to gaol for breaking their contracts.[4] A case is given of a young woman who was thus put in prison for a year, "brought back after a twelvemonth and worked for her meat; *and she had to pay the expenses that were incurred.* So she worked *two* years for nothing, to indemnify her master for the loss of her time."[5]

§ 230. *English Slavery.*

Here, again, is the story of a Huddersfield lad who was lame.[6] He lived a good mile from the mill, and it was painful for him to move, "so my brother and sister used, out of kindness, to take me under each arm, and run with me to the mill, and my legs dragged on the ground in consequence of the pain; I could not walk, and if we were five minutes too late, the overlooker would take a strap and beat us till we were black and blue." The worst of it was

---

[1] Alfred's *History*, Vol. I. i. 278.
[2] Evidence of James Paterson, quoted *ib.*, i. 283.
[3] *Ib.*, i. 283, 284.   [4] *Ib.*, i. 284.   [5] *Ib.*, i. 284.
[6] Evidence of Joseph Habergam, *ib.*, i. 286.

that the masters in many mills encouraged the overlookers in this kind of brutality. An eye-witness [1] relates : "I have seen them, when the master has been standing at one end of the room with the overlookers speaking to him, and he has said 'look at those two girls talking,' and has run and beat them the same as they beat soldiers in the barrack-yard for deserting." A Leeds girl,[2] who began her mill-work at six years old, and toiled then from five in the morning till nine at night, gives similar evidence : "When the doffers flagged a little or were too late, they were strapped, and those who were last in doffing were constantly strapped, girls as well as boys. I have been strapped severely, and have been hurt by the strap excessively. Sometimes the overlooker got a chain and chained the girls, and strapped them all down the room. The girls have many times had black marks upon their skin." [3] This was in a Yorkshire factory, and not upon a West Indian plantation; but the slaves were white. That the dreadful exertions, produced by this forced labour, often caused death from exhaustion among children is obvious. A Keighley overseer, in giving evidence, told the story [4] of a man who came to him, saying : "My little girl is dead." I asked, "When did she die ?" and he said : "In the night, and what breaks my heart is this; she went to the mill in the morning, but she was not able to do her work. A little boy said he would help her if she would give him a halfpenny on Saturday, but at night when the child went home, perhaps about a quarter of a mile, she fell down several times on the road through exhaustion, till at length she reached her door with difficulty. She never spoke audibly afterwards ; she died in the night." Tragedies like this, told in such simple, common-place words, happened in not a few homes ; or instead of death, a maimed and miserable life of ill-health and disease was slowly dragged along till the grave gave a merciful release. One might give a long list of such cases, and of various forms

[1] Same evidence, i. 287, 288.
[2] Evidence of Elizabeth Bentley, *ib.*, i. 297.   [3] *Ib.*, i. 298, 299.
[4] Evidence of Gillett Sharpe, *ib.*, i. 302.

of torture inflicted on children not daring to resist, but in this tender age one is not allowed to harrow even the feelings of a reader.   Yet we may perhaps be allowed to quote one more example from a speech of Richard Oastler's[1]: "I will not picture fiction to you," this brave reformer said, in the early days of the factory movement, "but I will tell you what I have seen.   Take a little female captive, six or seven years old; she shall rise from her bed at four in the morning of a cold winter day, but before she rises she wakes perhaps half-a-dozen times, and says, Father, is it time? Father, is it time?   And at last, when she gets up and puts her little bits of rags upon her weary limbs— weary yet with the last day's work—she leaves her parents in their bed, for their labour (if they have any) is not required so early.   She trudges alone through rain and snow, and mire and darkness, to the mill, and there for 13, 14, 16, 17, or even 18 hours is she obliged to work with only thirty minutes' interval for meals and play. Homeward again at night she would go, when she was able, but many a time she hid herself in the wool in the mill, as she had not strength to go.   And if she were one moment behind the appointed time; if the bell had ceased to ring when she arrived with trembling, shivering, weary limbs at the factory door, there stood a monster in human form, and as she passed he lashed her.   This," he continued, holding up an overlooker's strap, "is no fiction.   It was hard at work in this town last week.   The girl I am speaking of died; but she dragged on that dreadful existence for several years."

Such was the terrible nature of the evidence taken before the Sadler Committee of 1833; but even yet it was found impossible, for various reasons, to get a Bill passed.[2]   The Government appointed yet another Committee, which, however, reported so strongly in favour of legislation, that at length something had to be done.   The result was the famous Act of 1833.

---

[1] Speech at Huddersfield, Dec. 26, 1831, quoted in Alfred's *History*, i. 226
[2] *Cf.* Taylor, *Factory System and Factory Acts* (1894), p. 74.

§ 231. The Various Factory Acts.

But to gain a complete survey of Factory Legislation we must go back a few years. After the Act of 1802, already referred to, for improving the condition of apprentices, an Act[1] for the regulation of work in cotton mills was passed in 1819, allowing no child to be admitted into a factory before the age of nine, and placing 12 hours a day as the limit of work for those between the ages of nine and sixteen. The day was really one of 13½ or 14 hours, because no meal-times were included in the working day. Then, again, in 1831 an Act[2] was passed forbidding night-work in factories for persons between nine and twenty-one years of age, while the working day for persons under eighteen was to be 12 hours a day, and 9 hours on Saturdays. But this legislation only applied to cotton factories; those engaged in the manufacture of wool were quite untouched, and matters there were as bad as ever. But a spirit of agitation was fortunately abroad in the country. These were the days of the Reform Bill and of the rise of Trades Unions. The workmen cried out for the restriction of non-adult labour to 10 hours a day, and the Conservative party,[3] who were chiefly interested in the land and not in the mills, supported them readily against the manufacturers, who were mainly Liberals and Radicals. The long struggle against factory slavery was at last successful, and one of the most important Acts to prevent it was passed. The Act[4] of 1833, introduced by Lord Shaftesbury, prohibited night-work to persons under eighteen in both cotton, wool, and other factories; children from nine to thirteen years of age were not to work more than 48 hours a week, and young persons from thirteen to eighteen years were to work only 68 hours. Provision was also made for the children's attendance at school, and for the appointment of factory inspectors. Children under nine years of age were not to be employed at all. These restrictions in the employment of children led to a great

---

[1] The 59 Geo. III., c. 66.   [2] The 1 and 2 William IV., c. 39.
[3] Cf. Toynbee, Industrial Revolution, pp. 208, 209, 215.
[4] The 3 and 4 William IV., c. 103.

increase in the use of improved machinery to make up for the loss of their labour, and it is probable that they accelerated the use of steam instead of water power in the smaller and more old-fashioned mills, where also the worst abuses in children's employment had chiefly prevailed.[1] Then, after one or two minor Acts,[2] the famous Ten Hours' Bill[3] was passed in 1847, which reduced the labour of women and young persons to 10 hours a day, the legal day being between 5.30 A.M. and 8.30 P.M. Manufacturers tried to avoid the provisions of this Bill by working persons thus protected in relays, and making elaborate regulations to nullify the law,[4] but this was stopped by the fixing of a uniform working day in 1850, so that young persons and women could only work between the hours of 6 A.M. and 6 P.M., and on Saturdays only till 2 P.M.[5] Since the passing of these Acts many much-needed extensions of their provisions to other industries have been made, especially[6] in 1864, and in 1874 the minimum age at which a child could be admitted to a factory was fixed at ten years.[7] The limitation of the labour of women and young persons necessarily involved the limitation of men's labour, because their work could not be done without female aid.[8] Thus the Ten Hours' Day fortunately became universal in factories.

§ 232. How these Acts were Passed.

It is curious to notice how these Acts were passed. They all showed the steady advance of the principle of State interference with labour, a doctrine most distasteful to the old Ricardian school of economists, even when that interference was made in the interests of the physical and moral well-being, not only of the industrial classes, but of the community at large. Hence the economists of the day

[1] Cf. Cunningham, Growth of Industry, ii. pp. 626, 627.
[2] The 7 Victoria, c. 15; 8 and 9 Vic., c. 29; and others; see Taylor, Factory System and Factory Acts (1894), ch. iv.
[3] The 10 Vic., c. 29, and cf. Taylor, ib., pp. 88, 89.
[4] Cf. Taylor, u. s., pp. 89 and 78.   [5] The 13 and 14 Victoria, c. 54.
[6] By the 27 and 28 Victoria, c. 38; cf. Taylor, u. s., p. 95.
[7] The 37 and 38 Victoria, c. 44.   [8] Cf. Taylor, Factory Acts, p. 107.

aided the manufacturers in opposing these Acts to the utmost of their power, and the laws passed were due to the action of the Tories and landowners.[1] Lord Shaftesbury, Fielden, Oastler, and Sadler were all Tories, though they were accused of being Socialists. They were supported by the landed gentry, partly out of genuine sympathy with the oppressed, and partly out of opposition to the rival manufacturing interest.[2] But the millowners had their revenge afterwards when they helped to repeal the Corn Laws, in spite of the protest of the landlords, who did not mind the workmen having shorter hours at other people's expense, but objected to their having cheap bread at their own. It has been remarked by an economist,[3] who does not hesitate to point out the virtues as well as the vices of the landowners, that, where their own interests were not touched, they tried to use their power for the good of the people. The remark is so true that it is almost a truism. Most men are benevolent as long as benevolence costs them nothing. The working classes, however, seem to have a suspicion that each political party is their friend only in so far as they can injure their opponents, or at least do no harm to themselves. The Manchester School of Radical Economists bitterly opposed the Factory Acts, and John Bright especially distinguished himself (February 10, 1847) by his violent denunciation of the Ten Hours' Bill, which he characterised as " one of the worst measures ever passed in the shape of an Act of the legislature."[4] But when we look back upon the degradation and oppression from which the industrial classes were rescued by this agitation, we can understand why Arnold Toynbee said so earnestly: " I tremble to think what this country would have been but for the Factory Acts."[5] They form one of the most interesting pages in the history of industry, for they show how fearful may be the results of a purely capitalist and com-

---

[1] Toynbee, *Industrial Revolution*, p. 214. [2] *Ib.*
[3] Toynbee, *Industrial Revolution* (*Are Radicals Socialists?*), p. 215.
[4] As John Bright was always looked upon as "the people's friend," it may be well to observe that this extraordinary utterance is to be found in the records of *Hansard*, Third Series, Volume LXXXIX., p. 1148.
[5] *Industrial Revolution*, p. 215.

petitive industrial system, unless the wage-earners are in a position to place an effectual check upon the greed of an unscrupulous employer. It may be thought that too large a space has been devoted to them in this chapter, but when we consider the enormous and profound influence which the Factory System has had upon the life of the nation, it must be acknowledged that no outline of industrial history would be at all adequate that does not include a very marked reference both to the system itself and the Acts which now regulate it. The factory has so completely revolutionised the methods of industry in the last hundred years, and has thereby so completely altered the social and industrial life of the majority of the workers in this nation, that it is practically impossible to overestimate its importance as a feature in the national life. How far it has operated for good or for ill must be left to the historians of the future; but no one who has lived for any length of time (as the writer has done) amid the centres of a large manufacturing population, can fail to regard with considerable uneasiness the peculiar developments of life and character which this system has called forth. It has been acutely, if somewhat gloomily, remarked [1] that human progress is after all only a surplus of advantages over disadvantages, and that being so, one must attempt to regard the various disquieting features of the Industrial Revolution with philosophic equanimity. Its advantages have been great, but its drawbacks are great also, and the greatest drawback of all is probably to be found in the concentration of population in large towns, where the mill hand spends his life amid surroundings of repulsive ugliness, and engaged in an occupation of wearisome monotony. The fact that he has grown to like both his occupation and his surroundings is possibly a matter for even greater concern. But whatever we may think of the effects of the factory system, they form a striking example of the truth that the history of mankind is to be found written in the history of its tools, for there are few factors in modern English history more important than the inventions of the Industrial Revolution.

[1] Lecky, *History of the Eighteenth Century*, vi. 220.

CHAPTER XXIV

THE CONDITION OF THE WORKING CLASSES

§ 233. *Disastrous Effects of the New Industrial System.*

WE have already seen, in various preceding chapters, that the condition of the labourers deteriorated from the time of Elizabeth onwards, but in the middle of the eighteenth century it had been materially improved owing to the increase of wealth from the new agriculture and to the general growth of foreign trade. But then came the great Continental wars and the Industrial Revolution, and it is a sad but significant fact that, although the total wealth of the nation was vastly increased at the end of last century and the beginning of this, little of that wealth came into the hands of the labourers, but went almost entirely into the hands of the great landlords and new capitalist manufacturers, or was spent in the enormous expenses of foreign war.[1] We saw, too, that the labourer felt far more severely than any one else the burden of this war, for taxes had been imposed on almost every article of consumption,[2] while at the same time the price of wheat had risen enormously.[3] Moreover, labour was now more than ever dependent on capital, and the individual labourer was thoroughly under the heel of his employer. This was due to the new conditions of labour, both in agriculture and manufactures, that arose after the Industrial and Agricultural Revolution, and to the extinction of bye-industries.[4] The workman was now practically compelled to take what his employer offered him, either in the factory or the farm; for, as a mill-hand, he had nothing to fall back upon except the work offered at the mill, while for the agricultural labourer the increase

[1] Above, p. 373.   [2] Above, *ib.*; *cf.* also Rogers, *Six Centuries*, p. 489.
[3] Above, p. 375.   [4] Above, p. 386.

of enclosures, both of the common fields and the waste, had deprived him of the resources which he formerly possessed.[1] Few labourers had now a plot of ground to cultivate, or any rights to a common where they could get fuel for themselves and pasture for their cattle. The Assessment of Wages by the justices had indeed become inoperative, for it seems to have practically died out in the south of England at the close of the seventeenth century, and in the north at the beginning of the eighteenth.[2] But the low rates of pay which had been fixed thereby had become almost traditional,[3] and from a variety of causes, already alluded to, pauperism was growing with alarming rapidity. Moreover, it was impossible for the labourer to improve his position by agitating for higher wages, for all combination in the form now known as Trades Unions was suppressed, and his condition sank to the lowest depin of poverty and degradation.

§ 234. *The Allowance System of Relief.*

This state of things was aggravated by various misfortunes, among which the most prominent was the rise in the price of food. At the end of the seventeenth century there had been a succession of bad harvests, and the price of wheat, for the four years ending 1699, was between 64s. and 71s. a quarter,[4] or more than double the average [5] of the four years ending in 1691. This high price was maintained till 1710, when there was a considerable fall,[6] and the price of wheat continued, on the whole, fairly low till about 1751. But after that, and especially from 1765, the seasons were most unsatisfactory, harvests were poor, and the price of wheat rose enormously.[7]

The latter part of the eighteenth century was marked by almost chronic scarcity,[8] and after 1790 wheat was rarely below 50s. a quarter, and often double that price,

---

[1] Toynbee, *Industrial Revolution*, p. 101.
[2] Rogers, *Economic Interpretation of History*, p. 43.   [3] *Ib.*
[4] Prothero, *English Farming*, App. I. (p. 244).
[5] *Cf.* figures in Prothero, *u. s.*
[6] The prices were, in 1710, 78s. a qr.; in 1714, 50s.; in 1720, only 37s.
[7] Tooke, *History of Prices*, i. 66, 82, and i., ch. iii. generally.   [8] *Ib.*

as it was after the deficient harvest of 1795, when the price was 108s. a quarter.[1] The famine was enhanced by the restrictions of the Corn Laws. Meanwhile, population was growing with portentous and almost inexplicable rapidity. The factories employed large numbers of hands, but these were chiefly children whose parents were often compelled to live upon the labour of their little ones ; [2] and the introduction of machinery had naturally caused a tremendous dislocation in industry, which could not be expected to right itself immediately.[3] Poverty was so widespread that, in May 1795, the Berkshire justices, in a now famous meeting at Speenhamland, near Newbury,[4] declared the old quarter sessions assessment of wages unsuitable, besought employers to give rates more in proportion to the cost of living, but added that, if employers refused to do this, they would make an allowance to every poor family in accordance with its numbers. This is the celebrated " Speenhamland Act of Parliament," which never received the sanction of law, but was immediately followed in many counties, and obeyed much more cheerfully than is sometimes the case with the Acts of the Parliament at Westminster.[5] It is, therefore, worth while to notice the wording of the resolutions which the Berkshire Justices passed. They resolved (1) that the present state of the poor does require further assistance than has generally been given them ; (2) that it is not expedient for the magistrates to grant that assistance by regulating the wages of day-labourers, according to the directions of the Statutes of the 5th Elizabeth and 1st James ; but the magistrates very earnestly recommend to the farmers and others throughout the county to increase the pay of their labourers in proportion to the present price of provisions ; and, agreeable thereto, the magistrates now present have unanimously resolved that they will, in their several divisions, make the following calculations and allowances for the relief of all poor and industrious men and

---

[1] For prices (average) see Prothero, *English Farming*, App. I. (p. 244) and for 1795 and 1796 specially, Tooke, *Prices*, i. 182, 187.

[2] Above, p. 397.

[3] *Cf.* Rogers, *Six Centuries*, p. 485.   [4] Fowle, *Poor Law*, p. 65.

[5] *Ib.*, p. 66.

their families, who, to the satisfaction of the justices of
their parish, shall endeavour (as far as they can) for their
own support and maintenance—that is to say, when the
gallon loaf of seconds flour, weighing 8 lbs. 11 oz., shall
cost 1s., then every poor and industrious man shall have for
his own support 3s. weekly, either procured by his own or
his family's labour, or an allowance from the poor rates ;
and for the support of his wife and every other member of
the family, 1s. 6d.   When the gallon loaf shall cost 1s. 6d.,
then he shall have 4s. weekly for his own support, and
1s. 10d. for the support of every other of his family.   And
so, in proportion, as the price of bread rises or falls, that is
to say, 3d. to the man and 1d. to every other of his family
on every 1d. which the loaf rises above 1s." [1]

§ 235. *The Growth of Pauperism and the old Poor Law.*

Such were the celebrated Speenhamland resolutions.
The fact that the country justices felt compelled to pass
them shows how desperate the case of the labourer had
become. His position had grown steadily worse. Pauperism
had been slowly increasing in the course of the seventeenth
and eighteenth centuries, even when agriculture, manufactures, and commerce were improving, when the price of
corn was low, and money wages comparatively high ; [2] and
we may well ask what was the cause of this curious combination of progress and poverty ?   The answer is to be
found in the conditions which that progress created, and
especially in the case of agriculture.   It becomes increasingly evident that a very powerful cause of pauperism was
the system of enclosures,[3] accompanied by evictions [4] of
farmers and cottagers by landowners, eager to try new
agricultural improvements.

Sometimes, also, farmers sent off their labourers on
turning their fields into pasture ; at others the farmers
themselves were ejected, and sank into the condition of

[1] See Nicholls, *History of the Poor Law,* ii. 137.
[2] *Cf.* Toynbee, *Industrial Revolution,* p. 100.
[3] Eden, *State of the Poor,* ii. 30, 147, 384, 550.
[4] Laurence, *Duty of a Steward,* 3, 4 ; Toynbee, *u. s.,* 100.

labourers, or swelled the numbers of the unemployed.[1] The consolidation of farms[2] placed the labourer at the mercy of the capitalist farmer, who ground down his wages to the lowest possible point; and enclosures, though ultimately beneficial, contributed at first rather to the growth than to the removal of pauperism. The Act of Elizabeth, which provided that each new cottage should have four acres of land, was repealed, ostensibly on the ground that it made it difficult for the industrious poor to procure habitations; but, in reality, because it did not always suit the selfish interests of the landowners.[3] Its repeal was a great blow, which was further aggravated by the loss of bye-industries, and by the bad harvests already referred to; and the problem of poverty became so acute that the Legislature had to devise some method of dealing with it.

Hence we find several Poor Law Acts passed towards the close of the eighteenth century. The most noticeable of these was that known as Gilbert's Act,[4] in 1782. It alludes to the great increase of expenditure, and the equally great increase of pauperism, and, after blaming the parochial authorities for this state of things, takes away from them the administration of relief. The justices were constituted the guardians of the poor and the administrators of relief, and power was given to form Unions of parishes by voluntary arrangement, and to build a Workhouse for the Union.[5] The guardians were expressly forbidden to send any but the "impotent" to the workhouse, and were to find suitable employment for the able-bodied near their own homes. The main result of this well-meaning but fallacious measure was to increase the cost of relief some 30 per cent. Other Acts, dealing with minor details of administration, were subsequently passed, but the decisive step of legalising out-door relief to the able-bodied and giving it in aid of wages was not taken till 1796. The old workhouse test of 1722 was hereby[6] abolished as inconvenient and oppres-

---

[1] Eden, *State of the Poor*, i. 329, ii. 30, 384, 550.
[2] *Ibid.*, and Toynbee, *Indust. Rev.*, p. 101.
[3] Fowle, *Poor Law*, p. 68. Elizabeth's Act was the 31 Eliz., c. 7.
[4] The 22 Geo. III., c. 83.   [5] Fowle, *Poor Law*, p. 69.
[6] The Act 36 George III., c. 10 and c. 23.

sive, and parish authorities were empowered to give relief
to any industrious poor person at his own residence.
Refusal to enter a workhouse was not to be a reason for
withholding relief. The justices were also authorised to
order relief for a certain time to people who were "entitled
to ask and receive such relief at their own houses." By
this Act, therefore, an allowance was freely given to every
poor person who chose to ask for it, and the labourers'
wages were systematically made up out of the rates.[1] To
complete the history of this old code of Poor Laws, it may
be added that in 1801 the Justices were made the rating
as well as the relieving authority, while, to make them
"more safe in the execution of their duty," the nominal
penalty of 2d. only was to be imposed upon a justice who
made an illegal decision, unless it was plain that he was
actuated by improper motives.[2] The reason for this
measure is obvious: the landed gentry, from whom the
justices were chiefly chosen, were hereby allowed to fix the
rates, and even to amend them by altering names and
amounts; in other words, to adjudicate upon a question in
which they themselves were the most interested persons
present.[3] It is, of course, wrong to accuse them of consciously yielding to self-interest in their decisions; but no
one can be surprised to learn that the poor-rate was often
apportioned so as to fall most heavily upon others than
themselves, and upon parishes other than those in which
the rating justices had rateable property. Thus, for example, landowners would sometimes pull down every
cottage on their estate,[4] so as to compel surrounding
parishes to pay the poor-rates allowed to the labourers who
worked on their property; in other words, the labourers'
wages were paid half by the employer and half by the unfortunate non-employers in the next parish.

§ 236. *The Poor Law and the Allowance System.*

The burden upon non-employers was, in fact, sometimes
almost intolerable. The poor-rate, when levied upon house

[1] Fowle, *Poor Law*, 71, 87.
[2] *Ib.*, p. 71.   The Act was the 43 George III., c. 141.   [3] *Ib*
[4] Fowle, *Poor Law*, p. 88.

property, was simply a rate in aid of wages, paid by those who did not employ labour.[1] This was the case not only in agricultural districts, but even in manufacturing towns. Thus, at Nottingham, employers deliberately reduced the rate of wages for stocking making, and then gave their men a certificate to the effect that they were only earning (say) 6s. per week ; the men then applied to the parish, who allowed them 4s. or 5s. more.[2] Those manufacturers who employed parish apprentices sometimes even received annual payments from the parish for keeping its paupers at work.[3] Meanwhile, the poorer ratepayers, on whom the burden of rates fell most severely, often earned less and worked harder than the paupers whom they helped to support. One witness, before the Poor Law Commission of 1834, summed up their condition in the pregnant sentence : " Poor is the diet of the pauper, poorer is the diet of the small ratepayer, but poorest is that of the independent labourer."[4] Indeed, the independent labourer was in very evil case. Often he could not get work, because he was superseded by paupers, who were set to work by the overseers at the cost of the parish. If an industrious man was known to have saved money, he would be left without work till his savings were all spent, and then he could be employed as a pauper. Sometimes, even, men were discharged by their employers till they were reduced to the desired state,[5] so that the burden of maintaining them was cast upon the parish, while the employer had to pay only a nominal wage. The full working of this ingenious plan was seen in the "ticket system." Under this the parish sold "the commodity of labour" to the farmers, and made up the difference between the labourers' actual wages and the income supposed to be his due out of the rates. In one place there was a weekly sale of labour, at which an eyewitness saw ten men allotted to a farmer for five shillings.[6] It was called the "ticket system," because each pauper received a ticket from the overseer as a warrant for the farmer to employ him at the cost of the parish. It is not

---

[1] Fowle, *Poor Law*, p. 87.   [2] *Ib.*, p. 87.   [3] *Ib.*, and *cf.* above, p. 388.
[4] *Ib.*, p. 86.   [5] *Ib.*, p. 87.   [6] *Ib.*, p. 82.

surprising that the farmers supported this system, iniquitous though it was, and declared that "high wages and free
labour would ruin them."[1] But in the long run it often
caused even the farmer some pecuniary loss, not directly,
for he saved more in his wages-bill than he spent in poor-
rates, but indirectly, since the work of the labourers thus
employed was badly and inefficiently performed.[2]

Indeed, we may sum up by saying that the allowance
system, introduced by the Speenhamland resolutions and
made law by the Act of 1796, succeeded in demoralising
both employers and employed alike, taking the responsibility
of giving decent wages off the shoulders of the farmers, and
putting a premium upon the incontinence[3] and thriftlessness
of the labourers. This method of relief was general from
about 1795 to 1834, in fact, until the enactment of the
New Poor Law.[4] Employers of labour, manufacturing as
well as agricultural,[5] put down wages in many parts of the
country to what was simply a starvation point, knowing
that an allowance would be made to the labourers, upon the
magistrates' orders, out of the poor rates. The wages
actually paid to able-bodied men were frequently only five
or six shillings a week, but relief to the amount of four,
five, six, or seven shillings a week, according to the size of
the man's family, was given out of the rates. Such a
system could not fail to have a permanently disastrous
influence upon the moral and social condition of those who
suffered from it, taking from them all self-reliance, all hope,
all incentives to improving their position in life. This was
soon noticed by Arthur Young, who wrote : "Many authors
have remarked with surprise the great change which has
taken place in the spirit of the lower classes of the people
within the last twenty years. There was formerly found an
unconquerable aversion to depend on the parish, insomuch
that many would struggle through life with large families
never applying for relief. That spirit is annihilated ; appli-

[1] Toynbee, *Industrial Revolution*, p. 103.
[2] Fowle, *Poor Law*, p. 89, on *The Deterioration of Labour*.
[3] For the sad facts and for the bastardy laws, *cf.* Fowle, *Poor Law*,
pp. 89-92, summarising the evidence of the Commission of 1834.
[4] The 4 and 5 William IV., c. 76.   [5] Above, p. 413 (Nottingham)

cations of late have been as numerous as the poor ; and one great misfortune attending the change is that every sort of industry flags when once the parochial dependence takes place : it then becomes a struggle between the pauper and the parish, the one to do as little and to receive as much as possible, and the other to pay by no rule but the summons and order of the justice. The evils resulting are beyond all calculation ; for the motives to industry and frugality are cut up by the roots, whenever a poor man knows that if he do not feed himself the parish must do it for him ; and that he has not the most distant hope of ever attaining independency, let him be as industrious and frugal as he may. To acquire land enough to build a cottage on is a hopeless aim in ninety-nine parishes out of a hundred." [1] Unfortunately the last sentence of this remark is often true even to-day ; nor have the evil traditions of the Old Poor Law entirely disappeared. [2] Down to the reform of 1834, " the public funds were regarded as a regular part of the maintenance of the labouring people engaged in agriculture, and were administered by more than 2000 justices, 15,000 sets of overseers, and 15,000 vestries, acting always independently of each other, and very commonly in opposition, quite uncontrolled and ignorant of the very rudiments of political economy. The £7,000,000 or more [3] of public money was the price paid for converting the free labourer into a slave, without reaping even such returns as slavery can give. The able-bodied pauper was obliged to live where the Law of Settlement placed him, to receive the income which the neighbouring magistrates thought sufficient, to work for the master and in the way which the parish authorities prescribed, and very often to marry the wife they found for him." [4]

§ 237. *Restrictions upon Labour.*

What made the condition of the labourers worse still, was the fact that they could neither go from one place to

[1] Young, *Annals of Agriculture*, xxxvi. 504.
[2] The exhaustive *Reports* of the Poor Law Commission (1909) bring forward far-reaching proposals for dealing with the problems of poverty and unemployment. [3] For exact sum, *cf.* Porter, *Progress of the Nation*, i.82.
[4] Fowle, *Poor Law*, pp. 73, 74.

another to seek work, nor could they combine in industrial partnerships for their mutual interests. The Law of Settlement effectually prevented migration of labourers from one parish to another. It began with the Statute [1] of 1662, which allowed a pauper to obtain relief only from that parish where he had his settlement, "settlement" being defined as forty days' residence without interruption. The reason was that each parish, though ready to pay for its own poor, was not willing to pay for those of other parishes. There were many variations and complications of this Statute made in ensuing reigns, but it remained substantively the same [2] till it was mitigated by the Poor Law of 1834. Its main results were seen, as Adam Smith remarked,[3] in the "obstruction of the free circulation of labour," and consequently in the great inequality in wages which was frequently found in places at no great distance one from another. Nowhere else, he says,[4] does one "meet with those sudden and unaccountable differences in the wages of neighbouring places which we sometimes find in England, where it is often more difficult for a poor man to pass the artificial boundary of a parish than an arm of the sea or a ridge of mountains." Again he remarks [5] : "there is scarce a poor man in England of forty years of age, I will venture to say, who has not in some part of his life felt himself most cruelly oppressed by this ill-contrived Law of Settlements." [6]

§ 238. *The Combination Acts.*

The Law of Settlement was further strengthened by what are called the Combination Laws,[7] which forbade workmen to meet together in order to deliberate over their various

---

[1] The 13 and 14 Charles II., c. 12.

[2] Although it was nominally repealed. Fowle, *Poor Law*, 70, 84. For the whole question, see Adam Smith, *Wealth of Nations*, Bk. I., ch. x. (Vol. I., p. 144, Clarendon Press edn.).

[3] *Wealth of Nations, u. s.*, i. 148.   [4] *Ib.*   [5] *Ib.*, i. 149.

[6] *Cf.* also Toynbee's remarks, *Industrial Revolution*, p. 186.

[7] These date from the 2 and 3 Ed. VI., c. 15, prohibiting "all conspiracies and covenants not to do their work but at a certain price," under penalty of the pillory and loss of an ear. Other acts were passed, but all were summed up in the famous 40 Geo. III., c. 60.

industrial interests, or to gain a rise in wages. "We have no Acts of Parliament," said Adam Smith,[1] with justice, "against combining to lower the price of work, but many against combining to raise it." For "when masters combine together in order to reduce the wages of their workmen, they commonly enter into a private bond or agreement, not to give more than a certain wage under a certain penalty. Were the workmen to enter into a contrary combination of the same kind, not to accept a certain wage under a certain penalty, the law would punish them very severely; and if it dealt impartially,[2] it would treat the masters in the same manner." Elsewhere he describes the inevitable result of a strike as being "nothing but the punishment or ruin of the ringleaders."[3] The legislation of the close of the eighteenth century was all in favour of the masters, and after several acts had been passed regulating combinations in separate trades, the famous Act[4] of 1800 was applied to all occupations, and strictly forbade all combinations, unions, or associations of workmen for the purpose of obtaining an advance in wages or lessening the hours of work. All freedom of action was taken away from the workmen: "the only freedom," remarks an eminent and impartial judge[5] "for which the law seems to me to have been specially solicitous is the freedom of employers from coercion by their men." The reason is obvious; it was because the working classes had no voice in the government of the state, and were unable to check a measure inspired only by the self-interest of the employers. As yet they had no political influence whatever, except that unsatisfactory and unconstitutional influence which emanates from the violence of a riotous mob.[6] "The English statute-book was disfigured by laws which robbed the labourer as a wage-earner, and degraded him as a citizen,"

---

[1] *Wealth of Nations*, Bk. I., ch. viii. (Vol. I., p. 70).
[2] *Ib.*, Bk. I., ch. x. (Vol. I., p. 150).
[3] *Ib.*, Bk. I., ch. viii. (Vol. I., p. 71).
[4] The 40 Geo. III., c. 60; see Howell, *Trades Unionism New and Old*, p. 39.
[5] Justice Stephen, *History of the Criminal Law*, iii. 208.
[6] *Cf.* Toynbee, *Industrial Revolution*, p. 186.

for "the power of making laws was concentrated in the hands of the landowners, the great merchant-princes, and a small knot of capitalist-manufacturers, who wielded that power in the interests of their class rather than for the good of the people."[1] No doubt the action of these law-makers was natural, but it is only another example of the fact that no one class, and, for that matter, no single individual, is fit to possess irresponsible and absolute power over another. In spite of utopian theorists, selfishness is still the predominant factor in human nature ; and the most feasible, if not the most ideal, form of government is that in which the selfishness of one class is counteracted by the selfishness of another. But in 1800 the workmen had, of course, no political influence : they could only show their discontent by riots and rick-burnings. Yet the time of their deliverance was at hand.

I have already referred to the sympathy between the French Revolution and the Industrial Revolution. The former, it is true, frightened our statesmen and delayed reform, but it gave courage to the working classes, and made them hope fiercely for freedom. The latter Revolution concentrated men more and more closely together in large centres of industry, dissociated them from their employers, and roused a spirit of antagonism which is inevitable when both employers and employed alike fail to recognise the essential identity of their interests. Now, wherever there are large bodies of men crowded together, there is always a rapid spread of new ideas, new political enthusiasms, and social activities. And in spite of the lack of the franchise, the artisans of our large towns made their voices heard ; fiercely and roughly, no doubt, and often at first in riot and uproar, but they had no other means. There were found some statesmen in Parliament, chiefly disciples of Adam Smith,[2] who gave articulate utterance to the demands of labour, and owing to their endeavours the Combination Laws were annulled[3] in 1824. All previous statutes, so far as they related to combinations of workmen, were

---

[1] *Cf.* Toynbee, *Industrial Revolution*, p. 186.   [2] *Ib.*, p. 195.
[3] By the 5 Geo. IV., c. 95.

repealed, and those who joined such associations were to be no longer liable to be prosecuted for conspiracy. But the following year proved how insecure was the position of the labourers without definite political influence. The employers of labour were able to induce Parliament in 1825 to stultify itself,[1] by declaring illegal any *action* which might result from those deliberations of workmen which a twelvemonth before they had legalised. But still the workers were allowed to deliberate, strange as it may now seem that permission was needed for this, and their deliberations materially aided in passing the Reform Bill of 1832. For as soon as a class can make its voice heard, even though it cannot directly act, other classes will take that utterance into account.

§ 239. *Growth of Trades Unions.*[2]

But the Reform Bill, though a great step forward, somewhat belied the hopes that had roused the enthusiasm of its industrial supporters. The workmen found that, after all, it merely threw additional power into the hands of the upper and middle classes.[3] Their own position was hardly improved. Therefore they had to make their voice heard again, and, urged on by the misery and poverty in which they were still struggling, they demanded the Charter. The Chartist[4] movement (1838 to 1848) seems to us at the present time almost ludicrously moderate in its demands. The vote by ballot, the abolition of property qualifications for electors, and the payment of parliamentary members, were the main objects of its leaders, though they asked for universal suffrage as well. Nevertheless people were frightened, especially when the Chartists wished to present a monster petition at Westminster on April 10th, 1848 ; and

[1] In the Act 6 Geo. IV., c. 129. This Act rendered men liable to punishment for the use of threats, intimidation, and obstruction directed towards the attainment of the objects of Trade Unions ; *cf.* also Toynbee, *u. s.*, p. 195.

[2] For the history of these, *cf.* G. Howell, *Conflicts of Capital and Labour*, and *Trades Unionism New and Old* ; see also Note A.

[3] Toynbee, *Industrial Revolution*, p. 196.

[4] See Gammage, *History of the Chartist Movement* generally.

the aid of both military and police was invoked. The movement collapsed, and finally died away when the repeal of
the Corn Laws had restored prosperity to the nation. Many
have laughed at the working classes for trying to gain some
infinitesimal fraction of political power; but working men
are generally acute, especially where their own interests are
concerned, and they saw that this was the ultimate means
of material prosperity; nor has the event failed to justify
their belief.[1] In the somewhat quieter times which followed
the collapse of the Chartists, their influence went on extending, and though the workmen ceased to agitate they were
not idle, but continued steadily organising themselves in
Trades Unions. A large number of Unions were formed
between 1850 and 1860.[2] These institutions were not,
however, recognised by law till a Commission was appointed,
including Sir William Erle, Lord Elcho, and Thomas Hughes,
to inquire into their constitution and objects (February
1867). Their Report disclosed the existence of intimidation, with occasional outrages—as was natural when the
men had no other way of giving utterance to their wishes
—but on the whole the Report was in favour of the repeal
of the Act of 1825. This Act was accordingly repealed.[3]
The Unions were legalised by the Trade Union Act of 1871,
and this Act[4] was further extended[5] and amended in 1875
and 1876. The old law of master and servant had passed
away, and employer and employed were now on an equal
political footing. It has remained for the men by the
exercise of silent strength to place themselves on an equal
footing in other respects. Meanwhile the employers,
alarmed at Trades Unionism, had entered into a similar
combination by forming the National Federation of Employers[6] in 1873, and the long struggle of the working
classes for industrial freedom did not result in any lessening

[1] Toynbee points this out very clearly, and shows how political influence
led to the legalisation of Trade Unions; *Industrial Revolution*, p. 196.

[2] Howell, *Trades Unionism New and Old*, p. 59.

[3] By the 38 and 39 Victoria, c. 31 and c. 32.

[4] The 34 and 35 Victoria, c. 31 and 32; Howell, *Trades Unionism New
and Old*, p. 61.

[5] By the 38 and 39 Victoria, c. 86.

[6] *Cf.* Webb, *History of Trades Unionism*, pp. 312, 313.

of the feeling of class antagonism.[1] The formation in 1895 of the Industrial Union of Employers and Employed is a recent attempt to bring about better relations between master and man,[2] and if its objects were carried out on a wide scale, it would do much good. Apart from the question of antagonism, Trades Unions have done much to gain a greater measure of material prosperity for the working classes, and to give them a larger share than formerly in the wealth which the workers have helped to create. When we look back upon the last half-century, we are inclined to wonder that trades unionists have been so moderate in their demands, considering the misery and poverty amidst which they grew up.

§ 240. *The Working Classes Fifty Years Ago.*

For it must continually be remembered that the condition of the mass of the people in the first half of this century was one of the deepest depression. Several writers have commented upon this, and have taken occasion to remark upon the great progress in the prosperity of the working classes since that time. It is true they have progressed since then, but it has hardly been progress so much as a return to the state of things about 1760 or 1770. The fact has been, that after the introduction of the new industrial system the condition of the working classes rapidly declined ; wages were lower,[3] and prices, at least of wheat, were often higher ;[4] till at length the lowest depth of poverty was reached about the beginning of the reign of Queen Victoria. Since then their condition has been gradually improving, partly owing to the philanthropic labours of men like Lord Shaftesbury, and partly owing to the combined action of working-men themselves. To quote the expression of that well-known statistician, Mr Giffen :[5]

[1] *Cf.* Toynbee, *Industrial Revolution*, pp. 196-198.
[2] See the Report of the *Preliminary Industrial Conference* held at London, March 16, 1894 (Methuen, London).
[3] See the tables in Porter, *Progress of the Nation*, ii. 252, 253.
[4] Porter, *Progress of the Nation*, i. 156 ; Toynbee, *Industrial Revolution*, p. 101.
[5] *Essays in Finance, Second Series* (1886), p. 390, on *Progress of the Working Classes.*

" It is a matter of history that pauperism was nearly breaking down the country half a century ago. The expenditure
on poor law relief early in the century and down to 1830-31
was nearly as great at times as it is now. With half the
population in the country that there now is, the burden of
the poor was the same." The following table will show[1]
the actual figures of English pauperism at a time when the
wealth of the nation was advancing by leaps and bounds.

Year.	Population.	Poor Rate raised.	Rate per head of population.
			s. d.
1760	7,000,000	£1,250,000	3 7
1784	8,000,000	£2,000,000	5 0
1803	9,216,000	£4,077,000	8 11
1818	11,876,000	£7,870,000	13 3
1820	12,046,000	£7,329,000	12 2
1830	13,924,000	£6,829,000	10 9
1841	15,911,757	£4,760,929	5 11¾

It will be noticed that the rate was highest in 1818, which
was shortly after the close of the great Continental War,
but fell rapidly after 1830, and since 1841 the rate per
head of population has not been much more than six or
seven shillings.

But the mere figures of pauperism, significant though
they are, can give no idea of the vast amount of misery
and degradation which the majority of the working classes
suffered.[2] The tale of their sufferings may be studied in the
Blue-books and Reports[3] of the various Commissions which
investigated the state of industrial life in the factories,
mines, and workshops between 1833 and 1842 ; or it may
be read in the burning pages of Engels'[4] *State of the
Working Classes in England in* 1844, which is little more

---

[1] The first figure is from Toynbee, *Industrial Revolution*, p. 94; others
from Porter, *Progress of the Nation*, i. 82, 83; ii. 362, 363.

[2] " The fact is," said Toynbee (*Ind. Rev.*, p. 58), " the more we examine
the actual course of affairs, the more we are amazed at the unnecessary
suffering that has been inflicted on the people."

[3] *E.g.*, *Reports on Employment of Children in Factories*, 1816, 1833, and
(mines) 1842.

[4] This book, though avowedly Socialist, and written in a very one-sided
tone, is nevertheless accurate as to facts, which are all taken from the
above-mentioned Reports. It forms a convenient book of reference. It
was published in German in 1845, and in a new English edition in 1892.

than a sympathetic resume of the facts set forth in official documents. We hear of children and young people in factories overworked and beaten as if they were slaves;[1] of diseases and distortions only found in manufacturing districts;[2] of filthy, wretched homes, where people huddled together like wild beasts;[3] we hear of girls and women working underground in the dark recesses of the coal-mines, dragging loads of coal in cars in places where no horses could go, and harnessed and crawling along the subterranean pathways like beasts of burden.[4] Everywhere we find cruelty and oppression, and in many cases the workmen were but slaves, bound to fulfil their masters' commands under fear of dismissal and starvation. Freedom they had in name; freedom to starve and die; but not freedom to speak, still less to act, as citizens of a free state. They were often even obliged to buy their food at exorbitant prices out of their scanty wages at a shop kept by their employer, where it is needless to say that they paid the highest possible price for the worst possible goods. This was rendered possible by the system of paying workmen in tickets or orders upon certain shops, which were under the supervision of their employers. It was called the " truck system "; and was at length finally condemned by the law[5] (1887) after many futile attempts had been made to suppress it.[6]

But though, as a matter of fact, the sufferings of the working classes during the transition period of the Industrial Revolution were aggravated by the extortions of employers, and by the partiality of a legislature which

---

[1] See above, pp. 389, 400, 401.   [2] *Cf.* Engels (ed. 1892), pp. 151-164.
[3] Engels (ed. 1892), pp. 23-73, on *The Great Towns.* His evidence is really appalling.
[4] Engels, pp. 241-260; and *Report on Employment in Mines,* 1842.
[5] By the 50 and 51 Victoria, c. 46, amending the 1 and 2 William IV., c. 37.
[6] The 22 Geo. II., c. 27; the 57 Geo. III., cc. 115 and 122; the 1 Geo. IV., c. 93, were all measures passed against " truck," and all ineffectual. The system, however, has its apologists (*cf.* Cunningham, *Growth of Industry,* ii. 650) as being convenient, and the simplest way of providing workers with provisions in out-of-the-way villages. For a vivid description of a scene at a truck-shop, see Disraeli's novel *Sybil,* Bk. III., ch. iii. See also note in Rogers' edition of Adam Smith's *Wealth of Nations,* i. 150.

forbade them to take common measures in self-defence,
yet there was, in addition to the Revolution itself, one
great cause which underlay all these minor causes, namely,
the Continental war which ended in 1815. It has been
forcibly and accurately expressed by a great economist:
" Thousands of homes were starved in order to find the
means for the great war, the cost of which was really
supported by the labour of those who toiled on and earned
the wealth that was lavished freely—and at good interest
for the lenders—by the Government. The enormous taxation and the gigantic loans came from the store of
accumulated capital which the employers wrung from the
poor wages of labour, or which the landlords extracted
from the growing gains of their tenants. To outward
appearance the strife was waged by armies and generals;
in reality, the sources on which the struggle was based
were the stint and starvation of labour, the overtaxed and
underfed toils of childhood, the underpaid and uncertain
employment of men." [1]

§ 241. Wages.

And, indeed, if we examine some of the wages actually
paid at the beginning of this century, and again at the
beginning of Queen Victoria's reign, we shall find that
they were excessively low. The case of common weavers
was particularly hard in the years of the great war, and
affords an interesting example of the decrease of wages in
this period. For purposes of comparison I append the
price of wheat and of weekly wages in the same years;

YEAR.	Weavers' Wages.[2]	Wheat per qr.[3]
	s. d.	s. d.
1802	13 10	67 9
1806	10 6	76 9
1812	6 4	122 8
1816	5 2	76 2
1817	4 3½	94 0

[1] Rogers, *Six Centuries*, p. 505.
[2] Leone Levi, *History of British Commerce*, p. 146.
[3] Porter, *Progress of the Nation*, i. 156. The prices are averages from the
London Gazette, and were frequently far higher in the course of the year.

for the price of wheat forms a useful standard by which to gauge the real value of wages, even when it is not consumed in large quantities. It will be seen that wages were at their lowest point just after the conclusion of the war, while, on the other hand, wheat was almost at famine prices. After this, however, and till 1830, the wages of weavers rose again, for the new spinning machinery had increased the supply of yarn at a much greater rate than weavers could be found to weave it, and hence there was an increased demand for weavers, and they gained proportionately higher wages, the average for woollen cloth weavers from 1830-1845 being 14s. to 17s. a week, and for worsted stuff weavers 11s. to 14s. a week.[1] But even these rates are miserably low.

The wages of spinners were also very poor, the work being mostly done by women and children, though when men are employed they get fairly good pay. The following table [2] will show clearly the various rates, and it will be seen that here wages sink steadily till 1845, owing to the rapid

SPINNERS.	1808-15.	1815-23.	1823-30.	1830-36.	1836-45.
Men ...	24/ to 26/	24/ to 26/	24/ to 26/	24/ to 26/	24/ to 26/
Women ...	13/ to 14/	13/ to 14/	11/ to 12/	8/ to 10/	7/ to 9/

production of the new machinery. The women's wages exhibit the fall most markedly, the labour of children being already affected to some extent by the provisions of the Factory Acts. As for the agricultural labourer, he, too, suffered from low wages, the general average to 1845 being 8s. to 10s. a week, and generally nearer the former than the latter figure.[3] In fact, the material condition of the working classes of England was at this time in the lowest depths of poverty and degradation, and this fact must

[1] From a *Table of Wages and Prices*, 1720-1886, by Thomas Illingworth, Bradford (privately printed).

[2] *Ib. Cf.* also Porter, *Progress of the Nation*, ii. 253, where women's wages decrease from 10s. in 1805 to 8s. 5½d. in 1833.

[3] Rogers, *Six Centuries*, p. 510. According to the Parliamentary Report of 1822 (*Reports*, &c., 1822, v. 73) agricultural wages had sunk from 15s. or 16s. a week before 1815 to 9s. a week in 1822.

always be remembered in comparing the wages of to-day with those of former times. Some people who ought to know better are very fond of talking about the "progress of the working classes" in the last seventy years, and the Jubilee of Queen Victoria in 1887 afforded ample opportunity—of which full advantage was taken—for such optimists to talk statistics. But to compare the wages of labour properly we must go back more than a hundred years, not seventy, for seventy years ago the English workman was passing through a period of misery which we must devoutly hope, for the sake of the nation at large, will not occur again. It is interesting to note, though it is impossible here to go fully into the subject, that in trades where workmen have combined, since the repeal of the Conspiracy Laws in 1825 and the alteration in the Act of Settlement,[1] wages have perceptibly risen. Carpenters, masons, and colliers afford examples of such a rise.[2] But where there has been no combination, it is noteworthy how little wages have risen in proportion to the increased production of the modern labourer, and to the higher cost of living, nor does the workman always receive his due share of the wealth which he helps to create. Of the results of labour combinations we shall, however, have something to say in the final chapter of this book. But there was one class of people who happened to obtain a very large share of the national wealth, and who grew rich and flourished while the working classes were almost starving. In spite of war abroad and poverty at home, the rents of the landowners increased, and the agricultural interest received a stimulus which has resulted in a very natural reaction. The rise in rents and the recent depression of modern agriculture will form the subject of our next chapter.

[1] Above, p. 416.
[2] Thomas Illingworth's table, cited above. Carpenters' wages have risen from 23s. or 24s. in 1823-30 to 30s.-32s. in 1886; masons from 23s.-26s. to 32s.-34s.; colliers from 16s.-18s. to 22s.-28s.

CHAPTER XXV

§ 242. *Services Rendered by the Great Landowners.*

ALTHOUGH there have been occasions in our industrial history when one is compelled to admit that the deeds of the landed gentry have called for anything but admiration, we yet must not overlook the great services which this class rendered to the agricultural interest in the eighteenth century. It has been already mentioned that the development and the success of English agriculture in the half-century or more before the Industrial Revolution was remarkable and extensive; and this success was due to the efforts of the landowners [1] in introducing new agricultural methods. They took an entirely new departure, and adopted a new system. It consisted, as was mentioned before, in getting rid of bare fallows and poor pastures by substituting root-crops and artificial grasses. [2] The fourfold or Norfolk rotation of crops was introduced, [3] the landowners themselves taking an interest in and superintending the cultivation of their land and making useful experiments upon it. The number of these experimenting landlords was very considerable, and in course of time, though not by any means immediately, the tenant farmers followed them, and thus agricultural knowledge and skill became more and more widely diffused. [4] The reward of the landowners came rapidly. They soon found their production of corn doubled and their general produce trebled. [5]

---

[1] Rogers, *Six Centuries*, pp. 472-475; Prothero, *Agriculture in England* in *Dict. Pol. Econ.*

[2] Rogers, *Six Centuries*, p. 468.

[3] Toynbee, *Industrial Revolution*, p. 43.

[4] In 1836 Porter, *Progress of the Nation*, i. 149, mentions the various improvements in farming in a way which shows that by that time they were very widely employed.

[5] Rogers, *Economic Interpretation*, 269.

They were able to exact higher rents,[1] for they had taught
their tenants how to make the land pay better, and, of
course, claimed a share of the increased profit. About the
years 1740-50 the rent of land, according to Jethro Tull,
was 7s. an acre;[2] some twenty years or more afterwards
Arthur Young found the average rent of land to be 10s. an
acre, and thought that in many cases it ought to have been
more. Before very long it became more, indeed.[3] Between
1790 and 1836 rent was at least doubled in every part of
the country, and in many cases it was multiplied four or five
times.   Thus we are told, by a very competent authority,[4]
that in Essex farms could be pointed out which just before
the war of the French Revolution let at less than 10s. an
acre; but their rent rose rapidly during the war, till in
1812 it was 45s. to 50s. an acre; and though the rent
was subsequently reduced, it remained double the figure of
1790.   In Berkshire and Wiltshire, farms let at 14s. an
acre rose to 70s. in 1810, and after a reduction were still
30s. in 1836, which gives an advance of no less than 114
per cent. on the first figure.[5] In Staffordshire, again, several
farms on one estate are instanced, which in 1790 let at 8s.
an acre, and after having advanced to 35s., were afterwards
lowered to 20s., an advance of 150 per cent. within less
than half a century.[6] In Norfolk, Suffolk, and Warwick,
the same, or nearly the same, rise was experienced, and it
is more than probable that it was general throughout
the kingdom.   During the same period the prices of
most of the articles which constitute the landowners' expenditure fell materially, so that, this writer remarks, " if
his condition be not improved in a corresponding degree,
that circumstance must arise from improvidence or
miscalculation or habits of expensive living beyond even
what would be warranted by the doubling of income
which he has experienced and is still enjoying."[7]   In
fact, it is evident that the employment of the new

---

[1] Porter, *Progress of the Nation*, i. 164, gives some startling instances.
[2] Quoted by Rogers, *Economic Interpretation*, p. 268.
[3] *Cf.* Rogers, *Six Centuries*, p. 477.
[4] Porter, *Progress of the Nation*, i. 164.   [5] *Ib.*, i. 165.   [6] *Ib.*   [7] *Ib.*

methods in agriculture considerably benefited the landowners, though the rise in rent is not to be attributed solely
to this cause.[1] It is probable that the landowner would not
have done so much for agriculture if he had not expected to
make something out of his experiments; but the fact that
he was animated by an enlightened self-interest does not
make his work any the less valuable. The pioneers of this
improved agriculture came from Norfolk, among the first
being Lord Townshend and Mr Coke, the descendant of the
great Chief Justice. The former introduced into Norfolk
the growth of turnips and artificial grasses, and was laughed
at by his contemporaries as Turnip Townshend; the latter
was the practical exponent of Arthur Young's theories as to
the advantages to be derived from large farms and capitalist
farmers.[2] With improvements in cultivation, and the
increase both of assiduity and skill, came a corresponding
improvement in the live stock. The general adoption of
root crops in place of bare fallows, and the extended cultivation of artificial grasses, supplied the farmer with a great
increase of winter feed, the quality and nutritive powers of
which were greatly improved.[3] Hence with abundance of
fodder came abundance of stock, while at the same time
great improvements took place in breeding. This was
mainly due to Bakewell (1760-85), who has been aptly
described as "the founder of the graziers' art."[4] He was
the first scientific breeder of sheep and cattle, and the
methods which he adopted with his Leicester sheep and
longhorns were applied throughout the country by other
breeders to their own animals.[5] The growth of population
also caused a new impetus to be given to the careful rearing
and breeding of cattle for the sake of food, while the sheep
especially became even more useful than before, since, in
addition to the value of its fleece, its carcase now was more

[1] It was due, *e.g.*, also to the rise in the price of corn, which came from
(1) bad harvests, (2) growth of population, and (3) the great increase in
prices during the war.
[2] Prothero, *Agriculture in England*, in *Dict. Pol. Econ.*, and also *Pioneers
of English Farming* (1881), p. 79.
[3] Rogers, *Six Centuries*, p. 475.
[4] Prothero, *Agriculture in England*, in *Dict. Pol. Econ.*
[5] *Ib.*; *cf.* also his *Pioneers and Progress of English Farming* generally.

in demand than ever for meat. In various ways, therefore, the improvements in agriculture mark a very important advance, and the close of the eighteenth century witnessed changes in the field as great in their way as those in the factory.

§ 243. *The Agricultural Revolution.*

The new agriculture, indeed, brought with it a revolution as important in its way as the Industrial Revolution. One of the chief features of the change—the enclosures— has been already commented upon.[1]   The enclosure of the common fields was beneficial,[2] and to a certain extent justifiable, for the tenants paid rent for them to the lord of the manor.   But it was effected at a great loss to the smaller tenant, and when his common of pasture was enclosed as well, he was greatly injured,[3] while the agricultural labourer was permanently disabled.   Whereas between 1710 and 1760 only some 300,000 acres had been enclosed, in the period between 1760 and 1843 nearly seven million underwent the same process.[4]   The enclosure system, however, was only part of a great change that was passing over the country; it was but another sign of the introduction of capitalist methods into modern industry.   We have already noted the growth of the capitalist element in manufactures, and have seen how the small manufacturer died out, while his place was taken by the owner of one or more huge factories, who employed hundreds of men under him; and now we see very much the same process in agriculture.   The small farmer and the yeoman disappear, and the large capitalist takes his place.   The substitution of large for small farms is, in fact, one of the chief signs of the Agricultural Revolution.[5] It was both the cause and the effect of the enclosures;

---

[1] Above, pp. 274, 275; also Prothero, *Pioneers*, pp. 66-74.
[2] Above, p. 275; and Toynbee, *Industrial Revolution*, p. 89.
[3] *Ib.*, p. 89.
[4] *Ib.*, p. 89; *cf.* Prothero, *Pioneers*, p. 71, who mentions that from 1777 to 1793 only 599 Enclosure Acts were passed, but from 1793 to 1809 no less than 1052 Acts, involving some four-and-a-half million acres.
[5] Toynbee, *Industrial Revolution*, p. 89.

and, of course, as large farms could only be worked by men possessed of large capital, it marks very clearly the growth of capitalist methods.[1] It should be noted, however, that the reason for enclosures in the eighteenth and nineteenth centuries was quite different from that which caused them in the sixteenth century. The earlier were for the sake of pasture, and the later to get land for tillage.[2] That the changes induced by the new system have been beneficial to agriculture no one will attempt to deny, just as no one can dispute the benefits conferred upon industry by the use of machinery; but, at the same time, one cannot be blind to the fact that these great industrial changes, both in manufactures and agriculture, brought a great amount of misery with them, both to the smaller employers and the mass of the employed. "The change in agriculture brought with it a new agricultural and social crisis more severe than that of the Tudor period. The [eighteenth] century closed with the miseries that resulted from enclosures, consolidation of holdings, and the reduction of thousands of small farmers to the ranks of wage-dependent labourers. The result of the crisis was to consolidate large estates, extinguish the yeomanry and peasant proprietary, to turn the small farmers into hired labourers, and to sever the connection of the labourer from the soil."[3] In a comparatively short time the face of rural England was completely changed; the common fields, those quaint relics of primitive times, were almost entirely swept away, and the large enclosed fields of to-day, with their neat hedgerows and clearly-marked limits, had taken their places. There is a far wider difference between the rural England of the beginning of the nineteenth century, and the beginning of the seventeenth or even eighteenth, than between the England of William of Orange and of William of Normandy.

[1] Porter, *Progress of the Nation*, i. 181, remarks how both in England and Scotland "the tendency has been to enlarge the size of farms, and to place them under the charge of men possessed of capital."
[2] Prothero, *Pioneers*, p. 72.
[3] Prothero, *Agriculture in England*, in *Dict. Pol. Econ.*, p. 29, and *Pioneers of English Farming*, p. 73.

The improvements in agriculture, the enclosures, the consolidation of small into large farms, and the appearance of the capitalist farmer are, then, the chief signs of the Agricultural Revolution. They form an almost exact parallel to the inventions of machinery, the bringing together of workers in factories, the consolidation of small bye-occupations into larger and more definite trades, and the appearance of the capitalist millowner in the realm of manufacturing industry. Concurrently with these changes we notice certain contemporaneous events which, though not first causes,[1] were still important factors in the general Revolution. These are the increase of population, the growth of speculative farming by capitalists, and the high prices of grain. Upon the increase of population we have already [2] commented, and it is needless to point out how it encouraged agriculture by enlarging the home market for food products. The second and third facts—speculative farming and high prices of grain—are to some extent connected, and were due not only to the scarcity which marked the harvests at the close of the eighteenth century, and the consequent pressure of population upon subsistence, but also to the artificial conditions created by the Corn Laws.[3] Upon the Corn Laws we shall have something to say almost immediately; here it should be remarked that the bad harvests of 1765 to 1774, and the irregularity of the seasons from 1775 onwards, caused exceedingly violent fluctuations in the price of corn,[4] and these fluctuations were the opportunity of the speculative capitalist farmer. In March 1780, wheat was 38s. 3d. a qr., at Michaelmas of that year 48s., and in March 1781 it rose to 56s. 11d.[5] Now these violent fluctuations of price gave to those who could hold large stocks of corn the opportunity of gaining enormous profits, while the smaller men, who either worked in common fields or had small

---

[1] It is rather strange that Dr Cunningham (*Growth of Industry*, ii. 480) should say that these three minor facts were the chief causes " whereby the whole character of English agriculture was changed."

[2] Above, p. 349.   [3] *Cf.* Prothero, *Pioneers of English Farming*, p. 83.

[4] Cunningham, *Growth of Industry*, ii. 476, 477.

[5] Tooke, *Prices*, i. 76.

separate holdings, were generally compelled to realise their corn immediately after harvest, and consequently suffered severely when prices were low.[1] In 1779, for instance, many farmers were ruined by low prices,[2] and yet in other years prices were often excessively high. The nature of these violent fluctuations, caused partly by real scarcity and partly by the Corn Laws, was aggravated during the war by the fact that hardly any foreign supplies of corn were available owing to the interruption of commerce; and in any case there was not as yet that enormous import of foreign grain which to-day serves to steady the prices of the home market. But these alternations of high and low prices caused an amount of speculation which brought farming into the same category as the uncertainties of the Stock Exchange, and while it often brought huge profits to those who had capital enough to wait, led many of the smaller farmers into ruin. Thus the disappearance of small farms, already begun, was largely accelerated, and an important feature of the Agricultural Revolution became still more strongly marked. On the average, however, we find that the prices of grain, apart from these fluctuations, were steadily rising, and grain-growing continued to be very profitable to those who could afford to disregard sudden alterations in prices. The reason for the profits of agriculture at this period we can now examine.

§ 244. *The Stimulus caused by the Bounties.*

The real commencement of the system of imposing heavy protective duties upon the importation of grain from abroad in the interest of the landowners was the Act 22 Charles II., c. 13. This Act[3] practically prohibited import except when wheat was at famine prices, as it happened to be in 1662, when it was 62s. 9½d. a quarter, the ordinary average price being 41s.[4] But it did not reach this price again for many years afterwards. The Government of 1688, not

---

[1] Cunningham, *u. s.*, ii. 477-479.   [2] *Ib.*, ii. 477.
[3] By this law 16s. a qr. was imposed on wheat as long as it was at and below 53s. 4d., and 8s. a qr. when it was between 53s. 4d. and 80s.; Adam Smith, *Wealth of Nations*, Bk. IV., ch. v. (Vol. II., p. 113).
[4] Rogers, *Hist. Agric.*, v. 276, and *cf.* ch. vii. of Vol. V.

content with the foregoing protective measure, added a bounty of 5s. per qr. upon the export of corn from England.[1] But the effect of this bounty was not felt for several years, for, fortunately, soon after the passing of the Bounty Act, a series of plentiful harvests occurred, and corn was very cheap.[2] There were consequently loud outcries from the landlords about agricultural distress, which merely meant that the people at large were enjoying cheap food. The aim of the bounty on corn had been to raise prices by encouraging its export, and thus rendering it scarcer and dearer in England.[3] As a matter of fact, it had the opposite effect, for it served as a premium upon which the wheat-grower could speculate, and thus induced him to sow a larger breadth of his land with wheat. The premium upon production caused producers to grow more than the market required, and so prices fell.[4] Thus, happily for the consumer, the Corn Laws and the bounty were harmless during the greater part of the eighteenth century,[5] for farmers competed one against the other sufficiently to keep down prices, and with a small population the supply was generally sufficient to meet the demand. But the inevitable Nemesis of protective measures came at the end of the century, when population was growing with unexampled rapidity, and required all the corn it could get. Then the prices of corn rose to a famine pitch, while the duty upon its importation, even when it was lowered, prevented it coming into the country in sufficient quantities.

By a law of 1773, however, the importation of foreign wheat was allowed when English wheat was more than 48s. per qr.[6] In 1791 a duty of 24s. 3d. was imposed as long as English wheat was less than 50s. a qr.;[7] if English wheat was over 50s. the duty was 2s. 6d. The landed

---

[1] The 1 William and Mary, § 1, c. 12.

[2] Rogers, *Economic Interpretation*, p. 377.

[3] Adam Smith, *Wealth of Nations*, Bk. IV., ch. v. (Vol. II., 115).

[4] Rogers, *Economic Interpretation*, p. 378, who instances the similar result in the case of the premium on beet sugar abroad.

[5] *Ib.*, p. 378.

[6] The 13 Geo. III., c. 43; *cf.* Adam Smith, *Wealth of Nations*, Bk. IV., ch. v. (Vol. II., p. 119).

[7] By the 31 Geo. III., c. 30.

interest, however, was not satisfied yet. In 1804 foreign corn was practically prohibited[1] from importation if English wheat was less than 63s. a qr. ; in 1815 the prohibition was extended[2] till the price of English wheat was 80s. a qr.   Then came the agitations and riots of 1817-19, after which the country sank into despair till the formation[3] of the Anti-Corn Law League in 1839. During the operation of these laws the landlords received enormous rents,[4] so high, in fact, that with all the aid of artificial legislation, farmers, except in good years, could hardly pay them, and agriculture was often much distressed.[5] But meanwhile the mass of the people was frequently on the verge of starvation, and at length the country perceived that things could not be allowed to go on any longer in this way.   The manufacturing capitalists of the day supported the leaders of the people in their agitation, for they hoped that cheap food might mean low wages.[6] By their aid the landed interest was overcome, and in 1846 the Corn Laws, by the efforts of Cobden and his followers, were finally repealed. Nevertheless the British farmer and his landlords, forgetting, it seems, the days when they got high prices by the starvation of the poor, still frequently clamour for the re-imposition of the incubus of protection.

§ 245. *Agriculture under Protection.*

These years of Protection (1812-1845) comprised, in fact, one of the most disastrous periods through which British agriculture has ever had to pass.   The inflated prices created by the Continental War not only caused an enormous rise in rent, but also a more luxurious and com-

[1] By the 44 Geo. III., c. 109.
[2] By the 55 Geo. III., c. 26. By the 3 Geo. IV., c. 60, the price for duty was reduced to 70s. a qr.
[3] For this, see Morley's *Life of Cobden*, ch. vi.
[4] Porter, quoted above, p. 428.
[5] The distress of agriculturists in this period is carefully detailed in various Reports, and the whole subject has been ably dealt with by I. S. Leadam in his book, *What Protection does for the Farmer and Labourer* (1893). For the period 1812-1845 see also Prothero, *Pioneers of English Farming*, p. 87 *sqq.*
[6] *Cf.* Toynbee, *Industrial Revolution*, p. 207.

fortable mode of living among the higher agricultural classes ; but when the war was finally brought to a close by the Peace of 1815, there was a sudden fall in prices that caused widespread trouble.   The majority of landowners refused to reduce their rents, and many farmers were in consequence ruined.   Hence arose the cry for more stringent Protective laws, and these were duly passed.[1]   Encouraged by these enactments, farmers went on growing more corn than was necessary, in hopes that the former high prices would now be kept up artificially ; and, of course, they were inevitably doomed to the disappointment that awaits all ill-considered legislation.   Rent was paid, but it was paid out of capital, not out of profits ; and agricultural distress grew more and more bitter.   Select Committees and Commissions sat to inquire into it in 1814, and in 1821 and 1822 ; they sat again in 1835 and 1836 ; and terrible evidence of the widespread ruin of many farmers was brought before them.[2] It was shown that since 1790 rents had increased some 70 per cent., and yet distress was prevalent in all agricultural districts.[3]   The last ten years of this unfortunate period, however, were more prosperous than those which had gone before, partly because of the action of the New Poor Law [4] and the Tithe Commutation Act,[5] but chiefly, no doubt, owing to the marked improvements that were made in farming.   Of these improvements it is now time to speak.

§ 246. *Improvements in Agriculture.*

The advance made between the years 1812 and 1845 is remarkable, in view of the great distress which undoubtedly prevailed among agriculturists at the time.[6]   The first, and possibly the most important, of these was the greater attention paid to the drainage of agricultural land, a subject

---

[1] Especially in 1815 by the 55 George III., c. 26.

[2] This evidence is conveniently summarised in *What Protection does for the Farmer and Labourer*, by I. S. Leadam, pp. 5, 33, and *passim.* See also Prothero, *Pioneers*, p. 87.

[3] Prothero, *u. s.*, p. 87.   [4] The 4 and 5 William IV., c. 76 (1834).

[5] The 6 and 7 William IV., c. 71 (1836).

[6] See Prothero, *Pioneers of English Farming*, pp. 95, 96, for the following.

discussed as far back as 1641 by Blith, and strongly re-commended by Arthur Young. One of the first farmers to appreciate the importance of proper drainage was James Elkington, a Warwickshire man,[1] whose services were so markedly useful to his county that the Government gave him a grant of £1000 in recognition thereof. But it was Smith of Deanston[2] who proceeded in a really scientific manner, and from 1823 and 1834 onwards his suggestions were widely followed. The importance of the subject was recognised by Parliament, and loans for drainage purposes were allowed by the Act[3] of 1846.

Next to drainage comes the introduction of science into the use and application of manures. The chemical nature of the various soils, and the fertilisers which are most suit-able for them, were now more carefully studied. From about 1835 nitrate of soda and guano began to be used.[4] In 1840, Liebig, the great German chemist, recommended the use of superphosphate of lime, and Sir J. B. Lawes in England showed how this could be obtained by dissolving bone-dust in sulphuric acid.[5] Then phosphates and am-moniacal manures were gradually introduced; and marked strides were made by the beneficial action and inter-action of good drainage and suitable fertilising agents. Nor must we omit the advance made in agricultural implements and machines, such as Small's plough, the sub-soil plough, Meikle's threshing machine, and the drilling machine[6]—all of which have greatly assisted agricultural operations. More attention was also paid now to the proper cultivation of artificial grasses, agricultural plants, and the selection of seeds. The rearing and breeding of stock was carried on more scientifically, and the oil-cakes and other artificial foods, formerly introduced by Coke of Holkham,[7] were more

---

[1] Prothero, *Pioneers of English Farming*, p. 96.
[2] *Ib.*, p. 97.   [3] *Ib.*, p. 98.   [4] *Ib.*, p. 99.
[5] *Ib.*, p. 100. The value of bones for manure is said to have been dis-covered as early as 1772 by a Yorkshire foxhunter when clearing out his stables (Prothero, *Pioneers*, p. 80). According to Porter (*Progress of the Nation*, i. 149), bones were occasionally used for this purpose about 1800, but did not come into general use till 1820.
[6] Prothero, *Pioneers of English Farming*, p. 100.
[7] Prothero, *Pioneers*, p. 80.

and more widely used for cattle. This general advance in care and skill was greatly assisted by the work of the Royal Agricultural Society, which was founded in 1838, and held its first meeting the following year in Oxford,[1] the home of movements which have usually been of a somewhat different character from the operations of agriculture. The greater facilities of transit afforded by the introduction of railways, canals, and steam navigation should also be noted as contributing to the success of the farmer, by enabling him to bring his produce more readily to market, and it became no longer necessary for one parish to starve, while another in a different part of the country had to allow its surplus produce to rot.[2]

Altogether, therefore, English agriculture made great strides in the years before the repeal of the Corn Laws (1846); and although after that repeal many persons predicted ruin to the farmer, he continued to prosper. The fact was that the enormous development of trade and population, the stimulus given to all kinds of commerce by the use of steam, not only as a locomotive power but also for driving machinery, and the greater interchange of products due to modern facilities of transit, all had a beneficial effect upon the farmer. He shared also, in another way, in the general increase of trade and prosperity, for the population of England since 1840 has not only increased in actual numbers, but has taken to eating far more of the farmers' produce than ever it did before. The consumption of butter per head of the United Kingdom was only 1·05 lbs. in 1840, whereas in 1892 it was 6·14 lbs.; of cheese the figures are 0·92 lbs. in the earlier date, and 5·86 lbs. in the later ; of bacon 0·1 lbs., as compared with 13·11 lbs. in 1892.[3] Of course large quantities of produce now come from abroad, but, even allowing for this, it will be seen that a tremendous increase must have taken place in the consumption of the produce of British farms. In fact, English agriculture was in a very flourishing condition in the " fifties and sixties," reaching its most favourable point

---

[1] Prothero, *Pioneers*, p. 101.   [2] *Ib.*, 78.
[3] Leadam, *What Protection does for the Farmer and Labourer*, p. 81.

about the time of the Franco-German war (1871-73). But after that it began to decline, and has continued to do so for a period of twenty years, though it is to be hoped that now (1895) the depression has passed its most acute stage.

§ 247. *The Depression in Modern Agriculture.*

The causes of this modern collapse in English agriculture are many and varied, and it must be remembered that to a large extent agriculture has only suffered in common with the other industries of the country, from which it is impossible to separate it altogether.   Yet, we may distinguish two causes, which, more than any others, have tended to this depression, and these are, in the first part of the period, unfavourable seasons, and, in the second, low prices and foreign competition.   The autumn of 1872 was inclement, and the following spring unfavourable, so that the good effects of the fine harvest weather of 1873 were neutralised.[1]   The year 1874 was the last of a cycle of prosperous seasons.   From 1875 to 1877 the farmer had to contend against a succession of bleak springs and rainy summers,[2]—weather that produced short cereal crops of inferior quality, causing mildew in wheat, mould in hops, and blight in other cases, while sheep-rot and cattle disease became very prevalent.   The British farmer, thus enfeebled by bad seasons, was further attacked by an alarming increase in foreign competition, due partly to the increase of the wheat area in India and America, and perhaps even more largely to the constantly growing facilities for transport of agricultural produce from distant lands.   Meanwhile, his own harvests were going from bad to worse.   The summer of 1879, sunless and ungenial, caused the worst harvest of the century ; and though since 1882 the seasons have been less uniformly unfavourable, the effects of the previous lean years have been hard to neutralise.[3]

Moreover, the stress of foreign competition has been very

[1] Prothero, in *Dict. Pol. Econ.*, *s. v. Agricultural Depression*, Vol. I., p. 564.   [2] *Ib.*

[3] For the above, see Prothero, *u. s.*

severe. Between 1866 and 1883 the values of agricultural imports from abroad rose from £77,069,431 to double that figure, *i.e.*, £157,520,797. Again, in 1851, the supply of wheat was 317 lbs. per head per annum for a population of some 27 millions, and it cost £53,500,000; but in 1885 the supply was 400 lbs. per head for some 36 million people, and yet the cost was reduced to £43,700,000. No doubt the consumers, as a whole, profited by the low price of bread, but, nevertheless, the agriculturist was being steadily ruined; and it has been seriously doubted by some economists whether the wider interests of the nation at large do not suffer when the cheapness of food proves so disastrous to a respectable and important class.[1] The fall in prices may be further seen from the following table [2]:—

YEAR.	Wheat, per qr.	Barley, per qr.	Cattle, per stone of 8 lbs.		Sheep, per stone of 8 lbs.	
	s. d.	*s. d.*	*s. d. s. d.*		*s. d. s. d.*	
1873	58 8	40 5	5 1 to 6	4	5 8 to 6	11
1883	41 7	31 10	4 3 ,, 6	1	5 6 ,, 7	3
1893	26 4	25 7	2 10 ,, 4	9	3 8 ,, 5	5
1894	22 10	24 6	2 6 ,, 4	5	3 8 ,, 6	1
1895 (Sept. 28)	23 0	24 8	2 9 ,, 4	6	4 1 ,, 5	9
1911 (Sept.)	31 7	28 4	2 6 ,, 5	0	3 4 ,, 5	4

Other produce has fallen in proportion. Thousands of farmers have been ruined, agriculture generally has suffered a severe and prolonged depression, and much arable land has been laid down again as pasture,[3] while some has gone altogether out of cultivation.[4] Meanwhile political false prophets have been going about with their usual nostrums, and the flags of Protection and even of Bi-metallism are being waved before the bewildered eyes of the British farmer, as if they were signals of salvation.[5]

[1] Prothero, *Dict. Pol. Econ.*, i. 565, from which the above figures are taken.

[2] See Hazell's *Annual* for 1895, p. 15, and 1896, p. 11.

[3] See the *Agricultural Returns*. The arable land of 1893 was about 2,000,000 acres less than in 1873 (*cf.* also Hazell's *Annual*, 1895).

[4] Notably in Essex.

[5] This sentence was first written in 1890. There is no reason to alter it in 1895.

§ 248. *The Causes of the Depression.*

Now it is perfectly obvious, to an impartial observer of economic facts, that an industry, so flourishing as English agriculture was not very many years ago, could not have suffered so severe a collapse unless there had been some great underlying cause, besides the ordinary complaints of bad harvests and foreign competition already referred to. These must have due weight given them, but bad harvests are not peculiar to England, and foreign competition, however keen it may be, has first to overstep a very considerable natural margin of protection in the cost of carriage. It costs, for instance, according to a high American authority, 9s. per quarter to transport American wheat from Chicago to London.[1] It is clear that besides these, there must have been other influences of consider-able importance to cause English agriculture to have been, in spite of its apparent prosperity, in so insecure a position that it should have sunk to the depressed condition in which it even now remains. We have not to look far for the causes. There are several, and one among them is the lack of agricultural capital.

But how, it may naturally be asked, has it come about that the English farmer, after the very favourable period before the depression, should thus suffer from a lack of capital, a lack which renders it almost impossible for him to work his land properly ? The answer is simple. His capital has been greatly decreased, surely, though not always slowly, by an enormous increase in his rent. The landlords of the eighteenth century, it has been said, perhaps somewhat too severely, made the English farmer the foremost agriculturist in the world, but their successors of the nineteenth have ruined him by their extortions.[2] Such, at any rate, is the verdict of eminent agricultural authorities ; and landowners have been compelled, for their own sake, to reduce the exorbitant rents which they

[1] Mr David Wells, quoted by Thorold Rogers, in *The Relations of Economic Science to Social and Political Action*, p. 12. Mr Edward Atkinson puts it at 11s. This is about ¼d. per ton per mile.

[2] Thorold Rogers, *Economic Interpretation of History*, p. 182.

received in former years. Unfortunately, too, the attention of other classes of the community has been, till lately, diverted from the condition of our agriculture by the prosperity of our manufactures. But these two branches of industry, the manufacturing and the agricultural, are closely interdependent, and must suffer or prosper together. It is possible, also, that there are certain economic theories which have helped the decline of English agriculture. They are the Ricardian theory of rent, and the dubious "law of diminishing returns." [1] They have made many people think that this decline was inevitable, and have diverted their attention from a very important, though not the only, cause of the trouble—namely, the increase of rent. But putting the possible effect of these theories aside, we may employ ourselves more profitably in looking at the facts of the case. It has been mentioned before, that in Tull's time, at the beginning of the eighteenth century, the average rent of agricultural land was 7s. per acre, and by Young's time, towards the close of the century, it had risen to 10s. per acre. [2] Diffused agricultural skill caused an increase of profits, and the hope of sharing in these profits led farmers to give competitive rents, which afterwards the landlords proceeded to exact in full, and frequently to increase. The farmers were enabled to pay higher rents by the low rate of wages paid to their labourers, [3] a rate which the justices tended to keep down by their assessments. In 1799 we find land paying nearly 20s. an acre; in 1812 the same land pays over 25s.; in 1830, again, it was still at about 25s., but by 1850 it had risen to 38s. 8d., which was about four times Arthur Young's average. [4] Indeed, £2 per acre was not an uncommon rent for good land a few years ago (1885), [5] the average increase of English rent being no less than 26½ per cent. between

[1] I have dealt with them in an article in the *Westminster Review*, December 1888, but perhaps their importance is overrated.

[2] Both Tull and Young are quoted by Rogers, *Economic Interpretation of History*, p. 176.

[3] *Ib.*, p. 179; and *cf. Six Centuries*, p. 492.

[4] Rogers, *History of Agriculture and Prices*, v. 29.

[5] W. E. Bear, *The British Farmer and his Competitors*, p. 31. The calculation as to the increase in rent is Mr James Howard's.

1854 and 1879. Now, such rent as this was enormous, and could only be paid in very good years. In ordinary years, and still more in bad years, it was paid out of the farmer's capital.[1] This process of payment was facilitated by the fact that the farmer of this century did not keep his accounts properly, a fruitful source of eventual evil frequently commented upon by agricultural authorities,[2] and obvious enough to anyone who knows many farmers personally ; and, also, by the other fact, that even when the tenant perceived that he was working his farm at a loss, the immediate loss (of some 10 or 15 per cent.[3]) involved in getting out of his holding was heavy enough in most cases to induce him to submit to a rise in his rent rather than lose visibly so much of his capital.[4]

The invisible process, however, was equally certain, if not so immediate. The result has been that the average capital per acre now employed in agriculture is only about £4 or £5, instead of at least £10, as it ought to be,[5] and the farmer cannot afford to pay for a sufficient supply of labour, so that the agricultural population is seriously diminishing. Nothing in modern agriculture is so serious as this decline of the rural population, and we must, further on, devote a few words to a consideration of the agricultural labourer and the conditions of his existence. But before doing so it may be well to point out, for fear of misconception, that the high rent of English agricultural land is not the only cause of

[1] Prothero, on *Agricultural Depression*, in *Dict. Pol. Econ.*, i. 564, points out that even after 1874, "the last of a cycle of prosperous years," rent continued to rise for two years longer, and that farmers have lost their capital.

[2] Rogers, *Six Centuries*, 471, and *Relations of Economic Science*, p. 17.

[3] Rogers, *Relations of Economic Science*, p. 17.

[4] The state of the case is very clearly and forcibly put by Thorold Rogers in the pamphlet just quoted, p. 18.

[5] *Ib.*, p. 17. Elsewhere Rogers (*Six Centuries*, p. 471) remarks that Arthur Young, even in his time, set down £6 an acre as the minimum capital necessary for successful agriculture, which is equivalent to more like £12 at the present time. Rogers also mentions that on certain land known to him the capital was (in 1878) under £6 an acre. My own calculations on this head will be found in the *Economist* of April 28th, 1888, and they coincide closely, though independently, with the statements made by Professor Rogers.

the depression.   It is a very important cause, and operates
in more ways than are usually seen on the surface, nor is it
any argument to say, as some have done, that because land
will not pay for the expense of farming, even when it is let
rent free, that therefore the former high rent had nothing to
do with the matter.   For when a farmer has lost all his
capital in paying rent when he was not earning it, he is not
anxious to continue the experiment even at a reduction of
that rent, especially when he knows that, if successful, he
will only have to pay more rent again in the future.   But,
apart from this, the causes of the depression are manifold
and various.   Almost chief among them may be placed a
certain lack of adaptability to changed circumstances which
has characterised the British farmer as compared with his
foreign competitors.   This is very noticeable in the case of
dairy farming, where foreign producers have rapidly overtaken our own countrymen in supplying the British home
market.   Many an English farmer has gone on growing
wheat for years after it was obviously a loss to him, when
he might gradually have introduced some other crop.   Again,
he has neglected dairy farming, or only carried it on on
unscientific principles, while foreigners have been scientifically perfecting their methods.   He has certainly despised
the smaller industries of the farm, such as poultry-rearing
and egg-producing,[1] so that our home market is now largely
stocked with fowls and eggs from France, Germany, Denmark, and even Italy.   Again, as a nation, we have paid
too little heed to agricultural education, and though so-
called "technical instruction" is now given, it is conducted
in many places in a most chaotic manner, and money is
lavishly wasted with the minimum of result.   Dairy schools
are certainly at length being established, but not before
they had become familiar to every Danish cowherd and
Danish butter was ousting our own from the home market.
Here, as elsewhere in our educational system, the State has
neglected duties which every other great European nation

[1] It is only in the last two years (1895) that the farmers of a certain
parish which I know well in Wiltshire have paid attention to their poultry,
by placing fowl-houses for them in the stubble after harvest.

has long since taken upon itself, so that our British farmers are, like our British mechanics, the most sensible and yet the most ignorant of their kind.

But to enumerate all the causes of the present agricultural depression would exhaust both the patience of the reader and the industry of the writer, more especially as many of them are inextricably implicated in the general conditions of English industry.[1] Those already mentioned —high rents and low prices, foreign competition and domestic carelessness, lack of capital and want of education—are possibly among the chief. Everyone who knows much about agriculture will add others from his own experience, and those who know but little will add still more. It is, therefore, perhaps better to consider a subject which is closely connected with them, and of dangerous importance to the nation at large. I refer to the serious depopulation of the rural districts.

§ 249. *The Labourer and the Land.*

It has been previously mentioned[2] that the Industrial Revolution was accompanied by an equally important revolution in agriculture : the main features of the agrarian revolution being the consolidation of small into large farms, the introduction of new methods and machinery, the enclosure of common fields and waste lands, and discontinuance of the old open-field system, and, finally, the divorce of the labourer from the land. The consolidation of farms reduced the number of farmers, while the enclosures drove the labourers off the land, for it became almost impossible for them to exist on their low wages now that their old rights of keeping small cattle and geese upon the commons, of having a bit of land round their cottages, and other privileges, were ruthlessly taken from them.[3] They have retreated in large numbers into the towns, and taken up other pursuits, or helped to swell the ranks of English pauperism. Before the Industrial and Agrarian Revolu-

[1] See Prothero's excellent article in Vol. I. of Palgrave's *Dictionary of Political Economy.*

[2] Above, pp. 343, 430.

[3] Above, pp. 335, 408 ; and Prothero, *Pioneers, &c.*, p. 73.

tion, Arthur Young,[1] in 1769, estimated that out of a total population of 8,500,000, the agricultural class, " farmers (whether freeholders or leaseholders), their servants and labourers," numbered no less than 2,800,000— *i.e.*, over one-fourth of the total population—and, with others interested in agriculture, the number was 3,600,000. The number of those engaged in manufactures of all kinds he puts at 3,000,000. His figures may be taken as substantially correct, though perhaps not as accurate as a modern census. Now let us look at the agricultural population of more recent years. In 1871 the number of wage-earners in agriculture was just under one million (996,642) in England and Wales. In 1881 it had declined further to 890,174, in 1891[2] to just over three-quarters of a million (798,912), and in 1901 to 689,000. The proportion that these wage-earners bear to the class of agriculturists, as a whole, is 73 per cent., so that they are quite adequately representative of the general rural population. This decline in absolute numbers in twenty years is startling enough, but it is still more so when we take the proportion of the numbers to the total population of England and Wales, and find that the percentage of agricultural wage-earners was only 4·34 in 1871, 3·43 in 1881, and as low as 2·75 in 1891. Even if we include, besides wage-earners, the whole class of agriculturists, we shall find that the proportion has sunk from the one person in four employed in agriculture in Arthur Young's time to more like one in twenty-four. There is in these figures much cause for uneasiness, not only for the economist, but for the patriot and for the politician. Nor is that uneasiness lessened by the fact that the same phenomenon of rural depopulation may also be seen in other European countries.[3] The modern rush to the towns is not a healthy sign, nor can any nation rest on a firm and secure basis unless, to use a rustic metaphor, its roots strike deep into its native soil.

[1] Quoted above, p. 334.

[2] The figures are from the Official Reports of the Census, and are conveniently summarised in Hazell's *Annual* for 1895.

[3] See E. G. Ravenstein's interesting paper in Vol. LII. (1889), p. 241, of the *Journal of the Royal Statistical Society.*

§ 250. *The Condition of the Labourer.*

But not only have the numbers of the agricultural population decreased, but the labourer no longer has, as a rule, any share in the land. Certainly the agricultural labourer, at any rate in the South of England, was much better off in the middle of the eighteenth century than his descendants were in the middle of the nineteenth. In fact, in 1850 or so, wages were in many places practically lower in purchasing power, and not much higher in actual coin, than they were in 1750. But meanwhile almost every necessary of life, except bread, has increased in cost, and more especially rent has risen, while on the other hand the labourer, as we have seen, has lost many of his old privileges, for formerly his common rights, besides providing him with fuel, enabled him to keep cows or pigs and poultry on the waste, and sheep on the fallows and stubbles, while he could generally grow his own vegetables and garden produce. All these things formed a substantial addition to his nominal wages. From 1750 or so to about 1800 his nominal wages averaged 7s. 6d. or 10s. a week ; in 1850 they only averaged [1] 10s. or 12s., although in the latter period his nominal wages represented all he actually received, while in the former they represented only part of his total income. Since 1850, however, even agricultural wages have risen, the present average being about 14s. a week.[2] This, of course, represents in rural districts far more than the same amount of wages would in a town, since the agricultural labourer of to-day has been enabled to obtain allotments for his own use in many places, and only pays a low rent for his cottage. But even then it does not represent a large income, and though there is more than one honest South Country labourer who has brought up a family respectably on 10s. a week,[3] it can hardly be

---

[1] *Cf.* the figures in Rogers, *Six Centuries*, p. 510.

[2] The average weekly wages as based upon thirty-eight estimates of the mean rate for all the districts inquired into by the Assistant Commissioners on Agricultural Labour in the Labour Commission of 1891 was about 13s. 5d. per week. The average rate ascertained by the Richmond Commission of 1879-81 was 13s. 1d., and the estimate for 1867-70 was 12s. 3d. per week.

[4] I am speaking from my personal acquaintance with such.

contended that a higher rate of payment would not have been better both for himself and for his employers. At the same time, it cannot be denied the general condition of the agricultural labourer is far better now than it was twenty, or even fifty, years ago. The hours of work have been lessened, and machinery, although it has caused displacement in some cases, has yet relieved the labourer of much of the severe work which he had then to perform. In many counties the wives of the labourers have been entirely emancipated from field work for many years past, though, of course, in many counties also, they do light field work at harvest time. Greater opportunities for education have been given, and the dwellings of rural labourers, with all their defects, are generally better now than they used to be. "The labourer of the present day," it is said, "who is better fed, better clothed, better housed, than his father was, may not be fully conscious of the improvement that has taken place, because his ideas have expanded, and his wants, like those of persons in every other class, have grown; but none the less he lives in less discomfort, his toil is less severe, his children have a better prospect before them, and opportunities which he himself never enjoyed." [1]

Such is a fair, though not a roseate, statement of the present position, and at first glance it may seem satisfactory. But when we come to consider that, after all, the present tolerable position of the agricultural labourer is an improvement only when compared with the depth of degradation reached about the middle of the nineteenth century, and that his condition had till then been steadily declining, we may well stop and ask ourselves whether there is much cause for congratulation in the fact that the agricultural labourer of the end of the nineteenth century is not much worse off than he was a hundred or a hundred and fifty years ago. Considering the vast improvement that has taken place in the whole of our social and economic standard of living, and in the opportunities which are now

---

[1] Report of Mr W. C. Little, Assistant Agricultural Commissioner, in his *General Report on the Agricultural Labourer* to the Labour Commission (June 20, 1894).

opened up by modern culture, it is doubtful whether we can honestly say that the agricultural labourer has had his fair share of them. Statisticians rejoice because he has for some time no longer retrograded, but has even advanced; but this is but a poor advance compared with that of the nation as a whole. However, for whatever advance that has taken place, we shall do well to be thankful, for a sturdy and contented peasantry, where it exists, is the best backbone for a progressive nation.

The rise, such as it is, is due, among other causes, to the formation of Trades Unions, the leader and promoter of which among agricultural labourers was Joseph Arch. This active and energetic man, who has sat in more than one Parliament, was born in 1826, and in his youth and middle age saw the time when agricultural labour was at its lowest depth. Not only were wages low—being about 10s. or 11s. a week—but the evils of the factory system of child labour had been transferred to the life of the fields. Philanthropists seem to have overlooked the disgraceful conditions of the system of working in agricultural gangs, under which a number of children and young persons were collected on hire from their parents by some overseer or contractor, who took them about the district at certain seasons of the year to work on the land of those farmers who wished to employ them. The persons composing the gang were exposed to every inclemency of the weather, without having homes to return to in the evening, people of both sexes being housed while under their contract in barns, without any thought of decency or comfort, while the children often suffered from all the coarse brutalities that suggested themselves to the overseer of their labour.[1] Their pay was of

[1] For gang labour see the Report (*Reports*, xii., 1843) of the Committee of 1843 on this subject. The worst evils are said to have been corrected in 1816 by the 56 Geo. III., c. 139 (Cunningham, *Growth of Industry*, ii. 653), but *cf.* Rogers, *Six Centuries*, pp. 511, 512.

The following extract from one of the Rev. S. Baring-Gould's novels gives some idea of the conditions of gang labour. I am assured by the author that he derived the incident from a reliable authority in the district where it happened: "Twice or thrice the wheat had to be hoed, and the hoers were women. Over them the farmers set a 'ganger' armed with an ox-goad, who thrust on the lagging women with a prod between the shoulder-blades."—Baring-Gould, *Cheap Jack Zita*, p. 214.

course miserable, though gangs flourished at a time when farmers and landlords were making huge profits. But the degrading practice of cheap gang-labour was defended as being necessary to profitable agriculture ; which means that tenants were too cowardly or too obtuse to resist rents which they could not pay except by employing pauperised and degraded labour. Amid times like these Joseph Arch grew up, and the seed of Trade Unionism was sown, but it was not till 1872 (at which time it will be remembered that British farmers were doing very well)[1] that the agitation was begun which resulted in the formation of the National Agricultural Labourers' Union. The difficulties of organising the down-trodden labourers were enormous, but they were at length overcome by the leaders of the agitation, and their efforts have already done much to improve the material condition of their members. Wages have decidedly risen since the agitation began, but even now they certainly cannot be called high.

§ 251. *The Present Condition of British Agriculture.*

It remains to notice briefly the causes which are still influencing our agricultural industry, and to point out in what direction we may expect a revival from the present state of depression. Besides the fact of the increase of rents up to 1870 or 1875, we notice an increase of the foreign competition already alluded to—an increase which is of comparatively recent date. Our competitors are mainly Russia, America, and last, but by no means least, India.[2] At the time of the Crimean War, and for some years subsequently, Russian competition ceased to exist. Even when it began again, it was not very serious as long as it stood alone, for America had not yet entered the field, and was prevented from doing so by the sanguinary struggles of the Civil War. High prices for grain[3] prevailed, therefore, till some time after America had ceased her internal conflict, and it was only quite recently that much grain was grown for export in India. But since 1870 or so England has

[1] Above, p. 438.   [2] See the *Agricultural Returns* for recent years.
[3] Aided by the discovery of gold in California and Australia.

been supplied with grain from these three great agricultural countries, and the English farmer, no longer buoyed up at the expense of the rest of the community by protective measures, has found it impossible to grow wheat at a profit under the old rents. The consequence has been the ruin of many farmers, and a terrible loss of income for all classes in any way connected with agriculture.[1] But at the same time rents have decreased very slowly in spite of the frequent stories that are heard of wholesale reductions by sympathetic landlords. This may be seen from the official returns. The annual value of lands assessed under Schedule A in the United Kingdom was highest in 1879-80, when it was £69,548,793. It had decreased to £63,268,679 in 1885-86, and still further[2] declined to £57,694,820 in 1890-91, and to £51,894,826 in 1908-09. But it is surprising to find that even this figure is higher than the gross assessment[3] of 1852-53, before the Russian War, while, on the other hand, land is not worth nearly so much to farm as it was then, so that it is difficult to resist the conclusion that the fall in rents has not been so great as it should have been in proportion to the fall in the profits of the farmer.

In course of time it is certain that the economic action of supply and demand will bring rents down to something like their commercial value, as, indeed, it has been rapidly doing in some places lately (1895); meanwhile the English landlords, as an eminent agriculturist remarks, have the choice between allowing their old tenants to be ruined first, and then accepting reduced rents, or granting reductions soon enough to save men in whom they have hitherto had some confidence as tenants.[4] It will be necessary also to make important changes in the laws and customs of land

[1] It was estimated by Sir James Caird (Evidence before the Commission on Depression in Trade in 1886) that the loss of the agricultural community as a whole in *annual* income was £42,800,000 as compared with 1876. (C. 4715, Qu. 7673, and f. 7677, 7742, 7785).

[2] See Bear, *The British Farmer and his Competitors*, pp. 9, 10.

[3] The assessment for Great Britain under Schedule B was £46,571,887. A change in the assessment for Ireland renders the exact comparison difficult, but it is obvious that, even allowing for Ireland, there has not been so great a fall as might have been expected.

[4] W. E. Bear, *u. s.*, p. 12.

tenure, so that our farmers may have complete security for their capital invested in improvements, and freedom of enterprise (*e.g.*, in cropping and tilling), in order that they may do their best with the land. An extended system of small holdings and allotments[1] (which are fortunately increasing in spite of high rents), guaranteed by a thorough measure of Tenant Right, together with free trade in land as well as other commodities, would do much to place moderate farms within the reach of industrious and thrifty yeomen and labourers. Greater facilities for transit, including the encouragement of light railways and rural tram lines, together with the abolition of the system of preferential railway rates, would enable producers to put their produce with greater ease upon the home market; for the requirements of the English nation guarantee an enormous and steady demand at home for every scrap of food-stuff that the land is capable of producing. The farmer is slow to adapt himself to changed conditions, but a profitable future is yet open to him, even if he gives up wheat-growing, and betakes himself more to dairy-farming, market-gardening, and what may be termed the minor branches of agriculture. But it may not be necessary for him to give up wheat altogether, since foreign farmers are beginning to find out that they cannot put wheat on the English market at the present low prices. In course of time the nation will probably perceive that it is desirable, and that ultimately it will be profitable, to recall capital and labour back to the land which it is evident that they have left; and that it is the height of economic folly to rely, as some do, upon the extension of our manufacturing industries to counteract agricultural

---

[1] The steady increase in allotments is shown by the figures of British allotments under one acre :—In 1873, 246,398 ; in 1888, 357,795; in 1890, 455,005. Of these, the greater number (441,024 in 1890) were in England. Small holdings under fifty acres, and other than allotments, have also increased since 1875 (see Hazell's *Annual*, 1895). Mr W. C. Little, in the *Report* above referred to (Royal Commission on Labour, June 20, 1894), states that the rentals of allotments are very high, as everyone knows who has had experience of their working. Under the Small Holdings and Allotments Act (1907), County Councils up to 1910 have provided some 17,000 applicants with 89,253 acres of land, besides 27,000 acres provided by private landowners at the instance of the County Councils.

depression. Prosperous agriculture means for us prosperous manufactures, and from an economic point of view
the interests of the plough and the loom are identical.
Neither can be served by protective tinkering. Reforms of
a totally different character are needed, foremost among
which is a widespread reduction of rent, and a general re-
arrangement of the relations between landlord and tenant,[1]
together with the adoption of the best methods, both in
education and in agricultural practice, of our Continental
and foreign competitors. It is on the face of it ridiculous
to assert that, with an unequalled demand in the home
market for all he can produce, the English farmer cannot
find some means of making the land pay, and pay well.
But before he can do this he must spend more capital upon
it than he has lately been able to afford.

[1] *Cf.* W. E. Bear, *The British Farmer and his Competitors*, pp. 12-17,
and throughout the book generally. For the advantages possessed by the
British farmer (the chief of which is the unequalled home market), *cf.*
Mr James Howard's remarks quoted on p. 18 of the same book.

CHAPTER XXVI

MODERN INDUSTRIAL ENGLAND

§ 252. *The Growth of our Industry.*

WE have now traced the industrial growth of England
from the diffused beginnings of manufactures and agriculture in primitive times to the more settled period of the
manorial system, and have seen how, afterwards, towns
gradually grew up, commerce extended, and markets arose,
while manufactures became organised in various centres
and regulated by guilds. We have seen that for several
centuries the backbone of our national wealth was the
export of wool, but that in course of time we ceased to
export it, and worked it up into cloth ourselves, thereby
gaining great national wealth. We have seen, too, how our
foreign trade, after its petty beginnings in the Middle Ages,
made a new advance in the buccaneering days of the
Elizabethan sea captains, and then rapidly developed, by
means of the various great trading Companies, till England
became commercially supreme throughout the world. From
commercial beginnings we traced the rise of our Indian
Empire, and the growth of the American colonies. Meanwhile, at home, there came an Industrial Revolution, which,
happening as it did at the moment that was politically
most favourable to its growth, gave England a most
advantageous start over other European nations in manufacturing industries of all kinds, and thus enabled her to
endure successfully the enormous burdens of the great
Continental war. Now comes a time of still greater progress, economic as well as commercial, for the old restrictive
barriers to trade are to be swept away, and a new economic
policy is to be inaugurated.

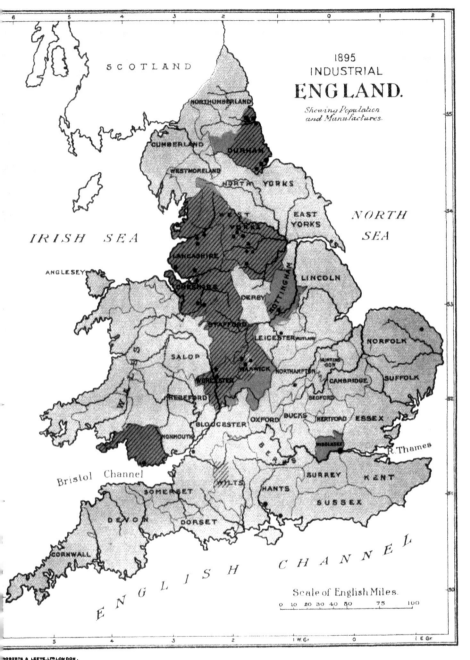

Manufacturing districts are shown by slanting lines, large manufacturing towns by black circles, and the most populous counties are coloured darker than the others. It will be noticed that population since 1750 has shifted very much to the North and North West of England, whilst manufactures are far more concentrated than formerly. (Compare the Map opposite page 350)

§ 253. *State of Trade in* 1820.

If we now endeavour to gain some idea of the trade of the country soon after the war, we may look for a moment at its condition[1] in 1820, just before Free Trade measures were begun. The official value[2] of the total imports was declared to be £32,438,650, while the exports amounted to £48,951,537. This gives a total trade of only £3, 15s. per head of the population then existing,[3] whereas in 1890 the proportion was no less than £18, 6s. per head.[4] The tonnage of shipping entering and leaving our harbours was about 4,000,000 tons, of which 2,648,000 tons belonged to the United Kingdom and its dependencies.[5] Steamers were, of course, as yet unknown. Professor Leone Levi calculates the trade of the country at not more than one-eighth or one-ninth of what it is at the present time. The wealth and comfort accessible to the people in general was much more limited, the consumption of tea, for instance, being only 1 lb. 4 oz. per head, and of sugar 18 lbs. a head.[6] In fact, if we compare the £327,880,676 worth of our exports in 1890 with the £48,951,537 worth in 1820, we see at once how gigantic has been the growth of our trade. In 1891, again, the imports[7] were £435,691,279, which is more than twelve times their value in 1820. In 1911 exports of British produce amounted to £454,282,460, and our total imports to £680,559,175. But even at the

[1] It may be well to tabulate briefly the figures of trade for the forty years previous to 1820 (Palgrave's *Dict. Pol. Econ.*, i. p. 344) :—

YEAR.	Imports.	Exports.	TOTAL.
1770	11,002,000	12,142,000	23,144,000
1780	9,956,000	11,363,000	21,319,000
1790	16,398,000	17,636,000	34,034,000
1800	28,258,000	34,382,000	62,640,000
1810	39,302,000	48,439,000	87,741,000

[2] *Accounts and Papers*, 1833, xli. 48.
[3] The population of the United Kingdom in 1821 included 12,000,236 in England and Wales, and 6,802,000 in Ireland—a total of nearly 19,000,000. *Accounts and Papers*, 1852-53, lxxxv. 23.
[4] The calculation is in the article *Commerce* in Palgrave's *Dict. Pol. Econ.*, p. 339, Vol. I.
[5] Leone Levi, *Hist. British Commerce*, p. 151.   [6] *Ib.*, p. 151.
[7] See the article on *Commerce* in *Dict. Pol. Econ.*, i. 339.

beginning of the century England was far ahead of her old rival France, for French imports were only worth £8,000,000 in 1815, and her exports only about double that amount, or less than half England's exports, which in that year rose to over £58,624,550 (official value).[1]

§ 254. *The Beginnings of Free Trade.*

The year 1820 has been chosen for comparison, not merely as showing the condition of our trade at that time, but for the great enunciation of Free Trade principles which it witnessed. The old Mercantile system was breaking up, and the ideas of Adam Smith were bearing fruit. A new era of commercial policy was beginning. For in that year the London merchants in the Chamber of Commerce formulated their famous Petition praying that every restrictive regulation of trade, not imposed on account of the revenue, together with all duties of a protective character, might be at once repealed.[2] At last the teachings of economists were being put into practice by men of business. The Edinburgh Chamber of Commerce sent up a similar petition; a Committee was appointed in Parliament to investigate the wishes of the petitioners of the Northern and the Southern capital; and it brought in a report[3] thoroughly in agreement with the Free Trade principles of the merchants. From that time onward these principles were gradually, but more and more widely, adopted.[4] In the following year Mr Huskisson, the President of the Board of Trade, proposed the first measures of commercial reform, and one by one the restrictions upon our trade were removed. The most important of the new measures was the gradual alteration[5] of the old Navigation Laws, finally culminating in their total repeal in 1849. It was also Huskisson who, in 1823, passed a "Reciprocity of Duties

---

[1] This is for the U. K., but of course the greater part came from England; *Accounts and Papers*, 1830, xxvii. 211, and, for French imports, *cf.* Levi, *u. s.*, p. 152.

[2] Leone Levi, *History of British Commerce*, pp. 150-153.

[3] The report was presented on July 18th, 1820.

[4] An excellent short account of the change of English commercial policy from 1815 to 1860 is given in Prof. Bastable's *Commerce of Nations*, ch. vi.

[5] By a series of five acts, all passed in 1822, viz. : the 3 Geo. IV., c 41, c. 42, c. 43, c. 44, c. 45; *cf.* Craik. *British Commerce*, iii. 234 235.

Bill," by which [1] English and foreign ships had equal advantages in England whenever foreign nations allowed the same to English vessels in their ports. The commerce of our colonies was thus thrown open, under certain restrictions, to other nations. In order to promote free trade in our manufacturing industries, he reduced the duties on silk and wool [2] in 1824, and in the same year the Act fixing wages for silk weavers was repealed.[3]

It is true that in the period 1821 to 1830 the foreign trade of the United Kingdom did not exhibit much material improvement, but still there was a steady increase. The official value of imports [4] rose from £30,000,000 to £46,000,000, and the value of British manufactures [5] exported from £40,000,000 to £60,000,000. But the declared value of exports remained fairly steady at about £37,000,000. Yet in the United Kingdom itself trade was growing rapidly,[6] and the increase of wealth gave an opportunity for a general diminution of taxes, so that our sorely strained finances were set in order.

Many of the injurious duties upon raw materials and articles of British manufacture, as e.g., those on raw silk, coal, glass,[7] paper, and soap, were taken off, to the great advantage of our manufacturing industries. The crisis of 1837, however, and the commercial depression [8] which

[1] The 3 and 4 Geo. IV., c. 37. In accordance with this Act, commercial treaties were made in 1824 with the Netherlands, Prussia, and Denmark; in 1825 with the Hansa Towns; in 1826 with France (for ten years) and Mexico; and in 1829 with Austria. The trade with the United States had been put on a reciprocal footing in 1815. *Cf.* Craik, *British Commerce*, iii. 237.

[2] See M'Culloch's *Commercial Dict.* (1844), *s. v. silk* and *wool.*

[3] *Ib., s. v. silk.*

[4] *Ib., s. v. Imports and Exports* for exact figures. [5] *Ib.*

[6] Yet many people believed it was decaying, till the evidence taken by a Committee of the Commons in 1833 disproved this idea. *Cf.* Tooke, *History of Prices*, ii. 242.

[7] For these see M'Culloch's *Dictionary of Commerce, s. v. coal, glass,* &c.; and see his most interesting tabular statement of the different English customs tariffs of 1787, 1819, and 1844, *s. v. Tariff.*

[8] Tooke, *History of Prices*, iv. 269, regards this as comparatively slight; but there were deficits in the budgets of 1838 (a million and a half), 1839 (half a million), 1840 (a million and a half), 1841 (a million and three-quarters), and in 1842 (two millions); Northcote, *Twenty Years of Financial Policy*, pp. 6, 12.

followed it, together with continual deficits in the Budget, prevented further financial reforms for a few years, though eventually circumstances rendered them imperatively neces- sary, and Sir Robert Peel courageously faced the difficulties of national finance in 1842.

§ 255. *Revolution in the Means of Transit.*

Meanwhile, too, another great industrial revolution was being effected. The introduction of railways, steam naviga- tion, and the telegraph, has done almost as much as the great inventions of the eighteenth century to revolutionise the commerce of the world. The Stockton and Darlington [1] railway was opened in 1825, and the Liverpool and Man- chester railway line in 1830. The first steamboat crossed the Atlantic, from Savannah to Liverpool, in 1825, in twenty-six days; and in 1838 ocean passages to New York by steamship were also accomplished by the *Great Western* from Bristol, and the *Sirius* from Cork, [2] although ever since the beginning of the century small steamers and tugs had been used for coasting purposes, and on the river Clyde. In 1837 Cooke and Wheatstone patented the needle telegraph, [3] and the Electric Telegraph Company was formed in 1846 for bringing the new inventions into general use. In 1840 the penny postage came into operation. [4] Yet more recently the Suez Canal (1869) has shortened immensely the distance to the East. Within the last fifteen years the telephone has become a business necessity, and the wireless telegraphy of Marconi has ex- tended our power of rapid intercourse even to mid-ocean. There has been an enormous increase in the size and speed of merchant vessels. Not only have the vast Atlantic liners reduced the passage between New York and Liverpool to a

---

[1] M'Culloch, *Commercial Dict.* (1844), *s. v.* " Railroads," and Leone Levi, *History*, p. 192.

[2] *Ib.*, *s. v.* " Steam Vessels," and Leone Levi, *History of British Com- merce*, p. 196.

[3] *Ib.*

[4] M'Culloch, *Commercial Dictionary, s. v.* " Postage," gives an account of its introduction.

length of about five days, but they are able to carry much larger cargoes, and thus doubly tend to swell the volume of trade. On land motor transport is now widely used both for goods and for passenger traffic, and the recent successes of aviation seem to foretell a new highway through the air. It is obvious to all how incalculably these inventions and appliances have aided the development, not only of English trade, but of the commerce of the whole world. But, owing to this development, commerce has become no longer national so much as international, and commercial history loses therefore many of its national characteristics.

§ 256. *Modern Developments.*

It is not therefore necessary, in the limits of a work like this, to go into a detailed account of the growth of commerce since these great modern inventions. There is ample material for the student in larger works; and the statistics of our progress may be consulted in the invaluable pages of Mr Giffen's and Professor Leone Levi's books. Here we need only indicate in the broadest outlines the chief features of the recent developments of industry. We have followed the industrial history of England up to a period more prolific in commercial events, and more remarkable for commercial progress, than any that preceded it. The experiments and tentative measures of Mr Huskisson and other statesmen paved the way for a bolder and more assured policy on the part of subsequent governments, till at length Sir Robert Peel, compelled to some extent by the deficits[1] in the Budgets of former years to adopt some drastic policy of finance, attacked seriously the great question of the reform of the tariff in his now famous Budget of 1842. In this,[2] tariffs were reduced wholesale, but soon Peel went still further. Urged on by the Anti-

[1] Above, p. 457, note 8.
[2] By the Tariff Act, 5 and 6 Victoria, c. 47. M'Culloch remarks: "The passing of this Act forms an important era in the history of commercial and financial legislation" (*Commercial Dictionary* (1844), *s. v.* "Tariff"); also *cf.* Prof. Bastable, *Commerce of Nations*, pp. 58-60.

Corn Law League,[1] and stimulated by a great famine in Ireland in 1845, he openly adopted the principles of Free Trade. Under his leadership the Corn Laws were repealed [2] (1846); the tariff was entirely remodelled, and the old pro tective restrictions were abolished, Mr Gladstone's Budget [3] of 1853 being particularly memorable in this direction. A great increase of trade followed the inauguration of the policy which is always associated with the famous name of Richard Cobden, and this increase was aided by various commercial treaties made between England and other countries.[4] Of these treaties, the most noticeable was that with France (1860), under which the prohibitive duties laid upon English goods were reduced by France to protective duties of fairly moderate amount, while England abolished all duties on the import of manufactured goods, and greatly reduced those on wine and brandy.[5] This treaty, which excited much controversy at the time, as raising the whole question of our commercial relations with foreign countries, was negotiated by Cobden.[6] In his efforts to form it Cobden was actuated by the hope that such treaties might lead to the gradual reduction of protective duties and the introduction of Free Trade; but in this, as in other cases, the enthusiasm of Free Traders has received a severe blow, and at the end of the nineteenth century there seems almost as small a chance of universal free trade as at the beginning of it. Some movement towards that enlightened policy has certainly been made, but progress has been very slow. Many wise statesmen deliberately continue to adopt a protective policy from an idea—which is far from being altogether baseless—that such a policy, though economically indefensible, is politically

[1] See Morley, *Life of Cobden*, ch. xi.

[2] By the 9 and 10 Victoria, c. 22.

[3] It reduced or abolished imports on 133 articles; Montgredien, *Free Trade* (1881), p. 171 ; Bastable, *Commerce of Nations*, pp. 63, 64.

[4] See list in Appendix to Leone Levi's *British Commerce*.

[5] See Morley's *Life of Cobden*, ch. xxvii. This treaty lasted till 1872, when it was denounced by Thiers, but was renewed in 1873, and so far modified in 1882 as to be practically useless.

[6] Morley's *Life of Cobden*, ch. xxvii. ; also *cf.* Bastable, *Commerce of Nations*, pp. 65, 66.

advantageous. Time may prove that politics and economics are too closely allied to allow political expediency to counterbalance economic error ; meanwhile it is somewhat doubtful whether protection, even from the political point of view, is worth the expense which it invariably entails.

Be that as it may, the wealth of England has undoubtedly increased enormously in the last fifty years.[1] The revolution in transit, the use of electricity and steam, the freedom of our country from protracted warfare, the growth of population, and the spread of our colonial dependencies, have all contributed to this result. The growth of commerce may be seen by comparing the figures of our exports and imports from 1855 to 1890, from which it will be seen that the most rapid increase went on until 1870 or 1872, and that since then it has not been so remarkable. On the other hand, it must be remembered that these figures are values only, and do not show the actual volume of trade. It is beyond doubt that, in spite of the groans of pessimists, the foreign commerce of England was greater in 1890 than in 1872, though, owing to a great depreciation in prices, the values may seem lower ; and that the actual commercial intercourse of this country with others has largely increased.[2]

TRADE OF THE UNITED KINGDOM.[3]

YEAR.	IMPORTS.	EXPORTS.		
		Produce of U.K.	Foreign Produce.	Total Exports.
1855	143,542,850	95,688,085	21,003,215	116,691,300
1860	210,530,873	135,891,227	28,630,124	164,521,351
1870	303,257,493	199,586,822	44,493,755	244,134,738
1880	411,229,565	223,060,446	63,354,020	286,414,466
1885	370,967,955	213,044,500	58,359,194	271,403,694
1887	362,227,564	221,414,186	59,348,975	280,763,161
1890	420,885,695	263,531,585	64,349,091	327,880,676
1911	680,559,175	454,282,460	102,720,799	557,003,259

[1] See Table xxvi. at end of Farrer's *Free Trade* v. *Fair Trade*.

[2] See the article *Commerce* in Palgrave's *Dict. of Pol. Econ.*, i. 339. It is there stated that the volume of our foreign commerce is 30 per cent. larger than in 1872.

[3] The table is from the article *Commerce* in Palgrave's *Dictionary of Pol. Econ.* (Vol. I.). Since 1854 "official" values were abandoned in favour of "computed" values for imports and "declared" values for exports.

Even before 1855, however, England was commercially far ahead of other countries. The great Exhibition of 1851, for instance, the precursor of several others, showed to all the world her immense superiority in productive and manufacturing industries. A certain stimulus to trade was given at the same time by the discovery of gold in California and Australia (1847-51), which supplied a much-needed addition to the currency of the world.

§ 257. Our Colonies.

But one of the most important causes of the growth of British trade has been the quite modern development of our colonies.[1] Since the war of American independence, England has been building up a great colonial empire, and she has been wise enough not to attempt again to levy taxes upon her unwilling offspring. India was taken over from the East India Company (1858). The colonies of Canada and the Cape were gained by conquest; those of Australia and New Zealand were the result of spontaneous settlement.[2] The two former were captured from the French and Dutch, but of South Africa at least we have not yet made a commercial or even a political success; nor are we likely to do so unless we have the sense to keep on good terms with the original settlers, and to allow no misplaced sentiment about native races to disturb cordial relations between Europeans. The recent activity in gold mining in South Africa will, however, have a beneficial influence upon that branch of our colonial trade. As regards our Australasian colonies, they have grown far beyond the expectations of former generations, and gained for themselves entire political freedom, though they have chosen to use it chiefly in carrying on a one-sided war of hostile protective tariffs against

[1] For the great question of colonial trade, see Farrer, *Free Trade* v. *Fair Trade*, on the one hand, and the publications of the Imperial Federation League on the other. A useful summary is found in Palgrave's *Dict. Pol. Econ.* (Art. *Trade and the Flag*, by A. Caldecott, i. 324-326); also my *British Commerce and Colonies*, ch. xvii.

[2] See Caldecott's *Colonisation and Empire* for a short summary of colonial history, and Lucas's *Historical Geography of the British Colonies.*

their mother-country.[1] As, however, they owe English capitalists a large amount of money, the interest on which is paid in colonial goods, there is a strong commercial bond of union between the old country and the new ; a bond which protectionists in England are strangely anxious to break, by placing unnatural obstacles upon the payment in goods of the interest due upon colonial loans. It is calculated that the amount of capital[2] borrowed from English investors by the colonies is some 250 millions at present outstanding, and unless some violent act of repudiation takes place, the interest alone on this vast sum guarantees a considerable trade between borrowers and lender.[3] But into this most interesting question of colonial commerce,[4] involving as it does colonial history and colonial industry, there is not space to enter in the limits of the industrial history of the mother-country. It can be studied at length in other works, and here is only noted as one element in the enormous foreign trade which our home industries have rendered possible.

In 1901 the various States of Australia united in a Federal Commonwealth with a highly protective tariff, and in 1911 Canada engaged in tariff negotiations with the United States, her nearest and most important market. These negotiations, however, broke down. Our colonies are thus rapidly developing into practically independent states, bound to us indeed by ties of filial affection and interest, but determined to shape their own careers. South Africa has just entered upon the most hopeful chapter of her chequered history by the federation of the four colonies in the Union of South Africa. The original settlements of Cape Colony and Natal and the two Boer States conquered in the late war form now a self-governing whole.

---

[1] *Cf.* Prof. Bastable, *The Commerce of Nations*. ch. x.

[2] Palgrave's *Dict. Pol. Econ.*, i. 324 ; and see paper on *Colonial Indebtedness*, by H. F. Billington, in *Journal of Institute of Bankers*, March 1889.

[3] *Cf.* Rogers, *Economic Interpretation of History*, 339-340.

[4] Very full statistics of its relation to British and foreign trade are given in Farrer's *Free Trade* v. *Fair Trade*, especially in Table V. of the Appendix.

§ 258. *England and other Nations' Wars.*

But besides the extension of our colonial relations, English trade has benefited by the quarrels of her competitors.[1] The prostration of Continental nations after 1815 precluded much competition till almost the middle of the century, and then the Crimean War broke out (1854-56). As mentioned before, this war gave a great stimulus to our agriculture,[2] and had a similar effect upon our manufactures. The Indian Mutiny, which followed it, did not much affect our trade, but it rendered necessary the deposition of the East India Company and the assumption of government by the Crown (1858), and thus eventually served to put our relations to that vast and rich empire upon a much more satisfactory and profitable basis. About the same time the Chinese wars of 1842 and 1857, regrettable as they were, established our commercial relations with the East generally upon a firm footing, and since then our trade with Eastern nations has largely developed. Then came the Civil War in America (1861-65), after which there was an urgent demand for English products to replace the waste caused by this severe conflict. The Civil War was succeeded by a series of short European wars, chiefly undertaken for the sake of gaining a frontier, as was the war waged by Prussia and Austria upon Denmark (1864), followed by another struggle between the two former allies (1866). Then in 1870-71 all Europe was shaken by the tremendous fight between France and Germany, and since then the Continental nations have occupied themselves in keeping up an armed peace at an expense which, though undoubtedly in the present state of affairs necessary, is almost equal to that of actual warfare. All their conflicts have arrested their industrial development, to their own detriment, but to England's great advantage. Not content, however, with that, they increase their difficulties by a dogged protectionism.[3]

---

[1] For the following brief summary, *cf.* Rogers, *Economic Interpretation,* pp. 292-294.   [2] *Ib.,* p. 293.

[3] Bastable, *The Commerce of Nations,* ch. ix. (on *European Tariffs,* 1865-1890).

As a result, they are far poorer in general wealth than our own land,[1] and only succeed in competing with us by means of underpaid and overworked labour. But the labourer will not always consent to be overworked and underpaid, and signs are not wanting that his discontent is fast ripening into something more dangerous.

Of late years the various quarters of the world have been visited by a series of calamities, natural and artificial. The Spanish-American War of 1898, the Russo-Japanese War of 1904-05, and the disastrous earthquakes at San Francisco (1906), Jamaica (1907), and Messina (1908), all caused not only loss of life and great physical suffering, but also widespread destruction of capital. Plague and famine in India and drought in Australia also checked at times the productive capacity and purchasing power of those great areas, and consequently affected our industries at home. But the closest influence was that of the South African War (1899-1903), which, after at first giving an apparent impetus to the trades supplying munitions of war, left behind it a legacy of debt, increased military and naval expenditure, and great depression in trade. Our recent rivalry in naval construction with Germany and our adoption of the *Dreadnought* type of battleship have also added to the burdens of taxation, while in the army, since the war, we have been maintaining practically a war establishment in time of peace.

§ 259. *Present Difficulties. Commercial Crises.*

But although English commerce has reached a height of prosperity considerably above that of other nations, it has not been, and is not now, without serious occasional difficulties. It has been throughout the century visited at more or less periodic intervals by severe commercial crises. Indeed, very soon after the conclusion of the Continental War, a severe commercial crisis passed over this country.[2] It happened partly because during the war our manufacturers

---

[1] *Cf.* Mulhall's *Dictionary of Statistics.*

[2] During the war there had also occurred a very severe crisis, that of 1810-11 ; *cf.* Tooke, *History of Prices,* i. 303 *sqq.*, and iv. 273.

2 G

had accumulated vast stocks of manufactured products, and could not get rid of them as quickly as they expected, owing to the financial exhaustion of those countries whom they expected to be their customers,[1] and partly also because foreign countries sought to protect their own almost ruined industries by imposing prohibitive duties upon English manufactures. The harvests of 1816 and 1817 were also very bad in England, and these, added to the causes just mentioned, produced a very severe crisis,[2] which reached its worst point in 1819. Once again, in 1825, a second crisis followed, caused by the too rapid importation of raw products that had been bought at a very high price, and by financial follies in speculation in the trade with the Spanish-American colonies, that seemed to recall the days of the South Sea bubble.[3] In fact, this panic is often called the second South Sea bubble. Ten years afterwards, in 1836 to 1839, another crisis occurred, owing chiefly to the formation of numerous joint-stock banks[4] and other companies, together with extravagant speculation in corn and tea. During the forties, however, our commercial condition continued to improve, and capital was rapidly accumulated, till the bad harvest of 1846, combined with speculations in grain, and the high price of cotton, caused another period of disaster,[5] in which the cotton industry, in particular, was severely damaged. The speculations in railways were also remarkable at this time, no less than £500,000,000 being raised in loans[6] in 1847. The country, however, recovered once more, and with the discoveries of gold in California and Australia in 1851, a renewed activity was seen in all branches of trade. As the supplies of gold increased, English exports increased also, since they were eagerly taken, especially by Australia, in

---

[1] *Cf.* Tooke, *History of Prices*, ii. 8 to 12.

[2] *Ib.*, ii. 77-79 ; Craik, *British Commerce*, iii. 219-224.

[3] These colonies required capital to work their silver mines, and this led to heavy speculation by English capitalists; *cf.* Tooke, *u. s.*, ii. 145, 147, 159.

[4] Tooke, *u. s.*, ii. 278, 303.

[5] *Ib.*, iv. 314 (railways) ; Leone Levi, *British Commerce*, p. 310 ; Palgrave's *Dict. Pol. Econ.*, i. 459.

[6] *Dict. Pol. Econ.*, i. 459.

return for the precious metals. Nevertheless, before very long another crisis [1] broke upon the commercial community (1857), having its origin in North America, but which extended over the whole commercial world, and proved very prejudicial to English interests on account of the close connection between our country and the United States. This time our iron and textile industries were specially affected; factories were closed, and blast furnaces extinguished, and the greatest distress prevailed amongst the working-classes. But once more the nation recovered as usual; and for another few years continued to prosper till the cotton industry was for a second time almost ruined by the effects of the Slavery War between the Northern and Southern States of America. A "cotton famine" occurred in Lancashire, when 800,000 wage-earners were deprived of their livelihood. This caused an increase of cotton-growing in India, which has continued since that time.[2]

§ 260. *Commercial Crises since* 1865.

But once again this industry recovered from what seemed to be a very severe blow, and the close of the American War in 1865 even gave a further impetus to new business, while, at the same time, considerable developments took place in our trade with China, India, and Australia. But the very next year the sudden and unexpected failure of the great bill-broking firm of Overend, Gurney & Co. caused much panic,[3] not only in financial but in industrial circles, though the ordinary symptoms of crisis were fortunately not apparent in the trade returns, and for some years our prosperity continued to increase, till a crisis [4] of truly international magnitude occurred in 1873. It was felt from New York to Moscow, and affected the trade industry and agriculture of all intervening countries. It was due to some extent to the great financial inflation which took place within the German Empire after the payment of

---

[1] *Dict. Pol. Econ.*, i. 464; Hyndman, *Commercial Crises*, ch. v.
[2] Hyndman, *Commercial Crises*, p. 93.
[3] *Ib.*, p. 95.   [4] *Ib.*, ch. vii.

£200,000,000 indemnity by the French to their conquerors, while a similar inflation prevailed in the United
States, owing to the rapid growth of business and the extension of railways after the Civil War.   England escaped
much of the severity of this international crisis (1873),[1] but
soon afterwards suffered from agricultural depression, and
has continued to do so since, from the causes mentioned in
a previous chapter.   During the last twenty years, the two
most severe periods of crisis[2] have taken place in 1882 and
1890, the former connected with the failure of the Union
Générale of France, combined with the low prices and
general stagnation of trade in Great Britain, which lasted
till 1888 ; and the latter due to the extravagant speculation, especially in South American securities, which termin-
ated in the difficulties experienced by the well-known firm
of Baring Brothers, and the panic which followed the
discovery of their unsafe situation.   More recently still,
the protective tariffs adopted by the United States and
other nations have had a depressing effect upon many
British industries.

§ 261. *The Recent Depression in Trade.*

Still more recently (1895) there has been an outburst of
speculative activity in the shares of South African gold-
mines, and some derangement has occurred, but we are
assured by an eminent authority[3] that there has been no
absolute panic since 1866.   There has been, however, a
very long period of depression, beginning about 1875 and
gradually growing worse till 1885, when a Commission was
appointed to take evidence on the subject.   The peculiarity
of this depression has been its gradual growth and continuance, in contrast to the former crises, which occurred

---

[1] Though two great failures—that of Collie & Co., in 1875, and the
Glasgow Bank, in 1878—showed that there was some uneasiness.

[2] Hyndman, *Commercial Crises*, chs. viii. and ix.

[3] Mr W. Fowler in his article on the *Crises of* 1857, 1866, and 1890, in
Palgrave's *Dict. Pol. Econ.*, i. 462.   The articles on *Crises* in this Dictionary should be compared with Hyndman's views in his book above
quoted.

after periods of sudden inflation, and passed away with comparative rapidity. The evidence of the Commission of 1885 showed that during this depression wages had, on the whole, remained firm, and that the incomes of those in trades and professions had actually increased, while, on the other hand, profits had been lowered, and the rate of interest reduced. It was agreed by most of the witnesses before the Commission that there had been much over-production, and though this is true to some extent, it would seem, on the whole, that at least one of the main causes of this prolonged depression was a slow but radical change in the relations of labour and capital, causing a closer approximation between the shares of the total product allotted to each. It is also probable that the term depression is only comparative in this case, and only shows a falling-off as compared with the abnormal activity of 1871-74, and also it should be borne in mind that, though English manufacturers have hitherto had a considerable start over their foreign neighbours, this advantage cannot be expected always to continue, as other countries will naturally tread more closely on the heels of our own in the race of international competition. In any case, however, there is no immediate fear for the future of English industry, although individual merchants or manufacturers may suffer, for it has already been seen above (p. 461) that the volume of our trade is by no means yet diminishing. But there are certain considerations on this subject of crises and depressions which are of a more general character.

The causes of such depressions in trade are various, and not always obvious. They are, so to speak, dislocations of industry, resulting largely from mistaken calculations on the part of those " captains of industry " whose *raison d'être* is their ability to interpret the changing requirements in the great modern market of the civilised world. A failure in their calculations, a slight mistake as to how long the demand for a particular class of goods will last, or as to the number of those who require them, results very soon in a glut of the market, in a case of what is called " over-production," but is in reality merely production of the wrong things; and this is as inevitably followed by a period of depression, occasionally enlivened by desperate struggles on the part of some manufacturer to sell his goods at any cost. With such a vast field as the international market, it is not to be wondered at that such mistakes are by no means rare, nor does it seem as if it were possible to avoid them under the present unorganised and purely competitive industrial system. They have been aggravated in England by a belief that our best customers are to be found in foreign markets, while the importance of a steady, well established, and well understood home market is not fully perceived. "A pound of home trade," it has been said,[1] "is more significant to manufacturing industry than thirty shillings or two pounds of foreign." The comparison may not be exact, but it is on the right lines. Now one of the most important branches of our home trade must be the supplying of agriculturists with manufactures in exchange for food. But when the purchasing power of this class of the community has sunk as much as £43,000,000 per annum,[2] it is obvious that such a loss of custom must seriously affect manufacturers. Again, no small portion of our home market must consist in the purchases made by the working-classes, yet it does not seem clearly understood that if a large proportion of the industrial classes is paid the lowest possible wages, and has to work the longest possible hours, while thus obtaining an ever-increasing production of goods, the question must sooner or later be answered: who is going to consume the goods thus produced?

1907 was a year of trade revival, abnormally high prices, and speculation, which culminated in an acute financial crisis in the United States. Vast quantities of gold were shipped thither, and though London at the time stood the shock to credit better than any other financial centre, the Bank of England was forced to raise its rate of discount to

---

[1] Thorold Rogers, *Relations of Economic Science to Social and Political Action*, p. 10.

[2] Sir J. Lawes, quoted above, p. 451, note 1.

seven per cent. The volume of our foreign trade was greatly reduced, and in 1908 the rate of unemployment was far higher than for many years past. The hardships of the workers have been increased by a period of rising prices, which still continues, as trade and employment have again revived.

§ 262. *The Present Mercantile System. Foreign Markets.*

The capitalist's answer to our question on the last page is—foreign customers in new markets. English manufacturers and capitalists have consistently supported that policy which seemed likely to open up these new markets to their goods. For a considerable time, as we saw, they occupied themselves very wisely in obtaining cheap raw material by passing enactments actuated by Free Trade principles, and removing protective restrictions. Cheap raw material having thus been gained, and machinery having now been developed to such an extent as to increase production quite incalculably, England sends her textile and other products all over the world. She seems to find it necessary to discover fresh markets every generation or so, in order that this vast output of commodities may be sold. The merchant and manufacturing classes have supported and still support this policy, from a desire, apparently, rather to find new customers than to keep the old ; and, it has sometimes appeared necessary to engage in foreign war for the purpose of promoting commercial, as well as political interests. At the present epoch, indeed, the industrial history of our country seems to have reached a point when production under a purely mercantile system is overreaching itself. It must go on and on without ceasing, finding or fighting for an outlet for the wealth produced, lest the whole gigantic system of international commerce should break down by the mere weight of its own immensity. Meanwhile, English manufacturers are complaining of foreign competition in plaintive tones, a complaint which really means that, whereas they thought some years ago that they had a complete monopoly in supplying the requirements of the world, they are now perceiving that they have not a monopoly at all, but only a good start, while other nations are already catching them up in the modern race for wealth.

§ 263. *Over-production and Wages.*

With all this, too, we hear cries of over-production, a phrase which economically is meaningless (except in so far as it indicates that production is proceeding in the wrong direction), more especially at a time when very large numbers of people in civilised communities are daily on the verge of starvation, when the paupers of every civilised country are numbered by thousands, and plenty of people who never complain have neither enough clothes to wear nor enough food to eat. Wages are certainly better than they were fifty years ago, but no one who knows the facts of the case will deny that for the average workman—without speaking of skilled artisans and the *élite* of the working-classes—it is practically impossible to save anything out of his wages that would form an adequate provision against old age or sickness. It is not the business of a historian to vituperate any particular class, but he may justly point out the mistakes to which classes have as a matter of history been liable. And the great mistake of the capitalist class in modern times has been to pay too little wages. It is an old agricultural saying—quoted, I believe, as Arthur Young's—that one cannot pay too much for good land, or too little for bad land. The same remark applies to labour. Capitalist employers rarely make the mistake of paying too much for bad labour, but they have constantly, as a matter of history, committed the worse error of paying too little for good labour. There are, however, signs at present that this state of things is being altered. But at the beginning of this century, as has been shown, the coming of the capitalists and of the capitalist factory system, beneficial as it was ultimately to England, was followed by a time of unprecedented misery and poverty for those whom they employed. The day of the capitalist has come, and he has

made full use of it. The day of the labourer will only
come when he has the strength and the wisdom to use
his opportunities.

§ 264. *The Power of Labour. Trades Unions and Co-operation.*

But the labourers of to-day are a very different class from
their ancestors of fifty or seventy years ago. They have
learnt, at least the most advanced among them, the power
of combination, a remedy which at one time was forbidden
them, but which is now legally once more theirs. The
steady growth of Trades Unions and of Co-operative
Societies has taught them habits of self-reliance and of
thrift, and has made them look more closely into the economic conditions of industry. These unions and societies
do not yet embrace more than a small fraction of English
workmen, but they contain the best and worthiest of them,
and their members are able to preserve a certain independence of attitude in treating with their employers. Even
as it is, the gigantic power of modern capital finds itself
occasionally confronted by the united forces of modern
labour. But these occasions are rare, and more often an
isolated body of workmen engages in a futile conflict with
superior strength. The great Dock Strike of 1889 showed,
indeed, what power the union of labour might possess, but
the success of that famous conflict was, after all, due
to other causes than the solidarity of labour, and many
subsequent events have shown the weakness of the workmen
who enter upon these unfortunate struggles. It may be
deplored that the relations of employer to employed are
such as to necessitate these combinations, but it has not
been always in the past the fault of the labourer if the
relations of labour and capital are somewhat strained.
Whether he looks back to the days of assessment of wages
and the Law of Settlement ; to the Statutes of Labourers
of the Middle Ages, or the Combination Laws of more
modern times ; whether he remembers the degradation and
horrors of the first factories and mines, or the grinding

misery of agricultural life after his common rights had been
taken from him, and he and his children worked in gangs not
so well cared for as foreign slaves—when he hears of all these
things he naturally does not credit the employer of his labour
with the best intentions towards him.   Nothing is so wasteful
and nothing so dangerous as industrial strife ; but the best
way to make the labourer desist from it is to give him
some guarantee of his own industrial freedom and safety.
This he is rapidly gaining, and when masters and men recognise alike the identity of interest and the equal rights of
Capital and Labour, the industrial history of England will
have entered upon a new era of more solid prosperity.

At present the position of the working-classes has been
vastly improved in their political relations, and there are
many signs that they are using political means—as other
classes have done—to gain economic ends.   The spirit of
democracy is gaining strength, and the wave of democratic
progress is washing down the ancient barriers of privilege
and rank.   Its advance has been welcomed by thinkers and
statesmen of no mean order, and the advent of political
power is hailed as bringing with it material posperity.   Yet
there must remain, even in the minds of many who sympathise with the industrial classes, grave doubts as to the
ultimate benefits of a popular government ; and the gravest
doubt of all arises when it becomes increasingly evident that
the advance of democracy practically involves the acquisition
of irresponsible power by the working-classes, who form
already the majority of parliamentary voters.   No man, and
no mass of men, has yet been found fit to be trusted for
long with such a power, for it is a weapon which wounds
equally those who use it and those against whom it is
directed.   And unless the working-classes of England can
learn a lesson from the errors of their former rulers in the
past, there can be but little hope that they will reach the
highest level of national prosperity in the future.

The modern movement for social reform and legislation
(exemplified in the establishment of Old Age Pensions and
a system of National Insurance) is due in part to the
pressure of the organised forces of labour upon politicians.

The membership of Trades Unions has risen from 1,688,531 in 1898 to 2,426,592 in 1910, and in the Parliament of 1911 the Labour Party consisted of 42 members, the majority of whom were nominated by Trades Unions. Recently, perhaps owing to improved trade conditions, there has been considerable unrest in the labour world, and much loss of time and money has accrued to both employees and employed through industrial disputes. We may instance the wide-spread strikes by dockers and railway workers in August 1911. Both the morality and the policy of these movements have been severely criticised, but it is admitted by most observers that the recent increase in the price of commodities and the general rise in the standard of life among the working-classes make the claim for higher wages and shorter hours a well-founded one.

§ 265. *The Necessity of Studying Economic Factors in History.*

For, hitherto, our prosperity, great as it is, has frequently had its drawbacks, and has passed through many vicissitudes. Our ancestors and ourselves have made many mistakes, and till recently, as we have seen, the growth of our national wealth has been slow. But a study of industrial history is not without its uses, if it helps us to-day to understand how we have come into our present position, and what faults and follies we must avoid in order to retain it. Unfortunately, few historians have thought it worth their while to study seriously the economic factors in the history of nations. They have contented themselves with the intrigues and amusements of courtiers and kings, the actions of individual statesmen, or the exciting feats of military heroes. They have often failed to explain properly the great causes which necessitated the results they claim to investigate. But just as it is impossible to understand the growth of England without a proper appreciation of the social and industrial events which rendered that growth possible, and provided the expenses which that growth entailed, so it will be impossible to proceed in the future without a systematic study of economic and industrial affairs. The story of industry is in reality the story of the fulfilment of those pressing material needs which occupy, and always must occupy, the bulk of mankind in the struggle for ordinary existence. It is one phase, and by no means the least important, in the evolution both of the individual and of the race, and it is because the satisfaction of our material wants is a matter of such continual urgency, that it becomes necessary to give it due consideration in a review of the history of mankind in general and of each nation in particular. The plain and simple issue may often be obscured, and political, religious and social considerations may from time to time have apparently greater weight, but in the long-run the economic factor in life and progress never fails to make itself felt, and sometimes it makes itself felt in curious and unexpected ways. It is one of the most interesting of studies to observe how the eloquence of the orator or the diplomacy of the statesman, the flash of the warrior's sword or the enthusiasm of preacher or patriot, have been swayed more or less unconsciously by the very considerations which they neglected or despised as too homely or too prosaic for consideration. More especially in the region of politics is it necessary to trace the economic factor as determining men's actions; and owing to the vast expansion of international commerce in modern times that factor has become, and will probably continue to be, more distinctly prominent than in previous epochs. The very existence of the British Empire is bound up with intricate commercial and industrial considerations, and though these are not by any means the only elements in our polity, they are too significant to be lightly set aside. The study of the industrial and commercia. features of history shows their far-reaching influence, and will amply repay a greater attention than has been accorded to it in the past.

NOTE A

In recent years some standard works on Domesday have been published, including Round, *Feudal England*; F. W. Maitland, *Domesday Book and Beyond*; Vinogradoff, *Villeinage in England*; and Ballard, *Domesday Inquest*, the last being an excellent summary. Webb, *Industrial Democracy* and *History of Trade Unionism*; Hobson, *Evolution of Modern Capitalism*; and Booth's monumental *Life and Labour of the People of London* are also useful. For special trades see Chapman, *Lancashire Cotton Industry*, and Clapham, *The Woollen and Worsted Industry*.

The Census returns, the current Statistical Abstracts, and other publications by Government Departments, and Royal Commissions on questions of trade, industry, and social progress, are indispensable. Bowley's *Elementary Manual of Statistics* affords valuable help in their interpretation.

M. E. H.

INDEX

A

Aboriginal races of Britain, 5
Accounts, agricultural, 113
Africa, South, 462, 463, 465
Agrarian difficulties (sixteenth century), 211, 217
Agriculture, Celtic, 13
—— in Roman period, 25 ; early influences in, 27 ; Saxon, 39 ; later, 99 ; mediæval, 112 ; (methods of), 113, 116, 185 ; (sixteenth century), 211, 247 ; (seventeenth century), 265 ; writers on, 268 ; (eighteenth century), 270 ; (agricultural population), 331, 335 ; (modern agric.), 427, ch. xxv. ; (revolution in), 430 ; (protection in), 435 ; (improvements), 436 ; (depression in), 439-445 ; (prices of produce), 440 ; (agric. capital), 443 ; (value of land), 451 ; (revival of), 452
Allowance system of relief, 408, 413
Alfred, 46
America, discovery of, 218 ; colonies in, 285, 289, 295, 366 ; war, 367-370 ; (civil war), 463
Antwerp, 228, 230
Apprentice system, 95 ; (Elizabethan law), 259 ; (in factories), 388
Arch, Joseph, 449
Arkwright, 343
Assessment of wages, 253-259, 281
Assiento contract, 289
Assize, 139
Australia, 462, 463
Aviation, 459

B

Bailiff, 114, 174
Bakewell, 429
Banking, 299 ; (Bank of England), 300, 322, 374
Barter, 43
Bordars, 72
Bounties on corn, 433
Brickmaking, 316
Bright, John, on factory acts, 405

Bronze age, 8
Bye-industries, 325, 329 ; (loss of), 385

C

Cabot, 193, 218
Canada, 295, 462, 463
Canals, 355
Cape Colony, 462
Capitalists, rise of, 324
Capitalist manufacturers, 325, 326, 381
Cattle, ancient, 7 ; improvements in, 271
Cartwright, 344
Celts in England, 5, 8 ; (Pytheas on), 11-14
Chancellor, Richard, 231
Changes in fifteenth century, 192
—— in sixteenth century, 220
Charters of towns, 91
Charter, the Great, 101
Chartists, 377
Children in factories, 388-402
Closes, 115
Clothiers, 147
Coal and coal mining, 310-312, 353, 423
Cobbett, 376
Cobden, 460
Cockayne's monopoly, 306
Coke of Holkham, 429
Colonies, 290, 293, 295 ; (policy towards), 364 ; (American), 366 ; (war with), 368 ; (trade with), 462
Columbus, 193, 218
Combination Acts, 416
Commendation, 53, 61
Commerce in sixteenth and following centuries, 284-304, and see Trade
Common fields, 115, 273
Communal ownership, see Manor
Communal land, 115
Communication, improvements in, 354 ; (recent), 458
Co-operative societies, 471
Copyholders, 38
Corn laws, 432, 435, 460
Cottars, 72
Cotton manufactures, 346

Counties, population and wealth of, 67-69
Crimean War, 464
Crises, commercial, 466-471
Crompton, 343
Cromwell, Oliver, 286
Crusades, 100
Cultivation, methods of (Saxon), 40
Currency (under Henry VIII.), 206 ; (Elizabeth), 235 ; (William III.), 300
Customary tenants, 56
Customs tariff, 375
Cuxham Manor, 79

D

Dairy, 115
Danes, 43-45, 61
Darby, Abraham, 314
Darien scheme, 301
Debasement of currency, 206
Defoe on commercial men, 322
Dock strike, 471
Domesday Book, 65-85
Domestic system of industry, 336
Drainage of fens, 268
Drainage, agricultural, 436, 437
Drake, 231, 232
Drawbacks of mediæval life, 177
Dudley and iron trade, 313
Dutch (in agriculture), 249 ; (in trade), 287 ; wars with, 287
Dunstan, St, 41
Dyeing, 131, 305

E

Early Britain, people of, 10 ; condition of, 11
East India Co., 285, 293, 463
Economic factors in history, 473
Edward III. and manufactures, 127 ; and staple, 136
Edward VI., 209 ; his ministers, 209, 234
Elizabethan seamen, 221, 231
Elizabethan England, 234-263
Enclosures, 119, 213, 215 ; results of (sixteenth century), 216-218 ; (seventeenth and eighteenth centuries), 274 ; (benefits of), 275 ; (number of), 335
Enumerated articles, the, 366
Exports, early, 15, 32 ; (Norman period), 100 ; (sixteenth century), 240 ; (later), 297, 455, 457, 461

F

Factory Acts, 391-406 ; (summary of), 403
Factory, germs of, 146
——, early, 347 ; increase of, 348 ; life in, 388
Factory system, results of, 381, 388 ; factory agitation, 391-405
Fairs, 42, 140
Famine, 151, 178
Farmers, see Agriculture
Fens drained, 268
Feudal system, 60, 98
Fifteenth century changes, 193
Finances (Ed. VI.), 210, 219, 220
Firma unius noctis, 54
Firma burgi, 90, 188
Fitzherbert, 171
Flanders, trade with, 229
Flemish weavers, 105, 121, 127, 129
Flemish immigrants, 241
Foreign trade (Saxon), 43 ; mediæval, 223-233 ; (sixteenth century), 240 ; (seventeenth century), 297 ; (later), 455, 457, 461
Forests, 17, 313
France, 291, 293, 460
Frauds, statute of, 277
Free and unfree, 38, 73, 76
Free Trade, 456, 460
Frobisher, 231
Fuggers, the, 210

G

Gang-labour in agriculture, 449
Geburs, 38
Geneat, 37
Gentry, country, 182
Gilds, 91 ; merchant, 93 ; craft, 94 ; functions of, 95 ; rural, 96 ; in cloth trade, 130 ; and towns, 189 ; lands, confiscation of, 207 ; revival of craft gilds, 246
Gold, 462
Greshams, the, 229
Grosseteste, 113

H

Halifax, 237
Hansa, the, 124, 227
Hargreaves, James, 343
Hawkins, 231
Henley, Walter de, 113
Henry VII., 193, 194, 196

Henry VIII., expenses of, 199 ; popularity of, 201 ; and monasteries, 202 ; and coinage, 206
Huguenots, in England, 308
Husbandry (book), 113, and *see* Agriculture
Huskisson, 456, 459

I

Imports, 16, 32, 45, 101, 143, 224-227, 229, 297, 366, 455, 457, 461
Income of different classes (eighteenth century), 334
Independence, American, 369
India, 285, 293
Indian Mutiny, 464
Industrial History, 3, 473
Industry, Celtic, 12-14
—— in Roman period, 31
Intercursus Magnus, 123
Inventors and inventions of eighteenth century, 343
Iron age, 9
Iron, 15 ; (iron trade), 313, 353
Isolation of villages, 41

J

Jack of Newbury, 147
Jews, 103

L

Labourers, statute of, 153, 165
Labourer, condition of (fourteenth and fifteenth centuries), 172-179 ; (Elizabethan period), 251 ; (eighteenth and early nineteenth centuries), 407, 421 ; (agricultural), 447
Land, sentiment about, 322
——, kinds of in a village, 82
——, labourers and the, 445
Landowners and the Plague, 156, 164
Landowners, services of, 427
Large and small holdings, 157
Lords of the manors, 70

M

Machinery and hand labour, 383-385
Manchester, 237 ; Manchester Massacre, the, 377
Manor and manorial system, 47-61, 70, 78 ; decay of, 85, 211
Manorial courts, 55, 80
Manual industry, 316
Manufacturers, small, 326

Manufactures, 104, 121, 125 ; (foreign), 126 ; (and politics), 132 ; (in Elizabethan period), 237 ; (later), 305, 309 ; (domestic system), 336
Manufacturing population, 327
Manures, 437
Marconi, 458
Markets, 42, 107, 138 ; (foreign), 469
Mark theory, the, 48 ; (criticism), 49
Marshes, 18
Mary, Queen, 234
Mayor, 188
Mercantile theory, the, 359-364
Mercantile system, the present, 469
Merchants and politics, 138
Merton, statute of, 214
Methuen treaty, 302
Middle Ages, close of, 180, 194
Migration of population from South to North, 350
Mining (early), 9 ; (Roman), 31 ; (mediæval), 315 ; (later), 316 ; (eighteenth century), 352
Monasteries, dissolution of, 202-205
Monopolies (of towns), 239 ; (other), 242-246 ; (Cockayne's), 306
Municipal institutions, 189

N

Navigation Acts, 287, 456
Neolithic age, 6
Nobles, 181
Norman period, summary of, 108
Norwich, 125, 129

O

Oastler, 393
Origin of the manor, 58
Over-production, 472

P

Papal exactions, 123
Paris, Treaty of, 293
Pauperism, 195, 205, 219, 260, 410, 422
Peel, Robert, 459
Physical features of early Britain, 17
Pilgrimage of Grace, 203
Plague, the Great, 151-160
Plagues, 178
Piers the Plowman, 162
Pigs, 39, 116
Piracy, 145

Pole, Wm. de la, 137
Politics and industry, 321, 358, 376, 418
Poor Laws, 205, 260, 411, 412
Population (in Domesday), 66, 106, 112; (Elizabethan), 263; eighteenth century), 332, 349-352; (decline of rural), 445, 446
Ports, 89, 107, 144
Pottery trade, 314, 338
Poultry, 116
Prehistoric influences, 4
Productivity of soil, 272
Progress, 149
Prices of provisions (mediæval), 175
Protection in agriculture, 434, 435
Pytheas, 11-14

Q

'Quia Emptores' Statute, 158

R

Railways, 458
Raleigh, 231
Reform, parliamentary, 379
Regulation of prices, 139
Rent (in kind), 75; rise of, 213; (in seventeenth century), 267; later, 279; (eighteenth and nineteenth centuries), 428
Revolt, the Peasants', 161-172
Revolution, the Industrial (eighteenth century), 323, 341; (and French), 342, 371, 379; (political results of industrial), 378, 418; (in agriculture), 430
Richard II., 166, 170
Roads and Rivers, 16
Roads, Roman, 22
——, mediæval, 354
—— (eighteenth century), 355
Romans in Britain, 21-31
Roses, Wars of the, 132, 195

S

Sadler, M. T., 397
Salt, 42
Saxon period, 34, 46
Scotland, Union with, 302
Seebohm, F., referred to, 51
Services of tenants, 74
Settlement, Law of, 415, 416

Shaftesbury, Lord, 399, 403
Sheep, 117
Sheep farming, 118, 185, 216, 248
Silures, 6
Six Acts, the, 377
Sixteenth Century, summary of, 220
Slave trade, 45
Slaves, 72
Social comforts, 250
Sokemen, 75
Somerset the Protector, 209
South Africa, 462, 463
South Sea Bubble, 303
Spain, wars with, 285, 289, 291
Speculation, 303
Spinning, 6, 14, 425
Speenhamland "Act," 409
Staple, the, 135, 136, 137
Steamboats, 458
Stock and land lease, 114, 186
Stock, 116
Stone age, 6
Stourbridge fair, 143
Strikes, 473-475
Supremacy of England, recent, 4
Survival of ancient population, 35

T

Taxation, 99; (on wool), 123; (in the Continental War), 373
Telegraphs, 458
Ten hours' day, agitation for, 397, 404
Tenants, classes of, 112
Thegen, 37
Tories, 321; (and factory acts), 405
Towns (Roman), 23; (Saxon), 42; (Domesday), 69; later, 86-97; origin of, 86; privileges of, 89; town life (mediæval), 90, 134; decay of, 145; constitution of, 187; decay of, 190; new, 191
Townshend, Lord, 429
Trade, Free, 456
Trade, early, 15; in Roman times, 31; foreign (Norman), 100; foreign (fourteenth to sixteenth century), 224; (sixteenth century), 240; (seventeenth century), 297; (in 1820), 455; (recent), 455, 457, 461; (depression in), 467
Trades Unions, 419, 449, 473-475

U

Union of Scotland and England, 302
Unions, Trades, see Trades Unions

V

Venetian fleet, 225
Verulamium, 33
Village life in eighteenth and early nineteenth centuries, 328-331
Village, Saxon, 37 ; (in Norman period), 80
Village communities, 57
Villages, industrial, 146
Villeins, 72, 77, 150, 159 ; (revolt of), 168, 171
Vinogradoff, referred to, 52

W

Wage-earning class, 111, 150
Wages, (mediæval), 173, 175 ; (sixteenth century), 253 ; (assessment of), 253 ; (in seventeenth and eighteenth centuries), 281 ; (in nineteenth century), 424 ; (agricultural), 447 ; (recent), 470
War, the Continental, 370, 372 ; cost of, 373, 424
Wars of nineteenth century, 464, 465
Watt, James, 345

Wealth, distribution of (counties), 67, 107
Wealth and wars of England, 356
Weaving, 6, 14 ; (Flemish), 105 ; (sixteenth century), 238 ; (inventions in), 344
Wedgewood, 315
Whigs and Tories, 321
Wiklif, 163
William III., 289
Willoughby, 231
Winchester fair, 142
Wool and politics, 121
Wool, 113, 120 (and ch. ix), 124, 305, 309
Woollen manufacture and trade, 120; (ch. ix), 305, 309
Working classes, see Labourers
Worsted trade, 129

Y

Yeomen, 157, 183 ; decay of, 276

Z

Zealand, New, 462